D1187765

Maren R. Niehoff

# Philo on Jewish Identity and Culture

Mohr Siebeck

*Maren R. Niehoff,* born 1963; studied Jewish Studies, Literature and Philosophy in Berlin, Jerusalem and Oxford; 1989–91 Junior Fellow at the Society of Fellows at Harvard University; since 1991 Lecturer in the Department of Jewish Thought at the Hebrew University in Jerusalem.

*CIP-Titelaufnahme der Deutschen Bibliothek*

*Niehoff, Maren:*
Philo an Jewish identity and culture / Maren R. Niehoff. - 1. Aufl., - Tübingen : Mohr Siebeck, 2001
  (Texts and studies in ancient Judaism ; 86)
  ISBN 3-16-147611-5

© 2001   by J.C.B. Mohr (Paul Siebeck), P.O. Box 2040, D-72010 Tübingen.

The book was typeset by Martin Fischer in Tübingen, printed by Gulde-Druck in Tübingen on non-aging paper and bound by Heinr. Koch in Tübingen.

Printed in Germany

ISSN 0340-9570

For Udi, Maya and Ayana

# Acknowledgements

This book had its beginning in the winter of 1995 when Professor Martin Hengel suggested that I contribute a volume to the series "Text and Studies in Ancient Judaism". It took some time until the theme of the present book took shape and work on the individual chapters could begin. Throughout this process, both editors of the series, Peter Schäfer and Martin Hengel, supported and encouraged me. Peter Schäfer's advise, from my first years of studying onwards, has in numerous ways guided my academic work.

I had the good fortune to share my work in progress with friends. I wish to thank especially Erich S. Gruen, Jonathan J. Price and Yehuda Liebes who read the entire manuscript of the book and provided comments distinguished by erudition and keen insight. Erich Gruen, who wrote at the same time a book on the Jewish diaspora in the Hellenistic world, also shared with me his work in progress. It was a pleasure to see that we share similar interests even though my perspective is more particular than his. Jonathan Price accompanied every stage of writing with keen friendship. Yehuda Liebes has been a colleague and friend since my arrival in Jerusalem a decade ago. Officially a master of Kabbalah, he has offered comments from the numerous fields of his expertise, including especially Philo and the Classical world. I also wish to thank John J. Collins, Martin Goodman, Daniel S. Schwartz and David Winston who read large portions of the manuscript and made detailed comments which substantially improved the book. Daniel Boyarin, Sylvie Honigman, Menahem Kister and David Satran read different chapters and suggested invaluable improvements. Gregory Sterling, Jan-Willem van Henten and Zeev W. Harvey discussed the final manuscript and offered extremely useful comments many of which could be incorporated into the printed version. I also profited immensely from reading the unpublished manuscripts of Katell Bertholet, Daniel Boyarin, Hannah Cotton, John Glucker, Gregory Sterling and Daniel S. Schwartz which the authors kindly gave me.

The Israel Science Foundation provided a generous research grant which allowed me, among other things, to hire two highly competent assistants, Nurit Shoval and Elke Morlok who has also compiled the indices with an unfailing eye for details and an ever reliable readiness to help.

I moreover wish to thank the editors of the Studia Philonica Annual and the Jewish Quarterly Studies for their permission to use earlier published material, which has in revised form been incorporated into chapters one and seven.

Last but not least I wish to thank the publisher Georg Siebeck, and Ms Ilse König, who saw the book through publication very speedily and efficiently.

This book is dedicated to my husband, Udi Rosenthal, and my two daughters, Maya and Ayana. Without them I would not be the person I now am and this book would consequently not have been written. Udi has also shared the exciting and often all-absorbing process of researching and writing.

Jerusalem, January 2001 Maren R. Niehoff

# Table of Contents

Introduction . . . . . . . . . . . . . . . . . . . . . . . . . . . . . . . . . . . . . . . . . . . . . . 1

## Part One: Jewish Identity

1. Jewish Descent: Mothers and Mothercities . . . . . . . . . . . . . . . . . . . . 17
2. The Egyptians as Ultimate Other . . . . . . . . . . . . . . . . . . . . . . . . . . . 45
3. Jewish Values: Religion and Self-Restraint . . . . . . . . . . . . . . . . . . . . 75
4. Roman Benefactors and Friends . . . . . . . . . . . . . . . . . . . . . . . . . . . . 111
5. Greeks and Greek Culture . . . . . . . . . . . . . . . . . . . . . . . . . . . . . . . . 137

## Part Two: Jewish Culture

6. Transforming New-Born Children into Jewish Adults . . . . . . . . . . . . . 161
7. The Textuality of Jewish Culture . . . . . . . . . . . . . . . . . . . . . . . . . . . 187
8. Parables as Translators of Culture . . . . . . . . . . . . . . . . . . . . . . . . . . 210
9. Inscribing Jewish Customs into Nature . . . . . . . . . . . . . . . . . . . . . . . 247

Bibliography . . . . . . . . . . . . . . . . . . . . . . . . . . . . . . . . . . . . . . . . . . . . 267
Indices . . . . . . . . . . . . . . . . . . . . . . . . . . . . . . . . . . . . . . . . . . . . . . . . 295

The translations of Philo are based on those of the LCL edition, with modifications and frequent corrections. For the Legatio I have usually preferred the translation by E. M. Smallwood.

# Abbreviations

## Journals and Series

| | |
|---|---|
| AJP | American Journal of Philology |
| AJS Rev. | Association for Jewish Studies Review |
| Ak. d. Wiss. u. Lit., Abhandl. Geist. u. Soz. Wiss. Kl. | Akademie der Wissenschaften und Literatur, Abhandlungen der Geistes- und Sozialwissenschaftlichen Klasse |
| Am. Jour. of Anc. Hist. | American Journal of Ancient History |
| Am. Phil. Assoc. Monogr. Ser. | American Philological Association, Monograph Series |
| Am. Philos. Quart. | American Philosophical Quaterly |
| ANRW | Aufstieg und Niedergang der Römischen Welt. Geschichte und Kultur Roms im Spiegel der neueren Forschung |
| APA | Abhandlungen der Preussischen Akademie der Wissenschaften |
| ASP | American Studies in Papyrology |
| Bull. Soc. Arch. Alex. | Bulletin. Societe archéologique d'Alexandrie |
| BZAW | Beihefte zur "Zeitschrift zur alttestamentlichen Wissenschaft" (ZAW) |
| Cambr. Phil. Soc. Suppl. vol. | Cambridge Philological Society, Supplement volume |
| CAH | Cambridge Ancient History |
| CBQ | Catholic Biblical Quaterly |
| CCSL | Corpus Christianorum, Series Latina |
| CJ | Classical Journal |
| CP | Classical Philology |
| CPJ | Corpus Papyrorum Judaicarum |
| CQ | The Classical Quaterly |
| CW | The Classical World |
| GLAJJ | Menachem Stern: Greek and Latin Authors on Jews and Judaism, Jerusalem: Israel Academy of Sciences and Humanities, 3 vols, 1974–1984. |
| HTR | The Harvard Theological Review |
| HUCA | Hebrew Union College Annual |
| JANES | Journal of the Ancient Near Eastern Society of Columbia University |
| JBL | Journal of Biblical Literature |
| JEA | The Journal of Egyptian Archeology |
| JHS | Journal of Hellenistic Studies |

| | |
|---|---|
| JJS | Journal of Jewish Studies |
| JPS | Jewish Publication Society (of America) |
| JQR | The Jewish Quaterly Review |
| JRS | The Journal of Roman Studies |
| JSJ | Journal for the Study of Judaism in the Persian, Hellenistic and Roman Periods |
| JSNT | Journal for the Study of the New Testament |
| JSOT | Journal for the Study of the Old Testament |
| JSQ | Jewish Studies Quaterly |
| JSS | Journal of Semitic Studies |
| JThS | Journal of Theological Studies |
| JStPs | Journal for the Studies of the Pseudepigrapha |
| | |
| LCL | The Loeb Classical Library |
| Mem. Am. Ac. in Rome | Memoirs of the American Academy in Rome |
| MH | Museum Helveticum |
| MJSt | Münsteraner Judaistische Studien |
| NT | Novum Testamentum |
| NTS | New Testament Studies |
| Pap. Mon. Am. Ac. Rome | Papers and Monographs of the American Academy in Rome |
| PBSR | Papers of the British School at Rome |
| Proc. XII. Intern. Congr. Pap. | Proceedings at the International Congress of Papyrology |
| Proceed. Mass. Hist. Soc. | Proceedings. Massachussets Historical Society |
| PT | Poetics Today |
| RB | Revue Biblique |
| REG | Revue des Études grecques |
| RIDA | Revue International des Droits de l'Antiquité |
| RHR | Revue de l'Histoire des Religions |
| SBL | Society of Biblical Literature |
| SBL Diss. Ser. | Society of Biblical Literature, Dissertation Series |
| SBLSP | Society of Biblical Literature, Seminar Papers |
| ScEs | Scienes Ecclesiastiques |
| SCI | Scripta Classica Israelica |
| SGRR | Studies in Greek and Roman Religion |
| Sitzungber. Kön. Pr. Akad. d. Wiss. | Sitzungebreicht der Königlich-Preussischen Akademie der Wissenschaften |
| SPhA | The Studia Philonica Annual |
| SP | Studia Philonica |
| TAPA | Transactions (and Proceedings) of the American Philological Association |
| TUGAL | Texte und Untersuchungen zur Geschichte der altchristlichen Literatur |
| VT | Vetus Testamentum |
| WUNT | Wissenschaftliche Untersuchungen zum Neuen Testament |

## Philo

| | |
|---|---|
| Abr. | De Abrahamo |
| Aet. | De Aeternitate Mundi |
| Agr. | De Agricultura |
| All. | Legum Allegoriae |
| Cher. | De Cherubim |
| Conf. | De Confusione Linguarum |
| Congr. | De Congressu quaerendae Eruditionis gratia |
| Cont. | De Vita Contemplativa |
| Dec. | De Decalogo |
| Det. | Quod Deterius Potiori insidiari soleat |
| Ebr. | De Ebrietate |
| Flac. | In Flaccum |
| Fug. | De Fuga et Inventione |
| Gig. | De Gigantibus |
| Her. | Quis Rerum Divinarum Heres |
| Hyp. | Hypothetica |
| Immut. | Quod Deus immutabilis sit |
| Jos. | De Josepho |
| Lib. | Quod Omnis Probus Liber sit |
| Leg. | De Legatione ad Gaium |
| Migr. | De Migratione Abrahami |
| Mos. | De Vita Mosis |
| Mut. | De Mutatione Nominum |
| Opif. | De Opificio Mundi |
| Plant. | De Plantatione |
| Post. | De Posteritate Caini |
| Praem. | De Praemiis et Poenis |
| Prov. | De Providentia |
| Q.E. | Questiones et Solutiones in Exodum |
| Q.G. | Questiones et Solutiones in Genesim |
| Sacr. | De Sacrificiis Abelis et Caini |
| Sobr. | De Sobrietate |
| Somn. | De Somniis |
| Spec. | De Specialibus Legibus |
| Vir. | De Virtutibus |

## Ancient Authors

*Aeschylus*
| | |
|---|---|
| Pers. | Persae |

Alexander A*phrodisiensis (Alex. of Aphrod.)*
| | |
|---|---|
| Met. | Metaphysica |

*Aristoteles (Arist.)*
| | |
|---|---|
| G.A. | De Generatione Animalum |

| Met. | Metaphysica |
| Nic. Eth | Nichomachea Ethica (Aristoteles) |
| Pol. | Politica |
| Rhet. | Rhetorica |

*Arrianus (Arrian.)*
| Anab. | Anabasis |

*Augustinus*
| De Cons. Evang. | De Consensu Evangelistarum |

*Augustus (Aug.)*
| R.G. | Res Gestae |

*Ben Sira (Sir.)*

*Cicero (Cic.)*
| Ad Her. | Ad Herennium (ascribed to Cicero) |
| De Benef. | De Beneficiis |
| De Div. | De Divinatione |
| De Fin. | De Finibus |
| De Off. | De Officiis |
| De Rep. | De Republica |
| Ep. Att. | Epistulae ad Atticum |
| Leg. | De Legibus |
| N.D. | De Natura Deorum |
| Pro Rabiro Post. | Pro Rabiro Postumo |
| Pro Flac. | Pro L. Valerio Flacco |
| Tus. Disp. | Tusculanae Disputationes |
| Verr. | In Verrem |

*Q. Curtius Rufus*
| H.A. | Historia Alexandri Magni |

*Cassius Dio (Dio)*
Roman History

*Dio Chrysostomos (Dio Chr.)*
| Or. | Orationes |
| Paus. | Pausanias |

*Diodorus (Diod.)*
| Bib. | Bibliotheces Historices |

*Diogenes Laertius (D.L.)*
Vitae Philosophorum

*Dionysus of Halicarnassus*
| A.R. | Antiquitates Romanae |

*Eusebius (Eus.)*
| Ec. Hist. | Ecclesiastes Historias |
| Praep. Ev. | Praeperatio Evangelica |

*Gaius*
| Inst. | Institutiones |

*Herodotus (Hdt.)*
Historiae

*Q. Horacius Flaccus (Hor.)*
Ep.                           Epistulae

*Iamblichus*
Vit. Pyth.                    De Vita Pythagorica

*Josephus (Jos.)*
A.J.                          Antiquitates Judaicae
B.J.                          Bellum Judaicum
Contr. Ap.                    Contra Apionem

*Juvenalis (Juv.)*
Sat.                          Saturae

*Livius (Liv.)*
Ab Urbe Condita

*Lucianus*
Quomodo hist.                 Quomodo historia conscribenda sit
  conscrib.

*Johannes Lydos*
De Mens.                      De Mensibus

*Cornelius Nepos*
Alc.                          Alcibiades

*Ovid*
Ars Amat.                     Ars Amatoria

*Philolaus (Phil.)*
In Nic.                       In Nicomachi Arithmeticam Introductionem
                              (apud Iamblichus)

*Plato*
Crat.                         Cratylos
Hip. Mai                      Hippias Maior
Leg.                          Leges
Men.                          Menon
Pol.                          Politicus
Rep.                          Respublica
Symp.                         Symposium
Theaet.                       Theaetetus
Tim.                          Timaius

*Plinius the Elder*
N.H.                          Naturalis Historia

*Plutarchus (Plut.)*
Alex.                         Alexandrus
Ant.                          Antonius
Cato Mai                      Cato Maior
De Is. et Os.                 De Iside et Osiride

| | |
|---|---|
| De Lib. Educ. | De Libris Educandis |
| Dem. | Demosthenes |
| Praec. Ger. Reip. | Praecepta Gerendae Reipublicae |

*Polybios (Polyb.)*

| | |
|---|---|
| Hist. | Historia |

*Pseudepigrapha*

| | |
|---|---|
| Ar. | Letter of Aristeas |
| G. Th. | Gospel of Thomas |
| Jub. | Jubilees |
| Jos. and As. | Jospeh and Aseneth |
| I. Macc. | I. Maccabees |
| II. Macc | II. Maccabees |
| Sib. Or. | Sybelline Oracle |

*Rabbinic Sources*

| | |
|---|---|
| b. Yeb. | Talumd Bavli Yebamoth |
| b. Kid. | Talmud Bavli Kidushin |
| b. Shab. | Talmud Bavli Shabbath |
| G.R. | Genesis Rabbah |
| K.R. | Kohelet Rabbah |
| m. Kid. | Mishna Kidushin |
| t. Kid | Tosephta Kidushin |
| Yalq. Shim. Numb. | Yalqut Shimoni on Numbers |

*Seneca the Elder*

| | |
|---|---|
| Contr. | Controversiae |

*Seneca the Younger (Sen.)*

| | |
|---|---|
| Cons. Helv. | Consolatio ad Helviam Matrem |
| Cons. Marc. | Consolatio ad Marciam |
| Cons. Pol. | Consolatione ad Polybium |
| De Brev. Vit. | De Brevitate Vitae |
| De Clem. | De Clementia |
| De Tranq. Anim. | De Tranquillitate Animi |
| De Vita Beat. | De Vita Beata |
| Div. Claud. Apocol. | Divii Claudii Apocolocyntosis |
| Ep. | Epistulae (morales) |
| N.Q. | Naturales Quaestiones |
| Oct. | Octavia |
| Prov. | De Providentia |

*Stobaeus*

| | |
|---|---|
| Anth. | Anthologion |
| Flor. | Florilegium |

*Strabo*

| | |
|---|---|
| Geogr. | Geographica |

*Suetonius (Suet.)*

| | |
|---|---|
| Aug. | Divus Augustus |
| Claud. | Divus Claudius |

Tib.                      Tiberius

*Tacitus (Tac.)*
Agr.                      Agricola
An.                       Annales
Hist.                     Historiae

*Pompeius Trogus*
Hist. Phil.               Historia Philippicae

*Vergilus (Verg.)*
Aen.                      Aeneis

*Xenophon (Xen.)*

# Introduction

> "Identity emerges as a kind of unsettled space,
> or an unresolved question in that space, be-
> tween a number of intersecting discourses.
> My purpose is to mark some of those points
> of intersection, especially around the question
> of cultural identity, and to explore them in
> relation to the subject of ethnicity in politics"
> S. Hall, Ethnicity 339.

This book is concerned with the ways in which Philo constructed Jewish identity and culture in first-century Alexandria. It deals with questions such as: what made Philo a Jew in his own eyes? Where did he draw boundaries between "us" and "them"? Furthermore, which features of cultural life did Philo distinguish as Jewish? What was for him a Jewish cultural discourse? All of these questions are patently modern. They derive from relatively recent theories and are closely related to a burgeoning literature on ethnic identity and nationhood. In an age which has witnessed both the collapse of seemingly stable categories and the re-emergence of hitherto obsolete ethnicities, questions of identity and culture naturally impose themselves. In Israel in particular such issues cannot be avoided by anyone consciously trying to understand his or her life in a wider intellectual context. Recent discussions, however, have often been informed by the specific conditions of modernity, such as printing, industrialisation and the nation-state.[1] This leads us to question their relevance to situations other than modern; to ascertain whether they apply exclusively to our own age or not. Close investigation does in fact reveal that modern scholarship has developed some theoretical categories which do transcend their particular time and are extremely useful for

---

[1] This is especially true for the so-called "modernist" school which has stressed the uniqueness of modern nationalism and its intrinsic connection to the conditions of modernity, see: E. Gellner, *Nations and Nationalism* (Oxford 1983); idem, *Culture, Identity, and Politics* (Cambridge 1987); B. Anderson, *Imagined Communities. Reflections on the Origin and Spread of Nationalism* (London 1991, 2nd revised ed.); for a systematic criticism of this approach, see: A. Hastings, *The Construction of Nationhood. Ethnicity, Religion and Nationalism* (Cambridge 1997); R. Poole, *Nation and Identity* (London and New York 1999) 18–23; D. McCrone, *The Sociology of Nationalism. Tomorrow's ancestors* (London and New York 1998) 1–21; see also: A.D. Smith, *The Ethnic Origins of Nations* (Oxford 1986), who emphasized the significant continuity between concepts of ethnicity in the past and notions of nationhood in the present.

a proper understanding of periods other than modern. They throw new light on Philo and uncover aspects of his writings hitherto overlooked.

The theoretical models underlying the present study concern the idea that identity and culture are social constructs. Benedikt Anderson has stressed the constructed nature of collective identity in his felicitous and by now famous phrase that a nation "is an imagined political community" which is rooted in large cultural systems.[2] As some commentators have noted, Anderson's definition implies an approval of national communities which are seen as products of positive intellectual creativity.[3] Each community is thought to be constituted in its own particular way. It can be distinguished from others by its rather unique form of creating both a sense of belonging and difference. Anderson assigned to written texts in vernacular languages a crucial role in the emergence of imagined communities. This type of literature creates in his view the necessary forum for addressing potential members and shaping their collective self-awareness (25–46). These theoretical notions are sufficiently general to be helpful in thinking about related issues in pre-modern societies as well. The creative role of texts in forming a public discourse about national identity and culture can, it seems, be investigated in most historical contexts. Anderson's own analysis of historical material, on the other hand, is highly problematic and leaves the reader without specific guidelines for further study.[4] Such guidelines may be gleaned from the works of scholars who have described general features of constructing ethnic identity and culture: Frederik Barth and Clifford Geertz.[5]

Barth stressed in a seminal paper that the decisive factor defining ethnic identity is the group's subjective sense of itself as belonging together and differing from others. He made scholars sensitive to the fact that "objective" criteria – such as geography, language and physical characteristics – do not by themselves constitute ethnicity. They only become relevant in so far as they are chosen by the group as ethnic markers. What ultimately matters is their symbolic value and not their physical existence. Barth therefore warned that com-

---

[2] Anderson, Imagined Communities 6, the cultural roots of these imagined communities are discussed ibid, 9–36; see also: Gellner, Culture, Identity, and Politics 6–17, who adopts with some qualifications Renan's voluntarist notion of a nation as involving a "daily plebiscite"; Hastings, Construction of Nationhood 26–7.

[3] See especially: Poole, Nation and Identity 10–11, 18.

[4] Anderson, Imagined Communities 47–65, argued that the South American Creole population created for the first time authentic concepts of nationhood, which were later phenomenologically repeated in Europe; this argument has rightly been criticized by Hastings, Construction of Nationhood 10–11.

[5] F. Barth, Introduction, in: idem (ed.), *Ethnic Groups and Boundaries. The Social Organization of Culture Difference* (Oslo/London 1969) 9–38; C. Geertz, *The Interpretation of Cultures. Selected Essays* (New York 1973) 33–54; see also: J. Assmann, *Das Kulturelle Gedächtnis. Schrift, Erinnerung und politische Identität in frühen Hochkulturen* (München 1992) 130–60.

ponents of ethnic identity must not be imposed from outside upon any group. A procedure which relies on "objective" and thus external factors only reflects the onlooker's perspective, while missing the real sense of community which holds the group together. Scholars truly wishing to understand identity therefore have to acknowledge the standards set by the group itself. Relativity and subjectivity have to be accepted. Apparently negligible differences may thus reveal themselves to be major dividing lines between groups. Seemingly substantial differences, on the other hand, may prove irrelevant to the group's self-awareness.

Barth furthermore identified certain strategies of constructing and maintaining identity. In his view the "Other" always plays a crucial and primary role. Barth did not refer by this term to the objective reality of other societies and states surrounding a given group. He rather suggested that a sense of collective self-awareness always emerges against the background of an imagined Other who is contrasted to one's own group.[6] Constructing the Other thus involves defining oneself. This may be done by pointing to a diametrical opposition between "us" and "them".[7] It may also take the form of describing semi-permeable boundaries which allow for certain similarities besides decisive differences. These types of boundaries, ranging from completely impervious to barely visible ones, are especially relevant in the context of multi-ethnic societies. Contacts between various groups are not only unavoidable here, but represent a part of daily life which is taken for granted or even welcomed. Ethnicity is in such a context constructed by distinguishing specialized tasks and particular social roles which are considered appropriate for "us", but not for Others.

Geertz's approach to culture is informed by a similar emphasis on the symbolic meaning which a group attributes to certain aspects of its environment. Following Max Weber, he defined culture as "webs of significance" which man has created for himself.[8] Understanding culture thus involves a search for socially established structures of meaning and signification. As Geertz put it, we are not concerned with the closing and opening of the eye, but with the winks that are potentially conveyed by such eye movements. Culture emerges as an interpretative framework which renders man's action meaningful and makes communication with others possible. It creates a public forum in which messages are exchanged and broader structures of significance attributed to specific human action. These social constructs provide man with crucial guidelines

---

[6] E. H. Erikson, *Identity. Youth and Crisis* (New York 1968); idem, *Childhood and Society* (New York 1950, 2nd. rev. ed. 1963), suggested a similar dynamics on the level of the individual.

[7] S. L. Gilman, *Difference and Pathology. Stereotypes of Sexuality, Race, and Madness* (Ithaca and London 1985), has shown that the construction of the Other is not only instrinsic to any formation of identity, but often goes so far as attributing pathological and abnormal qualities to the Other, which implicitly suggest the healthiness and normative values of one's own group.

[8] Geertz, Interpretation of Cultures 5.

without which his life would make no sense. Geertz indeed argued that human life would be unlivable without symbolic structures of meaning. These replace in his view the encompassing genetic codes with which animals are endowed, whose behaviour is largely determined from birth. Culture can thus be understood as an acquired code which has become as natural as inborn directives. This sense of naturalness is achieved by establishing a correspondence between the particular lifestyle of a group and a transcendental order rooted in the world as a whole. The formation of man's character in accordance with the specific customs of his nation is interpreted as an adjustment to larger, overall structures of meaning embedded in the universe. It is precisely the function of culture to draw that connection between the particular and the general, thus rendering man's life and customs meaningful on a much broader level.

The relationship between ethnic identity and culture is complex. Various interpretations have been offered. Often culture is seen as the driving force of national awareness. From this viewpoint, cultural distinction initially exists and then seeks self-expression in nationhood.[9] Anthony Smith distanced himself from this approach and suggested more cautiously that ethnic, and subsequently national groups, define themselves partly by cultural components.[10] Among the constructs which serve to define them is a myth of origin, a shared history with generally acknowledged heroes and a distinctive culture. Cultural components are in his view closely connected to the formation of ethnic identity, but do not precede it. Barth has taken a more radical view and criticized the very notion of culture engendering ethnic identity. He thinks that the relationship between cause and effect is precisely the other way round: identity comes first, culture second.[11] The latter results from the political and social choices which have previously been made in the context of defining the group's identity. There is, in other words, no culture without a specific ethnic context. The ways in which a group sets itself apart from others informs both its way of life and the meaning it attributes to its environment. Barth's approach seems to be correct. It is obvious that the emergence of culture cannot be divorced from the question of who we are. The politics and sociology of identity necessarily play a formative role in creating structures of meaning. As Stuart Hall has aptly formulated it:[12]

---

[9] See especially: Gellner, Nations and Nationalism 8–38; idem, Culture, Identity, and Politics 12–3.

[10] Smith, Origins of Nations 21–46.

[11] Barth, Introduction 11. This argument has provoked considerable controversy. In Jewish studies it has been the one element of Barth's theory which has been rejected even by those who generally applied his model, see especially: S. Stern, *Jewish Identity in Early Rabbinic Writings* (Leiden 1994 = Arbeiten zur Geschichte des antiken Judentums und des Urchristentums 23) 135–8; S. J. D. Cohen, *The Beginnings of Jewishness. Boundaries, Varieties, Uncertainties* (Berkeley 1999) 5–6.

[12] S. Hall, Ethnicity: Identity and Difference, in: G. Eley and R. G. Suny (eds.), *Becoming National. A Reader* (New York 1996) 347.

There is no way ... in which people of the world can act, can speak, can create ... can begin to reflect on their own experience unless they come from some *place* ... You have to position yourself *somewhere* in order to say anything at all. Thus, we cannot do without that sense of our own positioning that is connoted by the term ethnicity.

Constructs of ethnic identity must therefore be studied before culture can be properly appreciated. Culture indeed needs to be understood in the overall context of identity. Its importance, however, must not therefore be underestimated. As Ross Poole put it:[13]

If, as Renan argued, the existence of a nation is the 'daily plebiscite', then it is the national culture which secures the votes.

The notion of identity and culture as social constructs furthermore attributes a significant role to historical circumstances. If the idea of objective, stable identity and premordial culture is abandoned, relativity must be acknowledged. We must then accept the fact that concepts of identity and culture are constantly undergoing change. They are in a permanent flow and respond to the changing circumstances of history. The nature and outcome of a group's "daily plebiscite" naturally depend on the conditions of the day. Hall therefore rightly spoke about the construction of difference as "a never finished process" taking place in the changing narratives we tell about ourselves.[14]

These theoretical approaches to identity and culture provide new perspectives on Philo of Alexandria. They initially draw our attention to the fact that the views which transpire in his writings are constructs. They are the result of the author's creative imagination and particular choices, rather than a reflection of given facts. His discussions on Jewish identity and culture can therefore not be understood by reference to external criteria, such as the Bible and rabbinic literature. They must instead be appreciated by asking what made Philo a Jew in his own eyes. Where, in other words, did he himself decide to draw boundaries between "us" and "them"? Who were for him significant Others from whom he distinguished the characteristic features of being Jewish? Furthermore, what was for him a Jewish cultural discourse? How did he make sense of the specific customs of his people in a broader context of meaning?

Philo's views on Jewish identity and culture must moreover be appreciated as social constructs which have emerged under particular and changing circumstances. Neither internal stability nor detachment from the environment can be assumed. We must instead acknowledge that Philo wrote for a specific audience whom he addressed in terms meaningful at the time. His works had a definite

---

[13] Poole, Nation and Identity 35.

[14] Hall, Ethnicity 345; see also: idem, Cultural Identity and Diaspora, in: J. Rutherford (ed.), *Identity. Community, Culture, Difference* (London 1990) 222–37, where he discusses in a highly illuminating way the changing and creative constructions of Jamaican/Black identity in contemporary cinema.

social context and were grounded in contemporary concerns.[15] Philo himself moreover developed and changed in the course of his life, switching emphases as he encountered new circumstances. Justice must be done to these changes as far as the often undatable sources allow.[16] This holds especially true for Philo's construction of Jewish identity. In this area we can often distinguish significant developments both on external and internal grounds. These must be understood against the background of contemporary events.

Focusing on the immediate context of Philo's work leads us to a hitherto overlooked component: Rome. While her influence has increasingly been acknowledged regarding Palestinian figures, such as Herod, Josephus and Luke, it has thus far been neglected in the case of Philo.[17] To be sure, Philo's works have previously been analysed with a view to Roman rule. Yet such studies tended to concentrate almost exclusively on the *Legatio* and *In Flaccum* which were used as sources for the history of the Jews under Roman rule.[18] Rome's

---

[15] See also: G.E. Sterling, 'The School Of Sacred Laws': The Social Setting Of Philo's Treatises, *Vigiliae Christianae* 53.2 (1999) 148–64, who has suggested a useful reconstruction of some aspects of Philo's social environment.

[16] The chronology of Philo's works is notoriously difficult to settle and has been the subject of much scholarly controversy, see especially the divergent views of L. Cohn, Einleitung und Chronologie der Schriften Philos, *Philologus Suppl. Bd.* 7 (1899) 387–435, and L. Massebieau and E. Bréhier, Essai sur la chronologie de la vie et des oeuvres de Philon, *RHR* 53 (1906) 25–64, 164–85, 267–89. I have made no attempt to identify a specific order of works, but have relied on more limited and secure indications, such as Philo's reference to his old age in the opening of the *Legatio* (Leg. 1).

[17] Regarding Herod, see: J. Geiger, Herod and Rome: New Aspects, in: I.M. Gafni *et al.* (eds.), *The Jews in the Hellenistic-Roman World. Studies in Memory of Menahem Stern* (Jerusalem 1996) 133–45; regarding Josephus, see: M. Goodman, Josephus as Roman Citizen, in: F. Parente and J. Sievers (eds.), *Josephus and the History of the Greco-Roman Period. Essays in Memory of Morton Smith* (Leiden 1994) 329–38; M. Goodman, The Roman Identity of Roman Jews, in: Gafni, The Jews in the Hellenistic-Roman World 85–99; G. Haaland, Jewish Laws for a Roman Audience: Toward an Understanding of Contra Apionem in: J.U. Kalms and F. Siegert (eds.), *Internationales Josephus-Kolloquium Brüssel 1998* (Münster 1999 = MJSt4) 282–304; J.M.G. Barclay, Judaism in Roman Dress: Josephus' Tactics in the *Contra Apionem*, in: J.U. Kalms (ed.), *Internationales Josephus-Kolloquium Aarhus 1999* (Münster 2000 = MJSt 6) 231–45; regarding Luke, see: D.R. Schwartz, On Luke-Acts and Jewish-Hellenistic Historiography, unpublished paper based on a lecture delivered at the European Conference of the SBL (Lausanne 1997); M. Goodman, Jewish History and Roman History: Changing Methods and Preoccupations, in: A. Oppenheimer (ed.), *Jüdische Geschichte in hellenistisch-römischer Zeit. Wege der Forschung: Vom alten zum neuen Schürer* (München 1999 = Schriften des Historischen Kollegs. Kolloquien 44) 75–83, has generally emphasized the importance of Rome for a proper understanding of Jewish affairs during the Second Temple Period, without, however, specifically analyzing Philo in this context.

[18] See especially: E.M. Smallwood, *Philonis Alexandrini Legatio ad Gaium* (Leiden 1970); eadem, *The Jews under Roman Rule* (Leiden 1981); M. Hadas-Lebel, L'évolution de l'image de Rome auprès des Juifs en deux siècles de relations judéo-romaines –164 à + 70, *ANRW* II.20.2 (1987) 784–812, who makes very useful comments on Philo's pro-Roman position; in the past, however, Rome's presence was seen to be so oppressive that Philo had to become subversive and write in a political code which would escape Roman attention, see:

impact on Philo's overall ideas, on the other hand, has not yet become the subject of scholarly attention.[19] Even Koen Goudriaan, in his otherwise highly convincing and important study of Philo's "ethnical strategies" has overlooked this aspect.[20] The presence of Rome, however, is absolutely vital for a proper understanding of Philo's Jewish identity. This is so, because Egypt profoundly changed after Augustus' conquest which turned the country into a Roman province.[21] Direct Roman rule installed a new administration which significantly shaped the political, social, economic and cultural life of Egypt. Rome left an immediate imprint on the country, playing a substantial role in defining everybody's identity. Some Jews had already under Caesar become Roman *amicii* in Egyptian politics.[22] Others may have shared the greater reservation of

---

E.R. Goodenough, *The Politics of Philo Judaeus. Practice and Theory* (New Haven 1938) 21–41; while this interpretation has from the beginning been criticized (see especially: A.H.M. Jones, *JThS* 40 (1939) 182–5; and A. Momigliano, *JRS* 34 (1944) 163–5, it is now revived by J.G. Kahn, La Valeur et la Légimité des Activités politiques d'après Philon d'Alexandrie, *Méditerranées* 16 (1998) 117–27.

[19] Indicative of this trend is the fact that the *ANRW* series, which explores Rome's influence in culture, religion, literature and politics, deals only with Philo's political connections to Rome (*ANRW* II.21.1 (1984) 417–533). R. Barraclough, Philo's Politics. Roman Rule and Hellenistic Judaism, *ANRW* II.21.1 (1984) 417–553, even distinguishes between Roman rule and Hellenistic Judaism, treating all cultural and philosophical issues under the category of Hellenism as distinct from Rome. B. Schaller, Philo, Josephus und das sonstige griechisch-sprachige Judentum in *ANRW* und weiteren neueren Veröffentlichungen, *Theologische Rundschau* 59 (1994) 205, rightly criticized Barraclough for ignoring the connection between Philo's politics and his philosophy. A similar lack of attention to Philo's Roman context is visible in two other surveys: C. Mondésert, Philo of Alexandria, in: W. Horbury *et al.* (eds.), *The Cambridge History of Judaism* (Cambridge 1999) 3:877–900; J. Morris, The Jewish Philosopher Philo, in: E. Schürer, *The History of the Jewish People in the Age of Jesus Christ (175 B.C.-A.D.135) new engl. version rev. and ed. by G. Vermes, F. Millar and M. Goodman* (Edinburgh 1987) 3.2:817, briefly mentions Philo's position as a "well-born provincial with Roman citizenship" without, however, drawing further conclusions for his works and ideas.

[20] K. Goudriaan, Ethnical Strategies in Graeco-Roman Egypt, in: P. Bilde *et al.* (eds.), *Ethnicity in Hellenistic Egypt* (Aarhus 1992) 74–99. Goudriaan himself admits the anachronism implied in his exclusive consideration of Hellenistic circumstances under the Ptolemies (ibid. 80), without, however, being aware of its serious consequences.

[21] For a historical account of Augustus' victory at Actium and subsequent conquest of Alexandria as well as Egypt, see: Ch. Pelling, The triumviral Period, in: *CAH* (Cambridge 1996, 2nd ed.) 10:54–67; regarding the immediate and deep influence of Rome on the new province, see: A.K. Bowman, Egypt, *CAH* (2nd ed.) 10:676–702; idem and D. Rathbone, Cities and Administration in Roman Egypt, *JRS* 82 (1992) 107–27; M. Sartre, *L'Orient Romain. Provinces et sociétés provinciales en Méditerranée orientale d'Auguste aux Sévères (31 avant J.-C. – 235 après J.-C.)* (Paris 1991) 411–3; N. Lewis, "Greco-Roman Egypt": Fact or Fiction?, *Proc. XII. Intern. Congr. Pap.* (Toronto 1970 = ASP 7) 6–11; idem, The Romanity of Roman Egypt: a Growing Consensus, *Atti XVII Congr. Intern. Pap.* (Naples 1984) 1077–84; A. Stein, *Untersuchungen zur Geschichte und Verwaltung Aegyptens unter Römischer Herrschaft* (Stuttgart 1915) 119–31; V. Tcherikover in collab. with A. Fuks, *CPJ* (1957) 1:48–93.

[22] According to Josephus, Antipater supported Caesar's war in Egypt. He was rewarded by Roman *amicitia*, citizenship and exemption from taxes (A.J. 14:127–39; Contr. Ap. 2:58–60). It must stressed that H. Fuchs, *Der Geistige Gegenstand gegen Rom* (Berlin 1938) 62

many Alexandrians, such as Timagenes, who continued to admire Alexander the Great and believe in his superiority over Rome.[23]

Described by Josephus as a "man held in the highest honour, brother of Alexander the Alabarch and no novice in philosophy" (A.J. 18:259), Philo belonged to the rich provincial elite of the Greek East with whom the Romans entertained close political and cultural contacts.[24] Philo was probably a Roman citizen.[25] This would have been such a natural part of his status that he, like Plutarch, did not even bother to mention it.[26] Josephus' praise of Philo as ἀνὴρ τὰ πάντα ἔνδοξος furthermore suggests that he was successful in public affairs. He himself complained that his intellectual work had too often been interrupted by "civil cares" in which he seems to have been involved as a community leader (Spec. 3:3). This kind of complaint surely refers to regular political activity before Philo's participation towards the end of his life in the embassy to Gaius.[27] It indicates that he led the life typical of Greek intellectuals in the Roman empire. Nicolaus of Damascus, Plutarch and others characteristically divided their time between political responsibilities, philosophical conversations and their own research and writing.[28] They also entertained close

---

and *passim*, was fundamentally wrong in assuming that "das jüdische Volk hatte in der Zähigkeit, mit der es die Feindschaft gegen die Römer bei sich lebendig hielt, nirgends im Reiche seinesgleichen".

[23] Regarding Alexandrian views of Rome, see especially: P. M. Fraser, The Alexandrine View of Rome, *Bull. Soc. Arch. Alex.* 42 (1967) 1–16; R. Mac Mullen, Nationalism in Roman Egypt, *Aegyptus* 44.3–4 (1964) 179–99; for details on Timagenes, see below chapter five. Augustus' refusal to restore the Alexandrian *boule* certainly caused disappointment among the Alexandrians, see: *CPJ* no. 150; G. W. Bowersock, *Augustus and the Greek World* (Oxford 1965) 90.

[24] On the well-known Roman policy of supporting the local elites of the East and ruling through them, either directly in the framework of a provincial government or indirectly as "friends and associates", see: Bowersock, Augustus 1–13, 30–41; M. Goodman, *The Roman World. 44 BC – AD 180* (London 1997) 138–9; E. S. Gruen, *The Hellenistic World and the Coming of Rome* (Berkeley 1984) 1:54–95.

[25] On Roman policy regarding citizenship, see: A. N. Sherwin-White, *The Roman Citizenship* (Oxford 1973 2d ed.) 291–306; F. Vittinghoff, Römische Kolonisation und Bürgerrechtspolitik unter Caesar und Augustus *Ak. d. Wiss. u. Lit., Abhandl. Geist. u. Soz. Wiss. Kl.* (1951) 1217–1366; regarding Philo's Roman citizenship, see: G. Sterling, *The Jewish Plato. Philo of Alexandria, Greak speaking Judaism, and Christian Origins* (forthcoming) chap. one. J. Schwartz, Note sur la Famille de Philon d'Alexandrie, in: *Mélanges Isidore Lévy* (Bruxelles 1955 = *Annuaire de l'Institut de Philologie et d'Histoire Orientales et Slaves 13*) 591–602; idem, L'Egypte de Philon, in: *Philon d'Alexandrie. Colloques Nationaux du Centre National de la Recherche Scientifique* (Paris 1967) 38, 43; and the recent discussion of Schwartz' arguments by Barraclough, Politics 440–1.

[26] On Plutarch's reticence in this respect, see: C. P. Jones, *Plutarch and Rome* (Oxford 1971) 45.

[27] See also: Massebieau, Chronologie 35; E. R. Goodenough, Philo and Public Life, *JEA* 12.1–2 (1926) 77–9; *contra* Cohn, Einleitung 427.

[28] Regarding Nicolaus and Plutarch, see especially: B. Z. Wacholder, *Nicolaus of Damascus* (Berkeley 1962) 14–36; Jones, Plutarch 13–47.

friendships with the Roman elite of the empire, forming their ideas and identities in relation to these *amicii*. Philo's family background, wealth and education perfectly qualified him for a similar position. He may have counted among his friends Seneca the Younger who was related to a governor of Egypt and spent in his youth time in the province. The families of the two men belonged to the same social milieu and are likely to have known each other. Philo may have met Seneca already in Egypt and then again in Rome when he came there on his embassy to Gaius.[29]

The encounter between Rome and the Greek East is highly meaningful to a proper understanding of Philo's life and work. His views will often be found to correspond to those of other Eastern intellectuals who had been similarly brought up and then become involved in Roman affairs. In the present study of Philo this context has been carefully taken into account. The first section of the book, which deals with his construction of Jewish identity pays particular attention to the contemporary Roman discourse as reflected in the Greek East. The impact of Rome on political, social and cultural matters has in each instance been considered as an explanation for Philo's particular choice of boundaries. The way in which he constructed Jewish descent, significant Others and distinctly Jewish values are interpreted in light of contemporary Roman concerns. Changing circumstances, such as the crisis under Gaius, have furthermore provided important clues as to the developments of Philo's ethnic self-awareness. The second section of the book investigates how Philo's sense of identity translates into cultural structures. We examine here which distinctive activities, commitments and attitudes emerge from Philo's construction of ethnicity. More importantly, the characteristic features of Jewish life are analyzed with a view to the overarching meaning which he attributes to them. We shall see how he rooted Jewish customs in deeper structures of meaning which were in his view embedded in the overall order of the universe.

Philonic texts are not studied here as reflections of a given reality, but as creative constructions of an individual writer. They are understood as a means of communication aimed at shaping the identity and cultural awareness of potential readers. Philo imagined a community and outlined its features as he saw fit under the circumstances of his time. His narrative is evocative and meant to engender a certain mind-set among the elitist Jews who were his primary audience.[30] Philo's voice is distinct and to some extent even unique. It

---

[29] So far the connection between the two thinkers has been investigated from a purely philosophical perspective. Scholars tended to argue either for their dependence on a mutual source or for Seneca's dependence on Philo whose ideas he got to know when the latter came to Rome, see: H. Baumgarten, Vitam brevem esse, longam artem. Das Proömium der Schrift Senecas *De brevitate vitae*, *Gymnasium* 77 (1970) 299–323; G. Scarpat, Cultura ebreo-ellenistica e Seneca, *RB* 13.1 (1965) 3–30.

[30] For the most part Philo, as well as other Hellenistic Jews, wrote for a Jewish audience. His work must therefore be appreciated for its message in this context, rather than as

cannot be taken as representative of others and certainly not as typical of the whole Greek-speaking diaspora.[31] His constructs of identity and culture must instead be appreciated against the background of a considerable variety of Jewish positions in Egypt.[32] Despite the enormous loss of primary sources, some of this diversity can still be reconstructed from the extant works. Philo's failure to specify the names of other Jewish writers does not mean that he wrote his treatises without them in mind. Artapanus, for example, is an important point of reference. Even though his work survived only in most fragmentary form, we can see that his views were widely divergent from those of Philo. It indeed seems that Philo formulated at least some of his ideas in direct response to those expressed by Artapanus.[33] Philo's position on Jewish identity and culture can thus be fully appreciated only in the context of a vibrant and diverse community which formed many opinions on the burning issues of the day.

The specific objectives of the present book can further be clarified by distinguishing them from other approaches which have thus far prevailed in the study of Philo. It is from the outset conspicuous that my insistence on the connection between ideas and social realities sets this book apart from those primarily concerned with theological and philosophical perspectives on Philo. It is until now customary to appreciate him in the context of philosophical schools and to treat his ideas as detached *theologoumena*.[34] His writings tend to be discussed

---

apologetics for an outside world; see also: V. Tcherikover, Jewish Apologetic Literature Reconsidered, *Eos* 48.3 (1956); E. S. Gruen, *Heritage and Hellenism. The Reinvention of Jewish Tradition* (Berkeley 1998) XIII–XX. For a more detailed analysis of texts which have traditionally been taken to address a foreign audience, see below, especially chapter one.

[31] *Contra* G. E. Sterling, Recherché or Representative? What is the Relationship between Philo's Treatises and Greek-speaking Judaism", *SPhA* 11 (1999) 1–30; idem, Recluse or Representative? Philo and Greek-Speaking Judaism beyond Alexandria, *SBLSP* (1995) 595–616. Sterling's conclusion is problematic, because it is based on a too narrow sample of rather general ideas.

[32] The diversity of Ancient Judaism in general has been emphasized especially by V. Tcherikover, Apologetic Literature 185–6; A. T. Kraabel, The Roman Diaspora: Six Questionable Assumptions, *JJS* 33.1–2 (1982) 453–4; and with regard to Egypt especially by M. Pucci Ben Zeev, New Perspectives on the Jewish-Greek Hostilities in Alexandria During the Reign of Emperor Caligula, *JSJ* 21 (1990) 234–5. One of the Jewish groups which have recently been discussed as potentially important actors in Egypt are the Jews of Leontopolis. By the time of Philo, however, they seem to have lost their significance. For divergent interpretations of their role, see: E. S. Gruen, The Origins and Objectives of Onias' Temple, *SCI* 16 (1997 = Studies in Memory of Abraham Wasserstein) 47–70; D. R. Schwartz, The Jews of Egypt between the Temple of Onias, the Temple in Jerusalem, and Heaven (Hebrew), *Zion* 62.1 (1997) 5–22; G. Bohak, *Joseph and Aseneth and the Jewish Temple in Heliopolis* (Atlanta 1996 = *SBL* Early Judaism and its Literature 10).

[33] For details on Artapanus in comparison to Philo, see especially below chapters two, six and seven.

[34] See e.g. the recent article by D. T. Runia, Philo of Alexandria and the Greek *Hairesis*-Model, *Vigiliae Christianae* 53.2 (1999) 117–47. The over-emphasis on religion in the study of Ancient Judaism has been criticized before, see especially: Tcherikover, Apologetic Literature, 186–93; Kraabel, Roman Diaspora 454–56; J. M. G. Barclay, *Jews in the Mediterra-*

by reference to abstract ideas and as a form of "ism". All too often they have been interpreted as a spiritualization of Judaism, which severed national ties and thus became a kind of *preparatio evangelica*.[35] Even Alan Mendelson's important monograph on Philo's Jewish identity ultimately takes recourse to theological categories.[36] While social reality has sometimes been taken into account, as for example in the discussion of Philo's attitude towards the Egyptians,[37] Mendelson overall relies on the categories of "orthodoxy" and "orthopraxy". He argues that Philo's Jewish identity should be understood as a form of orthodox belief and praxis. These terms, however, are patently anachronistic. They presuppose the existence of mainstream orthodoxy and a form of Jewish dogma analogous to that of the Christian Church. Daniel Boyarin and others have recently shown that such categories developed only in subsequent centuries in rabbinic circles.[38] Their application to a writer living prior to that period inevitably incurs distortions.

My emphasis on Philo's individual construction of Jewish identity and culture furthermore removes the present study from numerous other investigations into his Jewishness. The latter have characteristically taken external criteria as their point of departure. The Hebrew Bible and rabbinic literature served in this context as decisive points of reference. If and to the extent that Philo's views could be interpreted as conforming to these corpuses of Classical Jewish literature, they were identified as proper Jewish concepts.[39] In cases, however, where

---

*nean Diaspora. From Alexander to Trajan (323 BCE – 117 CE)* (Edinburgh 1996) 402–13, with regard to Philo, however, the author takes recourse to rather more traditional categories 163–80, 406.

[35] See recently: N. Umemoto, Juden, "Heiden" und das Menschengeschlecht in der Sicht Philons von Alexandria, in: R. Feldmeier und U. Heckel (eds.), *Die Heiden: Juden, Christen und das Problem des Fremden*, (Tübingen 1994 = WUNT 70) 22–51.

[36] A. Mendelson, *Philo's Jewish Identity* (Atlanta 1988 = Brown Judaic Studies 161); Mendelson's views have been adopted with minor modifications by G. Graesholt, Philo of Alexandria. Some Typical Traits of his Jewish Identity, *Classica et Mediaevalia* 43 (1992) 97–110.

[37] Mendelson, Identity 35–7, 116–22.

[38] D. Boyarin, *Making a Difference: How Christianity created Judaism*, forthcoming at Stanford University Press; idem, A Tale of Two Synods: Nicea, Javneh, and Ecclesiology, *Exemplaria* 12.1 (2000) 21–62; idem, Justin Martyr invents Judaism, forthcoming in the *Journal of Church History*; M. Goodman, The Function of Minim in Early Rabbinic Judaism, in: H. Cancik, H. Lichtenberger, P. Schäfer (eds.), *Geschichte – Tradition – Reflexion. Festschrift für Martin Hengel zum 70. Geburtstag* (Tübingen 1996) 1:501–10; N. Janowitz, Rabbis and their Opponents: The Construction of the "Min" in Rabbinic Anecdotes, *Journal for Early Christian Studies* 6.3 (1998) 449–62; Barclay, Mediterranean Diaspora 83–88, has similarly criticized the labels "orthodoxy" and "deviation" in the context of Ancient Egyptian Jewry.

[39] See especially: H. A. Wolfson, *Philo. Foundations of Religious Philosophy in Judaism, Christianity, and Islam* (Cambridge MA 1947); N. G. Cohen, *Philo Judaeus. His Universe of Discourse* (Frankfurt 1995), whose approach can be traced back to the work of Z. Frankel and H. Graetz, both of whom were committed to modern orthodoxy and felt ambivalent

a departure from them was recognized, the verdict was clear: Philo succumbed to foreign influence. The paramount foreign influence which has been detected in Philo's work is that of Greek culture. Assuming a diametrical and intrinsic opposition between Judaism and Hellenism, modern scholarship from the late 18th century onwards has regularly conceived of Greek culture as an inevitable threat to Philo's Jewishness.[40] Hellenism has usually been taken to symbolize rationality, aesthetics and universal humanism, while Judaism stood for faith, revealed ethics and national particularism.[41] This archetypal distinction, however, is ultimately rooted in Christian theology which defined itself as a perfect synthesis of these supposed opposites.[42] It is therefore an external impetus which placed Philo in the context of an existential conflict between his respective loyalties to the Greek and the Jewish world. Erich S. Gruen rightly criticized the widespread application of such dichotomies to the study of Greek-speaking Jews:[43]

"Judaism" and "Hellenism" were neither competing systems nor incompatible concepts. It would be erroneous to assume that Hellenization entailed encroachment upon Jewish traditions and erosion of Jewish beliefs. Jews did not face a choice of either assimilation or resistance to Greek culture.

As we have seen above, the present study is not based on external criteria, but searches instead for the factors which Philo himself chose as markers of Jewish identity and culture. It is not his "objective" Jewishness which concerns us here, but his subjective sense of being a Jew and engaging in Jewish culture. This approach allows for considerable complexity. We might, for example, encounter items which were central to Philo's construction of Jewish identity,

---

about Hellenistic Judaism, but nevertheless wished to incorporate it into the "normative" tradition of Judaism; on Frankel and Graetz in this context, see: M. R. Niehoff, Alexandrian Judaism in 19th Century *Wissenschaft des Judentums*: Between Christianity and Modernization, in: Oppenheimer, Jüdische Geschichte 9–28.

[40] For more details, see: Niehoff, Alexandrian Judaism 9–28.

[41] M. Hengel emphazised in his classic study, *Judaism and Hellenism. Studies in their Encounter in Palestine during the Early Hellenistic Period* (London 1974, Germ. orig.) that Judaism and Hellenism constituted opposites which were synthesized by the Jewish reform party in Palestine; see also: M. Hengel, Die Begegnung zwischen Judentum und Hellenismus im Palästina der vorchristlichen Zeit, in: idem, *Judaica et Hellenistica. Kleine Schriften I* (Tübingen 1996) 151–70.

[42] See also: Gruen, Heritage XIV–XVII; M. Goodman, Jewish Attitudes to Greek Culture in the Period of the Second Temple, in: G. Abramson and T. Parfitt (eds.), *Jewish Education and Learning. Published in Honour of Dr. David Patterson on the occasion of his Seventieth Birthday* (Chur 1994) 167–74; J. Goldstein, Jewish Acceptance and Rejection of Hellenism, in: E.P. Sanders *et al.* (eds.), *Jewish and Christian Self-Definition* (London 1981) 2:64–87; Barclay, Mediterranean Diaspora 88–102, 161.

[43] Gruen, Heritage XIV; see also: G.E. Sterling, 'Thus are Israel': Jewish Self-Definition in Alexandria, *SPhA* 7 (1995) 1–18, who emphasized that Greek culture was an integral part of the self-awareness of Alexandrian Jews (he does, however, not go into any details of Philo's particular construction of identity).

yet derived from the point of view of *Traditionsgeschichte* from Greek or Roman culture. Such a situation gives rise to interesting questions concerning ethnic boundaries. It also enhances our awareness of the intricate nature of identity in a multi-ethnic and multi-cultural society, such as first century Alexandria.

Shifting the emphasis away from the supposed dichotomy between Judaism and Hellenism does not imply a total disregard of Greek culture. Neither Philo's own construction of identity nor the impact of Rome can be properly appreciated without recourse to the Greek traditions which Philo both knew and loved.[44] At the same time, however, Greek traditions as such will not be used as criteria for evaluating Philo's sense of identity and culture. They are only taken into account in so far as he himself referred to them and made them relevant. It is highly significant that such references will usually be found to resonate also in the contemporary Roman discourse. It emerges that Philo's active engagement in his contemporary world decisively informed his choice of Greek traditions and his views on the culture as a whole. His construction of Jewish identity and culture are therefore best understood in a broad context which does justice to the multi-ethnic reality of Alexandria. His views thus have to be appreciated not only vis-à-vis Greek culture, but also in relation to the discourse among Romans, Egyptians and other Jews of various political colours.

Finally, the approach of the present book differs sharply from those studies which see in Philo nothing but an apologist. He has all too often been interpreted as a writer who addressed a foreign audience and presented his tradition in a somewhat opportunistic mode. Such assumptions have long been criticized by Victor Tcherikover who, in his seminal article "Apologetic Literature Reconsidered", stressed that the laborious way of reproducing texts in Antiquity, namely by preparing handwritten copies, prevented their spread to a wide and anonymous audience. Each author wrote for his immediate friends and intellectual community. This holds true for Philo as well. Apart from a few specific studies, such as the *Life of Moses*, he does not indicate any awareness, let alone hope, that his readers be anything other than congenial Jews. It is with them in mind that he wrote his treatises and formulated his ideas. These deserve to be taken seriously even today.

---

[44] For details on Philo's attitudes towards Greek culture, see below chapter five.

Part One

# Jewish Identity

# 1. Jewish Descent: Mothers and Mothercities

> "my handmaiden ... is ... an Egyptian by race
> but a Hebrew by her rule of life"    (Abr. 251)

Philo paid attention to descent and made it a crucial factor in his construction of Jewish identity. Common origins, whether real or imagined, defined the Jews as a distinct ethnic group. As Barth and Smith have emphasized, biology and other objective factors matter little in this context.[1] It is instead decisive which places and figures are chosen as meaningful markers of origin. Tracing oneself back to a particular situation in the past becomes a formative part of one's identity. Such roots define one's place in the present and determine the cultural, social, religious and political objectives of the future. The past explains who "we" are and what "we" are destined to do. *Vice versa*, present concerns and experiences are rendered more meaningful by grounding them in bygone times. They are thus provided with a sense of continuity and long-standing value.

By reshaping the past, Philo made an important contribution to the definition of Jewish identity in first century Alexandria. He suggested a new construction of Jewish descent which indicated his particular understanding of Jewish ethnicity. Philo proceeded in two ways, applying both law and myth to distinguish the Jews from their multi-ethnic environment. His discussion of the Jewish mother determined the status of each person wishing to be considered a Jew by birth. His criteria in this respect were more stringent than those of the Bible or other Egyptian Jews. Philo moreover provided a myth of origins for those who could in his view properly identify as Jews. He constructed Jerusalem as a "mother-city" to which he traced the roots of every Jew. These stories of Jewish descent were meant to create a strong sense of community and played an important role in the politics of Jewish identity during the fateful years 38–41 C.E.

The biological mother became for Philo a basic, yet hitherto unrecognized factor in Jewish identity.[2] In this regard Philo was not concerned, as he might

---

[1]  Barth, Introduction; Smith, Ethnic Origin 21–46; for more details, see above Introduction.

[2]  The role of the mother has as yet not been sufficiently explored by feminist scholars, but has been considered by: D. Sly, *Philo's Perception of Women* (Atlanta 1990); J.R. Wegner, Philo's Portrayal of Women – Hebraic or Hellenic?, in: A.-J. Levine (ed.), *"Women like this". New Perspectives on Jewish Women in the Greco-Roman World* (Atlanta 1991) 41–66; S.L. Mattila, Wisdom, Sense Perception, Nature, and Philo's Gender Gradient, *HTR* 89.2 (1996)

theoretically have been, with issues of purity, but instead focused on a mother's civil status.[3] Her Jewishness made the transmission of Jewish status to her children possible, while her Gentile status prevented it. The question of who was a Jew was thus to a considerable extent determined by reference to her. Philo's emphasis on correct lineage furthermore indicates that he saw the Jews as an ethnic group. As far as he was concerned, they were a large family united by a distinct pedigree and common ancestors.

Philo's definition of Jewish identity by reference to maternal pedigree conferred a new status on women who had, as Shaye Cohen has shown, been rendered virtually irrelevant in the patrilineal legislation of the Pentateuch.[4] These matrilineal aspects, however, were introduced within a strictly patriarchal framework which was not generally questioned. Philo even embraced patriarchal principles to the extent that he used Aristotelian biology to prove the father's innate superiority.[5] He argued that the male role in procreation is active, while the

---

103–29; R. S. Kraemer, Monastic Jewish Women in Greco-Roman Egypt: Philo Judaeus on the Therapeutrides, *Signs: Journal of Women in Culture and Society* 14.2 (1989) 342–70.

[3] This is surprising, if one argues, as does D.R. Schwartz, Philo's Priestly Descent, in: F.E. Greenspahn *et al.* (eds.), *Nourished with Peace. Studies in Hellenistic Judaism in Memory of Samuel Sandmel* (Chico 1984) 155–71, that Philo was a priest. The especially stringent nature of the halacha on *post-partem* impurity in the MMT from Qumran has been discussed by Y. Sussman, The History of Halakha and the Dead Sea Scrolls – Preliminary Observations on Miqsat Ma'ase Ha-Torah (4QMMT) (Hebrew), *Tarbiz* 59.1 (1990) 11–76. Sussman identified these regulations with Sadducean halacha – a conclusion which has recently been challenged by M. Kister, Studies in 4QMiqsat Ma'ase Ha-Torah and Related Texts: Law, Theology, Language and Calender (Hebrew), *Tarbiz* 68.3 (1999) 325–30. Philo does not mention Qumranic legislation on purity and even ignores Biblical injunctions concerning post-menstruant women (Lev. 15:19–24). Together with Hippocrates he instead recommended intercourse immediately after the individual termination of the monthly period, those days being considered particularly fertile (Spec. 3:33); cf. Hippocrates, Women's Diseases 1.17 (ed. Littré 8.56–57); idem, The Nature of the Child 15 (ed. Littré 7.494–5); idem, The Eight Months Fetus 13 (ed. Littré 7.458–9).

[4] S.J.D. Cohen, The Origins of the Matrilineal Principle in Rabbinic Law, *AJS Review* 10.1 (1985) 19–53, an updated version of this article can be found in: idem, Jewishness 241–307; see also: idem, Solomon and the Daughter of Pharaoh: Intermarriage, Conversion, and the Impurity of Women, *JANES* 16–17 (1984–5 = Ancient Studies in Memory of Elias Bickerman) 23–37; J. Ch. Exum, *Fragmented Women. Feminist (Sub)Versions of Biblical Narratives* (Sheffield 1993 = JSOT Suppl. Ser. 163) 94–147; *contra* V. Aptowitzer, Spuren des Matriarchats im Jüdischen Schrifttum, *HUCA* 4–5 (1927–8) 207–240, 261–297; L.H. Schiffman, Jewish Identity and Jewish Descent, *Judaism* 34.1 (1985) 78–84.

[5] Philo acquired some biological and medical knowledge as part of his general education, thus continuing a Classical tradition, on which see: W. Jaeger, *Paideia. The Ideals of Greek Culture* (New York 1944, Germ. orig.) 3: 3–45, and anticipating to some extent the typical connection between medicine and philosophy in the Second Sophistic, on which see: G.W. Bowersock, *Greek Sophists in the Roman Empire* (Oxford 1969) 59–75; M. Foucault, *The Care of the Self* (New York 1986 = The History of Sexuality vol. 3) 97–123. Philo acquired considerably more medical knowledge than Ben Sira, who first discussed the physician's place within Jewish theology (Sir. 38: 1–15). His exposure to medical notions was certainly facilitated by the environment of Alexandria which had become the capital of medicine under Herophilus (for more details, see below).

mother fulfills merely the secondary role of a passive and nursing vessel.[6] He even warned her not to regard herself as the "cause of generation", because her part is in reality entirely "passive".[7] This is so, because she is like a field, only receiving the sperm and nourishing it.[8] It was implied that the father's sperm contained all the necessary genes for the later human being. It only required a supporting environment to develop its full potential, and was not actually dependent on maternal genes. A mother's part in procreation consisted of "receiving the seed for safekeeping" (Aet. 69). Philo indeed seems to have agreed with the Classical Greek view that "the mother is not the begetter of that which is called the child, but only the nurse of the newly implanted seed. It is the one who mounts who is the true begetter".[9]

How did a man, who held such views, confer more legal status on the mother and make Jewish identity dependent also on her? For an answer we have to look to the social and cultural reality of Philo's Alexandria. The Romans had established here a new administration which left a particularly manifest impact on the realm of family law.[10] As a leading intellectual and community leader, Philo

---

[6] Regarding the Aristotelian background of this doctrine, see: Aristotle, G.A. (2.1) 732a8–10. On Aristotle's gender biases in his "scientific" work, see: R. J. Hankinson, Philosophy of Science, in: J. Barnes (ed.), *The Cambridge Companion to Aristotle* (Cambridge 1995) 109–39; on the general shortcomings of Hellenistic medicine, which still lacked rigorous and independent experiments, see: P. Green, *Alexander to Actium. The Historical Evolution of the Hellenistic Age* (Berkeley 1990) 480–96. Note that Hippocrates is the only physician whom Philo mentioned by name and praised as an "expert in the processes of nature" (Opif. 124). Yet this tribute to the most famous physician of Antiquity seems to have been largely rhetorical. Philo adopted hardly any of his views and altogether ignored his theories about the womb as well as the pangenesis of the seed, on which see: A. E. Hanson, The Medical Writers' Woman, in: D. M. Halperin *et al.* (eds.), *Before Sexuality. The Construction Of Erotic Experience in the Ancient Greek World* (Princeton 1990) 314–20. Philo probably avoided Hippocrates' overall gynaecological approach, because he lived in Alexandria, where these doctrines had been revised in the influential school of Herophilus, on which see: H. von Staden, *Herophilus. The Art of Medicine in Early Alexandria* (Cambridge 1989) 1–31, 67–88; P. M. Fraser, *Ptolemaic Alexandria* (Oxford 1972) 1.338–76; R. Garland, *The Greek Way of Life. From Conception to Old Age* (New York 1990) 18–105. Philo's remarks on the physician in Agr. 142 indeed suggest his familiarity with Herophilus' work which was famous for its dissections of corpses and even vivisections. Herophilus was so influential that his doctrines left a mark even on the halachic discussions in Palestine, see: M. Bar-Ilan, Medicine in Eretz Israel in the First Centuries C.E. (Hebrew), *Cathedra* 91 (1999) 31–78, J. Geiger, Cleopatra the Physician (Hebrew), *Cathedra* 92 (1999) 193–8.

[7] πάσχουσα (Ebr. 73); see also All. 2.39. Philo characteristically treated mothers in the animal kingdom differently: here, where gender distinctions obviously did not apply, he regarded them precisely as the "cause of generation" (Vir. 134).

[8] Aet. 69, Opif. 14, Ebr. 211 etc. The metaphor of the field for the female body and sexuality was common in Antiquity, for a survey of Classical Greek sources, see: P. duBois, *Sowing the Body* (Chicago 1988) 39–64.

[9] Aeschylus, *Eumenides* 2:658–60 (quoted in Garland, Way of Life 28).

[10] See also: Stein, Untersuchungen 119–31; R. Taubenschlag, Die Geschichte der Rezeption des römischen Privatrechts in Aegypten, in: idem, *Opera Minora* (Warsaw 1959) 1:194–209; J. Modrzejewski, La Règle de droit dans l'Egypte Romaine, Proc. *XII Intern. Congr.*

was highly aware of the details of the Roman administration in Egypt.[11] One of its prominent characteristics was a rigorous segregation of ethnic groups, with each group belonging to a different social class and being taxed at a different rate. Lowest in the Roman scale were the Egyptians, who were charged a heavy poll tax (*laographia*). Metropolitans paid somewhat lower rates, while Greek citizens were altogether exempted. Official affiliation with a particular group thus became a prime concern. Registers were introduced, which not only identified Alexandrian citizens, but also Metropolitans. *Epikrisis* and status declarations, already known under the Ptolemies, became now an all-pervasive practice with considerable financial consequences.[12] Ethnicity and social status became far more decisive than they had been during the Ptolemaic period, when the different national groups had increasingly mingled and identified with the Greco-Egyptian ethos of the Ptolemies.[13] In order to prove affiliation with the upper classes the candidate had to prove that both his mother and his father belonged to that class and that he himself was their legal offspring. The latter pertained, if his parents had been legally married at the time of his birth.[14] At the top level of society civil rights and official marriage were thus linked, while the lower class Egyptians were free to marry whom they wanted, since they had in any case no status to lose. They inevitably formed the third estate and lacked civil rights, whether or not their parents had been formally engaged.

---

*Pap.* (To Pronto 1970) 346; Lewis, "Greco-Roman Egypt" 6–11; Sartre, *Orient* 423–30; Bowman, *Egypt* 676–702; idem and Rathbone, *Cities* 113.

[11] For details on Philo's position as intellectual and community leader vis-à-vis Roman rule, see above Introduction.

[12] Regarding the social tensions caused by the *laographia*, see *CPJ* no. 150 l.1–6, no. 151; *The Gnomon of the Idios Logos* § 43–4 illustrates the kind of frauds which occurred as a consequence of the high social tension; see also: Bowman and Rathbone, *Cities* 120–25; C. A. Nelson, *Status Declarations in Roman Egypt*, *Am. St. Pap.* 19 (Amsterdam 1979); M. Hombert et C. Préaux, *Recherches sur le Recensement dans l'Egypte Romaine* (Leiden 1952); F. Zucker, Verfahrensweisen in der Einführung gewisser Einrichtungen des Augustus in Ägypten, *RIDA* 8 (1961) 155–64.

[13] While S. K. Eddy, *The King is Dead. Studies in the Near Eastern Resistance to Hellenism 334–31 B.C.* (Lincoln 1961) 257–323, stresses the initial aversion of the Egyptians to the Ptolemies, whom they experienced as a foreign and imposed dynasty, he convincingly shows how the new regime became an integral part of Egypt. This change of attitudes among the local population was a gradual process led by the priestly upper-class, who benefitted most from cooperating with the Ptolemies.

[14] This regulation corresponded to the legal practice in Rome, where children of a citizen father and a non-citizen mother were classified as non-citizens. Even if both parents were citizens, but lacked a formal marriage engagement, their children would be considered bastards, see: Gaius, *Inst.* 1:104, 1:55; P. R. C. Weaver, The Status of Children in Mixed Marriages, in: B. Rawson (ed.), *The Family in Ancient Rome. New Perspectives* (New York 1986) 145–47; S. Dixon, *The Roman Family* (Baltimore 1992) 123–30; S. Treggiari, *Roman Marriage. Iusti Coniuges from the Time of Cicero to the Time of Ulpian* (Oxford 1991) 5–13, 43–49. The law in Rome, however, lacked the ethnic implications it carried in Egypt.

The *Gnomon of the Idios Logos*, which provided basic instruction in Roman law for officers in Egypt, indicates the role mothers were assigned in determining status and ethnic affiliation.[15] The *Gnomon* imposed a financial penalty on a Greek citizen or a Syrian who married an Egyptian woman (§ 51).[16] For an Alexandrian freeman it was illegal to marry an Egyptian (§ 49). Roman citizens, on the other hand, as the rulers of the world were permitted such unions. Their offspring, however, remained Egyptian and could make no claims on their father's status.[17] In such cases of intermarriage the mother's status was crucial, but only in a negative or regulating sense. If her status was inferior to that of the father, she prevented her children from inheriting his status. If her status was however superior, she could not transmit it. Paragraph 13 of the *Gnomon* stipulates that the offspring of a citizen mother and a foreigner was not granted citizenship. Rome was similarly stringent regarding the offspring from a citizen mother and an Egyptian (§ 38).[18] The social situation in Egypt was further exacerbated by the fact that Roman soldiers were not allowed to enter a formal marriage during their time of service. They consequently produced numerous illegitimate children, who were declared "fatherless" and considered bastards. They had to pay the poll-tax until their father was released from his military service, which enabled him to marry their mother and adopt his biological children.[19]

The impact of Rome on Egyptian Jewry has been the subject of a prolonged scholarly controversy. Victor Tcherikover established the influential view that

---

[15] The *Gnomon* dates back to Augustan times and has, as far as can be ascertained, not been significantly changed since then, see: Bowman, Egypt 684; E. Seckel und W. Schubart, *Der Gnomon des Idios Logos* (Berlin 1919 = Ägyptische Urkunden aus den staatlichen Museen zu Berlin. Griechische Urkunden V. Band) Teil I, 7. The segregating force of the *Gnomon* has already been noted by its editor, see: W. Schubart, Rom und die Ägypter nach dem Gnomon des Idios Logos, *Zeitschrift für ägyptische Sprache und Altertumskunde* 56 (1920) 80–95.

[16] The degree to which even a secondary union with an Egyptian woman was discouraged can be gathered from the *Gnomon*'s legislation concerning a citizen, who took an Egyptian wife after he had been married to another citizen. Concerning his inheritance, clear priority is given to the offspring from the first union (§ 45).

[17] While § 52 states that "it is allowed for a Roman to marry an Egyptian", § 46 indicates how unattractive such an engagement would be: only if the Roman had married in ignorance of his wife's Egyptian status, would his offspring be able to inherit his status. This regulation clearly assumes that in all other cases, i. e. under normal circumstances when the true status of each partner is known, the offspring follow the Egyptian mother. § 39 is even harsher and stipulates, in contrast to § 46, that even if the marriage was contracted in ignorance of the true status, the children follow the parent of the lower status.

[18] This situation seems to have changed later on. The evidence from the Papyri suggests that the mother could during the 2nd century C.E. transmit her status as a free person even if the father was a slave; see: J. A. Straus, L'esclavage dans l'Égypte Romaine, *ANRW* (1988) II.10.1 878–79.

[19] H. C. Youtie, ΑΠΑΤΟΡΕΣ: Law vs. Custom in Roman Egypt, in: J. Bingen *et al.* (eds.), *Le Monde Grec. Hommages à Claire Préaux* (Bruxelles 1975) 723–40.

the status of the Jews dramatically deteriorated as a result of direct Roman rule.[20] He argued that most of them were no longer considered part of the hitherto large and rather heterogeneous class of "Greeks". Jews were instead counted together with the Egyptians and charged the *laographia*. Generally devoid of citizenship, they became in his view part of the third estate. This situation not only implied a significant financial loss, but also a severe social and political demotion with ethnic connotations. This was the background to the subsequent civil rights battle among the Jews and their violent conflict with the Egyptians who were competing for the same status improvement. This interpretation has never been accepted by Aryeh Kasher and was recently challenged by Erich S. Gruen.[21] The latter highlighted the neglected evidence from the *Acta Isidori* which puts the following revealing statement into Agrippa's mouth: "The Egyptians have taxes levied on them by their rulers ... but none has imposed tributes on the Jews".[22] Yet even if the Jews were not directly implied in the *laographia* and succeeded in maintaining an independent status, they were nevertheless influenced by the increasing social tension under Roman rule.

As an upper-class intellectual Philo was especially sensitive to the new situation. He intensely disliked the lower-class Egyptians and wished to dissociate his own people from them.[23] He asserted the superior standing of the Jews by constructing their descent in a way which conformed to Roman perspectives and policies. In this context the status of the mother began to matter for him. Philo determined that only someone born to a Jewish mother as well as a Jewish father was a Jew by birth. Egyptian mothers, by contrast, would give birth only to Egyptian children, even if the father was Jewish. While the Jewish community of Elephantine might already have assumed some degree of matrilineality in matters of social status, there is no evidence that this became an ethnic factor which concerned Jewish identity.[24] Jews of the Ptolemaic era had indeed far

---

[20] V. A. Tcherikover, The Decline of the Jewish Diaspora in Egypt in the Roman Period, *JJS* 14 (1963) 1–32; idem, CPJ 1:63, 2:79n. 25–7; see also: J. Mélèze-Modrzewski, *The Jews of Egypt. From Ramses II to Emperor Hadrian* (Philadelphia 1995, Fr. orig.) 161–4; J. Barclay, The Jews in the Diaspora, in: idem and J. Sweet, *Early Christian Thought in its Jewish Context* (Cambridge 1996) 28–30.

[21] A. Kasher, *The Jews in Hellenistic and Roman Egypt. The Struggle for Equal Rights* (Tübingen 1985) especially 233–309 (for a summary criticism of Kasher's position, see: Barclay, Meditarrenean Diaspora 60–71); E. S. Gruen, The Jews in Alexandria, chap. in forthcoming book, tentatively entitled *Diaspora as Construct and Reality. Jewish Experience in the Second Temple*.

[22] Acta Isidori, *CPJ* no. 156c l. 25–30. Tcherikover focused in his interpretation on Isidorus' preceding rhetorics: "They [the Jews] are not of the same nature as the Alexandrians, but live rather after the fashion of the Egyptians. Are they not on a level with those who pay the poll-tax?" (*CPJ* 2:79), arguing that it points to a status problem of the Jews.

[23] For details on Philo's construction of the Egyptians, see below chapter two.

[24] Regarding evidence for the matrilineal principle among the Elephantine Jews, see: B. Porten, *Archives from Elephantine* (Berkeley 1968) 207–9; idem and H. Z. Szubin, The

less reason to concern themselves with their ethnicity since this was generally not a prominent issue at their time. Ezekiel the Tragedian betrays a highly significant innocence in this respect. He casually mentions that Moses' wife Zipporah was an alien from the dark-skinned Ethiopians.[25] Ezekiel obviously lacked any awareness that such a match would be unsuitable for the principal hero of the Israelite past. He still thought in the strictly patrilineal terms, which pertained during Biblical times, and assumed that the mother was irrelevant in determining the status of her offspring. Under the Ptolemies Moses was therefore still free, like the Biblical Solomon, to choose a spouse from any nation he liked. Under the Roman administration, by contrast, such mixed marriages became a source of concern. Ethnic segregation became anchored in a tax system based on the differentiation of national groups. These contemporary concerns also left traces on Philo. He became sensitive to the issue of proper descent, from the mother's side as well, and reinterpreted Biblical stories in light of the social reality of his time.

Philo defined a Jew by birth as someone born to two Jewish parents, who had been legally married at the time of his or her birth. He required the mother of a Jew not only to be Jewish but also free. He made the latter mandatory, because according to Roman law only a free woman had *conubium* and could enter a formal marriage. The formality of such an engagement can be gathered from Philo's recommendation to his readers (Spec. 3:67):

Go to her parents, if they are alive, or, if not, to her brothers or guardians or others who have charge of her, lay bare before them the state of your affections, as a free man should, ask her hand in marriage and plead that you may not be thought unworthy of her.

The woman's legal representatives would then examine the candidate's credentials and, should they be satisfied, agree to his formal union with their *protegée*. Such an official engagement was emphatically distinguished by Philo from sexual relations without official license.[26] He insisted that the latter amounted

---

Status of the Handmaiden Tamet: A New Interpretation of Kraeling 2 (TAD B,3.3), *Israel Law Review* 29.1–3 (1995) 43–64.

[25] Exagoge 60–7; Ezekiel thus harmonizes two Biblical references to Moses' wives: on the one hand, Ex. 2:21 mentions the marriage between Moses and Zipporah, Jethro's daughter, and, on the other hand, Num. 12:1 briefly mentions that Moses took an otherwise undefined "black wife".

[26] On the formalities of the Philonic marriage engagement, see also: I. Heinemann, *Philons griechische und jüdische Bildung* (Breslau 1932) 292–313; see also: H.M. Cotton, A Cancelled Marriage Contract From The Judean Desert (XHev/Se Gr.2), *JRS* 84 (1994) 64–86; eadem, The Archive Of Salome Komaise Daugher Of Levi: Another Archive From The 'Cave Of Letters', *Zeitschrift für Papyrologie und Epigraphik* 105 (1995) 171–208; eadem, The Rabbis and the Documents, in: Goodman, Jews in a Graeco-Roman World 167–79, who convincingly argued that Jews of the Second Temple Period were deeply influenced by Greco-Roman law, as is especially visible in the extant marriage contracts, and applied even in Palestine the same juridical principles as in Egypt, for example; J.J. Collins, Marriage,

to treating "free women as though they were servant maids".[27] This was so, because servants had no *conubium* and were their masters' unprotected prey. Philo moreover deplored children from adulterous relationships. Lacking the official recognition of their parents' union, they were considered as "most unfortunate, unable to be classed with either family, either the husband's or the adulterer's".[28] In contrast to the *mamzer* in rabbinic legislation, such a bastard in the Roman sense was considered "fatherless" and could inherit neither his biological father's status nor his property.[29] His situation in a way corresponded to that of a harlot's offspring in whose case, too, one "cannot recognize or distinguish their real father" (Spec. 1:326).

As mentioned above, Philo required the mother of a Jew to be Jewish. While he did not formulate an explicit law on this matter, he assumed it in his Bible exegesis. He is the first extant exegete for whom the foreign mothers mentioned in Scripture became problematic. Given Roman policy in Egypt, Philo could no longer accept them in the pedigree of Israelite heroes. They would have stained such central figures as the heads of some tribes and the Davidic line. Philo did not hesitate to offer an exegetical solution to this problem: he converted the foreign mothers and raised the social status of those who were handmaids as well.

The case of Isaac and Ishmael was intriguing for Philo. The Biblical story describes a problem of succession which resulted from the fact that Abraham had offspring from two different women. The Biblical narrator, as well as other Jewish interpreters of the Second Temple period, did not consider Hagar's status to be relevant to this issue. On the contrary, patrilineality was assumed and the Biblical narrator suggested that Abraham himself equally loved and accepted Hagar's child (Gen. 21:11). Ishmael had to be expelled in order to annul his claims to his father's inheritance and status.[30] Isaac's ultimate prevalence had in the Bible to do with his mother's personal determination which was sanctioned by God (Gen. 21:12). Philo, by contrast, disqualified Hagar and her offspring in principle, while insisting that Isaac was Abraham's only legitimate son. He could thus afford to drop the story of Ishmael's expulsion, because he had already dismissed him on new legal grounds. Philo focussed for this

---

Divorce, and Family in Second Temple Judaism, in: L. G. Perdue *et al.* (eds.), *Families in Ancient Israel* (Westminster 1997) 104–62.

[27] Spec. 3:69. Philo insists in the same vein that a captive woman must not be treated as a harlot, but taken as a legitimate wife (Vir. 110–4). Moses introduced this regulation, he explains, in order to curb irrational and uncontrolled passion.

[28] Dec. 130. Note that Philo characteristically assigned the role of "adulterer" to the woman, while the man was respectfully described as the "husband"; cf. Ex. 20:14 where the role of adulterer applies to the male.

[29] On the rabbinic *mamzer* see: b.Yeb. 22b, b.Kid. 68a.

[30] On the rivalry between Sarah and Hagar over the primogeniture of their respective sons, see: J. Levenson, *The Death and Resurrection of the Beloved Son. The Transformation of Child Sacrifice in Judaism and Christianity* (New Haven 1993) 92–110.

purpose on his mother's lower status and argued that this determined his own status as well. In order to highlight the difference between the two mothers, Philo initially intimated that a formal marriage engagement had taken place between Isaac's parents. Sarah had become Abraham's legitimate wife and her offspring was Abraham's lawful son. As Philo put it, "to the sage was born from his wedded wife a lawful son, beloved and only".[31] Legal terminology abounds in this short sentence so as to justify Isaac's status. The adjective μόνος furthermore indicates that his half-brother's situation was fundamentally different. This was so, because his mother Hagar was not only an Egyptian, but also a slave (Gen. 16:1). Philo suggested an exegetical solution to one of these debilitating factors, while using the other as a decisive argument for disqualifying her son.

Hagar's Egyptian origins were modified by Philo. He showed that she adopted her master's life-style and joined the Israelite community. Sarah praised her transformation when proposing her as a mate to her husband (Abr. 250–1):

And therefore I shall not be backward to lead to you a bride who will supply what is lacking in myself. And if our prayers for the birth of children are answered the offspring will be yours in full parenthood, but surely mine also by adoption. But to avoid any suspicion of jealousy on my part take if you will my handmaiden, who is a slave in the body, but free and nobly born in the spirit, proved and tested by me for many years from the day when she was first brought to my house, an Egyptian by race but a Hebrew by her rule of life.

This passage addresses the two problematic aspects of Hagar's status: her Egyptian origins and her menial status. Philo was concerned to attenuate the gravity of both in order to justify Sarah's proposal. He could obviously not accept the idea of a union between Abraham and Hagar which was in his view illegitimate and automatically produced bastard offspring. He had on other occasions inveighed against unions between Jewish men and Egyptian women, stressing that their children were nothing but bastards (Mos. 1:147). Philo could hardly fathom that Sarah would have suggested such a worthless union to her dear husband. He therefore presented both of Hagar's flaws as potentially amendable. He argued that Hagar's Egyptian origins had by the time of Sarah's proposal already been superseded by her Hebrew "life style" (προαίρεσις). The distinction between a Jew by birth and a Jew by life-style, introduced during the Maccabean period, enabled Philo to argue that Hagar had become Jewish by personal choice.[32] The dimension of her own individual decision is well re-

---

[31] υἱὸς ἐκ τῆς γαμετῆς γίνεται τῷ σοφῷ γνήσιος, ἀγαπητὸς καὶ μόνος (Abr. 168).

[32] On the emergence of the notion of Jewish lifestyle as opposed to Jewish origins, see: S. J. D. Cohen, Religion, Ethnicity, and 'Hellenism' in the Emergence of Jewish Identity in Maccabean Palestine, in: P. Bilde *et al.* (eds.), *Religion and Religious Practice in the Seleucid Kingdom* (Aarhus 1990) 204–223; idem, 'Ἰουδαῖος τὸ γένος' and Related Expressions in Josephus, in: F. Parente and J. Sievers (eds.), *Josephus and the History of the Greco-Roman Period. Essays in Memory of Morton Smith* (Leiden 1994) 23–38; R. S. Kraemer, On the Meaning of the Term "Jew" in Greco-Roman Inscriptions, *HTR* 82.1 (1989) 35–53; see also:

flected in the Greek term προαίρεσις, which Philo contrasts to her γένος, her Egyptian origins. While the latter was a given, the former was a question of choice and could therefore be changed. Hagar's passage to Jewish society and culture is furthermore indicated by the fact that her new commitment had been found satisfactory over a long period of acquaintance. In comparison to the famous conversions of Abraham and Tamar, however, Philo did not emphasize the religious dimension of Hagar's transformation. He did not even mention her insight into the special nature of the Jewish God, let alone any spiritual experience that might have accompanied it. This should, however, not surprise us. Philo's minimal description is entirely appropriate to Hagar's menial status. As a slave she would have been predominantly concerned with the practical arrangements of the household. On the basis of Gen. 17:12–3 Philo would in any case have preferred her to become Jewish in order to guarantee the observation of Jewish ritual in her master's house.[33] The concise account of Hagar's conversion is furthermore not surprising, because the boundaries between the different communities were still rather more fluid during the Second Temple period. No official rite of passage seems yet to have existed, let alone a universally recognized or institutionalized process of conversion. Becoming Jewish primarily meant to become part of a specific Jewish community, or as Philo formulated it, of the Jewish *politeia*.[34] A perfect way to do that would have been to join a Jewish family. This is precisely what Philo suggested Hagar did.

While Hagar's Egyptian origins could thus be moderated, her menial status proved harder to shake off. It became detrimental both to her and her son. The nobility of her spirit, which Sarah praised in the above-quoted passage, did not actually annul her inferior status. It only indicated the future possibility of a change for the better. After all, Joseph who had similarly been a slave only in body but not in spirit later became the first governor of Egypt. As we shall see below, Philo occasionally manumitted Biblical handmaids, if he wanted to justify their status as Jewish matriarchs. Sarah's proposal to Abraham thus sounded like a suggestion which could, if necessary, lead to an official union.

---

P. Borgen, Some Hebrew and Pagan Features in Philo's and Paul's Interpretation of Hagar and Ishmael, in: idem and S. Giversen (eds.), *The New Testament and Hellenistic Judaism* (Aarhus 1995) 151–64, who suggested that Hagar and Ishmael "are to be seen within the context of Jewish proselytism", representing borderline figures who could be treated both positively and negatively.

[33] Gen. 17:12–3 generally seems to have encouraged expectations of Jews during the Second Temple period that their slaves convert, see: M. Goodman, *Mission and Conversion* (Oxford 1994) 65.

[34] See also: S. J. D. Cohen, Crossing the Boundary and Becoming a Jew, *HTR* 82.1 (1989) 13–33; J. J. Collins, A Symbol of Otherness: Circumcision and Salvation in the First Century, in: J. Neusner and E. S. Frerichs (eds.), *"To see Ourselves as Others see us". Christians, Jews, and "Others" in Late Antiquity* (Chico 1985) 171–6; T. Rajak, The Jewish Community and its Boundaries, in: J. Lieu *et al.* (eds.), *The Jews among Pagans and Christians in the Roman Empire* (London/New York 1992) 9–28.

For the benefit of Isaac, however, Philo disqualified Hagar on account of her menial status. He stressed several times that she remained a child-like slave and Abraham's "concubine", much inferior to his lawful wife.[35]

Hagar's continued menial status had serious consequences for her son Ishmael. Philo referred to him in no uncertain terms as a "bastard", who arrogantly "claimed to play on equal terms with the lawful son".[36] Ishmael remained childish like his mother and was never able to attain Isaac's virility and moral vigour (Sobr. 9). Philo highlighted his bastardy by contrasting his character to authentic Jewish features: while Isaac was truly wise, Ishmael remained a rather worthless sophist; while the Jews were generally city-dwellers, he belonged to the uncivilized countryside; while they perceived God by the highest sense, namely the eyes, he merely heard Him with his ears like Balaam.[37] Philo could thus conclude with a sigh of relief that "from slaves (come) slaves" (Fug. 212). The application of Roman provincial law to Scripture enabled him to interpret Ishmael as a bastard who had no claims on his father's status. He was consequently excluded from the Israelite pedigree. The low status of his mother proved decisive in this process. Ishmael was disqualified, because he was the son of Hagar, a slave woman who had formerly been an Egyptian.

Rome's impact on Philo's definition of Jewish descent can especially be appreciated by considering the fact that his matrilineal legislation contradicted his medical doctrine. While he enhanced the mother's civil status and introduced a degree of matrilineality, he virtually denied her genetic contribution to her offspring. As we have seen above, she was in his view virtually irrelevant in the process of procreation. Her passivity certainly did not justify an increase in her importance in determining the status of her offspring. On the contrary, Philo's medical doctrine supported the Biblical notion of strict patrilineality. Egyptian practice, as observed by Diodorus just before the Augustan period, may highlight this point. The Hellenistic historian reported that the Egyptians did not "hold any child a bastard even though he was born of a slave mother; for they have taken the general position that the father is the sole author of procreation and that the mother only supplies the foetus with nourishment and a place to live" (Bib. 1.80:3–4). Whether or not faithful to his sources, Diodorus explained the strictly patrilineal legislation of the Egyptians in terms of Aristotelian biology. Since the father is the sole generator of the child, only his status matters. The identity and status of the mother, on the other hand, are as irrelevant as the nature of her union with the father. Medicine and law complemented each other. Not so in the case of Philo. While he shared the medical doctrine of Diodorus' Egyptians, he defined the mother's legal status from an

---

[35] παλλακή (Congr. 23), similarly in Congr. 154–6.
[36] νόθος (Sobr. 8).
[37] Sobr. 9; Cher. 8–9; Fug. 204–8.

entirely different perspective – the perspective of Roman law as applied in Egypt since the beginning of the Augustan period.

The Biblical story of Zilpah and Bilhah presented another challenge to Philo's construction of Jewish descent. These two women became mothers of important Biblical heroes even though they were handmaids (Gen. 30:3–13) and, as Philo added, foreigners from beyond the Euphrates (Vir. 223). Their sons even became the heads of four Israelite tribes. For Philo, this was a contradiction in terms. The children of non-Jewish handmaids were by his definition nothing but bastards and could obviously not be counted among the prestigious Israelite forefathers. Yet Philo reacted to the problem of these mothers with considerably greater sympathy than he had done in the case of Hagar. He could obviously not simply disqualify the heads of four Israelite tribes as bastards. Yet a legal solution to the status of Zilpah's and Bilhah's sons was not easily at hand. Philo once confessed to being unable to decide how they should be classified. He was especially concerned whether Zilpah's offspring should be counted among Jacob's sons: "of those born of Leah Issachar is Jacob's fifth lawfully begotten son, or if Zilpah's two sons are included, he is the seventh. But Jacob's fifth son is Dan from Bilhah, Rachel's handmaid" (All. 2:94). This statement indicates Philo's difficulty. At this point he was hesitant and inconsistent, obviously lacking an answer to the tricky question.[38]

A solution was, however, suggested in another and probably later discussion. Philo had now made up his mind. He decided to accept the handmaids' sons among the Israelite forefathers, suggesting that a change of their mothers' status led also to their own legitimation. While giving birth as handmaids, Bilhah and Zilpah subsequently improved their status and "passed on from mere concubinage to the name and role of wedded wives".[39] This change of status enabled Philo to acknowledge the Biblical information about their menial status, while suggesting at the same time a way of legitimating their sons (Vir. 223–4):

But when they [Zilpah and Bilhah] had been considered worthy to pass onto the wise man's bed, they initially passed on from mere concubinage to the name and position of wedded wives and no longer being treated as handmaids they were almost equal in rank to their mistresses, who indeed – incredible as it seems – promoted them to the same dignity as themselves … Secondly, the illegally born children (νόθοι παῖδες) from them were treated like the legitimate ones (γνησίων), not only by their begetter – for it

---

[38] Another Jewish writer of presumably Egyptian origin living apparently in the same Roman context as Philo, discovered a status problem in the Joseph story. The author of *Joseph and Aseneth* has Joseph claim that "they are not my brothers … lest they share the inheritance with us because they are children of maidservants" (*Jos. and As.* 24:1–10); on the date and provenance of *Joseph and Aseneth*, see three recent and radically divergent views: Schürer 3.1 546–50; Bohak, Joseph and Aseneth XII–III, 83–7; R. S. Kraemer, *When Aseneth Met Joseph. A Late Antique Tale of the Biblical Patriarch and His Egyptian Wife, Reconsidered* (New York 1998) 245–93.

[39] ἐκ παλλακίδων εἰς γαμετῶν ὄνομα καὶ σχῆμα (Vir. 223).

is not at all surprising that he being the common father of all would show the same kindness to the children of different mothers – but also by their stepmothers.

Philo applied in this passage a contemporary Roman procedure to the case of the Biblical handmaids. He suggested that the mothers' status was enhanced after they had given birth to bastard offspring. This rendered their union with Jacob lawful and solved the problem of their children, who could now be retroactively acknowledged. Jacob in Philo's Midrash was in the same position as many Roman soldiers in Egypt, who had produced illegal children whom they could later adopt.[40] In both cases the mother's status was decisive for the child. Only after she had been legitimated could her children claim to be the legal sons of their biological father. Philo emphasized this point by insisting on the consent of Jacob's other wives to whom he had been lawfully married from the beginning. Even Rachel and Leah accepted the improved status of the former handmaids and their sons, who now became equal to their own children.

While Philo offered a legal solution to the problem of Zilpah's and Bilhah's menial status, he apparently left another issue unresolved: their foreign origin. As mentioned before, he considered them to be aliens from "the extreme parts of Babylonia". In the above-quoted passage this matter does not seem to have been treated at all. It was, on the face of it, irrelevant to the process of their legitimation. Did Philo then suppose that a Gentile could become the lawful mother of an Israelite hero? Did he thus revert here to Biblical patrilineality? The answer is no. Philo rather assumed the conversion of these handmaids, too. This can be gathered from the fact that he drew a direct analogy between them and Tamar, a woman of foreign background, who converted and became the mother of an Israelite tribe. In Philo's view Bilhah and Zilpah were parallel to Tamar, who was also ἀλλόφυλος, but in contrast to them at least free born.[41] This comparison is highly suggestive. It raises the possibility that Philo's vague formulation about the handmaids "being considered worthy to pass onto the wise man's bed" implies a similar process of assimilation and conversion as Hagar had undergone. Hagar had also been found worthy by her masters. She had changed her lifestyle and become a Jew before she "passed onto the wise man's bed". As a slave she had naturally become part of her master's household, including affiliation with the Jewish *politeia*. The same seems to have happened in Philo's view to Bilhah and Zilpah in Jacob's house. This conjecture is strengthened by the fact that Philo gave a detailed description of Tamar's conversion just before discussing their parallel transfer from the status of foreign servants to that of lawful wives and mothers of legitimate Israelite sons.

Tamar is the foreign mother whose conversion Philo described in greatest detail. He interpreted her as the female equivalent of Abraham, who was during

---

[40] For details, see: Youtie, ΑΠΑΤΟΡΕΣ.
[41] ἐλευθέρα καὶ ἐξ ἐλευθέρων (Vir. 222).

the Second Temple Period generally regarded as the first believer in the God of Israel.[42] Tamar's conversion included two steps in the crossing of boundaries: she initially denounced idolatry and then became a member of the Jewish *politeia*.[43] According to Philo, Tamar went through a similar spiritual experience as Abraham (Vir. 220–1):

> To this nobility [of Abraham] aspired not only godloving men but also women who unlearnt the willful blindness of their upbringing concerning the worship of handmade artifacts and became schooled in the knowledge of the monarchical principle by which the cosmos is governed. Tamar was a woman from Palestinian Syria, bred in a house and city believing in many gods and full of wooden images and statues and generally images of gods. However, when so to speak passing out of the deep darkness, she was able to see a little ray of truth. She deserted to the pious [city] at the peril of death, caring little about life if it were not to be a good life. This good life she held to mean nothing other than to be a servant and suppliant to the One Cause.

Tamar is in this passage explicitly compared to Abraham, who out of love for God experienced true spiritual elevation even though he had been raised in a polytheistic environment. The key issue in her conversion is the "unlearning" of her ancestral idolatry. While Abraham took a distinctly active role in recognizing the God of the Jews, Tamar remained more passive and enjoyed a more limited experience. Philo had thus mentioned Abraham's zeal and eager desire to "be obedient to His commands" even before the Divine voice reached him (Abr. 60). The moment of his highest religious insight was described by Philo in the following terms (Abr. 70):

> Then opening the soul's eye as though after a profound sleep, and beginning to see the pure beam instead of deep darkness, he followed the ray and discerned what he had not behold before, a charioteer and pilot presiding over the world and directing in safety his own work, assuming the charge and superintendence of that work and of all such parts of it as are worthy of the Divine care.

Abraham's experience culminated in his vision of God. As Philo put it, He "came forward to meet him and revealed His nature, so far as the beholder's power of sight allowed" (Abr. 79). Tamar's conversion was very similar. She

---

[42] See for example the account of his religious insight in Jub. 11:14–12:21; on Abraham's conversion in Philo, see: P. Borgen, *Philo of Alexandria: Exegete for His Time* (Leiden 1997 = *Suppl. Nov. Test.* 86) 217–8. Regarding the similarity between Abraham's and Tamar's conversion in Philo's account, see also: M. Petit, Exploitations non bibliques des Thèmes de Tamar et de Genèse 38. Philon d'Alexandrie; textes et traditions juives jusq'aux Talmudim, in: *ΑΛΕΞΑΝΔΡΙΝΑ. Mélanges offerts à Claude Mondésert* (Paris 1987) 80.

[43] Regarding the nature of the Philonic conversion, consider especially the following passage: "... the equal privilege and equal rank which He grants them [the προσηλύτους] because they have denounced (κατεγνωκόσι) the delusion of their fathers and ancestors", thus joining the "new and godloving πολιτεία" of the Jews (Spec. 1:51–3, especially 1:53). See also Vir. 102, 219; Spec. 4:178; and Cohen, Crossing the Boundary 13–34. A similar view of conversion is shared by the author of *Joseph and Aseneth*, discussed by V. Aptowitzer, Asenath, the Wife of Joseph, *HUCA* 1 (1924) 239–306.

also emerged from the deep darkness to the light of belief in the One creator God. Philo said that she became schooled (παιδευθεῖσαι) and saw a "little" ray of truth. While Tamar's conversion was obviously more limited and of a more passive character, as befits a woman, she essentially went through the same experience as Abraham. Philo conspicuously spoke about both conversions as a social process which primarily involved a change of city affiliation.[44] In Abraham's case he stressed his ability to sever his bonds to family, home and customs (Abr. 66–67). Philo appreciated the difficulty of such a step and praised Abraham for the speediness of his obedience to God's command.[45] Tamar likewise left her original city in favour of a more pious one. Philo even used the term ηὐτομόλησεν to stress the danger and breach of loyalty involved in such a step. Yet Tamar's courage was rewarded: she became a servant of the Jewish God. From Philo's point of view she gained another significant advantage: as a Jew she was now able to be recognized as the legitimate ancestor of an illustrious line of Israelites. In the same way as Abraham became exemplary for all potential male converts, and indeed for the average Jew, she must have become exemplary for all Gentile women who came into contact with Jews and their religion. This might also have been one of the reasons why Philo dwelt to such an extent on the details of her conversion.

The cases of foreign mothers discussed so far have produced rather clear results. Philo assumed a degree of matrilineality and made the status of children dependent also on their mother. Her status was no longer as irrelevant as it had previously been, although he did not yet grant her positive rights to transmit her status if the father was not Jewish.[46] Applying contemporary Roman concerns to the Biblical stories, Philo began to pay attention to the maternal pedigree of important heroes. He was the first Jewish exegete who retroactively improved the status of foreign mothers in order to protect their offspring. This involved conversion, manumission and a written marriage contract. Philo's reaction to

---

[44] The connection between city and religion is rooted in Classical traditions, on which see: F. de Coulanges, *The Ancient City. A Study on the Religion, Laws, and Institutions of Greece and Rome* (Boston 1901) 205–221; the Hasmoneans' forced conversion of their conquered subjects has been interpreted as an application of the notion of *politeia*, see especially: Goodman, Mission 76; Cohen, Religion 218–9; M. Smith, Rome and the Maccabean Conversions – Notes on I Macc. 8, in: E. Bammel *et al.* (eds.), *Donum Gentilicium: New Testament Studies in Honour of David Daube* (Oxford 1978) 1–7.

[45] Philo assumed here with the Stoics that the wise man must disconnect himself from his biological and emotional affiliations in order to join the ideal city of wise men. On the Stoic notions implied here, see especially: M. Schofield, *The Stoic Idea of the City* (Cambridge 1991) 57–92.

[46] The offspring from a union between a Jewish mother and an Egyptian father was still Egyptian (Mos. 2:193). Philo's position differed in this respect from later rabbinic law as recorded in m.Kid. 3:12, m.Yeb. 7:5, t.Kid. 4:16, b.Yeb. 16b, 23a, 44b–45b, b.Kid. 70a. Cohen, Matrilineal Principle, has shown that rabbinic law changed in this respect over time: in the Mishna the offspring of a Jewish mother and a gentile father was still regarded by most rabbis as a lower-status Jew (*mamzer*), while Talmudic rabbis agreed that he was a regular Jew.

one Biblical figure, however, seems to question these results: Joseph's wife was the daughter of an Egyptian priest, yet Philo did nothing to modify this incriminating fact. More seriously, he did not dismiss her two sons as bastards.[47] On closer inspection, however, this case proves too anomalous to challenge our previous conclusions. While Joseph's sons from his Egyptian wife were not disqualified as mere Egyptians, they were in fact allegorized out of historical existence.[48] Menasseh and Ephraim were exclusively treated as symbols of remembering and forgetting. Philo altogether repressed their historical reality as well as their share in the inheritance of the Promised Land. As far as he was concerned, there was no historical continuity to the union between an Israelite and an Egyptian woman. On the merely allegorical level, on which he was willing to acknowledge Menasseh and Ephraim, the question of their status was obviously irrelevant. Symbols do not require social legitimation.

Philo's definition of Jewish descent had important implications for Jewish identity in first century Egypt. It has become evident that he accepted Roman policies of segregation and constructed Jewish descent along the same lines as contemporary Roman law. As an upper-class citizen he emphatically asserted the high social status and proper Jewishness of the Biblical matriarchs. He accepted neither slaves nor foreigners in the pedigree of the Jews. While Philo could easily rewrite the Biblical stories to suit his construction of Jewish descent, he must have faced greater difficulties with regard to living Jews. Did he judge them by the same standards? It is intriguing to speculate what Philo might have thought about the Jewishness of the many poor Jews of Egypt. If they were slaves like the otherwise unknown Johanna mentioned in the papyri and lacked *conubium*, did they produce in his view nothing but bastards?[49] Probably not. Philo's references to the vast number of Jews and synagogues in Alexandria preclude such a radical conclusion. He could not have recruited their number only from the upper-classes. His views were nevertheless so much based on upper-class and distinctly Roman values that he came dangerously close to ignoring the Jews of the third estate. Philo furthermore frowned upon intermarriages by contemporary Jews.[50] If a friend of his married an Egyptian woman, who did not follow in Tamar's footsteps, would he welcome her son in the synagogue? The stringency of Philo's position may have come as

---

[47] On Joseph's wife, see Jos. 121; on his children from her: All. 3:90–94; Sobr. 28; Migr. 205; Congr. 40; Mut. 97–102.

[48] On other occasions Philo suggested that the allegorical meaning may complement the literal one (e.g. Abr. 52–5). Regarding Menasseh and Ephraim, however, he replaced the literal by the allegorical sense in the same way as he occasionally did, when a passage seemed too mythological to him. On the latter, see also: M. R. Niehoff, Philo's Views on Paganism, in: G. N. Stanton and G. G. Stroumsa (eds.), *Tolerance and Intolerance in Early Judaism and Christianity* (Cambridge 1998) 149–50.

[49] Johanna is mentioned in *CPJ* no. 7; cf. also the situation of Martha (*CPJ* no. 148).

[50] Spec. 3:29; see also: Mendelson, Identity 71–5.

a surprise to fellow Jews. Some of them perhaps disagreed, while others may simply have socialized in other Jewish circles.

Philo complemented his construction of Jewish descent via the biological mother by a myth of Jewish origins in Jerusalem. He hoped that those whom he acknowledged as Jews would accept his story of their common past and consequently define their identity in a certain way. Philo's myth of Jewish origins centres on Jerusalem as the "mothercity" (μητρόπολις) of world Jewry. It provides a highly positive explanation for Jewish life abroad and reverses both the Exodus account as well as traditional exile theology.[51] Philo realized that in contrast to other nations the Jews were not defined by a "dwelling-place set apart" and a "land cut off from others" (Mos. 1:278). They rather lived, as he proudly asserted, throughout the entire *oikoumene*. While Judea was thus not the physical homeland of most Jews, Philo made its capital the symbolic centre of Jewish ethnicity. To be sure, the physical existence of the city and especially the Temple are of special importance to him.[52] Yet Jewish identity could not be defined by actually living there. Jews differed, in other words, from Judeans.[53]

---

[51] See e.g.: Ez. 11:14–25, 20:5–44, 36:16–35, and 3 Macc. 6:3. As I. Pardes, Imagining the Promised Land: The Spies in the Land of the Giants, *History and Memory* 6.2 (1994) 5–23, has forcefully argued, the positive appreciation of the Promised Land is already in Scripture balanced by critical counter-views. Philo's positive attitude to diaspora life has been noted before, see especially: J.J. Collins, *Between Athens and Jerusalem* (New York 1983) 111–17; cf. W.C. van Unnik, *Das Selbstverständnis der jüdischen Diaspora in der hellenistisch-römischen Zeit* (Leiden 1993 = Arbeiten zur Geschichte des antiken Judentums und des Urchristentums 17) 127–37 (reviewed by D. Winston in *AJS Rev.* 20.2 (1995) 399–402), who stressed Philo's apologetic concerns; Borgen, Philo of Alexandria 19–21; idem, Philo of Alexandria, in: M.E. Stone (ed.), *Jewish Writings of the Second Temple Period. Apocrypha, Pseudepigrapha, Qumran Sectarian Writings, Philo, Josephus* (Assen 1984 = Compendia Rerum Judaicarum ad Novum Testamentum II) 269; idem, Philo, Luke and Geography, in: idem, *Philo, John and Paul. New Perspectives on Judaism and Early Christianity* (Atlanta 1987 = Brown Judaic Studies 131) 273–85, who stressed Philo's alleged sense of exile and inferiority vis-à-vis Palestine.

[52] See also: D.R. Schwartz, Temple or City: What did Hellenistic Jews See in Jerusalem? in: M. Poorthuis and Ch. Safrai (eds.), *The Centrality of Jerusalem. Historical Perspectives* (Kampen 1996) 120; the importance of the Temple worship for Jews of the intertestamental period has also been stressed by M. Goodman, The Emergence of Christianity, in: A. Hastings (ed.), *A World History of Christianity* (Michigan 1999) 9–10. This physical dimension has been overlooked by those scholars who focused rather exclusively on Philo's allegory, see e.g.: V. Nikiprowetzky, La Spiritualisation des Sacrifices et le Culte Sacrificiel au Temple de Jérusalem chez Philon d'Alexandrie, *Semitica* 17 (1967) 97–116; B. Halpern Amaru, Land Theology in Philo and Josephus, in: L.A. Hoffman (ed.), *The Land of Israel: Jewish Perspectives* (Notre Dame 1986 = Studies in Judaism and Christianity in Antiquity 6) 65–93.

[53] Philo himself attached only minimal importance to his own visit to Palestine (Prov. 2:64); see also: B. Schaller, Philon von Alexandreia und das "Heilige Land", in: G. Strecker (ed.), *Das Land Israel in biblischer Zeit* (Göttingen 1983) 174. On the origins during Herod's reign of world-wide Jewish pilgrimage to the Jerusalem Temple, see: M. Goodman, The Pilgrimage Economy of Jerusalem in the Second Temple Period, in: L.I. Levine (ed.), *Jerusalem – Its Sanctity and Centrality to Judaism, Christianity, and Islam* (New York 1999) 69–76.

Philo nevertheless wanted Jerusalem to play an important role for Jews living abroad and encouraged them to define their identity by reference to their alleged origins in that city.

Let us initially consider the most famous and detailed of Philo's discussions of Jerusalem as mothercity. It is preserved in one of his later treatises (Flac. 46):

> For so populous are the Jews that no one country can hold them. Therefore they settle in very many of the most prosperous countries in Europe and Asia both on the islands and on the mainland, and while they hold the Holy City where stands the sacred Temple of the most high God to be their mothercity (μητρόπολιν), yet those which are theirs by inheritance from their fathers, grandfathers and ancestors even farther back, are in each case accounted by them to be their fatherland (πατρίδας) in which they were born and reared, while to some of them they have come at the time of their foundation as immigrants to the satisfaction of the founders.

Philo addresses in this dense passage fundamental issues of Jewish life abroad: its historical origins, the relationship to Jerusalem and the Temple and, finally, the right balance between the Jews' loyalty to their place of residence and their "place of origin". Some Classical Greek motifs of colonization immediately catch the reader's attention.[54] Initially, Philo's purely demographic explanation of Jewish migration is striking. It completely lacks the theological criticism of Biblical writers who usually describe the process of leaving Jerusalem as going into exile and receiving punishment for previous sins. The tone and contents of Philo's account are instead surprisingly neutral. They echo the Classical Greek ideology of colonization. Greek settlers had been known to leave their home when the latter became too overcrowded.[55] Their departure from their place of origin did not carry any negative undertones and was, on the contrary, often perceived as a pioneering step worthy of admiration. Applying this ideology to the case of the Jews, Philo replaces the paradigm of exile and return according to which life outside the land of Israel is a dreadful, transitional situation.[56] Philo departs to such an extent from prominent Biblical views that he can even

---

[54] See also: Y. Amir, Philo's Version of Pilgrimage to Jerusalem (Hebrew), in: A. Oppenheimer *et al.* (eds.), *Jerusalem in the Second Temple Period. A. Schalit Memorial Volume* (Jerusalem 1980) 154–65, reprinted in: Y. Amir, *Die hellenistische Gestalt des Judentums bei Philon von Alexandrien* (Neukirchen 1983 = Forschungen zum jüdisch-christlichen Dialog 5) 52–64, who pointed to some parallels between Classical Greek notions of colonization and Philo's description of Jerusalem as mothercity; Amir's argument has been repeated almost *verbatim* by H.-J. Klauck, Die heilige Stadt. Jerusalem bei Philo und Lukas, *Kairos* 28.3–4 (1986) 129–36; and been embraced with certain moderations by J. M. Modrzejewski, How to be a Jew in Hellenistic Egypt?, in: S.J.D. Cohen and E.S. Frerichs (eds.), *Diasporas in Antiquity* (Atlanta 1993 = Brown Judaic Studies 288) 70. An excellent study of the role of the mothercity in Classical Greek colonization can be found in: A.J. Graham, *Colony and Mother City in Ancient Greece* (Chicago 1983, 2nd revised ed).

[55] A. Gwynn, The Character of Greek Colonisation, *JHS* 38 (1918) 88–98.

[56] Some motifs of the Biblical exile theology have nevertheless resurfaced in Philo's writings, see: Praem. 164–5, which refers, however, only to the messianic age.

speak of the Exodus as a colonial expedition "from Egypt to another home".[57]
Moses, when approaching the land of Israel, was moreover shocked by the
Jewish population which had remained there. Although Moses naturally treated
them as kinsfolk (συγγενεῖς), he quickly discovered that they had abandoned
all their ancestral customs and sense of belonging (Mos. 1:239). Philo stresses
in this context that the group of inauthentic Jews "had been attached to the soil"
(ἐφιλοχώρησεν), while the virtuous ones had gone abroad.[58]

Philo's construction of Jerusalem as mothercity implied further Classical
features of colonisation. He underlined the importance of the metropolis by
pointing to the "sacred Temple of the most high God" in her midst (Flac. 46).
This Temple should, as he occasionally stressed, be considered as the one
temple of the one God (Spec. 1:67). This meant that Jerusalem possessed the
central sanctuary to which all Jews should be looking. It furthermore implied
that the Jews should construct their identity in analogy to Greek colonists, who
looked up to the cult of their mothercity and modelled their own religious
practice on it. The colonists' sense of loyalty to their city of origins was usually
symbolized by the *oikist*'s transfer of a significant cultic item to the new
colony.[59] More generally, Philo wished to convey the idea of faithfulness to
one's place of origin. While independent, Classical Greek colonists were expected to recognize the special status of their mothercity. Aware of their obligations to the past, they would usually act as her ally rather than her rival and
support her especially in times of emergency and war.

Philo demanded that Jerusalem be considered as mothercity even by those
Jews, who had been living abroad for several generations and saw themselves
as the founders of their respective "fatherlands". It is crucial to realize the
normative nature of Philo's statement. He neither described a given reality, as
some scholars have assumed, nor did he engage in mere apologetics which do
not reflect his real views.[60] Philo instead suggested a particular way in which
Jews should define their identity. On other occasions he expressed a keen
awareness of the fact that remembering one's mothercity was anything but self-
evident. The colonist differed in this respect from the occasional traveller who
always longs to return home. Philo acknowledged that for "men [who] found a

---

[57] ἀποικίας (Mos. 1:71); see also Mos. 1:170; cf. Hyp. 6:1. This view is anticipated by
Hecataeus (GLAJJ 1:26 ἀποικίας).

[58] (Mos. 1:240–2, especially 240). Philo similarly praised the wise man for being able to
transcend his fatherland and find refuge in wisdom alone (Agr. 65); see also the discussion
above of Abraham's and Tamar's conversion.

[59] On the transmission of the cult from mothercity to colony, see especially: I. Malkin,
*Religion and Colonization in Ancient Greece* (Leiden 1987 = SGRR 3)17–134.

[60] The former view has been advocated by A. Kasher, Jerusalem as a 'Metropolis' in
Philo's National Consciousness (Hebrew), *Cathedra* 11 (1979) 45–56; idem, Jews in Egypt
236–8; the latter by I.M. Gafni, *Land, Center and Diaspora. Jewish Constructs in Late
Antiquity* (Sheffield 1997 = JStPs Suppl. Ser. 21) 47.

colony, the land which receives them becomes their native land instead of the
mothercity" (Conf. 78). It was implied that colonists usually change their
identity after some time. While they start out as settlers from a place afar, they
increasingly identify with their place of residence, which eventually becomes
their primary point of reference. Philo sought to counter this natural process.
When insisting on the continuous relevance of Jerusalem as the mothercity of
world Jewry, he encouraged Egyptian Jews to assert themselves as a distinct
group among others. Philo wanted them to remember their particular origins
and behave like ideal Greek colonists, who continued to live with an emotional
attachment to their roots. In this way they would maintain a distinct identity in
the multi-ethnic environment of first century Egypt.

Philo furthermore implied an unmistakably Roman dimension in his notion
of mothercity. This is most visible in his emphasis on the universal distribution
of the Jewish colonists.[61] In the above-quoted passage Philo said that they
settled "in very many of the most prosperous countries in Europe and Asia, both
on the islands and the mainland" (Flac. 46). He emphatically repeated this
statement in Leg. 283. Jerusalem was thus constructed as a mothercity in the
broadest sense. Colonists all over the world could trace their origins to her.
Philo's association of Jerusalem with the ends of the earth echoes the famous
Roman identification of *Urbs* with *Orbis*. This play on words referred from late
Republican times onwards to Rome's domination in an ever-expanding empire,
which was thought to emcompass the whole *oikoumene*. Augustan poets in
particular relied on this image when celebrating the Actian victory.[62] As Ovid
put it, "Romanae spatium est urbis et orbis idem" (Fasti 2:684). Philo thus
modelled the role of Jerusalem on the position of Rome in the empire. He hoped
to render the idea of Jerusalem's centrality attractive for educated contemporary Jews. Loyalty to Jerusalem would provide them with the same kind of
identity as Roman citizenship – an identity which, though ethnic in origin,
transcended the narrow boundaries of a specific state and created the sense of
world-wide community.[63] Philo might in this context also have thought of the

---

[61] See also: Schwartz, City 124.

[62] See: J. S. Romm, *The Edges of the Earth in Ancient Thought. Geography, Exploration,
and Fiction* (Princeton 1992) 121–2; C. Nicolet, *Space, Geography, and Politics in the Early
Roman Empire* (Ann Arbor 1991 = Jerome Lectures 19) 29–56; L. Storoni, *The Idea of the
City in Roman Thought. From Walled City to Spiritual Commonwealth* (London 1970, Ital.
orig. 1967) 173–81; P. R. Hardie, *Virgil's Aeneid. Cosmos and Imperium* (Oxford 1986) 364–
6; F. Bömer, *P. Ovidius Naso. Die Fasten* (Heidelberg 1958) 2:131–2; on the role of Rome in
the emerging ideology of empire, see: Gruen, Hellenistic World 1:273–87, especially 274–5,
281–2.

[63] See especially: Cicero, Leg. 2:5–8, where he discusses the problem of integrating the
sense of local attachment cherished by Italians in a general Roman identity; for a discussion
of this issue in Latin literature, especially Horace, see: Th. N. Habinek, *The Politics of Latin
Literature. Writing, Identity, and Empire in Ancient Rome* (Princeton 1998) 88–102.

cosmic city in Stoic political theory. This city was an ideal, which replaced the organisation of the concrete state and referred to the universal community of all rational beings.[64]

In the *Legatio* Philo added another Roman dimension to his image of Jerusalem. In contrast to his earlier treatments of the subject, he described here the sacred moneys from the first fruits as money sent not to the Temple, but to the city of Jerusalem (Leg. 156).[65] This was precisely the formulation used in the Augustan letters, quoted by Philo, which acknowledged the Jews' right to send "envoys to Jerusalem according to their ancestral practice" (Leg. 313). These were also the words used in a similar Augustan letter which Josephus quoted in confirmation of Jewish rights in Asia Minor (A.J. 16:163–71).[66] Cicero as well had spoken in this way about the Jewish Temple donations (Pro Flacco 69). Philo clearly echoed a Roman perspective when speaking in the *Legatio* about Jewish donations to the city rather than the Temple of Jerusalem. He might well have been inspired by the contemporary veneration of the city of Rome. The capital of the empire received numerous envoys with financial dedications and offerings, which were collected by the priests of the goddess Roma all over the world.[67] These features of Rome's position in the empire were assimilated by Philo and transposed to Jerusalem. This new construction of the Jewish mothercity would, he hoped, not fail to make an impression on his readers and encourage them to define themselves in analogy to Roman self-perceptions.[68]

It is striking that the motif of mothercity was originally not part of Philo's myth of origins. Jerusalem did not always have the central importance it acquired in the *Legatio* and *In Flaccum*. References to her were a relatively late development. Philo's earlier accounts of Jewish origins made no mention of Jerusalem. This surprising fact cannot be attributed to a lack of familiarity at an earlier stage with the motif of metropolis. Philo used it as a philosophical metaphor already in his earlier treatises.[69] At this stage, however, he did not yet

---

[64] See also: Schofield, Stoic City 57–92.

[65] It is only in the *Legatio* that Philo described the Temple donations in such city-centred terms. In earlier discussions he had spoken of them in the exclusive context of the Temple (Spec. 1:76–78).

[66] The nature and status of the Augustan confirmation has been disputed; see especially T. Rajak, Was there a Roman Charter for the Jews?, *JRS* 74 (1984) 107–23; C. Saulnier, Lois romaines sur les Juifs selon Flavius Josèphe, *RB* 88.2 (1981) 161–98. Given the nature of imperial rule in the provinces and especially the predominance of case law it seems clear that the acknowledgement of Jewish rights solicited by a specific community carried wider significance; on the style of imperial rule in the provinces, see especially: F. Millar, Empire and City, Augustus to Julian: Obligations, Excuses and Status, *JRS* 73 (1983) 76–96.

[67] R. Mellor, The Goddess Roma, *ANRW* II, 17:2 (1981) 950–1030.

[68] The image of the Jews as colonists indeed became so common in the Roman world that a little later Josephus naturally described them thus in his brief sketch of the events of 38 C.E. (A.J. 19:281).

[69] See: Conf. 78–82; Somn. 1:41, 181.

apply it to Jerusalem and the issue of Jewish identity. Philo's myth of Jewish origins rather focused on the country as a whole (Mos. 2:232):

For settlers abroad and inhabitants of other regions are no wrongdoers who deserve to be deprived of equal privileges, particularly if the nation has grown so populous that a single country cannot contain it and has sent out colonies in all directions.

The parallels between this passage and Flac. 46 are obvious. Philo points here as well to the demographic factor of Jewish settlement abroad and highlights the neutral, if not positive status of the colonist. In the present context he uses this story to explain the absence of Jews from Jerusalem and to justify their equal treatment. This passage, however, lacks the motif of mothercity so central to the later account. Neither Jerusalem nor the Temple are even alluded to.

What prompted Philo to change the emphasis of his story and focus at a later stage on the city of Jerusalem? Why would he no longer have been satisfied with his original version? For an answer we have to look at the historical context of the passages in which Philo's myth of origins appears. It is initially conspicuous that the motif of Jerusalem as mothercity appears only in two late works, namely in *In Flaccum* and the *Legatio*. It was thus added at a time of crisis, when the local synagogues had been desecrated and the purity of the Jerusalem Temple been threatened by Gaius' plan to set up his statue there.[70] During the difficult years between 38–41 C.E. Egyptian Jews were confronted with both a local and an international Jewish issue. Philo headed the first Jewish embassy to Gaius to solve the local problem, which emerged first, but the embassy ended up devoting much, if not all of its time to the international issue.[71] For Philo, the tension between the two was a difficult matter which overshadowed even his personal career. He himself gave priority to the Jerusalem Temple and argued that the local issue was only a derivative of the larger international one. For most Alexandrian Jews, however, the ethnic violence in the city was itself a crucial subject. It may have been connected to issues of civic status and certainly deserved in their view not only independent treatment, but priority.[72] These Jews wanted the embassy to discuss the local issue

---

[70] For details regarding the local synagogues in the context of Philo's image of the Egyptians, see below chapter two; for details regarding Gaius' plans to set up his statue in the Jerusalem Temple, see below chapter three.

[71] The best discussions of the chronological problems still are: J. P. V. D. Balsdon, Notes concerning the Principate of Gaius, *JRS* 24 (1934) 19–24; P. Bilde, The Roman Emperor Gaius (Caligula)'s Attempt to Erect his Statue in the Temple of Jerusalem, *Studia Theologica* 32 (1978) 67–93. Note that the subject of Jewish *politeia* in Alexandria was hardly touched in the meeting between Philo's embassy and Gaius (Leg. 363–4).

[72] On the roots of the conflict, see especially the recent controversy between P. Schäfer, *Judeophobia. Attitudes toward the Jews in the Ancient World* (Cambridge MA 1997) 136–60, and W. Bergmann and Ch. Hoffmann, Kalkül oder "Massenwahn"? Eine soziologische Interpretation der antijüdischen Unruhen in Alexandria 38 n. Chr., in: R. Erb and M. Schmidt (eds.), *Antisemitismus und jüdische Geschichte. Studien zu Ehren von Herbert A. Strauss*

in a more aggressive manner, which would produce concrete results and improve their lives in the city. Many of them may have belonged to lower echelons of society than Philo and perhaps cherished some anti-Roman sentiments.[73] Such Jews took to street violence after Gaius was assassinated in 41 C.E., when Philo was presumably still in Rome (Jos., A.J. 19:278–9). It is probably from circles sympathetic to such expressions of despair that a second Jewish embassy was dispatched to the new emperor Claudius.[74] In contrast to the street rioters, its members still believed in negotiation, but presented the case of the Jews from a very different perspective to Philo.[75] They asserted the rights of the Jews in the city and must, under the immediate impression of the events, have had a much more pessimistic perspective on Rome's rule over the multi-ethnic population of Egypt. They were presumably part of the rising hostility towards Rome among all parts of the population – a fact which Philo must have found highly alarming. Ultimately, the controversy between the two Jewish embassies to Claudius revolved around the question of Jewish identity. At stake was the question whether the Jews were to be defined by reference to Jerusalem and Rome or primarily with regard to Alexandria.

Both the *Legatio* and *In Flaccum* aimed at defending Philo's pro-Roman politics. He wished to convince his Jewish readers back home that the more radical positions, which had been adopted by many Jews during his stay in Rome, were unwise and doomed to failure. Street violence would only bring disaster. Philo moreover had a personal stake in these matters. He had to account for the fact that, as Tcherikover put it, his embassy was "a complete failure" (*CPJ* 1:69). It is generally acknowledged now that the *Legatio* and *In Flaccum* were never designed as pieces of detached historiography.[76] Nor were they intended for a Roman audience, as Goodenough and others following him have assumed.[77]

---

(Berlin 1987) 15–46, who have stressed the role of the civic rights issue to the extent that the violence was interpreted as an organized, rational move on the part of the Greek population, especially of the clubs associated with the gymnasium in Alexandria.

[73] See also: V. Tcherikover, *CPJ* 1:66–9. The perspective of the lower classes, who were not represented by Philo, has recently also been emphasized by Pucci Ben Zeev, New Perspectives 234–5. The role of anti-Roman sentiments in the unrest of 38 C.E. has been altogether denied by Bergmann/Hoffmann, Kalkül 20–21, 45–7, who consider them merely the result, but not the cause of the tension.

[74] The best discussion of the two embassies is still: Tcherikover, *CPJ* 2:51–3; see also: Barclay, Mediterranean Diaspora 55–60.

[75] Claudius' Letter to the Alexandrians (*CPJ* no. 153, l. 90–92) indicates that he was anything but pleased with the existence of two embassies and two Jewish perspectives, which differed so much that they seemed to represent two different cities.

[76] See especially: D. R. Schwartz, On Drama and Authenticity in Philo and Josephus, *SCI* 10 (1989–90) 113–20; P. Borgen, Philo's *Against Flaccus* As Interpreted History, in: K.-J. Illman *et al.* (eds.), *A Bouquet of Wisdom. Essyas in Honour of Karl-Gustav Sandelin* (Abo 2000) 41–57; Schäfer, Judeophobia 138.

[77] Goodenough, Politics 19–20; Smallwood, Legatio 182; Barraclough, Politics 450–1, who stresses that he agrees only partially with Goodenough's views, but is nevertheless

Since the assumption of a Jewish audience for the *Legatio* and *In Flaccum* is crucial to the present argument, the evidence for it must be briefly reviewed. Initially, both treatises lack the features characteristic of an apologetic work addressed to the new Roman emperor. Neither of them stresses the merits of the Jews which would have made their claims more plausible in Roman eyes. These treatises significantly differ in this respect from Philo's biography of Moses, which explicitly took a non-Jewish audience into account (Mos. 1:1–3). The *Legatio* moreover includes a passage describing in detail how the Roman mob sided with Gaius and justified his murders of three alleged rivals (Leg. 67– 73). If Philo had indeed addressed Claudius, he would hardly have mentioned plebeian support in Rome for the kind of tyranny from which he endeavoured to discourage the new emperor.

The Jewish audience of Philo's two "historical" treatises can be asserted more positively. In the opening of the *Legatio* Philo criticizes those who "have come to disbelieve (ἄπιστοι) that God takes forethought for men" (Leg. 3). Who else but the Jews would have entertained a belief in Divine providence which had been shaken by Gaius and the pogrom in Alexandria? Furthermore, both the subtitle of the *Legatio,* "On the Virtues", and its lost palinode, as far as can be established, made such a strong theological claim that nobody but Jews can have been anticipated as readers. Hans Leisegang has shown long ago that the subtitle of the *Legatio* refers to the virtues of the Jews, who remained faithful to their customs despite the calamities that had befallen them.[78] The palinode, as its name suggests, illustrated the Divine reversal of Gaius' fate, who probably ended like Flaccus repenting his policy vis-à-vis the Jews and confessing their God.[79]

Philo also interpreted Flaccus' downfall from an unmistakably Jewish perspective. He unhesitatingly presented it as divine punishment for his actions

---

strongly influenced by his interpretation of the *Legatio* as an apologetic work. Even Tcherikover, who generally discouraged the reading of Jewish Hellenistic literature as apologetic works, followed Goodenough in this matter and thought of Philo's *Legatio* and *In Flaccum* as exceptional treatises addressed to the Roman authorities (Tcherikover, Apologetic Literature 182); Barclay, Mediterranean Diaspora 422, recently suggested a compromise solution, arguing that while Flac. 45–6 is a piece of apologetics, it nevertheless reflects Philo's real feelings.

[78] H. Leisegang, Philons Schrift über die Gesandtschaft der Alexandrinischen Juden an den Kaiser Gaius Caligula, *JBL* 57 (1938) 377–405.

[79] Ibid. 404–5; Leisegang furthermore suggested that a Christian writer omitted the palinode, because he wished to suppress material challenging the Christian image of Judaism as a defunct religion which had been replaced by Christianity (ibid. 385). This explanation, however, is challenged by the fact that the palinode of Flaccus with its emphatic assertion of Divine providence over the Jews was not omitted. It is more likely that the palinode of the *Legatio* got lost, because the notion of Gaius' repentance did not agree with Christian martyrology which was based on a radical opposition to the imperial cult and its representatives; on the latter see especially: G. W. Bowersock, *Martyrdom and Rome* (Cambridge 1995 = Wiles Lectures 1993).

against the Jews. Flaccus is explicitly described as an "indubitable proof that the help which God can give was not withdrawn from the nation of the Jews" (Flac. 191). Divine providence is in Philo's view especially visible in the direct correspondence between the details of Flaccus' career and downfall: he was arrested at a banquet, precisely because he had previously destroyed numberless hearths (Flac. 115); on his way to exile he was watched by the same people who had on his way to Egypt boasted his pride (Flac. 152); he was killed by as many strikes as the number of Jews whom he had killed (Flac. 189).[80] It is moreover conspicuous that Philo does not convey any material from the actual proceedings of Flaccus' trial. He merely mentions the fact that he was accused and condemned (Flac. 147), while the specific charges of the Roman court are entirely omitted. These probably differed significantly from Philo's own interpretation. For this very reason the Roman proceedings were committed to oblivion. It required Jewish eyes to see a connection between Flaccus' trial and his earlier treatment of the Jews. Philo himself indicated the subjective nature of his own interpretation when explaining that Flaccus' violent end had come upon him, "I am convinced", as a result of "his treatment of the Jews".[81] The Romans themselves had different reasons for accusing him of incompetent administration in Egypt. Certainly only Jewish readers would have appreciated Philo's portrayal of him as a repentant sinner acknowledging the Jewish God and His providential care for His people (Flac. 170).

The *Legatio* furthermore contains some passages which throw direct light on the background of Philo's myth of Jewish origins. In the middle of the treatise the purpose of the embassy is discussed. Philo defends himself against what must be considered Jewish charges of inefficiency. It emerges between the lines that he had been criticized for spending too much time in Rome chasing Gaius from one engagement to another, hardly succeeding to obtain even a minimal hearing, while the Jews in Alexandria were daily suffering the ethnic tension in the city. Philo replied to such allegations that a more aggressive style of negotiation would hardly have brought improvement. He shares in this spirit some of the deliberations among the members of his embassy (Leg. 192–3):

Shall we be allowed to come near him [Gaius] and open our mouths in defense of the houses of prayer to the destroyer of the all-holy place? For clearly to houses less conspicuous and held in lower esteem no regard would be paid by one who insults that most notable and illustrious shrine whose beams like the sun's reach every whither, beheld with awe both by East and West. And even if we were allowed to approach him unmolested, what have we to expect but death against which there is no appeal? Well so

---

[80] For another example of the providential reversal of Flaccus' life, see Flac. 125–6, where Philo stresses the significance of the fact that Flaccus was accused in court precisely by those who had previously been his subjects.

[81] Flac. 116; for further details on Philo's interpretation of Flaccus, see below chapter four.

be it, we will die and be no more, for the truly glorious death, met in defense of the laws, might be called life. But if our decease brings no advantage, is it not madness to let ourselves perish as well, particularly as we are supposed to act as ambassadors, so that the disaster would fall more on those who sent us than on the actual sufferers? Indeed those among our fellow nationals who most detest wickedness will accuse us of impiety in selfishly pleading for something which concerns us in particular, when the existence of all is tottering in extreme danger.

This passage indicates that Philo was pressed to respond to Jewish allegations from Alexandria. His reaction was straightforward: he pointed to the overriding importance of the Jerusalem Temple which had to take precedence over local issues of synagogue desecration and street violence. Only after Gaius would give up his plans regarding the Jerusalem Temple could he be expected to show respect for the local synagogues. Action in this respect was to be taken by God, not by human beings.[82] As Philo insisted, even the ambassadors' self-sacrifice would not have effected anything. He therefore recommended sitting still and waiting for divine providence. In this vein he also mused that "perhaps these things are sent to try the present generation, to test the state of their virtue and whether they are schooled to bear dire misfortunes with a resolution which is fortified by reason and does not collapse at once" (Leg. 196). Philo thus asserted that he had chosen the path of leniency not out of cowardice, but out of real piety and a proper understanding of Jewish priorities. Incidentally, this piety also corresponded to Roman interests.

Against this background it becomes clear why Philo began to focus his myth of origins on Jerusalem, the mothercity of world Jewry. He hoped that this Greco-Roman motif would appeal to educated upper-class readers, who did not yet support the more radical course of other Jewish parties. Philo's appeal to Jerusalem was intended to counter rival views and divergent constructions of Jewish identity. He suggested a different approach, recommending an orientation towards Jerusalem. Jews should in Philo's view make the city and the Jerusalem Temple their first priority. Local issues should not unduly engage their attention and evoke dissatisfaction with Rome. Philo asserted that God would solve their problems just as He had previously done in the case of Flaccus and Gaius.[83]

---

[82] Even Philo admits that Gaius had been moved by King Agrippa to cancel his plans, giving Petronius respective instructions (Leg. 333). However, in contrast to Josephus who highlights this point in A.J. 18:300–1, Philo suggested that the reversal was only half-hearted and depended on conditions which were in Philo's view impossible to fulfil (Leg. 334–5). According to his account, Gaius even made secret preparations for another statue to be built and set up in the Jerusalem Temple (Leg. 337). Philo thus attributes the rescue of the Jerusalem Temple wholly to Gaius' assassination, which was in his view due to God's providential action. On the discrepancy on this important point between Josephus and Philo, see especially: Bilde, Gaius' Attempt 83–89; for further details, see below chapter three.

[83] For more details on the role of providence and the character of these two figures, see below chapters three and four.

Philo summarized these points in a speech which he attributed to Agrippa on the occasion of meeting Gaius. The Jewish king expressed here his overriding loyalty to his mothercity Jerusalem. All other concerns for his country, such as taxation, were subordinated to his wishes for the welfare of Jerusalem on which all Jewish colonies depended (Leg. 281–4):[84]

> While she, as I have said, is my native city she is also the mother city not only of one country Judea but of most of the others in virtue of the colonies sent out (ἀποικίας ἅς ἐξέπεμψεν) at diverse times to the neighbouring lands ... So that if my home-city is granted a share of your goodwill the benefit extends not to one city but to myriads of the others situated in every region of the inhabited world whether in Europe or in Asia or in Lybia, whether in the mainlands or on the islands, whether it be seaboard or inland. It well befits the magnitude of your great good fortune that by benefiting one city you should benefit myriads of others also so that through every part of the world your glory should be celebrated and your praises mingled with thanksgiving resound.

Philo also used a stylistic device in order to guarantee his reader's emotional acceptance of his myth of origins in Jerusalem. He inserted into his narrative three highly dramatic scenes in which tears were shed for the Temple. Detailed accounts were provided of the physical revulsion which proper Jews experienced at the very thought of Gaius erecting his statue in Jerusalem. The messenger, who told Philo's embassy about Gaius' plans, was actually prevented from speaking "as a flood of tears streamed from his eyes" (Leg. 186). The Jewish demonstration before Petronius was similarly "accompanied with much gasping and spasmodic breathing, the sweat streaming over every limb amid a flood of ceaseless tears" (Leg. 243). King Agrippa was even said to have reacted to the news of Gaius' plans with an immediate fainting fit (Leg. 267).[85] Philo dwelled on the details of his shuddering, convulsions, trembling and palpitation. In his case the dramatisation is especially obvious, since Agrippa cannot really have been taken by surprise. He surely met Gaius already knowing what everybody else in Palestine knew at the time. Philo thus created these scenes primarily to arouse strong emotions in his readers. They should become as concerned about the Jerusalem Temple as Agrippa had been and define their identity by reference to the mothercity of all Jews.

Philo's myth of Jewish origins in Jerusalem thus complements his construction of Jewish descent via the biological mother. Both stories suggest that the Jews could look back to a noble past which conformed to Roman values and norms. Both place the Jews in a decidedly Roman context, while extracting

---

[84] Regarding the Philonic authorship of "Agrippa's" speech, see: D. R. Schwartz, *Agrippa I. The Last King of Judaea* (Tübingen 1990 = Texte und Studien zum Antiken Judentum 23, revised Hebr. orig.) 200–2.

[85] The dramatic quality of this account has been noted before, while its connection to Philo's myth of origins has not yet been recognized, see: Schwartz, Drama 117–8, following H. Willrich, Caligula 42–3; Schwartz, Agrippa 85–7.

them from Egyptian soil. The past, whether constructed biologically or mythologically, shapes Jewish identity in the present and defines important objectives for the future. Having a proper Jewish mother and considering oneself a colonist from the mothercity Jerusalem meant more than just being aware of one's descent. It implied that one belonged to an elite group of Egyptian Jews, who identified with Rome and looked beyond the boundaries of their country of residence.

## 2. The Egyptians as Ultimate Other

> "Things which Egyptians reckon as profane
> are called sacred in the estimation of the keen-
> sighted"                                        (Fug. 19)

In this chapter we will be concerned with ethnic boundaries which Philo constructed by way of binary opposition. Suggesting a basic division between "us" and "them", Philo characterized the Jews by reference to their ultimate Other. We will investigate his image of the Egyptians following Barth's insight that boundaries are social constructs which are not primarily based on objective factors, such as geographic isolation. They are instead created by ascription and agreement among the members of a group. We furthermore agree with Barth that constructing the Other is a primary constituent of ethnic identity.[1] For Philo this was an especially complex task, because he sought to define a minority group within a multi-ethnic environment where contacts with members of other groups were pervasive and unavoidable. Ethnic boundaries were thus permeable in many respects. The image of the Egyptians became vital in defining impervious spans of a boundary which clearly separated the Jews from their environment. Philo described the Egyptians, as has often been noted, in the most negative terms.[2] His exasperated and untiring criticism of them played a keyrole in his construction of Jewish identity.[3] The Egyptians emerge as the

---

[1] Barth, Introduction 11–3; for further details regarding Barth's argument that the construction of the Other precedes and shapes culture, see above Introduction.

[2] See especially: D. I. Sly, *Philo's Alexandria* (London and New York 1996) 19–21, 111–4; Borgen, Philo of Alexandria an exegete 23–5, 179–88; Mendelson, Identity 116–22; Goudriaan, Ethnical Strategies 85–86. Notable exceptions are Philo's references to the Egyptians in Mos. 1:21 and Spec. 1:2. These passages have been highlighted by K. Bertholet, The Use of Greek and Roman Stereotypes of the Egyptians by Hellenistic Jewish Apologists, with special reference to Josephus' *Against Apion*, in: Kalms, Internationales Josephus- Kolloquium Aarhus 1999 107–9, who identifies Philo predominantly as a continuation of the positive Greek ethnography on the Egyptians, while Josephus' account is interpreted as corresponding to Roman stereotypes. This argument, however, relies on a few highly exceptional passages in Philo, which must not obscure the otherwise overwhelmingly negative image of the Egyptians.

[3] This point has been most seriously taken into account by S. Pearce, Belonging and Not Belonging: Local Perspectives in Philo of Alexandria, in: S. Jones and S. Pearce (eds.), *Jewish Local Patriotism and Self-Identification in the Graeco-Roman Period* (Sheffield 1998 = *JSPS* Suppl. Ser. 31) 79–105. Her analysis, however, must be completed in numerous aspects and also corrected with regard to Philo's audience.

ultimate Other whose perversion implicitly defines the positive characteristics of the Jews. Distancing oneself from the Egyptians is for Philo a crucial factor in becoming and remaining an authentic Jew.

The Egyptians are the only ethnic group which Philo places in diametrical oppositon to the Jews. While being Jewish, Roman and Greek are for him complementary identities, one can in his view never be both a Jew and an Egyptian. Philo leaves no doubt about the fact that these are mutually exclusive terms. The more one is Egyptian, the less one is Jewish and *vice versa*. Being Jewish thus involves the permanently renewed choice to avoid the Egyptians and their ways. Yet precisely because Egypt is a constant threat, she has also become a prime constituent of Jewish identity. Philo speaks of Jews who betray Jewish values as unstable persons who have adopted Egyptian traits. The worshippers of the Golden Calf, for example, are for the first time in Jewish exegesis interpreted as having undergone a "change of [ancestral] habits"[4]. They began "to emulate Egyptian counterfeits ... having fashioned a golden bull, in imitation of the animal held most sacred in that country, they offered sacrifices which were no sacrifices, set up choirs which were no choirs, sang hymns which were nothing but funeral chants".[5] While Philo obviously does not yet think in terms of the later Christian concept of "True Israel", he nevertheless suggests uncommonly stringent boundaries of Jewish identity.[6] It is striking that the worshippers of the Golden Calf are no longer described as sinful Jews, but as deserters to another nation which is characterized by sheer negatives ("no sacrifices", "no choirs"). An inner Jewish conflict has thus been interpreted as an encounter between two diametrically opposed ethnicities. The Levites were in Philo's view right to kill those "Egyptians", because they thus prevented the further spread of alien customs.

---

[4] ἐκδιαίτησιν (Mos. 2:167). This process is strikingly similar to Hagar's inverse adoption of a "Hebrew life style", on which see above chapter one.

[5] Mos. 2:161–2; see also Mos. 2:270; see also: K.-G. Sandelin, The Danger of Idolatry according to Philo of Alexandria, *Temenos* 27 (1991) 131–2. The Biblical account does not associate the Golden Calf with Egypt even though the book of Exodus establishes the Egyptians as the constitutive Other of the Jews and the prophets subsequently translated this historical narrative into an eternal typology, Egypt now representing all the elements seducing Israel away from God (Ez. 20:7–9, 23:19–21; Is. 19:1–3; Jer. 43:12–3). It is likely, but not certain that Philo knew these prophetic passages. On the image of Egypt in Biblical literature, see especially: Assmann, Gedächtnis 196–202; S. E. Loewenstamm, *The Evolution of the Exodus Tradition* (Jerusalem 1992, transl. of Heb. orig.); J. J. Collins, The Exodus and Biblical Theology, *Biblical Theology Bulletin* 25.4 (1995) 152–60. Josephus altogether omitted this story which subsequently became a central issue in Christian-Jewish polemics, on which see especially: Stephen's speech in Acts 7:39–42; L. Smolar and M. Aberbach, The Golden Calf Episode in Postbiblical Literature, *HUCA* 39 (1968) 91–116.

[6] On the Christian origin of the notion of True Israel, see: G. Harvey, *The True Israel. Uses of the Names Jew, Hebrew and Israel in Ancient Jewish and Early Christian Literature* (Leiden 1996), regarding Philo see especially 219–24 and 43–6.

The rebellious son is also interpreted by Philo as someone who went over to the Egyptian side. He crossed the boundaries by having "made a god of the body, a god of the vanity most honoured among the Egyptians, whose symbol is the image of the golden bull" (Ebr. 95). The rebellious son also warrants the death penalty which Philo fully expects to be carried out.[7] Yet Egypt challenges the average Jew as well. Philo suspects that Egyptian elements are lurking in everyone, including even himself, and demands to destroy "the part of us that … pines for the dwellings in Egypt" (All. 2:77). The choice between being either Egyptian or Jewish is thus not an issue pertaining only to the past or to the exceptionally wicked. It rather concerns every contemporary Jew. The Exodus is not only a historical event, but an ever topical demand.

Philo uses numerous techniques to describe the negative characteristics of the Egyptians. The details of their national character are important, because they demarcate a sharp boundary vis-à-vis a people among whom Philo and his readers were actually living. Philo's strategies are diverse. Blatant and noticeable is open polemics: he never tires of emphasizing just how materialistic, impious and untrustworthy the Egyptians have always been.[8] A particular effect is achieved by placing them on the opposing side to civilized humanity. Philo suggests that the Egyptians have degenerated to such an extent that they can no longer be counted as normal human beings. Their character and customs are instead akin to those of animals. In Philo's view they are nothing but perverse and pathological. These qualities are especially conspicuous in the areas of food, sex and religion.

Egyptian food is described by Philo as appalling and disgusting. The Egyptians, he reports, consume "the onions and the garlic, which give great pain and trouble to their eyes and make them close, or the other ill-smelling things, the leeks and dead fishes" (Her. 79). Philo obviously expects his readers to shudder at the very thought of such dishes. He can imagine no civilized person touching this beastly food.[9] The sexual customs of the Egyptians appear equally perverse to him. Their lawgiver has (Spec. 3:23–4):

produced a fine crop of lewdness. With a lavish hand he bestowed on bodies and souls the poisonous bane of incontinence and gave full liberty to marry sisters of every degree … For twins are often born who although separated and disunited by nature at

---

[7] For details on the death penalty for the rebellious son, see below chapter six.

[8] Among numerous passages, see especially: Congr. 83; Migr. 77; Post. 156; Cont. 8–10; Somn. 2:255; Q.G. 4:177; All. 2:59; see also: Pearce, Belonging 89–92; Goudriaan, Ethnical Strategies 82; P. Carny, Biblical Egypt as a Symbol in Philo's Allegory (Hebrew), *Shnaton. An Annual for Biblical and Ancient Near Eastern Studies* 5–6 (1982) 197–204; D. Zeller, Das Verhältnis der alexandrinischen Juden zu Ägypten, in: M. Pye and R. Stegerhoff (eds.), *Religion in fremder Kultur. Religion als Minderheit in Europa und Asien* (Saarbrücken-Scheidt 1987 = Schriften zur internationalen Kultur- und Geisteswelt 2) 80.

[9] Philo's polemics may partly respond to Egyptian attacks on Jewish food laws, such as voiced by Apion, apud Jos., Contr. Ap. 2:137.

birth, enter at the call of concupiscence and voluptuousness into a partnership and wedlock which are neither in the true sense of the words.

This passage indicates that Philo has constructed his Egyptian Other as a perversion of what is familiar and natural. The Biblical marriage laws serve here as the standard by which the Other is measured. Moses is said to have established healthy standards of sexuality, which inculcate true values and civilized self-restraint.[10] The Egyptians are projected onto this screen as a sick nation. Their laws are "poisonous" and encourage a subversion of humanity. Philo's stereotyping follows here the same pattern as in the dietary context: he draws an unsurpassable line between the camps of the good and the pathological Other.[11] The Egyptians have come to serve as a peg onto which Philo hangs anything that arouses horror and anxiety.

Philo moreover ridicules the zoolatry of the Egyptians and suggests that it has reduced them to subhumans (Dec. 79–80):

What could be more ridiculous than all this [Egyptian zoolatry]? Indeed strangers on their first arrival in Egypt before the vanity of the land has gained a lodgement in their mind are like to die with laughing at it, while anyone who knows right instruction, horrified at this veneration of things so much the reverse of venerable, pities those who render it and regards them with good reason as more miserable than the creatures they honour, as men with souls transformed into the nature of those creatures, so that as they pass before him, they seem beasts in human shape.

This statement confirms our impression that Philo identifies the boundary between Jews and Egyptians with the boundary between humanity and subhumans. The Egyptians are not only contrary to "us", but to everything that is worthy to be counted among mankind. "We" thus emerge as the spearhead of human civilization from which the Egyptians are excluded. Philo stresses that aversion to Egyptian zoolatry conforms to the values of the enlightened world.[12] Any civilized tourist to Egypt will feel that way. A famous stranger who had on his first visit to Egypt expressed the kind of scorn Philo expected was Augustus. According to Dio Cassius, he had refused to "enter the presence of Apis …, declaring that he was accustomed to worship gods, not cattle".[13] Philo may

---

[10] For details on Philo's interpretation of Spec. 3:23–4 in the context of Jewish values, see below chapter three.

[11] Gilman, Difference and Pathology 22–5, has shown that the category of the pathological is a typical component of stereotyping. The sexual aspects of this construct are especially pervasive and enduring. They also appear in numerous modern guises, see e.g. Gilman, Difference and Pathology 109–27, 188–9; see also: D. Boyarin, *Unheroic Conduct. The Rise of Heterosexuality and the Invention of the Jewish Man* (Berkeley 1997) 189–270.

[12] Note that Aristeas also presented the Egyptians as archetypal idolators from whom God has separated the Jews by surrounding them with "unbroken palisades and iron walls" (Ar. 137–9).

[13] Dio, 51.16:5; on other Roman criticism of Egyptian zoolatry, see especially: Tacitus, who spoke of Egyptian religion as "superstitione ac lascivia" (Hist. 1:11); Juv., Sat. 15:44–

have had this incident in mind when stating that strangers on their first visit to Egypt will naturally be repulsed by the local religion.

Philo's reference to foreign perspectives on Egypt moreover suggests that he wished to enlist wide support for his stereotypes. He wrote on the assumption that his rhetorics will easily meet with approval. He could indeed count on the fact that much of Roman discourse supported his construction of the Egyptians as Other. Augustus had made special efforts to present the civil war against Antony as a clash between Rome and Egypt. Official war had been declared against Cleopatra, not Antony.[14] Augustus' prewar propaganda proved so successful that popular sentiment identified the Egyptian queen as the cause of the civil conflict.[15] Antony himself was presented as a renegade to the Egyptian side.[16] He emerged as someone who foresook his Roman identity by adopting the barbarian customs of the Egyptians. He was accused of having enslaved himself to an Egyptian woman for whose sake he "abandoned all his ancestors' habits of life".[17] Parallel to Philo's worshippers of the Golden Calf, Antony was said to have "emulated all alien and barbaric customs" and to pay no honour to "us or to the laws or to his fathers' gods".[18] Augustus concluded

---

6; Strabo, Geogr. 17:801; Cic., Tus. Disp. 5:78, N.D. 1:81–2, 1:101, 3:39 had already made disparaging remarks about Egyptian animal worship and in N.D. 1:43 called Egyptian mythology "insane"; on tourism to Egypt, see: L. Friedländer, *Darstellungen aus der Sittengeschichte Roms in der Zeit von Augustus bis zum Ausgang der Antonine* (Leipzig 1922) 1:423–446; J.G. Milne, Greek and Roman Tourists in Ancient Egypt, *JEA* 3 (1916) 76–80; K.A.D. Smelik and E.A. Hemelrijk, "Who knows not what monsters demented Egypt worships?" Opinions on Egyptian animal worship in Antiquity as part of the ancient conception of Egypt, *ANRW* (1984) II 17.4 1938–45.

[14] On the circumstances and justification of Rome's declaration of war on Cleopatra, see: M. Reinhold, The Declaration of War against Cleopatra, *CJ* 77.2 (1981–2) 97–103.

[15] See also: R.A. Gurval, *Actium and Augustus. The Politics and Emotions of Civil War* (Ann Arbor 1995) 24–5, 28–30. The following means of Augustan propaganda have been especially noticed by ancient historians: after illegally seizing Antony's will, Augustus publically announced that his adversary wished to be buried in Alexandria and acknowledged his children from Cleopatra (Plut., Ant. 58:4; Suet., Aug. 17:1; Dio 50.3:4–5). Dio Cassius observed that this step had been highly effective in stirring up xenophobic fears in Rome and associating Antony with the foreign Other. "This", he reported, "caused the Romans in their indignation to believe that the other reports in circulation were also true, to the effect that if Antony should prevail, he would bestow their city to Cleopatra and transfer the seat of power to Egypt" (50.4:1).

[16] Virgil characteristically celebrated Actium as a victory over a barbarian renegade, who had gone over to the Egyptian woman (Aen. 8:685). On Augustan propaganda, see: K. Scott, The Political Propaganda of 44–30 B.C., *Mem. Am. Ac. in Rome* 11 (1933) 35–49; I. Becher, Oktavians Kampf gegen Antonius und seine Stellung zu den ägyptischen Göttern, *Das Altertum* 11.1 (1965) 40–7; M. Malaise, *Les Conditions de Pénétration et de Diffusion des Cultes Egyptiens en Italie* (Leiden 1972), 385–9; J.P.V.D. Balsdon, *Romans and Aliens* (Chapel Hill 1979) 68–9; Smelik and Hemelrijk, Egyptian Worship 1852–2000.

[17] Dio, 50.25:3 νῦν πάντα μὲν τὰ πάτρια τοῦ βίου ἤδη ἐκλελοιπότα; cf. also 50. 5:1, 50.26:3.

[18] Dio, 50.25:3; see also Verg., Aen. 8:685–8; echoes of the Augustan propaganda are

his famous speech against Antony by a fervent appeal to the audience: "therefore let no one count him a Roman but rather an Egyptian" (Dio, Aug. 50.27:1). The diametrical opposition between "us" and the Egyptians had thus become part of the Roman discourse. The conquest of Egypt became a watershed. Augustus' triumph commemorating it far surpassed his Illyrian and Actian triumphs in lavishness and ostentation. It celebrated the importance of this conquest for the ushering in of a new era of world-wide dominion and peace.[19] To be sure, the Roman discourse on Egypt reached neither the same level of hostility as we encountered in Philo nor did it assume an equally central role.[20] Yet it was certainly congenial to Philo's cause and enhanced his sense of belonging to an elite of humanity which distanced itself from the primitive, disgusting and zoolatrous Egyptians.

Philo moreover uses ethnographic models to explore the Egyptian national character. He investigates the origins of their traits and points to an intrinsic connection between a nation and the geography of its homeland. The features of the land shaped in his opinion the character of its people. Living by the Nile, the Egyptians have assimilated the features of this unusual river. Philo points out that in contrast to all other streams, the Nile does not dwindle during the summer, but "rises and overflows, and its flood makes a lake of fields which need no rain but every year bear a plentiful crop of good produce of every kind" (Mos. 1:6). Egypt is thus watered from below and requires no effort to produce an exceptionally rich harvest. Philo continues to review a number of known explanations for this unusual phenomenon, concluding with his own suggestion that no rain falls in Egypt, because "Nature is no wastrel in her work, to provide rain for a land which does not want it" (Mos. 1:117). Egyptian soil thus rejects heavenly favours and produces an abundance independent from the Divine gift of rainfall.

So far Philo's discussion of the Nile echoes Herodotus' account.[21] The latter had as well noted that the Nile is "contrary in nature to all other rivers" and stressed the fertility of the land (Hdt. 2:19). Herodotus suggested that thanks to the Nile the Egyptians hardly need to work for their harvests: "the river rises of itself, waters the fields and then sinks back again; thereupon each man sows his field ... and waits for the harvest" (2:14). Various explanations for this pheno-

---

evident also in Plutarch's generally more favourable portrait of Antony, see: Plut., Dem. and Ant. 3:4.

[19] Gurval, Actium and Augustus 28–33

[20] Gurval, Actium and Augustus *passim*, has consistently warned not to overemphasize the importance of Actium in post-war Roman ideology.

[21] D. Winston, *Philo of Alexandria. The Contemplative Life, The Giants, and Selections* (New York 1981) 362 n. 385, notes the similarity between Philo's account of the Nile and typically Egyptian views. These would then also seem to underlie Herodotus' account. It must at the same time be remembered that both Hellenistic writers imposed their own ethnographic perspective and value system on Egyptian geography and – if available to them – on Egyptian interpretations of that geography.

menon, similar to the ones Philo subsequently mentioned, are discussed (2:20–24). Herodotus' real interest, however, lay in identifying a connection between Egypt's geography and the character of its people. A close correlation existed in his view between the two: "as the Egyptians have a climate peculiar to themselves, and their river is different in nature from all other rivers, so have they made all their customs and laws of a kind contrary for the most part to those of all other men" (2:35). The Egyptians are thus constructed as the inversion of the rest of humanity. Yet Herodotus meant this in a neutral, if not positive sense. He mentions Egyptian customs, such as the women's shopping in the market, with astonishment, but without overt criticism. To quote Hartog, the Egyptians served as a mirror to the Greeks, not as their ultimate Other.[22] Herodotus even cherished a deep admiration for their religion and was convinced that many Greek practices and beliefs originated from the Nile valley (2:37–64).

Philo has adopted Herodotus' ethnographic strategy. He also draws a parallel between the land and its people. For him, as well, the Egyptians differ from all other nations because their river is contrary to all other rivers. This difference, however, is not described with empathy. Philo rather judges it in negative terms. The Nile has now become indicative of Egyptian materialism and impiety. Philo explains this matter on two occasions. In Fuga 180 he states the following:

For what the sky is in winter to other countries, this the Nile is to Egypt in the height of summer: the one sends the rain from above upon the earth, the other – most contrary to expectation (τὸ παραδοξότατον) – rains from below and waters the fields. This urged Moses to declare the Egyptian character as godless (ἄθεον)[23] in its preference for earth above heaven, for the things that live on the ground above those that dwell on high and the body above the soul.

Returning to this issue in Mos. 2:194–5, Philo adds:

For the Egyptians almost alone among the nations have set up earth as a power to challenge heaven. Earth they held to be worthy of the honours due to a god, and refused to render to heaven any special tribute of reverence, acting as though it were right to show respect to the outermost regions rather than to the royal palace. For in the universe heaven is a palace of the highest sanctity and earth is the outer region ... as far inferior to it as darkness is to light and night to day and corruption to incorruption and mortal man to God. Since the land [of Egypt] is not watered like other countries by the downpour of rain but regularly every year becomes a standing water through the flooding of the river, the Egyptians speak of the Nile as though it were the counterpart of heaven and therefore to be deified and talk about the land in terms of high reverence.

---

[22] F. Hartog, *The Mirror of Herodotus. The Representation of the Other in the Writing of History* (Berkeley 1988, transl. Fr. orig. 1980 = The New Historicism. Studies in Cultural Poetics 5) 212–24; P. Cartledge, *The Greeks. A Portrait of Self and Others* (Oxford 1993) 38, 58–9; Smelik and Hemelrijk, Egyptian Worship 1873–4; C. Préaux, La singularité de l'Egypte dans le monde gréco-romain, *Chronique d'Egypte* 25 (1950) 110–5.

[23] This expression might echo Ex. 5:2 where Pharaoh declares that he does not know the God of the Israelites; see also Philo's discussion of this passage in Mos. 1:88.

In these two passages the Egyptians are constructed as the archetypal people of the soil who revere the earth and its river. Philo agues that they have thus turned the ideal of religiosity upside down. The inverse and indeed perverse nature of their worship is highlighted by the adjective "godless". Philo moreover proposes pairs of opposites, which locate the Egyptians in the areas of darkness, night, corruption and mortality. While it is proper to turn to light, the Egyptians turn to darkness. While it is natural to worship the incorruptible and immortal, they worship the corruptible and mortal.[24] Egyptian religion emerges as a complete non-religion. Their corrupt materialism is the absolute inversion of human civilization.

The extreme attachment of the Egyptians to the soil, to the extent that they are shaped by its geography, indicates their complete Otherness. They are the exact opposite of the Jews, who have left their homeland and retained a largely emotional attachment to their mothercity Jerusalem.[25] While the Egyptians are literally and metaphorically flooded by their river, the Jews have transcended their original homeland. The Egyptians have consequently become the personification of materialism and impiety, whereas "we" represent transcendental values. This image of the Egyptians reinforces Philo's construction of Jerusalem as the mothercity analogous to Rome's position in the empire. By identifying the Egyptians with the soil of Egypt, Philo suggests that Jews together with Romans are on the opposite side of an existential divide. Both "civilized" nations trace their origins to an eminent city, while living all over the world. The Egyptians, on the other hand, are not part of this international community, but remain bound to the very earth of their homeland.

Additional strategies were used by Philo to construct the Egyptian national character. One of them was to suggest that they are Barbarians in the Classical Greek and topical Roman sense. This primarily meant that they were in Philo's eyes irrational, slavish and savage.[26] Philo especially attributed to the Egyptians those traits which Aeschylus had in his influential drama ascribed to "the Persians".[27] By describing the Egyptians in such terms Philo has significantly integrated himself into a contemporary Roman discourse which revived those Classical images. Augustus had already used these motifs in his own propaganda and stigmatized both the Egyptians and the Parthians as barbarian "Per-

---

[24] Rabbinic interpreters similarly identified the unusual nature of the Nile as a potential source for irreverence, see: G.R. 13:9; A. Marmorstein, *The Old Rabbinic Doctrine of God* (London 1937 = Jews' College Publications 14) 152.

[25] For more details on this subject, see above chapter one.

[26] For a discussion of a wide range of historical writings expressing these stereotypes, see: Cartledge, Greeks 36–62.

[27] See: E. Hall, *Inventing the Barbarian. Greek Self-Definition through Tragedy* (Oxford 1989) *passim*, especially 56–159; J. M. Hall, *Ethnic Identity in Greek Antiquity* (Cambridge 1997) 34–66. On the importance of "The Persians" for establishing an ethnocentric discourse, see also: Cartledge, Greeks 39–40.

sians". Philo extended the images of this discourse to the definition of Jewish boundaries and assimilated the historical Exodus to the battle at Salamis. In this way he suggested that the victory at the Red Sea had the same foundational significance as both the Greeks' maritime victory over the Persians and Rome's supremacy over her "barbarian" enemies.

Philo was apparently familiar with Aeschylus' interpretation of the Persian Wars. His brief references to these events echo Aeschylus' tragedy. Following the Greek dramatist, Philo describes Xerxes as an arrogant and foolish ruler who attempted to reverse the order of Nature by crossing over into Europe. When building the famous bridge over the Hellespont, he is said to have done so "by creating a revolution in nature; for he converted two elements, earth into sea and sea into earth, giving dry land to the ocean and ocean in exchange to the dry land" (Somn. 2:117–8). Aeschylus had similarly presented Xerxes' effort as "forcing his route to take a shape against its nature", thus offending Poseidon and other gods.[28] In Philo's portrait Xerxes moreover appears as a voluptuous man, who is caught in grandiose fantasies without realistically appreciating the limits of his power. He emphasizes that "the feats he hoped to do were ... utterly unholy" and to his discredit (Somn. 2:120). Aeschylus had likewise criticized Xerxes, because he "foolishly thought that he could master all gods" (Pers. 749–50). Both authors sarcastically commiserate with Xerxes and speak of him as an unhappy "wretch".[29] Most importantly, however, Philo embraces Aeschylus' interpretation of the Persian Wars as a foundational event, which pushed the Barbarians back into their natural borders and secured Greek freedom. He recalls that the Greeks were inspired to defend the freedom of their homeland (Lib. 133). This emphasis echoes the war slogan of the Greek soldiers in Aeschylus' play: "O sons of Greeks, go on, bring freedom to your fatherland, bring freedom to your children, wives and seats of your ancestral gods, and your forefathers' graves; now the struggle is for all" (Pers. 402–4).

It is of interest that imperial Rome also adopted this Greek self-image. Augustus publically presented himself as an Alexander-type conqueror, who brought Greek civilization to the *oikoumene*.[30] Increasingly aware of his historical role in the East, he suggested that his military expeditions corresponded

---

[28] Pers. 747–8, transl. A.J. Podlecki, *The Persians by Aeschylus* (Englewood Cliffs 1970).

[29] Both Philo and Aeschylus use the term δύστηνος, see Somn. 2:119; Pers. 909, similarly Pers. 733.

[30] D. Kienast, Augustus und Alexander, *Gymnasium* 76 (1969) 446–7; A. Heuss, Alexander der Grosse und die politische Ideologie des Altertums, *Antike und Abendland* 4 (1954) 83–9; R. Syme, The Crisis of 2 B.C., in: idem, Roman Papers 3:921–3 (originally published in: *Bayer. Ak. d. Wiss. Phil.-Hist. Klas. Sitzungsber.* (1974.7) 3–34); Bowersock, Augustus and the East: The Problem of the Succession, in: Millar and Segal, Caesar Augustus Succession 174–5 (repr. in: Bowersock, Studies 27–46); Gurval, Actium and Augustus 70–72. For more details on Philo's views on Alexander, see below chapter five.

to and even surpassed that of the Macedonian king.[31] The Romans were thus cast into the role of the enlightened Greeks, while their respective enemy had to play the role of the Barbarian Persians. The Egyptians were the first to be assigned that role by Augustus. After his victory over Egypt two cities by the name of Nicopolis were founded in analogy to Alexander's Nicopolis established after the latter's victory over the Persians at Issus.[32] Augustus thus indicated that he had triumphed over the present-day Persians. Cleopatra had in this spirit been stigmatized as the personification of barbarism: she was said to be licentious, tyrannical in her style of rule, overly feminine, cowardly in war and politically manipulative.[33] Her companion Antony was paraded as a renegade to barbarian Egyptian customs. The civil war, in which Egypt supported the opposite candidate, thus appeared as a confrontation between the civilized West and the "Persian" uncivilized East. This interpretation was highly publicized and reached Philo as well. He seems to have adopted it, speaking of Augustus' ascendancy as a unification of "Europe and Asia".[34] This West-East typology was especially exploited in the context of the Parthians. In preparation for the planned Parthian campaign, which never actually took place, Augustus cast his adversaries in the role of the Persians. He staged for this purpose a naval battle between "Persians" and "Athenians" in the Circus of Rome, thus repeating the fateful victory at Salamis.[35] This spectacle was obviously meant as a rehearsal for Rome's imminent triumph over the Parthians.[36]

Aware of both the Greek construction of the Persians and its Roman adaptations, Philo assimilates the Egyptians to the Western stereotype of the Barbarian. He thus adheres to and expands their Augustan interpretation. Most indicative of the Egyptians' role as Persians is their military equipment. When confronting

---

[31] E. S. Gruen, Rome and the Myth of Alexander, in: T. W. Hillard et al. (eds.), *Ancient History in a Modern University* (Grand Rapids, Michigan and Cambridge 1998)1:190–1, forcefully argued for Augustus' intention to impress Parthia and her Eastern admirers with his public gestures of *Imitatio Alexandri*.

[32] Gurval, Actium and Augustus 69–73 and 81, stresses the relative lack of attention paid to these cities by the Roman public. They mainly played a role vis-à-vis the Greek East where Alexander's symbols would resonate.

[33] Tyrannical rule: Dio, 50.5:1–2, 50.26:5; luxurious indulgence and ostentation: Dio, 50.5:3, 50.27:4; manipulation and untrustworthiness: Dio, 50.5:4; femininity and sexuality: Dio, 50.23:3–7, 50.27:7, 50.28:3; cowardice: Dio, 50.33:2. Cleopatra's traits are discussed in these passages in the context of her relationship with Antony.

[34] Leg. 144; for more details on this passage in the context of Philo's construction of the Romans, see below chapter four. Philo does, on the other hand, acknowledge that the different countries had been led by "Romans in great positions who stood foremost in repute" (Leg. 144).

[35] R.G. 23; see also: Dio, 55.10:7; Ovid., Ars Amat. 1:171–2.

[36] As mentioned above, there was no military victory over the Parthians. Yet Augustus presented his diplomatic success as though it was military in nature. As E. S. Gruen, The expansion of the empire under Augustus, *CAH* (Cambridge 1996, 2nd ed.) 10:163, has put it: "The behaviour was marked by restraint, but the public posture was one of aggressiveness".

the fleeing Israelites at the Red Sea, Philo stages them as riding on "scythed chariots".[37] These vehicles neither appear in the Biblical Exodus account nor are they mentioned by any extant interpreter before Philo. He is the first to equip the Egyptians with this particular martial accessory. His choice is not accidental. Scythed chariots had in Greek literature become the proverbial weapons of the Persians. Xenophon, Polybios and Diodorus mention them as representing *pars pro toto* the Persian war machinery.[38] Philo has thus ascribed to the Biblical Egyptians the most stereotypical marker of Persian warfare. The opponents of the Israelites at the Red Sea thus looked like the arch-enemies of the Ancient Greeks. Not surprisingly they also behaved like them.

Philo accommodates numerous details of the Biblical Exodus account to the stereotype of a historical confrontation between East and West.[39] It is initially conspicuous that he emphasizes the theme of political liberty (ἐλευθερία). While the Biblical account stresses liberty from slave labour and religious freedom, Philo highlights the value of a liberal regime as opposed to tyranny.[40] In his story the Israelites were motivated by their innate passion for liberty just as Aeschylus' Greeks. Both were able to triumph over an enemy far outnumbering their own forces (cf. Pers. 338–45). Pharaoh played in this context the role of a Persian tyrant. Philo explicitly describes him as an incontinent and savage-hearted master and a true "despot".[41] This implies that he was a ruler who brutally subdued freedom of speech, reduced his own fatherland to slavery and greedily longed for ever more territory and wealth.[42] Philo's Pharaoh did indeed rule by exercising terror over his subjects and operating a comprehensive system of controls (Mos. 1:10). He did not tolerate any form of democratic freedom and, like Xerxes, reduced guests and subjects to slavery.[43] In contrast to the simple democratic government of the Israelites (Mos. 1:86), rule in Egypt is said to have been based on stereotypical Persian traits: "treasuring up gold

---

[37] δρεπανηφόρα ἅρματα (Mos. 1:168); note that the LXX translates the Biblical רכב simply as τὰ ἅρματα, see for example LXX Ex. 14:6–7.

[38] See especially: Xen., Cyropaedeia 7.1:47, 8.8:24; Polyb., Hist. 5.53:10; Diod., Bib. 14.22:7, 17.39:4.

[39] For a recent analysis of other aspects of Philo's Exodus story, see: P. Borgen, The Crossing Of The Red Sea As Interpreted By Philo. Biblical Event – Liturgical Method – Cultural Application, in: J. V. Hills et al. (eds.), *Common Life in the Early Church. Essays Honoring Graydon F. Snyder* (Harrisburg 1999) 77–90.

[40] Mos. 1:86 and 140; cf. Ex. 3:17–9, 4:1–5:2; on the wide-spread motif of freedom in Ancient Greek constructions of identity, see: Cartledge, Greeks 118–51; regarding subsequent interpretations of the Exodus in terms of liberal revolutions, see: M. Walzer, *Exodus and Revolution* (New York 1985).

[41] τύραννος (Mos. 1:9); cf. Pers. 213, where the queen mother emphasizes that Xerxes is answerable to no city, whatever the dimension of the disaster he had brought on the Persians.

[42] Spec. 3:138–9; regarding Philo's characterisation of tyranny, see also: Barraclough, Politics 529–33.

[43] Mos. 1:36. Philo stresses that the inimical behaviour of the Egyptians was not limited to the Jews (Spec. 2:146); cf. Pers. 233, 213, 584–90.

and silver, levying tributes ... and any other accompaniment of costly and opulent living".[44] Joseph's chariot is moreover said to symbolize the character-istic pomp and vanity of Egyptian rule (Migr. 160–1). Persons in inferior positions are so awestruck that they immediately perform "*proskynesis* in the old fashioned style" (Jos. 164). This submissive gesture was a Classical marker of Persian political culture, which Aeschylus did not fail to ridicule on numer-ous occasions in his drama.[45] Finally, Philo suggests that Abraham could not defend his wife at Pharaoh's court and had to leave her "at the mercy of a licentious and cruel-hearted despot", because he was "menaced ... by the terror of stronger powers" (Abr. 95). Parallel to the behaviour of Aeschylus' Xerxes vis-à-vis the Persian and Dorian ladies, Philo's Pharaoh planned to "bring her [Sarah] to shame" and subdued the freedom of speech of those who might have come to her aid.[46] The positive image of Pharaoh in Genesis has thus been translated not only into negative, but also distinctly political terms.[47] None of the earlier interpreters of Abraham's visit to Egypt, such as the author of the *Genesis Apocryphon*, anticipated Philo's language even though they similarly wished to improve the protagonist's reputation. He was the first who applied to the Biblical Pharaoh political categories echoing the Greek image of the Per-sian king.

Philo's Pharaoh resembles Aeschylus' Xerxes in another important respect: he acts on emotion rather than rationally planning his steps. Pharaoh is pos-sessed by "relentless wrath".[48] His "harshness and ferocity and obstinacy of temper" make him act as wilfully and cruelly as the impetuous and "furious" Xerxes.[49] To be sure, the Biblical Pharaoh by no means lacked cruelty, but this

---

[44] Mos. 1:152; cf. Pers. 159, 213, 241–2, 754–6, 608, 586–7.

[45] Pers. 499, 152, 684–6, 584–94; see also: Hall, Barbarian 96–100.

[46] Cf. Aeschylus' portrayal of Xerxes in Pers. 595, 181–99. Xerxes' greediness is both political and sexual as Atossa's dream about his violation of a Persian and a Doric lady illustrates.

[47] The Biblical narrator provided a positive portrait of Pharaoh in the book of Genesis, while Abraham was described in highly ambivalent terms. Pharaoh had honest intentions concerning Sarah and wished to marry her. When he discovered Abraham's trick, he was rightly angry with his guest (Gen. 12:18–9). Abraham, on the other hand, passed his wife off as his sister and did not interfere in Pharaoh's liaison with her. He did so not only because he feared for his life, but also because he expected material compensation for Sarah's services (Gen. 12:13, 16). The latter aspect has already been stressed by the Medieval commentator Nahmanides *ad. loc.*, who highlights the meaning of Abraham's double justification of his request to Sarah "Say you are my sister so that it may be well with me because of you and that my life may be spared on your account". The Biblical narrator repeated the reference to Abraham's welfare when reporting on the benefits he received in return for Sarah's sexual services to Pharaoh (Gen. 12:16); on early Jewish and rabbinic interpretations of the Biblical story, see: M. R. Niehoff, Associative Thinking in the Midrash Exemplified by the Rabbinic Interpretation of the Journey of Abraham and Sarah to Egypt (Hebrew), *Tarbiz* 62.3 (1993) 339–59.

[48] ὀργὴν ἀμείλικτον βασιλέως (Mos.1:49).

[49] Mos. 1:89; cf. Pers. 718.

characteristic had not been analysed in terms of temper and emotionality. Philo's Pharaoh is particularly savage in war. In contrast to the Biblical figure, Philo has him pursue the Israelites with the clear intention of "slaying them from the youth upwards" should they refuse to return.[50] Like Xerxes, who recklessly sacrificed the whole "flower of Persia" to his personal *hybris* and easily killed disobedient sailors, he obviously had no qualms about destroying human life.[51] On the contrary, he seems to have taken pleasure in it. Philo's Pharaoh shares another personal trait with Xerxes: like the Persian king on the verge of the historical battle at Salamis, Pharaoh expected an "uncontested victory" at the Red Sea.[52] This expectation was obviously unrealistic and indicates the foolishness of the tyrant, who was greedy rather than clever. Philo has Pharaoh run into battle and tells how "with unabated rapidity he rushed to the attack, and pushed on eagerly, wishing to come upon them [the Israelites] suddenly and unforeseen" (Mos. 1:168). Pharaoh's tactics prove illusionary and entirely inappropriate to cope with the heroes of the story. He was mistaken like Xerxes, who sought to surprise the Greeks by an ambush, but was unaware "what was about to come from the gods" (Pers. 373). His father Darius bemoaned his rashness and wished his son had followed his more cautious advice (Pers. 782–6).

The Egyptians themselves are in Philo's story similar to Aeschylus' Persians. They are given to the same excessive mourning and cowardice in battle. Philo initially dwells on their overly emotional reaction to the loss of their first-born sons. They are depicted as giving exaggerated expression to their grief. Philo expresses his view on the matter when he has Abraham dismiss too much mourning over Sarah as "out of keeping with wisdom" (Abr. 258). In poignant contrast to Abraham's stoicism, Philo's Egyptians engaged in "a united outcry, one single dirge of wailing" and upon learning that everybody had been struck "lost even the hope of consolation".[53] Philo's description echoes Aeschylus, who had stressed the Persians' overly emotional reaction to the disaster at Salamis. Aeschylus criticized their excessive weeping, crying and breast-beating on numerous occasions, using sound effects and repetition to highlight the foolish weakness of these barbarians.[54] The same emotionality characterizes Philo's Egyptians when the loss of the battle dawns on them. While the Biblical Egyptians simply said: "let us flee from before Israel; for the Lord fights for them against the Egyptians" (Ex. 14:25), Philo dramatizes the scene. He reports that "tumult and confusion prevailed everywhere among them. In their terror their ranks fell into disorder. They tumbled over each other and sought to

---

[50] Mos. 1:167; cf. Ex. 14:3–9.
[51] Concerning Xerxes' cruelty, see especially Pers. 353–4, 782–6, 909–1001; the sailors are ordered to be killed in Pers. 369–71.
[52] Mos. 1:169, cf. Pers. 361–73.
[53] Mos. 1:136–7, cf. Ex. 11:6, 12:30.
[54] Pers. 268–83, 465–71, 537–45, 909–1076; Hall, Barbarian 83–4, 131–2.

escape" (Mos. 1:178). His Egyptians clearly behaved in a far more barbarian and uncontrolled manner. They resemble Aeschylus' disorganized Persians, who were already panic-stricken at the very sound of the Greek war paean. They were confused to the extent that they even violated each others' ships.[55] When the dimension of the catastrophe dawned on them, they "leapt from their ships just as they were ... And at a loss for where to turn, they were pummelled by rocks".[56] It thus emerges that Philo's Israelites were at the Red Sea confronted with a Persian type enemy, who lacked the "Western" virtues of courage, military discipline and strategic thinking. The Egyptians instead acted like true barbarians. They were chaotic, emotional and prone to panic.

Philo's construction of the Biblical Egyptians as Persians has important implications for Jewish identity. It is initially obvious that this is the way he integrates the Jews among the civilized Western nations. Greeks and Jews, united by their common opposition to barbarism, stand on the same side of a basic division between East and West. Both defend freedom and rational dignity. The Jews appear now as a spearhead of the democratic and enlightened world. Philo has in addition rewritten Jewish history in analogy to the Greek national myth. He argues that "we" had the same formative experience in a battle equivalent to Salamis, and that this constituted "our" political and ethnic identity. This interpretation was of crucial importance in the contemporary Roman world where the Classical myth had been revived and become far more significant than in the Greek culture of the time. Philo thus applied the same typology to Jewish history as Augustus had done to Roman history. Both assimilated the events of their own nation to the Greek national myth, casting themselves in the role of the ancient Athenians, while their respective Other played the role of the Barbarian. By describing the Egyptians as Persians Philo has integrated himself into the Roman discourse. He uses the same language and the same stereotypes as they had done to speak about the Jewish past and Jewish identity. Augustus had indeed provided him with the keymotif, when celebrating his victory at Actium as a repetition of Alexander's victory over the Persians. Reading the Exodus story from such a distinctly contemporary perspective, Philo merely had to embellish an existing typology and add further details from prevailing stereotypes. The Jews consequently emerge as a nation sharing Rome's barbarian Other.

The last strategy Philo employs to construct the national character of the Egyptians is to portray them as a most dangerous source of political unrest. They, and they alone, are responsible for having upset the peaceful order of

---

[55] Pers. 388–92, 413–28, 465–71, 480–1.

[56] Pers. 457–60; Xerxes himself "shrieked ... tore his robes and let out a shrill and piercing cry", rushing away "in disordered flight" (Pers. 465–70); similarly the remaining ships' commanders "raised their sails in haste and fled in disarray wherever the wind might lead" (Pers. 480–1).

Roman rule in contemporary Alexandria. They caused the crisis under Gaius Caligula.[57] It is striking that no other political factor is considered by Philo: not Roman rule as such, nor the Jews, some of whom had destroyed a pagan altar in Jamnia and behaved provocatively in Alexandria, nor the Greeks whose *gymnasiarchoi* led the anti-Jewish politics in Alexandria.[58] Philo instead explained all aspects of the crisis by pointing to the innate hatred of the Egyptians for the Jews and their irredeemable tendency for political strife. Their political agitation against the Jews was not seen as a response to a specific and real conflict, but as a one-sided problem of their national character.

Philo dwells on the political flaws of the Egyptians at considerable length. He says that they are jealous by nature (Flac. 29) and most excitable among all nations, "accustomed … to blow up the tiniest spark into grave seditions" (Flac. 17). "The Alexandrians", Philo continues, "are adepts at flattery and imposture and hypocrisy, ready enough with fawning words but causing universal disaster with their loose and unbridled lips".[59] On another occasion he ridicules the "lazy and unoccupied mob of the city, a multitude well practiced in idle talk, who devote their leisure to slandering and evil speaking" (Flac. 33). These descriptions agree to a striking extent with Roman views on the Egyptians, which were overwhelmingly negative since Augustus' propaganda campaign. Tacitus criticized them in the same manner as Philo for their propensity to civil strife and political unrest. Cicero and Seneca the Younger complained about the loose tongue and insolent speech of the Alexandrians.[60] Seneca, who had in his youth spent some time in Egypt, related specific cases of Romans being murdered in Egypt. This confirmed his views about the "incestuous", unstable and "faithless" nature of this country.[61] This convergence of opinion between Philo

---

[57] The anti-Egyptian tendency of Philo's account of contemporary events has often been noticed, see especially: Goudriaan, Ethnical Stategies 86–9; Pearce, Belonging 92–4; Schäfer, Judeophobia 143–5; Tcherikover, *CPJ* 1:66–7.

[58] On Philo's views on Roman rule, see below chapter four; Philo's tendency to downplay the Jewish part in the crisis has often been noted, see most recently: Barclay, Mediterranean Diaspora 54–5; Schäfer, Judeophobia 143–4; on Isidorus and Lampon as *gymnasiarchoi*, see: Tcherikover, *CPJ* 2:69–70. To be sure, the gymnasiarchal setting of the anti-Jewish agitation is mentioned by Philo (e.g. Flac. 34, 37), but he does not connect this fact to "the Greeks". Goudriaan, Ethnical Strategies 85–87 is therefore right in stressing the descrepancy between Isidorus' self-image as a Hellene (attested in the *Acts of the Alexandrian Martyrs*) and Philo's inclination to disconnect the Greeks from the political and anti-Semitic opposition to the Jews; for further details on Philo's construction of the Greeks, see below chapter five.

[59] Leg. 162; see also Flac. 41; Leg. 120.

[60] Tac., Hist. 1:11; Cic., Pro Rabiro Post. 34–5 (Alexandria is the home of "every deceit" and its inhabitants provide the writers of farces with plots); Sen., Cons. Helv. 19:6, discusses the wife of the governor of Egypt – his aunt – who never went out in order to avoid the calumnies of "a province that was gossipy and ingenious in devising insults for its rulers, one in which even those who shunned wrong-doing did not escape ill fame"; see also Dio 39.58:1–2; M. Reinhold, Roman Attitudes towards the Egyptians, *Ancient World* 3.3–4 (1980) 97–103.

[61] Sen., Oct. 519–21; Cons. Marc. 14:2.; Cons. Helv. 9:8; De Brev. Vit. 13:7.

and Roman intellectuals reinforces the profile which has emerged so far: Philo constructs the Egyptian Other in a way that integrates the Jews into the contemporary Roman world and suggests a profound Roman-Jewish congeniality. It now becomes clear that in political matters, too, both nations stand side by side.[62]

In the same spirit Philo goes one step further and identifies the Egyptians as the source of religious and cultural anti-Semitism. They cherish in his view "an old and in a way innate hatred for the Jews".[63] The nature and origin of this hatred are nowhere discussed. Philo takes its existence for granted and uses it as an explanation for the "Egyptian" opposition to events such as Agrippa's parade through the city. He locates the beginning of the deterioration at the point when the Egyptian agitators succeeded in endearing themselves to the new emperor Gaius Caligula. Flattering his vanity and aspirations to divinity, they managed to gain political influence and thus an opportunity to implement anti-Jewish measures. We saw in the previous chapter how Philo, for inter-Jewish purposes, linked the local crisis in Alexandria with the issue of Gaius' statue in the Jerusalem Temple. He suggested that the real and original conflict revolved around Gaius' deification.[64] The pogrom in Alexandria was to a significant extent a derivation of this larger issue. An intrinsically local conflict involving civic issues is hardly ever alluded to.[65] Philo argues that the Egyptians' innate wickedness caused both the Alexandrian riots and the general crisis.

According to Philo's story of the events, everything began with the shameless flattery of the Alexandrians. They encouraged Gaius to think of himself as a regular god (Leg. 162) and thus gave "birth to ... the idea of godship which occupied his dreams" (Leg. 338). Even though the crisis around Gaius' statue in the Jerusalem Temple broke out as a result of the incident in Jamnia and was therefore a separate as well as later issue, Philo rewrote history and linked the Alexandrian riots to Gaius' deification.[66] He suggests that Gaius' claim to divinity served the Alexandrians as a pretext for demolishing the Jewish syna-

---

[62] Pearce, Belonging 94–5, also points to the Roman background of Philo's seditious Egyptians. In her opinion, however, his message was mainly directed to an outside audience: he wanted to convince the Romans that the Jews, not the Egyptians, are loyal to the Romans. As we have seen in the previous chapter, however, both *In Flaccum* and the *Legatio* addressed a Jewish audience and therefore need to be appreciated in the context of inter-Jewish discussions.

[63] τὴν παλαιὰν καὶ τρόπον τινὰ ⟨φύσει⟩ γεγενημένην πρὸς Ἰουδαίους ἀπέχθειαν (Flac. 29).

[64] On Philo's views of Gaius in the context of the imperial cult, see below chapter three.

[65] Flac. 53–4, 172. The political roots of the conflicts have been emphasized especially by: I. Heinemann, Ursprung und Wesen des Antisemitismus im Altertum, in: *Festgabe zum zehnjährigen Bestehen der Akademie für die Wissenschaft des Judentums 1919–1929* (Berlin 1929) 76–91; Bergmann and Hoffmann, Kalkül 34–46.

[66] On Philo's one-sided reconstruction of the events, see also: Bilde, Gaius' Attempt 70–76; J.P.V.D. Balsdon, *The Emperor Gaius (Caligula)* (Oxford 1934) 135–7.

gogues. Initially, however, they succeeded to get Flaccus under their control (Flac. 19–20):

the ruler became the subject, the subjects leaders, who put forward very pernicious proposals ... [they] took Flaccus like a masked dummy on the stage, with the title of government inscribed upon him merely for show, to be an instrument in the hands of a popularity-hunting Dionysius, a paper-poring Lampo, an Isidorus, faction leader, busy intriguer, mischief contriver ...

These statements perfectly suit Philo's overall construction of the Egyptians: their leaders are mere agitators without any serious political agenda. Their influence is most detrimental to the generally peaceful order of Roman rule. The Egyptians are thus said to have used the new power vacuum for their anti-Jewish machinations. They ridiculed Agrippa by letting "a certain lunatic named Carabas" personify him on stage (Flac. 36). Then they "called out with one accord for installing images in the synagogues ... using the name of Caesar as a screen" (Flac. 41–2). Philo indicates that the Alexandrians pretended to honour Gaius by setting up images in the Jewish synagogues (Flac. 51). This interpretation of the events presupposes the prior existence of a conflict between Gaius and the Jews, who refused to pay him the expected honours. Only on this assumption does it make sense to claim that the setting up of images in Jewish synagogues could be justified before Flaccus as a measure to force the Jews into the right kind of respect for the emperor.

The way, however, in which Philo has inserted this interpretation into his narrative arouses doubt as to its historicity. It is initially striking how brief Philo's reference to this argument is. No explanations. No background information. His readers, it seems, can fully grasp his point only after reading the *Legatio*. Philo himself seems to have looked on the Alexandrian riots from the significantly later perspective of that book. He has adapted the events of *In Flaccum* to the plot of the *Legatio* which revolves around Gaius' deification.[67] Amalgamating these two stories, Philo attributes the worst character to the Egyptians. They incited Gaius and affected religious indignation which was not even based on genuine piety. Philo comments sarcastically on their alleged concerns for Gaius' deification: "how much reverence is paid by them to the title of God is shown by their having allowed it to be shared by the indigenous ibises and venomous snakes and many other ferocious wild beasts" (Leg. 163). Philo moreover emphasizes that under the Ptolemies the Egyptians never made similar demands to set up the ruler's image in the synagogues. Their claim to honour Gaius was thus nothing but hypocricy, a rather transparent camouflage for their innate hatred of the Jews. Devoid of genuine political or religious motivation, the Egyptians were thus nothing but dangerous trouble-makers and agitators.

---

[67] For further details on Philo's change of the chronological order of the events and his overall focus on the issue of Gaius' deification to which other subjects are subordinated, see: Smallwood, Legatio 3–4, 206–7.

Cunning Egyptians receive particular attention in Philo's account, while serious political opponents like Apion, who led the Alexandrian embassy to Gaius, are never even mentioned. Helicon and Isidorus especially stand in Philo's spotlight. Helicon is described as a slave at Gaius' court, who used his private access to the emperor for propaganda against the Jews. He is said to have transmitted the most malicious parodies about their customs, which he had as a child heard by "the noisiest element in the city of the Alexandrians" (Leg. 170). Philo even calls him a "scorpion in the form of a slave, [who] vented his Egyptian venom on the Jews" (Leg. 205). Similarly, "the virulent sycophant Isidorus" is said to have stirred up Gaius against the Jews by suggesting that they are an oppositional element: "my lord, you will hate still more these people here present, and the rest of their compatriots, too, when you learn of their ill-will and disloyalty towards you" (Leg. 355). The terrible violence of the pogrom itself is for Philo the ultimate expression of the Egyptians' national character (Flac. 66). They indeed showed "no pity for old age nor youth, nor the innocent years of childhood" and instead destroyed everything they could lay their hands on (Flac. 68). Egyptian violence towards the Jews thus appears as an inevitable consequence of their general character. Essentially nothing but slanderers and flatterers, they lack any serious political agenda and are entirely given to jealousy and innate hatred. Conflict can therefore not be avoided. In Philo's opinion a strong Roman government is necessary to keep the Egyptians under control and limit the effects of their inherent weaknesses.

What are the implications of Philo's multi-faceted construction of the Egyptians? How does their image as subhuman idol-worshippers, paramount people of the soil, Persian-type barbarians and political trouble-makers shape Jewish identity? Moreover, what is the broader meaning of this negative construction in the politics of Jewish identity throughout Egypt? Some implications are immediately obvious and have already been mentioned. Philo constructs them as the complete Other of the Jews, whose perversion dialectically highlights "our" positive qualities. Egyptian zoolatry thus emphasizes the aniconic and moral character of Jewish religion. Egyptian attachment to the soil stresses the value of diaspora life, which transcends the physical homeland, but remains loyal to the mothercity. The Persian features of the Egyptians moreover suggest that the Jews share the Classical Greek and Roman values of freedom, rationality and discipline. Finally, the demagogic agitation and physical violence of the Egyptians imply that the Jews are politically mature as well as peaceful citizens. In all of these respects the Jews emerge as spearheads of Western civilization. They are most congenial to the Romans with whom they share their scorn for the Egyptians.

The absolute dichotomy between Egyptians and Jews has further consequences for Jewish identity in Egypt. It is indeed striking that Philo speaks so negatively about the Egyptians, while actually living in their midst. Jews had lived there for many generations in relative harmony with the local population.

They had appreciated Egyptian culture and religion, setting up their own temple at Leontopolis next to the famous Egyptian sun temple. Artapanus even celebrated Moses as the founder of Egyptian zoolatry.[68] Other Jews of the Ptolemaic period are known to have integrated firmly into Greco-Egyptian culture. Dositheus, son of Drimylos and memorandum writer of Euergetes I, made a career as "priest of Alexander and the gods Adelphoi and the gods Euergetai".[69] Ptolemaios, the son of Dionysius the Jew, and Theodotus, son of Dorion the Jew, dedicated inscriptions praising Pan in his temple at El-Kanais.[70]

To Philo all this was anathema. He was a fervent opponent of Jewish-Egyptian symbiosis, which had in any case become far more difficult because of political tension and the circulation of negative Exodus stories.[71] Philo insisted on a complete segregation from the Egyptians. This implied a thorough reorientation of Egyptian Jewry. As far as Philo was concerned, Jews should no longer see themselves as Egyptians. If they identified with Egyptian values and culture, they lost something essential of their Jewish character. Philo's demand for segregation becomes especially conspicuous in his interpretation of two Biblical figures who assumed leadership roles in Egypt: Joseph and Moses. These were now enlisted to support Philo's new construction of Jewish identity, thus revising earlier Jewish exegesis on them.

The figure of Joseph had for a long time engaged the attention of Egyptian Jews. Joseph became a favourite name during the Ptolemaic period. Its exceptional frequency among Egyptian Jews stands in contrast to Palestine where Maccabean names were much preferred. This phenomenon indicates the interest Egyptian Jews took in the career of a Jew in the land of their residence. Sylvie Honigman rightly identified this moment as a sign of an independent and self-conscious Egyptian-Jewish identity.[72] The Biblical Joseph story naturally

---

[68] On Artapanus' tolerant attitude towards Egyptian polytheism, see also: C. R. Holladay, Jewish Responses to Hellenistic Culture, in: Bilde, Ethnicity in Egypt 145–6; M. R. Niehoff, Philo's Views on Paganism, in: G. N. Stanton and G. G. Stroumsa (eds.), *Tolerance and Intolerance in Early Judaism and Christianity* (Cambridge 1988)135–6; for further details, see below.

[69] *CPJ* no. 127d; see also: Mélèze-Modrzejewski, How to Be a Jew 65–92; Barclay, Mediterranean Diaspora 104–6; on the identity of the Dositheos of the papyri and the Dositheos of 3 Macc. 1:3, see Tcherikover, *CPJ* 1:230–1.

[70] W. Horbury and D. Noy, *Jewish Inscriptions of Graeco-Roman Egypt* (Cambridge 1992) nos. 121–2.

[71] On the influence of such Egyptian stories on Philo's attitude to the Egyptians, see especially: Goudriaan, Ethnical Strategies 87–90; Pearce, Belonging 84–7. Gruen, Heritage 41–72, and J. Assmann, *Moses the Egyptian. The Memory of Egypt in Western Monotheism* (Cambridge MA 1997) 23–55, have independently shown that these Egyptian stories must not be understood as reactions to the Biblical Exodus account, but as originally independent stories which have been associated with the Jews only at a relatively late stage.

[72] S. Honigman, The Birth of a Diaspora: The Emergence of a Jewish Self-Definition in Ptolemaic Egypt in the Light of Onomastics, in: Cohen and Frerichs, Diasporas 93–127; on common names in Palestine, see: T. Ilan, The Greek Names of the Hasmoneans, *JQR* 78.1–

concerned Egyptian Jews and must have expressed the aspirations of many of them. It is therefore only to be expected that the battle over Jewish identity in Philo's Egypt should be fought, among other things, over this figure. Philo decisively changed the way Jews were to see their forefather.

Philo's interpretation of Joseph has until today remained a puzzle for scholars. He left two rather contradictory views, a positive one in *De Josepho* and a critical one mainly in *De Somniis*. This dichotomy between the two treatises has at times been ignored, explained away or simply acknowledged. At other times historical and exegetical explanations have been advanced.[73] Jaques Cazeaux recently suggested the importance of Egypt in Philo's interpretation of Joseph. He argued that *De Josepho* and *De Somniis* are mirror treatises in a geographical sense: while the former looks at Joseph in an Egyptian context and from an Egyptian perspective, the latter presents Joseph from the point of view of Palestine.[74] Judged by Egyptian standards Joseph is a positive character, while measured by Israelite values he is rather more disappointing. This line of inquiry is highly suggestive and needs further exploring. It will become clear that Joseph is interpreted by Philo with one central question in mind: did he compromise with Egyptian ways? This question is treated with a view to contemporary issues. Joseph thus becomes an examplary test-case for the extent Jews could and should integrate in Egypt. Philo's interpretation of the Biblical figure serves two ends. It demonstrates the ideal of segregation, while at the same time expressing criticism of contemporary Jews who failed to live up to the ideal and assimilated too much. This double bind gave rise to Philo's different interpretations of Joseph. In the biographical narrative he outlines the model, whereas on other occasions he uses Joseph as an allegory for contemporary Egyptian Jews. *De Josepho* thus indicates how Egyptian Jewry should in Philo's view behave and *De Somniis* the rather more gloomy reality.[75]

---

2 (1987) 1–20; eadem, Notes on the Distribution of Jewish Women's Names in Palestine in the Second Temple and Mishnaic Periods, *JJS* 40.1 (1989) 186–200.

[73] The dichotomy has been ignored by M. Niehoff, *The Figure of Joseph in Post-Biblical Jewish Literature* (Leiden 1992 = Arbeiten zur Geschichte des antiken Judentums und des Urchristentums 16) 54–83; explained away by J.M. Bassler, Philo on Joseph. The Basic Coherence of *De Josepho* and *De Somniis II*, *JSJ* 1.26 (1985) 240–55; and been acknowledged by Gruen, Heritage 81–7, see also bibliography there to which may be added: D. Sills, Strange Bedfellows: Politics and Narrative in Philo, in: S. D. Breslauer, *The Seductiveness of Jewish Myth. Challenge or Response?* (New York 1997) 171–90.

[74] J. Cazeaux, Nul n'est prophète en son pays: Contribution à l'étude de Joseph d'après Philon, in: J. P. Kenney (ed.), *The School of Moses. Studies in Philo and Hellenistic Religion. In Memory of Horst R. Moehring* (Atlanta 1995 = Brown Judaica Studies 304) 61–6.

[75] After formulating this argument I saw that Sandelin, Idolatry 137, briefly suggested a topical context for the allegorical interpretation of Joseph. He, however, interpreted this as referring to the dangers of assimilation to Roman culture.

The key to *De Josepho* is paragraph 254, where Jacob reacts to the news of Joseph living in Egypt. While happy to hear that his son is still alive, Jacob is immediately concerned about his Jewish identity:

But joy also straightway begat fear in his soul at the thought of leaving his ancestral way of life. For he knew how natural it is for youth to lose its footing and what license to sin belongs to the stranger's life, particularly in Egypt where things created and mortal are deified and in consequence the land is blind to the true God. He knew what assaults wealth and renown make on minds of little sense, and that left to himself, since his father's house supplied no monitor to share his journey, alone and cut off from good teaching, he would be readily influenced to change to alien ways.

Philo shows that Jacob's fears are unfounded. The patriarch receives a most warm-hearted welcome by his son. Even Pharaoh, the highest representative of Egyptian culture, was "overcome by his venerable appearance, ... welcomed him with all modesty and respect, as though he were the father not of his viceroy but of himself" (Jos. 257). Egypt, it seems, is assimilating to the Israelites rather than the other way round. Jacob sees for himself that Joseph, despite his high position, has remained honest and reverent of "truly genuine riches rather than the spurious" (Jos. 258). Joseph moreover assures his brothers of the stability of his character which remains the same even under changing circumstances (Jos. 262). It is significant that Philo limits Joseph's influence on Egyptian culture and life. As a ruler over the land he could have introduced many innovations and established forms of Jewish-Egyptian symbiosis. Yet the reader learns nothing of the sort. Philo's Joseph instead focused on crisis management (Jos. 258–9). The only mention of Joseph's cultural contribution to Egypt concerns dining customs and reflects the blurred perspective of the brothers who have not yet recognized Joseph (Jos. 204). It is precisely this non-involvement in Egyptian culture which Philo likes about his Biblical Joseph.

Highlighting the ideal of preserving Jewish identity in Egypt, Philo gives paramount importance to Joseph's rejection of Potiphar's wife. Unlike other commentators, he interprets this incident for the first time as a paradigmatic refusal of Egyptian values. The author of the book of *Jubilees* had identified adultery as the main issue of Genesis chapter 39; the *Testaments of the Twelve Patriarchs* were shocked by the shamelessness and idolatry of the woman and Josephus subsequently constructed the incident as a stereotypical encounter between a rational male and an over-emotional, unrestrained female.[76] Philo's interpretation, however, highlighted the confrontation between Egyptian and Jewish values. Potiphar's wife personifies Egyptian licentiousness and vice. Joseph, by contrast, represents Jewish virtue. When he rejects her advances, he

---

[76] Jub. 39:6–8; regarding the *Testament of the Twelve Patriarchs*, see: H.W. Hollander, *Joseph as an Ethical Model in the Testaments of the Twelve Patriarchs* (Leiden 1981); Jos., A.J. 2:50–9.

stresses that "we children of the Hebrews follow laws and customs which are especially our own" (Jos. 42). These customs, Joseph continues, are diametrically opposed to those of the Egyptians. Philo draws his readers' attention directly to the ethnic significance of Joseph's steadfastness. His chaste reply is said to be "worthy of his race" (Jos. 42).

In *De Somniis* and other tractates, however, it becomes clear that the issue of Joseph in Egypt is not yet settled. Philo has thoughts about him which were not expressed in the idealizing biography. These thoughts which burst from Philo's lips in a far more fragmentary and precipitated manner are most negative: Joseph is accused of vainglory, opportunism and licentiousness.[77] The most striking aspect of these passages is the change of perspective from Joseph's point of view in the biography to the brothers' point of view in *De Somniis*. While *De Josepho* presents the events through Joseph's eyes, Philo identifies in *De Somniis* with his brothers. Radically changing the Biblical facts, Philo even speaks of their reconciliation with him instead of Joseph's reconciliation with them (Somn. 2:108). The reader will immediately ask which sins they forgave him. What had disturbed the brothers about Joseph? In Philo's story his sin is no longer personal arrogance in the family, but assimilation to Egypt. He adopted the Egyptian vices of vainglory and licentiousness, thus abandoning his father's customs. The brothers could forgive Joseph only after he repented and rejected Egypt. Philo explains Joseph's assimilation and subsequent return to Jewish tradition in the following terms (Somn. 2:106–8):

When moved by a yearning for continence and a vast zeal for piety he rejects bodily pleasure, the wife of the Egyptian, as she bids him come in to her and enjoy her embraces (Gen. 39:7); when he claims the goods of his kinsmen and father from which he seemed to have been disinherited and holds it his duty to recover that portion of virtue which falls to his lot, when he passes step by step from betterment to betterment and, established firmly as it were on the crowning heights and consummation of his life, utters aloud the lesson which experience has taught him so fully: "I belong to God" (Gen. 50:19) ... – then his brothers will make with him covenants of reconciliation, changing their hatred into friendship, their ill-will to good-will and I, their follower and servant, who have learnt to obey them as masters, will not fail to praise him for his repentance (μετανοίας).

This is in many ways a remarkable passage. It initially emerges that Philo identifies Joseph's character flaws with Egypt. His shortcomings are no longer seen as inherent features of an individual, but as changes of character due to assimilation. Joseph is, in other words, no longer seen as a problematic personality, because he was spoilt and selfish. He rather develops vice by leaving ancestral ways and assuming Egyptian features. Philo may even have implied that Joseph's youthful arrogance, when he related visions of his own glory, is due to his Egyptian leanings (Somn. 2:98–100).

---

[77] See e.g. Somn. 1:210–20; 2:10–4; 2:42–7, 2:63–6.

Yet Joseph's assimilation is reversable. He gradually recovers his ethnic identity by rejecting Potiphar's wife, confessing God and requesting the transfer of his bones to Palestine. It is this return to Jewish customs which makes a reconciliation with his brothers possible. They can now forgive him and become his friends. Philo emphasizes that their previous hatred of him had nothing of a "misanthropic and unbrotherly character", but was dictated by pure virtue (Somn. 2:98). Their judgemental behaviour was entirely justified. Philo identifies to such an extent with Joseph's brothers that he openly declares himself to be their "follower and servant". This is a highly exceptional statement of personal commitment on Philo's part, occasioned by the urgent matter at stake. The danger of Jewish assimilation to Egyptian values was an issue of highly topical concern. Philo's unusually personal remarks create a direct link between the Biblical Joseph and contemporary Egyptian Jewry. They indicate that Joseph is also read as an allegory for Egyptian Jews in the first century. While the Biblical figure was in *De Josepho* rewritten as an ideal model of segregation from Egyptian culture, an allegorical interpretation indicates Philo's ambivalence about contemporary affairs. He himself identified with the brothers and seems to have had other Jews in mind, who in his view associated too much with Joseph's successful integration in Egypt.

These conclusions are confirmed in other passages in *De Migratione*. The tone here is again critical and Joseph is once more accused of vainglory, opportunism and licentiousness. On one occasion Philo states his interpretation with particular emphasis (Migr. 160):

Do you notice that this politician [Joseph] takes his position in the midst between the house of Pharaoh and his father's house? that his object is to be equally in touch with the concerns of the body, which is Egypt, and those of the soul which are kept as in a treasury in his father's house? For when he says "I belong to God" (Gen. 50:19) and other things of this kind, he is abiding by the customs of his father's house. But when he mounts "the second chariot" of the mind that fancies itself a king, even Pharaoh (Gen. 49:43), he again sets up the idol Egyptian vanity.

The exegesis of Gen. 50:19 in this passage follows the same pattern as in *De Somniis*. Philo interprets the moment of Joseph's reunification with his brothers, when he confesses God, as an indication of his return to a self-conscious Jewish identity. His high position in the Egyptian hierarchy, by contrast, is condemned as a compromise with Jewish tradition. Joseph's riding in the second chariot behind Pharaoh was a grave mistake. He thus imbibed Egyptian vanity and succumbed to foreign values. The reason for Philo's ambivalence towards Joseph is clearly his integration into Egyptian society. Philo could not avoid expressing his disapproval, especially in light of the repetition of Joseph's flaws in his own time.

Philo's interpretation of Joseph seems to have been revolutionary. As far as the extant sources can tell, he was the first Jew who constructed him with such ambivalence and a view to the totally negative Egyptian Other. Philo's Midrash indicates an important turning-point in the tradition of Egyptian Jewry and counters earlier commentaries on Joseph. Such an earlier and distinctly pro-Egyptian interpretation of Joseph is conspicuous in Artapanus' work. Philo might even have written his Joseph story in order to negate the kind of Jewish identity which that author from the Egyptian countryside had publicized.[78] Artapanus had used the Biblical Joseph to celebrate an irenic Jewish-Egyptian symbiosis. No word about his rejection of Potiphar's wife. No word either about his imprisonment in Egypt. On the contrary, the highlight of Artapanus' story is Joseph's marriage to "Aseneth, the daughter of a Heliopolitan priest".[79] It is implied that Joseph deserved this union with one of the most noble Egyptian ladies after having introduced various agricultural innovations which gained him general popularity and esteem. The engagement thus crowned a successful career of a Jew who had come to live in Egypt. Upon marrying, Artapanus continues his story, Joseph settled his recently arrived family in Helioplis and Sais (Praep. Ev. 9.23:2–3). The geographically undefined Goshen of the Biblical account has thus been replaced by the famous Egyptian site next to the Jewish temple of Onias. As if this were not enough, Artapanus has Joseph's clan build a temple in Heliopolis and Athos (Praep. Ev. 9.23:4). These features of Artapanus' Joseph story place the author in the context of a Jewish party which supported acculturation to the Egyptian environment.[80] Artapanus could not have been further removed from Philo's subsequent position of complete segregation. He reflected a totally different sense of Jewish identity during the Ptolemaic period. Its very rootedness in Egyptian soil and Egyptian culture subsequently became anathema to Philo. As a Jewish leader in close contact with Roman rule, Philo constructed a counter-image to Artapanus' Joseph. In an attempt to reverse this kind of assimilatory exegesis, he stressed Joseph's

---

[78] On the geographical setting of Artapanus, see: Fraser, Ptolemaic Alexandria 704–6; Collins, Athens and Jerusalem 32–3; C.R. Holladay, *Fragments from Hellenistic Jewish Authors* (Chico 1983 = *SBL* Texts and Translations 20) 1:189–90.

[79] Artapanus, apud Eusebius, Praep. Ev. 9.23:3; the LXX had already modernized the term אֹן in Gen. 41:45, translating it as Ἡλίου πόλεως.

[80] G. Sterling, *Historiography and Self-Definition. Josephus, Luke-Acts and Apologetic Histporiography* (Leiden 1992) 184–6, rightly stresses Artapanus' contribution to Jewish-Egyptian identity; cf. the less appreciative interpretations of Holladay, Fragments 1:190 Gruen, Heritage 155. Some scholars have suggested Artapanus' connection to Leontopolis; see: M. Hengel, Anonymität, Pseudepigrahie und Literarische Fälschung in der Jüdisch-Hellenistischen Literatur, *Entretiens sur l'Antiquité Classique XVIII*, Pseudepigrapha (1972) 1:239; C.R. Holladay, *Theios Aner in Hellenistic Judaism. A Critique of the Use of This Category in New Testament Christology* (Missoula 1977 = SBL Diss. Ser. 40) 217. In his discussion of Artapanus in Fragments 1:184 n. 25, however, Holladay suggests that the reference to Heliopolis may simply derive from the Septuagintal notice of Joseph's marriage to the daughter of the high-priest of Heliopolis.

segregation from Egyptian culture and criticized any sign of his personal integration as a warning to contemporary Jews.

In comparison to Joseph, the figure of Moses lends itself more easily to Philo's agenda. There was no need to feel ambivalent about him, because he was precisely the leader who took the Israelites out of Egypt. Moses could thus easily personify the ideal of a cultural Exodus from Egypt and support Philo's demand that the Jews keep a mental distance from the country of their residence. Philo's interpretation of Moses again seems to have countered earlier exegesis, this time also taking into account rumours about his Egyptian origins.[81] Philo could obviously not accept the idea of his hero's Egyptian descent, even if this was suggested in a sympathetic spirit.[82] Philo's biography of Moses was thus meant to correct all such stories about Moses, especially Jewish ones, which identified him to varying degrees with Egypt.

Philo's Moses was indeed isolated from Egyptian culture. Philo insists that he never became an integral part of the Egyptian court even though he was raised there. From infancy onwards Moses was self-sufficient and never inclined towards luxury or idleness (Mos. 1:20, 25–9). His teachers, some "unbidden from the neighbouring countries and the provinces of Egypt" (Mos. 1:21), left hardly any impression on him, because he quickly advanced beyond their capacity. His intellectual progress "seemed a case rather of recollection than of learning" (Mos. 1:21). Knowledge came to him from within, his mind being "incapable of accepting any falsehood" (Mos. 1:24). Even the Egyptian courtiers immediately recognized the Otherness of Moses. They were "struck with amazement at what they felt was a novel spectacle" (Mos. 1:27). Summarizing Moses' youth, Philo highlights his hero's awareness of the Egyptians' Otherness and leaves no doubt about the implications for contemporary Jews (Mos. 1:30–3):

---

[81] Gruen, Heritage 41–72, convincingly argued that accounts of Moses' Egyptian origins and/or conquest of Egypt cannot be simply attributed to anti-Semitic fabrications. They did not even emerge as counter-history to the Biblical Exodus account, but may instead have derived from Jewish writers who wished to inscribe their people into the history of their land of residence. The question remains whether such Jews would have gone as far as identifying Moses as an Egyptian. Such a move would have undermined the very process of integration, which always assumes the mingling of different entities.

[82] Philo emphatically states this point in Mut. 117. A positive view of Moses the Egyptian is expressed by Strabo, Geogr. 16.2:35–6 = GLAJJ 1:299–300; see also: Assman, Moses 23–55; Schäfer, Judeophobia 19–21; S. Freud, *Der Mann Moses und die monotheistische Religion* (1934–38, available also in the Engl. Standard transl. of Freud's works by J. Strachey (New York and London 1966). It emerges from Mos. 1:2–4 that Philo anticipated an isolated circulation of his biography of Moses. He opens here with a summary of previous Israelite history meant obviously for those who were familiar with neither his other treatises nor even the book of Genesis; see also: E. R. Goodenough, *An Introduction to Philo Judaeus* (Oxford 2nd ed. 1962) 33–4.

Now, most men, if they feel a breath of prosperity ever so small upon them, make much ado of puffing and blowing ... [and] look down on their relations and friends and set at naught the laws under which they were born and bred, and subvert the ancestral customs to which no blame can justly attach, by adopting different modes of life and in their contentment with the present, lose all memory of the past.

But Moses, having reached the very pinnacle of human prosperity, regarded as the son of the king's daughter .... was zealous for the discipline and culture of his kinsmen and ancestors. The good fortune of his adopters, he held, was a spurious one, ... that of his natural parents, though less distinguished for the nonce, was at any rate his own and genuine; and so, estimating the claims of his real and his adopted parents like an imperial judge, he requited the former with good feeling and profound affection, the latter with gratitude for their kind treatment of him.

This passage highlights the merely external nature of Moses' sojourn at the Egyptian court. Besides an appropriate sense of gratitude Moses did not develop any emotional attachments. His values were not challenged and his foster parents never became real parents. Philo especially emphasizes that Moses did not act like many others in a similar situation. This remark sounds conspicuously general and distinctly topical. It is probably an indirect reference to contemporary Jews, who quickly assimilated and forgot their ancestral ways. Philo's Moses, by contrast, never succumbed to the temptation of Eygpt and never forsook either his origins or ancestral traditions. It is implied that Moses was actually familiar with the Jewish heritage and remained faithful to it during his stay at Pharaoh's court. This assumption is striking. Philo constructs here a *curriculum vitae*, which attributes familiarity with Jewish traditions to a child who had in the Bible never been exposed to them. Egypt is thus excised from the biography of Moses, while Jewish customs are added to the early stage of his life. The result is an ideal hero, who was nourished by Jewish traditions and preserved them through dramatically changing circumstances. In this respect he was a model of crucial importance whom Philo held up to his contemporaries.

The incident of Moses' killing the Egyptian who had beaten a fellow Hebrew, is rewritten in the same spirit. While the Biblical narrator pointed to the underlying ethnic issue by describing the beaten Hebrew as "one of his brothers" (Ex. 2:11–2),[83] he also indicated the complexity of national loyalties. Indeed, Moses was most severely judged for his action by other Israelites, who rejected his leadership and feared that he might kill them just like the Egyptian (Ex. 2:14). Pharaoh's reaction to this incident is recorded with utmost brevity: "when Pharaoh heard of it, he sought to kill Moses" (Ex. 2:15). It is up to the reader to fill in the gap and conjecture Pharaoh's precise motives. Philo completely

---

[83] This tendency is reinforced in the LXX by the expression "his brother from the children of Israel".

rewrites this incident in Moses' life. He omits entirely any reference to Israelite criticism of Moses' killing. On another occasion he even stresses that Moses' leadership was most willingly accepted by the Israelites (Praem. 54). Pharaoh's reaction to the rumours of Moses' killing, by contrast, is significantly expanded. Philo ascribes to him a sudden awareness of Moses' complete Otherness. The issue of ethnic identity becomes paramount in this context. Philo emphasizes that what Pharaoh "felt so strongly was not that one man had been killed by another whether justly or unjustly" (Mos. 1:45). Pharaoh was after all an Egyptian with no moral decency. He was rather concerned with one fact alone, namely (Mos. 1:45):

that his own daughter's son did not think with him, and had not considered the king's friends and enemies to be his own friends and enemies, but hated those of whom he was fond and loved those whom he rejected, and pitied those to whom he was relentless and inexorable.

Philo constructs here Moses' Jewish identity through Pharaoh's eyes. While Moses was said to have killed the Egyptian out of primarily humanitarian considerations, Pharaoh judges him on grounds of personal and ethnic loyalty. It suddenly dawns on Pharaoh that Moses is not "one of us". For Philo, this is of course the greatest compliment a Jew ever can receive from an Egyptian.

Finally, it is of interest to note that Moses' leadership is described in distinctly philosophical terms.[84] Philo emphasizes his superior virtue and natural modesty. It was God who installed him in his position and appointed him together with his more eloquent brother. Ruling by the force of superior insight and virtue, Moses personifies the ideal of a philosopher king (Mos. 2:2). Philo is furthermore concerned to distinguish Moses from military leaders. He is said to behave in exact contrast to those, who "thrust themselves into positions of power by means of arms and engines of war and strength of infantry, cavalry and navy" (Mos. 1:148). According to Philo, Moses neither pushed himself into power nor used any kind of military equipment.

The force of Philo's interpretation becomes especially clear when we consider Artapanus' Moses story. It emerges that Philo has once more constructed a counter-image to that earlier and distinctly pro-Egyptian exegesis. Artapanus presents Moses primarily as a military leader. He credits him with having invented "the Egyptian arms and the implements for drawing water and for warfare" (Praep. Ev. 9.27:4). Moses saw his role as firmly preserving the monarchy for Chenephres (Praep. Ev. 9.27:5). He was the kind of military leader who mediated between the ruler and the people and guarded the stability of the regime. Most importantly, Moses was sent "as a general with an army" to campaign against Ethiopia (Praep. Ev. 9.27:7). Artapanus is especially inter-

---

[84] See also: D. L. Tiede, *The Charismatic Figure as Miracle Worker* (Missoula 1972 = SBL Diss. Ser. 1) 101–37.

ested in this campaign and provides many details. He tells how Moses came to
the district of Hermopolis with about one hundred thousand farmers, how he
pitched camp there, how he sent his generals to blockade the region and how
these generals gained notable advantage in the battles which lasted ten years.
Moses was a benign conquerer, who founded a city and was so beloved by his
new subjects that they adopted the custom of circumcision (Praep. Ev. 9.27:9–
10). Unfortunately, Moses was also involved in a plot initiated by Chenephres
at the end of which he slayed Chanethothes whilst defending himself with a
sword (Praep. Ev. 9.27:18). Moses' appointment to lead the Israelites out of
Egypt is again phrased in distinctly military language: God bade him to "campaign against Egypt" (Praep. Ev. 9.27:21).

Artapanus' use of popular Egyptian sources in his portrait of Moses has often
been discussed.[85] David L. Tiede recently argued at length that Artapanus'
Moses is modelled on the Egyptian hero Sesostris.[86] Both Herodotus and
Diodorus describe this figure as a military leader who conquered Ethiopia for
the first time and then made further conquests in the Far East. He was plotted
against and escaped. Being a benign conquerer, he was loved by his subjects who
adopted the Egyptian custom of circumcision. The parallels between Sesostris
and Artapanus' Moses are conspicuous and indicate the latter's sources. They
furthermore carry important, yet hitherto overlooked implications for Artapanus'
Jewish identity. It is striking that Moses has been subsumed to the character of
the most popular Egyptian hero who anticipated Alexander the Great. Diodorus
stresses that "not only did he [Sesostris], in fact, visit the territory which was
afterwards won by Alexander of Macedon, but also certain peoples into whose
country Alexander did not cross" (1.55:2). Sesostris was thus the same type of

---

[85] See especially: H. Willrich, *Judaica. Forschungen zur hellenistisch-jüdischen Geschichte und Literatur* (Göttingen 1900) 112–5; Y. Gutman, *The Beginnings of Jewish-
Hellenistic Literature* (Hebrew, Jerusalem 1963) 2:120–35; Collins, Athens and Jerusalem
33–5; Holladay, Theios Aner 204–14; A.J. Droge, *Homer or Moses? Early Christian Interpretations of the History of Culture* (Tübingen 1989) 25–35, whose conclusion regarding
Artapanus' use of Hecataeus is not substantiated by his discussion. Some authors have given
exaggerated emphasis to Artapanus' polemics against Manetho, see: J. Freudenthal, *Hellenistische Studien*, 2:160–2 (Breslau 1875 = *Jahresbericht des jüdisch-theologischen Seminars "Fraenkel'scher Stiftung"*); M. Braun, *History and Romance in Graeco-Oriental Literature* (Oxford 1938) 26–31; Fraser, Ptolemaic Alexandria 1:706, suggests more cautiously
that Artapanus wished "to refute that or a similar narrative, by a form of revision which
enabled him to adopt material present in the earlier version"; cf. also T. Rajak, Moses in
Ethiopia: Legend and Literature, *JJS* 29.2 (1978) 111–22, who over-emphasizes the exegetical impetus of these Moses' legends, to the extent that she interprets allegedly Artapanus
moving away from the original Midrash as preserved in Josephus.

[86] Tiede, Charismatic Figures 153–67; the "propagandistic intention", which Tiede ascribes to Artapanus (p. 147) cannot, however, be asserted. Artapanus seems rather to have
addressed a Jewish audience, which was concerned about its place in the Ptolemaic empire.
See also: Sterling, Historiography 176–8, 180.

leader as Alexander the Great, yet excelling him in the seize of territory he brought under his influence. The Egyptians celebrated Sesostris as a hero of their own who was superior even to the founder of the Hellenistic empire. By attributing his features and achievements to Moses, Artapanus has integrated him into the distinct climate of the Ptolemaic period. His portrait of Moses expresses a Jewish identity firmly rooted in Greco-Egyptian culture, which cherished a profound veneration for Alexander and his type of military leadership.

In the same vein, albeit with greater cultural emphasis, Artapanus celebrates Moses as the teacher of Orpheus (Praep. Ev. 9.27:4). This is significant because Orpheus was, according to Diodorus, the founder of Greek culture who had imbibed Egyptian traditions.[87] By tracing Orpheus' contribution ultimately back to Moses, Artapanus has not only claimed Jewish origins for Western civilization, but also suggested a profound congeniality between Jewish and Greco-Egyptian culture. In Artapanus' story Moses furthermore "divided the state into 36 nomes and appointed for each of the nomes the god to be worshipped, for the priests the sacred letters, and that they should be cats and dogs and ibises" (Praep. Ev. 9.27:4). This is undoubtedly the most quoted sentence of Artapanus, which has often been noted for its surprising tolerance of the Egyptian cult. In complete contrast to Philo, Artapanus did not abhor Egyptian religion, but subordinated it to his own tradition, thus again suggesting a deep congeniality between the two. Finally, Moses is in Artapanus' story so "loved by the masses" that he was "deemed worthy of godlike honor by the priests and called Hermes, on account of the interpretation of the sacred letters" (Praep. Ev. 9.27:6). Reading the hieroglyphics, Moses thus played a central role in Egyptian culture – a role which was otherwise associated with Hermes and Isis.[88]

Artapanus' story of Jewish integration into Greco-Egyptian culture is only overshadowed by Chenephres' jealousy. His envy provokes increasing tension and ultimately leads to the Exodus. For Artapanus this is an unfortunate accident, which explains in rather universal terms why the Jews left. Their departure had in his view nothing to do with a broader ethnic conflict, but was grounded in the personal emotions of a particular ruler. Such envy as Chenephres harboured towards Moses was typical of many rulers in other countries and other chronological circumstances, to the extent that it had become a standard topic in political biographies. The Exodus thus remained for Artapanus a peculiar incident. He seems to have thought that Jewish-Egyptian symbiosis could and should naturally continue once an envious ruler like Chenephres had been replaced.

---

[87] 1.23:2–3, 6–7; see also Gutman, Beginnings 121–2; Droge, Moses 25–6; Tiede, Charismatic Figures 151–3.

[88] Tiede, Charismatic Figures 155.

Artapanus' highly pro-Egyptian position subsequently became anathema to Philo. In political, cultural and religious respects he was diametrically opposed to the kind of Jewish identity Artapanus expressed. Partly in response to the latter's Midrash, he constructed a negative counter-image of the Egyptians. They were now reduced to subhuman zoolators, paramount people of the soil, "Persians" and political trouble-makers with no genuine agenda. Jews would do best to avoid any contact with them. Joseph and Moses pointed the way and indicated how contemporary Jews should physically live in Egypt, while being on a mental exodus from the country. In all these aspects Philo's portrait of the Egyptian Other closely corresponds to their Roman image. He clearly wished to integrate the Jews into Roman culture and directly associated them with the rulers of the world.

# 3. Jewish Values: Religion and Self-Restraint

> "the Jewish nation has none to take its part, as
> it lives under exceptional laws which are nec-
> essarily grave and severe, because they incul-
> cate the highest standard of virtue. But gravity
> is austere, and austerity is held in aversion by
> the great mass of men because they favour
> pleasure"                                    (Spec. 4:179)

We have so far seen that Philo's construction of Jewish descent and the Egyptian national character created significant boundaries of Jewish identity. These
boundaries distinguished the Jews by reference to their pedigree, their common
origins in the mothercity Jerusalem and their distance from anything Egyptian.
Philo implied that this definition of Jewish identity was similar to that of the
Romans. The latter shared to a considerable degree "our" Egyptian Other, "our"
orientation towards a prominent city of origins and "our" concern for proper
pedigree. Jewish identity was thus defined in both positive and negative terms,
setting the Jews apart as well as placing them among the elite of world civilization. Before we investigate how the image of the Romans and Greeks complements Philo's construction of Others, the more directly positive sides of Jewish
identity have to be appreciated. We have to examine the values by which Philo
characterized the Jews. In particular, how did their being different from the
Egyptians translate into a positive agenda of Jewish identity?

We will investigate Philo's construction of Jewish values following Barth's
insight that values play a significant role in shaping and strengthening ethnic
boundaries.[1] This is so because different population sectors are regularly associated with different value standards. The Otherness of other groups is anchored in the assumption of a disagreement over basic principles. "They" do
not share "our" values. Ethnic identity is more easily maintained by a sense of
one's own moral superiority. Philo is an especially interesting case in this
respect because he makes no secret of his pride in the excellence of Jewish
values. He explicitly argues that in matters of religion and ethics nobody equals
the Jews. Their standards are of such high quality that they often provoke the
animosity of lower-minded nations. Philo made such statements with a view to
specific groups. He had especially the Egyptians in mind when praising the

---

[1] Barth, Introduction 17–8; for more details on Barth's theory, see above Introduction.

Jews' elevation above vulgar polytheism and materialism. He also looked to the Romans and Greeks, assessing their values more favourably. Philo maintained that "we" as a people are far more stringent in the implementation of principles shared to some degree by the Greek and especially the Roman elite of the world. Philo's construction of Jewish values positioned the Jews within a distinctly contemporary and Roman discourse. Ethnic boundaries were thus shaped and reinforced by a sense that the Jews are congenial and in certain respects superior to the leading nation of the whole *oikoumene*.

Religion was crucial to Philo's distinction of the Jews. He argued that they are no "ordinary" nation because they make "the greatest of all professions, namely that it is the suppliant of Him who truly exists and is the Maker and Father of all".[2] "The larger part of mankind", he lamented, has been befallen by "a great delusion" and has deified the elements of Nature (Dec. 52). Most men ignore the transcendent cause of everything and have thus hidden from sight "the highest and the most august, the begetter, the ruler of the great world-city, the commander-in-chief of the invincible host, the pilot who ever steers all things in safety".[3] While unknowable in His essence, this Creator God was the God of one particular people.[4] As Philo once formulated it in typically Biblical language, "one God ... has taken all the members of the nation for His portion" (Spec. 4:159). The Jews are "dearest to God", "chosen" and "holy".[5] They are a priestly people, a function which involves mediation on behalf of the rest of mankind.[6] As confessors and servants of the superior Creator God they fulfill a duty which, though incumbent on everybody, was neglected by virtually all other nations (Spec. 2:167). Philo's belief in the election of the Jews involved especially the notion of Divine providence. The cases of Gaius, Flaccus and others had in his view clearly shown that the Jews enjoyed God's special beneficence and protection.[7]

---

[2]  Vir. 64; in a similar vein, see also: Dec. 81; Spec. 1:28, 332; Opif. 9. Throughout this chapter I have relied also on Smallwood's translation of the *Legatio*, which I have often found preferable to Colson's standard rendition. I have not been consistent in this matter, however, selecting in each case the translation closer to the original.

[3]  Dec. 53–9, especially Dec. 53.

[4]  Immut. 62; Post. 169; Mos. 1:75–6; Mut. 11; see also: D. T. Runia, Naming and Knowing. Themes in Philonic Theology with special reference to the *De Mutatione Nominum*, in: R. van den Broek *et al.* (eds.), *Knowledge of God in the Graeco-Roman World* (Leiden 1988 = Etudes preliminaires aux Religions orientales dans l'Empire Romain 112) 69–91; G. Stellin, Gotteserkenntnis und Gotteserfahrung bei Philo von Alexandrien, in: H.-J. Klauck (ed.), *Monotheismus und Christologie. Zur Gottesfrage im hellenistischen Judentum und im Urchristentum* (Freiburg 1992 = Quaestiones Disputatae 138) 19–21.

[5]  See especially: Abr. 56; Conf. 56; Abr. 98.

[6]  See especially: Mos. 1:149 ("a nation destined to act as priest (ἱερᾶσθαι) above all others to offer prayers for ever on behalf of the human race that it may be delivered from evil and participate in what is good"); Spec. 2:163; Abr. 98.

[7]  For more details on Philo's interpretation of these characters, see above chapter one and below chapter four.

Becoming a Jew moreover involved leaving one's country, kinsfolk and friends "for the sake of virtue and religion (δι᾽ ἀρετὴν καὶ ὁσιότητα)". Candidates who wished to join the Jewish *politeia* and serve the one God were to denounce "the vain imaginings of their fathers and ancestors".[8] We may infer from the case of Tamar that this often implied, at least in the case of free and educated proselytes, a perhaps public statement to the effect that the statues worshipped so far were in fact idols.[9] These indications of some kind of *rite-de-passage* may suggest that Philo distinguished the Jews by a clear set of beliefs. Such a conclusion, however, is challenged by other Philonic statements. He often makes considerable efforts to argue for the Jews' religious integration into their pagan environment. Proselytes were, for example, warned not to "deal in idle talk or revile with blasphemous speech the gods whom others acknowledge, lest they on their part be moved to utter words not established by custom about the truly existing one" (Spec. 1:53). Philo's language here betrays a surprising degree of respect for pagan deities. He even calls denouncing references to them "blasphemous speech" (γλώσσῃ βλασφημοῦντας).[10] This tolerance is undoubtedly based on LXX Ex. 22:27, which prohibits the cursing of "gods",[11] and also on Deut. 4:19 which recognizes the worship of the elements of Nature by other nations, while forbidding the Jews to bow down to such deities. Philo himself justifies his position by clearly political considerations. Tolerance, he suggests, is based on mutuality. It is therefore wise for Jews to respect the religion of others so as to be respected by them. Yet caution does not seem to have been Philo's only motivation. He repeats his views in the neutral context of the first commandment, insisting that one must acknowledge God as the "most noble source of everything which exists ... either to the exclusion of or above all others" (Dec. 52). It is implied that the superiority of the Creator God must be acknowledged and only He should be worshipped. At the same time, however, the existence of other, subordinate deities does not seem to have been denied.

---

[8] Spec. 1:52–3; see also: A.J. Guerra, The One God Topos in Spec. Leg. 1:52, *SBLSP* 29 (1990) 148–57, who stresses the double function of the One God topos: internally unifying and excluding 'outsiders'.

[9] Vir. 220–1. Philo described Tamar's previous life by reference to "images and wooden busts and idols in general". For further details on the conversion of Tamar and foreign handmaids, see above chapter one.

[10] Colson *ad. loc.* ascribes the "blasphemous" speech to pagan denouncements of the Jewish God, while I. Heinemann, Über die Einzelgesetze Buch I–IV, in: L. Cohn (ed.), *Die Werke Philos von Alexandria in deutscher Übersetzung* (Breslau 1910) 2:25, captures the original intention of the text by translating "verbietet er, die Götter, an welche andere glauben, mit frechem Munde und zügelloser Zunge zu lästern, damit nicht auch jene in ihrer Erregung gegen den wahrhaft Seienden unerlaubte Reden führen".

[11] LXX Ex. 22:27 translates the Masoretic expression (לא תקלל) אלהים by a definite plural: θεοὺς (οὐ κακολογήσεις). See also: V. Tcherikover, *Hellenistic Civilization and the Jews* (Philadelphia 1959; rep. New York 1970) 352; P.W. van der Horst, "Thou shalt not Revile the Gods": the LXX Translation of Ex. 22:28 (27), its Background and Influence, *SPhA* 5 (1993) 1–8.

More importantly, Philo even acknowledged a secondary god within the Jewish religion. He explicitly spoke about the Logos as a δεύτερον θεόν (Q.G. 2:62). Similarly, the planets are occasionally called "divine natures".[12] Philo once stated that "all Greeks and barbarians unanimously acknowledge the supreme Father of gods and men and the Maker of the whole universe" (Spec. 2:165). This suggests that he, like the author of the Letter of Aristeas (Ar. 16,) thought of the Jewish God in typically Stoic terms, distinguishing between one divine essence and its different names.[13] Philo thus admitted that polytheistic pagans worship in their own particular way the true God whom also the Jews know. Varro, the eminent scholar of Republican Rome, had made a similar point. He "thought the God of the Jews to be the same as Jupiter, thinking that it makes no difference by which name he is called, so long as the same thing is understood".[14]

The above statements indicate that Philo's views on the nature and role of religion in shaping ethnic boundaries varied considerably. He often suggests that the religion of the Jews, and especially their form of worship, separated them from others, while sometimes stressing a similarity verging on identity between the Jews and their pagan environment. How are we to understand this discrepancy? What role did religion ultimately play for Philo in distinguishing the Jews from others? The very fact that such a descrepancy exists initially shows that Philo's thoughts on the matter lacked conscious systematisation. This is an important insight. It emerges that Philo neither thought yet in terms of "orthodox" beliefs nor did he formulate stringent principles of monotheism.[15] Jewish orthodoxy was not even in the making in the first century C.E. and had to await its crystallisation until the firm establishment of the rabbinic

---

[12] θεῖαι φύσεις (Opif. 144; Q.G. 4:188).

[13] See especially J. Glucker, God and Gods in Stoicism (Hebrew), forthcoming in: M. Kister (ed.), title to be determined, who emphasized the connection between Stoic theology and linguistics. Another item of religious language which Philo shares with the Stoics and which renders his position tolerant towards others is his account of Abraham, who discovers the Creator God in the superior, more abstract principle of the world responsible for both nature's regularity and the harmony of the elements (Abr. 70–1); cf. Cic., N.D. 2: 16–8, 77, 85–97 and note especially the following expressions in N.D. 2:19: "nothing exists that is superior to god" (nihil est autem praestantius deo) and "a single pervading spirit" (uno divino et continuato spiritu). Note furthermore that Josephus departed from this strictly Stoic line of argumentation and made Abraham recognize God in the irregularities contained in the general regularity of the world (A.J. 1:154–7). Josephus' proof of God thus approaches the traditional notion of a miracle, see also: L. H. Feldman, *Josephus' Interpretation of the Bible* (Berkeley 1998) 228, 261–3.

[14] Varro apud Augustinus, De Cons. Evang. 1.22:30, translation Stern, GLAJJ 1:210.

[15] It is indeed impossible to discuss Philo in terms of an existing "orthodox monotheism", whether this is meant in the sense of Philo representing such orthodoxy, as Mendelson, Identity 1–50, has argued, or in the sense of Philo deviating to some extent from such an orthodoxy, as has been argued by Y. Amir, Monotheistic Problem of Hellenistic Jewry (Hebrew), *Da'at* 13 (1984) 22–3; L. H. Feldman, The Orthodoxy of the Jews in Hellenistic Egypt, *JSS* 22.4 (1960) 220–9.

movement.[16] To be sure, Philo did sometimes express himself in terms which can be identified as monotheistic.[17] Yet he was neither consistent in this matter nor did he attribute overriding importance to a theological definition of religion.[18] For Philo different and indeed more complex issues were at stake.

The intricate nature of Philo's position on religion can be clarified by an investigation into his interpretation of the imperial cult and especially the conflict with Gaius Caligula. The imperial cult represents the nodal point of all the issues concerning us here. It raises the question whether Philo had religious reservations about this Roman institution and, if so, of what nature they were and which limitations they created for the Jews. The crisis under Gaius moreover created extreme tensions and highlighted the underlying issues. It therefore provides an excellent opportunity to study how Philo perceived of the nature and relative importance of each of them.

The tension between Gaius and the Jews reached a climax in the year 40, probably in early June, after Gaius gave the order to set up his statue in the Temple of Jerusalem.[19] One gathers from Philo's account that Gaius had done so in reaction to the Jews of Jamnia demolishing an imperial altar, an act which the emperor regarded as a dangerous sign of political disloyalty.[20] Gaius' order provoked a strong and very successful Jewish resistance which was even noted by Tacitus (Hist. 5.9). Thanks to the intervention of Agrippa I Gaius revoked his order in October of the same year.[21] Philo devotes much attention to these

---

[16] This point has been forcefully argued by Boyarin, Two Synods 21–62; Janowitz, Rabbis and their Opponents; in a similar vein, yet with no view to contemporary developments in Christianity, see also: P. Hayman, Monotheism – A Misused Word in Jewish Studies?, *JJS* 42 (1991) 1–15; R. K. Gnuse, *No Other Gods. Emergent Monotheism in Israel* (Sheffield 1997 = *JSOT* Suppl.Ser. 241).

[17] See esp. in All. 2:1 "God, being one, is alone and unique, and like God there is nothing".

[18] See also: Barclay, Mediterranean Diaspora 429–33.

[19] Leg. 203; see also: Balsdon, Principate of Gaius 19.

[20] Leg. 200–2. Philo himself minimizes the significance of this incident for the unleashing of the crisis, but in contrast to Josephus he nevertheless mentions it; its importance as a cause of the subsequent events has been stressed by Schwartz, Agrippa 80–3; Bilde, Gaius' Attempt 71–4; Willrich, Caligula 442–3.

[21] Jos., A.J. 18:289–304, describes Gaius' revocation as final, while Philo suggests that Gaius only feigned abandoning his plans, while secretly preparing for another statue to be set up in Jerusalem (Leg. 333–7). Bilde, Gaius' Attempt 83–9, has convincingly argued that Josephus' account is more reliable than Philo's which is strongly influenced by his overall interpretation of Gaius, on which see below. Schwartz, Agrippa 87–88, rejects Bilde's conclusion and argues instead for the basic congruence of Josephus' and Philo's account. For this purpose he emphasizes Josephus' reference to Divine providence in A.J. 18:305–6 and its similarity to Philo's account. Schwartz' argument, however, is problematic on two accounts: 1) Josephus' reference to Divine providence in A.J. 18:305–6 does not speak of Gaius' revoking his revocation. It merely explains that Gaius' providential death saved Petronius from having to kill himself as Gaius had angrily ordered him. Josephus thus differs in this respect from Philo; 2) Schwartz himself argues that Josephus' story of Agrippa's intervention and banquet are based on a source which he has identified as *Vita Agrippa* (Agrippa 87, 18–23). This source stresses the importance of Agrippa and is independent from

events and leaves no doubt that the conflict revolved around religion. He himself suggests that it had to do with the issue of deifying a human being. Gaius' order to set up his statue in the Temple violated one of the most important Jewish principles (Leg. 117–8):

> But one single nation, the chosen people of the Jews, was suspected of being likely to resist, since it was used to accepting death as willingly as if it were immortality in order not to allow any of their ancestral traditions, even the smallest, to be abrogated … But the change being effected [by Gaius' order to set up his statue in the Jerusalem Temple] was not a small one, but an absolutely fundamental one, namely the apparent transformation of the created, destructible nature of man into the uncreated, indestructible nature of God, which the Jewish nation judged to be the most grievous impiety, for God would change into man sooner than man into God.

Philo suggests in this passage that the Jews' principal refusal to worship a human being created not only significant boundaries, but a fundamental conflict. Gaius resented them, and only them, on this account. Wanting to be regarded as a god, he was willing to wage "war" against them and desecrate their Holy Temple.[22] Even some gentiles noticed, according to Philo, "how enthusiastic Gaius was about his own deification and the extreme hostility he felt towards the whole Jewish race".[23] These Philonic statements are usually discussed in terms of a clash between monotheism and the Roman imperial cult. As Jean Juster put it in a famous formulation, the latter was a "cauchemar" for the Jews, because it always negated the "principe fondamental du judaïsme, du monothéisme".[24] From this viewpoint, the imperial cult challenged from out-

---

Philo's account on which Josephus, according to Schwartz, generally relies in the matter of Gaius and the Temple. Schwartz' own analysis of the sources of A.J. thus suggests significant differences between the accounts of Josephus and Philo. For more details on the significance of Philo's version, see below chapter four.

[22] Leg. 119, 198, 208.

[23] ὅση σπουδῇ κέχρηται Γάιος περὶ τὴν ἰδίαν ἐκθέωσιν καὶ ὡς ἀλλοτριώτατα διάκειται πρὸς ἅπαν τὸ Ἰουδαϊκὸν γένος (Leg. 201). In the second half of the sentence I have preferred Colson's translation over Smallwood's, because he is more sensitive to the superlative form of ἀλλότριος and Philo's emphasis on ἅπας.

[24] J. Juster, *Les Juifs dans L'Empire Romain. Leur Condition Juridique, Economique et Sociale* (Paris 1914) 1:339; similarly: F. Taeger, *Charisma. Studien zur Geschichte des Antiken Herrscherkultes* (Stuttgart 1957) 1:434–8, who furthermore suggested that Jewish opposition to the imperial cult implied a general opposition to Rome; G. Delling, Philons Enkomium auf Augustus, *Klio* 54 (1972) especially 172–3, 190–1; Smallwood, Legatio 209; P. Borgen, Emperor Worship and Persecution in Philo's *In Flaccum* and *De Legatione ad Gaium* and the Revelation of John, in: Cancik *et al.*, Geschichte – Tradition – Reflexion 3.493–509; P. Borgen, *Early Christianity and Hellenistic Judaism* (Edinburgh 1996) 91–2, while stressing that Philo's opposition to Gaius did not imply a generally negative attitude towards the Romans, Borgen identifies as the source of the crisis Gaius' enforcement of the (regular) imperial cult. Momigliano, on the other hand, sounded a different tone and argued that the "imperial cult (except under Gaius) was no serious problem" for the Jews, see: A. Momigliano, Some Preliminary Remarks on the "Religious Opposition" to the Roman Empire, in: A. Giovannini (ed.), *Opposition et Résistances à l'Empire d'Auguste à Trajan*

side a previously established monotheism which was unconditionally cherished by all Jews. This interpretation, however, overlooks the great complexity of the situation. As far as Philo is concerned, there did not exist beforehand a consistent formulation of a monotheistic dogma which then clashed with the very institution of the imperial cult. On the contrary, the imperial cult under Augustus was remarkably acceptable to Philo. He praised Augustus for his more than human nature,[25] and enthusiastically discussed the Alexandrian *Caesareum* which was dedicated to Augustus in his cultic function as protector of sailors.[26] Philo also expected the Jews to go through the regular motions of the imperial cult and express in the synagogues "εὐσέβεια to their benefactors" and "ὁσιότης to the whole Augustan house" (Flac. 48–9). He took for granted that "gilded shields and crowns, monuments and inscriptions" were set up in Egyptian synagogues.[27] These indicated that the respective place of worship was dedicated to the emperor, following the pattern of pagan temples in honour

---

(Genève 1987 = *Fondation Hardt* 33) 114–5 (in his earlier work, however, *Claudius. The Emperor and his Achievement* (Cambridge 1961; Engl. transl. Ital. orig.) 30–1, Momigliano expressed a more traditional view). This suggestion, however, has largely gone unnoticed, partly perhaps because Momigliano restricted himself to a brief statement, discussing neither the nature of Jewish tolerance nor the source of the conflict with Gaius. These are indeed crucial issues which deserve further investigation.

[25] ὁ τὴν ἀνθρωπίνην φύσιν ὑπερβαλὼν ἐν ἁπάσαις ταῖς ἀρεταῖς (Leg. 143). Philo furthermore describes Augustus as the quintessential σωτὴρ καὶ εὐεργέτης (Flac. 74). He was in his view "the first and the greatest and the common benefactor" (Leg. 149) – a widespread title in the ideology of the imperial cult, on which see: V. Nutton, The Beneficial Ideology, in: P. D. A. Garnsey and C. R. Whittaker (eds.), *Imperialism in the Ancient World* (Cambridge 1978) 209–221. According to Philo, the name Augustus was given to this emperor on account of the "vastness of his imperial sovereignty as well as the nobility of his character" (Leg. 143). His exceptional virtues justified that "he has himself become the source of veneration" (Leg. 143) and that "the whole *oikoumene* voted him Olympian-like honours" (Leg. 149; Colson's translation *ad. loc.* "voted him no less than celestial honours" reflects a rather pervasive tendency to minimize the pagan connotations of Philo's language). For further details on Philo's views on Augustus, see below chapter four.

[26] Leg. 150–1. The detailed nature of Philo's account is especially noteworthy in view of the fact that pagans like Strabo mentioned it merely in passing. While Strabo dwelt on other aspects of the city of Alexandria, he only mentions the Καισάριον in one word besides the Emporium and the warehouses of the Great Harbour (Geogr. 17. 1:9); on the term Καισάριον as a designation for temples dedicated to Augustus (not Julius Caesar) and Strabo's reference to the one in Alexandria (which was the first of its kind, established yet not entirely completed already in 30 B.C.E), see: H. Hänlein-Schäfer, *Veneratio Augusti. Eine Studie zu den Tempeln des ersten römischen Kaisers* (Roma 1985 = *Archaelogica* 39) 10–6, 205–9. On the cultic meaning of the title ἐπιβατήριος in Leg. 150–1, see: Smallwood, Legatio 92; Hänlein-Schäfer, Veneratio Augusti 206–8; A.C. Merriam, The Caesareum and the Worship of Augustus at Alexandria, *TAPA* 14 (1883) 20–5; F. Blumenthal, Der ägyptische Kaiserkult, *Archiv für Papyrusforschung und verwandte Gebiete* 5 (1913) 319; H.I. Bell, Alexandria, *JEA* 13. 3–4 (1927) 175; Colson's translation *ad loc.* "a temple to Caesar on shipboard" clearly ignores this cultic dimension of the Philonic text. For further details on Philo's views on the *Caesareum*, see below chapter four.

[27] Leg. 133, on which see also: Smallwood, Legatio 220–1.

of Augustus. The Jews would furthermore mourn over deceased members of the imperial household and offer sacrifices marking such events as the accession to the throne of a new emperor or his recovery from illness or his embarkation on a military campaign (Leg. 356).[28] King Agrippa is once more made to summarize Philo's views. He emphatically states that the Jews have "not lagged behind any Asian or European nation in expressions of reverence, … that is in prayers, the dedication of offerings, and numerous sacrifices – not only the sacrifices offered at public festivals but the regular daily sacrifices as well".[29] It is furthermore remarkable that Philo nowhere indicates a need for exceptional legislation regarding the imperial cult. While Jewish privileges concerning the Sabbath observance and the Temple taxes required official acknowledgement, the imperial cult does not seem to have demanded a similar charter.[30] In light of the generally relaxed atmosphere around the imperial cult the question arises what precisely was at stake in the conflict with Gaius. Why did Philo trace this clash back to a fundamental difference in religious values, focusing on the issue of man's deification?

It is initially obvious that Gaius posed a new problem for the Jews, because his plan to set up his own statue in the innermost part of the Jerusalem Temple represented a new dimension of intrusion into Jewish religious life. This intention impinged on the central institution of the Jews and directly threatened the nature of their worship.[31] No one before had ever considered desecrating the Jerusalem Temple by a statue dedicated to a human being under the name of Zeus (Leg. 188, 292). Aniconism may have played a considerable, yet hitherto overlooked role in this conflict. Philo indicates on various occasions that the Jewish resistance to Gaius' plans was seriously concerned about the violation of a particular form of ritual. Aniconism seems to have been a significant factor.[32] Philo has Agrippa state this point with particular emphasis (Leg. 290):

My Lord Gaius, this Temple has never from the beginning admitted any man-made image, because it is the dwelling-place of the true God. The works of painters and sculptors are copies of gods perceived by the senses. But the making of any picture or sculpture of the invisible God was considered by our forefathers to be blasphemous.

---

[28] On Jewish perspectives of sacrifices in honour of Gentiles, see: D. R. Schwartz, On Sacrifice by Gentiles in the Temple of Jerusalem, in: idem, *Studies in the Jewish Background of Christianity* (Tübingen 1992) 102–16.

[29] Leg. 280, see also: Leg. 317, 157, 152. As Gaius himself noted, these sacrifices were made in honour of the emperor, not to him (Leg. 357).

[30] Philo lists twice the privileges recognized by Augustus; the shorter version can be found in Leg. 156–8, while the extended one appears in Leg. 309–18.

[31] See especially Leg. 306–8.

[32] T. N. D. Mettinger, *No Graven Image? Israelite Aniconism in Its Ancient Near Eastern Context* (Stockholm 1995 = Coniectanea Biblica Old Testament Series 2), has forcefully argued that aniconism refers to a type of ritual, which does not presuppose any particular theology. This form of worship had indeed been shared by other Near Eastern cultures which did not subsequently develop a monotheistic religion

The Jewish demonstrators before Petronius similarly made a petition for the maintenance of their traditional ritual, pleading that their Temple may not be "deprived of its ancestral tradition of worship".[33] The term θρησκεία suggests that these Jews were concerned about their particular rites and sacrificial customs. Aniconism seems to have been a central issue. This impression is confirmed by Philo's emphasis on the fact that nobody before Gaius ever thought of setting up images, busts, statues or paintings in Jewish places of worship.[34] He praises Augustus in the same vein for recognizing the uniqueness of aniconic worship in the Jerusalem Temple.[35] Petronius significantly attributed Jewish resistance to "zeal for the Temple". He was especially impressed by the provision of the death penalty for any non-Jew entering its inner precincts (Leg. 212). In Petronius' view, too, the Jews were more concerned with their particular form of worship than with theology. This interpretation of the conflict cannot simply be dismissed as an outsider's ignorant speculation. Philo himself praised Petronius for his profound insight into Jewish philosophy which rendered him a kind of intuitive convert (Leg. 245).

The relative importance of aniconism, however, cannot fully account for Philo's explanations in Leg. 117–8. As we saw above, he stressed there that the Jews are distinguished by their refusal to accept the deification of a human being. The "created, destructible nature of man", Philo insisted, cannot be transformed "into the uncreated, indestructible nature of God". While we saw that this statement does not defend a monolithic creed of monotheism vis-à-vis the outside world, it certainly amounts to a distinct religious principle. This principle has crystallized over considerable time and results from prolonged internal negotiation. It ultimately represents a preference for one particular voice within the Philonic discourse which emerged both under the impression of the historical events and in dialogue with contemporary Roman culture. In the final analysis Philo even suggests that "we" share the values of the Romans, but practice them with far greater rigidity, being willing even to risk our lives for them.

It is striking how flexible Philo was in his earlier works concerning the deification of human beings. He evidently did not yet feel the need to formulate

---

[33] Leg. 232; I have slightly departed from Smallwood's translation "traditional ways of worship", which does not bring out the important nuance of τὸ πάτριον.

[34] Leg. 138 regarding Ptolemaic rule; Leg. 148 regarding Augustan rule.

[35] "When he was told about our Temple and heard that no man-made image, no visible representation of the invisible Being, was to be found in it, did he not marvel and worship?" (Leg. 310). On another occasion Philo says of Augustus that he was a "philosopher second to none", who realized that "it was essential for a special place to be consecrated to the invisible God to be set apart in the earthly regions and for it to contain no visible representation" (Leg. 318). Philo thus distinguishes the invisibility of the Jewish God and the aniconic nature of His worship. Like other pagan philosophers, he is concerned with the issue of anthropomorphism, cf. e.g. Cicero, N.D. 1:45, 63–70. For further details on Augustus' recognition of the Jewish God according to Philo's *Legatio*, see below chapter four.

a consistent and uncompromising position on this issue and could therefore entertain a variety of views. In his earlier treatises he himself even spoke of human rulers as gods. Moses is the most famous example. Philo praised him for having attained divinity, describing him as a "partner of His own possessions" who was "named god and king" (θεὸς καὶ βασιλεύς).[36] Moses had thus not only been endowed with a divine nature, but had actually become a god who was, to be sure, subordinate to the creator God and did not apparently enjoy any direct worship (Lib. 43). He had transcended the role of Divine agent and personified himself something of the Divine. Moses' outstanding beneficience as ruler as well as his exceptional mind elevated him to the realm of minor deities. According to Philo, the elements of Nature obeyed him as their "master" and "god".[37] It is even more striking that the role of king and god is not restricted to Moses the unique hero of the past. Rather Philo expected, in a surprisingly encompassing way, that outstanding rulers would reach the same degree of divinity and become gods by virtue of their beneficience. He did not hesitate to speak of such rulers, his own contemporaries as well, in terms of θεός.[38] Philo moreover considered the High Priest to be beyond the human. "He is not a man", he insisted, "but a Divine Word and immune from all unrighteousness whether intentional or unintentional" (Fug. 108). Wendy E. Helleman has furthermore

---

[36] Mos. 1:155–8, especially 1:158; see also: Sacr. 8–9; Mut. 125–9. Moses' status as god has been emphasized by W. A. Meeks, Moses as God and King, in: J. Neusner (ed.), *Religions in Antiquity. Essays in Memory of Erwin Ramsdell Goodenough* (Leiden 1968 = Suppl. to *Numen* 14) 354–71; idem, The Divine Agent and His Counterfeit in Philo and the Fourth Gospel, in: E. Schüssler Fiorenza (ed.), *Aspects of Religious Propaganda in Judaism and Early Christianity* (Notre Dame 1976) 45–9. P. Borgen, Moses, Jesus, and the Roman Emperor. Observations in Philo's Writings and the Revelation of John, *NT* 38 (1996) 145–59, also embraces this view with some reservations.

[37] δεσπότῃ (Mos. 1:156); θεὸν (Sacr. 9).

[38] Consider especially: Mut. 125–9, where Philo says on the basis of Ex. 7:1 that rulers who have attained divine virtue and function as benefactors and mediators for their community are rightly called god. According to the manuscript traditon, Philo repeats twice in Mut. 125–9 that such a ruler is or is called god, yet Colson *ad. loc.* characteristically corrects one instance of θεός to θεοῦ, translating "God's man". Colson justifies this radical change of the text only by reference to a note by Wendland, who suggested "that ἄνθρωπος θεοῦ seems the right reading", which he himself, however, has not adopted. See also Spec. 4:188 "these things good rulers have to imitate if they have any aspiration to be assimilated to God (ἐξομοιώσεως τῆς πρὸς θεόν)"; and Philo's comments on the *theios aner* in Vir. 177 and on Isaac in Q.G. 4:188. On the background of these Philonic statements in the ideals of Hellenistic kingship, see especially: E.R. Goodenough, The Political Philosophy of Hellenistic Kingship, *Yale Classical Studies* 1 (1928) 55–102; E. Kornemann, Zur Geschichte der antiken Herrscherkulte, *Klio* 1 (1901) 56–75; L.R. Taylor, *The Divinity of the Roman Emperor* (Middletown 1931 = APA Monograph Ser. 1) 1–34. Cf. also Cicero, N.D. 2:62, where Romulus is counted among the benefactors, who "were duly deemed divine, as being both supremely good and immortal, because their souls survived and enjoyed eternal life; J.R. Fears, The Cult of Virtues and Roman Imperial Ideology, *ANRW* II.17.2 (1981) 827–948.

shown that humanity in general is endowed by Philo with the potential of assimilating to God and becoming like Him.[39]

These statements indicate Philo's acceptance of the idea, common among pagans as well, that exceptional men transcend human nature and become either deities in their own right or immanations of a god. This approach to the issue of deification, however, is balanced by other Philonic remarks. Sometimes he expressed himself in a considerably different spirit. He then insisted that Moses' appointment as "god to Pharaoh", mentioned in Ex. 7:1, did not imply that he has "become such in reality, but only by a convention is supposed to be such".[40] Philo concludes that "the wise man is said to be a god to the foolish man, but that in reality he is not god just as the counterfeit four-drachma piece is not a tetradrachma" (Det. 162). As Carl Holladay has observed, Philo moreover uses Num. 23:19 to stress that God is not like man.[41] Philo once formulated this idea from the inverse point of view, emphatically rejecting the very thought that the created can be transformed into uncreated, the mortal into immortal and man into god (Mut. 181). But this statement is not, as Holladay implied, "a cliché" universally advocated throughout Philo's writings. It is rather one of a variety of views on the issue of man's deification. It now remains to be seen precisely why Philo later gave exclusive attention to this particular view and identified it as a principle value of the Jews which distinguished them from others.

It is initially noteworthy that Philo formulated conclusive views on the issue of man's deification at a time when he was describing the conflict with Gaius up to his assassination and while presumably still in Rome.[42] These circumstances shed light on the remarkable consolidation of his views. The first clue to Philo's motivations is provided by the fact that he associates Gaius' deification with the Egyptians. They had encouraged the vanity of the new emperor and given "birth to ... the idea of godship which occupied his dreams" (Leg. 338). When

---

[39] W. E. Helleman, Philo of Alexandria on Deification and Assimilation to God, *SPhA* 2 (1990 = Brown Judaic Studies 226) 51–71.

[40] μὴ πρὸς ἀλήθειαν γεγενῆσθαι, δόξῃ δὲ μόνον ὑπολαμβάνεσθαι (Det. 161). The importance of this passage has been emphasized by D. T. Runia, God and Man in Philo of Alexandria, *JThS* 39 (1988) 48–75; and Holladay, Theios Aner 103–198; similarly Delling, Enkomium 190–1.

[41] See e.g. Immut. 53–9; Q.E. 2:54; Mos. 2:194, 1:283; see also: Holladay, Theios Aner 105–6; followed by L. W. Hurtado, *One God. One Lord. Early Christian Devotion and Ancient Jewish Monotheism* (London 1988) 59–63.

[42] Philo must have written the *Legatio* after Gaius' assassination in 41 C.E. because he refers to his successor (Leg. 206) and promises an account of the "reversal" of Gaius' fortune (Leg. 373). Even though the *palinode* is unfortunately lost, it must have dealt with the emperor's violent death as an appropriate punishment for his earlier hatred of the Jews (see also: Leisegang, Legatio; Bilde, Gaius' Attempt 71). It is moreover likely that Philo wrote the *Legatio* while still in Rome and under the immediate impression of the new emperor Claudius whom he met as the head of the first Jewish embassy.

Gaius began "not only saying but thinking that he was a god", he found most sympathetic supporters in the Alexandrians.[43] Being "adepts at flattery and imposture and hypocrisy", they confirmed his "unmeasured passion which craves for more than is natural to mankind".[44] This was according to Philo in line with the national character of Egyptians, who worshipped animals and were thus altogether devoid of religion in a real sense (Leg. 138–9). It was moreover the Egyptian Helicon who gave Gaius the advice to set up his own statue in the Jerusalem Temple.[45] Virtuous Romans, by contrast, continued to relate to Gaius as a fallible human being who required instruction in the art of government. Macro and Silanus sacrificed their life in their commitment to this approach (Leg. 32–65). The acute discrepancy between Egyptian and Roman reactions to Gaius' aspirations provides the first indication that Philo aligned the Jews with the Romans. These two nations once more found themselves on the same side of a basic divide.

Philo's views on Gaius are indeed to a large extent a Roman construct which is not fully consistent with his own story of the events.[46] His explanation of the Jewish role in the conflict must therefore be appreciated in this Roman context. It is initially conspicuous that there is a descrepancy between the "wild and frenzied μανία" which Philo attributes to Gaius and the signs of apparently realistic policy pursued by him. Philo gives the impression that Gaius was obsessed with his own deification to the extent that he hated anybody not fully submitting to it.[47] The reader of the *Legatio* is likely to get the impression that affairs of government were seen as secondary to the personal issue at stake. At the same time, however, Philo provides some details of Gaius' rule which do not quite support this image.

It emerges that, whatever his interest in self-deification may have been, Gaius was nevertheless not totally oblivious to the political needs of the day. It

---

[43] Leg. 162. According to Philo, Gaius' *hybris* did not immediately manifest itself. He rather guarded his megalomaniac thoughts until his rule became more consolidated (Leg. 76–7).

[44] Leg. 162. I have again preferred to use Colson's translation because it brings out Philo's expression ὑπὲρ φύσιν ἀνθρωπίνην.

[45] Leg. 203. Philo emphasizes that this piece of advice was an expression of Helicon's "Egyptian venom" (Leg. 205). For further details on Philo's construction of the Egyptians, see above chapter two.

[46] The inconsistencies in Philo's account and his bias against Gaius have often been noted, but not properly analysed in the context of his Roman orientation and his construction of Jewish identity, see especially: Willrich, Caligula 439–43; Bilde, Gaius' Attempt 71–4; A. A. Barrett, *Caligula. The Corruption of Power* (London 1989) 182–91. Others have accepted Philo's image of a mad emperor, see recently: A. Ferrill, *Caligula. Emperor of Rome* (London 1991). A somewhat intermediate position with emphasis on Gaius' exceptionally negative character has been assumed by Z. Yavetz, *Tiberius and Caligula. From Makebelieve to Insanity* (Hebrew), (Tel Aviv 1995).

[47] Leg. 78–93, especially Leg. 93.

was actually he who speedily replaced Flaccus when things got out of hand (Flac. 108–24). One gathers from the margins of Philo's report that the Jewish community of Alexandria was grateful for this intervention in their favour which immediately eased the tension between them and the Egyptians. There is moreover little in Philo's account to support the claim that Gaius was madly obsessed with his deification. It is not clear to what extent the emperor took active steps to impose it on his subjects. While he did give instructions to set up his statue in the Jerusalem Temple, he promptly backed down in the face of Jewish resistance.[48] This bespeaks a realistic politician rather than a blind ideologist. Philo himself moreover admits that Gaius was rather amused by the Jewish ambassadors and confronted them in the same provocative manner as he did virtually everybody else.[49] It is significant that they were not on the spot forced to worship him. They had of their own accord bowed down before him and addressed him as Σεβαστός Αὐτοκράτωρ.[50] More than this voluntary gesture was apparently not required. Philo does not mention any coercion on this occasion and he had good reason to look for it. It is equally striking that Philo never even alludes to an official cult of Gaius in Rome.[51] If a temple in the capital had been dedicated to Gaius, he would surely have known about it and can certainly be trusted to have mentioned it in corroboration of his argument. The very fact that he cannot rely on such evidence indicates that there was no cult of Gaius in Rome. Philo's account of Gaius' mad drive for self-deification evidently relied on sources other than the factual presence of a cult.

It furthermore emerges from the account in the *Legatio* that *proskynesis* was not imposed from above. Philo admits that it was practiced on a spontaneous level by some individuals (ἔνιοι) who were given to political flattery.[52] Very little thus remains by way of evidence for Gaius' mad occupation with his own deification. The main material illustrating his aspirations is the report about his impersonation of different gods. Philo complains that Gaius imitated the outfit and appearance of increasingly important gods, moving from various demigods up to Dionysus (Leg. 78–85). Philo's venom, however, is mainly directed against Gaius' failure to imitate the virtues of the respective gods (Leg. 92–8). Impersonating gods was not an occasion for affront and was indeed no novelty

---

[48] Leg. 188, 333–7, see also n. 21.

[49] Leg. 352–67. Cf. especially the story in Dio 59.26:8–9 of a Gallic cobbler who confronted Gaius when the latter masqueraded as Jupiter. When asked what he thought of these ostentations, he retorted: "a great humbug" – a confession for which he was not punished.

[50] Leg. 352; see also Philo's comments on this title in connection with Augustus (Leg. 143).

[51] See also: Barrett, Caligula 149; C. J. Simpson, The Cult of the Emperor Gaius, *Latomus* 40.3 (1981) 490.

[52] Leg. 116; Philo's account corroborates the image of *proskynesis* under Gaius in other sources, on which see: Barrett, Caligula 150–1.

at the Roman court. Augustus had already in 40 B.C.E. attended a fancy dinner party at which each of the guests appeared in the outfit of one of the Olympians, Augustus himself appearing as Apollo.[53] This party had become famous in Antiquity and can hardly have escaped Philo's attention. Why then did he hold such behaviour against Gaius, while ignoring it in the case of Augustus?

The key to this question may be found in the circumstances at Rome after Gaius' assassination and Claudius' accession to the throne.[54] Philo was then in the capital and imbibed the cultural as well as political climate of that turbulent period. His views on Gaius were shaped by the contemporary *post-mortem* discourse about him. His interpretation of the dead emperor's conflict with the Jews also consolidated at this time. Both of these were closely connected to the issue of Jewish identity and the propaganda of the new emperor Claudius.

Even before Claudius' formal accession to the throne, when he was still negotiating with the Senate over the right form of government, the legacy of Gaius became a critical issue. The Roman senate on the whole wished to use the opportunity of Gaius' assassination to "escape a slavery brought upon them by the *hybris* of the tyrants" (Jos., A.J. 19:227). The senators reminded Claudius of the "perils" they had undergone, especially at the hands of Gaius, and urged him to respect their authority. They even hinted that the fate of Gaius might befall any ruler suppressing political freedom.[55] While assuming power under military threat, Claudius nevertheless sought to appease the senatorial opposition. For this purpose he projected his own rule as a complete break with Gaius' ways. The result was a devastating image of his predecessor.[56] Claudius argued that only Gaius, and not the imperial system *per se,* must be blamed for the suffering in Rome. Assuring the senators of his sympathy for their criticism of the assassinated emperor, he "promised to behave with such propriety that they would taste for themselves the savour of an era of fair dealing" (Jos., A.J. 19:246). Claudius declared that he would "govern the empire as a virtuous ruler and not as a tyrant" (Jos., B.J. 2:208). By nature "moderate", he would act with discretion and share his power.[57]

---

[53] Suet., Aug. 70; see also: Balsdon, Gaius 160, 168–70; Gurval, Actium and Augustus 94–8, who emphasizes that Augustus had not intended a public statement regarding his aspirations to divinity and regretted the unexpected political consequences; on the rather innocent nature of Gaius' impersonations of the gods, see also: Simpson, Cult 492; Barrett, Caligula 146.

[54] In Leg. 206 Philo mentions a measure taken by "Claudius Germanicus Caesar". This statement proves that Philo was alive after Claudius came to power.

[55] Jos., A.J. 19:230–3; see also: M. Swan, Josephus, A.J,. XIX, 251–252: Opposition to Gaius and Claudius, *AJP* 91.2 no. 362 (1970) 149–64.

[56] See also: Barrett, Caligula XVII; Willrich, Caligula 459–63.

[57] Jos., B.J. 2:208; A.J. 19:246.

While publically undoing "the unjust acts performed by Gaius" (Dio 60.5:1), Claudius also sought a positive model which could consolidate his power. The natural choice was Augustus. Claudius cast himself in the role of a successor to the first emperor. It was his style of government he wished to emulate and his success he hoped to achieve. Suetonius records a number of symbolic actions Claudius undertook "as soon as his power was firmly established" (Claud. 11:1–2). They included an oath "by Augustus", divine honours for Livia and the imitation of Augustus' chariots drawn by elephants in the procession at the circus. More importantly, Claudius sought to create the impression that he was "modest and unassuming, … refusing excessive honours" (Suet., Claud. 12:1). This slogan of moderation implied a notion crucial for understanding Philo. Claudius embraced the Augustan formula of refusing divine honours.[58] In his famous letter to the Alexandrians of 41 B.C.E. Claudius declared:[59]

But the establishment of a high-priest and temples of myself I decline, not wishing to be offensive (φορτικός) to my contemporaries and in the belief that temples and the like have been set apart in all ages for the gods alone (μόνοις τοῖς θεοῖς).

This gesture repeated Germanicus' refusal of "divine acclamations" by the Egyptians (ἰσόθεοι ἐκφωνήσεις). Tiberius had also insisted on his own mortality and declared that human, not divine honours were appropriate for him.[60] These imperial statements followed Augustan precedent. Christian Habicht has convincingly reinforced Charlesworth's earlier argument that Augustus allowed the province of Asia in 30–29 B.C.E. to build a temple in honour of Dea Roma and himself, while explaining to the Roman citizens there that he was not a god, but merely a mortal human being who did not deserve such honours on his own.[61] This position is echoed in the official Augustan ideology. In response to

---

[58] On the Augustan formula, see especially: M.P. Charlesworth, The Refusal of Divine Honours. An Augustan Formula, *PBSR* 15 (1939) 1–10; Ch. Habicht, Die augusteische Zeit und das erste Jahrhundert nach Christi Geburt, in: *Le Culte des Souverains dans l'Empire Romain* (Geneva 1972 = Entretiens sur l'Antiquité Classique 19) 76–85; J. Pollini, Man or God: Divine Assimilation and Imitation in the Late Republic and Early Principate, in: K.A. Raaflaub and M. Toher (eds.), *Between Republic and Empire. Interpretations of Augustus and His Principate* (Berkeley 1990) 339–54, who stresses the ambiguity which was purposely left between the official image of the emperor as a mediator between man and the gods, and the emperor as a god himself.

[59] Text and translation *CPJ* 2:39–43 (no. 153, 3.48–51).

[60] Germanicus' speech is preserved on a Berlin papyrus, published by U. v. Wilamowitz-Moellendorff und F. Zucker, Zwei Edikte des Germanicus auf einem Papyrus des Berliner Museums, *Sitzungsber. Kön. Pr. Akad. d. Wiss.* 1911, 794–821, especially 797; quoted also by Charlesworth, Divine Honours 3; Tiberius' words are transmitted by Tac., An. 4:38 "Ego me, patres conscripti, mortalem esse et hominum officia fungi satisque habere, si locum principem impleam, et vos testor et meminisse posteros volo"; quoted also by Charlesworth, Divine Honours 2; see also: L.R. Taylor, Tiberius' Refusal of Divine Honours, *TAPA* 60 (1929) 87–101.

[61] Habicht, Augusteische Zeit 80–3; Charlesworth, Divine Honours 5–6, reached his conclusion on the basis of an inscription from Cyme in honour of the benefactor Labeo, who

Republican sensitivities, Augustus had created a public self-image, which presented his autocratic measures as a restoration of the old, more egalitarian
order.[62] He had therefore officially rejected the dedication of temples in Rome
to his person, while later accepting them in Italy and the provinces.[63] Notwith-
standing popular enthusiasm for his beneficience, which might sometimes have
amounted to direct worship, Augustus equally rejected the proposal to be named
among the gods of the pantheon.[64]

Intellectuals in the Roman empire typically shared this interpretation of the
imperial cult.[65] They preferred to think of the emperor as a human being with
perhaps divine qualities and praised Augustus for his outward moderation.
After Claudius' accession to the throne Gaius became the anti-type of this ideal.
He was blamed for excessive claims to divinity. Suetonius made this point with
particular emphasis. The two emperors emerge in his account as mirror-images,
representing extreme opposites. Augustus' humility is praised and illustrated
by the following incident:[66]

---

had "deprecated the honour both of the consecration of the temple and of the title of Founder
as excessive and suited only to gods and heroes ...; but he joined in assenting to the honours
that were fitting for good men" (ibid 5).

[62] See especially R.G. 6:1, 34:1–3; Z. Yavetz, The Res Gestae and Augustus' Public
Image, in: F. Millar and E. Segal (eds.), *Caesar Augustus. Seven Aspects* (Oxford 1984) 1–
36, emphasized that the addressee of such propaganda was an upper-class audience, especially young people still forming their position in the political arena; idem, *Julius Caesar.
The Limits of Charisma* (Hebrew), (Tel Aviv 1992) 190–5, dealing with the increasing
personality cult of Caesar as a preparation to Rome's more comprehensive acceptance of
Eastern forms of ruler worship.

[63] Scholars differ in their views about the way the imperial cult became institutionalized.
While both S.R.F. Price, *Rituals and Power. The Roman imperial cult in Asia Minor* (Cambridge 1984); and Taylor, Divinity 205–23, stress the active part of Rome in the deification
of Augustus in the East, Nock and Bowersock see the cult as a spontaneous reaction in the
East which was welcomed and manipulated by Augustus, see: A.D. Nock, Religious Developments from the Close of the Republic to the Death of Nero, *CAH* 10 (1934) 481–89; G.W.
Bowersock, The Imperial Cult: Perceptions and Persistence, in: B.F. Meyer and E.P. Sanders
(eds.), *Jewish and Christian Self-Definition in the Graeco-Roman World. Self-Definition in
the Graeco-Roman World* (London 1982) 3:171–82 (repr. in: G.W. Bowersock, *Studies on
the Eastern Roman Empire. Social, Economic and Administrative History. Religion. Historiography* (Goldbach 1994), 327–42); idem, Augustus 112–21.

[64] Goodman, Roman World 129–33; Nock, Religious Developments 483–88; D. Fishwick,
Genius and Numen, *HTR* 62 (1969) 356–67; K. Galinsky, *Augustan Culture. An Interpretative
Introduction* (Princeton 1996) 325–6; J. Geiger, The Ruler Cult as an Ideology of the Roman
Empire (Hebrew), in: I. Gafni and G. Motzkin (eds.), *Priesthood and Monarchy. Studies in the
Historical Relationships of Religion and State* (Jerusalem 1987) 51–60, stressed the possibil-
ity of a religious and emotional dimension of the imperial cult on a popular level.

[65] See also: G.W. Bowersock, Greek Intellectuals and the Imperial Cult in the Second
century A.D., in: *Le Culte des Souverains* 179–206 (repr. in: G.W. Bowersock, Studies 293–
320).

[66] Aug. 53:1; see also: Aug. 52:1; A. Wallace-Hadrill, *Suetonius. The Scholar and his
Caesars* (London 1983/ New Haven 1984) 163; W. Steidle, *Sueton und die Antike Biographie*
(München 1951 = Zetemata. Monographien zur klassischen Altertumswissenschaft 1) 76–80.

He always shrank from the title 'Lord' (dominus) as reproachful and insulting. When the words 'o just and gracious Lord' were uttered in a farce at which he was a spectator and all the people sprang to their feet and applauded as if they were said of him, he at once checked their unseemly flattery by look and gesture and on the following day sharply reproved them in an edict.

Gaius, on the other hand, is described as an arrogant tyrant. He is accused of assuming absolute rule and generally having become a "monster" violating all norms of decent conduct and morality.[67] His worst crime, however, was to "lay claim to divine majesty".[68] He is said to have erected a temple to his own Numen in Rome, demanded his statue to be worshipped like that of Castor and Pollux and to have punished a tragic poet, who was too slow to assert his superiority over Jupiter.[69] Gaius is thus condemned as a kind of counter-figure to Augustus. He neither shared the virtue nor the modesty of the ideal *princeps*. All of his faults can be summarized by his claim to divinity, which breach of official Roman policy amounted to the utmost expression of his *hybris*.

Suetonius' image of Gaius was an elaboration of a view which emerged immediately after the latter's assassination. Seneca, who had been ridiculed by Gaius for his loose style, but otherwise seems to have fared quite well under him, substantially contributed to the bad reputation of the dead emperor.[70] Flattering the new ruler, he suggested that Claudius emulated the divine Augustus, while

---

[67] Suetonius attributed to him the demand: "let there be one lord, one king!" and described him as a "monstro" (Gaius 22:1); among his crimes were the following: incest (Gaius 23–24), murder of friends (26:1), innate brutality (27–28), sadistic speech (29–31), plan to destroy the poems of Homer (34:2).

[68] "divinam ex eo maiestatem asserere sibi coepit" (Suet., Gaius 22:2).

[69] Gaius 22:2–4 (Suetonius further noted with horror that Gaius fabricated statues of his own person by replacing the heads of those of traditional gods), Gaius 33:1. On the historical unreliability of Suetonius' suggestion that a temple to Gaius' numen was erected in Rome, see: Barrett, Caligula 146–50; Simpson, Cult 500–9.

[70] Himself a "first-rate orator" (Jos., A.J. 19:208), Gaius was known for his low opinion of Seneca, on which see: J. Stroux, Vier Zeugnisse zur römischen Literaturgeschichte der Kaiserzeit, *Philologus* 86 (1931) 349–55. Some scholars have suggested a connection between Seneca and the conspiratory circle around Sejanus, see: Z. Stewart, Sejanus, Gaetulicus and Seneca, *AJP* 74 (1953) 70–85; and more hesitantly G. W. Clarke, Seneca the Younger under Caligula, *Latomus* 24.1 (1965) 62–9. Their arguments, however, rest only on most indirect evidence, mostly on Tacitus' note about Seneca's gratitude towards Agrippina (An. 12.8). A. A. Barrett, *Agrippina. Sex, Power, and Politics in the Early Empire* (New Haven 1996) 68–9, convincingly argued that active opposition to Gaius would have been out of character for Seneca who generally preferred rather opportunistic strategies. Barrett, Caligula 236, therefore suggested that Seneca himself may have invented the story of his imminent execution under Gaius, which was prevented by an unnamed lady. Like Lucius Vitellius' story in a similar vein, this episode may have been designed to cover a silent collaboration with a dead emperor now fallen out of favour; cf. M. T. Griffin, *Seneca. A Philosopher in Politics* (Oxford 1976) 54–5, who argued that Seneca betrayed "no tendency to inflate his past dangers or to pose as a heroic"; H. Lindsay, *Suetonius. Caligula. Edited with Introduction and Commentary by Hugh Lindsay* (London 1993) 9–10, who stresses Seneca's influence in shaping the negative image of Gaius.

Gaius was dutifully reduced to an anti-hero whose violation of Roman norms had provoked his assassination. Seneca celebrated Claudius as an emperor analogous to the "divus Augustus".[71] He showed that he possessed similar virtues and could be expected to "bring peace" to all parts of the empire (Cons. Pol. 13:2–3). It was implied that he also shared the princeps' modesty. Augustus himself was praised, among other things, for the fact that, even though considered to be of divine descent, he made it "his deepest concern that no man should make complaint of the gods".[72] Augustus thus maintained the distinction between man and god, stressing that humans must act with appropriate modesty towards the heavenly realm. Gaius, by contrast, was presented as someone (Cons. Pol. 17:3):

whose name ought to be torn from every list of the Caesars, whom Nature produced to be the ruin and the shame of the human race, who utterly wasted and wrecked the empire that is now being restored by the mercy of the kindliest of princes.

Seneca left little doubt as to what he meant by this generalisation. He characterized Gaius as outright mad, unspeakably ugly as well as arrogant and barbarically brutal.[73] His tyranny had imposed a foreign style of government on Rome and he himself showed the same *hybris* as Xerxes.[74] Seneca's outspoken criticism of Alexander's tyrannical measures which involved the killing of former friends, such as Callisthenes, was only a thinly veiled arrow directed against what he regarded as analogous practices under Gaius.[75] More importantly, Seneca accused his anti-hero of being "swollen with pride beyond all human decency" (Cons. Pol. 17:5). His arrogant challenge of Jupiter had literally fatal consequences (De Ira 1.20:8–9):

… he [Gaius] challenged Jove to fight, even to the death, shouting in the words of Homer 'Or uplift me or I will thee'. What madness ("dementia")! He thought that not even Jove could harm him, or that he could harm even Jove. I suppose that these words of his had no little weight in arousing the minds of the conspirators; for to put up with a man who could not put up with Jove seemed the limit of endurance.

While Simpson is surely right that this passage does not suggest Gaius' identification with Jupiter (Cult 494), it nevertheless indicates a religious source for Gaius' downfall. Seneca traced his assassination to his lack of modesty vis-à-vis the gods. A man who did not acknowledge Jupiter's superiority was clearly

---

[71] Cons. Pol. 12:3–5; see also: Div. Claud. Apocol. 9:5.

[72] Cons. Marc. 15:2; for other aspects of Seneca's idealized picture of Augustus himself, see e.g.: De Clem. 1.9:1–11:3; De Brev. Vit. 4:2–5; Cons. Pol. 15:3; De Benef. 2.25:1, 2.27:2, 3.27:1–4, 3.32:5; De Ira 3:23:4–8, 3.40:2–5.

[73] Seneca, De Const. 18:1–5; De Ira 3.18:3–19:5; De Tranq. Anim. 14:4–10; Cons. Pol. 13:1.

[74] Seneca, De Brev. Vit. 18:5–6; Ep. 94:65–6.

[75] Seneca, N.Q. 6.23:2–3; regarding Seneca's assimilation of Gaius to Alexander, see below chapter five.

oblivious to the principle distinction between humans and gods. Gaius had confused his own status and powers with those of the immortals.[76] This was the root of his "dementia" as well as the cause of his death.[77]

The similarities between Seneca's and Philo's interpretation of Gaius are striking. This is not surprising. They were not only contemporaries, but formulated their views under the same circumstances in Rome. To be sure, Philo gave more exclusive attention to Gaius' self-deification which was only one of the points on Seneca's agenda. It remains clear, however, that Philo formulated his invective against the dead emperor very much in the spirit of his time. His report in the *Legatio* undoubtedly integrated him in a prevalent Roman discourse. This is especially true of his interpretation of the Jews' role. Philo's argument that the Jews in principle refused the deification of any human being suggests that they shared the values and political culture of contemporary Roman intellectuals. They emerge as defenders of a Classical Roman tradition which had been neglected and abused under Gaius. It is therefore not surprising that Philo himself points to an agreement between Augustus and the Jews in matters of deification. As he put it, when Augustus rejected "ever to be addressed as a god", being rather "annoyed if anyone so addressed him"[78], he heartily approved of the Jews "who, as he knew very well, eschewed all such language on religious grounds".[79] Philo moreover says explicitly that by refusing Gaius divine honours the Jews protected "the high tradition of Roman freedom" (Leg. 116). As a nation they made the same sacrifice as the Roman intellectuals Macro and Silanus (Leg. 32–65). Like Seneca and Lucius Vitellius they had been victimized by the tyrant and could now proudly look back on their resistance.[80]

Both the events of the year 40 and the climate in Rome after Gaius' assassination thus shaped Philo's position. They led him to favour one of his earlier views on the deification of human beings. He now formulated rigid value standards for the Jews, while ignoring his own statements on the divinity of exceptional rulers in his earlier treatises. In this way he has provided a mean-

---

[76] Seneca once ironically referred to Gaius as "deus noster" in order to highlight the gap between the vulgar illusions of this emperor and the nobility of his victim Canus (De Tranq. Anim. 14:9).

[77] It is interesting that Musonius Rufus suggested a similar ideal of kingship. Reviving Augustan ideology, he urged the king to study philosophy so that he could reach an exceptional degree of self-control as well as justice and become truly beneficial to his subjects (frgm. 8 *apud* Stobaeus, Floril. 46.67; edition and Engl. tr. by C.E. Lutz, Musonius Rufus "The Roman Socrates", *Yale Classical Studies* 10 (1947) 60–3). This was in his view also the way for a king to become "godlike and worthy of reverence" (θεοπρεπής τε καὶ αἰδοῦς ἄξιος [ibid.]).

[78] The verb προσειπεῖν suggests a public declaration of Augustus' divinity (Leg. 154).

[79] Leg. 154. Colson *ad loc.* translates "the Jews, who he knew full well regarded all such things with horror". The verb ἀφοσιόω implies both the notion of horror and sacrilege.

[80] On their story of vicitimisation, see above n. 70.

ingful and highly topical interpretation of the conflict with Gaius, which initially revolved to no small degree around the issue of aniconism. Philo's interpretation associated the Jews once more with the Roman elite, while reinforcing the Otherness of the Egyptians.

A similar picture emerges in the field of ethics. Here, too, Philo stresses the high quality and rigidity of Jewish principles which he defines in terms congruent with Roman culture. He constructs a hierarchy ranging from "barbarian" to civilized nations. The Jews are placed at the top. They represent the elite of the Western world which promotes the value of virile self-restraint. Philo argues that *enkrateia* informs all of Mosaic legislation and distinguishes the Jews in virtually every aspect of daily life. This boundary of Philo's Jewish identity is usually overlooked because scholars tend to focus on the nature and sources of Philo's ethics.[81] Little attention has thus been paid to another question, namely the role of ethics in defining the specific character of the Jews. Philo himself left no doubt about the importance of self-restraint for Jewish identity. He argued that *enkrateia* is the basis of all Pentateuchal legislation. Moses, he explained, always "exhorted them [the Jews] to show this [ἐγϰϱάτεια] in all the affairs of life, in controlling the tongue and the belly and the organs below the belly" (Spec. 2:195). This austerity isolated the Jews. Philo lamented that "we" live as an orphan, who "is held in aversion by the great mass of men because they favour pleasure".[82]

The centrality of self-restraint for Jewish identity is furthermore indicated by the fact that Philo traces the different names of the Jews to their transcendence of wordly matters. The term "Hebrew" is interpreted as referring to a migrant "quitting the objects of sense-perception and going after those of the mind".[83] The name "Israel" is taken to indicate those who have left behind everything

---

[81] See especially the examplary studies by D. Winston, Philo's Ethical Theory, *ANRW* II. 21.1 (1984) 372–416; J.M. Dillon, *The Middle Platonists, 80 B.C. to A.D. 220* (New York 1977) 146–55. The role of Philo's ethics as an ethnic boundary has been noted very briefly by O.L. Yarbrough, *Not like the Gentiles. Marriage Rules in the Letters of Paul* (Atlanta 1985 = *SBL* Diss. Ser. 80), 7–25; S.K. Stowers, *A Rereading Of Romans. Justice, Jews, and Gentiles* (New Haven and London 1994) 57–61.

[82] Spec. 4:179; see also Spec. 1:163.

[83] Migr. 20; see also Jos. 42–48. Philo's explanation derives from the Hebrew etymology of the word "Hebrew" (עבֿרי), which conveys the notion of passing and migrating. Philo himself does not seem to have been fluent in Hebrew. Like other upper-class intellectuals in the Greek East, he may have employed Hebrew speaking assistants who provided more direct access to texts which he himself could not master in the original. Cf. Jones, Plutarch 84–6, who suggests a similar situation for Plutarch regarding the Latin sources of the *Parallel Lives; contra* A. Strobach, *Plutarch und die Sprachen. Ein Beitrag zur Fremdsprachenproblematik in der Antike* (Stuttgart 1997 = Palingenesia 64) 33–9, who argues for Plutarch's reading knowledge of Latin which allegedly enabled him to read the necessary sources by himself. For more details regarding Philo's access to the Hebrew Bible, see below chapter seven.

material in preparation for the vision of God.[84] *Ioudaioi* are identified as those who have "passed over all created objects" (Spec. 2:166). Self-restraint and sublimation thus set the Jews apart as a group of individuals who are called to become moral agents. To put it in Foucault's famous words, Philo expected each Jew to "act upon himself, to monitor, test, improve and transform himself".[85]

Philo uses the sixth commandment against adultery for an extended discussion on the nature of pleasure and its unique restraint by Mosaic legislation. He initially stresses that "pleasure is a mighty force felt throughout the whole inhabited world, no part of which has escaped its domination" (Spec. 3:8). Even animals succumb to it and live by its principles. More importantly, Philo acknowledges the satisfaction of hunger and sexual desire as "a pleasure in accordance with nature".[86] He probably meant with contemporary Roman and Classical Greek writers that such pleasure serves to ensure the survival of the species.[87] It thus fulfills a higher, rational purpose and is not intrinsically self-indulgent. Philo consequently suggests that pleasure becomes a moral issue when excess is involved. Gluttony is forbidden even if only permitted food is consumed. A "craze for sexual intercourse" must not be allowed even within marriage (Spec. 3:9). Simple food in reasonable measure should instead be eaten, while married life should be governed by a gentle rhythm of alternating periods of sexual fulfilment and abstention.[88] It is moreover significant that

---

[84] E. Birnbaum, *The Place of Judaism in Philo's Thought: Israel, Jews, and Proselytes* (Atlanta 1996 = Brown Judaic Studies 290, Studia Philonica Monographs 2) summarized also in *SBLSP* 32 (1993) 54–69, argued that Philo distinguished between the Jews as an ethnic group worshipping a particular God and Israel, a nationally undefined group which enjoyed the vision of God and included any respected philosopher whether Jewish or not. Such a radical distinction between Jews and Israel, however, is unwarranted. Statements such as "the suppliants' race which the Father and King of the Universe and the source of all things has taken for his portion ... is called in the Hebrew tongue Israel, but, expressed in our tongue, the word is 'he that sees God' " (Leg. 3–4) demonstrate the intrinsic connection between Jews and Israel. Birnbaum dismissed the importance of such statements in the *Legatio*, because she held this treatise to be an apologetic work for a foreign audience. As we saw above, however, the *Legatio* addressed the Jewish community in Alexandria. Philo's view of Abraham similarly suggests a deep connection between Israel and the Jews: this patriarch is interpreted as both the founder of the Jewish nation and the paradigmatic visionary of God (ἀρχηγέτου τοῦ ἔθνους (Abr. 276); Abr. 77; Her. 279). Similarly, Moses the paradigmatic *nomothetes* of the Jews enjoyed a most perfect vision (Mos. 1:158).

[85] Foucault, *The Use of Pleasure* (New York 1980, Fr. orig. = *The History of Sexuality* vol. 2) 28.

[86] ἡ κατὰ φύσιν ἡδονή (Spec. 3:9).

[87] Musonius, ed. Lutz fragms. 12–14, pp. 84–97 = Stobaeus, Anth. 3.6:23, Flor. 69.23, 70.14, 67.20; Plato, Leg. 1:636c; Arist., Nic. Eth. 3. 1118b.

[88] The appetites for food and sex were commonly discussed together as analogous expressions of the same drive which required control; on the nature of this pagan discourse, especially in the second century C.E., and its continuation in early Christian sources, see: G. P. Corrington, The Defense of the Body and the Discourse of Appetite: Continence and Control in the Graeco-Roman World, *Semeia* 57 (1992) 65–74.

Philo explains immoderation by reference to the moisture and fire of the body. These tend to produce effects which are not easily under the control of the mind, because fire is insatiable and constantly demands further nourishment, whereas moisture causes diseased irritations in the genital organs. Following Plato and anticipating Galen, Philo thus discusses pleasure within the overall context of a pathology of excess.[89] Finally, the main argument against adultery which Philo advances in these preliminary remarks is the havoc and disorder it creates in society. He is anxious that adultery will bastardize widespread family connections and ruin whole households (Spec. 3:11). The excess of pleasure is thus judged from a distinctly social perspective. In this context Philo does not dwell on the inherent wickedness of pleasure. He is rather concerned with its right measure which will ensure order and harmony in the individual person as well as in society at large.

Philo proceeds on the basis of these theoretical considerations to distinguish Mosaic marriage laws. It is striking that there is no other field of *Halacha* where so many explicit comparisons are drawn to other legal codes. In each case Philo shows how a particular law left a deep impact on the overall culture and history of that nation. He was clearly interested in ethnicity and, like Herodotus, explicitly used marriage laws and customs as a way of identifying national character.[90] He may have been inspired in this respect by the introductory remarks in Lev. 18:3–4, which contrast the Mosaic legislation on incest to Egyptian and Canaanite customs. Yet Philo went far beyond the Biblical *Vorlage* and suggested Jewish superiority, if not uniqueness, on more general moral grounds. Mosaic legislation on self-restraint thus emerges as an absolute norm by which human civilization must be appreciated.

Philo's first example is the Mosaic law against unions between mothers and sons.[91] Moses, he explains, not only forbade such unions *per se*, but also objected to a related yet minor offense, namely the union between the son of a first marriage with his stepmother after his father's death. This additional regulation served as a precaution in order to ensure that mother-son unions will not occur. The significance of this Biblical legislation is highlighted by contrast to the Persians and Greeks. Both of them are assigned the role of a significant Other, the Persians staging as the archetypal barbarian and the Greeks as a nation of culture.[92] Philo insists that both remain far below the standards of

---

[89] Spec. 3:10; cf. Plato, Tim. 86C–E; on Galen and the generally increasing concern about the body in the first century C.E., see: Foucault, Care of Self 39–68, 105–23.

[90] Cartledge, Greeks 76–86, showed that Herodotus used common Greek constructions of the male-female dichotomy to create ethnographic accounts of other nations which highlight "our" normative values.

[91] Spec. 3:12–21, which is based on Lev. 18:6–8.

[92] For details on Philo's construction of the Persians as barbarians, see above chapter two. Regarding Philo's notion of the Greeks as a nation of culture, see below chapter five.

Mosaic law because they allow unions between mothers and sons. He initially explains the case of the Persians. Repeating ancient opinions, he suggests that they considered mother-son unions to be especially prestigious:[93]

To the Persian custom it [the Mosaic law] at once shows its aversion and abhorrence and forbids it as a very grave offense against holy living. For the Persian magnates marry their mothers and regard the children of the marriage as nobles of the highest birth, worthy, so it is said, to hold the supreme sovereignty.

Philo adds his own interpretation to this known custom. Instead of merely reporting it, he constructs it as the essence of the Persians' Otherness. It expresses their barbaric character and accounts for the terrible disorder in their society. Philo initially illustrates this by pointing to the confusion caused by the Persian mother-son unions: the men are both son and husband to the same woman, while the women are both mother and wife to the same man. Even worse is the situation of their offspring: they are brothers to their father and grandsons to their mother. Yet the disaster is in Philo's view not confined to the private sphere. He argues that the Persian mother-son unions have caused devastation on a broader national level. They involved the whole country in constant warfare and sedition directed both against external and internal enemies. This is typical, as Philo does not fail to point out, of the "barbarian nature" which "can never remain in quietude" (Spec. 3:17).[94] It is thus intimated that the Persians are sexually and politically perverted, while the Jews subdue excessive pleasure, avoid mother-son unions and consequently enjoy inner peace.

Not satisfied with merely contrasting the Jews to the inferior Persians, Philo also distinguishes Mosaic legislation by comparison to the Greeks. He presents them as similarly perverted as the Persians, lamenting that "even among the Greeks these things were done in old days in Thebes in the case of Oedipus the son of Laius" (Spec. 3:15). This example is astonishing. Philo himself admits its weakness, acknowledging that Oedipus acted in ignorance. One may add that the case of Oedipus belongs to the realm of fiction and can certainly not claim to represent Greek marital law. The tragedy moreover conveys the sense that mother-son unions, even if perpetrated in ignorance, are a devastating curse. The story of Oedipus could thus even have been used to show a basic congeniality between Jews and Greeks. Yet Philo refers to it as a point of contrast illustrating Greek inferiority. One can therefore not escape the impression that Philo made rather artificial efforts to construct the Greeks in contrast to the Jews. Relying on a Roman stereotype of Greek licentiousness, he was

---

[93] Spec. 3:13; for similar views in Antiquity, see: Colson, Philo 7:632.

[94] Regarding the Greek stereotype of the Persians as constantly engaged in battle, see: Aeschylus, Pers. 93–106.

overly eager to place their values below Jewish ones.[95] Oedipus' tragic error has thus become an important element in Philo's overall argument about the superiority of Jewish values.

Philo's second example is the Mosaic prohibition of sibling marriages (Spec. 3:22–5). This law is praised for promoting "both continence and orderly conduct (ἐγκράτειαν ὁμοῦ καὶ εὐκοσμίαν)". Those nations who allow sibling unions consequently encourage the opposite, namely incontinence and licentiousness. The Egyptians are Philo's foremost example of such a nation. Being generally materialistic, barbaric and even bestial, they are also guilty of sanctioning unions between siblings of the same parents on both sides.[96] Philo vehemently condemns them, accusing their lawgiver of having (Spec. 3:23–4):

produced a fine crop of lewdness. With a lavish hand he bestowed on bodies and souls the poisonous bane of incontinence and gave full liberty to marry sisters of every degree ... For twins are often born who although separated and disunited by nature at birth, enter at the call of concupiscence and voluptuousness into a partnership and wedlock which are neither in the true sense of the words. These practices our most holy Moses rejected with abhorrence as alien and hostile to the blameless commonwealth ...

The Egyptians are here once more assigned the role of the complete Other. Their legislation is not only the opposite of Mosaic law, but contradicts Nature herself, thus amounting to a complete denial of all true values. As far as Philo is concerned, Egyptian sibling unions such as the Ptolemies practiced were sheer non-unions. The very perversion of the Egyptians, however, highlights the perfect standards of the Jewish commonwealth which altogether avoids such unions. Yet the contrast to the Egyptians proves insufficient. Philo highlights the uniqueness of Jewish self-restraint by another comparison to the Greeks. While their moral standards are admittedly higher than those of the Egyptians, their partial permission of sibling unions reinforces the superiority of Mosaic law. Philo especially mentions the Solonic and Spartan codices which respectively allow unions with either paternal or maternal sisters, but not with full siblings (Spec. 3:22). This example from Greek culture is again somewhat astonishing. While more convincing than Oedipus in the above discussion, it provides only a very partial picture. Philo must have been familiar with Plato's *Leg.* 8:838a–b, where sibling unions are principally forbidden. Had he wished, he could thus have presented Greek and Mosaic legislation as congruent and even analogous. Philo did not do so, however, because such a step would have undermined his overall argument about the superiority and uniqueness of Jewish self-restraint. He therefore selected such examples from Greek law which supported his construction of Jewish identity. Their allegedly

---

[95] For details on Philo's use of Roman stereotypes in his construction of the Greeks, see below chapter five.

[96] For more details on Philo's image of the Egyptians, see above chapter two.

inferior values complement the overall image of a hierarchy in which the Egyptians and Persians figure lowest as barbaric nations, the Greeks occupy the centre and the Jews are the leading nation with the highest standards. It is striking that the Romans are not mentioned in this context. No place is assigned to them in Philo's hierarchy. Roman values, however, do inform his discussion. A sense of moral superiority over the "barbarians" as well as the "licentious" Greeks is a position well known among Roman intellectuals.[97] Philo adopts it here in order to highlight the superiority of Jewish values. Frowning upon Greek morality, he constructed Jewish identity in close analogy to Roman self-definitions.

Philo paid particular attention to a group of Biblical laws which he understood to reject sexual relations not promoting the natural purpose of procreation (Spec. 3:32–63). Besides adultery, such prohibited sex included intercourse within marriage during the wife's menstruation, pederasty, sodomy and prostitution.[98] Philo himself added to this list unions with women who are known to be sterile. All of these were condemned for aiming at mere pleasure, while impeding the continuation of the human species. Philo used these largely Mosaic prohibitions to distinguish Jewish self-restraint in sexual matters from the customs of other nations. He especially pointed out that pederasty had become pervasive and even honourable, thus isolating the more modest Jews.[99] Many other nations awarded in his view prizes to "licentiousness and effeminacy" (Spec. 3:40). Only the Jews, Philo insisted, were singularly devoted to procreation. As he has Joseph say to Potiphar's wife: "the end we seek in wedlock is not pleasure but the begetting of lawful children" (Jos. 43).[100]

---

[97] For further details on Roman constructions of the "barbarian" and Greek Other, see above chapter two and below chapter five.

[98] Regarding the prohibition of prostitution, Philo relies on LXX Deut. 23:18, which translates קדשה (temple prostitute) by the general term πόρνη (harlot); see also: M.J. Gruber, The Hebrew qedeshah and Her Canaanite and Akkadian Cognates, in: idem, *The Motherhood of God And Other Studies* (Atlanta 1992) 22–4. L.M. Epstein, *Sex Laws and Customs in Judaism* (New York 1948) 152–7, 164–7; and S. Belkin, *Philo and the Oral Law. The Philonic Interpretation of Biblical Law in Relation to the Palestinian Halakah* (Cambridge MA 1940) 256–61, have already emphasized that the death penalty for prostitution which Philo assumes not only in Spec. 3:51, but also in Hyp. 7:1, was neither enjoined by Scripture nor other Jewish sources. On the contrary, some Biblical passages show a remarkably positive attitude towards prostitution. Nothing seems to have been wrong with Tamar playing the prostitute or with Judah visiting one (Gen. 38:15–6). The prostitute Rahab even became a national hero (Josh. 2:1–21).

[99] As Colson, Philo 7:634, has suggested, there is no evidence for the prominence of male prostitutes in the mysteries of Demeter. Philo once more seems to have exaggerated in order to strengthen his argument.

[100] Philo's interpretation of the encounter between Joseph and Potiphar's wife is exceptional in the context of other exegetes in the Second Temple Period. Only he interpreted these figures as representatives of their respective national ethos. Cf. for example Josephus who interpreted these figures as typical of their sex: while Joseph demonstrated manly rationality, Potiphar's wife was given to "feminine" emotionality and vengeance (A.J. 2:39–59).

The austerity of Philo's position on sex has often been noted. K.L. Gaca recently reinforced earlier suggestions of his Pythagorean sources.[101] The latter prohibited any sexual act not specifically aimed at procreation and enjoined men to direct their thoughts during orgasm to that overall aim. Philo, however, does not seem to have embraced such extreme ideals. While he, as many other Hellenistic writers, often stressed the procreational purpose of marriage, he made his polemical statements against wasting the seed in very specific contexts.[102] Unlike the Pythagoreans and later Babylonian rabbis, Philo was not concerned with the life-containing potency of the sperm itself.[103] He rather objected to sexual relations that were devoid of any procreational context and thus only served to satisfy physical pleasures. This position clearly emerges from his discussion of the various forms of wasting the seed.

Philo criticizes the husband for wasting his seed when sleeping with his wife during her menstruation. This is a mistake a good sower would never make.[104] The context of this statement has often been overlooked. Philo interprets here a Biblical injunction in contemporary terms, translating distinctly ritual notions into general ideals of sexual morality. He obviously opposed sex whenever there was no chance of conception. This may, however, say little about a couple's conduct during the remaining periods. Philo's criticism of sex during menstruation does not apply to times when the woman is not menstruating. It is highly significant that he, unlike the more Pythagorean Musonius, makes no general statement about the "unjust and unlawful" nature of any sexual act which is not specifically directed to procreation.[105] It would thus appear that the

---

[101] K.L. Gaca, Philo's Principles of Sexual Conduct and their Influence on Christian Platonist Sexual Principles, *SPhA* 8 (1996) 21–7. See also *pars pro toto* D. Boyarin, *Carnal Israel. Reading Sex in Talmudic Literature* (Berkeley 1993) 78–80, who places Philo in the opposite camp of the pro-sex rabbis; D. Winston, Philo and the Rabbis on Sex and the Body, *PT* 19.1 (1998) 41–2, nuances Boyarin's conclusions by stressing that Philo's views on the body were not wholly negative and that he did not reduce women to mere vehicles of procreation. Philo's ambivalence in this matter resembles his view the rabbis' position.

[102] Philo refers to the procreational purpose of marriage in Cher. 43; Congr. 12; Abr. 137, 248; Her. 164; Praem. 108–9; Q.G. 3:21. Philo's contemporary Musonius expressed himself in similar terms, thus following a long tradition of Classical Greek and Hellenistic writers, see also: A.C. Van Geytenbeek, *Musonius Rufus and Greek Diatribe* (Assen 1963) 62–71.

[103] M.L. Satlow, "Wasted Seed", The History of a Rabbinic Idea, *HUCA* 65 (1994) 137–75, has convincingly shown that concern with the seed itself and condemnation of its waste have emerged only in the Babylonian Talmud, while the earlier Palestinian rabbis opposed masturbation on the grounds that it was a sign of mental weakness and lacking self-control. Satlow moreover noted that Philo shares the earlier concern for self-restraint (163–4). He identified this, however, as typical of Graeco-Roman ethics, without considing the exceptionally stringent position of the Pythagoreans. For details on Philo's Aristotelian notions of the seed and procreation, see above chapter one.

[104] For details on the parable of the sower in this context, see below chapter eight.

[105] Musonius, On Sexual Indulgence, frgm. 12 apud Stobaeus, Anth. 3.6:23 = ed. Lutz 86–7; in light of this difference Geytenbeek, Musonius 73, has overemphasized the parallel between Musonius and Philo.

married couple was left in peace by Philo during all the days of the month that the woman was not directly bleeding.[106]

Philo's polemics against both pederasty and unions with women known to be sterile reflect the same position on sexuality. These relations are condemned because they cannot lead to procreation. Philo accuses homosexuals of rendering cities desolate and "destroying the means of reproduction" (Spec. 3:39). The man who ploughs "a hard and stony land" is similarly criticized for destroying "the procreative germs with deliberate purpose" (Spec. 3:34). Yet it does not follow from these two cases that a lawful, "natural" couple must direct every single act of intercourse to procreation. It is on the contrary striking that Philo's most vehement condemnation of the "pleasure-lovers", who "mate with their wives, not to procreate children and perpetuate the race, but like pigs and goats in quest of enjoyment", appears in the context of his sharp polemics against child exposure (Spec. 3:113). Philo is concerned here to uproot a widespread custom which retroactively annuls the natural fruits of marriage.[107] He thus insists on the general possibility of procreation as a criterion for legitimizing sex. Exposing the offspring obviously negates the overall aim of marriage and is therefore condemned in the strongest terms. The procreative purpose, however, only sets the general framework for sexuality and does not govern every single act.[108] It may even be theoretical as in the case of a couple who discovers the woman's sterility during the course of their marriage. Philo encourages them to stay together and continue their companionship.[109]

Consistent with these views, Philo never expresses concern for the individual sexual act as such. Unlike the Pythagoreans, he neither prescribes how it should be performed nor does he tell the male what to think while copulating. He did not embrace the Pythagorean belief that "wretched offspring" comes from intercourse "that fails to be temperate and purposeful".[110] On the contrary, Philo even admits that it is through pleasure that "begetting and the coming of life is brought about" (Opif. 161). Sexual pleasure was thus acknowledged as long as it was not divorced from the overall purpose of procreation. Long periods of sexual abstention, as recommended by Pythagoras, were by no

---

[106] Regarding Philo's limitation of the woman's impurity to the actual days of her bleeding, which implies ignoring certain Biblical legislation, see above chapter one.

[107] For further details on child exposure, see below chapter six.

[108] A similar conclusion has been reached on different grounds by G. Delling, *Paulus' Stellung zu Frau und Ehe* (Stuttgart 1931 = Beiträge zur Wissenschaft vom Alten und Neuen Testament 5) 55.

[109] See also: Winston, Philo and the Rabbis 53–5, emphasizing the importance in Philo's discussion of companionship within marriage.

[110] Iamblichus, *Vit. Pyth.* 211, quoted by Gaca, Sexual Conduct 24; for similar Pythagorean statements on sexuality, see: C. J. De Vogel, *Pythagoras and Early Pythagoreanism. An Interpretation of Neglected Evidence on the Philosopher Pythagoras* (Assen 1966) 110–1, 132–3, 237–8.

means required or even suggested.[111] The Jews, Philo implies, are masters in the art of the *aphrodisia*. Striking the right balance, they direct the sexual impulse to a noble purpose.[112] By altogether avoiding certain unions and limiting sexual activity to the right *kairos* each month, they create a unique framework for the development of true continence.

Philo's ideal of sexual restraint also translates into a complete seclusion of Jewish women. These were to be confined to the women's quarters of the house.[113] Philo even prides himself that they "never even approached the outer doors" and were so rigorously kept inside that their exposure to unfamiliar eyes was a major disaster (Flac. 89). The younger women were "for modesty's sake" restricted to the inner chambers of the *gynaikon*. They entirely avoided the sight of men "even of their closest relations" (Flac. 89). Philo moreover hoped that his upper class audience would shudder at the very thought of their wives going "like a vagrant in the streets before the eyes of other men" (Spec. 3:171). They should not be allowed to do the shopping and not go on their necessary religious errands at a time when other people could be expected in the streets (Spec. 3:171). Philo was equally anxious that women might interfere in state affairs which, he was convinced, would corrupt the whole community. Such a woman, who "unsexes" herself, was caricatured by him as someone who "overcome by wifely feeling" rushes to assist her husband. In the process she behaves in the most vulgar fashion, cursing and catching hold of her opponent's genitals (Spec. 3:173–5). Jews, Philo insisted, must not allow their women to behave thus and intrude upon the male domain.

This picture of the totally secluded Jewish woman is undoubtedly an "ideal" portrait drawn by Philo.[114] It can hardly have applied to the numerous women

---

[111] Diod. 10. 9:3 quotes Pythagoras as advising "people to abstain from sexual intercourse during summer and not to practice it except with great moderation during the winter" (quoted from Vogel, Pythagoras 179).

[112] See also Philo's praise of Moses as someone who submitted his impulses to the guidance of reason (Mos. 1:26–9).

[113] Spec. 2:207; All. 3:40, 98; Somn. 2:9; in metaphorical use in Agr. 79–80; Migr. 96. See also: D. Sly, The Plight of Woman: Philo's Blind Spot?, in: W.E. Helleman (ed.), *Hellenisation Revisited. Shaping a Christian Response Within the Greco-Roman World* (Lanham and London 1994) 178. Those Jewish synagogues, which explicitly anticipated female participation, boasted of a clear separation between men's and women's quarters (Cont. 32–3); on the exceptionally active role of the Therapeutrides in the religious life of their community, see: Kraemer, Monastic Jewish Women 342–70; *eadem*, Women's Authorship of Jewish and Christian Literature in the Greco-Roman Period, in: Levine, "Women like this" 221–42. Philo's remark about women having to fulfil their necessary religious errands at a time when the streets are empty and the place of worship totally silent (Spec. 3:171), suggests that he did not approve of their participation in the regular service. The Therapeutrides were therefore highly exceptional upper class women, who were allowed to act "like men"; see also: J.E. Taylor and Ph. R. Davies, The So-Called Therapeutae of *De Vita Contemplativa*: Identity and Character, *HTR* 91.1 (1998)16–7.

[114] See also: Barclay, Mediterranean Diaspora 117. Philo's ideal of women's seclusion even contradicts the image of Biblical women on which see especially: P.L. Day (ed.),

who belonged to the lower classes, where separate women's quarters could presumably not be afforded. Rather than staying at home, such women had to earn a living outside the house. This fact, however, must not obscure the importance of Philo's construction in the context of Jewish identity. It initially implies that Jewish *enkrateia* was an exclusive virtue of men. Women were kept outside the realm of this ideal because they were not trusted to develop rational self-control. Philo confined them to the *gynaikon* precisely because he considered them incapable of mastering their passions. He even identified man's succumbing to the passions with submission to feminine weakness and disease, while rationality was associated with manliness.[115] Men aspiring to *enkrateia* thus had to be protected from feminine laxity. Attaining sexual restraint and self-control implied masculinity which involved valour and stern determination. One had to fight like an athlete in order to achieve these virtues.[116] The Jew who implemented this ideal consequently became a true man in the broader cultural sense. Unlike the homosexual, who has in Philo's view fallen prey to the "disease of effemination" and transformed "male nature to the female" (Spec. 3:37), the authentic Jew is distinctly virile. He is not penetrated, but assumes an active and rational control over his sexual drives, getting married for the purpose of procreation and keeping the female members of his family under firm control in the *gynaikon*.

Philo's particular construction of sexual self-restraint and its contingent seclusion of women has important implications for Jewish identity in first century Egypt. His immediate environment seems to have been far more permissive. In Hellenistic Egypt women had been given a more active and visible part in public life. Queens and female heads of the Neopythagorean school at Alexandria were a fact of life. Women were moreover active, if not dominant in the local Isis cult.[117] They even enjoyed a considerable degree of sexual licence,

---

*Gender and Difference in Ancient Israel* (Minneapolis 1989); A. Brenner, *The Israelite Woman. Social Role and Literary Type in Biblical Narrative* (Sheffield 1985 = *JSOT Suppl. Ser.* 21).

[115] See especially: Abr. 136; Ebr. 55; consider also Philo's statement in Q.E. 1:7 "the male is more perfect than the female. Wherefore it is said by the naturalists that the female is nothing else than an imperfect male"; see also: H. Szesnat, 'Pretty Boys' in Philo's *De Vita Contemplativa*, *SPhA* 10 (1998) especially 103–5; on the gender-biases in Philo's views on education, see below chapter six.

[116] See also: D.D. Gilmore, *Manhood In The Making. Cultural Concepts Of Masculinity* (New Haven and London 1990) 9–29, who has compared constructions of masculinity in different Mediterranean cultures and pointed to the pervasive notion of manhood as something not given, but acquired by special efforts.

[117] Heinemann, Bildung 232–5, noticed already the discrepancy between Philo's position and the customs of Hellenistic Egypt. On the status of women in Hellenistic Egypt, see: S.B. Pomeroy, *Women in Hellenistic Egypt. From Alexander to Cleopatra* (New York 1984) 13–28, 60–70; C. Préaux, Le Statut de la Femme à l'époque hellénistique, principalement en Egypte, *Recueils de la Societé Jean Bodin* 11.1 (1959) 171–74; R.S. Kraemer, *Her Share of*

especially during religious festivals.[118] If Philo's ideal was indeed implemented, it would considerably isolate the Jews from many of their countrymen. At the same time, however, the very nature of Philo's construction integrated them into the discourse of the Roman elite in the province. The Romans had been horrified by Cleopatra's role in politics and public life.[119] Her person and feminine allurements had been condemned in the strongest terms. Antony's coalition with her had been interpreted as an expression of weakness and submission to female frailty. A Roman had thus lost his manliness. Moreover, Seneca's famous note on his aunt indicates how the ideal of secluded women contributed to Roman identity in Egypt. Seneca's aunt had been the wife of the Roman governor in Alexandria. She was generally praised by him for her moral strength and even held up as a model for weaker men to master their emotions (Cons. Helv. 19:3–4). Her modesty in Egypt earned her special respect. Throughout the sixteen years of her husband's appointment, Seneca insists, "she was never seen in public, never admitted a native to her house and sought no favour from her husband nor suffered any to be sought from herself" (Cons. Helv. 19:6). This Roman matron kept herself distant both from the Egyptians themselves and from their effeminate customs. Rather than succumbing to their gossipy and unstable character, she maintained traditional Roman values. Implementing the conservative Augustan ideals of female modesty, she stayed in her house, gave absolutely no cause for gossip and never intruded upon the male domain of state-affairs.[120] The image of this woman perfectly corrobo-

---

*the Blessings. Women's Religions among Pagans, Jews, and Christians in the Greco-Roman World* (New York 1992) 71–9.

[118] D. Montserrat, *Sex and Society in Graeco-Roman Egypt* (London and New York 1996) 83, 163–79.

[119] For more details, see above chapter two.

[120] On the Augustan ideal of female modesty, see especially: Dio 54.16:1–5, who presents it as a hypocritical statement of policy which was not even adhered to by Augustus himself; Liv. 34.2:1–4:3, who projects Augustan values onto Cato, on the Augustan context of "Cato's" speech, see: E. S. Gruen, *Culture and National Identity in Republican Rome* (New York 1992 = Cornell Studies in Classical Philology 52–70; A. E. Astin, *Cato The Censor* (Oxford 1978) 25–6; D. Cohen, The Augustan Law on Adultery: The Social and Cultural Context, in: D. I. Kertzer and R. P. Saller (eds.), *The Family in Italy from Antiquity to the Present* (New Haven and London 1991) 113–5. The manliness of the Augustan ideal has been emphasized by J. Walters, Invading the Roman Body: Manliness and Impenetrability in Roman Thought, in: J. P. Hallett and M. B. Skinner (eds.), *Roman Sexualities* (Princeton 1997) 29–43; it becomes a conspicuous theme in Roman discussions on Greek homosexuality, on which see below chapter five. Similar values had earlier been advocated by Cic., Verr. 2.1:140 and in Classical Athens, on which see: S. B. Pomeroy, *Goddesses, Whores, Wives, and Slaves. Women in Classical Antiquity* (New York 1975) 79–81; D. Cohen, Seclusion, Separation, and the Status of Women in Classical Athens, in: I. McAuslan and P. Walcot (eds.), *Women in Antiquity* (New York and Oxford 1996 = *Greece and Rome Studies* III) 134–45. The Roman context of Philo's ideal of manly *enkrateia* has been briefly noted by Stowers, Romans 50–1; M. L. Satlow, "Try To Be a Man": The Rabbinic Construction of Masculinity, *HTR* 89.1 (1996) 23; idem, Rhetoric and Assumptions: Romans and Rabbis on

rated Seneca's general advocation of manly self-restraint.[121] Philo shared his position. He wanted Jewish women to play a similar role as Seneca's idealized aunt. They, too, should keep away from the eyes of men other than their husbands and especially avoid the treacherous mores of the Egyptians. They, too, should leave public space to the men and enable them by their own abstinence to run wordly affairs with manly *enkrateia*. The Jews, like the Romans, would thus not "resemble an Eastern procession" exhibiting "weakness and lack of endurance", but would instead act as the valiant leaders of the rational Western world.[122]

Philo's ideal of Jewish *enkrateia* also pertained to food. He understood the Biblical injunctions regarding a proper diet in the same spirit as the prohibitions concerning sexuality. The Mosaic limitations on food consumption were in his view informed by the same purpose, namely to teach the Jews proper self-restraint. Philo insists that neither to food nor to drink "did he [Moses] give full liberty, but bridled them with ordinances most conducive to self-restraint and humanity" (Spec. 4:97). The yearly donation of the first-fruits and temple taxes initially prevented the Jews from recklessly consuming everything at their disposal (Spec. 4:98–9). The more important lesson, however, was taught by the restriction of daily food. Anything which arouses the appetite and uncontrolled pleasures was forbidden so as to withdraw the fuel and regulate desire (Spec. 4:100–18). Pork must be especially avoided, Philo explains, because "among the different kinds of land animals there is none whose flesh is so delicious as the pig's, as all who eat it agree".[123] This interpretation of the kosher food regulations strikingly corresponds to the contemporary Roman ideal of frugality. Musonius Rufus similarly condemned gluttony and high living, criticizing them as expressions of "intemperance" and "excess".[124] Like Philo, Musonius was concerned that desire for food could become an obsession which would disturb the rational conduct of life. He therefore recommended that one accustom oneself "to chosing food not for enjoyment but for nourishment".[125] Valour was required to combat weaker inclinations.

---

Sex, in: Goodman, Jews in a Graeco-Roman World 135–44, who emphasized the continuity of this ideal in rabbinic culture in Palestine.

[121] See e.g. Prov. 1.6; on Seneca's discourse on manly self-restraint and its subversion, see also: Habinek, The Politics of Latin Literature 143–5.

[122] For senatorial objections during the Tiberian principate to women accompanying their husbands into the provinces, which would make Roman magistrates look like "an Eastern procession", see Tac., An. 3:33. Juv., Sat. 6:82–104, significantly criticizes Eppia for abandoning her senator husband in favour of dubious pleasures in Egypt and for thus ignoring her country.

[123] Spec. 4:101. The author of Ar. 143–57 advanced a similar argument. Jewish abstinence from pork was generally known, if not despised in Antiquity (see: Schäfer, Judeophobia 71–81; Philo, Leg. 361; Flac. 96).

[124] Fragm. 18B = Stobaeus, Anth. 3.18:17. (ed. Lutz 116, l. 9–12).

[125] Fragm. 18B = Stobaeus, Anth. 3.18:17 (ed. Lutz 118, l. 6–7).

Philo believed that the Mosaic dietary regulations struck a perfect balance between indulgence and the total abnegation of pleasure. In his view only such a balance led to true *enkrateia* and distinguished the Jews from other nations (Spec. 4:102):

> He [Moses] approved neither of rigorous austerity like the Spartan legislator, nor of dainty living, like him who introduced the Ionian and Sybarites to luxurious and voluptuous practices. Instead he opened up a path midway between the two. He relaxed the overstrained and tightened the lax, and as on an instrument of music blended the very high and the very low at each end of the scale with the middle chord, thus producing a life of harmony and concord which none can blame.

Mosaic law thus created the perfect framework for the cultivation of temperance. Each individual Jew was called upon to implement the values underlying these laws and to transform himself into a moral agent who actively controls his impulses. The Jews, Philo believed, distinguish themselves in this respect. Their life is governed by an overall harmony and more rational principles than that of other nations. Abiding by the kosher food laws enables them to reach a healthy balance which regulates the natural impulses rather than altogether subduing them. Instead of being overwhelmed by the appetites the Jews take an active part in selecting the right dish at the right time. Their diet thus habituates them to a considerable degree of self-control. Their *enkrateia* in dietary matters moreover integrates them into the elite of their country. While the Egyptians indulged in Philo's view in all kinds of detestable foods, the upper classes advocated self-restraint.[126]

Finally, the Jewish holidays are also discussed by Philo in the context of *enkrateia*. They, too, are teachers of self-restraint.[127] Their impact on daily life slightly differs from the effect of a kosher diet. The Jewish holidays, Philo argues, regulate the experience of time. They create a separate temporal space where Jews can withdraw from the concerns of daily life and return to their authentic values.[128] The whole people inhabits in regular intervals a higher spiritual realm which is in the Gentile world only occasionally reached by exceptional individuals.[129] This spiritual space provides the Jews with moments of recreation, which have a significant therapeutic effect on the rest of

---

[126] Philo expresses his views on Egyptian food especially in Her. 79; for the role of this passage in his construction of the Egyptian Other, see above chapter two.

[127] Another aspect of the Jewish holidays which Philo highlights is their conformity to Nature, on which see below chapter nine.

[128] For a similar model of holidays in different cultural settings, see: J. Assmann, Der Zweidimensionale Mensch: das Fest als Medium des kollektiven Gedächtnisses, in: idem and Th. Sundermeier (eds.), *Das Fest und das Heilige. Religiöse Kontrapunkte zur Alltagswelt* (Gütersloh 1991) 13–30.

[129] Philo admitted that individual wise men "either in Grecian or barbarian lands" are capable of celebrating authentic holidays, namely spiritual feasts not devoted to material indulgence (Spec. 2:42–48).

their life. In Philo's view the halachic provisions for the Jewish holidays create that special framework where *enkrateia* is cultivated.

Philo's discussion of the Sabbath, the Passover and the Day of Atonement illustrate his strategy. His interpretation of the Biblical injunctions concerning these holidays reinforces ethnic boundaries and stresses the high standards of Jewish *enkrateia*. The Sabbath was by all accounts a central marker of Jewish identity. Philo records distinct ethnic behaviour, such as tucking the right hand inside the garment and leaving the left held close to the flank under the cloak.[130] When challenged by an Egyptian official, the Jews refused to abandon the Sabbath observance and were "as mournful and disconsolate as they would were their native city being sacked and razed".[131] The Romans moreover repeatedly acknowledged special Jewish privileges concerning the Sabbath (Leg. 156–7). While Philo suggested that some form of Sabbath was celebrated by others as well, he distinguished the Jewish practice as far superior.[132] His interpretation of the holiday rested on two complementary arguments: inversion of daily life and spiritual recreation. Philo initially stresses that on the Sabbath the regular routine breaks down and social status is abandoned (Spec. 2:66–70). As a result every Jew is at least momentarily brought back to the level of basic human needs. The master is not served on this day and must therefore do the menial work by himself.[133] In Philo's view this experience is crucial because it keeps the master courageous in the face of life's unavoidable vicissitudes. It teaches the rich what is in reality superfluous and dispensible.[134] Inversely, the servant who does not have to submit to his master on the Sabbath recovers his full human dignity. He tastes of the freedom he might in the future

---

[130] Somn. 2:126; Cont. 30.

[131] Somn. 2:124. Both D. R. Schwartz, Philonic Anonyms of the Roman and Nazi Periods: Two Suggestions, *SPhA* 1 (1989) 63–73, and R. A. Kraft, Philo and the Sabbath Crisis: Alexandrian Jewish Politics and the dating of Philo's Works, in: B. A. Pearson *et al.* (eds.), *The Future of Early Christianity. Essays in Honor of Helmut Koester* (Minneapolis 1991) 131–41, independently argued that the officer mentioned in this context was in reality Philo's nephew Ti. Julius Alexander. The chronological problems of this suggestion have been stressed by Gruen, Heritage 85–6.

[132] Philo explains in Dec. 96 that "some other states celebrate this day as a feast once a month". As H. Weiss, Philo on the Sabbath, in: D. T. Runia *et al.* (eds.), *Heirs of the Septuagint. Philo, Hellenistic Judaism and Early Christianity. Festschrift for Earle Hilgert* (1991 = *SPhA* 3) 99, already pointed out, it is not clear whom Philo refers to; see also: Y. D. Gilat, The Sabbath Laws in the Writings of Philo, in: R. Link-Salinger (ed.), *Torah and Wisdom. Studies in Jewish Philosophy, Kabbalah, and Halacha. Essays in Honor of Arthur Hyman* (New York 1992) 62; R. Goldenberg, The Jewish Sabbath in the Roman World up to the Time of Constantine the Great, *ANRW* II. 19.1 (1979) 429.

[133] Gilat, Sabbath 65, noted that Philo's Halacha differs in this respect from rabbinic legislation: while he principally exempted the servant from any work, they exempted him only from such works as were specifically forbidden on the Sabbath. The non-Jewish servant was permitted to perform any work this rabbinic master might request.

[134] See also: T. E. Schmidt, Hostility to Wealth in Philo of Alexandria, *JSNT* 19 (1983) 85–97, who convincingly argued that Philo's attitudes towards wealth are typical of his class.

achieve, thus preparing himself to become a self-responsible moral agent. The Sabbath indeed trains the Jews, both from the upper and the lower end of the social stratum, to live by the standards of true frugality.

The Sabbath furthermore inverses the relation of body and soul. While the body works during the week, but rests on the Sabbath, the soul is at rest during the week, but resumes its activity on the Sabbath.[135] The day of physical rest thus serves as a weekly opportunity for spiritual recreation. Like Nicolaus of Damascus (Jos., A.J. 16:43), Philo argued that it was devoted to study and the restoration of virtue:[136]

For the law bids us to take time for studying philosophy and thereby improve the soul and the dominant part of the mind. So each seventh day there stand wide open in every city thousands of schools of good sense, temperance, courage, justice and the other virtues in which the scholars sit in order quietly with their ears alert and with full attention ..., while one of special experience rises and sets forth what is the best and sure to be profitable and will make the whole of life grow to something better.

Philo suggests here that the Sabbath creates a special space which enables the Jew to recover the "dominant part of the mind (τὸν ἡγεμόνα νοῦν)". Receiving instruction from the elders, he reinstalls the mind in its proper place. In this way he regains a position of active control over himself which may have elapsed during the week. Virtue and *enkrateia* are thus regularly strengthened by the gentle rhythm of Jewish life.

The Passover played in Philo's view a similar role. The Jews remember and re-enact on this occasion "that great migration" from Egyptian materialism and idolatry (Spec. 2:146). The Passover, too, is characterized by the double function of inverting daily life and providing spiritual recreation. Social hierarchies are temporarily abandoned, all male Israelites carrying out the sacrifices. Philo stresses that "the whole people, old and young alike, [are] raised for that particular day to the dignity of priesthood" (Spec. 2:145). They perform what is otherwise an exclusively priestly prerogative. This inversion of status re-enacts the spontaneous initiative of the Biblical Israelites who were so enthusiastic to leave Egypt that they sacrificed without waiting for the priest.[137] The annual

---

[135] Spec. 2:64. Philo stresses that the physical rest on the Sabbath does not indicate idleness, but on the contrary produces refreshment and guarantees a more energetic resumption of work after the Sababth (Spec. 2:60). These statements were probably made with a view to Roman prejudices concerning the Sabbath. Seneca is the first known Roman writer who criticizes the Sabbath as a day of idleness. This motif subsequently became a typical feature of Roman views on Jews, on which see: Schäfer, Judeophobia 86–9.

[136] Spec. 2:61–2; see also: Dec. 98 (with greater emphasis on the individuals' examination of his sins during the previous six days of the week); Leg. 156 (from the perspective of Augustus); Hyp. 7:10–14 (with emphasis on the communal acquisition of expertise in Torah and customs).

[137] Spec. 2:146. Philo's explanations reflect the original idea of Passover as described in Ex. 23:14–5, 17, 34:23, which was subsequently revised in the book of Deuteronomy; see

performance of the Passover holiday thus revives in the Jews a hope for liberation from the material realm as well as from rigid social hierarchies.

Philo moreover assigned a special role to the Passover banquet and the
subsequent Feast of Unleavened Bread.[138] Both of them create a festive atmosphere, but demand modesty in matters of food and drink.[139] The unleavened
bread especially evokes images of perfect frugality. Philo interprets it as the
original food in the Garden of Eden. The connection between the holiday and
the beginning of the world is drawn both on chronological and Scriptural
grounds: the feast occurs in the spring season when the New Year was originally celebrated and Ex. 12:2 explicitly dates the Exodus celebrations to the
first month of the year.[140] For Philo this means that the Passover and the Week
of Unleavened Bread are days of remembrance celebrating the creation of the
world. The unleavened bread consequently restores the Jews to the primary and
unadulterated state of humanity (Spec. 2:160):

Since, then, the spring-time feast ... is a reminder of the creation of the world and its
earliest inhabitants, children of earth in the first or second generation, must have used
the gifts of the universe in their unperverted state before pleasure had got the mastery,
he [Moses] ordained for use on this occasion the food most fully in accordance with the
season. He wished every year to rekindle the embers of the serious and rigorous mode
of life and to employ the leisure of the festal assembly to confer admiration and honour
on the old life of frugality and economy and, as far as possible, to assimilate our
present-day life to that of the distant past.

The Day of Atonement epitomizes in Philo's view all of Moses' teaching on
*enkrateia*. Taking place during the harvest season, when man is naturally inclined
to taste of the new fruits, it demands a day of complete abstinence. The rigour of
the fast both highlights the central message of Mosaic legislation and raises the
Jew's awareness to what is essential rather than superfluous (Spec. 2:195):

---

also: B. M. Levinson, *Deuteronomy and the Hermeneutics of Legal Innovation* (New York
and Oxford 1997) 53–97. J. G. McConville, Deuteronomy's Unification of Passover and
Massot. A Response to Bernard M. Levinson, *JBL* 119.1 (2000) 47–58, criticizes Levinson's
argument, but ignores the particular nature of ancient Midrash on which it is based. For more
details on the relationship between the Feast of Passover and the Feast of Tabernacles, see
below chapter nine.

[138] Philo differentiated between the Passover proper and the Feast of Unleavened Bread
(Spec. 2:150); for further details on the latter, see below chapter nine.

[139] Philo stresses that the participants "are not there as in other festive gatherings, to
indulge the belly with wine and viands, but to fulfil with prayers and hymns the custom handed
down by their fathers" (Spec. 2:148). Similar symposia are described in Jos. 201–6 and Cont.
36–75. For further details on the revival of the original, spiritual symposion, see: F. Ullrich,
Entstehung und Entwicklung der Literaturgattung des Symposion, *Programm des Kgl. Neuen
Gymnasiums zu Würzburg* (Würzburg 1908–9) 1:3–49, 2:3–73; W. Rösler, *Mnemosyne* in the
Symposion, in: O. Murray (ed.), *Sympotica. A Symposium on the Symposion* (Oxford 1990)
230–7. Regarding Philo's views on the Classical symposia of Plato and Xenophon, see below
chapter five.

[140] Regarding Philo's calendar, see below chapter nine.

Always and everywhere indeed he [Moses] exhorted them to show this [self-restraint] in all the affairs of life, in controlling the tongue and the belly and the organs below the belly, but on this occasion especially he bids them do honour to it by dedicating thereto a special day. To one who has learnt to disregard food and drink which are absolutely necessary, are there any among the superfluities of life which he can fail to despise, things which exist to promote not so much preservation and permanence of life as pleasure with all its powers of mischief?

The Day of Atonement thus exemplifies the inculcation of *enkrateia*, the central Jewish value which informs all parts of Mosaic legislation. By demanding extreme abstinence this holiday strengthens the Jew's awareness of essential needs and prepares him for a continent life. This day significantly contributes to the rhythm of Jewish life throughout the year and restores the spiritual dimension of man which enables him to gain a rational control over daily affairs.

All of the above discussed aspects of *enkrateia* – Jewish holidays, kosher food regulations and sexual restraint – are paramount to Philo's construction of Jewish identity. They distinguish the Jews both in their everyday life and on special occasions, while at the same time integrating them among the Roman elite of the world. The values of the Jews thus emerge as superior to those of other nations and place them at the top of a distinctly masculine Western civilization. In the field of ethics the Jews play the same leading role as in the realm of religion, where they refused to accept Gaius' statue in their Temple and thus staunchly defended what Philo recognized as traditional Roman principles which had, however, been temporarily abandoned by the Romans themselves.

# 4. Roman Benefactors and Friends

> "He [Tiberius] held sway over land and sea for
> twenty-three years without allowing any spark
> of war to smoulder in Greek or barbarian lands,
> and he gave peace and the blessings of peace
> to the end of his life with ungrudging bounty
> of hand and heart"                                    (Leg. 141)

The centrality of Rome for Philo's construction of Jewish identity has emerged
repeatedly over the previous chapters. Virtually all aspects of his discussion
related in one way or another to contemporary Roman notions. Philo described
Jewish descent, the Egyptian Other and Jewish values in a way that suggested
a deep affinity between Jews and Romans. The similarities between the two
became increasingly conspicuous in Philo's later works, reaching a climax in
the *Legatio* and *In Flaccum*. While close to each other, the two ethnic groups
nevertheless remained distinct. Philo constructed boundaries between Jews and
Romans as well. These were obviously not oppositional as in the case of the
Egyptians, but suggested what Barth has called a "complementarity of the
groups".[1] By this term he referred to the fact that in multi-ethnic societies,
where interaction between different groups is pervasive, boundaries are created
by assigning particular roles to each of them. Certain constraints are thus
imposed on social behaviour as well as on cultural and political functions. The
result is an agreement, reached at least by the majority if not by all of the
population, about the place of each ethnic group within the larger society.

For Philo the task of characterizing the Romans was complex and challenging. It involved, among other things, interpreting the pogroms in Alexandria
under Roman rule and Gaius' plan to set up his statue in the Jerusalem Temple.[2]
Philo at this time was in Rome as an ambassador and became increasingly
familiar with its culture. It is perhaps not surprising that his views on Rome
were explicitly formulated in the early forties C.E. when he described the
fateful events for a Jewish audience back home.[3] Philo's discussions in the
*Legatio* and *In Flaccum* thus reflect a far more tense time than, for example,

---

[1] Barth, Introduction 18; for further details on Barth's theory, see above Introduction.

[2] For details on this crisis from Philo's point of view, see above chapters one and three.

[3] It is significant that all explicit references to Romans and Roman customs, with the
exception of one reference to the Latin language in Opif. 127, occur in *In Flaccum* and the
*Legatio*; regarding the Jewish audience of the latter two, see above chapter one.

Plutarch's *Parallel Lives* which were written in a more relaxed atmosphere.[4] Philo's writings are of special value because they are the first detailed expression of a sustained pro-Roman attitude on the part of a Jewish intellectual. Doubtless, Jews before Philo had supported Rome.[5] Yet these left only fragmentary accounts which do not sufficiently explain the nature of their position.[6] While Philo's pro-Roman attitude has recently been acknowledged, scholars have continued to read the *Legatio* and *In Flaccum* mainly as sources for Jewish history. The question of identity has been virtually ignored in this context. Even raising the issue has become difficult because Philo's statements have so often been dismissed as mere apologetics aimed at a foreign audience.[7] Traditional interpretations thus have to be set aside in order that Philo's own voice may be heard. For him, politics, culture and self-definition converged. The task is to understand exactly how Philo saw the Romans and how this shaped his sense of being a Jew in first century Alexandria.

The starting-point of Philo's discussion on the Romans is remarkably broad. Instead of focussing on the immediate problems of the Jews under Gaius, he introduces general observations on Roman rule. In contrast to the critical account in the third *Sibylline Oracle*, Rome emerges as a positive force which has greatly contributed to the whole *oikoumene*.[8] Philo's position in this respect resembles that of other upper-class intellectuals in the Greek East, who were also involved in mediating between Rome and their local communities.[9] For

---

[4] Regarding the circumstances of Plutarch's writings, see: Jones, Plutarch 103–9, 122–30. Regarding the relevance of this author for a proper understanding of Philo, see above Introduction.

[5] Consider especially the Jewish *amicii* of Caesar and Augustus mentioned by Jos., A.J. 14:127–39, 15:328–39; Contr. Ap. 2:58–61. On the well-known Roman policy to support the local elites of the East and rule through them, either directly in the framework of a provincial government or indirectly as "friends and associates", see: Bowersock, Augustus 1–13, 30–41; R. Syme, The Greeks under Roman Rule, in: idem, *Roman Papers* (Oxford 1979) 2:571 (orig. Proceed. Mass. Hist. Soc. 72 (1957–63) 3–20); Goodman, Roman World 138–9; for examples see: A. H. M. Jones, *The Greek City. From Alexander to Justinian* (Oxford 1940) 170–1 and *passim*.

[6] I Macc. 8:1–32 briefly describes the conceptions of Rome held by Judas the Maccabee and his informants. The Romans mainly emerge here as mighty and reliable friends with whom it is worthwhile to make an alliance.

[7] For more details on the *status questionis* in Philonic scholarship, see above Introduction.

[8] On the anti-Roman position of the third *Sibylline Oracle* and its awareness of Rome's exploitation, see: E. S. Gruen, Jews, Greeks, and Romans in the Third Sibylline Oracle, in: Goodman, Jews in a Graeco-Roman World 15–36; J. J. Collins, Sibylline Oracles, in: J. H. Charlesworth (ed.), *The Old Testament Pseudepigrapha* (New York 1983) especially 1:356, 360.

[9] Described by Josephus as a "man held in the highest honour, brother of Alexander the Alabarch and no novice in philosophy" (A.J. 18:259), Philo belonged to the rich provincial elite of the Greek East with whom the Romans entertained close political and cultural contacts. He led the life typical of Greek intellectuals in the Roman empire; on the latter see also: F. L. Vatai, *Intellectuals in Politics in the Greek World. From Early Times to the Hellenistic Age* (London 1984) 124–29. For further details, see also Introduction.

Philo as well the Romans primarily represented the leading nation of the world, which had swiftly appeared on the stage of history and replaced earlier empires.[10] Roman ascendancy differed in his view from the dominion of other nations. Greeks, Macedonians, Persians and Lybians were all subject to the vicissitudes of fortune. Their power rose and fell seemingly at whim. As Philo put it, these nations were "tossed up and down and kept in turmoil like ships at sea, subject now to prosperous, now to adverse winds" (Immut. 175). The empires of Alexander and the Ptolemies were especially drastic examples (Jos. 135–6):

The Macedonians in their day of success flourished so greatly that they held the dominion over the whole inhabitable world, but now they pay to the tax-collectors the yearly tributes imposed by their masters. Where is the house of the Ptolemies, and the fame of the several diadochs, whose light once shone to the utmost boundaries of land and sea?

Roman rule, by contrast, seemed far more stable to Philo. This was because it stretched even further than the dominion of earlier empires. More importantly, it was morally deserved. Philo's praise of the extent of Roman dominion was exuberant. As far as he could see, there were literally no limits to her rule (Leg. 10):

a dominion not confined to the really vital parts which make up most of the inhabited world, and indeed may properly bear that name, a world, that is, which is bounded by the two rivers, the Euphrates and the Rhine, the one dissevering us from the Germans and all the more savage nations, the Euphrates from the Parthians and from the Sarmatians and Scythians, races which are no less savage than the Germans, but a dominion extending, as I said above, from the rising to the setting sun both within the ocean and beyond it.

This description of Roman dominion echoes an imperial Roman slogan which we have encountered before, namely the identification of *urbs* with *orbis*.[11] Philo suggests that Roman rule has cosmic dimensions, stretching "from the rising to the setting sun both within the ocean and beyond it". Rome thus reaches beyond the limits of the inhabited world and incorporates areas which had not even been part of Alexander's empire. As Philo explained above, the latter only held "the dominion over the whole inhabitable world" (Jos. 135).

---

[10] In contrast to historians and ethnographers, Philo pays no attention to the details of Rome's early history. Unlike Polybios, Dionysius of Halicarnassus, Strabo and others, he neither discussed historical figures before Augustus nor mentioned the founding of Rome; on these events as interpreted by Eastern intellectuals, see: J.-L. Ferrary, *Philhellénisme et Impérialisme. Aspects Idéologiques de la Conquete Romaine Du Monde Hellénistique, de la Seconde Guerre de Macédoine à la Guerre contre Mithridate* (Rome 1988) 223–9, 265–76; D. Dueck, *The Geography of Strabo as an Augustan Work* (Jerusalem 1996, Diss. in Hebrew) 1:202–63.

[11] As we saw above in chapter one, Philo had applied this notion to his description of Jerusalem as mothercity.

Rome, on the other hand, extends beyond the natural borders marked by the Euphrates and the Rhine. Even the savage nations of the Germans, Parthians and Scythians are in her domain.[12] This statement is somewhat surprising. It overlooks the fact that neither the Parthians nor the Germans ever fully submitted to Rome. Certain Eastern intellectuals were highly aware of these limitations of Roman rule. Livy complained that the "most light-minded of the Greeks" expressed their opposition to Rome by exalting Parthia.[13] Even Strabo, who advocated the notion of Roman world dominion, stressed the gradual pace of the conquests which often met with local resistance. Occasionally he even pointed out that Parthia remained an independent power equal to Rome.[14]

Philo's assumption of literally universal and unchallenged Roman dominion reflects imperial ideology. Augustus had in his *Res Gestae* elegantly passed over the fact that the Germans and Parthians had not been truly conquered.[15] He instead advertized military expeditions "by land and by sea throughout the world"[16] and proudly entitled his account "rerum gestarum divi Augusti, quibus orbem terrarum imperio populi Romani subiecit". In the same spirit Virgil created the poetic image of inhabitants from all parts of the world, including the Rhine and the Euphrates, marching among the conquered nations in Augustus'

---

[12] The Scythians had been meaningful Others of the Greeks (Hartog, Mirror 12–33 and *passim*), while the Germans and Parthians were identified as barbarians especially by the Romans, see: D. Lührmann, The Godlessness of Germans Living by the Sea according to Philo of Alexandria, in: B.A. Pearson (ed.), *The Future of Early Christianity. Essays in Honor of Helmut Koester* (Minneapolis 1991) 57–63; Balsdon, Romans and Aliens 60–4.

[13] Liv. 9.18:6; on this passage see also: T.J. Luce, The Dating of Livy's First Decade, *TAPA* 96 (1965) 227–9, suggesting that Livy wrote before 20 B.C.E when the lost Roman standards were recovered from Parthia – a fact, if already known to Livy, would have provided him with welcome ammunition against the *levissimi ex Graecis*; H.R. Breitenbach, Der Alexanderexkurs bei Livius, *MH* 26.3 (1969) 156–7; most scholars interpret Livy's reference to include also Timagenes, see: Bowersock, Augustus 109–10; M. Sordi, Timagene di Alessandria: uno storico ellenocentrico e filobarbaro, *ANRW* II.30.1 (1982) 775–97; cf. also Pompeius Trogus, Hist. Phil. 41.6:8, who expresses a similar view which might reflect the attitude of Timagenes of Alexandria; regarding Trogus' reliance on Timagenes, see: Nicolet, Space 33; C. Wachsmuth, Timagenes und Trogus, *Rheinisches Museum für Philologie* 46 (1891) 465–79.

[14] In Geogr. 6.4:2, 16.1:28, 17.3:2 Strabo describes Parthia's full submission to Roman influence, thus suggesting that Rome virtually ruled over the entire *oikoumene*; in Geogr. 11.9:2–3, 1.2:1, 11.6:4, 11.13:2, however, he suggests that the world was divided between two empires, the Parthian in the East and the Roman in the West; see also: Dueck, Strabo 227–33.

[15] R.G. 3:1; 6:1; 8:5, 26:3–4, 32:2, 34:1; see also: Yavetz, Public Image *passim;* on Augustus' policy to present negotiated compromises with the Parthians as (military) victories, see: E.S. Gruen, The Imperial Policy of Augustus, in: Raaflaub and Toher (eds.), Between Republic and Empire. 396–9.

[16] "toto in orbe terrarum" (R.G. 3:1); see also: R.G. 31–32; R.G. 26:4 where Augustus prides himself in the fact that his fleet "sailed ... to the territory of the Cimbri, a country which no Roman had visited before".

Actian triumph.[17] Ovid similarly spoke about the cosmic dimensions of Roman rule (Fasti 2:684). Such views of the empire were also embraced by intellectuals who had come to Rome from the Greek East. Dionysius of Halicarnassus is a striking example. He praised Roman supremacy as surpassing "all those that are recorded from earlier times" (A.R. 1.2:1). Anticipating Philo's formulations, he stressed that while Assyrians had been replaced by the Medes, and these by the Persians, and these by the Macedonians, Rome was destined for uncontested rule.[18] She had become "mistress of every sea" and was "the first and the only state recorded in all times that ever made the risings and the settings of the sun the boundaries of her dominion" (A.R. 1.3:3).

Philo interpreted the unprecedented dimensions of Rome's dominion as an expression of her moral and cultural superiority. He stressed that Gaius inherited an empire which was "at peace with itself, under good laws, and experiencing complete harmony between all its regions" (Leg. 8). It was therefore "a joy" to all the nations of both Europe and Asia (Leg. 10). It was especially remarkable in Philo's eyes that inherently contradictory elements of the empire had been brought into harmony. Full agreement had thus also been reached between Greeks and barbarians (Leg. 8). This was due to Augustus who (Leg. 147):

civilized all the unfriendly, savage tribes and brought them into harmony with each other, who enlarged Greece with many other Greek lands and who hellenized (ἀφελληνίσας) the most important parts of the barbarian world.

Rome's hellenizing role placed her on the side of civilisation. She was an agent of culture and superior morality. Philo implied that the leading nation of the world should not be judged from a traditional Greek perspective as belonging to the barbarian realm. He himself had frequently spoken of the world as being divided into Greeks and barbarians.[19] He assumed that the latter were uncivilized persons who "have never had a taste of human culture".[20] Given the

---

[17] Aen. 8:714–31; discussed by Gurval, Actium 240–47, as a contribution to Augustan ideology rather than as a mere reflection of it.

[18] A.R. 1.2:1–2; see also: J.M. Alonso-Núñez, Die Abfolge der Weltreiche bei Polybios und Dionysios von Halikarnassos, *Historia* 32.4 (1983) 411–26; E. Gabba, *Dionysius and The History of Archaic Rome* (Berkeley 1991) 192–3, who both compare Dionysius' succession of world empires to Polybius', arguing that while the latter used this historiographical model to foretell the decline of Rome, Dionysius stressed the breadth and duration of the Roman empire as a proof of its enduring superiority and guarantee of future expansion. Cf. also Cic., Ad Her. 4:34 where the rhetorical figure of *gradatio* is illustrated by the following succession of empires: "The empire of Greece belonged to the Athenians; the Athenians were overpowered by the Spartans; the Spartans were overcome by the Thebans; the Thebans were conquered by the Macedonians; the Macedonians in a short time subdued Asia in war and joined her to the empire of Greece".

[19] See e.g. Opif. 128; Cher. 91; Plant. 67; Ebr. 193; Abr. 136, 180–1; Jos. 30; Lib. 94; see also: Goudriaan, Ethnical Strategies 82–3.

[20] Spec. 3:163; on other occasions, however, he could use the term "barbarian" in a

existential nature and the pervasiveness of this dichotomy it was important to establish where Rome belonged. Philo's answer was unambiguous. The Romans, he insisted, brought Greek culture to barbarian countries. Augustus and the Roman empire thus succeeded where Alexander had in Philo's opinion failed.[21] Rome had created a common cultural framework for the whole empire. This unified the different regions and enabled Philo to consider himself, as well as other members of the Eastern elites, as serious partners in a far-reaching and beneficial project of government.[22]

Dionysius of Halicarnassus expressed remarkably similar views. In his account of Roman origins he argued that Roman ascendancy was not fortuitous. He even saw the main purpose of his own historiography in uprooting anti-Roman positions supported by "barbarian kings". He wished to replace these by showing that Rome morally deserved her power.[23] Eastern intellectuals, Dionysius insisted, should "neither feel indignation at their present subjugation, which is grounded on reason (... superiors shall ever govern their inferiors) nor rail at Fortune for having wantonly bestowed upon an undeserving city a supremacy so great".[24] In Dionysius' opinion Rome's success was grounded in her superior virtue which had not been equalled by anyone else (A.R. 1.5:3). Those "malicious" Greeks who accused the Romans of being "the basest of barbarians" who wantonly robbed them of their blessings were mistaken.[25] Dionysius not only hoped to show that the Romans were not barbarians, but that they could even boast of proper Greek descent. Their city had been founded, he explained, by Greek colonists, who had introduced to Italy their traditional lifestyle.[26] This

---

neutral linguistic sense, including among the latter even the Hebrew tongue of his ancestors (e.g. *Conf.* 6, 190).

[21] For details on Philo's view on Alexander, see below chapter five.

[22] See also: E. Gabba, The Historians and Augustus, in: Millar and Segal, *Caesar Augustus* 63–4, who pointed out that Greek culture served in Philo's view as a harmonizing factor throughout the Roman empire.

[23] A.R. 1.4:3; see also: Gabba, *Dionysius* 16–7, 36–9, 191–2, 195–9, who forcefully argued that Dionysius aimed his account against Mithridatic historiography which was outspokenly anti-Roman, while idealizing Alexander the Great; see also: St. Usher, The Style of Dionysius of Halicarnassus in the 'Antiquitates Romanae', *ANRW* II.30.1 (1982) 819, who argued for a more general Greek audience, while H. Hill, Dionysius of Halicarnassus and the Origins of Rome, *JRS* 51 (1961) 88–93, suggested a Roman audience beside a Greek one.

[24] A.R. 1.5:2. On the possibly Stoic origin of this position, see: W. Capelle, Griechische Ethik und römischer Imperialismus, *Klio* 25 (1932) 86–105; H. Strasburger, Poseidonios on Problems of the Roman Empire, *JRS* 55 (1965) 40–53; Ferrary, *Philhéllenisme* 363–94.

[25] A.R. 1.4:2; the rhetoric on the part of Dionysius' opponents corresponds to the position initially expressed by mainland Greeks around the turn of the third century B.C.E., on which see: J. Deininger, *Der politische Widerstand gegen Rom in Griechenland 217–86 v.Chr.* (Berlin and New York 1971) 13–37.

[26] For a summary statement of his view, see especially A.R. 1.11–13, 1.60:3, 7.70–72. Dionysius attributed the differences between Roman and Greek culture, which were nevertheless obvious even to the most prejudiced eye, to the subsequent mixing of Romans with barbarians (A.R. 1.10:1–2). See also Diod. Sic. 1:4.

was the reason why Rome in his days spread not barbarian, but civilized and beneficial customs over the whole world.[27] While Philo did not address the issue of Roman origins, he intended to convey a similar message to that of Dionysius. The Romans, he told his Jewish audience in Alexandria, are not to be seen as barbarians who fortuitously gained power, but as the leaders of Greek civilization who introduce superior values to the savage parts of the world. Philo, like Dionysius, hoped in this way to overcome traditional Greek views and prepare his readers for a positive appreciation of the contemporary world power. His readers should ultimately see themselves as important partners in a multi-national empire, which provided Greek culture as a common framework for an immense diversity of traditions.

Philo's reference to Rome's hellenizing function reflects a prevalent Roman self-image. Augustus had presented himself as a protector of Greek culture, thus hoping to win the allegiance of the affluent and educated classes in the newly subdued territories of the Greek East.[28] He also tried in this way to transfer the loyalty of Antony's former supporters to his own person. For this purpose he prided himself on having "replaced in the temples of all the cities of the province of Asia the ornaments which my late adversary, after despoiling the temples, had taken into his private possession" (R.G. 24:1). In Alexandria Augustus made special efforts to address the crowd in Greek, to show himself a friend of the local philosopher Arius Didymos and to express his respect for Alexander the Great.[29] When visiting the latter's tomb, he touched his body so vigorously that, according to Dio, "a piece of the nose was broken off".[30] Such gestures and rhetoric, however, did not meet with universal approval. Timagenes, for example, who had been deported from Alexandria to Rome, remained hostile to the empire. He continued to believe in the superiority of Greek culture proper and admired Alexander the Great as its true representative. If only the Macedonian conqueror had lived longer, he lamented, Rome would have surrendered.[31] Strabo also remained considerably more reserved than Philo and

---

[27] A.R. 7.70:5; 1.33:4; see also: Gabba, Dionysius 10–6, who showed that Dionysius based his claim of Rome's Greek origins on numerous earlier writings, both Greek and Roman, but went further than these by arguing that the Greek character of Rome underlay her whole history and culture until his own days.

[28] See also: Bowersock, The Problem of the Succession 169–88; Kienast, Augustus und Alexander 446–7; Gruen, Alexander 190–1.

[29] Plut., Ant. 80:1; Praec. Ger. Reip. 814d; Dio, 51.16:3–4; see also: Bowersock, Augustus 33–4, Fraser, Alexandrian View 15–6; Ferrary, Philhéllenisme 435–86. Augustus' speech in Greek was a special effort, because he never became fluent in that language. As Bowersock suggested, his speech may well have been translated from Latin into Greek by Arius Didymus. It is also noteworthy that Suet., Aug. 89:1 mentioned Augustus' particular interest in "Greek studies".

[30] Dio. 51.16:5; for further details on Augustus' and Roman attitudes in general to Alexander, see above chapter two and below chapter five.

[31] Liv. 9.18:6; see also: Bowersock, Augustus 109–10; Sordi, Timagene.

Dionysius. While admitting that Rome had "taught the more savage how to live under forms of government" (Geogr. 2.5:26), he still assumed the separate status and superiority of Greek culture.[32] Like Erastothenes he was concerned to identify noble barbarians who might eventually qualify as Greeks in a cultural sense (Geogr. 1.4:9). Rome was in his eyes a barbarian nation. Despite her humble origins she had adopted Greek ways. Unlike Philo and Dionysius, however, Strabo was not willing to speak explicitly about Rome's hellenizing function.[33] Only the former two demonstrated literally no sign of ambivalence towards Rome's role in the realm of the Greek East.[34]

It is against this general background that Philo appreciates the different representatives of Roman rule and their relationship to the Jews. His exuberant praise of Augustus has often been noted. Scholars agree that it plays a rather central role in the *Legatio* and indicates Philo's attitude towards the Romans. So far, however, its purpose has been appreciated on the assumption that Philo wrote an apologetic encomium for either a foreign audience in general or for the new emperor Claudius in particular.[35] In this context the positive image of Augustus appeared to function as the ideal model of a ruler, in contrast to the wicked Gaius, whose memory would encourage the Romans to adopt a favourable policy towards the Jews. If, however, the *Legatio* addresses a Jewish audience back home, as has become clear in the first chapter, this interpretation must be reassessed. We then have to ask what role the image of Augustus played in explaining the Romans to Alexandrian Jews. In order to grasp Philo's overall construction of the Romans, however, we initially have to understand another figure: Tiberius. This may initially seem surprising. Philo, like Strabo, pays

---

[32] See Geogr. 1.4:9, 3.3:8, where Strabo speaks about rendering remote nations "peaceful and πολιτικούς"; Strabo refers to the separate and superior nature of Greek culture in Geogr. 3.4:19; see also: Dueck, Strabo 236; B. Forte, *Rome and the Romans as the Greeks saw them* (Rome 1972 = *Pap. Mon. Am. Ac. Rome* 24) 185–6; Sherwin-White, Racial Prejudice 1–32. Strabo's greater reservation in comparison to Dionysius has been overlooked by Gabba, Dionysius 48–52, who mistakenly compared Strabo's praise of Alexander's integrative policies, irrespective of his subjects' Greek or barbarian origins, to Dionysius' explicit attribution of that hellenizing role to Rome.

[33] Nicolaus of Damascus held views similar to Strabo's. He praised Augustus for his world-wide rule, including Greeks and barbarians (frgm. 125, FrGrH 2:391). While he may have implied a parallel to Alexander, as Gabba, Historians 63–4; Wacholder, Nicolaus 74, have argued, he did not explicitly refer to Augustus' hellenizing agency.

[34] Similarly positive attitudes are subsequently expressed by Aelius Aristides, Appian and Dio, on which see: Gabba, Historians 67–70.

[35] See especially: Barraclough, Politics 453–4; Delling, Enkomium *passim.* V. Guignard, Le Rapport De Philon D'Alexandrie A La Philosophie Grecque Dans Le Portrait Des Empereurs, in: C. Levy (ed.), *Philon D'Alexandrie Et Le Langage De La Philosophie* (Brepols 1998) 459–69, argued that Philo's portrait of Augustus and Tiberius must not be understood as mere flattery, but as an honest attempt to draw the attention of the intended Roman audience to the duties of the emperor as defined by Greek philosophy. This argument, however, is problematic, because the Greek philosophical notions which Guignard has identified in the *Legatio* are rare and must not be overemphasized.

only little attention to him, presenting him as Augustus' successor who faith-fully continued his step-father's policies.[36] Philo has Agrippa stress this conti-nuity especially with regard to their respect for the religious sensibilities of the Jews (Leg. 299–310). Tiberius thus appears to deserve little attention in his own right. Philo's brevity, however, is deceptive. It obscures a significant story which explains Philo's construction of the Romans in the context of Jewish identity.

Initially, the laconic nature of Philo's remarks on Tiberius is astonishing, because he is speaking of the man who was Roman emperor for much of his adult life (14 C.E. – 37 C.E). One would therefore expect more detail, perhaps even some personal reminiscences as in the case of Gaius. Furthermore, Philo's brevity does not allow for a nuanced portrait of Tiberius. He only says good things about him, but in a rather general way and without providing specific examples. Philo's approach differs considerably in this respect from his de-scription of both Augustus and Gaius whose images emerge far more vividly. His style regarding Tiberius indicates, as we shall see, a rather defensive posi-tion. Philo's portrait is carefully designed in response to the latter's negative reputation among other intellectuals. This idealized image of the controversial emperor was needed in order to distinguish authentic Roman rule from Gaius' deplorable perversion of it.

In Philo's account Tiberius' death represents a crucial turning point. Before that fateful event Roman rule was characterized by "moderation and observ-ance of the law" (Leg. 119); after it leading Roman politicians succumbed to Egyptian vice. As we saw in the second chapter, Philo emphatically stresses Egyptian influence on both Gaius and Flaccus. The Alexandrians were in his view guilty of encouraging Gaius to think of himself as a god (Leg. 162). They had given "birth to ... the idea of godship which occupied his dreams" (Leg. 338). They had also gained control over Flaccus to the extent that "the ruler became the subject, the subjects leaders" (Flac. 19–20). These tragic changes were occasioned by Tiberius' death. Philo identifies this event as the trigger which rapidly led to the corruption of Roman standards and gave way to a pathology of excess. The dramatic career of Helicon, a most "damnable and abominable slave" from Alexandria (Flac. 166), illustrates the dimension of the change (Leg. 167–9):

Now at that time he [Helicon] did not enjoy any privileged position, since Tiberius detested childish jokes; he had been inclined to seriousness and austerity almost from childhood. But when he died and Gaius inherited the empire, Helicon attended his new master, who was relaxing into loose living and sensual luxury of every kind, and said to

---

[36] Strabo briefly speaks of Tiberius as Augustus' successor and imitator especially in matters of military and cultural conquest (Geogr. 3.3:8, 6.4:2). He consequently appeared as a great benefactor in the East (Geogr. 13.4:8). On Strabo's view of Tiberius, see also: F. Lasserre, Strabon devant l'Empire romain, *ANRW* II. 30.1 (1982) 885–7.

himself: "Now is your chance, Helicon. Rouse yourself .... If you put some slightly malicious sting into your mockery, so as to arouse bitterness based on suspicion as well as laughter, then you have your master completely in your power ...

Tiberius' death thus signifies an absolute change from better to worse. Philo highlights the rupture by producing an immaculate portrait of Tiberius to which he constrasts Gaius. He initially praises him as a man "of profound prudence and the cleverest of all his contemporaries at knowing a person's secret intentions", surpassing everybody "as much in sagacity as in rank" (Leg. 33). Tiberius therefore noted the "unsociable and uncooperative disposition" of Gaius as well as "the inconsistency of his character" (Leg. 34). He even doubted the latter's suitability for the imperial office, but Macro's manipulative lobbying prevented him from acting on his misgivings.[37] It is clear, however, that Tiberius did not approve of the man who would overturn the tradition of "Roman freedom" (Leg. 116). With Gaius the excellence of Roman rule came to an abrupt, albeit temporary end. Philo indicates which blessings were thus eclipsed (Leg. 141–2):

He [Tiberius] held sway over land and sea for twenty-three years without allowing any spark of war to smoulder in Greek or barbarian lands, and he gave peace and the blessings of peace to the end of his life with ungrudging bounty of hand and heart. Was he inferior in birth? No, he was of the noblest ancestry on both sides. ... Was he inferior in education? Who among those who reached the height of their powers in his time surpassed him in wisdom or eloquence? Was he inferior in age? What other king or emperor enjoyed a happier old age? Why, even when he was still young, he was called "elder" out of respect for his perspicacity.

E. Mary Smallwood took this portrait of Tiberius to be somewhat idealistic, yet historically true. She confirmed the notice of Tiberius' learning by parallels from other sources and, in other cases of discrepancy, preferred Philo's account. The reference to Tiberius' happy old age consequently appeared to indicate Philo's ignorance "of the alleged orgies on Capri" and ultimately to disprove "the pictures drawn by Tacitus, Suetonius, and Dio of the old Emperor wallowing in debauchery and sensuality during his retirement".[38] A careful

---

[37] Leg. 35–40; Flac. 11–5. In Leg. 24 Philo mentions a different interpretation proposed by "some people" according to which Tiberius would indeed have disposed of Gaius, had he not been snatched away by death. Josephus presents Tiberius' dislike of Gaius as a preference for his biological grandson Gemellus. He even suggests that Gaius was the natural successor by describing him as "a young man who had gained a thorough education" and profited from his father Germanicus' popularity (A.J. 18:205–10, especially 18:206). On the divergent views of Philo and Josephus regarding Tiberius, see further below.

[38] Smallwood, Legatio 227, 164. The only feature which Smallwood recognizes as an idealization is Philo's reference to worldwide and absolute peace without faction (Smallwood, Legatio 158–9, 227); on this see below. F.B. Marsh, *The Reign of Tiberius* (Oxford 1931) 222, similarly took Philo's account at face value and used it as a basis for his theory of a change in Tiberius' reputation under Domitian: while he was seen favourably by his

reading of the above passage, however, reveals that Philo was anything but ignorant of Tiberius' bad reputation. The very style of his writing indicates that he was responding to critical queries about the emperor's character. It is significant that Augustus is nowhere presented by way of refuting allegations concerning his person. Regarding Tiberius Philo is clearly more on the defensive. His exposition aimed at replacing a widely known, negative image with a more favourable one.

In the above passage Philo initially stresses the peacefulness and bounty of Tiberius' rule. He insists that there was no suggestion of war throughout his long reign and that he gave ungrudgingly to the territories under his domain. These statements reflect the official aims of Tiberius' policy, but overlook a more dire reality. It is no accident that there are close parallels between the views of Philo and Velleius, who served as Tiberius' cavalry prefect in the German campaign and became his enthusiastic admirer.[39] Velleius praised the Tiberian principate as a period of unsurpassed "safety, order, peace and tranquility" for all mankind (2.103:5). He also recounted how Tiberius shared his royal equipment, kitchen and physicians with any needy soldier (2.114:1–2). This indicated the emperor's ungrudging generosity and true empathy for his subjects. These qualities were most clearly expressed by two measures: the *pax augusta* which Tiberius brought to "the regions of the east and of the west and to the bounds of the north and of the south" and the imperial "munificence" to provinces, cities and private persons (2.126:3–4). Philo thus agreed with Velleius on the blessings of peace and prosperity which Tiberius had brought to the whole empire. He may have been encouraged to hold such views by the emperor's resolution not to extend the borders of the empire beyond the limits established by Augustus' conquests (Tac., Agr. 13). Another official report confirmed this peaceful and beneficient line: Tiberius reassured the prefect of Egypt that he wanted his sheep shorn, not shaved (Suet., Tib. 32:2). Philo should, however, have been cautioned in his enthusiasm at least by the case of Germanicus who at a time of emergency lowered the price of corn in Egypt, but was rebuked by Tiberius for interfering in the affairs of the province (Tac., An. 2:59). Yet Philo chose to overlook such oppressive aspects of Tiberius' rule. Certain facts well known at the time were simply ignored. The officially postulated peace, for example, was throughout Tiberius' reign disturbed by local resistance and military uprisings.[40] The provinces had moreover been syste-

---

contemporaries, he was increasingly criticized by later generations who had no direct acquaintance with him and wrote under the influence of their own time.

[39] G. Alföldy, La politique provinciale de Tibère, *Latomus* 24.4 (1965) 827, identified Velleius' account as reflecting Tiberius' official policies; *contra* A.J. Woodman, *Velleius Paterculus. The Tiberian Narrative (2.94–131). Edited With An Introduction and Commentary* (Cambridge 1977) 51–4, who argued for the not more than average panegyric in Velleius' writings.

[40] See e.g. the revolts of Thrace, Gaul, and the Frisians as described by Tac., An. 3:44, 38,

matically exploited.[41] Particularly corrupt governors were usually not even prosecuted and if they were, then mainly on other grounds such as *maiestas*.[42] Tiberius himself expressed considerable reluctance to investigate cases of corruption and exploitation, arguing that it was impossible to foresee the further development of a governor (Tac., An. 3:69).

There is a major discrepancy between Philo's description of Tiberius' immaculate rule and the far more gloomy picture in Tacitus' *Annals*. The immediate context and motivation of Philo's interpretation can best be appreciated when Josephus' account is also taken into account. The latter's views on Tiberius have been surprisingly overlooked given that they throw crucial light both on the emperor's early *Rezeptionsgeschichte* and on Jewish attitudes towards him. Josephus expresses a highly negative opinion about Tiberius which overlaps in significant points with Tacitus' account.[43] Tiberius emerges in the *Jewish Antiquities* as nothing less than a tyrant. He is described as a ruler, who (A.J. 18:226):

had inflicted fearful wrongs in greater number on the Roman nobles than any other one man, for he was quick to anger and relentless in action, even if his grounds for conceiving hatred of a man made no sense. It was his bent to turn savage in every case that he decided and he inflicted the death penalty even for the slightest offences.

Josephus moreover complains that Tiberius inflicted great damage on the provinces. He tended towards excessive procrastination and was slow even to give an initial hearing to embassies and court cases (A.J. 18:168–78). Injustice and corruption thus prevailed. Parallel to Tacitus, Josephus suggests that Tiberius was reluctant to replace unsuitable governors and accepted their extortion of the provinces "as a law of nature" (A.J. 18:172). More importantly, the *Jewish Antiquities* indicate that the Jews of Rome were in severe discord with Tiberius. Josephus relates how Tiberius gave orders to expell all the Jews from Rome on

---

4:46–7, 72–3. The shortcomings of Tiberius' rule in the provinces have been most critically and perceptively discussed by Alföldy, Politique provinciale, 824–44; see also: B. M. Levick, *Tiberius The Politician* (London 1976) 125–47; R. Seager, *Tiberius* (London 1972) 162–70; D. Shotter, *Tiberius Caesar* (London and New York 1992) 57–8.

[41] Suet., Tib. 48, remarks that the provinces received no financial benefits or special aid under Tiberius except the cities of Asia which had been hit by an earthquake; see also: Alföldy, Politique provinciale 830–1, who points to the exaggerated publicity which Tiberius' aid to the cities of Asia has received by both ancient and modern authors. For cases of brutal exploitation under Tiberius, see Tac., An. 1:76, 2:5, 3:40–4, 4:45.

[42] See e.g. Tac. An. 1:74, 3:66–8, 4:18–20, 4:34–5.

[43] The similarities between Josephus' and Tacitus' views on Tiberius have rarely been noted. R. Syme, *Tacitus* (Oxford 1958) 1:420–34, 271–86, 2:688–92; M. Baar, *Das Bild des Kaisers Tiberius bei Tacitus, Sueton und Cassius Dio* (Stuttgart 1990 = Beiträge zur Altertumskunde 7) 232–45, do not mention them at all; Seager, Tiberius 172, occasionally notes a similarity without, however, discussing its implications for Tacitus' possible sources; only D. Timpe, Römische Geschichte bei Flavius Josephus, *Historia* 9 (1960) 474–502, refers to them and draws important conclusions about the prior history of many of Tacitus' motifs.

account of only one case of corruption involving a Jewish resident of Rome (A.J. 18:81–4). Agrippa I furthermore incurred Tiberius' anger because he had given special attention to young Gaius rather than "cultivating" the emperor's grandson Tiberius Gemellus, as he had been ordered (A.J. 18:188). The Jewish prince paid court to Gaius and supported his accession to the throne to the extent that he was accused of plotting against Tiberius.[44] Agrippa I was consequently arrested and received the news of Tiberius' death with overwhelming joy (A.J. 18:225–37). Josephus describes how the new emperor swiftly released him and took personal care of his physical as well as political welfare (A.J. 18:237). Agrippa's early loyalty to Gaius later enabled him to make an appeal on behalf of the Jerusalem Temple. Josephus significantly suggests that Gaius granted Agrippa's request because he remembered that he had for his sake been imprisoned by Tiberius (A.J. 18:292).

Philo was familiar with this negative image of Tiberius which may have been based on an oral account by Agrippa II or on a *Vita* of Agrippa I.[45] It was in any case an image which apparently circulated among Roman Jews long before Josephus committed it to writing.[46] Philo, who portrayed Tiberius both from the distinctly provincial perspective of Alexandria and after the crisis under Gaius, was eager to correct it. This tendency clearly emerges from his references to Tiberius' negative legacy as preserved in Josephus' *Antiquities*. It is initially

---

[44]  A.J. 18:167–9, 186–91.

[45]  H. Bloch, *Die Quellen des Flavius Josephus in seiner Archäologie* (Leipzig 1879) 121, briefly suggested Agrippa II as an oral source for Josephus in bk. 18; Schwartz, Agrippa 2–11, argued at length that the relevant passages on Agrippa and Tiberius in A.J. 18:126–55 are based on an assumed *Vita* of Agrippa. The sources of A.J. book 18 have been given relatively little attention in comparison to book 19. The scholarly insights into the latter, however, are also useful for the present context. L. H. Feldman, The Sources of Josephus' 'Antiquities', Book 19, *Latomus* 21.2 (1962) 323 suggested that Agrippa II may have been one of Josephus' oral informants. He based his conjecture on the important notice in Jos., Vita 361–6, where Josephus says that he gave a personal copy of his *Jewish War* to Agrippa II. The latter praised the work and promised in a letter: "when you meet me, I will myself by word of mouth inform you of much that is not generally known". A similar, yet more general argument has recently been made by Yavetz, Tiberius and Caligula 233. Feldman's suggestion modified Hölscher's thesis of a Herodian written source which, prior to Josephus, combined Cluvius Rufus' Roman history with a Jewish history, see: G. Hölscher, *Die Quellen des Josephus für die Zeit vom Exil bis zum Jüdischen Kriege* (Leipzig 1904) 59–60; Hölscher in turn modified Mommsen's suggestion that Cluvius was Josephus' direct source, see: Th. Mommsen, Cornelius Tacitus und Cluvius Rufus, *Hermes* 4 (1870) 320–2. This discussion on A.J. book 19 and especially Feldman's contribution are highly relevant to book 18 where Agrippa I is given an overriding role.

[46]  *Contra* Timpe, Flavius Josephus 502, who conjectured that Josephus' heavier reliance in the *Jewish Antiquities* on a Roman source or a Jewish mediator of such a Roman source indicates that this source had not yet been composed during the writing of the *Jewish War*. Yet if we assume with Feldman that Josephus received information from Agrippa II concerning events in which the latter's family had been directly involved, Agrippa I himself could obviously have influenced Jewish public opinion on Tiberius to which Philo was exposed at the latest during his stay in Rome.

striking that Philo nowhere indicates that it was Tiberius who had imprisoned Agrippa. To be sure, the imprisonment itself is mentioned (Leg. 324). Yet Philo severs it from any explicit link to Tiberius and refers only to Gaius' liberation of Agrippa. This is the best he could do to cover the clash between the Jewish prince and Tiberius given the inconvenient fact that everyone knew the story. Philo himself admits as much when putting the following words into Agrippa's mouth: "You [Gaius] set me free when I was fettered with iron chains – who does not know it?" (Leg. 324). Philo wrote here with a clear awareness that he skipped over a well-known fact. His readers were obviously familiar with Agrippa's imprisonment and must have known its background. While Philo could not altogether argue the facts away, he obscured the tension between Agrippa and Tiberius as much as possible. He especially left out the embarrassing fact that the Jewish prince had been one of Gaius' earliest and staunchest supporters, a political commitment which directly led to his alienation from Tiberius.

The same hermeneutic strategy is visible in Philo's treatment of the Jews' expulsion from Rome. The fact itself was apparently too well-known to be left out of the account altogether. Yet a more favourable interpretation of it had to be forthcoming. Philo provided it and thus exculpated Tiberius from a responsibility which Josephus and later also Tacitus, Suetonius and Dio unanimously attributed to him.[47] Responding to the charges against Tiberius preserved in A.J. 18:81–4, Philo refers to a crisis "in Italy" which revolved around certain Jews found guilty of some unspecified crime (Leg. 159–61). Philo explains that Sejanus, Tiberius' infamous praetorian prefect, used this crisis as a pretext for larger measures against the Jews. Tiberius, however, was well aware of Sejanus' agitation and the false accusations which had been made against "the Jewish inhabitants of Rome". The emperor consequently reassured the Jews of their rights, insisting that "the penal measures did not extend to all but only to the guilty" (Leg. 161). Philo thus refutes precisely the charge preserved in Josephus, namely that Tiberius expelled the Jews from Rome only on account of a few guilty individuals found among them. He thus uses the same strategy as before, namely referring rather vaguely to the embarassing facts, which incriminated Tiberius and undermined his own argument, while advancing a version which he intended to replace the well-known story.[48] In this case Philo reinforces his favourable description of Tiberius by relegating the responsibility to his subordinates. In this way he could praise the emperor himself as a just ruler protecting the Jews.

---

[47] The expulsion of the Jews from Rome is mentioned by Tac., An. 2:85; Suet., Tib. 36:1 and Dio, 57:18.

[48] The relative vagueness of Philo's reference has sometimes been mistaken for an indication that he is in fact speaking about a different incident, see: E. M. Smallwood, Some Notes on the Jews under Tiberius, *Latomus* 15.3 (1956) 314–29; E.T. Merrill, The Expulsion of Jews from Rome under Tiberius, *CP* 14.4 (1919) 365–72.

The same technique is also conspicuous in Philo's story about Tiberius reprimanding Pilate for dedicating golden shields in Herod's palace.[49] In this case, too, Tiberius' subordinate is presented as corrupt and hostile towards the Jews, while the emperor himself emerges as a staunch defender of their special customs.[50] Philo accuses Pilate of malicious intent when setting up the shields. He acted "not so much to honour Tiberius as to annoy the multitude" (Leg. 299). When Jewish complaints reached him, he responded with stubborn intransigence (Leg. 301). Philo stresses that this position sharply deviates from Tiberius' own policies. He has the Jews of Palestine warn Pilate not to "take Tiberius as your pretext for outraging the nation; he does not wish any of our customs to be overthrown" (Leg. 301). Moreover, Tiberius himself is said to have been driven to violent anger, even though he was generally of a mild temper, and to have promptly corrected Pilate's mistakes (Leg. 304–5). This behaviour indicated in Philo's view his worthiness as a true successor to Augustus who also respected the Jewish religion.

Philo similarly reinterprets the known complaints about Tiberius' tacit acceptance of corruption and exploitation in the provinces. Josephus, as we saw above, lamented the emperor's extreme procrastination and lack of initiative in tracking cases of corrupt Roman governors. Philo was aware of this criticism. He mentions a trial under Tiberius "which had dragged on for two years" (Flac. 128). Instead of joining the complaints about the emperor's procrastination, however, Philo explained the advantages of this delay. Tiberius, he insisted, had intentionally acted thus in order to punish the suspect with the fear of an uncertain future which is an even greater torment than death itself (Flac. 129). Philo furthermore suggested that other cases of corruption in the provinces were speedily and earnestly prosecuted. While he admits that some governors had "spread hopeless misery through their territories" and had not been replaced until the end of their official appointment (Flac. 105), he praises Tiberius as well as Augustus for dispensing full justice in such cases (Flac. 105–6). Both saw to it that such governors accounted for their doings upon their return to Rome. Throughout the trials, Philo stressed, they proved "impartial judges".

The only issue in Josephus' account which Philo does not mention is Tiberius' maltreatment of Roman nobles. He does not make any attempt to explain the tyrannical measures taken by the emperor in the capital. This, however, is not surprising in view of the authors' different audiences. Josephus and his source, as well as Tacitus who expresses similar criticisms, addressed the ruling class of the Empire and especially readers in Rome, while Philo wrote for Alexan-

---

[49] This story appears in Leg. 299–305 as part of "Agrippa's letter" to Gaius. On this incident, see also: P. S. Davies, The Meaning of Philo's Text about the Gilded Shields, *JThS* 37.1 (1986) 109–14.

[50] In Leg. 302 Philo lists his faults as a governor of the province.

drian Jews.[51] The latter would obviously take less interest in matters pertaining to the rights of the Roman aristocracy. They could instead be expected to pay special attention to the effects of the emperor's personality on the empire at large and the provinces in particular. Philo caters precisely to those provincial interests when stressing in *Leg.* 141 that Tiberius ruled for "twenty-three years without allowing any spark of war to smoulder in Greek or barbarian lands", but instead provided "peace and the blessings of peace to the end of his life with ungrudging bounty of hand and heart". Philo thus responded to characteristically provincial queries by enthusiastically repeating the official aims of the imperial policy.

In the above-quoted passage in *Leg.* 141–2 Philo furthermore makes special efforts to explain Tiberius' old age. His rhetorical questions and long-winded answers show that this point was important to him: "Was he inferior in age? What other king or emperor enjoyed a happier old age? Why, even when he was still young, he was called "the elder" out of respect for his perspicacity." The issue of Tiberius' old age was obviously sensitive. Without going into details, Philo wished to convince his readers that nothing had been wrong with the emperor's last years. This point was made amid vivid rumours to the contrary. Ancient authors unanimously agreed that Tiberius degenerated in his retirement on Capri "into crime and into ignominy" (Tac., *An.* 6:51). Suetonius especially dwelt on Tiberius' fall at the end of his life. He criticized Tiberius for utterly neglecting the conduct of state affairs and instead engaging in unspeakable pleasures with "the licence of privacy" on Capri.[52] Suetonius was moreover convinced that this conduct only brought out Tiberius' real character which had so far remained somewhat obscure (*Tib.*, 42:1). It showed that Tiberius had always been a tyrant running the state by barbarous measures (*Tib.*, 61:2–4). The news of his death was consequently welcomed by widespread jubilation (*Tib.*, 75:1). Josephus similarly suggests that Tiberius became more tyrannical in his old age (*A.J.* 18:179–89). He as well speaks of an overwhelming joy at Tiberius' death which could initially not be freely expressed for fear of retaliation.[53] In light of these reports about Tiberius' dishonourable end it is clear that Philo presented an apologetic interpretation. He wished to uproot the idea of a decline into tyranny and crime before Gaius' accession to the throne. In his account the worldwide joy over Gaius' accession had therefore nothing to do with a sense of relief from Tiberius' tyranny. The population was instead de-

---

[51] Regarding Tacitus' criticism of Tiberius' hypocritical dealings with the Senate, which covered a rather dictatorial inclination, see e.g.: Tac., *An.* 1:72–77.

[52] Suet., *Tib.* 40:1–75, the quotation is taken from *Tib.* 42:1.

[53] *A.J.* 18:225–35; Tacitus' version is again similar to Josephus': upon the news of Tiberius' death a gratulatory crowd gathered around Gaius, but was surprised by the old emperor's sudden recovery. A panic prevailed in view of the consequences such a betrayal might bring (Tac., *An.* 6:50).

lighted with Gaius "as they had been with no previous emperor" (Leg. 11). By insisting that Tiberius had enjoyed a happy old age Philo emphatically rejected the suggestion of a continuity between his reign and that of Gaius. As far as he was concerned, there existed a total rupture between beneficent Roman rule, as exemplified by Tiberius up to his very last day, and the complete perversion of it by Gaius. Philo reinforces this point in Agrippa's letter to Gaius, which stresses once more the latter's departure from Roman precedents (Leg. 294–310).

Rejecting the negative image of the controversial emperor Philo focused on Tiberius' noble birth and outstanding wisdom. In the above-quoted passage in Leg. 141–2 he elaborated on these two points: "Was he inferior in birth? No, he was of the noblest ancestry on both sides. Was he inferior in education? Who among those who reached the height of their powers in his time surpassed him in wisdom or eloquence?". Tiberius' noble birth was beyond doubt and his education in both Latin and Greek literature a known fact.[54] For Philo the emperor's wisdom was connected to additional highly laudable qualities: he "detested childish jokes" and "had been inclined to seriousness and austerity almost from childhood ".[55] These were precisely the qualities by which Philo distinguished also the Jews. We saw in the previous chapter that he characterized them by their *enkrateia* in every area of life. The Jewish nation, he insisted, was isolated like an orphan because of its "austerity" (Spec. 4:179). The close similarity between Philo's descriptions of Tiberius and the Jews has important implications. It suggests that the two were in his eyes complementary and congenial to each other. Tiberius shared Jewish values and promoted them from the top of the political hierarchy. In Philo's account Tiberius himself was fully aware of the Jews' complementary role and overall benefit to the Roman empire. He requested that the Jews be held as a "sacred trust" because they were of a "peaceful disposition" and their laws "conducive to public order" (Leg. 161). This role is confirmed also from a distinctly Jewish perspective. Philo shows indignation when Jewish houses were searched for weapons by Roman authorities. Rejecting the very thought of militant Jews, he insists on his nation's contribution to the peaceful order of the empire: "When were we not thought to be peacefully inclined to all? Were not our ways of living which we follow day by day blameless and conducive to good order and stability in the state?" (Flac. 94).

The analysis of Tiberius' portrait has yielded important insights into Philo's overall construction of the Romans. He looks to them from a distinctly provincial perspective, emphasizing issues which would be of particular interest to an

---

[54] See e.g. Suet., Tib. 70; Tac., An. 4:58.

[55] Leg. 167; Tacitus as well distinguishes Tiberius by his "duriora" from Augustus' more sociable personality which took the crowd's desire for pleasure into account (An. 1:54).

Alexandrian audience. The idealized picture of Tiberius' personality and rule furthermore supports Philo's underlying argument about the exceptional beneficence of Roman dominion both for the commonwealth in general and the Jews in particular. Only Gaius, he argued, perverted Roman government by succumbing to Egyptian vice. Once the death of Tiberius is established as a crucial turning-point, Augustus' image naturally fits into the overall framework of Philo's story. The first *princeps* now makes his appearance as Tiberius' perfect predecessor who established the high standards of Roman rule throughout the *oikoumene*. In some sense the figure of Augustus lent itself more easily to Philo's agenda than Tiberius. By the time the *Legatio* was composed the first *princeps* had become a popular symbol of the glorious past. Claudius made special efforts, as we saw in the previous chapter, to revive the memory of Augustus' exemplary virtue and moderate style of government. Other Jewish writers do not seem to have had particular complaints about Augustus either. Josephus, for example, dwells on the friendship between him and the Herodian house and furthermore conveys numerous Augustan letters guaranteeing Jewish rights in various regions of the Empire.[56] The image of Augustus did thus not require the same kind of substantial reinterpretation as did that of Tiberius. Philo could instead heap rather stereotypical praise on him, adding a specifically Jewish-Alexandrian perspective.[57]

Philo's portrait of Augustus is characterized by the same dual focus as his description of Tiberius: imperial beneficience to the whole *oikoumene* and special congeniality with the Jews. Philo opens with praise of Augustus' character. His virtues "transcended human nature" and he showed "nobility of character" (Leg. 143). These, together with his imperial sovereignty, earned him the title "Augustus" or venerable (Leg. 143). Philo justifies this nomenclature by reference to his exceptional acts of beneficence. The items now listed reflect the perspective of a man from the Greek East. While Josephus was mostly concerned with Augustus' relationship to the Herodian house and Roman intellectuals showed an interest also in Augustus' dealings with the senate, Philo exclusively focused on the emperor's contribution to the realm in which he lived.[58] Augustus' suppression of war between the continents and especially between Europe and Asia is mentioned first (Leg. 144–5). Philo speaks in superlative terms, stressing the exhaustion of the entire human race by mutual

---

[56] See especially: A.J. 15:187–201, 16:160–73, 19:282–3, Contr. Ap. 2:61. On the status and effect of these letters, see above chapter three.

[57] The stereotypical nature of Philo's praise has been emphasised by Delling, Philo's Encomium 171–92. If indeed Qumranic circles developed their figure of the anti-Messiah on the model of Augustus, as I. Knohl, On 'The son of God', Armillus and Messiah Son of Joseph (Hebrew), *Tarbiz* 68.1 (1998) 13–9, conjectured, Philo sharply differed from them.

[58] The only exception is perhaps Leg. 149 where Philo justifies Augustus' assumption of absolute power.

slaughter and Augustus' subsequent healing of "the pestilences common to the Greeks and barbarians". In the context of Alexandria this referred especially to the end of the civil war waged between Augustus and Antony. We saw above in chapter two that Philo accepted Augustus' tendentious presentation of this war as a defense of Roman values against barbarian Egypt and Asia. Philo obviously greeted Augustus' victory and welcomed direct Roman rule over Egypt. In his view "Asian" forces had thus been subdued and the empire harmoniously united. He invited his Jewish readers in Alexandria to share his view and accept Augustus as a worldwide benefactor who had established peace in their country.

Philo's following notices on Augustus also had a special appeal to an Alexandrian audience. He presented Augustus as someone who had cleared the sea of pirates, reclaimed every state to liberty and hellenized the outer regions of the empire (Leg. 146–7). Control over the pirates was an achievement of which Augustus himself had been proud. He advertised it in his *Res Gestae* even though his success had in fact been partial and involved the subjugation of Republican forces as well.[59] Strabo joined in the praise and spoke enthusiastically about Roman clearance of piracy (Geogr. 10.4:9). Philo's appeal to this *topos* of the imperial ideology will have resonated among Alexandrian readers. Generally dependent on the city's maritime trade, they were likely to feel gratitude for Augustus' measures. The slogan of liberty to each city in the empire must have been equally attractive. Philo thus showed how Augustus respected an intrinsically Greek value which in his view also characterized the Jews.[60] The theme of liberty had also been a prominent item of the imperial agenda in the Greek East.[61] It served as a catch-word to integrate the elites of territories either conquered or submitted to Roman influence, while at the same time covering the more oppressive aspects of Roman rule. Other intellectuals from the East had adopted the slogan of liberty and become reconciled with Rome. Strabo, for example, praised Augustus and the Romans in general for protecting the freedom of the cities.[62] When Philo appealed to this standard theme, he wished to convince his readers that Augustus had introduced to their country a rule which was in harmony with their own values and traditions. Rome should not be seen as a foreign tyranny imposing herself on native

---

[59] R.G. 25:1; see also: P.A. Brunt and J.M. Moore (eds.), *Res Gestae Divi Augusti. The Achievements of the Divine Augustus* (Oxford 1967) 102 n. 52.

[60] Philo mentioned the theme of *eleutheria* especially in Greek contexts, see e.g.: Lib. 114–41. We moreover saw above in the second chapter how Philo applied the Greek national myth of defending liberty against the barbarian Persians to the Exodus account, thus suggesting that the Jews share the same values and the same glorious past.

[61] See also: Gruen, Hellenistic World 1:132–57; Bowersock, Augustus 84–100; Ferrary, Philhellénisme 45–209; Forte, Rome 26–7; R. Bernhardt, *Imperium und Eleutheria. Die römische Politik gegenüber den freien Städten des griechischen Ostens* (Hamburg 1971).

[62] See e.g.: Geogr. 8.5:5 (referring to Augustus), 9.1:20; 8.7:3 (referring to the Romans in general); similarly Dionysius, A.R. 2:16, 3:9, 6:19, 6:54.

cultures, but rather as a liberator who restored each nation to its original independence.[63] Finally, the theme of Augustus' hellenizing role suggested, as we saw above, that Roman rule brought culture and civilization. The Romans, Philo asserted, belonged to the Greek side of the existential divide between Greeks and barbarians.

Philo's praise of Augustus as "the first and greatest universal benefactor" (Leg. 149) culminates in his description of the Alexandrian *Caesareium*. He professes to join the worldwide veneration of Augustus priding himself in the special honours which "our own Alexandria" is offering (Leg. 149):

It was because the whole world voted him Olympian-like honours. Temples, gateways, vestibules, and colonnades bear witness to this, so that the imposing buildings erected in any city, new or old, are surpassed by the beauty and size of the temples of Caesar, especially in our own Alexandria (τὴν ἡμετέραν Ἀλεξάνδρειαν). There is no precinct like our so-called Sebasteion, temple of Caesar, the protector of sailors.[64] It is situated high-up, opposite the sheltered harbours, and is very large and conspicuous; it is filled with dedications on a unique scale, and is surrounded on all sides by paintings, statues, and objects of gold and silver. The extensive precinct is furnished with colonnades, libraries, banqueting-halls, groves, gateways, open spaces, unroofed enclosures, and everything that makes for lavish decoration. It gives hope of safety to sailors when they set out to sea and when they return.

Philo's enthusiasm for the Alexandrian *Caesareium* is truly remarkable. This first temple of its kind dedicated to Augustus was mentioned only in passing by pagan authors like Strabo.[65] Philo evidently visited the site and was intimately acquainted with the appearance of its different parts. He even seems to have encouraged his Jewish readers to appreciate this specifically Alexandrian expression of veneration for Augustus. It is only in this context that he speaks of "our own Alexandria". Philo's position significantly differed in this respect from Josephus' reaction to the equivalent temple in Caesarea. The latter had also been constructed right at the harbour, "visible a great way off" to those sailing in and hoping for Augustus' protection (A.J. 15:339). Josephus condemned such cultic sites in no uncertain terms and regretted that Herod had thus bowed down to Roman tastes and power (A.J. 15:328). He emphasized that such temples were a severe violation of Jewish custom, since they were of a nature that belonged to Greek religion (A.J. 15:329). Philo, by contrast, does

---

[63] "Eleutheria" thus meant antononomy. See also: D.R. Schwartz, *Rome and the Jews, Freedom and Autonomy*, forthcoming in: A.K. Bowman *et al.* (eds.), *Rome and the Mediterranean* (Oxford 2002), who showed that Josephus knew both this Roman notion of *eleutheria* and the original Greek term which implied freedom in the sense of political independence.

[64] On the translation and cultic connotation of the expression ἐπιβατηρίου Καίσαρος νεώς, see above chapter three.

[65] Strabo merely says that "then one comes to the Caesarium" (καισάριον, Geogr. 17.1:9); on the nature and construction of the Alexandrian *Caesareion*, see especially: Hänlein-Schäfer, Veneratio Augusti 10–6, 205–9, and above chapter three.

not draw such a distinction between "us" and "them". For him the boundaries were much more blurred. The cultic veneration of Augustus in the Alexandrian *Caesareium* was in his view compatible with Jewish values and Jewish identity.[66]

Augustus, like Tiberius, appears in the pages of Philo's *Legatio* as a ruler most akin to the Jews. He shared "our" values and protected "our" rights. In chapter three we have already discussed Augustus' most important quality in this respect: "he was never elated or made vain by extravagant honours" and refused "ever to be addressed as a god" (Leg. 154). He was therefore annoyed at anyone thus relating to him, while approving of the Jews "who, he knew very well, eschewed all such language on religious grounds" (Leg. 154). As we saw above, Philo embraced here an Augustan self-image denoting political modesty, which subsequently became a model for Tiberius and Claudius.[67] Philo used this image to highlight the compatibility of Jews and Romans. Both shared the value of *enkrateia* and were not swept away by vanity. Even when enjoying ultimate veneration by the whole empire, Augustus valiantly acknowledged the limitations of his humanity and persevered in taking care of his imperial duties. This position indicated his manly self-control, which did not give way to feminine weakness and his affinity with the Jews who also held fast to authentic values.[68] Augustus appeared to Philo as someone who generally respected "the native customs of each particular nation no less than of the Romans" (Leg. 153), but gave special attention to Jewish rights. Through the Jewish residents of Rome he had become aware of the synagogues and the Sabbath observance as well as the regular donations to the Jerusalem Temple (Leg. 156). Augustus not only tolerated these Jewish customs, but also "showed such a reverence" (ὡσίωτο) for them that, supported by virtually his whole family, he "enriched our Temple with expensive dedications" and ordered "regular sacrifices of holocausts to be made daily in perpetuity at his own expense as an offering to the Most High God (τῳ ὑψίστῳ θεῷ)" (Leg. 157). These sacrifices were in Philo's eyes a most telling "proof of his truly imperial character" (Leg. 157).

This description of Augustus' support for Jewish customs shows a tendency both to establish his behaviour as the essence of Roman rule and to draw him

---

[66] This fact has been unacceptable to some scholars who suggest that Philo simply reiterated a Gentile source, see e.g. Barraclough, Politics 453–4. Yet the very idea of Philo quoting a text of which he vehemently disapproved, without in fact saying so, is highly problematic. Philo's position, as it emerges from a literal reading of Leg. 149–51, instead makes sense in the context of his position on the imperial cult, on which see above chapter three.

[67] Augustus publicised his modesty not only in the strictly political terms, which we investigated in chapter three, but also in the field of ethics where he presented himself as the counterpoint to Antony's Oriental licentiousness and lack of manly willpower; on the latter aspects, see: K. Scott, Octavian's Propaganda and Antony's *De Sua Ebrietate*, CP 24 (1929) 133–41.

[68] For details on the manly self-restraint of the Jews, see above chapter three.

spiritually near to the Jewish religion. Philo explicitly presented Augustus as the model of an imperial ruler, implying that any successor departing from the norms he established was no emperor in the true sense. Philo moreover imputed Augustan respect for Jewish customs to the whole imperial household. The emperor was not alone, but represented the sympathetic attitude of the entire imperial family. In another context Philo even provides a specific example. Julia Augusta is said to have "adorned the temple with golden vials and libation bowls and a multitude of other sumptuous offerings" (Leg. 319). The affinity which Philo felt existed between the Augustan house and the Jews was so deep that he began to speak about the Roman emperor in terms akin to those of a convert to Jewish beliefs. In Leg. 157 he says that Augustus ordered regular sacrifices to "the Most High God". It is not clear whether Philo was expressing his own religious feelings or attributing them also to Augustus. The emperor's "reverence" for Jewish customs would warrant the latter.

This conclusion is underlined in other contexts where Philo speaks of Augustus in exaggerated terms as a "philosopher second to none" with special insights into the principles of the Jewish religion.[69] Initially Augustus is heralded as a philosopher-king in the style of Moses. Philo asserted that "he had more than a merely superficial taste of philosophy but had feasted on it deeply" (Leg. 310). Like the paramount *nomothetes* of the Jews, he made spiritual progress partly thanks to his own recollection and partly as a result of instruction which he received in his daily conversations with literary men. His philosophical standing enabled him to appreciate the true nature of the Jewish Sabbath and the Jerusalem Temple. Philo has Augustus recognize that the Jews in their synagogues were not engaged in "drunkenness and disorderliness", but received on the Sabbath "instruction in their national philosophy" and training in "sobriety and justice" (Leg. 156, 312). Augustus became moreover convinced that (Leg. 318):

it was essential for a special place consecrated to the invisible God to be set apart in the earthly regions, and for it to contain no visible representation ...

Philo's construct of Augustus has important implications for Jewish identity. It initially ignores signs that the Roman emperor may have been far more selective in his tolerance of foreign rites. Suetonius reports in a famous note that he had only respect for customs that were recognized to be ancient, but "held the rest in contempt", especially the Jewish and the Egyptian cults (Aug. 93). Philo's construct moreover establishes a distinct pattern for appreciating the Roman empire. Its founder and benevolent representatives became mirror-images of the Jews themselves and were to a significant degree assimilated to

---

[69] Leg. 318; Suetonius speaks more moderately about Augustus' interest in "Greek studies" in which "he excelled greatly" (Aug. 89:1); see also: Bowersock, Augustus 31–4.

Jewish ethnicity. Augustus became a Jew in spirit and acknowledged the true nature of the most high God. Petronius was equally said to have acquired philosophical knowledge and been directly guided by God both to understand the Jewish religion and to protect the Temple against Gaius.[70] Philo's emphasis on the affinity between true Romans and the Jews was meant to inspire in his readers confidence in their safe and lofty position in the empire. Under both Augustus and Tiberius, Philo insisted, "the whole population of the empire, even if not instinctively well-disposed towards the Jews, was afraid to tamper with any Jewish practice" (Leg. 159).

Given Philo's overwhelmingly positive construction of the Romans as benefactors and friends, he owes an explanation for cases of extreme deviation. How, in other words, did Gaius and Flaccus fit into the picture? Philo had two answers to the question of bad Romans. He initially suggested that their vice was rooted in a typically Egyptian pathology of excess. He also showed that their deviation from truly Roman standards was only temporary. Guided by divine providence they were brought back to their senses and ultimately returned to the authentic values shared by Jews and Romans. In the case of Flaccus we still possess Philo's full account showing his initial fall and subsequent repentance. Regarding Gaius, however, whose *palinode* is painfully missing, we have only part of the story and must conjecture the rest.

A pathology of excess is well attested in the fall of both Gaius and Flaccus. Gaius is said to have succumbed to a "severe disease" shortly after Tiberius' death.[71] While this emperor had initially been hailed by the whole commonwealth (Leg. 8–13), he subsequently "exchanged the more moderate, and therefore healthier, mode of life which he had followed hitherto, during Tiberius' life-time, for a life of luxury" (Leg. 14). Gaius lost self-control in three central areas: food, sex and religion (Leg. 14, 76–114). Body and soul were thus destroyed, giving way to "weakness and mental illness bordering on death".[72] Philo stresses that Gaius gave himself over to "savagery" and became an altogether different person, unrecognizable to those who had known him before (Leg. 22; Flac. 14). This decline ultimately led to his "cult of illegality" and rendered him a true "despot" (Leg. 119). The overriding importance which Philo attributes here to Gaius' disease is somewhat surprising. We saw above that in another context he pointed out that Tiberius had been well aware of his successor's inconsistent character. The change of Gaius' personality can thus not have been as dramatic as Philo now wishes his readers to believe. It furthermore emerges from Philo's account that Gaius completely recovered before he began to behave tyrannically (Leg. 18). His illness can therefore hardly have

---

[70] Leg. 209–12, 245.
[71] κατασκήπτει βαρεῖα νόσος (Leg. 14).
[72] ἀσθένεια καὶ νόσος γειτνιῶσα θανάτῳ (Leg. 14).

been the direct cause of his aberrant policies.[73] Yet Philo needed the motif of Gaius' disease. It helped him to argue that Gaius' fall was a case of succumbing to Egyptian pathology. The emperor shared their sickness of effemination with regard to food, sex and religion. Gaius thus falls into the same category as the worshippers of Golden Calf and the rebellious son, who had betrayed Jewish values by defecting to the Egyptian side.[74] Like the priests, who had tried to prevent the worship of the Golden Calf, Gaius had true Romans at his side who reminded him of his duties. Philo shows how Macro and Silanus rebuked the emperor. Macro especially drew his attention to the dangers of licentiousness and warned him not be overcome by superficial pleasures (Leg. 44, 51). The model which he held up against his eyes was the "Augustan family" (Leg. 48). Silanus made similar efforts to "obstruct the torrent of his lusts" (Leg. 63–5).

Flaccus similarly fell from the "high excellence" which characterized his administration during Tiberius' life-time (Flac. 2). As Philo put it (Flac. 9):

… in the last year when Tiberius was dead and Gaius had been appointed Emperor he began to let everything slip from his hands. This may have been due to his profound grief at the death of Tiberius. For how greatly he mourned the loss of one whom he looked on as his closest friend was shown by his constant depression and the stream of tears which poured ceaselessly from him as from a fountain.

Flaccus' pathology is put forward more tentatively. Philo presents it as one possible interpretation and not as the decisive factor as he had done in the case of Gaius. Yet his description of Flaccus' excessive grief suggests the same malaise. This Roman governor, too, had succumbed to his passions and given them full licence. The tears "which poured ceaselessly from him as from a fountain" indicated a severe lack of *enkrateia*. Philo develops this motif further. He has Flaccus virtually loose his wits when hearing of the murder of Tiberius' grandson. Flaccus then "threw himself down and lay speechless" and "at the same time as his reasoning powers deteriorated made changes in all his recent policy" (Flac. 10, 18). From that moment onwards he let Egyptian agitators rule the province and became a mere puppet-figure implementing their anti-Jewish agenda (Flac. 19–25). Philo has Flaccus later recognize his state as a case of mental derangement. His mind, he admitted, had been clouded by a "phantom" and he had been "asleep and dreaming", seeing "figments of a soul which recorded as we may suppose things which had no existence as though they were" (Flac. 164). Flaccus professes to have been utterly "deluded" (Flac. 165).

---

[73] See also: T. E. J. Wiedemann, Tiberius to Nero, *CAH* (Cambridge 1996, 2nd ed.) 10:224; Barrett, Caligula 73–4; M. G. Morgan, Caligula's Illness again, *CW* 66 (1973) 327–9; idem, Once Again Caligula's Illness, *CW* 70 (1977) 452–3; *contra* R. S. Katz, The Illness of Caligula, *CW* 65 (1972) 223–5; M. P. Charlesworth, Gaius and Claudius, *CAH* 10 (1934, 1st ed.) 656.

[74] For details on the worshippers of the Golden Calf and the rebellious son as well as Egyptian pathology in the areas of food, sex and religion, see above chapter two.

He defected so much from true Roman values that he even violated the custom of taking dead prisoners off the cross on the emperor's birthday (Flac. 83). This clearly indicates the degree to which he had become an "Egyptian".

The motif of Divine providence in the *Legatio* and *In Flaccum* has often been noted.[75] It can hardly be overlooked because Philo opens the *Legatio* with an emphatic note on it. He laments here that too many of his contemporaries have become like children who see only outer appearances, while disregarding God's benevolent presence in history (Leg. 1–3). Philo returned to this theme throughout his treatise and showed how Divine providence had been acknowledged by virtuous Jews. When the ambassadors had been dismissed by Gaius, they "went forth to supplicate the true God that He should restrain the wrath of the pretender to that name" (Leg. 366). Their faith was rewarded. God, Philo recalls, "took compassion on us" and calmed Gaius who now turned to mocking the Jews rather than punishing them for *maiestas* (Leg. 367). The readers of the *Legatio* are furthermore encouraged to emulate the ambassadors' piety (Leg. 196):

Perhaps these things are sent to try the present generation, to test the state of their virtue and whether they are schooled to bear dire misfortunes with a resolution which is fortified by reason and does not collapse at once. So then what man can do is gone, and let it go. But let our souls retain indestructible the hope in God our Saviour who has often saved the nation when in helpless straits.

These Philonic references to Divine providence obviously suggest that the Jewish God passionately guides human affairs. He even has control over the world power of the day and regulates the behaviour of Roman politicians. This has evident implications for Jewish identity. Jews, Philo suggests, could and should be more self-confident than the external events of history gave credence. They could trust their personal guardian to work in their favour and effect changes for the better. This position had further implications for Philo's construction of the Romans. The "reversal" of Flaccus indicates their nature.[76]

Philo not only suggests that Flaccus was providentially punished by penalties corresponding exactly in type and degree to his previous crimes, but attributed an awareness of God to the convict himself.[77] Philo stages Flaccus at the end of his days as a repentant sinner (Flac. 170):

---

[75] See especially: Leisegang, Gesandtschaft 377–405.

[76] μεταβολή (Flac. 159).

[77] Flac. 115, 125, 152, 189; Philo moreover summarizes Flaccus' life-story in the following words: "an indubitable proof that the help which God can give was not withdrawn from the nation of the Jews" (Flac. 191). Philo's explanations of Flaccus' punishment differ from Roman perceptions of his failure in the province and its adequate penalty. It is highly significant that Philo merely mentions the fact of Flaccus' trial and condemnation without ever providing any details of the proceedings (Flac. 147). See also: P. Borgen, Two Philonic Prayers And Their Contexts: An Analysis of *Who is the Heir of Divine Things* (*Her.*) 24–29 and *Against Flaccus* (*Flac.*) 170–75, NTS 45.3 (1999) 302–8.

"King of gods and men", he cried, "so then you do not disregard the nation of the Jews, nor do they misreport your providence, but all who say that they do not find in you a champion and defender, go astray from the true creed. I am a clear proof of this, for all the acts which I madly committed against the Jews I have suffered myself".

Flaccus' confession of the Jewish God placed him in a similar role as Augustus and Petronius who, however, never departed from the path of righteousness. Even though Flaccus' turn of mind came late, in fact too late to keep him alive, he nevertheless proved to have zealously returned to truly Roman and Jewish standards. Had he been given a further chance, he too would have acted as a benefactor and friend of the Jews. The same was probably true of Gaius. After his reversal he, too, would have aligned himself with the Jews and supported them.

The exceptional cases of Flaccus and Gaius thus prove the rule: true Romans are beneficient and friendly towards the Jews. They bring peace and civilization to all regions of the empire and are to a high degree congenial to the Jews. Philo thus suggests that the Temple incident and the Alexandrian pogroms must be seen in a broader context, i.e. as temporary crises which have already been alleviated by God and not indicative of the real nature of Roman rule. His readers should therefore not be distracted by them from the essentials.

# 5. Greeks and Greek Culture

> "We are not like those philosophers of the
> Greeks who practice words for a festal assembly.
> With us deeds accord with words and words with
> deeds." (Lib. 96)

In this final chapter on Jewish identity Philo's construction of the Greeks must be considered. This is a daunting task given the pervasive influence of Greek literature on Philo's writings. It is, however, important to remember that his assessment of the Greeks is not equivalent to an appreciation of his indebtedness to Greek sources. The extent to which he used these sources will not be investigated here because the results would not indicate his identity nor his attitudes towards the Greeks. These two issues have in the past often been conflated, with the result that many scholars took Philo's reliance on Greek sources as a sign of his identification as a Greek.[1] It has been assumed that if he adopted a Platonic motif, for example, he thereby assumed Greek ethnicity and gave up something of his Jewish identity. Following this line of argument any serious engagement with Greek culture would inevitably result in a loss of one's original sense of self. The famous example of Cato, however, challenges the accuracy of this assumption. Though highly versed in Greek letters, this Roman aristocrat openly polemicized against the Greeks and certain aspects of their culture. He alerted his fellow Romans to their shortcomings in philosophy and medicine as well as culture, warning them not to fall totally under the spell of the Greeks while abandoning clearly superior Roman values.[2] It is thus clear that being influenced by Greek literature is not tantamount to adopting Greek identity. The engagement of an individual writer with Greek culture is usually far more complex.

Following Barth's theory of ethnic identity, emphasis will be given to what Philo himself said about the Greeks and their culture. Modern stereotypes about the nature of Hellenism thus have to be put aside. It has often been taken for granted that an inherent antagonism exists between Judaism and Hellenism. Hellenism symbolizes in the eyes of many a commitment to rationality, aesthet-

---

[1] For an overview of Philonic research with emphasis on this assumption, see: E. Hilgert, Philo Judaeus et Alexandrinus: The State of the Problem, in: Kenney, School of Moses 1–15.

[2] See also: Gruen, Culture and National Identity 52–83; Astin, Cato 157–81; D. Kienast, *Cato der Zensor* (Heidelberg 1954) 101–16; Balsdon, Aliens 31–3; N. Petrochilos, *Roman Attitudes to the Greeks* (Athens 1972) 39–40, 43–5; R. Syme, Greeks 569–70.

ics and universal humanism, while Judaism stands for faith, revealed ethics and national particularism. "Hebraism" and "Hellenism" have thus come to be seen as the two archetypal components of Western civilization. According to this view any Jewish encounter with the Greeks must result in deep existential conflict. As the differences between the two cultures are too substantial to be bridged, each author has to decide to which side he belongs.[3] While the dichotomy between Judaism and Hellenism is undoubtedly a prominent motif in modern literature and received beautiful poetic expression in Heinrich Heine's work, it remains to be seen whether and in what form it existed in Ancient Jewish sources.[4] Did Philo, in other words, sense an inherent contrast between the two cultures? Did he moreover see the Greeks as representatives of secular rationalism, aestheticism and universal humanism or did he see them in a different and perhaps more similar light?[5]

The most striking feature of Philo's construction of the Greeks is the discrepancy between his open admiration for specific philosophers and playwrights of the Classical period, on the one hand, and his open criticism of Alexander the Great and Greek philosphical culture on the other. Philo suggests a deep affinity between the Jews and Plato, for example, while contrasting "us" to "the Greek philosophers" in general. Both aspects of this equivocal position reflect a clear sense of superiority over the Greeks and their culture. The specific characteristics which are ascribed to the Greeks moreover correspond, as we shall see, to distinctly Roman views on them.

Certain Classical Greek philosophers and writers enjoyed Philo's enthusiastic praise. Plato was in his view "most holy", an adjective otherwise attributed only to Moses.[6] Zeno is appreciated for having "lived under the direction of virtue to an unsurpassed degree" (Lib. 53). Homer is identified as "the greatest and most reputed of poets".[7] The words of Sophocles are in Philo's eyes "as true

---

[3] The idea of an existential conflict has generally been emphasized in M. Hengel's classic study Judaism and Hellenism; L. H. Feldman, Hebraism and Hellenism Reconsidered, *Judaism* 43.2 (1994) 115–26; and with regard to Philo by Hilgert, Philo Judaeus et Alexandrinus *passim*. The assumption of an inherent conflict between Jews and Hellenism has increasingly been criticized, see especially: F. Millar, The Background to the Maccabean Revolution: Reflections on Martin Hengel's Judaism and Hellenism, *JJS* 29.1 (1978) 1–21; Goldstein, Jewish Acceptance and Rejection 167–74; Gruen, Heritage XIV–XVII.

[4] On Heine's construction of Hellenism, see: Y. Shavit, *Athens in Jerusalem: Classical Antiquity and Hellenism in the Making of the Modern Secular Jew* (London 1997, Hebr. orig.) 40–5.

[5] Philonic studies have so far remained surprisingly oblivious to the new questions which have been raised by Millar, Goldstein and others. Even Sterling, Jewish Self-Definition 1–18, who stresses that Alexandrian Jews regarded Greek culture as an integral part of their identity refers only briefly to Philo.

[6] ἱερώτατος (Lib. 13); Plato is moreover called "great" in Aet. 52 and a true philosopher in Cont. 57 (where he is mentioned together with Xenophon).

[7] Conf. 4; Homer is also called "the poet" *per se* (Abr. 10); cf. Sen., Ep. 58:17 for a similar expression.

as the Delphic oracle" (Lib. 19), while Euripides is frequently quoted as the quintessential tragedian whose pieces provoked overwhelming applause among the audience in the theatre (Lib. 141).[8] The poets in general are spoken of as "educators through all our days" who teach wisdom to the public in the same way as parents do their children (Lib. 143). Philo hardly treats these writers as representives of a foreign or even other culture. Their works rather form a natural part of his intimate intellectual environment. Their lines are quoted in support of his own ideas which he is in the process of expounding.[9] Sophocles is even adduced as a witness to the doctrine that God alone is the leader of the truly free man.[10] In the same vein it is highly significant that many of Philo's references to Ἑλλάς, Ἕλλην and Ἑλληνικός deal with surprisingly general matters. Twenty-one out of ninety-one deal with Greek language, mostly Septuagintal expressions in comparison to Biblical Hebrew, and twenty-five others discuss features of the whole world under the rubric of "Greeks and barbarians". More than half of Philo's references to things Greek thus lack a sense of the Greeks as Other. Philo identified with the Greek language to such an extent that he once called Hebrew speakers "barbarians".[11] Did Philo then not construct any boundaries with regard to the Greeks and simply become absorbed in their culture without clearly distinguishing between "them" and "us"?

On closer examination it becomes clear that Philo relates to the above-mentioned Greek writers and philosophers with a distinct sense of superiority. He has in fact assimilated them into Jewish ethnicity. As far as he is concerned, they either directly derived their ideas from Scripture or reached the same insights as Moses. Plato, for example, is frequently quoted in support of the Biblical creation account.[12] Like Moses, he is said to have defended the true doctrine of a created, yet indestructible world. Plato's *Timaeus* is moreover quoted to show that "the Father and Maker of all is good", ungrudgingly sharing His blessings with His creatures.[13] Philo further assimilates the Classical Greek heritage to the Jewish tradition when he attributes Plato's ideas to Moses himself. He thus argues that Moses "could not fail to recognize that the

---

[8] Regarding Euripides, see also: Aet. 30, 144.

[9] See especially Philo's quotation of Euripides' lines on freedom and honesty of speech in All. 3: 202, Jos. 78, Lib. 25, 99–104; his quotation of Homer in support of frugality (Cont. 17), his reference to him in support of the idea that kings are shepherds of men (Lib. 31, Jos. 2 where he is referring more generally to "the order of poets"), and his reference to Homer's description of the Egyptian Proteus which he applies to Gaius (Leg. 80).

[10] Lib. 19; Philo originally seems to have quoted Sophocles' line as Ζεύς ἐμὸς ἄρχων ..., later scribes substituting the clearly pagan term Ζεύς by θεὸς (see note by Colson *ad. loc.*).

[11] Mos. 2:27; *Contra* J.A. Fishman, Language and Ethnicity, in: H. Giles (ed.), *Language, Ethnicity and Intergroup Relations* (London 1977) 15–57, who argued for the overwhelming centrality of Hebrew for Jewish identity.

[12] See especially Aet. 13–5, 25–7, 38, 52, Opif. 119, 133; see also: Runia, Timeaus *passim*.

[13] Opif. 21, Philo refers here to Plato more indirectly as "one of the men of old"; on the identity of this figure, see Runia, Timeaus 109.

universal must consist of two parts, one part active Cause and the other passive
object" (Opif. 8). The Israelite *nomothetes* emerges as an advocate of Platonic
principles expounded in the *Timaeus*. This indicates an astonishing degree of
convergence between the two thinkers. More importantly, it implies Philo's
sense of Moses' originality. It was in his view Moses who initially formulated
ideas which subsequently also surfaced in Plato's work.[14]

In the case of Zeno Philo explicitly speaks about the derivation of his ideas
from the Hebrew Scriptures. He was convinced that the stringent ethics of the
Stoics were based on a reading of the Torah (Lib. 57):

> We may well suppose that the fountain from which Zeno drew this thought was the law-
> book of the Jews, which tells of two brothers, one wise and temperate, the other
> incontinent, how the father of them both prayed in pity for him who had not attained to
> virtue that he should be his brother's slave.

Philo suggests here that Zeno took his moral theory from the Biblical story of
Jacob and Esau. Interpreted in a Stoic vein, this Biblical story indeed parallels
Stoic ethics. Far from admitting Stoic influence, however, Philo interprets this
similarity in the opposite way, namely as a sign of Zeno's dependence on
Scripture. This is a striking statement. It implies that Stoicism is in reality part
of "our" heritage. Their theory of ethics is perceived as nothing but an extension
of Jewish values and is said to have derived from "our" Scripture. According to
Philo, other Greeks also studied and adopted the Torah. "Some Grecian legisla-
tors", he insists, copied the Mosaic regulation regarding the unacceptability of
hearing as legal evidence (Spec. 4:61). Even Socrates may have been taught by
Moses (Q.G. 2:6). The Greeks in general were moreover among the Gentiles
who imitated the Jewish Sabbath (Mos. 2:20–1). Such borrowings were natural,
Philo argues, because knowledge of the Torah had spread widely among the
Gentiles who showed an exceptionally keen interest in the beauties of Mosaic
law.[15] King Ptolemy, who initiated the actual translation of the Hebrew Bible

---

[14] To be sure, Philo does not explicitly claim Mosaic origins for Plato's ideas, see also:
D. Winston, Philo And The Hellenistic Jewish Encounter, *SPhA* 7 (1995) 127; D. Runia,
Timaeus 528–9; G. Sterling, Platonizing Moses: Philo And Middle Platonism, *SPhA* 5 (1993)
101–3.

[15] Mos. 2:27; Philo stresses the exceptional nature of Greek attraction to Mosaic law by
pointing out that generally each nation follows only its own laws, while rejecting those of
others (Mos. 2:17–20). Philo's position clearly emerges in his interpretation of the circumstances which led to the translation of the Hebrew Bible into Greek. In contrast to Aristeas,
who assumed a purely academic impetus, Philo suggested a pervasive Greek demand for the
translation. Aristeas as well as Josephus thus traced the LXX back to the initiative of
Demetrius the librarian, who wished to complete the ambitious holdings of the Alexandrian
library (Ar. 29–31; Jos., A.J. 12:12–118); see also: V. Tcherikover, The Ideology of the Letter
of Aristeas, *HTR* 51.1 (1958) 59–85; M. Hadas, *Aristeas to Philocrates (Letter of Aristeas)*
(New York 1951) 59–66; E.S. Gruen, Fact and Fiction: Jewish Legends in a Hellenistic
Context, in: P. Cartledge *et al.* (eds.), *Hellenistic Constructs. Essays in Culture, History, and
Historiography* (Berkeley 1997) 81–3. Philo, by contrast, speaks of Gentile attraction to the

into Greek, thus making it available for the eagerly awaiting Hellenic world, is even said to have cherished an "ardent affection for our laws".[16]

Philo's claim about the derivation of Greek thought and culture from Mosaic law has often been compared to Aristobulus' statements in a similar vein.[17] The latter argued long before Philo that "the Greeks begin from the philosophy of the Hebrews". Plato was said to have "imitated our legislation" and Pythagoras "transferred many of our doctrines and integrated them into his own system of beliefs".[18] This approach seems to have been rather prevalent among Egyptian Jews and is visible also in Artapanus.[19] Moses Hadas suggested in an influential study that this strategy must be understood in the context of a broader Oriental appropriation of Greek culture.[20] He initially pointed to significant parallels among other Eastern nations. Homer had been claimed by Syrians, Egyptians and other countries, while Plato, Aesop, Orpheus and Alexander the Great were predominantly traced back to Egyptian origins.[21] This claim was apparently so common and widely accepted, not only in the East, that Diogenes Laertius felt

---

beauties of the Mosaic law (Mos. 2:27–31). The discrepancies between Aristeas and Josephus, on the one hand, and Philo, on the other hand, suggested to L. Cohn, Philo von Alexandria, *Neue Jahrbücher für das Klassische Altertum, Geschichte und Deutsche Literatur und Pädagogik* 1 (1898) 521–2, that Philo was unfamiliar with the account preserved in the *Letter of Aristeas*. The differences between them can, however, equally be explained as expressions of the authors' different interests.

[16] Mos. 2:31; cf. the Ptolemaic king in the *Letter of Aristeas*, who became a student of the seventy-two Bible translators (Ar. 187–300) and respected kosher food regulations (Ar. 181).

[17] D. Dawson, *Allegorical Readers and Cultural Revision in Ancient Alexandria* (Berkeley 1992) 78–82, 113–26; Collins, Athens and Jerusalem 219–22; Holladay, Fragments 3:58, 208–9; Gruen, Jewish Constructs of Greeks and Hellenism, forthcoming in: idem.

[18] Aristobulus, Fragment 3, apud Eusebius, Praep. Ev. 13.12:1, translation by A. Yarbro Collins in: J. H. Charlesworth, The Old Testament Pseudepigrapha (New York 1985) 2.839; for a more detailed discussion of Aristobulus' appropriation of Greek traditions, with further examples and bibliography, see: Gruen, Heritage 246–53; idem, Jewish Constructs; N. Walter, *Der Thoraausleger Aristobulos. Untersuchungen zu seinen Fragmenten* (Berlin 1964 = TUGAL 86) 44–50; Dawson, Allegorical Readers 78–82.

[19] For details on Artapanus' interpretation of Moses as teacher of Orpheus, see above chapter two. The Church Fathers moreover preserve fragments of anonymous, yet obviously Jewish-Hellenistic appropriations of Classical writers to whom traditional Jewish ideas are attributed; on these fragments, see: A.-M. Denis, *Fragmenta pseudepigraphorum quae supersunt Graece* (Leiden 1970) 161–74; Gruen, Jewish Constructs of Greeks and Hellenism.

[20] M. Hadas, *Hellenistic Culture. Fusion and Diffusion* (New York and London 1959) 72–4, 82–4.

[21] Homer was claimed to be a Syrian by Meleager of Gadara, Athenaeus 157b, to be an Egyptian by Heliodorus, Ethiopica 3:14, and had according to Dio Chr. 47:5, 55:7 and Paus. 10.24:3 been claimed by many other countries. Egyptian origins for known Greek figures were suggested by Heliodorus, Ethiopica 3:14; Ps.-Callisthenes 1:4; see also: Hadas, Hellenistic Culture 83–4; T. Whitemarsh, The Birth of Prodigy: Heliodorus and the Genealogy of Hellenism, in: R. Hunter, *Studies in Heliodorus* (Cambridge 1998 = Cambr. Phil. Soc. Suppl. vol. 21) 105; cf. also the appropriation of Greco-Egyptian culture by modern Africans, discussed by Y. Shavit, Up the River or Down the River? An Afrocentrist Dilemma, in: H. Erlich and I. Gershoni (eds.), *The Nile. Histories, Cultures, Myths* (London 2000) 79–104.

a need to refute it. He began his account of Greek philosophy by an explicit rejection of the idea that "the study of philosophy had its beginning among the barbarians" (Prol. 1:1–11). Claiming native roots for foundational Greek writers was thus a common device. Hadas argued that it served to strengthen the self-confidence of the conquered nations in face of the overwhelming Greek civilization. This strategy ultimately facilitated Eastern acceptance of Hellenism, rendering possible a profound and large-scale integration of cultures.

Philo undoubtedly stands in this Eastern and earlier Jewish tradition. He, too, assimilated Plato, Zeno and others to the Jewish heritage. Yet the similarity between the strategies of Aristobulus, for example, and Philo must not be overemphasized. Philo added an important new dimension to the discourse which deserves our attention. In his overall work the claim to Scriptural origins for Greek thought occupies only a limited amount of space.[22] It appears beside a well thought out and openly competitive discussion on the relationship between the Jewish and the Greek heritage. Rather than merely absorbing Greek culture, Philo appreciated it with a new sense of distance. For the first time among Jews the model of Greek dependence on Scripture has thus been enlarged by a discourse of explicit comparison. Such comparison was characteristic of Roman intellectuals, who tended to look upon Greek culture from the point of view of a clearly separate and rival nation. Parallel to Cato, Cicero, Seneca and Josephus, Philo made some favourable and some unfavourable comparisons as suited his own agenda of highlighting pristine Jewish values. Cato had praised Pericles and Themistocles, while on other occasions dismissing Socrates and the Greeks in general for mere loquacity.[23] Cicero similarly acknowledged Socrates as the "father of philosphy" and devoted much of his work to expounding "the profound learning" of Greek philosophers, while dismissing the Greeks in general because of their irresponsible talk and fickleness.[24] In the same spirit Seneca expressed high respect for Socrates, Plato, Zeno and Cleanthes, but ridiculed the "hairsplitting logic" of the Greeks and their "unrestrained style" of speech.[25] Josephus also embraced this equivocal approach, supplementing it by earlier Jewish strategies of cultural appropriation. He appreciated the "wisest of the Greeks" for having either derived their philosophy directly from Scripture or reached similar ideas about God, while at the same time condemning the eloquence and unreliability of the Greeks as historians and writers.[26]

---

[22] The precise place and larger context of Aristobulus' statements within his overall work can, of course, no longer be established due to the very partial survival of his writings. It is nevertheless clear that his surviving discussions lack the very dimension which is conspicuous in Philo's writings.

[23] Plut., Cato Mai. 8:8, 12:5, 23:1.

[24] Cic., De Fin. 2:2, 1:1, Pro Flac. 59, 61–2, cf. Runia, Timaeus 548.

[25] Sen., Ep. 64:10, 44:3–4, 58:30, De Vita Beat. 18:1, Ep. 82:8–9, 40:11.

[26] Jos., Contr. Ap. 2:168, 2:257, 1:6–14, 1:27, 1:44–6.

Philo needs to be appreciated precisely in this context of Roman writers defining their identity vis-à-vis the Greeks and their culture. He, too, assumed certain similarities between the Jewish and the Greek tradition, sometimes assimilating the latter to his own heritage, while on other occasions formulating critical generalizations about "the Greeks". To be sure, Jews before Philo had expressed critical views about the Greeks. In the *Letter of Aristeas*, for example, they had been explicitly associated with idolatry.[27] Philo's position, however, is of a different nature. He does not argue on traditional religious grounds, extending Biblical polemics against idolatry to the Greeks. He, on the contrary, avoids any explicit link between polytheism and Hellenism of the kind which Aristeas had suggested.[28] Furthermore, unlike the author of II *Maccabees* Philo never expresses any concern that Hellenism may threaten Jewish law observance.[29] Nor does he criticize Greek imperialism in the way the author of the third *Sibylline Oracle* had done.[30] Philo's discussion of "the Greeks" rather betrays a keen sense of cultural competition, which was based on a comparison between the achievements of the two nations.

The new tone of Philo's discussion can be appreciated in his treatment of Heraclitus. While he had at one point spoken about him in a friendly tone as a follower of Mosaic teachings (All. 1:108), he also made the following rather snide comments on the Greeks' mistaken pride in his alleged inventiveness (Her. 214):

---

[27] See especially Ar. 134–7, where the author complains that idol worshippers "who have invented these fabrications and myths are usually ranked to be the wisest of the Greeks"; on the attitudes towards Greek culture expressed in the *Letter of Aristeas*, see also: R. Feldmeier, Weise hinter 'eisernen Mauern'. Tora und Jüdisches Selbstverständnis zwischen Akkulturation und Absonderung im Aristeasbrief, in: M. Hengel and A.M. Schwemer (eds.), *Die Septuaginta zwischen Judentum und Christentum* (Tübingen 1994 = *WUNT* 72) 20–37; Gruen, Heritage 218, idem, Jewish Constructs of Greeks and Hellenism. Aristeas' position was later continued by Paul and through his writings in the subsequent Christian Church, on which see also: K.L. Gaca, Paul's Uncommon Declaration in Romans 1:18–32 and Its Problematic Legacy for Pagan and Christian Relations, *HTR* 92:2 (1999) 165–98.

[28] The best example of Philo's approach is his discussion of the Decalogue. While he specifically identifies the Egyptians as idolators, holding their national character responsible for their religious aberrations (Dec. 76), he speaks only in general terms about the features of Greek polytheism (Dec. 52–71). The names of the gods are mentioned, but only the sculptors and myth-makers in general are directly accused. For similar examples, see: Spec. 1:28 where Philo again speaks about "the myth-makers" in general; Spec. 2:164–5 where he complains about idolatrous practices throughout the Greek and barbarian world.

[29] II Macc. suggests that the Jews may abandon their traditional way of life either voluntarily (4:10–17) or by external force (6:9). The literature on the encounter between Judaism and Hellenism as described by the author of II *Maccabees* is vast; see especially two recent discussions and bibliography there: Gruen, Heritage1–40; M. Himmelfarb, Judaism and Hellenism in 2 Maccabees, *PT* 19.1 (1998) 19–40.

[30] Sib. Or. 3:171–4, 381–400; on the critical view of the Greeks expressed in the third Sib. Or., see also: Gruen, Third Sibylline Oracle; idem, Jewish Constructs of Greeks and Hellenism.

Is not this the truth which according to the Greeks Heraclitus, whose greatness and art they celebrate so loudly, put in the fore front of his philosophy and vaunted it as a new discovery? Actually, as has been clearly shown, it was Moses who long ago discovered the truth that opposites are formed from the same whole, to which they stand in the relation of sections or divisions.

Philo stresses here Mosaic precedence from a new point of view. Instead of smoothly assimilating Heraclitus to the Jewish heritage, he speaks with considerable distance about "the Greeks" and mocks their pride in the alleged innovations of their scientist. Philo clearly expresses himself more aggressively than in previous passages, where he showed profound sympathy for Greek writers and advocated their dependence on Scripture in a self-confident, yet friendly spirit. Now he appears more critical of Greek culture and writes with a new sense of open competition. No longer satisfied with merely showing Heraclitus' dependence on Scripture, he triumphantly announces his nation's superiority and originality. This and other Philonic statements in the same spirit are foreign to Artapanus and Aristobulus.[31] They instead anticipate the position of Josephus who also wrote in a distinctly Roman context.[32] The latter introduced his *Contra Apionem* with a harsh criticism of Greek pride in their own writers, who were in his view not as trustworthy as generally assumed (Contr. Ap. 1:4). This is followed by a categorical statement: "For in the Greek world everything will be found to be modern, and dating, so to speak, from yesterday or the day before" (Contr. Ap. 1:7). This holds especially true, Josephus asserts, for the invention of arts, the compilation of law codes and historiography. In all of these fields other nations, foremost among them the Jews, are more ancient and thus far worthier.

Socrates is submitted to an interpretation in a similar vein. We saw above that Philo once suggests the possibility of Socrates' dependence on Scripture. Now, however, he compares him to Terach and stresses his philosophical inferiority (Somn. 1:58–9):

This character [who advocates self-knowledge] the Hebrews call Terach, the Greeks Socrates. For they say that "know yourself" was likewise the theme of life-long ponder-

---

[31] Cf. two additional statements: 1) Philo insists on the superiority of the Mosaic designation for supernatural beings. While "Greek philosophers" called them heroes, Moses identified them as angels (Plant. 14). The Mosaic term is in his view more accurate, because it captures the angels' nature as messengers between God and humanity; 2) Philo also claims Jewish superiority with regard to philosophy of language. In his view Moses "did better (ἄμεινον)" than "the Greek philosophers" in explaining the origin of language (All. 2:15). While they had attributed the first assignment of names to a number of wise men, Moses recognized that the first man alone performed this task. Philo preferred the Mosaic account, because it explained the natural connection between an object and its one intrinsic name (All. 2:15). For further details on Philo's philosophy of language, see below chapter seven.

[32] The Roman context of Josephus' statements on the Greeks has been stressed by Goodman, Jewish Attitudes 171–3; Haaland, Jewish Laws for Roman Audience.

ing to Socrates, and that his philosophy was concerned exclusively with his own self. Socrates, however, was a human being, while Terach was self-knowledge itself ... Such do we find those to be whose part it is to explore good sense, but more perfect than theirs is the nature with which those are endowed who train themselves to contest for it [fruit of moral knowledge]. These, when they have thoroughly learned in all its details the whole study of the sense-perceptions, claim it as their prerogative to advance to some other greater object of contemplation, leaving behind them those lurking-places of sense-perception to which the name Haran is given.

Philo compares here two figures, one from the Hebrew and the other from the Greek tradition, who represent in his view parallel principles. Both Terach and Socrates are said to personify self-knowledge. While Socrates was known for this maxim (D.L. 2:21), Terach's portrait is clearly made up in this fashion so as to promote a comparison between the two cultures. It is clear from the very beginning that Philo aims at demonstrating the superiority of his own tradition. He immediately stresses that Socrates was only a human being, while Terach, a minor figure in the Bible, is supposed to be "self-knowledge itself". Philo is furthermore eager to diminish the ideal represented by Socrates and expose it as a merely preliminary stage which was dialectically superseded in the Mosaic tradition. For this purpose he insists on the limitations of self-knowledge. The Socratic ideal is shown to boil down to inferior sense-perception which lacks proper moral application. The Greeks are thus associated with the realm of changing appearances and self-centred thinking which is useless to society at large. Their ideal is said to have been overcome by Abraham who reached insight into eternal truth (Somn. 1:60):

for when he [Abraham] most knew himself (ἔγνω), then most did he despair of himself (ἀπέγνω ἑαυτόν), in order that he might attain to an exact knowledge (εἰς ἀκριβῆ γνῶσιν) of Him who in reality is. And this is nature's law: he who has thoroughly comprehended himself, thoroughly despairs of himself (ἀπέγνωκε), having as a step to this ascertained the nothingness in all respects of created being. And the man who has despaired of himself (ἀπογνοὺς ἑαυτὸν) is beginning to know (γινώσκει) Him that is.

Abraham represents in this passage the philosophical breakthrough embraced by the Hebrews. Not content with mere appearances and self-centred contempla- tion, he left Haran and reached God "who in reality is". Philo highlights the contrast between the positions of Socrates and Abraham by a repeated play on the words γιγνώσκω and ἀπογιγνώσκω, implying that the renunciation of the kind of knowledge Socrates represents leads to the only true knowledge of Him who in reality is. The Jews who follow Abraham are thus associated with authen- tic and unchanging values which have a high moral relevance. Their philosophi- cal orientation differs significantly from that of the Greeks who have remained loyal to Socrates and thus stayed behind in ultimately futile ratiocination.

These distinctions between Greeks and Jews echo familiar Roman themes. Philo was indeed not the first to argue for his nation's superiority over the self-centred and unrealistic philosophy of the Greeks. Cato had become famous for making similar comparisons between Romans and Greeks. He thought that "the words of the Greeks were born on their lips, but those of the Romans in their hearts" (Plut., Cato Mai. 12:5). Socrates had been criticized by him as a "mighty prattler" who had betrayed the interests of his country.[33] Cato was especially shocked by the "magic eloquence" of Carneades, who easily persuaded Rome's best youth to acquire a "reputation based on mere words".[34] The Greeks were generally suspected of pursuing reputation at all costs, being even ready to commit murder for this purpose.[35] True Romans, Cato insisted, rather distinguish themselves by virtuous actions and an oratory rooted in moral performance.[36] These images of the Greeks became common coin to the extent that even Strabo occasionally repeated them, speaking of the Greeks as "the most talkative of all men" (Geogr. 3.4:19). Philo's Socrates in the above-quoted passage has absorbed these themes to a considerable extent. He, too, represents unreal values which only lead to self-centred ratiocination, while lacking moral application. This, however, is exactly what the Greeks liked – or so Philo tells us.

Roman categories have been applied with particular consistency in the discussion of the Therapeutae and the Essenes. These two groups of quintessential Jewish philosophers were represented as the direct opposite of their Greek counterpart.[37] Philo initially contrasts "our" pristine values to the merely talkative Greeks:[38]

Such are the athletes of virtue produced by a philosophy free from the futile wordiness of the Greeks (περιεργίας Ἑλληνικῶν), a philosophy which sets its pupils to practice

---

[33] Plut., Cato Mai. 23:1; see also: Gruen, Culture and National Identity 64–5, who argued that Cato's criticism of Socrates was intended to distinguish philosophical chicanery from the true discipline, thus implying approval of the established Hellenistic institutions rather than a general criticism of Hellenism. In the case of Philo, however, a national typology is clearly intended, because an explicit link is established between Socrates and "the Greeks".

[34] Plut., Cato Mai. 22:1–5; Pliny, N.H. 7:112. Cato similarly criticized Greek philosophical training for its long duration, which precluded in his view any meaningful application (Plut., Cato Mai. 23:2).

[35] Pliny, N.H. 29:14.

[36] "vir bonus dicendi peritus" (Sen., Contr. 1:9).

[37] On the historical identity of the Therapeutae and Essenens, see especially: G. Vermes and M. D. Goodman (eds.), *The Essenes According to the Classical Sources* (Sheffield 1989) 15–7; Taylor and Davies, Therapeutae; P. Bilde, The Essenes in Philo and Josephus, in: F. H. Cryer and T. L. Thompson (eds.), Qumran between the Old and the New Testament (Sheffield 1998 = *JSOT* Ser. 290) 32–64, who stresses the congruence between the sources and the two groups themselves; P. Wendland, *Die Therapeuten und die Philonische Schrift vom Beschaulichen Leben. Ein Beitrag zur Geschichte des Hellenistischen Judentums* (Leipzig 1896), who pointed to the idiosyncratic nature of Philo's account. It is precisely Philo's subjective perspective and values transpiring in his description of the Therapeutae which are of interest here.

[38] Lib. 88; cf. also Acts 17; 18:15 where Luke makes similar statements about talkative Greeks; Schwartz, Luke-Acts and Jewish-Hellenistic Historiography, pointed to the Roman context of Luke' polemics.

themselves in laudable actions, by which the liberty which can never be enslaved is firmly established.

The Therapeutae, Philo moreover insists, do not practice philosophy for mere ostentation (Cont. 75):

In doing this he [the interpreter of Scripture] has no thought of making a display, for he makes no effort to get a reputation for clever oratory but desires to gain a closer insight into some particular matters and having gained it not to withhold it selfishly from those who if not so clear-sighted as he have at least a similar desire to learn.

The negative image of the talkative and ostentatious Greeks serves in these passages as a screen onto which Philo projects the excellence of Jewish philosophers. This contrast highlights "our" commitment to moral action and real concern for others. Jewish philosophy emerges as relevant to life and society, aiming at real progress rather than self-centred ratiocination. The Therapeutae and Essenes have thus been assigned the same role as Roman intellectuals assumed for their own philosophers. Philo's strategy becomes especially conspicuous in his comparison between the Therapeutae and two philosophers admired by the Greeks (Cont. 14):

The Greeks extol Anaxagoras and Democritus because smitten with the desire for philosophy they left their fields to be devoured by sheep. I too myself admire them for showing themselves superior to wealth, but how much better are these [the Therapeutae] who did not let their estates serve as the feeding-ground for cattle but made good the needs of men, their kinsfolk and friends, and so turned their indigence to affluence. Of the two actions the first was thoughtless, I might say mad (μανιῶδες), but that the persons concerned have the admiration of Greece, the second showed soberness and careful consideration and remarkable good sense.

Philo points in this passage to a significant clash between the philosophical orientations of Jews and Greeks. While the Greeks have chosen selfish, ostentatious and indeed "mad" action as their ideal, the Therapeutae represent the practical wisdom of the Jews. Philo's vehement criticism of the Greek philosophers is surprising in view of the fact that they nevertheless share his overall rejection of material values. He himself admits to a partial appreciation of their action and acknowledges that they have shown themselves "superior to wealth". Why then did Philo criticize them as virtually mad principles admired by the Greeks? Plato's attitude towards Anaxagoras may provide a clue to this question. He, too, disapproved of Anaxagoras and his "senseless wisdom". Plato did so, however, without suggesting that this was a typically Greek trait.[39] He rather discussed them as philosophers belonging to his own nation. Their faults were thus interpreted as personal shortcomings. Philo seems to have used this earlier Greek tradition for his own purposes. He no longer speaks of Anaxagoras and

---

[39] Hip.Mai.. 283a; Cicero, Horace and Seneca, by contrast, expressed admiration for Anaxagoras and Democritus (Cic., Tusc. Disp. 5:115; Hor., Ep. 1:12; Sen., Prov. 6:2).

Demetrius as individuals, but as types, and integrates them into his overall construction of "the Greeks". Despite the considerable degree of affinity between their action and Philo's general rejection of material values, they consequently emerge as quintessential representatives of the Greek Other. The regard in which the Greeks hold them indicates their overall inclination towards irresponsible ostentation, which lacks "foresight and consideration for the interest of others" (Cont. 15). Their example serves as a point of contrast in which the advantages of Jewish philosophy stand out even more sharply.

Philo moreover uses the banqueting customs of the Therapeutae to highlight the contrast between Jewish and Greek philosophy. The Therapeutae, he insists, celebrate spiritual and frugal kinds of banquets. They use only a minimum of material expenditure and devote their symposiac gatherings to intellectual conversation as well as study. Exhibiting a solemn cheerfulness, they do not recline on costly and soft couches, but on "plank beds of the common kind of wood" (Cont. 66, 69). No slaves, but the junior members of the group wait on them (Cont. 70–2). Neither wine nor meat is served, the Therapeutae being content with mere bread and water (Cont. 73–4). The women who participate in these banquets are usually "aged virgins who have kept their chastity not under compulsion, like some of the Greek priestesses, but of their own free will in their ardent yearning for wisdom" (Cont. 68). This distinction alludes to an important difference between the Therapeutides and Greek priestesses. The latter are not truly spiritual, but accept celebacy only under compulsion.

This inclination towards licentiousness is not limited to the women. Rather, it characterizes the Greek Other as a whole. Philo stresses this point by juxtaposing the Therapeutic banquet to Greek practices. He even introduces his discussion by an explicit contrast to "the banquets held in Greece".[40] Plato's and Xenophon's symposia are singled out for this purpose. Philo complains that even these two philosophers described and engaged in banquets deserving nothing but "supreme contempt" by the "disciples of Moses" (Cont. 63). Plato's and Xenophon's banquet revolved in his view only around forbidden pleasures (Cont. 58–61):

Yet even these if compared with those of our people who embrace the contemplative life will appear as matters for derision. Pleasure is an element in both, but Xenophon's banquet is more concerned with ordinary humanity. There are flute girls, dancers, jugglers, fun-makers proud of their gift of jesting and facetiousness and other accompaniments of more unrestrained merry-making. In Plato's banquet the talk is almost entirely concerned with love, not merely with the love-sickness of men for women, or women for men, passions recognized by the laws of nature, but of men for other males differing from them only in age … The chief part is taken up by the common vulgar love which robs men of the courage which is the virtue most valuable for the life both of peace and war, sets up the disease of effeminacy in their souls and turns into *androgynoi*

---

[40] ἀντιτάξω (Cont. 64).

those who should have been disciplined in all the practices which make for valour. And having wrought havoc with the years of boyhood and reduced the boy to the grade and condition of a girl besieged by a lover it inflicts damage on the lovers also in three most essential respects: their bodies, their souls and their property.

The severity of Philo's criticism is astonishing. As Colson *ad. loc.* noted, Philo generally seems to have relied rather heavily on Plato's *Symposion*, especially on the idea of the spiritual *Eros* in Diotema's speech.[41] In the present context, however, he pursues different objectives. Busy constructing the Greek Other as a point of contrast to the Therapeutae, he explores the theme of licentiousness and pederasty which had in the Roman discourse become closely associated with "the Greeks". *Pergraecari* essentially meant to indulge in these vices.[42] While pederasty had within certain limits been accepted in Greek culture and sometimes even been extolled, in Rome seduction of a young male citizen constituted a *stuprum*, an offense subject to criminal punishment.[43] Part

---

[41] Symp. 206C–212A; see also: Winston, Philo of Alexandria 320. Philo refers to the idea of the soul's spiritual offspring for example in Sacr. 102; Cher. 42–50; Poster. 135; Immut. 137; Mut. 134–5. On the connection between Philo and Plato in this respect, see: Ch. Riedweg, *Mysterienterminologie bei Platon, Philon und Klemens von Alexandrien* (Berlin 1987) 71–107. Philo was not singular in adapting the Platonic idea of the Eros, regarding other authors, see: D. Winston, The Sage as Mystic in the Wisdom of Solomon, in: J.G. Gammie and L.G. Perdue (eds.), *The Sage in Israel and the Ancient Near East* (Winona Lake 1990) 383–97; H.E. Goldberg, Torah and Children: Symbolic Aspects of the Reproduction of Jews and Judaism, in: idem (ed.), *Judaism Viewed from Within and from Without. Anthropological Studies* (New York 1987) 107–30.

[42] See also: C.A. Williams, Greek Love at Rome, *CQ* 45.2 (1995) 517–39, who stresses in contrast to earlier scholarship that Roman criticism was not directed at homosexuality in general, but against pederasty involving free boys. Only the latter was dismissed as typically Greek and appears only as one of several Greek characteristics in Roman writings.

[43] The status of Greek homosexuality in comparison to Roman practice has been debated: while M.B. Skinner, *Quod multo fit aliter in Graecia*, in: J.P. Hallett and M.B. Skinner (eds.), *Roman Sexualities* (Princeton 1997) 11, recently repeated the view of a distinct dichotomy between Greece and Rome, D. Cohen, *Law, Sexuality, and Society. The enforcement of morals in Classical Athens* (Cambridge 1991) 171–202, tried to argue for social and even legal restrictions on homosexuality in Ancient Greece; the most balanced view is still to be found in: Foucault, Use of Pleasure 187–225, who stressed that even though homosexuality was accepted in Ancient Greece as a natural pleasure, which was judged by the standard criteria of self-restraint versus indulgence, it was problematized when it concerned a free boy, who should not accept a role too passive and feminine for his (future) status. This problem, Foucault argued, was subsequently solved in Rome by legislation which excluded free boys from homosexual engagements, which were relegated to male slaves (Foucault, Care of the Self 198–90); see also: J.N. Bremmer, Adolescents, *Symposion,* and Pederasty, in: O. Murray, *Sympotica. A Symposium on the Symposion* (Oxford 1990) 135–48; E. Fantham, *Stuprum*: Public Attitudes and Penalties for Sexual Offenses in Republican Rome, *Echos du Monde Classique* 35 (1991) 267–91; A. Richlin, Not before Homosexuality: The Materiality of the *Cinaedus* and the Roman Law against Love between Men, *Journal of the History of Sexuality* 3 (1993) 561–66; A. Rousselle, Personal Status and Sexual Practice in the Roman Empire, in: M. Feher (ed.), *Fragments of the Human Body* (New York 1989) 3:317–21.

of the ideal of the Roman *vir* was his impenetrability.[44] Nepos, Cicero and Tacitus condemned pederasty as a Greek vice.[45] Referring to all aspects of *pergraecari*, Livy put into Cato's mouth a sharp criticism of the Greeks as indulging in luxury, allurements and pederasty.[46] Polybios similarly warned against Rome's "infection with Greek laxity" (31.25:4). This Roman discourse provides a meaningful background to Philo's discussion of the Classical banquets. His harsh criticism of Plato and Xenophon repeats Roman rhetoric on the Greeks and their flaws. Philo identifies the same vices of indulgence and pederasty, treating the latter in typically Roman fashion as a violation of the boy's manly valour.[47] Philo has thus once more adapted an ancient Greek tradition, this time the Classical symposion, to his overall construction of the Greeks in a distinctly Roman spirit. In this way he has redrawn an important ethnic boundary, which originally distinguished the Romans from the Greeks, but has now been used to define the Jews. It is implied that Jewish philosophers played a parallel role as Roman intellectuals. Both consciously refrain from *pergraecari*. Avoiding luxurious indulgence and pederasty, the Therapeutae have been cast precisely into the role which the Roman elite had assumed for itself in relation to "the Greeks". Philo obviously intended the image of the Therapeutae to extend to all Jews. He repeated the dichotomy between the frugal Jews and the licentious Greeks also in halachic contexts where he highlighted "our" superiority over the licentious Greek Other.[48]

Another milestone in Philo's construction of the Greeks is the figure of Alexander the Great. Philo lived in the city which had since the Ptolemies most proudly born his name and cherished his memory.[49] His bones were preserved here and shown to Augustus after his victory over Antony (Suet., Aug. 18:1).

---

[44] See also: Walters, Invading the Body 29–43; see also the discussion on Roman ideals of virile morality and self-restraint in chapter three.

[45] Nepos, Alc. 2:2; Cicero, Tusc. Disp. 5:58; Tacitus, An. 14:20; see also: Williams, Greek Love 523–6.

[46] Livy, N.H. 34.4:1–4; Cato's speech in Livy's account has been identified as unoriginal, reflecting Livy's own rather than Cato's ideas, see: Gruen, Culture and National Identity 70; Astin, Cato 25–6.

[47] Classical Greco-Roman categories are conspicuous also in Philo's general discussion of pederasty and homosexuality in Spec. 3:37–42, on which see above chapter three.

[48] Philo contrasted the Day of Atonement to "the Holy Month of the Greeks" during which "untempered wine flows freely" (Mos. 2:23–4). He also criticized the Greeks for permitting certain incestuous unions (Spec. 3:15–22 ); for further details on these two issues, see above chapter three.

[49] On the memory of Alexander in Alexandria, see especially: P. Goukowsky, *Essai Sur Les Origines Du Mythe D'Alexandre (336–270 av. J.-C.)* (Nancy 1978) 1:131–3, 136–41; Kornemann, Herrscherkulte 56–75. Indicative of a continuous Alexandrian admiration for Alexander is the *Alexander Romance*, on the Greco-Egyptian background of which see especially: Braun, History and Romance 31–43; U. Wilcken, *Alexander der Grosse* (Leipzig 1931) 304. Eddy, King 257–323, stressed the initial antagonism between the Egyptian population and the Greek conquerors, yet admits that the two increasingly mingled, thus preparing the way for a Greco-Egyptian identity revolving around Alexander the Great.

Alexandrian intellectuals like Timagenes saw in Alexander a symbol of Greek superiority over the Romans which provided hope for the future.[50] Popular Alexander stories continued to glorify this hero.[51] Many Egyptian Jews seem to have joined in the praise. Artapanus appreciated the Macedonian to the extent that he modelled his figure of Moses on Sesostris, Alexander's Egyptian counterpart.[52] Josephus moreover conveys legends of probably Jewish-Egyptian origin which portray Alexander most favourably as visiting the Jerusalem Temple and confessing God.[53] Philo, as usual, departed from the ways of his Greco-Egyptian countrymen and embraced a distinctly more Roman position.[54] Alexander the Great was in his eyes nothing but an "immature and childish soul" (Cher. 63). He was accused of yielding to his passions and material attractions. An anecdote about the Macedonian king is told to illustrate the superficiality and vulgarity of his character: "when it seemed to him that he had gained the mastery of Europe and Asia, he stood in some commanding spot and, looking at the view around, said: this way and that all is mine" (Cher. 63). Philo condemns Alexander's gesture as an expression of arrogance and "unreasoning pride" (Cher. 63). The reader is expected to frown upon this foolish king who died at a very young age, leaving behind an empire on the verge of disruption.[55]

---

[50] See also: Heuss, Alexander der Grosse 77–79; Bowersock, Augustus 108–10; Sordi, Timagene 776–97.

[51] The popular elements of the Alexander-Romance have been especially pointed out by Braun, History and Romance 31–43

[52] For details on Artapanus' interpretation of Moses, see above chapter two.

[53] A.J. 11:302–47; the Egyptian-Jewish sources of Josephus' account have been suggested by A. Momigliano, Flavius Josephus and Alexander's Visit to Jerusalem, *Athenaeum* 57.3–4 (1979) 442–8; see also: G. Delling, Alexander der Grosse als Bekenner des Jüdischen Gottesglaubens, *JSJ* 12.1 (1981) 24–5; R. Stoneman, Jewish Traditions on Alexander the Great, *SPhA* 6 (1994) 39–45; for divergent opinions see: Gruen, Heritage 189–202; S.J.D. Cohen, Alexander the Great and Jaddus the High Priest according to Josephus, *AJS Review* 7–8 (1982–3) 67.

[54] On Rome's ambivalent, often outright negative attitude towards Alexander, see: J.R. Fears, The Stoic View of the Career and Character of Alexander the Great, *Philologus* 118.1 (1974) 113–30, *contra* J. Stroux, Die Stoische Beurteilung Alexanders des Grossen, *Philologus* 88.2 (1933) 222–40. Fears' views have been repeated by A.B. Bosworth, *A Historical Commentary on Arrian's History of Alexander* (Oxford 1980) 1:12–4; more hesitantly also by U. Ortmann, Cicero und Alexander, in: W. Will (ed.), *Zu Alexander d. Gr. Festschrift G. Wirth zum 60. Geburtstag* (Amsterdam 1988) 2.801–63; see also: P. Green, Caesar and Alexander: Aemulatio, Imitatio, Comparatio, *Am. Jour. of Anc. Hist.* 3.1 (1978) 1–26; Gruen, Alexander *passim*, who forcefully argued for the consistency of Roman ambivalence towards Alexander from the earliest contacts onwards. Delling, Bekenner *passim*; Stoneman, Jewish Traditions 39–45, have overlooked the crucial difference between the Greek and the Roman receptions of the Alexander legacy, mistakenly arguing for Philo's integral place among the Greco-Egyptian Alexander traditions.

[55] On the circumstances of Alexander's death, see especially: A.B. Bosworth, The Death of Alexander the Great: Rumour and Propaganda, *CQ* 21.1 (1971) 112–36. If Alexander was indeed assassinated, as ancient rumour had it and Bosworth suggests, his illusion about his power was obviously even greater than if he succumbed to some bodily ailments.

Philo's position emerges even more forcefully in his reinterpretation of some Eastern traditions about Alexander. Philo adapts a story about the king encountering on his conquest of the East a group of Indian gymnosophists to his overall construction of the Greeks. Alexander emerges in this context as the quintessential representative of Greek shortcomings, while his opponent, the Indian gymnosophist Calanus, defends a typically Roman and Philonic self-image vis-à-vis the Greeks. This is Philo's version of the encounter (Lib. 93–5):

> ... combining virtuous actions with laudable words, he [Calanus] gained the admiration not only of his fellow countrymen, but of men of other races, and, what is most singular of all, of enemy sovereigns.
>
> Thus Alexander of Macedon, wishing to exhibit to the Grecian world a specimen of the barbarians' wisdom, like a copy reproducing the original picture, began by urging Calanus to travel with him from India with the prospect of winning great fame in the whole of Asia and the whole of Europe; and when he failed to persuade him declared that he would compel him to follow him. Calanus' reply was as noble as it was apposite: "what shall I be worth to you, Alexander, for exhibiting to the Greeks if I am compelled to do what I do not wish to do?" What a wealth of frankness there is in the words and far more of freedom in the thought.

Philo relies here on what has been described as "perhaps the most resonant of all Alexander stories" which is mentioned in the fragmentary histories of Alexander as well as the Alexander Romance and later Medieval stories.[56] Different versions of it were available from the beginning and circulated also in Alexandria. Philo has significantly chosen the more critical one as his model, following Aristobulus' rather than Onesicritus' account. While the latter wrote such an encomiastic history that he was later dismissed by Lucian as a dilitant flatterer, Aristobulus expressed considerably more ambivalence about Alexander's imperialism.[57] Onesicritus has left behind a story of a cordial encounter between Alexander and the Indian gymnosophists. He relates how the king sent the historian himself to the Indians, not with any intention of imperialistic ostentation, but for honest intellectual purposes, namely "to converse with these sophists" and "to learn the wisdom of the sophists and report it to him".[58] One of them, Mandanis by name, praised the Macedonian conquerer as the "only philosopher in arms". He and his colleague Calanus honoured him by explaining Indian philosophy to Alexander's envoy. This is done with a view to supporting Alexander's civilizing role in the *oikoumene*: he is an ideal ruler who spreads wisdom among his subjects, transforming even the ignorant and un-

---

[56] R. Stoneman, *Alexander the Great* (London and New York 1997) 66.

[57] Lucianus, Quomodo hist. conscrib. 40. On the different styles of Onesicritus and Aristobulus, see: L. Pearson, *The Lost Histories of Alexander the Great* (Chico 1983 = reprint of 1960 ed. in Am. Phil. Assoc. Monogr. Ser. 20) 86–7, 97–99, 150–87; U. Wilcken, Alexander der Grosse und die indischen Gymnosophisten, *Sitzungsber. d. Preuss. Ak. d. Wiss. Phil.-Hist. Klasse* 1923, 174–7.

[58] This and the following quotations are taken from Strabo, Geogr. 15.1:63–5.

willing.[59] Mandanis moreover appreciates the overall congeniality between Indian and Greek principles, remarking that the Greeks are "sound-minded in general". Onesicritus' Indians feel alienated from the Greeks only with regard to their clothes. Their broad-brimmed hats and boots provoke Calanus to laughter and open criticism.[60] But these are clearly external features, which cannot seriously challenge the overall picture of harmony between East and West which Alexander has established.

Aristobolus, by contrast, shifts the focus of the story to the reserved nobility and national self-awareness of the Indian philosophers. He introduces them as well respected authorities who enjoy special privileges in their homeland and serve as advisors. Two of them "came up to the table of Alexander, ate dinner standing, and taught him a lesson in endurance" (Strabo, Geogr. 15.1:61). The Indians emerge here as representatives of indigenous values superior to the conqueror. Aristobolus moreover describes a conflict which resurfaces in Philo's account: should the Indian gymnosophists follow Alexander on his expedition and become his personal counsellors? While the younger philosopher initially accepts the invitation, yet quickly returns home, the elder, probably Calanus, accompanied the king.[61] Aristobolus frowns upon Calanus' behaviour and dismisses it as sheer opportunism. The younger philosopher, on the other hand, is praised for "showing a far greater self-mastery than the elder" (Strabo, Geogr. 15.1:61). Megasthenes, another early historian of Alexander, similarly criticized Calanus, whose name he explicitly mentions, for accompanying Alexander. He insists that he was "a man whom the wise men themselves regarded as most uncontrolled in his desires, ... because he deserted the happiness which they had, while he served a master other than God" (Arrian, Anab. 7.2:4). Calanus emerges here as an unauthentic gymnosophist whom even his own colleagues criticize. The true ethos of the Indian philosophers was instead

---

[59] Plut., *Fortune of Alexander* 328–9 reflects the same idea: Alexander is praised here as a politician who provided philosophy with practical authority. He is said to have civilized countless savage tribes and therefore to be rightly regarded as "a very great philosopher".

[60] This image has given rise to earlier scholarly speculations about the Cynic origins of Onesicritus' story, see: Wilcken, Indische Gymnosophisten 175–77; T.S. Brown, Onesicritus. A Study in Hellenistic Historiography (Berkeley 1949); R. Merkelbach, *Die Quellen des Griechischen Alexanderromans* (München 1954 = Zetemata 9) 50–3; W. Hoffmann, *Das literarische Porträt Alexanders des Grossen im griechischen und römischen Altertum* (Leipzig 1907) 7–14; recently this interpretation has rightly been criticized and replaced by suggestions of the story's Indian origins, see: Pearson, Lost Histories 98–9, R. Stoneman, Who are the Brahmans? Indian Lore and Cynic Doctrine in Palladius' *De Bragmanibus* and its Models, *CQ* 44.2 (1994) 505–6; idem, Naked Philosophers: the Brahmans in the Alexander Historians and the Alexander Romance, *JHS* 115 (1995) 99–114; A. B. Bosworth, *Alexander and the East. The Tragedy of Triumph* (Oxford 1996) 94–6, on the other hand, stresses that the image of the Brahmans as a class of philosophers reflects a strictly Greek image, which does not conform to the social reality of the Indian caste system.

[61] On the identity of this courtier, see: Bosworth, Alexander and the East 92–7; U. Wilcken, *Alexander the Great* (New York 1967, transl. of Germ. orig.) 180–1, 257

personified by Dandamis who refused Alexander's invitation.[62] The reasons given for the Indian's resistance are especially relevant to Philo's story. Dandamis is said to criticize Alexander as arrogant and expecting the same divine honours as Zeus. The king is exposed as a camouflage who has nothing of authentic value to offer. Alexander's response to such severe criticism from his subject is nevertheless generous. He "had no mind to compel him, realizing that the man was indeed free" (Arrian, Anab. 7.2:2–4). Aristobolus' and Megasthenes' accounts of Alexander's encounter with the Indian gymnosophists thus convey an image of a disliked foreign conqueror who is morally inferior to his subjects.

Philo's story reflects precisely the same perspective. He, too, presents Alexander as an arrogant "enemy sovereign" whose company is rightly shunned by the Indian philosophers. Calanus plays in this context an unprecedented role. He is not only freed from the charge of betraying his homeland, which Aristobolus had levelled against him, but emerges now as the paramount defender of indigenous values vis-à-vis Alexander. Plutarch also spoke favourably of Calanus' opposition to the Macedonian. He mentions him as a teacher of Alexander who criticized his imperialism in a parable (Plut., Alex. 65:8). Plutarch may have relied here on an earlier Alexandrian source. If this is the case, a tradition sympathetically focusing on Calanus may already have been available to Philo. His portrait of the Indian gymnosophist nevertheless remains distinct. Philo set his own accents and created a new version of the old story. Calanus and Alexander have under his pen become ciphers for a broader cultural distinction between "the Greeks" and "us". This distinction was formulated in conspicuously Roman terms, which appear to have been anticipated in Cicero's fragment about Alexander and Calanus. We get here nothing but a glimpse of Alexander, who generally suffers from a highly negative reputation in Cicero's work, turning to Calanus when the latter was about to burn himself on the pire.[63] Directed "to speak if he wished to say anything to him", Calanus replied: "thank you, nothing, except that I shall see you very soon" (De Div. 1:47). Cicero stresses the accuracy of Calanus' prophecy and his heroism by a dry comment of his own: "so it turned out, for Alexander died in Babylon a few days later" (ibid.).

Philo juxtaposes Calanus to Alexander mainly on two grounds: culture and politics. The Indian represents Eastern honesty and freedom, while Alexander is an ostentatious Greek tyrant. The king is not genuinely interested in philoso-

---

[62] Dandamis' story appears in Arrian, Anab. 7. 2:2 before Megasthenes is mentioned. It is therefore possible that Arrian relied for this information on other sources.

[63] For details on Cicero's Alexander image, see especially De Off. 1:90, where Cicero criticizes his illusionary arrogance, recommending instead that "the higher we are placed, the more humbly should we walk" and moreover speaks of him as "often infamously bad"; and De Rep. 3:24, where Cicero compares the villany of Alexander's imperialism to that of pirates; see also: Gruen, Alexander 187.

phy, but merely wishes "to exhibit to the Grecian world a specimen of the barbarians' wisdom". He offers nothing but "the prospect of winning great fame" and attempts to compel his subjects when encountering resistance. Unlike Aristobulus and Megasthenes, Philo is not concerned with the issue of loyalty to the Indian homeland. He rather shifts the focus of the story to more general cultural as well as political matters: ostentation versus authenticity, the Greek world in relation to barbarian wisdom, tyranny vis-à-vis simple freedom. These issues are further brought out in a letter which Philo has Calanus send to Alexander (Lib. 96):

> Calanus to Alexander
> Your friends urge you to apply violence and compulsion to the philosophers of India. These friends, however, have never even in their dreams seen what we do. Bodies you will transport from place to place, but souls you will not compel to do what they will not do, any more than force bricks or sticks to talk. Fire causes the greatest trouble and ruin to living bodies: we are superior to this, we burn ourselves alive. There is no king, no ruler, who will compel us to do what we do not freely wish to do. We are not like those philosophers of the Greeks who practice words for a festal assembly. With us deeds accord with words and words with deeds. Deeds pass swiftly and words have short-lived power: virtues secure to us blessedness and freedom.

While the Alexander Romance also preserves a letter in which the Indians warn the approaching Macedonian not to use violence against them,[64] Philo has added the detail about the "philosophers of the Greeks who practice words for a festal assembly". In this way he has associated Alexander with the stereotypical image of the Greeks which we have encountered above. Calanus, by contrast, who insists upon the accordance of words with deeds defends exactly the same value as Philo's Therapeutae and Essenes. We saw above that the practical prudence of the latter had been contrasted to the "wordiness of the Greeks" (Lib. 88). The teacher of the Therapeutae did not seek "a reputation for clever oratory", but wished to gain and transmit true insight (Cont. 75). Philo had moreover accused "the Greeks" of celebrating Heracleitus' alleged discoveries "so laudly" and ostentatiously (Her. 214). These constructs of the Greek Other in relation to "us" had, as we saw above, been directly inspired by a distinctly Roman discourse on them. Philo has adopted an ethnic boundary of the Romans and applied it to Jewish identity. This same boundary is also brought to bear on the Eastern Alexander traditions, which are now assimilated to Philo's overall construction of the Greeks in a Roman spirit.

The significance of Philo's interpretation of Alexander can hardly be overestimated. In the stronghold of support for the Macedonian his legacy has been reversed. The anti-Roman invective which had been attached to Alexander by

---

[64] Pseudo-Callisthenes 3:5 (ed. C. Müller, *Reliqua Arriani et Scriptorum de Rebus Alexandri M. Fragmenta (collegit); Pseudo-Callisthenis Historiam Fabulosam* (Paris 1877); see also: Merkelbach, Alexanderroman 119; Wilcken, Indische Gymnosophisten 176.

Timagenes and others is now turned against him. The pro-Greek message associated with his person is replaced by a Roman-style critique of him. The figure of Alexander thus comes to symbolize Judeo-Roman rather than Greek superiority. The hero has turned anti-hero. Appreciating Alexander from Philo's perspective, the reader gains distance from the Greek heritage, while simultaneously becoming aware of the value of his own tradition.

The extent to which Philo's interpretation of the Macedonain king inscribes him and his readers into the contemporary Roman discourse can be appreciated by a comparison with his treatment by Seneca. Alexander personified in the latter's eyes a tyranny completely alien to Rome. Seneca accused him of "beastly" brutality, "savagery" and unlimited greed. Alexander was in his view a "puffed-up creature", who gave "most stupid" speeches and robbed the world he had conquered.[65] Alexander was indeed a "madman ... incapable of conceiving any plan that was not grandiose".[66] These traits are contrasted to the personality of Callisthenes, a man "of outstanding intelligence" who did "not submit to the rage of the king" (N.Q. 6.22:2). Alexander's murder of Callisthenes and Clitus signified the victory of barbarian tyranny over sound reason. Seneca feared that a similar fate may befall contemporary Rome (De Ira 3.17:1–18:1):

Such was the ferocity of barbarian kings when in anger – men who had no contact with learning or the culture of letters. But I shall now show you a king from the very bosom of Aristotle, even Alexander, who in the midst of a feast with his own hand stabbed Clitus, his dearest friend, with whom he had grown up, because he withheld his flattery and was reluctant to transform himself from a Macedonian and a free man into a Persian slave ... Would to heaven that the examples of such cruelty had been confined to foreigners, and that along with other vices from abroad the barbarity of torture and such venting of anger had not been imported into the practices of Romans!

Philo obviously uses the image of Alexander in a similar way to Seneca to define the Other. Both writers dismiss him as a tyrant lacking any genuine interest in learning and philosophy. Both project onto him everything that is contrary to "our" own pristine values. While Seneca focuses on political issues and stresses the barbarian dimension of Alexander's shortcomings, Philo gives equal weight to cultural matters and suggests his distinctly Greek weaknesses. The aspects which Philo raised had special relevance for Jewish identity in contemporary Alexandria.

Philo's portrait of Alexander initially implies that the Greeks were denied any significant political role. Their idealized leader has been exposed as a fraud, who could certainly not provide hope for the future. Philo stresses on other occasions, too, that the empires of Hellas and Macedonia belong to a

---

[65] Ep. 94:62–3; N.Q. 2:praef. 5; Clem. 1.25:1–26:4; Benef. 2.16:1–2 "tumidissimum animal!"; see also: Willrich, Caligula 459–60; Fears, Alexander the Great 121–3.
[66] Benef. 2.16:1 "vesanus et qui nihil animo nisi grande conciperet".

bygone world. Their fall from power has even become proverbial. Philo mentions their change of fortune in rhetorical passages where he laments the vicissitudes of external goods. The Greeks are listed together with the Persians, Lybians and others who were once powerful, but are now defunct (Immut. 173–5):

Greece was once at its zenith, but the Macedonians took away its power. Macedonia flourished in its turn, but when it was divided into portions it weakened until it was utterly extinguished.

The rise and fall of Hellas and the Hellenistic empire serve here as a rhetorical *exemplum*. Their passing glory demonstrates how the whole civilized world is "tossed up and down and kept in turmoil" (Immut. 175). Philo was aware of the topical implications of his views (Jos. 135–6):

The Macedonians in their day of success flourished so greatly that they held the dominion over the whole inhabitable world, but now they pay to the tax-collectors the yearly tributes imposed by their masters. Where is the house of the Ptolemies, and the fame of the several diadochs, whose light once shone to the utmost boundaries of land and sea?

Philo stresses here with a sense of *Schadenfreude* the submission of both Macedonians and Ptolemies to their new masters, the Romans. He clearly lacks empathy for the Greek powers who have lost in the historical race for supremacy. His rhetorical question "where is the house of the Ptolemies?" must have been especially painful for many Alexandrians. Not everybody can have accepted Roman taxation as happily as the brother of Alexander the Alabarch. Philo's rhetoric thus seems exceptional in his Alexandrian environment and clearly echoes Roman gestures. It is significant that Curtius equally celebrated the replacement of Alexander's empire by Rome (H.A. 10.9:1–6). Augustus himself had set the tone of the discourse by a famous bon-mot. After his conquest of Egypt he "declined to view the remains of the Ptolemies though the Alexandrians were extremely eager to show them" (Dio, 51.16:5). His explanation, according to Suetonius, was that he did not wish to see mere corpses (Aug. 18:1). Augustus thus refused to recognize the living memory of the Ptolemies and pointed the Alexandrians to the irreversible death of their admired leaders. He made it clear that as far as he was concerned the Ptolemies belonged to a bygone world and were utterly meaningless for present times. As Willrich with characteristic terseness put it: "Die Ptolemäer sollten tot sein und tot bleiben, so wollte es Augustus" (Caligula 91). Philo's comments about the demise of the Ptolemies repeat this Augustan gesture. He, too, wanted the Ptolemies to be dead and to remain dead. The Greeks had in his view not survived as a political entity, but only as a culture.

The consequences of Philo's position can hardly be overestimated. He denied the political dimension of Hellenism and severed it as much as possible from the contemporary Egyptian context. Philo systematically ignored the

Greek identity and culture of many figures, such as Isidorus and Lampo who were involved in the administration of the Alexandrian gymnasium, and treated them as mere Egyptians (Flac. 130, 138). Furthermore Philo never even mentioned Apion, the head of the Alexandrian delegation to Gaius, who was a Greek citizen of Egyptian descent and a leading scholar of Homer.[67] His Greek identity was apparently too known and too established to be altogether denied. Philo therefore found it convenient to commit his memory to oblivion. Only once does Philo mention "Greek men of letters" in a clearly Greco-Egyptian context, namely when he refers to the negative "Exodus stories" which he is about to correct in his biography of Moses (Mos. 1:1–3).

While the Egyptians were denied Greek identity and culture, the Romans were identified with it. We saw in the previous chapter that Philo associates the positve role of hellenization with the Romans. Augustus had brought civilization and culture to primitive nations. This interpretation not only enabled Philo to accept Roman dominion in the Greek East, but also to define the place of the Jews in relation to the Greeks and Hellenism in contemporary Alexandria. His sense both of affinity with Greek culture and superiority over it aligned him with the leading class of his country.

---

[67] See: V. Pirenne-Delforge, Apion, in: Der Neue Pauly (1996) 1:845–7; see also: Willrich, Caligula 400–1, 413–4; Smallwood, Legatio 227, 246; Goudriaan, Ethnical Strategies 87–90; regarding the implications of this phenomenon for Philo's views on the Egyptians, see above chapter two.

Part Two

# Jewish Culture

# 6. Transforming new-born Children into Jewish Adults

> "For all men guard their own customs, but this is especially true of the Jewish nation. Holding that the laws are oracles vouchsafed by God and having been trained in this doctrine from their earliest years, they carry the likenesses of the commandments enshrined in their souls"
>
> (Leg. 210)

In this part of the book we shall investigate how Philo's construction of Jewish identity translates into cultural discourse.[1] The nature of his position on culture can initially be appreciated by examining his views on childhood, since children are born with an immense, yet unspecified potential which needs to be shaped by culture. Children are, for example, born with the ability to speak, but need to learn a specific language in order to articulate themselves. Early impressions are therefore formative. They create deep-rooted patterns of thought and behaviour which mould the rest of life. To put it in Geertz' terms, man only becomes a full human being by absorbing the specific features of the culture he or she happens to grow up in.[2] Man as such does not exist, only specific persons formed by a particular environment. In light of these insights it becomes clear that raising children is an important means of transmitting culture.[3] Each society and family perpetuate in their children the structures of meaning they have created for themselves. An investigation into notions of childhood and child rearing therefore reveals the patterns of culture embraced by a particular society, family or individual writer.

---

[1] For further details on culture as a social construct and the relationship between culture and identity, see above Introduction.

[2] Geertz, Interpretation of Cultures 33–7; for more details on Geertz' theory of culture, see above Introduction. My interest in Philo's notion of childhood thus differs from the fine studies of A. Reinhartz, who interpreted aspects of the subject from a primarily historical perspective, see: A. Reinhartz, Parents and Children: a Philonic Perspective, in: S.J.D. Cohen (ed.), *The Jewish Family in Antiquity* (Atlanta 1993 = Brown Judaic Studies 289) 61–88; eadem, Philo On Infanticide, *SPhA* 4 (1992) 42–58.

[3] This insight also guides modern scholarship on children's literature in a cultural context, see especially: Z. Shavit, *Poetics of Children Literature* (Athen, Georgia 1986); eadem, *A Past Without Shadow. The Construction of the Past Image in the German "Story" for Children* (Hebrew, Tel Aviv 1999).

Philo was highly aware of the key role childhood played in the formation of human beings and the transmission of culture. He realized that new-born children lack specific characteristics and are to a large extent formed by their environment. He spoke about the "age of childhood" as a time when the soul is still fluid and shapeless.[4] During the first seven years of life, he insisted, the child "possesses only the simplest elements of the soul, a soul which closely resembles smooth wax and has not yet received any impression of good or evil".[5] It is only in the second stage of life, during adolescence, that the "soul begins to associate with evils".[6] On the other hand, early imprints on the soul were in his view lasting. Philo acknowledged an intrinsic connection between a person's upbringing and his or her later character. Pharaoh, for example, was blind because his "soul from the earliest years was weighed down with the pride of many generations" (Mos. 1:88). The Egyptian slave Helicorn was similarly corrupt and hated the Jews because he had "right from the cradle" been exposed to the slanderous rumours of "the noisiest element in the city [of Alexandria]" (Leg. 170). Philo considered the Egyptians to be a particular example of a general tendency. Virtually all nations, he believed, neglected proper child education. He complained that they "destroy the souls of their offspring right from the cradle by failing to imprint on their still tender souls truth-giving conceptions of the one, the truly existing God" (Spec. 1:313).

The Jews alone were in Philo's view an exception. He believed that they paid careful attention to child rearing and inculcated the right values from the earliest stage. Philo proudly asserted that the Jews trained their offspring from the cradle "to acknowledge one God who is the Father and Maker of the world" (Leg. 115). "The diligence which parents devote to rearing their children", he continued, "has trained us in this practice [of being peaceable] from the very beginning" (Leg. 230). These sentences express Philo's confidence in the special purpose of Jewish culture. He expected the Jews to be devoted to transmit-

---

[4] ἐν ἡλικίᾳ τῇ παιδικῇ (Her. 295); see also: Opif. 103–5; regarding Philo's division of life into different ages, see also: A. Mendelson, *Secular Education in Philo of Alexandria* (Cincinnati 1982 = Monographs of the Hebrew Union College 7) 40–2; J. Laporte, The Ages of Life in Philo of Alexandria, *SBLSP* 25 (1986) 279–86, who, however, mistakenly compared Philo to Augustine, suggesting that the former also believed in the notion of original sin.

[5] Her. 294; see also Lib. 15. Childhood is for Philo furthermore a time when "the reason is not yet able to see good and evil ..., but is still slumbering, its eyes closed as if in deep sleep" (Congr. 81); see also Lib. 160 where the child is said to possess a naked soul which "as yet got nothing of either kind, neither that which enslaves nor that which establishes freedom"; similarly in All. 2:53; Praem. 62.

[6] Her. 295–6; Philo bases himself in this context on LXX Gen. 8:21, which refers to man's wickedness from his youth (ἐκ νεότητος); see also: Congr. 82 . The only place where Philo interprets the Biblical expression "youth" as a reference to the swaddling age is of dubious textual quality (Q.G. 2:54; see R. Marcus' comments *ad. loc*).

ting their particular values and customs. As he once put it, parents should "find the consummation of their own happiness in the high excellence of their children" (Spec. 2:236). They should be gladdened "by nothing so much as by the virtues of their children" (Somn. 2:178).

Philo highlighted the importance of child education by grounding it in religion. Assuming that the child's life was divinely generated, he demanded not only that its life be preserved, but by extension also that it be brought up in a God-pleasing way. Raising children was thus not merely a human virtue, but a divinely given obligation.[7] Philo was not concerned with the experience Plutarch called "the joy we have in our children".[8] He rather cared about the transmission of culture which would transform new-born children into authentic Jews.

Ex. 21:22–3 provided Philo with an occasion to outline his views on child rearing. To be sure, the Masoretic text has nothing to do with this subject. It discusses the injury of a pregnant woman in light of the question whether the injury had fatal consequences for her. The possible abortion of her foetus is treated merely under the rubric of compensating the father for his loss of property.[9] The LXX transformed these Biblical verses into a law protecting the unborn foetus. The verse in the Greek translation no longer focused on the violation of the mother's body and the father's property rights, but on the injury

---

[7] This implied a considerable degree of child-orientation. As we shall see, however, Philo's position must not be confused with the modern psychological idea of cherishing individual personality in children. Cf. L. deMause, The Evolution of Childhood, in: idem (ed.), *The History of Childhood* (New York 1974) 1–73,who argued that attitudes towards children must be measured by modern psychoanalytic standards. A society is thus child-oriented only if it shows true empathy. This means that both society at large and individual parents should seek to fulfil each child's special needs and support the growth of personality. DeMause suggested that a distinct humanity gradually developed such empathy and increasingly moved away from the view that children are their parents' exclusive property to be treated as mere objects. Child exposure and beating were identified as characteristics of the primitive attitude, whereas modern parents are expected to see themselves as supportive companions to their children's individual development. By these standards Philo can hardly be described as child-oriented. Although he was the first known author in antiquity to reject in principal child exposure, he advocated severe beating and even the death penalty as educational measures. More importantly, he lacked an awareness of individual personality in the modern sense and did not appreciate each human being as a unique configuration of traits which emerged in singular psychological circumstances. He rather conceived of human beings as character types who must be judged against the background of objective norms and virtues; Philo's views in this matter were widely shared in antiquity, see especially: Ch.Gill, The Question of Character and Personality in Greek Tragedy, *PT* 7 (1986) 251–73; idem, The question of character-development: Plutarch and Tacitus, *CQ* 33.2 (1983) 469–87; cf. Ch. Pelling, Childhood and Personality in Greek Biography, in: idem (ed.), *Characterization and Individuality in Greek Literature* (Oxford 1990) 213–44.

[8] Plut., De Amore Prolis 495C, 496C.

[9] The question of the foetus' own value and status is not raised. Unlike Hittite law, the Biblical legislator did not determine the amount of the fine in relation to the age of the foetus; see also: N.M. Sarna, *The JPS Torah Commentary. Exodus* (Philadelphia – New York 1991) 125.

done to the foetus itself. The LXX distinguished in this context between an unformed foetus and one that had already assumed human shape. The former was treated in the same way as in the Masoretic text, namely as mere property. If it was, however, "fully shaped" (ἐξεικονισμένον) and had assumed human form, the offender was liable to the death penalty on account of his having caused the abortion and the death of a being already considered human. Abortion was tantamount to murder. The neologism ἐξεικονίζειν suggests that the LXX associated the human features of the unborn foetus with its creation in the image of God. According to Gen. 9:6 the killing of such a human creature constitutes murder and is liable to the death penalty.[10] Procedures of criminal law applying to adults have thus been extended to the foetus who already looks human. The latter's status has been considerably been improved. In contrast to the Masoretic text, the LXX protects the foetus. No connection, however, is yet made to questions of man's destiny and culture. It was Philo who made this important contribution.

While maintaining the Septuagintal distinction between a humanly-shaped and an unformed foetus, Philo introduced a completely new perspective to the discussion. He insisted for the first time that an abortion at any stage of the pregnancy constituted a criminal interference with the process of nature. The protection of the foetus thus no longer depended on its developmental stage. Whether human-looking or not, it was to be saved. The injurer of a pregnant woman, who caused the abortion of her foetus, is accused by Philo of "obstructing the artifex Nature in her creative work of bringing to life the fairest of living beings, man".[11] It is striking that Philo no longer refers to the father's rights of compensation. The issue of his "living property" has become obsolete.[12] The nature of the offense is explained with particular clarity in the context of a humanly shaped foetus. Philo insists here that the injurer must die "for that which answers to this description is a human being, which he has destroyed in the workshop of Nature who judges that the hour has not yet come for bringing it out into the light" (Spec. 3:109).

Philo moreover links the issue of accidental abortion to intended abortion and child exposure. This enables him to distinguish a particular Jewish custom and contrast it to the norms of other nations. While child exposure is prohibited among the Jews, this "sacriligious practice" has come to be regarded with complacence by "many other nations through their ingrained inhumanity" (Spec. 3:110). Philo derived the prohibition of child exposure, which is nowhere explic-

---

[10] On the exegetical connection between LXX Ex. 21: 22–3, Gen. 1:26 and Gen. 9:6, see also: A. Le Boulluec et P. Sandevoir, *La Bible d'Alexandrie. L'Exode* (Paris 1989) 2:219–20; R. A. Freund, *Understanding Jewish Ethics* (San Francisco 1990) 245–7.

[11] Spec. 3:108. To be sure, Philo also speaks of the injurer in the Biblical sense as someone who has committed an "outrage (ὕβρις)". The term ὕβρις is used here in its technical legal sense, i.e. covering all the more serious senses of injuries done to the person (Liddell and Scott, Lexicon 9th ed. p. 1841).

itly stated in the Pentateuch, by a complex exegesis of Ex. 21:22–3. His argumentation relies on the previous discussion of accidental abortion, the conclusions of which he extends to the graver offense of child exposure (Spec. 3:111–2):

For if on behalf of the child not yet brought to the birth by the appointed conclusion of the regular period thought has to be taken to save it from disaster at the hands of the evil-minded (μὴ ἐξ ἐπιβουλῆς τι δεινὸν πάθοι), surely still more true is this of the full-born babe sent out as it were to settle in the new homeland assigned to mankind, there to partake of the gifts of Nature ... If the guardians of the children rob them of these blessings (τοσούτων ... ἀποστεροῦντες ἀγαθῶν), they must rest assured that they are breaking the laws of Nature and stand self-condemned on the gravest charges, love of pleasure, hatred of men, murder and, the worst abomination of all, murder of their own children.

This is in several respects a remarkable passage. It is initially significant that Philo's gradual move from accidental abortion by injury to child exposure includes also intended abortion. This clearly emerges from his reference to the "hands of the evil-minded" who have prematurely terminated pregnancy. Philo obviously deals here with malicious intention rather than accidental injury. Abortion is thus included in the offenses against Nature from which the Jews are called upon to abstain.[13] This conclusion is supported by another statement in an allegorical context. Philo speaks here about the impious mind "which has either failed to welcome divinely-bestowed power to bear children, or, after welcoming it, has subsequently chosen to bring about an abortion" (Det. 147). Philo condemns such mental abortions in no uncertain terms, suggesting once more that one must not interfere in the growth of the "germs of life" he has been granted.

Philo's position on abortion was exceptional at the time. In contemporary society abortion was permitted on condition of paternal consent.[14] The different philosophical schools which argued over the desirability of the practice considered various reasons, none of which, however, corresponded to Philo's fundamental objections. While the Pythagoreans opposed abortion because the em-

---

[12] This is so even though Philo once mentions the father's compensation in a metaphoric context (Congr. 137).

[13] Philo's argument presumably implied also a prohibition on contraceptives. While Philo never makes an explicit statement on this issue, his reservations towards contraceptives can nevertheless be gathered from his comparison between those despising rationality and those who render the rational mind "barren and unproductive of noble doings" by sterilizing and blocking it (Somn. 1:106–7). Philo did not even anticipate the use of contraceptives in order to delay pregnancy in cases of wives who were still minors and thus likely to be physically incapable of sustaining a pregnancy and giving birth. Rather, he regarded the frequent deaths of (usually very young) women in labour as a natural part of the female condition (Aet. 65). On contraceptive methods in the Ancient World see: J. M. Riddle, *Contraception and Abortion from the Ancient World to the Renaissance* (Cambridge MA 1992) 16–23; Garland, Way of Life 23–5; J. Preuss, *Biblical and Talmudic Medicine* (Northvale and London 1993, Germ. orig. transl. and ed. by F. Rosner) 381, 406–18.

[14] See also: Riddle, Contraception; J. F. Gardner, *Women in Roman Law and Society* (London and Sydney 1986) 158–9; Garland, Way of Life 53–55.

bryo was endowed with a human soul from the moment of its conception, the Stoics generally approved of it even during the later stages of pregnancy, holding that the embryo was part of its mother until birth.[15] Aristotle recommended the performance of abortion in the early stages of pregnancy "before the embryo has developed sensory perception and life".[16] Philo, by contrast, argued from the transcendental principle of nature. In his view it was neither the human look nor the human soul of the foetus which commanded its survival, but the fact that it was part of the divine scheme of creation to which parents were answerable. He thus suggested an overall religious and cultural purpose for child rearing, the meaning of which is further explained in the context of child exposure.

In the above-quoted passage Philo objects to child exposure mainly on the grounds that every new-born infant is entitled to enjoy the gifts of Nature. Children are thus invested with specific rights which must be respected by their parents. Those who expose their offspring are "robbing them of these blessings" and fail in their role as guardians. Parents do not possess absolute rights of property over their children, but receive them as a kind of deposit. They are consequently accountable for their behaviour and must provide for their offspring in a way that accords with Nature. Departure from these norms equals "love of pleasure, hatred of men, murder and, the worst abomination of all, murder of their own children".

Philo returns to the topic of child exposure in Vir. 128–33, this time with renewed emphasis on nature. He now derives the "Mosaic" prohibition from Lev. 22:27, which protects new born kids and lambs for seven days from being slaughtered for sacrificial purposes. Philo argues that this law was motivated by the "idea of moderation and gentleness" even in the sphere of non-rational animals, which must not be snatched away from their mothers (Vir. 125–6). This Biblical context provides him with additional motifs for his rhetoric against child exposure. He now stresses that the natural bond between parents and children resembles that between animals.[17] In order to highlight nature's urge, Philo initially draws attention to the stressful biological consequences of child exposure for the mother. If deprived of her offspring immediately after delivery, she will be left with "breasts, whose flowing fountain is obstructed through lack of its suckling, [and which will] grow indurated and strained by the weight of the milk coagulated in them and suffer a painful oppression".[18]

---

[15] See also: Garland, Way of Life 53–59; Riddle, Contraception 62–64.

[16] Pol. 335b24–6; on Aristotle's theories of foetal development, see especially: G.A. 2:1:734a.

[17] For the use of similar comparisons among Epicureans and Stoics, see: J. Brunschwig, The cradle argument in Epicureanism and Stoicism, in: M. Schofield and G. Striker (eds.), *The Norms of Nature. Studies in Hellenistic Ethics* (Cambridge and Paris 1986) 113–44.

[18] Vir.128; Philo's emphasis on the mother's biology is especially remarkable in comparison to Xenophon who praised her exceptional patience and intuition into the infant's often unclear desires (Memor. 2:2.5).

Maternal milk is furthermore praised as "the fountain which Nature has rained into the breasts" and as a "happily timed aliment which flows so gently fostering the tender growth of every creature".[19] Philo insists that it provides perfect nourishment for the new-born child, who is thus saved from "those bitter mistresses, hunger and thirst" (Vir. 130).

These statements draw a forceful analogy between the new-born offspring of humans and animals. Both, Philo suggests, survive thanks to their mother's suckling and must therefore not be severed from their natural source of nourishment.[20] This argument is striking because it implies that mothers generally breastfed, while Philo himself assumed the pervasive employment of wet-nurses. Upper-class women would not perform this time-consuming task themselves.[21] In contrast to Musonius and Plutarch, Philo did not encourage mothers to breastfeed.[22] He had no objections to wet-nurses. His argument about the mother's physical pain after her baby's exposure is thus mostly theoretical. The analogy between animals and humans was evidently not as close as Philo suggested.[23] The argument itself, however, must not be dismissed on these grounds. By referring to the nursing of new-born animals Philo wished to illustrate that raising one's children accords with nature. He thus suggested in an almost metaphorical way that children have a natural right to their parents' love and care (Vir. 133):

Can you not see that our all-excellent lawgiver was at pains to ensure that even in the case of non-rational animals, the offspring should not be separated from their mother so long as it is being suckled? Still more for your sake, good sirs, was that order given, that if nature does not, instruction may teach you the duty of family love. Learn it from the sight of lambs and kids, who are not hindered from feasting on abundant supplies of what they need.

Philo's argumentation from Nature in the context of family relations has often been identified as Stoic.[24] Cicero indeed stressed that the Stoics were the first

---

[19] Vir. 129–30. On other occasions Philo similarly asserts that "Nature has provided every mother as a most essential endowment with gushing breasts, thus preparing in advance food for the child to be born" (Opif. 133) and that already towards the end of pregnancy "springs of milk" are produced (Plant. 15).

[20] Philo disagreed in this respect with Soranus, who argued that mother's milk immediately after birth is not healthy, since it was produced by a weakened body (*Gynecology* 89). Soranus therefore recommended the use of a wet-nurse for the first twenty days of a child's life after which its mother could nurse it.

[21] See e.g.: Somn. 2:204; Spec. 2:233. In Palestine breastfeeding seems to have been both a greater economic necessity and a more developed social ideal, see: T. Ilan, *Jewish Women in Greco-Roman Palestine. An Inquiry into Image and Status* (Tübingen 1995 = Texte und Studien zum antiken Judentum 44) 119–21.

[22] Musonius, frgm. 3 apud Stobaeus, Anth. 2.31 126 = ed. Lutz 42–3; Plut., De Lib. Educ. 3.

[23] Philo himself occasionally admitted that surrogate figures could cherish motherly feelings towards someone else's child or a findling; see for example his comments on the nurse (Aet. 67) and Pharaoh's daughter (Mos. 1:15).

[24] See e.g. Heinemann, Bildung 254–5.

philosophers who taught "that the love of parents for their offspring is a provision of Nature".[25] This could in their view be gathered from two facts: the constitution of the human body which is obviously designed to procreate and the attitude of lower animals towards their offspring (De Fin. 3:62). Cicero himself stressed that "when we observe the labour that they [lower animals] spend on bearing and rearing their young, we seem to be listening to the actual voice of Nature". Therefore, he continued, "we derive from Nature herself the impulse to love those to whom we have given birth".[26] The argument of the Stoics, however, applied to surviving children only. Nature did in their view not protect unborn or new-born life. Indeed, child exposure was legally practiced in the Roman Empire until 374 C.E. During the first century C.E., the Greek population of Roman Egypt in particular frequently exposed their offspring on the assumption that they were under their father's absolute authority.[27] Children still needed to be officially acknowledged before they legally counted as their father's offspring.[28] Child exposure before this formal act was acceptable. Even the Stoic philosopher Musonius, who in the second half of the first century began to criticize child exposure in Rome, did not argue on the same fundamental grounds as Philo. He rather spoke in the spirit of Augustan family policy about the usefulness of large families both for the city and the individual.[29] In this context he once vaguely referred to the responsibility adults have towards Zeus "guardian of the family".[30] Musonius obviously cherished the ideal of "raising many children" which required a limitation of child exposure. He was not yet concerned, however, about the rights of every single child to survival.[31]

What then prompted Philo to extend the traditional Stoic argument about parents' natural love for their surviving children to every unborn and new-born life?[32] To answer this we have to look at Philo's interpretation of Gen. 1:26–8.

---

[25]  De Fin. 4:17; see also Cic., Ep. Att. 7:2

[26]  "sic apparet a natura ipsa ... ut eos quos genuerimus amemus" (De Fin. 3:62); see also De Fin. 1:23.

[27]  On the plentiful evidence of child-exposure among Egyptian Greeks around the turn of the era, see especially: W. V. Harris, Child-Exposure in the Roman Empire, *JRS* 84 (1994) 7–8. Harris also mentions Philo as the "first explicitly disapproving voice" (ibid. 15), subsequently followed by Musonius and other Stoics.

[28]  Garland, Way of Life 84–93; Gardner, Women 143–56.

[29]  Musonius, frgm. 15 apud Stobaeus, Floril. 79.51 = ed. Lutz 96–101. On Augustan family policy, see especially: Dixon, Roman Family 119–23, 69–70; Dio 56.3:3–5, 56.8:2–3. In Vir. 132 Philo expressed himself in similar terms, stressing the detrimental effect of child exposure on the demography of the cities.

[30]  Both quotations are taken from Musonius, frgm. 15 l. 25–7 (transl. Lutz).

[31]  Lutz, 98, l. 1–2; see also Lutz, 97, l. 25–6.

[32]  The novelty of Philo's argumentation must not be obscured by the fact that he himself refers in support of his ideas to the doctrines "current both among natural philosophers whose life study is concerned with the theoretical side of knowledge and also among physicians of the highest repute" (Spec. 3:117). All of these agree, he insists, that the new born child is no longer an integral part of his mother, but has become an independent creature.

These verses dealing with the creation of Adam in God's image provided him with important ideas concerning the existential status of every individual. The above-quoted passage from Spec. 3:111–2 seems to have been inspired by it. Philo refers there to the "new homeland" for which every new-born infant is destined. This homeland is the earth which provides for all its needs. Philo emphasizes nature's gifts which are drawn "from earth and water and air and heaven". While nature grants contemplation of the heavenly things, she assigns to man "sovereignty and dominion" over earthly things (Spec. 3:111). These formulations echo Gen. 1:28 where Adam is commanded to rule over creation. Philo interpreted this verse in the following sense:[33]

> God, when He made man partaker of kinship with Himself in mind and reason best of all gifts, did not begrudge him the other gifts either, but made ready for him beforehand all things in the world … since it was His will that when man came into existence he should be at a loss for none of the means of living and of living well.

It is highly significant that the abundant beneficience which Philo assigned in Spec. 3:111–2 to Nature is now attributed to God Himself (Opif. 79). This suggests that these two terms were for him in certain respects synonymous. "Nature" could, in other words, represent God's providential care in the world. The close proximity, if not identity of these two, is further confirmed by Vir. 128–33, where Philo explicitly identifies Nature's abundant provisions for the new-born infant with divine gifts (Vir. 133):

> Nature has provided this abundance in places best suited for the purpose, where those who require it will easily find means of enjoyment, while the lawgiver greatly careful for the future looks to see that none interferes with the gifts of God, which bring welfare and safety.

This passage, too, has presumably been inspired by Gen. 1:26–8 which Philo applied to every human offspring. Philo took very seriously the connection, adumbrated in Gen. 1:26–8, between Adam's own creation in the image of God and the subsequent command of procreaction. For him this subtle link implied the idea that every individual man following Adam was also created by God and in His image.[34] Each human being must therefore be acknowledged as God's personal possession (Dec. 132–4). Philo furthermore concluded that God is the true creator of every individual person. It is He, Philo insists, who "causes all things to be sown and come into being, through whom it is that mother and

---

This was part of the Stoic doctrine on pregnancy which was, however, used to justify abortion (see above).

[33] Opif. 77; regarding the parable which Philo provides in this context, see below chapter eight.

[34] Opif. 69. Philo is not the only exegete to perceive this link; for subsequent examples, see: J. Cohen, *"Be Fertile and Increase, Fill the Earth and Master It". The Ancient and Medieval Career of a Biblical Text* (Ithaca and London 1989).

father appear to generate, though they do not really do so, but are the instruments of generation".[35] Philo occasionally spoke of parents as "puppets" invisibly moved by God and as "servants of God for the task of begetting children".[36] Philo warned them not to become too bold and equate their own reproduction with divine creativity (Dec. 119–20). The difference between God and parents was too obvious to be overlooked: while He truly created, they only seemed to do so. Philo was moreover convinced that circumcision had been commanded, among other reasons, in order to curb the father's arrogant assumptions about his own imput.[37] Philo thus left no doubt about the fact that human offspring is ultimately God's own creation. Human beings are unique in this respect. In the case of animals, Philo unhesitatingly acknowledged the parents' generative role. He openly spoke of the mother as "the cause of generation" and assumed that her invulnerability also protected her unborn offspring (Vir. 134–8). Animal offspring undoubtedly belongs to its parents. The situation of human children differs considerably because Adam alone has, according to Scripture, been created in the divine image. Philo therefore insisted on divine rights over man. Nobody, he stressed, must be "denied any stage of life that God has assigned to the human race" (Praem. 110).

This interpretation of humanity in the scheme of divine creation has important consequences for Philo's overall construction of Jewish childhood and culture. It emerges that his view of Jewish culture expresses a strong sense of self-awareness and is anchored in religion. Philo makes the transmission of Jewish culture mandatory by rooting it in the divine command to procreate and raise children. He called Jews to respect every potential and new-born life. Pregnancy, birth and child-rearing were not to be seen as purely personal matters which could be manipulated or anulled at will, but as integral aspects of God's overall design. Jewish parents were expected to submit to His plan and accept responsibility for every new child. Infants thus enjoyed considerable importance in Jewish culture. They were not left to the arbitrary disposal of adults, but were regarded as the fulfillment of God's overall scheme. They carried the promise of the future in a specific religious sense, namely the reproduction of God's image on earth. This interpretation of childhood irreversibly defined the role of parents. Adults were in Philo's view account-

---

[35] μήτηρ τε καὶ πατὴρ γεννᾶν ἔδοξαν, οὐ γεννῶντες, ἀλλ' ὄργανα γενέσεως ὄντες (Her. 171).

[36] Q.G. 3:48; Dec. 119.

[37] Q.G. 3:47; other aspects of circumcision in Philo's work have been usefully discussed by J.J. Collins, A Symbol of Otherness: Circumcision and Salvation in the First Century, in: J. Neusner and E.S. Frerichs (eds.), *"To see Ourselves as Others see Us". Christians, Jews, "Others" in Late Antiquity* (Chico 1985) 171–6; R.D. Hecht, The Exegetical Context of Philo's Interpretation of Circumcision in: Greenspahn *et al.*, Nourished with Peace 51–79; J.Z. Smith, Fences and Neighbors: Some Contours of Early Judaism, in: idem, *Imagining Religion. From Babylon to Jonestown* (Chicago 1982) 14–5.

able to God for their child's care. They were not only obliged to raise each infant, but also to bring it up in a certain way. These stringent requirements could, as we shall see, occasionally have gruesome implications.

Before the aims of Jewish education can, however, be properly discussed, two further aspects of Philo's construction of childhood have to be noted. It is initially conspicuous that Philo himself was keenly aware of the fact that his Jewish readers would not easily accept his criticism of child exposure. Many of them obviously practiced it. Philo therefore made special efforts to convince his readers, employing rhetoric rather than his usual style of writing. Suspecting them of exposing their children, he sarcastically addressed them as "you good and highly prized parents" and showed them the "monstrous cruelty and barbarity" involved in this practice.[38] He spoke in detail of how parents "stifle and throttle the first breath which the infants draw or throw them into a river or into the depths of a sea, after attaching some heavy substance" (Spec. 3:114). Philo moreover unmasked child exposure in a desert place as murder. Even though parents may claim or perhaps even convince themselves that their offspring may thus be saved, he reminded them that they actually commit it to an almost certain death by carnivorous birds (Vir. 115). This rhetoric indicates that Philo was conscious of a reality not corresponding to his own convictions. His argument about rearing children as a natural duty anchored in God's overall plan of creation was evidently normative rather than descriptive. It suggested how he personally saw the role of Jewish children and, ultimately, of Jewish culture.

Furthermore, Philo's assumption of infants' rights must not be confused with absolute human rights. Since the parents' obligation towards their offspring was rooted in a duty towards God, it was also subject to substantial limitations. The most significant of these is the possibility of child sacrifice. The idea of sacrificing the first-born son was, as Jon Levenson has shown, originally part of Biblical religion and was only gradually transformed, but never completely erased.[39] A striking reflection of the ancient practice is LXX Ex. 22:28. This

---

[38] Vir. 131; Spec. 3:114; see also: Reinhartz, Infanticide passim, who has stressed that Philo responds to the historical reality of child exposure among Jews. Two Jewish authors, possibly writing before Philo's time, also objected to child exposure: Ps.-Phocylides 184 and Syb. Or. 2:281. Ps.-Phocylides, however, speaks of exposure only in the context of an offence committed by the mother. This implies that he still thought of it in Classical terms, namely as an acceptable practice on condition of paternal consent. The author of Syb. Or. 2:281 is more general in his condemnation of child-exposure, criticizing those who "cast forth their offspring unlawfully". Yet he provides no explanation and does not elaborate the point. Josephus, by contrast, was subsequently very explicit about the distinctly Jewish command to raise all children (A.J. 4:278; Contr. Ap. 2:202). His argumentation, however, was Classical: it focused on the mother's duty towards her husband and on demographic considerations.

[39] Levenson, Beloved Son, especially 3–52.

verse explicitly demands the donation of all first-born sons as sacrificial gifts to God. A similar remnant of the oldest tradition is the story of Isaac's binding (the Akedah). Levenson has shown that Genesis chapter twenty-two assumes the positive acceptance of child sacrifice. Abraham is the hero of the story precisely because he is willing to give up his son. The angels preventing him from doing so say nothing about abolishing the practice in principal. On the contrary, they praise him for his exemplary and unconditional obedience to God.[40] The sacrifice of the first-born son subsequently became problematic and was replaced by the obligation to pay the priests a redemption fee (Ex. 34:20). The process of substitution was completed by the institution of consecrating the Levites to the Temple. An explicit link was in this context drawn to the earlier sacrificial practice. The Biblical legislator explains that the Levites are consecrated "instead of every first-born of the Israelites" (Num. 8:18). Later on, the prophets Ezekiel and Jeremiah expressed for the first time a fundamental opposition to any form of child sacrifice (Ez. 20:25–6, Jer. 19:5–6). They remained, however, rather lonely voices which did not succeed in completely uprooting the custom of child sacrifice in ancient Israel.

Given the fact that Philo lived in the first century C.E., he expressed surprisingly few reservations about child sacrifice. Generally reluctant to refer to the prophets, he did not even repeat the content of Ezekiel's and Jeremiah's outcry.[41] His interpretations of Ex. 22:28 and the Akedah even indicate a considerable degree of sympathy for the practice. Philo speaks in this context about parents having "their first-born male children consecrated as a first-fruit, a thank-offering for the blessings of parenthood" (Spec. 1:138). Moses, he further explained, thus showed his wish "that the marriages, the first produce of which is a fruit sacred to His service, should not only be blameless but worthy of the highest praise" (Spec. 1:138). These comments sound as if child sacrifice was not only a reality in Philo's time, but also approved by him. It is only in the subsequent paragraph of the above Philonic passage that the reader learns about Biblical procedures of substitution. These are explained by remarkable considerations. Philo insists that child sacrifice was abandoned so as to ensure that parents and children are not separated (Spec. 1:139). No word is in this context said about the intrinsic problems of child sacrifice. No word either about children's natural rights.

---

[40] Levenson, Beloved Son 111–42, has shown that there is no evidence in the Biblical text itself for the prevalent interpretation of the Akedah as an etiology of substituting child sacrifice by animal sacrifice. Instead, the Akedah tests whether Abraham is willing to put "obedience to God ahead of every possible competitor" and to "surrender his son to the God who gave him" (ibid. 126).

[41] Philo generally focused on the Pentateuch which presumably was the only part of Scripture he recognized as canonical; for more details on his notions of Scripture, see below chapter seven.

A similar picture emerges from Philo's interpretation of the Akedah. He defended the original idea of a trial even though many other Jews criticized it as a pagan atrocity.[42] Some of these critics had apparently suggested that the Akedah violates Deut. 12:31 which forbids the burning of one's children for idolatrous purposes (Abr. 179–81). While Philo was keen to distinguish the Akedah from pagan practices, he wholeheartedly defended the idea of parental willingness to sacrifice the first-born son.[43] Faithful to the Biblical story, he defined Abraham's test as a choice between two competing demands: complete obedience to God, on the one hand, and paternal love, on the other.[44] Abraham was praised for his unconditional devotion to the deity. As Philo put it, he remained:[45]

steadfast as ever with a judgement that never bent or wavered. Mastered by his love for God, he mightily overcame all the fascination expressed in the fond terms of family affection.

Philo identifies here with the Biblical ideal of complete obedience to God, even if this implies a sacrifice of one's own child. Parental love which he defined as natural and thus authoritative in other contexts is evidently a lower priority in relation to this overall duty. If there was a conflict between the two, obedience to God had to be preferred. Ideally, as in the case of Abraham, one should identify to such an extent with the divine command that no conflict would arise. Philo in this context makes the following extraordinary statement: "For a father to surrender one of a numerous family as a tithe to God is nothing extraordinary, since each of the survivors continues to give him pleasure".[46] To be sure, this

---

[42] Philo speaks of these critics as "quarrelsome people who represent everything negatively" (Abr. 178). These critics must have been Jewish for two main reasons: 1) there is no indication that the story of Abraham was known outside Jewish circles before the Christian era; reponses to it would therefore naturally have arisen in Jewish circles; 2) they argue from another Pentateuchal verse. The verb διαβάλλω does not necessarily imply malicious intent; these Jewish critics differed from the "Greek men of letters" who, according to Philo, distorted the Exodus story and "abused the powers which education has given them, by composing in verse or prose comedies and pieces of voluptuous licence" (Mos. 1:2–3).

[43] In Abr. 176 Philo stresses that Abraham had raised the sword "with the intention of killing him" (ὡς ἀναιρήσων), thus closely paraphrasing LXX Gen. 22:10 σφάξαι τὸν υἱὸν αὐτοῦ. In Abr. 177 Philo further explains that Abraham's real intention could not have been implemented because "a voice from the air" interfered (εἰ καὶ μὴ τὸ τέλος ἐπηκολούθησεν), yet his complete willingness counted as though the deed had actually been committed.

[44] P.R. Davies and B.D. Chilton, The Aqedah: A Revised Tradition History, *CBQ* 40.4 (1978) 519–21, rightly identified Philo's exclusive focus on Abraham's obedience as a proof for the absense of a full Akedah theology in the later Christian and rabbinic sense of an expiatory sacrifice. Philo indeed remained close to the Biblical story and attributed no role whatsoever to Isaac.

[45] Abr. 170; see also Abr. 198.

[46] Abr. 196; commenting only on the text of the Torah, Philo did not explain the case of Yiphtah's daughter in Judg. 11:30–40, on the significance of which see: Levenson, Beloved Son 14–6; C.A. Brown, *No Longer Be Silent. First Century Jewish Portraits of Biblical Women* (Westminster 1992) 93–139.

statement is a rhetorical reply to those contemporary critics of the Akedah who denied its uniqueness and compared it to any other child sacrifice in the pagan world. Philo responded, among other things, by insisting that Abraham deserved praise because he was willing to sacrifice his only son. This was in his view extraordinary, because he would thus be left without any other offspring compensating him and giving him pleasure. Despite the polemical context of these statements it is striking how lightly Philo spoke about the possibility of sacrificing children under normal circumstances, namely when siblings were available to replace the victim. This indicates his mental proximity to the original notions of the Akedah. Philo was clearly more sympathetic to the idea of child sacrifice than both Josephus and the rabbis. Josephus expressed his awareness of the gruesome nature of Abraham's test by disclosing at the very beginning of the story that the end would be a happy one. In this way the readers of his account were reassured that sacrifical blood was no longer spilt.[47] The rabbis suggested in a similar vein that Abraham had rather good grounds for refusing the Divine order.[48] They, too, expressed uneasiness about the Biblical idea of child sacrifice as an expression of unconditional obedience to God. Philo, by contrast, seems to have approved of it theoretically even though the practice had already become obsolete by his time.

Philo's position on child sacrifice underlines the conclusions we have reached so far. Parents' obligations vis-à-vis their children were in his view primarily dictated by God. Under normal circumstances this meant that parents had to fulfil their task in the divine scheme of creation by producing children and raising all of them in accordance with His plan. Children, and especially Jewish children, were considered a God-given task. This implied the parents' complete submission to His will even to the extent of accepting the theoretical possibility of child sacrifice.

Philo extended these notions of childhood to the field of education. Here, too, man's generation by God and in His image implied concrete obligations. Children should in his view primarily be raised to live according to the specific values of the Jews. This demanded a considerable degree of austerity and discipline from the early stages of life. Philo advocated rather stringent forms of education even though he was willing to acknowledge the special nature of early childhood. The first seven years of life were for him a period when the

[47] Jos., J.A. 1:223–4; for an analysis of this passage, see; M.R. Niehoff, Two Examples Of Josephus' Narrative Technique in His "Rewritten Bible", *JSJ* 27.1 (1996) 35–6.

[48] See especially: G.R. 56:3–4, for comment on these passages, see: M.R. Niehoff, The Return of Myth in Genesis Rabbah on the Akeda, *JJS* 46. 1–2 (1995) 83–5.

[49] All. 2:53; see also Spec. 3:119 where Philo discusses the innocence of new-born children. Similar ideas as Philo's can later be found in Christianity, see: P. Ariès, *Centuries of Childhood: A Social History of Family Life* (New York 1962, Fr. original 1960) 100–27; DeMause, Childhood 47; J.Z. Smith, The Garments of Shame, *History of Religions* 5.2 (1966) 233–38.

mind was still fluid. On one occasion he even associated infants' immaturity with Adam's and Eve's nakedness which he allegorized as "the mind that is clothed neither in vice nor in virtue, but absolutely stripped of either".[49] Philo's notion of a child's innocence differs considerably from the typical views on early childhood held by Classical Greek writers.[50] Plato, for example, judged children merely by adult standards and dismissed their immaturity in no uncertain terms. He complained that children lacked rationality and therefore were "treacherous, sly and most insolent" (Leg. 7:808d). Philo's sympathy instead corresponds to the more enthusiastic mood with which Roman authors of the imperial age discovered the charms of childhood. Michel Manson has shown in a number of pioneering studies that the Roman elite began at this time to pay more attention to its infants.[51] The Latin language developed neutral and even positive terms for the young child who was now described as sweet, innocent and deserving of parental love. Philo shared to some extent in this new spirit. Unlike Classical writers such as Plato, Aristotle and Chrysippus, Philo deferred systematic instruction until the age of seven.[52] One should wait, he insisted, until the mind had become sufficiently firm to retain meaningful impressions. Otherwise too much of the teacher's effort would be wasted. At the initial stage attention should rather be directed towards protecting the child from bad influences. For Philo this primarily meant that "nurses and mothers and the rest of the company, slaves and free" must neither tell infants mythological fables nor act in their presence in an unexemplary way.[53] Even though the child's mind is still flexible it should not be exposed to corrupting influence. Philo feared that if falsehood was perpetually welded to the young soul, it would eventually become part of it (Spec. 4:68).

---

[50] Garland, Way of Life 127–31; M. Golden, *Children and Childhood in Classical Athens* (Baltimore and London 1990) 1–22.

[51] M. Manson, *Puer bimulus* (Catulle, 17, 12–13) et l'image du petit enfant chez Catulle et ses prédécesseurs, *Mélanges de l'Ecole Française de Rome* 90.1 (1978) 247–91; idem, The Emergence of the Small Child in Rome (Third Century BC-First Century AD), *History of Education* 12.3 (1983) 149–59; idem, La 'Pietas' et le Sentiment de l'enfance à Rome d'après les monnaies, *Revue Belge de Numismatique et de Sigillographie* 121 (1975) 21–80 (relating to the coinage of imperial age from Caligula onwards). Manson's conclusions have recently been affirmed by the following authors: Dixon, Roman Family 98–132; J.K. Evans, *War, Women and Children in Ancient Rome* (London and New York 1991) 166–209; cf. B. Rawson, Adult-Child Relationships in Roman Society, in: eadem (ed.), *Marriage, Divorce, and Children in Ancient Rome* (Oxford 1991) 7.

[52] Congr. 121; in All. 1:10 Philo speaks of the development of reasoning in the child as a process connected to verbal expression. Other ancient thinkers recommended an earlier beginning of schooling: Plato age six, Aristotle age five and Chrysippus as early as age three; see also: H.I. Marrou, *A History of Education in Antiquity* (London 1956, Fr. orig.) 143.

[53] Spec. 4:68; Vir. 178; see also: Reinhartz, Parents and Children 74, who pointed to the gender bias involved in Philo's statement. He never referred specifically to the father's negative influence on his children, but asserted, on the contrary, that a true father will never give any instruction contrary to virtue (Spec. 2:236).

While sympathetic to children's immaturity until the age of seven, Philo focused on the positive tasks of education, namely the inculcation of manly *enkrateia* and the acquisition of knowledge. Their attainment was crucial for him and indicated educational success. Philo insisted on the pursuit of these goals and demanded harsh measures of discipline, including beating, in order to guarantee their implementation.[54] Children who forgot the "teaching of their race and their father in which they have been trained from earliest youth" deserved in his view severe punishment (Praem. 162). The most extreme case in this respect was the "rebellious son" who was ultimately liable to the death penalty, which Philo actually assumed would be carried out.[55] Philo supported capital punishment because the "rebellious son" had foresaken his ancestral traditions and thus lost any right to live within the Jewish community.[56] Since he had, as Philo formulated it, "made a god of the body, a god of the vanity most honoured among the Egyptians" (Ebr. 95), he deserved death. The following measures led up to his final verdict (Spec. 2:232):

And therefore the fathers have the right to upbraid their children and to admonish them most severely, and if they do not submit on hearing threats to beat and disgrace them (προπηλακίζειν) and to bind them. And further, if in the face of this they refuse to obey the reins, and by the force of uncorrected wickedness shake off the yoke, the law entrusted (ἐπέτρεψεν) them [the parents] to use even the death penalty. However, here neither the father nor the mother alone are sufficient, because the magnitude of the punishment demands that it be decided not by one alone, but by both parents. For it is improbable that both parents would be of one mind to kill their child, if his offences were not sufficiently weighty and drawing down the scales strongly enough to over-come the affection for the child naturally present in them.

This passage indicates the extent to which Philo was willing to use discipline. Departure from the Jewish way of life forfeitted in his view the natural love of

---

[54] He believed with Prov. 3:11–2 that beating children indicates love and concern (Congr. 177); see also: Spec. 2:240–1; All. 2:89–90; Sacr. 63; Post. 97; Det. 143–7; Jos. 74. Philo furthermore distinguished between the physical chastisement of a slave by his master and the "educational" beatings delivered to a son. While the latter in his view served the youth's best interest and ensured his improvement, the former only resulted in humiliation and fear of a powerful person (All. 3:84).

[55] Philo's position corresponds to the halacha in the *Temple Scroll*, 11 QT, col. 64, while differing from rabbinic circumventions of this last consequence. On the latter, see especially: M. Halbertal, *Interpretative Revolutions in the Making. Values as Interpretative Considerations in Midrashei Halakhah* (Hebrew) (Jerusalem 1997) 46–67; M. Bar-Ilan, "Childhood" and its Status in Biblical and Talmudic Society (Hebrew), *Beit Mikra* 40.1 (1994–5) 19–32; D. Kraemer, Images of Childhood and Adolescence in Talmudic Literature, in: idem (ed.), *The Jewish Family. Metaphor and Memory* (New York and Oxford 1989) 65–80.

[56] Other rebels whose execution Philo welcomes are the builders of the Golden Calf, on whom see above chapter two. See also: T. Seland, *Establishment Violence in Philo And Luke. A Study of Non-Conformity to the Torah and Jewish Vigilante Reactions* (Leiden 1995) 103–81, who drew attention to Philo's "zealous" spirit which led him to accept the spontaneous execution of "rebels from the holy laws" (Vir. 182).

parents for their offspring and justified the initial beating and ultimate execution of the "rebellious son". His parents were not only entitled, but in a way
morally obliged to dispose of him. While their son's life had originally been
given by God, it now had to be extinguished because it no longer conformed to
His will. Philo was so adamant about this matter that he ignored the Biblical
requirement of a counsel of elders as a control mechanism and left the judgement to the parents alone. The execution would thus be more spontaneous and
faster. Philo did so on the assumption of contemporary Roman law which still
extended paternal authority to the *ius necis*, while also demanding maternal
consent.[57]

Given Philo's determination to perpetuate the Jewish way of life in children,
we must investigate how he described the contents of education which would
transform new-born children into authentic Jews. A survey of his discussions
on this topic immediately reveals a striking fact: while Philo says little about
specifically Jewish ways of education, he assumed general and especially Greek
forms of *paideia*. All of these were in remarkable harmony with each other and
furthered the aims of Jewish education.

To be sure, Philo expected Jews to be instructed "from their earliest years" in
the doctrine that Scripture is a Divine oracle and consequently to "carry the
likenesses of the commandments enshrined in their souls" (Leg. 210). As he
once formulated it (Spec. 1:314):

… we who, born as citizens of a god-loving community, reared under laws which incite
to every virtue (ἐντραφέντες νόμοις ἐπὶ πᾶσαν ἀρετὴν ἀλείφουσι), trained from our
earliest years under divinely gifted men (παρὰ θεσπεσίοις ἀνδράσι), show contempt
for their teaching [the corrupting teaching of other nations] …

These statements clearly assume a distinct form of Jewish education, apparently given by professionals, which aimed at transmitting separate values not
shared by other nations. Philo speaks in this context about instruction in "the
laws which incite to every virtue". This undoubtedly refers to Mosaic law

---

[57] See also: Heinemann, Bildung 250–51; E.R. Goodenough, *The Jurisprudence of the
Jewish Courts in Egypt: Legal Administration by the Jews under the Early Roman Empire as
Described by Philo Judaeus* (New Haven 1929) 69, Reinhartz, Parents and Children 76–77.
Originally, Roman law gave absolute authority to the father who could on his own decide
upon the execution of his children. Subsequently, around the turn of the era, *patria potestas*
was restricted by the requirement of a *consilium domesticum* which basically amounted to
the requirement of maternal consent; for further details of Roman law in this context, see:
R.P. Saller, *Patriarchy, property and death in the Roman family* (Cambridge 1994) 114–30;
J. Plescia, *Patria Potestas* and the Roman Revolution, in: S. Bertman (ed.), *The Conflict of
Generations in Ancient Greece and Rome* (Amsterdam 1976) 143–69; R. Taubenschlag, Die
*patria potestas* im Recht der Papyri, in: idem, *Opera Minora* (Warsaw 1959) 2:261–321;
idem, Die *materna potestas* im gräko-ägyptischen Recht, ibid. 2:323–337; N. Lewis, On
Paternal Authority in Roman Egypt, *RIDA* 17 (1970) 251–58; Dixon, Roman Mother 61–62.
Consider also Josephus' description of Herod's attempts to legally dispose of his sons (B.J.
1: 534–43, A.J. 16: 361–2).

which taught the Jews in Philo's view to lead a life of perfect *enkrateia*.[58] He moreover insisted on another occasion that Jewish children acquire from their earliest days the notion of one truly existing God (Spec. 1:332). Sarah, for example, had "from the cradle" been taught the notion of divine omnipotence (Abr. 112). At the same time, however, Philo said virtually nothing about the gradual process of such education. He provided hardly any details about the kind of experience a Jewish child should in his view go through. Unlike Aristotle, he did not specify how character could be formed by the persistant acquisition of virtuous habits.[59] Philo neither discussed the boy's training in the synagogue and Torah reading nor anticipated such child-centred rituals as the reading of the Passover Haggadah.[60] Sometimes the reader rather gets the impression that growing-up involved for Philo a swift and unmediated passage from infancy to adulthood (Cher. 114).

Philo's interpretation of children in the Bible indicates that, ideally at least, a good measure of personal effort and individual insight were involved. His Biblical heroes attained the goals of Jewish education virtually from the cradle onwards, thus setting an example for contemporary Jews. Moses once more represented the ideal.[61] Driven by exceptional spirituality, he showed perfect *enkrateia* already as a young child. Philo's Moses never delighted in the "fun and laughter and sport" of children (Mos. 1:18–20). He even weaned himself prematurely.[62] Moses was thus praised for leaving behind childhood more

---

[58] For further details, see above chapter three.

[59] While Philo occasionally mentions "exercise in the principles of virtue" (e.g. Praem. 64), he did not make this aspect the focus of his educational programme. On Aristotle's approach to education, see especially: M.F. Burnyeat, Aristotle on Learning to Be Good, in: A. Oksenberg Rorty (ed.), *Essays on Aristotle's Ethics* (Berkeley 1980) 69–92.

[60] For Philo, the Passover meal was mainly celebrated as a symposion with strong mystical overtones; see especially: Sacr. 58–64, which echoes the terminology of the Eleusinian mystery cults, on which see: Riedweg, Mysterienterminologie 30–69, 71–107; K. Dowden, Grades in the Eleusinian Mysteries, *Revue de l'Histoire des Religions* 197.4 (1980) 409–27. As B.M. Bokser, *The Origins of the Seder. The Passover Rite and Early Rabbinic Judaism* (Berkeley 1984) 22–4, has shown, the Passover Haggadah had not yet emerged in Philo's time. Another child-oriented ritual, which became prominent in Medieval Judaism (see: I.G. Marcus, *Rituals of Childhood. Jewish Acculturation in Medieval Europe* (New Haven 1996), the school initiation rite was unknown to Philo – not least because he anticipated private instruction rather than proper schools. Philo's lack of reference to the boy's early instruction in Torah reading contrasts with the rabbis who provided ample information on this subject, see especially: S. Safrai, Education and the Study of the Torah, in: idem and M. Stern (eds.), *The Jewish People in the First Century. Historical Geography, Political History, Social Cultural and Religious Life and Institutions* (Philadelphia 1976) 2: 945–70; H. Lichtenberger, Lesen und Lernen im Judentum, in: A.T. Khoury and L. Muth (eds.), *Glauben Durch Lesen? Für Eine Christliche Lesekultur* (Freiburg 1990) 32–8.

[61] For other aspects of Philo's Moses as an ideal figure, see above chapter two.

[62] Mos. 1:18–20; for a survey of known toys and games in Antiquity, see: M. Bar-Ilan, Children's Games in Antiquity (Hebrew), *Proceedings of the Eleventh World Congress of Jewish Studies* (Jerusalem 1994) 2:1:23–30.

speedily than his peers and intuitively embracing the values of adults. This was noteworthy because Philo felt ambivalent about the games and pleasures of childhood. He suggested that children's "games and merriment" fall short of the spiritual joy of adults.[63] They were in his view more material forms of pleasure and therefore bound to encourage the growth of the passions.[64] He nowhere discussed them as a form of early education. The vision of a suckling baby could occasionally arouse Philo's uneasiness. He once compared it to a man of incontinence who "presses hard on the fountain from which the curse of wine-bibbing pours like rain, to find in the squeezed droppings a nourishment of delicious sweetness" (Somn. 2:204). When the infant Moses avoided the typical food and games of his age, he thus shunned the lures of licentiousness. His abstinence prefigured the adult ideal of *enkrateia*.[65] Moses in fact mentally became an adult, while physically still a child. His precocity was exemplary and meant to serve as a guide for Philo's readers and their children. As Philo once formulated it in more general terms, the virtuous ranks "from the cradle ... as an elder in the senate of prudence".[66] Moses had thus become a hero who represented the austerity of Jewish culture in contrast to the far more permissive life-style of Egypt.

This interpretative pattern recurs in Philo's construction of Isaac's and Joseph's early years. While the former resembles Moses, the latter symbolizes a departure from Jewish culture. Isaac characteristically disdained "any use of soft and milky food suited to infants and little children", using instead "only strong nourishment fit for grown men" (Somn. 2:10). Philo's Isaac furthermore lacked any interest in toys and games.[67] He was instead naturally stalwart and vigorous – the opposite type of Joseph who assimilated to Egyptian culture, cared about children's games even as an adult and was given to the more material pleasures of life.[68]

---

[63] παιδιὰ καὶ γέλως (Plant. 168).

[64] In Congr. 81 and Opif. 161–2 Philo explicitly associates early childhood with the passions. These views correspond to a prevalent attitude in Classical Athens, on which see: Gill, The Question of Character; Garland, Way of Life 141; Golden, Children 1–22. Plato occasionally recognized the educational value of children's games (Leg. 7:792a–797b, 1:643d–644b), see also: Marrou, Education 143.

[65] Philo's portrait of the childhood of Biblical heroes corresponds to the norms of Ancient biography which aimed, as far as can be reconstructed, at showing the consistency of character from early childhood to the climax of the hero's career, see also: Pelling, Childhood and Personality 213–44. For details on *enkrateia* as a distinctly Jewish value, see above chapter three.

[66] Sobr. 24; see also: Q.G. 4:14, where Philo compares the foolish man to a child, while the wise behaves already in his youth like an elder. On another occasion he said of the gifted soul that it does not "stay in childish thoughts", but "seeks to gain a condition of serenity and pursues the vision of the excellent" (Abr. 26).

[67] Cher. 8. Philo insisted several times that Isaac's name referred to nothing but spiritual enjoyments suitable for adults, see especially: Cher. 8; Abr. 201; Plant. 169.

[68] See especially Jos. 204; for further details on Philo's interpretation of Joseph in relation to Egypt, see above chapter two.

While the outstanding heroes of Jewish culture took the initiative and early
weaned themselves of the dubious pleasures of childhood, such personal strength
could not be expected from average children. The question arises how these
were socialized to Jewish culture and moved from cradle to adulthood. Philo
suggests that parents played a key role in this process even though he took
tutors and teachers for granted.[69] He described the parents as the child's natural
guide (Det. 145) and acknowledged their formative influence on their offspring
(Spec. 2:228):

> They [the parents] are also in the position of instructors because they impart to their
> children from the earliest years everything that they themselves happen to know, and
> give them instruction not only in the various branches of knowledge which they impress
> upon their young minds, but also on the most essential questions of what to choose and
> avoid, namely to choose virtues and avoid vices and the activities to which they lead.

Philo suggests that parents play a formative role because they have immediate
access to the child, thus shaping it both morally and intellectually. They are the
child's "birth-fellows" who accompany it from the beginning and provide
"good archetypes" which can be directly emulated (Vir. 197). While Philo often
spoke about parents in general, fathers were clearly more important. By virtue
of being the child's engenderer, the father entertained in his view a more
profound and enduring tie to his "artifact".[70] Philo was convinced that there
could be no closer relationship than that "of a father to a son, or a son to a
father" (Congr. 177). A "true father", he insisted, "will give no instruction to his
son that is foreign to virtue".[71] He distinguished several patriarchs who had

---

[69] Spec. 2:233. It is not clear whether Philo assumed any institution of schooling, which
was according to Marrou, Education 144–6, widespread in the Hellenistic world. Note that
Philo's emphasis on the parents' role in child education is anticipated by traditional Israelite
wisdom literature, such as Sir. 30:13.

[70] For details on Philo's medical doctrine of procreation, see above chapter one. The
father thus resembles to some extent God who cherishes a tender affection for the products
of His creation (Opif. 9–10, 21–22; cf. Plato, Tim. 29E; see also: Runia, Timaeus 132).

[71] Spec. 2:236. Philo says in this context that the children "will be willing to hearken to
their [parents'] commands and to obey them in everything that is just and profitable". This
phrase may imply that children do not hearken to instructions which are not profitable and
just. Reinhartz, Parents and Children 79, has understood Spec. 2:236 in this sense. This
reading, however, is rather unlikely, because Philo nowhere anticipates a discrepancy between virtue and paternal instruction. Even in Vir. 178 where he accuses "the parents" of
introducing "mythical fables" to their children, he does not primarily refer to the father, but
to the mother (as we saw above). Philo's idealization of the father differs from Musonius'
more realistic appreciation: The latter envisioned incompetent fathers acting like someone
who, though not a physician, prescribes a medicine which turns out to be harmful. In such a
case, Musonius insisted, disobedience is not only permitted, but even mandatory. An obedient son is therefore someone who "listens to anyone who counsels what is fitting and follows
it voluntarily" (frgm. 16 apud Stobaeus, Flor. 79,51 = ed. Lutz 102–3). Refusing the father's
immoral instruction, by contrast, was in his view nothing but the inverse side of proper
obedience to the call of virtue.

shown exceptional love and care for their sons. Philo's Abraham was moved "not merely by a feeling of natural affection [for Isaac], but also by such deliberate judgement as a censor of character might make" (Abr. 168). Combining spontaneous emotion with a moral sense, Abraham "cherished for him a great affection" (Abr. 168). Jacob was similarly praised for his natural love and sound judgement of character. Interpreting Gen. 37:3, Philo stressed that he held "high admiration and respect" for Joseph (Jos. 4). Jacob distinguished in his late-born son a potential for exceptional virtue: "by special and exceptional attentions he fostered the fire of the boy's nature, in the hope that it would not merely smoulder but burst rapidly into flame" (Jos. 4). The Biblical matriarchs, on the other hand, were nowhere assigned a similar role by Philo. On the contrary, Joseph's imitation of Rachel turned out to be harmful and led to his materialistic proclivities (All. 3:180).

Philo furthermore expected Jewish children to go through the Classical Greek curriculum. Strikingly, these are the only studies he discussed in any detail. In his view they not only complemented Jewish education, but directly strengthened faith in the Jewish creator God. As Philo formulated it on one occasion (Spec. 2:230):

grammar and arithmetic and geometry and music and the whole of philosophy which lifts on high the mind lodged within the mortal body and escorts it to the very heaven and shows it the blessed and happy beings therein and creates zeal and yearning for the unchangeable and the harmonious arrangement, which they never forsake because they rely on their captain.

This is in several ways a remarkable passage. Philo initially lists the Classical Greek disciplines of education and then speaks of heavenly vision as well as reliance on God.

While grammar is the most basic learning, philosophy represents the climax of studies.[72] Philo himself went through the hierarchy of such a curriculum (Congr. 74–6). He began with grammar, namely writing and reading, and then moved on to geometry by whose "beauty" he was "charmed, for she showed symmetry and proportion in every part". Music was the third discipline Philo engaged in. While he appreciated the contribution of each of these subjects, he stressed that they were mere handmaids. His "lawful wife" was philosphy, of which the other studies gave him but dim foretastes. This curriculum is distinctly Greek and distinctly upper-class. It prepared Jewish children for participation in the high culture of Alexandria which was dominated by Greek tastes and traditions. The culture and education of the lower classes looked very different. As Diodorus reports, their children were taught the paternal trade, but

---

[72] See also: Congr. 15–16; Agr. 18; Mendelson, Secular Education 1–46. On the centrality of philosophy, which is according to Philo the true basis of all the other disciplines, see especially: Congr. 146–50, Post. 101–102.

spared the Classical Greek disciplines of which especially music was considered too effeminate (1:81, 1–7).

The above-quoted passage also suggests that Greek *paideia* was in Philo's view an integral part of Jewish culture. It posed no threat for him and did not challenge Jewish values. On the contrary, Philo felt that the encyclical studies naturally led to Jewish commitments. This was so because he believed, as we saw above in chapter five, that the best of Greek philosophy is nothing but an imitation of the Torah. The highest insights of Greek philosophy thus coincide with the principles conveyed by the Hebrew Scriptures. As far as Philo was concerned, religious insight is the loftiest aim of all education. As he put it in a famous passage (Congr. 79–80):

And indeed just as the school subjects (ἐγκύκλια) contribute to the acquisition of philosophy, so does philosophy to the getting of wisdom. For philosophy is the practice or study of wisdom, and wisdom is the knowledge of things divine and human and their causes. And therefore just as the culture of the schools is the bond-servant of philosophy, so must philosophy be the servant of wisdom. Now philosophy teaches us the control (ἐγκράτειαν) of the belly and the parts below it, and control also of the tongue. Such powers of control are said to be desirable in themselves, but they will assume a grander and loftier aspect if practised for the honour and service of God.

Philo describes here a hierarchy of studies, leading from the more concrete and ancillary to the ethereal. The pinnacle of education is the acquisition of wisdom which Philo defines as "the knowledge of things divine and human and their causes". Even though Stoic philosophers had similarly expressed themselves, Philo meant something specifically Jewish by this phrase.[73] Wisdom is characteristically said to be based on philosophy which inculcates *enkrateia* in all aspects of human life. As we saw above in chapter three, self-restraint was in Philo's view a quintessential Jewish virtue which some other nations approximated, but never fully implemented. Philo moreover associates wisdom with the service of God. He explains in the above-quoted passage that "a grander and loftier aspect" is added to the ideal of philosophy and *enkrateia* if they are practiced "for the honour and service of God". Pursued thus, general Greek studies lead to religious insight and, more importantly, to a renewed commitment to the Jewish God. This is a remarkable position on the part of Philo. Jewish culture in fact turns out to be composed to a significant extent of Classical Greek studies. For Philo there is no contradiction in this. Nor does he perceive any tension between the two kinds of heritage. This is so because of

---

[73] Cic., De Off. 2.2:5 defines wisdom as "rerum divinarum et humanarum causumque ... scientia". Y. Amir, *Die hellenistische Gestalt des Judentums bei Philon von Alexandrien* (Neukirchen 1983) 118–28, and Dillon, Middle Platonists 141, conclude from such similarities that Philo's ideal of education was purely Stoic, lacking any Jewish dimension. Wolfson, Philo 1:145–7, by contrast, argued for the ancillary function of general philosophy in Philo's work.

the way he constructed ethnic boundaries vis-à-vis the Greeks and Greek culture. As we saw above in chapter five, Philo was convinced that the best of Greek philosophy derived from Scripture or imitated Mosaic principles. His interpretation of the relationship between Greeks and Jews enabled him to construct a cultural discourse which absorbed Greek studies into the educational programme of Jewish children. The latter were thus instructed in the Classical Greek disciplines as part of their own heritage.

Finally, the cultural discourse constructed by Philo was distinctly male-oriented. This emerges from the way in which young children were socialized into a culture which relied primarily on male roles. Boys were assigned a clear place in it, while the girls were not. This tendency is conspicuous from the very beginning of life. Philo already saw the parents as mediators of public male-roles. They were compared to seniors, teachers, benefactors, rulers and masters (Spec. 2:226–7). All of these positions refer to an exclusive male domain to which women had no access.[74] In other contexts they were, not surprisingly, associated exclusively with the father.[75] The father moreover represented the more reliable avenue to true values. He transmitted in Philo's view "reason, masculine, right reason", while the mother stood for "the lower learning of the schools".[76] This distribution of roles implied distinct calls: "the father bids us follow in the steps of nature and pursue truth in her naked and undisguised form; education, the mother, bids us give ear to rules laid down by human ordinance".[77] Educational progress thus implied a move from the mother to the father or from a feminine to a masculine way of relating to the world. The erotic imagery Philo used in his description of the Classical Greek disciplines shows the dominance of the masculine voice at the stage of formal education and higher learning. Only boys were expected to receive instruction in the encyclical studies. They alone would be able to engage the different "handmaids" and finally commit themselves to their "lawful wife", philosophy.

Philo furthermore recommended a physical education "by means of the gymnasium and the training there given, through which it [the body] gains muscular vigour and good condition and the power to bear itself and move with ease marked by gracefulness and elegance" (Spec. 2:230). This training is both highly gender biased and highly elitist. The gymnasium was the exclusive domain of rich men. Philo praised the managers of gymnastic competitions for

---

[74] See also: Adele Reinhartz, Parents and Children 66–69.

[75] E. g.: Post. 68, Immut. 134, Spec. 4:184.

[76] Ebr. 33; see also: Ebr. 34–6, 64, 95; on other occasions the father is identified as the mind, see especially: Det. 52, Conf. 43. For similar evaluations of parental roles in Ancient wisdom literature, see: Prov. 1:8, 4:3–4, 10:1, 23:22–25.

[77] Ebr. 34. In Ebr. 54–55 Philo stresses that women tend more towards the rule of convention. He nevertheless insists that the instructions of both parents need to be heeded (Lib. 36, Ebr. 35, Vir. 208).

"barring women from the spectacle, in order that they may not be present when men are stripping themselves naked" (Spec. 3:176). When Philo thus appreciates gymnastic education given by "parents" to their "children", he is in reality speaking about fathers enabling their sons to attend the training ground of the body which served as a *billet d'entrée* into higher society. This avenue was open to the boys, but closed to the girls who did not require culturally conditioned gracefulness in the privacy of the *gynaikon*.[78]

Philo mentioned the education of girls only once. Orphans, he said in a general way, must be provided by the magistrates with an "education that befits maidens".[79] It is not specified what this may have implied. One can therefore only speculate. Philo probably referred to a basic education in Jewish values, such as Sarah's instruction in the principle of God's providence (Abr. 112). Girls' education must also have involved a knowledge of all the things required to function in the house and fulfil female duties vis-à-vis the family. Philo nowhere suggests that this required any kind of philosophical training or formal education. While needy parents were to be assisted in order to "marry their daughters and provide them with an ample dowry" (Fug. 29), no help was given to ensure the girls' education. Girls were presumably expected to learn their mothers' expertise by emulating their work in the *gynaikon*. The female domain was fundamentally different from the public sphere of the men. While the latter acted in the marketplaces, council-halls, law-courts, gatherings and meetings, the woman was in Philo's view (Spec. 3:169):

best suited to the indoor life which never strays from the house, within which the middle door is taken by the maidens as their boundary, the outer door by those who have reached full womanhood.

A woman must therefore not be "a busy-body, meddling with matters outside her household concerns" (Spec. 3:171). Philo looked with horror on women intruding upon the male domain.[80] He confined them to the *gynaikon* which he characterized by a "softer and more luxurious way of life" as opposed to the austerity of the men's world (Somn. 2:9). While it was in his view proper for women to lead a soft life without intellectual demands, and strict control over their sexuality,[81] Jewish boys and men should avoid the smoothness of the *gynaikon* and turn to more challenging functions in the outside world. This strict segregation of the sexes implies that Jewish culture was for Philo an exclusive male affair. Women were not to be seen in the public arena of culture

---

[78] On the seclusion of Jewish women as a Philonic ideal, see above chapter three.

[79] παιδείαν τὴν ἁρμόττουσαν κόραις (Spec. 2:125).

[80] Spec. 3:172–5. Regarding the exceptional nature of Philo's position within the context of Hellenistic Egypt, see above chapter three.

[81] Philo suggests that the women's tight supervision especially during adolescence was necessary so as to guarantee her virginity on her wedding day (Spec. 3:81).

nor to participate in serious spiritual life. Neither should they leave any traces on their boys who were destined for greater tasks.

We saw already above in chapter three that Philo's ideal of female seclusion conformed to conservative Roman views. He shared Augustan visions of women's modesty and shuddered, as did many imperial writers, at the very thought of women politicians like Cleopatra. Seneca was especially close to his way of thinking. Seneca's praise of his aunt's exceptional modesty in Egypt as well as his ideal of manly *enkrateia* suggested that these two men constructed a similar cultural discourse which was heavily gender-biased.[82] Philo was distinctly conservative in this respect and did not preempt any of the more progressive positions subsequently held by Musonius. The latter introduced some measure of equality between the sexes in an essentially patriarchal society and culture. While embracing the traditional division of labour, assigning indoor work to women and outdoor activities to men, Musonius recommended some philosophical education for girls as well.[83] He initially insisted that the female role required exactly the same virtues as that of men. Both could only implement their respective tasks if they cultivated courage, self-control and justice.[84] Women were moreover regarded as blessed with the same talents and inclinations for philosophy and as morality.[85] Girls were therefore in Musonius' view entitled to a philosophical education. As he put it, "if then men and women are born with the same virtues, the same type of training and education must of necessity befit both men and women".[86] While daughters were nevertheless excluded from the more theoretical training in "technical skill and acuteness in argument", they were exposed to the same moral philosophy.[87] This, Musonius hoped, would transform them into good wives and exemplary mothers.[88] While separate, the male and female realms were grounded in the same values. The world of the women was thus subordinated to that of the men, but not totally isolated from it. Philo, by contrast, consigned Jewish girls to a much gloomier realm. They were not recognized as agents of culture and morality. Their contribution to the perpetuation of Jewish life was indirect and mostly physical: they produced offspring which would, if it was male, carry Jewish culture into the next generation.

Philo's views of children and childhood have produced important insights into his construction of Jewish culture. It intially became apparent that he had a clear sense of Jewish culture, to whose preservation he was firmly committed.

---

[82] For more details on parallels between Philo and conservative Roman views on women, especially those held by Seneca, see above chapter three.

[83] Frgm. 4 apud Stobaeus, Anth. 2.31.123 = ed. Lutz 46–7.

[84] Frgm. 3 apud Stobaeus, Anth. 2.31.126 = ed. Lutz 39–43.

[85] Ibid. Lutz 40–1.

[86] Fragm. 4, ed. Lutz 46–7.

[87] Fragm. 4, ed. Lutz 48–9.

[88] Fragm. 3, ed. Lutz 40–41.

Children, he realized, played a vital role in this process. Educated in the right way, they would perpetuate Jewish values and thus ensure the continuity of a specifically Jewish way of life in a multi-ethnic and multi-cultural environment. Philo therefore expected Jewish parents to pay more careful attention to the upbringing of their children than was customary among other nations. He suggested on the basis of Gen. 1:26–8 that raising children was a God-given task, which demanded not only that every pregnancy be carried to term and every new-born child be raised, but also that all offspring be moulded in the image of God to lead a virtuous life. This obligation was so important for Philo that he approved of executing the "rebellious sons" who failed to live up to this expectation.

An investigation into the contents of Philo's educational programme yielded further remarkable conclusions. While taking for granted a training in the Hebrew Scriptures from early childhood, he said hardly anything about the specific requirements of such instruction. The modern reader is left with no clear idea of how this ideal should be implemented. The Classical Greek disciplines, on the other hand, are described in some detail. They are indeed warmly recommended on the assumption that they promote Jewish values and perpetuate Jewish culture. Philo's discourse thus absorbed Classical *paideia* and integrated the Jews into the elitist culture of first century Alexandria.

# 7. The Textuality of Jewish Culture

> "'Book' is Moses' name for God's Logos,
> in which have been inscribed and engraved
> the composition of all else"    (All. 1:19)

We saw in the previous chapter that Philo socialized Jewish children to a culture which was based on Torah learning, on the one hand, and on Greek *paideia* on the other. While these two branches of knowledge complemented each other, with Greek learning leading in Philo's view to Jewish values, he said surprisingly little about the boys' instruction in Scripture. He took it for granted that "we who, born as citizens of a god-loving community, [are] reared under laws which incite to every virtue, trained from our earliest years under divinely gifted men" (Spec. 1:314). The reader, however, was left with virtually no details about this process in Jewish education. On the other hand, Philo was considerably less reticent concerning the role of Scripture in the broader context of adult culture. It will now be our task to explore these aspects of his discourse.

For Philo, the role of Scripture took on unprecedented importance in Hellenistic and Roman Egypt. None of the extant writers prior to him had focused their literary activity on the interpretation of the Torah. While Artapanus and Ezekiel the Tragedian, for example, referred to Biblical heroes, they related to Scripture mainly as a storehouse of meaningful stories and formative events. The text itself was not important to them, but its contents. Scripture remained so much in the background that Artapanus never even mentioned Moses' achievements as a lawgiver. Philo, by contrast, praised Moses primarily for his role as *nomothetes*. He himself devoted most of his vast literary output to exegesis. The vast majority of his work can be described as Midrash, i.e. a creative reading of Scripture. More importantly, Philo was the first to explain the centrality of the text in philosophical terms. This is highly significant because he thus made a major, yet hitherto overlooked contribution to the process of canonization. His argument for what Jan Assmann has called the "textual coherence" of Jewish culture is indeed a milestone.[1] It gives for the

---

[1] Assmann, Gedächtnis 87–129. Assmann contrasts textual coherence with ritual coherence, distinguishing a culture based on the precise repetition of oral texts from a culture focussing on a written text, which may be interpreted in different ways and whose meaning may thus be changed over time. The canonization of the Hebrew Bible is in his view a prime example of a move from ritual to textual coherence.

first time a comprehensive explanation for assumptions and ideas about the Biblical text which had, in a rather unsystematic fashion, informed such passages as Kg. 2:22:2–13, Neh. 8:1–8 and Deut. 4:1–8.[2] Philo developed a comprehensive theory of language which accounted for the logo-centricity and textuality of Jewish culture.

The basis of Philo's theory is the assumption of a Divine meta-language. This language is natural, without grammar and serves as the archetype for human language which is always to some degree conventional.[3] On the level of the Divine language there is no gap between a name and its referent. God's names for the various objects are identical to their respective essence. Human language, by contrast, is characterized by an inherent gap between a name and its referent.[4] Giving names to objects, man can only hope to approximate their essence. Man will succeed to provide true mimetic names, Philo argues, if his language imitates the Divine Logos. This is so because God's meta-language is the archetype of human utterance. It contains both the pattern of the specific human languages and the perfectly accurate names for all objects. The question of how and to what extent human language can reflect metaphysical realities has thus been transferred from the field of secular epistemology to religion. The accuracy of a name is no longer measured by reference to man's insight into the nature of an object. The relevant criterion has instead become the degree to

---

[2] On the nature and emergence of the Hebrew Canon, as reconstructed from these passages, see especially: J. Barr, *Holy Scripture. Canon, Authority, Criticism* (Oxford 1983); R. H. Pfeiffer, Canon of the Old Testament, in: G.A. Buttrick *et al.* (eds.), *The Interpreter's Dictionary Of The Bible. An Illustrated Encyclopedia* (Nashville 1962) 1:498–520, who pays a little more attention than others to the evidence of Hellenistic Judaism.

[3] While Philo's construct of a Divine meta-language has thus far escaped scholarly attention, his discussion of human language has been examined before, see especially: D. Winston, Aspects of Philo's Linguistic Theory, *SPhA* 3 (1991 = Heirs of the Septuagint. Philo, Hellenistic Judaism and Early Christianity. Festschrift for Earle Hilgert) 109–25; D. Chidester, *Word and Light. Seeing, Hearing and Religious Discourse* (University of Illinois Press 1992) 25–43; R. Mortley, *From Word to Silence. The rise and fall of logos* (Bonn 1986) 1:39–44; cf. also P. A. K. Otte, *Das Sprachverständnis bei Philo von Alexandrien* (Tübingen 1967), who mistakenly applies Heideggerian terms to the discussion of Philo.

[4] Platonists and Stoics paid particular attention to this question, both arguing for a close connection between names and the nature of the named objects, while Aristotle and the Peripatetics argued for the conventional nature of language and thus for an arbitrary connection between a name and its referent; on Hellenistic theories of language, see especially: D.M. Schenkeveld and J. Barnes, Language, in: A. Keimpe *et al.* (eds.), *The Cambridge History of Hellenistic Philosophy* (Cambridge 1999) 177–84; A. A. Long and D. N. Sedley, *The Hellenistic Philosophers* (Cambridge 1987) 1:97–101; M. Pohlenz, Die Begründung der abendländischen Sprachlehre durch die Stoa, *Nachrichten von der Gesellschaft der Wissenschaften zu Göttingen*, philologisch-historische Klasse 1 N. F. 3.6 (1939) 151–98; regarding Plato, see especially: Plato, Crat. 424a–426b; J. Annas, Knowledge and Language: the Thaetetus and the Cratylus, in: M. Schofield and M.C. Nussbaum (eds.), *Language and Logos. Studies in ancient Greek philosophy presented to G. E. L. Owen* (Cambridge 1982) 95–114; P. Friedländer, *Plato* (New York 1964, Germ. orig.) 2:196–215; I.M. Crombie, *An Examination of Plato's Doctrines* (London 1963) 2:475–86

which human language is a mimesis of the Divine language in which the essence of everything is inscribed.[5]

These statements are based on a number of assumptions about the nature and role of language. We must initially appreciate that for Philo, as well as for Plato, language had mainly to do with names.[6] The faculty of naming was associated with the inferior sphere of the senses, because it relies on speaking. In contrast to other senses, such as hearing, however, naming does not involve a merely passive reception of external stimuli, but was instead recognized to be anchored in the mind, man's most active and spiritual part.[7] Speech therefore occupies an intermediary position between the higher, intellectual and the inferior, external realm. It contains the potential for both ascent to true spirituality and decline into merely material and inauthentic existence. Naming moreover implies an epistemological process, signifying a move from a situation of ignorance to full apprehension of a particular object the essence of which is then captured by giving it an appropriate name.[8] Things which cannot be fully grasped can therefore not be named either (All. 1:91–2). No proper name can thus be assigned to God whose nature escapes precise definition and cannot be grasped by distinguishing separate features.[9] Conversely, God who is omniscient does not engage in naming in the usual sense of the word because He does obviously not undergo the respective epistemological process (Mut. 63–5). Philo stresses that after the creation of the world God left the task of naming material objects to Adam, who was supremely qualified for this task because he possessed foremost wisdom.[10]

---

[5] This central aspect of Philo's theory of language resurfaces in Kabbalistic literature. In contrast to the rationalist thinkers of the Middle Ages, the Kabbalists assumed a divine metalanguage, without grammar, which provides the structure of the universe and emanates into the material, human realm. The letters and numbers of Scripture were consequently identified with the Divine *Sefirot*. On Kabbalistic theories of language, see especially: G. Scholem, Der Name Gottes und die Sprachtheorie der Kabbala, *Neue Rundschau* 83 (1972) 470–95, reprinted in: idem, *Judaica. Studien zur jüdischen Mystik* (2nd ed. Frankfurt 1977) 3.7–70, Engl. transl. in: *Diogenes* 79 (1972) 59–80, 80 (1972) 164–94; Y. Liebes, The Seven Double Letters *BGD KFRT*, On the Double *REISH* and the Background of Sefer Yezira (Hebrew), *Tarbiz* 61.2 (1992) 237–47, whose analysis is especially relevant to Philo because Liebes argues for an Alexandrian contemporary setting of the *Book of Yezira*; M. Idel, *Language, Torah, and Hermeneutics in Abraham Abulafia* (New York 1989, Hebr. orig.).

[6] On Plato's overall emphasis on names, see N. Kretzmann, Plato on the Correctness of Names, *Am.Philos. Quart.* 8 (1971) 126–38; T. M. S. Baxter, *The Cratylus. Plato's Critique of Naming* (Leiden 1992). While the Stoics were also interested in the mimetic value of the name, they paid at least equal attention to other aspects of grammar, as Schenkeveld and Barnes, Language; Pohlenz, Sprachlehre, have shown.

[7] Mut. 69; Opif. 69, 145–6; see also: Winston, Linguistic Theory 123–5; Chidester, Word 32–33.

[8] See especially Opif. 149–50, where Philo describes Adam's naming of objects, stressing that it corresponded to his understanding of their nature.

[9] See also: Runia, Naming and Knowing 76–9; regarding Philo's sense of the evasiveness of God's nature, see especially: Mut. 11–2; Mos. 1:75; Immut. 62; Somn. 1:40; All. 1:36.

[10] Mut. 11–2. Philo interpreted those verses in Gen. chap. one, which speak about God's

If language consists of names, yet God essentially refrains from naming, how does Philo conceive of the Divine language? According to Philo God's language is entirely different from its human counterpart. Whereas human language is composed of "names, verbs and the parts of speech in general", Divine language is not composite, but simple and homogeneous (Migr. 48–9). Referring to LXX Ex. 20:18, where the Israelites are said to have "seen the voice" of God,[11] Philo explains the distinct characteristics of the Divine language (Migr. 47–8):

> For this reason, whereas the voice of mortals is judged by hearing, the sacred oracles intimate that the words of God are seen as light is seen, for we are told that "all the people saw the voice", not that they heard it. For what was happening was not an impact of air made by the organs of mouth and tongue, but the radiating splendour of virtue indistinguishable from a fountain of reason. And this is also indicated elsewhere in this way: "you have seen that I have spoken to you out of Heaven" (Ex. 20:22) – not you have heard, and this is for the same reason. Therefore he [Moses] distinguishes the audible from the visible and hearing from seeing, as when he says "you have heard a voice of words and saw no similitude, but only a voice" (Deut. 4:12), making a very subtle distinction, for the voice dividing itself into name and verb and the parts of speech in general he [Moses] naturally spoke of as audible, for it is recognized by hearing; but the voice of God, which is not that of verbs and names, yet seen by the eye of the soul he rightly introduced as visible.

Despite its apparent faithfulness to the Scriptural prooftexts, Philo's interpretation contains a radical proposition. He suggests that in contrast to human language there exists a language which is ideal in the Platonic sense of the word: it is undivided, uncomposed and belongs entirely to the ethereal realm which is governed by reason and vision rather than by hearing. The Divine language is moreover said to be virtue itself and to be comparable to the radiance of light as well as a fountain of reason. These two metaphors indicate its active rather than passive nature. The Divine language effects rather than being moulded. This image of God's ideal language is completed on other occasions. Philo sometimes identifies the Divine Logos with the Ideas and stresses that it serves as an archetype.[12] He moreover insists that the "Divine Logos is an organ of pure and unalloyed speech, too subtle for hearing to catch it, but visible to the soul which is single in virtue of its keenness of sight" (Migr. 52). The Divine language is said to be "incorporeal" and thus by implication

---

naming of his creation, as referring to the ethereal realm of the intelligible world. In his view they do thus not imply a naming of material objects in the regular human sense. See also Opif. 149–50, where Adam is said to name the animals in the Garden of Eden in accordance with their essence as conceived by God.

[11] While the Masoretic text has the plural קֹלֹת, the LXX translates in the singular τὴν φωνήν.

[12] Mos. 2:127; see also: W. Theiler, *Die Vorbereitung des Neuplatonismus* (Berlin 1930) 29–30.

ideal as well as uncomposed (Somn. 1:127). These characteristics suggest a close analogy between the Divine Logos and God Himself, who is also described as undivided, incorporeal and unalloyed.[13]

The implications of Philo's concept of Divine language can hardly be overestimated. In order to appreciate the significance and originality of his contribution, it is initially important to remember that Plato himself, though mentioning the notion of the gods' language, intentionally refrained from investigating into its nature because he considered it beyond human reach (Crat. 400d-401a). Divine words are thus not at all part of his theory of language. It would moreover be out of characer for Plato to assign the role of the Forms to language. For him vision and contemplation are the best and indeed the only ways to truth. In this scheme there was much space for the vision of ideal Forms by the individual soul, as well as for music and mathematics, yet considerably less for words and texts.

Philo's concept of the Divine language represents a considerable philosophical achievement. He has thus complemented the system of Platonic Forms, raising language to the level of an Idea. In this way he has not only attributed utmost importance and real existence to language, but also suggested in Middle-Platonic fashion that this ideal language serves as a general pattern for specific languages.[14] Philo's construction of language parallels to a certain extent his notion of the ideal man whom he describes as "an idea or type or seal, an object of thought only, incorporeal, neither male nor female, by nature incorruptible" (Opif. 134). As Thomas H. Tobin has shown, Philo platonizes here the double account of man's creation in the book of *Genesis*, supplying the notion of an ideal, pre-Adamic model.[15] Philo stresses also in this context the simple and undivided nature of the ideal type. He does so even to the extent of explicitly denying Gen. 1:27, which asserted man's creation as male and female. While the similarities between Philo's concepts of language and man are significant, the former is far more impressive. This is initially so because Philo does not seem to have had a Middle-Platonist model for his definition of the Divine language. His originality in this area differs from his more recipient role regarding the notion of an ideal man which he apparently adopted from Arius Didymus (Eus., Praep. Ev. 11:23). More importantly, Philo idealizes language more than man. For him the ideal language does not belong to the realm of createdness. It rather seems to have preexisted with God Himself. It entirely

---

[13]  See for example: All. 2:2.

[14]  Regarding the Middle-Platonic interpretation of Platonic Forms as generic paradigms, see especially: Theiler, Vorbereitung; *idem, Untersuchungen zur antiken Literatur* (Berlin 1970) 484–501; R. E . Witt, *Albinus and the History of Middle Platonism* (Cambridge 1937 = Transactions of the Cambridge Philological Society 7); Dillon, Middle-Platonists 47–8, 91–6.

[15]  T. H. Tobin, *The Creation of Man: Philo and the History of Interpretation* (Washington 1983 = The Catholic Biblical Quarterly Monograph Series 14) 108–24.

pertains to the realm of the eternal, unchanging, most real and most true. In comparison to the ideal man, Divine language also plays a far more active and generative role. As far as Philo is concerned, the most important function of the Divine language is to provide the hidden code of the universe, which is made explicit in the Hebrew Bible. It is through this code and this text that human beings have access to ultimate truth, including a knowledge of aspects of God's nature.

Philo argues that the Divine language shapes human language. God's Logos contains in his view the pattern of all specific languages and is the basis for their accuracy. Special efforts are therefore made to explain the connection between these two realms. This is by definition an impossible task because man cannot properly speak about the ideal language of God. Philo nevertheless attempts an explanation by employing allegories, which allow for a more tentative and suggestive approach. These allegories are the figures of the water, the light and the seal. They initially indicate a connection between man's utterance and his thought. Their importance ultimately lies in the fact that they describe an emanational relationship between God's Logos, the source of all utterance, and human language as captured in Scripture. Divine language is thus said to transpire into human language, Moses' mind fulfilling an intermediary function and translating ethereal notions into concrete words. This process of transmission culminates in the text and interpretation of Scripture which Philo regards as the closest reflection of the Divine Logos.

The first allegory which deserves our attention is the image of the spring water. Philo distinguishes its purity from the more defective water of the rain and the river.[16] The rain symbolizes for him the onslaught of sense impressions.[17] It lacks deeper sources and is therefore only superficial and deceptive. Man is somewhat helplessly exposed to its influence, because he cannot altogether avoid the reception of sense impressions.[18] The river, too, often symbolizes for Philo the realm of the unreal and transitory.[19] He frequently uses the image in connection with gluttony and drowning in the passions.[20] Not surprisingly, the Nile epitomizes all the inherent dangers of river water.[21] Water in general moreover symbolizes for Philo words and speech. This is sometimes

---

[16] Cf. also: F. Manns, Le symbole eau-Esprit dans le Judaisme ancien, *Studium Biblicum Fransciscanum Analecta* 19 (1983) 152–68, who lists many relevant passages without, however, analysing their function and significance.

[17] See especially: All. 1:25–6; Somn. 2:262.

[18] See especially: All. 2:39, 56; Cher. 116–7.

[19] Philo's emphasis on the river's transitoriness follows the famous statement by Heraclitus, on whom see: J. Barnes, *The Presocratic Philosophers* (London 1982) 65–9; D. Wiggins, Heraclitus' conceptions of flux, fire and material persistence, in: Schofield and Nussbaum, Language and Logos 1–32.

[20] See especially: Fug. 49; Mut. 214; Somn. 2:109, 258, 278.

[21] Somn. 2:258; Conf. 70. On Philo's negative construction of the Nile in the context of the Egyptian Other, see below chapter two.

meant in a negative sense, but most often in a positive. Philo refers on the one hand to the Nile as representing that kind of speech which is "ill-trained, ignorant and practically soulless" (Somn. 2:259). It is transformed into blood "since it cannot provide nourishment, for the speech of indiscipline none can drink" (Somn. 2:259). This kind of speech is ultimately antagonistic to rational thought which is killed like fish in the blood-stream (Somn. 2:260). Philo, however, uses the image of the water also in a neutral and even distinctly positive sense, namely to indicate the outflow of words from the mind through the lips. He says that the lips provide man with the possibility to "give expression to thought, for the stream of words flows through the lips".[22] Using the figures of Moses and Aaron, Philo furthermore explains the following (Det. 38–40):

[Scripture] says that Moses is not "eloquent" (Ex. 4:10), which is equivalent to saying that he has no gift for an oratory which suggests probable truth by fair and persuasive words. Afterwards he follows this up by emphatically stating that he is not merely not eloquent, but absolutely "speechless" (ἄλογος, Ex. 6:12). He is speechless, not in the sense in which we use the word of animals who do not speak, but of him who does not judge it right to pronounce himself through the word uttered by the vocal organ, rather only stamping and impressing on his mind the lessons of true wisdom, the direct opposite of false sophistry. And he will not go down to Egypt and engage in dispute with its sophists until he has been fully trained in the speech, God having shown and perfected all the hermeneutic notions by the election of Aaron who is Moses' brother and of whom he is used to speak as his "mouth" and "spokesman" and "prophet" (Ex. 4:16, 7:1), for all of these belong to speech and word, which is the brother of mind. For mind is the fountain of words (πηγὴ γὰρ λόγων) and speech is its mouth; for all the thoughts, like a stream from a spring, flow and pour forth into the open through speech, and speech is the interpreter of the plans which understanding has formed in its own council-chamber.

Philo uses here the metaphor of the spring-water to indicate how authentic thought is accurately expressed by words. Speech is defined here as an external expression of inner thoughts which have so far been hidden in man's "own council-chamber". The internal and external aspects of the logos are thus intrinsically connected, being two sides of the same coin.[23] Philo's metaphor moreover alludes to the transcendental sources of man's authentic speech. He stresses that Aaron, the interpreter of Moses the mind, has been appointed by God. The accuracy of Moses' utterance through Aaron's mouth is highlighted. In contrast to shallow sophistry this language reflects the real lessons of wisdom and is connected to the mind rather than the sense perceptions. It derives from a deeper, Divine source.

The significance of Philo's allegorization of Moses and Aaron as mind and speech can be appreciated by comparing it to Classical uses of the image of the

---

[22] Somn. 2:262; similarly in Spec. 1:147.
[23] See also: Migr. 71; Congr. 33; Mos. 2:127.

water. Plato had already employed it to describe the continuity between thought and speech (Theaet. 206d):

The first would be making one's own thought clear enough speech by means of verbs and names, imaging the opinion in the stream that flows through the lips, as in a mirror of water.

The Stoics maintained a similar distinction, describing it less poetically as the inward and the uttered Logos.[24] The Stoics, however, tended to focus rather exclusively on spoken language and largely ignored the question of its origin in the mind.[25] Their philosophy of language as well as Plato's probably served as Philo's starting-point, but cannot fully account for the details of his ideas. Indeed, Philo's notion of language is considerably more transcendental. He generally avoids speaking about man's inward logos and instead stresses the Divine origins of man's authentic speech.[26] In the aforementioned context of Moses and Aaron Philo thus concludes that human "speech is furthermore the prophet and public messenger of the oracles which the understanding never ceases to utter from a depth unseen and unapproachable" (Det. 40). Philo must mean by this that the stream of human words originates from man's mind only in a transitional sense. It ultimately derives from deeper Divine sources. The stream indeed emerges from a spring in the Divine realm and culminates in Aaron's utterance, while the human mind fulfills a merely intermediary function. It is not the real source of the word and its independent conceiver, but instead transmits higher notions given by God to the level of human expression and communication.

Philo's allegory of the river in the Garden of Eden further explains the process whereby the Divine word emanates into human terms (Somn. 2:242–5):

The Divine Word descends from the fountain of wisdom like a river to lave and water the Olympian and celestial shoots and plants of virtue-loving souls which are as a garden. And this Holy Word "is separated into four heads" (Gen. 2:10), which means that it is split up into the four virtues ...

It is this Word which one of Moses' company compared to a river, when he said in the Psalms "the river of God is full of water" (Ps. 65:10), where surely it were absurd to use that word literally with reference to rivers of the earth. Instead, as it seems, he represents the Divine Word as full of the stream of wisdom, with no

---

[24] The Stoics called these respectively the λόγος ἐνδιάθετος and λόγος προφορικός.

[25] See also: Pohlenz, Sprachlehre 191–98.

[26] The word ἐνδιάθετος appears only eight times in Philo's work, referring among other things to the inward source of tears (Migr. 157), to Isaac's inward laughter (Mut. 131), and once in the Stoic sense to the inward word (Abr. 83). In Gig. 64 Philo stresses that reason, the father of speech, "has the one and only God for its owner"; in Opif. 149 he similarly says that Adam's innate ability to name things had been implanted by God.

part empty or devoid of itself ... inundated through and through and lifted up on high by the community and unbroken sequence from that everflowing fountain.

This passage reflects Philo's view that the Divine word inundates and nourishes the human soul. The relationship between God's word and wisdom is analogous to that of man's word to his mind: both kinds of logos flow from a spiritual fountain.[27] In the case of God, however, the word is a virtually unmediated mirror-reflection of an autonomous mind, while man's thought and speech are dependent on an external source, namely God. Philo clearly thought of the Divine language in terms of an "inward" and an "outward" Logos, thus applying a notion which he had only very partially used with regard to man. God's language is therefore a natural language in which the idea of an object perfectly corresponds to its name. As a result of this the Divine Logos is highly effective. It flows into man's soul, providing it with right insight which may in turn be translated into human virtue.

The relationship between the fountain of Divine language and the human sphere is desribed in another allegory of the paradisal river (Post. 127–9):

It is in this way that the word of God waters the virtues, for the word of God is the source and spring of noble conduct. The lawgiver intimates as much by the words "a river goes out from Eden to water the Garden. Thence it is separated into four heads" (Gen. 2:10).

For there are four main virtues, wisdom, courage, temperance and justice ... These have sprung from the Divine word as from a single root, and that word is likened to a river because of the unbroken flow of the constant stream of words and doctrines ever sweet and fresh by which it brings nourishment and growth to the souls that love God.

Philo clarifies in this passage how God's word is transmitted into the human soul and translated into words and doctrines. This process implies a transformation of ethereal and absolute notions into humanly graspable units.[28] It can be illustrated by the image of the water, which suggests continuity between God and man. The water thus flows from Him to man, transferring patterns from one realm to the other, while preserving the essence of the transmitted patterns. The authenticity of the Divine language is expressed by its morally beneficient effect. When translated into human language, it plants virtue in the soul, thus communicating the nature of the Divine Logos which is said to be "pure virtue".[29]

---

[27] See also All. 1:63–5, where Philo allegorizes the paradisal river as generic virtue which is derived from God's reason; similarly in All. 2:87.

[28] See also Sacr. 131, where the Divine flow is said to be conceived by man in the form of laws.

[29] Philo also develops this aspect in the context of the matriarchs drinking spring-water. He praises Leah and Rebecca for drinking from the "springs of moral beauty" and from "God's wisdom, that never-failing spring" (Post. 135–6). They are contrasted to Hagar who draws water from a skin bottle which represents sense-perception and the imperfect wisdom of the sophists (Det. 137–40). Philo makes similar statements in Fug. 195–202.

Another allegorization of Moses and Aaron in the context of Ex. 4:10 also argues this point. This time Philo expains Moses' lack of eloquence as follows (Mos. 1:84):

God, finding delight in Moses because of his modesty, said to him: "do you not know who it is that gave man a mouth and formed his tongue and throat and all the organisms of reasonable speech? It is I myself, therefore fear not, for a sign from Me will become articulate and be brought over to metrical speech, so that none can hinder the stream of words from flowing easily and smoothly from a fountain undefiled. And if you should need an intepreter, you will have in your brother a mouth to assist your service, to report your words to the multitude, as you report those of God to him".

Philo suggests here through the image of the water a direct line of continuity stretching from God through Moses to Aaron. While God is the undefiled source of speech, Moses represents the human mind through which the Divine Logos is filtered, while Aaron symbolizes the interpretation of that word to a wider audience. As the lawgiver of the Jews, Moses undoubtedly stands for the Torah, which Philo thus identifies as the human script reflecting most authentically the Divine Logos. Aaron, on the other hand, stands for the authentic and authoritative exegesis of the Torah.

It is highly significant that Philo associates both figures with the priesthood. Moses was in his view a high-priest, while Aaron was not only the founder of the priestly line as in the Bible, but also the incarnation of the Divine Logos.[30] Philo generally praises the priests for their exemplary spirituality, their water purifications and their cleansing of the people.[31] Philo's above interpretations of Moses and Aaron place the foremost representatives of the priesthood in the centre of Torah transmission and exegesis. Moses indicates the priestly framework of the text's revelation, whereas Aaron signifies the priests' leading role in the study and explanation of Scripture.[32] Philo's priestly sympathies further become apparent in his interpretation of the Garden of Eden as the Temple. He calls Paradise a "Divine Park" (Opif. 153), a "sacred spot" (All. 1:62) and associates the Tree of Life exegetically with the altar and sacrifices (All. 1:48–52). He moreover says that no defiling thought could penetrate into this holy space just as Aaron, taken to mean mountainous and referring to Mount Zion, represents lofty and sublime thoughts "which will not let him cherish any

---

[30]  Mos. 2:66–186; Fug. 108–10; Somn. 1:215.

[31]  Regarding the priests' spirituality, see especially: Mos. 2:138; All. 3:144; Cher. 14–7; Spec. 1:188, 191, 2:163; Post. 182.

[32]  Philo thus strengthens a claim of the priests which became increasingly challenged by the Pharisees towards the end of the Second Temple Period and was ultimately replaced by the rabbinic leadership which established itself step by step after the destruction of the Temple. On the relatively late date of the rabbinic ascendance and the initial persistence of the priests after the destruction of the Temple, see especially: S. D. Fraade, *From Tradition to Commentary. Torah and Its Interpretation in the Midrash Sifre to Deuteronomy* (Albany 1991 = SUNY Series in Judaica: Hermeneutics, Mysticism, and Religion).

reasoning that is mean and low" (Ebr. 128). This identification of Paradise with the Mountain of God is probably based on Ez. 28:11–4, where this connection is first suggested. Given the dominance of the image of the paradisal river in Philo's theory of language, it is clear that he generally associates the revelation and transmission of Scripture with the priestly circles.

It is remarkable that another Jewish thinker of the Second Temple Period, who shared Philo's sympathies for the priesthood, similarly allegorized the paradisal river in terms of the Torah and the Temple. Ben Sira interpreted the four rivers of the Garden of Eden as a reference to the wisdom flowing forth from the mouth of God into the Torah.[33] He even used the same metaphor of water as Philo to describe the emanation of the Divine word: it pours forth from God's mouth like mist, settles in the Jerusalem Temple and finally transpires into the Torah, culminating in prophetic exegesis. Ben Sira defined his own role in the same way as Philo had described Aaron's. He, too, transmitted water from a higher source and served as a canal delivering it to a wider audience (Sir. 24:30).[34] The outflow of Divine wisdom into the paradisal river and its subsequent canalisation through the Torah closely corresponds to the process Philo described. Both writers had in mind the emanation of Scripture from the mouth of God and its interpretation by a priestly exegete. Both writers moreover established in this way the utmost centrality of Scripture for Jewish culture. The Torah was for them not just a foundational text as understood in other cultures, but the only text which contained the whole truth to which man can aspire.[35] Reading Scripture provided access to that truth and gave a focus to Jewish life. While Ben Sira made this point rather more allusively, Philo firmly stated and justified it on the basis of an elaborate theory of language.

Light is the second metaphor which deserves our attention. Philo borrowed this image from the Platonic dialogues, thus adopting its transcendental dimension and its physiological conception. Based on the simile of the sun in the sixth and seventh book of the *Republic*, light represents for Philo a source of highest truth and insight.[36] God is spoken of as the sun, who replaces the Form of the

---

[33] Sir. 24:1–12, 23–34; on Ben Sira's sympathies for the priesthood, see especially: S. M. Olyan, Ben Sira's Relationship to the Priesthood, *HTR* 80.3 (1987) 261–86; L. G. Perdue, *Wisdom and Cult. A Critical Analysis of the Views of Cult in the Wisdom Literature of Israel and the Ancient Near East* (Missoula 1977) 184–90.

[34] Regarding the transmission of the Divine language through the Temple and the Torah, see especially Sir. 24:10–15; wisdom's priestly function is stressed by the verb λειτουργέω; see also: R. Smend, *Die Weisheit des Jesus Sirach* (Berlin 1906) 2:218–20; Hengel, Judaism and Hellenism 1:131–38; J. Marböck, *Weisheit im Wandel. Untersuchungen zur Weisheitstheologie bei Ben Sira* (Bonn 1971, repr. 1999 in BZAW Bd. 272) 63–68.

[35] On the difference between a canonical book in Greek literature and the Hebrew canon, see especially: Assmann, Gedächtnis 103–29.

[36] See also: F. N. Klein, Die Lichtterminologie bei Philon von Alexandrien und in den hermetischen Schriften. Untersuchungen zur Struktur der religiösen Sprache der hellenistischen Mystik (Leiden 1962) 13–33; V. Nikiprowetzky, Thèmes et traditions de la lumière

Good in the Platonic system.[37] Philo stresses that God is "not only light, but the archetype of every other light, prior to and high above every other light, holding the position of the model of a model".[38] The radiating beams of the light moreover suggest that the Divine realm of ultimate truth can also penetrate into the lower, material world. This function of descending is identified with the Logos which is sometimes equated with the sun itself (Somn. 1:85–6). On other occasions the Logos is said to be the "images" of the Divine rays (Somn. 1:115) and to "contain His fullness, namely light" (Somn. 1:75). Philo also speaks of the Divine words as "lesser luminaries" (Somn. 1:72). It emerges that the Logos transmits the fiery essence of God. Its flame can *pars pro toto* illuminate the material world and enlighten man.

Philo also accepts Plato's physiological conception of light. This means that he, too, thinks of the process of seeing as a real physical encounter between the beams of light radiating from the subject of vision, on the one hand, and the beams of light emitted or reflected from the object of vision on the other.[39] Seeing actually implies a special kind of touching and can take place only between similar types of stuff. Philo has thus embraced Plato's physiological model of vision, but applies it mainly to the realm of spirituality where Plato had hardly ever used it. Plato had focused on simple human perception, while treating spiritual enlightenment in a distinctly metaphorical sense. When speaking of the soul's contemplation of the Forms, he did not therefore mention any physiological process or direct contact between the light beams of the soul and the Ideal Forms.[40] Philo, on the other hand, cherished only minimal interest in the physiological process of regular vision, but paid special attention to the vision of man's "spiritual eyes".[41] Physiological terms were thus appropriated for entirely new purposes.

Philo suggested that God, as the supreme source of light, possesses also perfect vision. The Divine light is so strong that it reaches everywhere and sees everything. All secrets will be exposed as in the sunlight. Philo significantly

---

chez Philon d'Alexandrie, *SPhA* 1 (1989) 6–33; cf. Plato, Rep. 6:507d-517a; Crombie, Examination 1:111–21.

[37] Somn. 1:73, 90; see also: E.R. Goodenough, *By Light, Light; The Mystic Gospel of Hellenistic Judaism* (New Haven 1935) 7–8, 19, 243; R. Bultmann, Zur Geschichte der Lichtsymbolik im Altertum, *Philologus* 97 (1948) 1–36 (repr. in: *idem, Exegetica* (Tübingen 1967) 323–55).

[38] Somn. 1:75; see also: P. Borgen, Logos was the True Light, *NT* 14 (1972) 115–30, especially 120, where he stresses the importance of Somn. 1:75 in the context of the exegesis of Gen. 1:3.

[39] Cf. Plato, Tim. 45b-d; see also: Chidester, Word 35.

[40] See especially: Plato, Phaedo 66e-69e, 79a-84b; cf. Symp. 212a; see also: B. McGinn, *The Foundations of Mysticism* (New York 1992) 24–35.

[41] See especially: Abr. 76 where Philo explains the vision of God in terms of the eyes "touching" (ψαύειν) the Eternal; see also: G. Delling, The "One Who Sees God" in Philo, in: Greenspahn, Nourished with Peace 27–41. Note also that in comparison to Plato, Philo limits the active and light-emitting function of man's physical eyes (All. 3:108).

says also of the Divine Logos that it has the "keenest sight", being "able to survey all things" (All. 3:171). This applies to language as well. The image of the light indicates how the Divine language transpires into the human words and how God's voice can be seen by the Isrealites. This vision implies intimate contact, even a touching of each other. Moses and Aaron are again used to explain this process (Det. 125–7):

God is an author in whose work you will find no myth or fiction, but truth's inexorable rules all observed as though graven on stone. You will find no metres and rhythms and tuneful verses charming the ear with their music, but nature's own consummate works, which possess a harmony all their own. And even as the mind with its ear tuned to God's poems, rejoices, so the word in harmony with the meanings of thought and in a way approaching it, is necessarily glad. This will be shown by the Divine oracle to the all-wise Moses, in which these words are contained: "look, is there not Aaron your brother, the Levite? I know that he will speak for you. And look, he shall come forth to meet you and on seeing you he shall rejoice" (LXX Ex. 4:14).

The Creator says that He knows that the uttered word, being brother to the mind, can speak, for He has made it like an instrument of sound to be an articulate utterance of our whole complex being. This Logos, both for me and for you and for all men, sounds and speaks and announces our thoughts and, more than this, goes out to meet that which reason has thought.

Philo establishes in this passage the unique status of Divine poetry, namely the Torah. This text, he argues, is not guided by a wish to amuse the readers, as other types of literature are, but by an earnest desire to instruct. The Torah is a perfectly mimetic text, directly reflecting the reality of nature as arranged by God.[42] Philo moreover specifies how the Divine word is received and interpreted by the human mind. For this purpose Moses and Aaron are again allegorized as different parts of human speech. Moses represents once more the human mind which receives the Divine word, while Aaron is again said to spread the word to a broader audience. The text of the Torah thus contains an ethereal truth which waits to be made manifest in human terms. The continuity between the Divine Logos and the priestly exegesis of the Torah is this time not expressed by the image of water flowing from one end to the other. Philo instead suggests that vision and thus direct contact play a crucial role. The human word is in this context exceptionally active. In contrast to the mouth, which merely received the Divine word-stream, the human word is now accredited with the ability to capture the Divine thought informing Scripture. Philo stresses its vigour by pointing to its outgoing nature: it actually meets and touches the thought.[43]

---

[42] Concerning the unique status of the Torah according to Philo, see also: Niehoff, Philo's Views on Paganism 139–42; for a detailed discussion of Torah as law of nature, see below chapter nine.

[43] The Septuagintal term συνάντησις suggests that a physical contact is involved in this encounter.

This dimension is fully explored in the subsequent passage where Philo initially stresses that the human mind "bursts forth", receiving an "impulse towards some congenial object" (Det. 127). After reading Divine poetry it becomes "pregnant" with thoughts which are in the "womb" of the mind and can only be delivered by human utterance. This delivery takes place in the following way (Det. 127–9):

This sound produced by the tongue and other organs of speech receives the thoughts and like mid-wives brings them forth to the light. For just as things laid up in darkness are hidden until a light shine on them and show them, in the same way conceptions are stored in the understanding, an invisible place, until the voice illumine (ἐναυγάσασα) them like a light and uncover them all. It is therefore correctly said that the word goes forth to meet the thoughts and running in its eagerness to lay hold of them (καταλαβεῖν), yearning to announce them. For to each one his proper work is the most desired and speaking is the proper work of the logos and so it hastens to it, by nature treating it as a friend. And it rejoices and is glad, when, as though illumined it sees and fully grasps the sense of the matter manifest to it, for when grasping it with the hands (περιδραξάμενος), it becomes a perfect interpreter.

The human word, it emerges, experiences a mystical vision in the process of grasping the underlying thoughts of Scripture. Philo describes this vision in terms of light beams radiating from the word and uncovering the idea. He stresses that the word's grasping of the thought is a most natural process appropriate to its innate qualities. The expression οἰκειώσει moreover suggests a deep affinity between the word and the thought. It reflects Philo's conviction, based on Plato's physiological concepts, that only such things can meet in vision which are essentially of the same stuff. The human word is thus akin to God's Logos, being able to grasp it literally and metaphorically in the process of reading the text.

Philo's notion of logo-vision attributes a far more forceful role to the word than to the soul, which is also to some extent capable of vison and ascent to the intelligible world (Opif. 69–70). Like Plato's soul it must initially liberate itself from the material chains of the senses and can then begin to rise "on soaring wing". Yet the soul remains rather passive in the vision of ethereal truths and is ultimately overwhelmed by the onslaught of Divine light (Opif. 71). While active in the first phase, the soul cannot behold God because it is dazzled and blinded. Philo does not even mention the light which might be projected from "the eyes of the soul". If existent at all, it is far too weak and dissimilar to take an active part in the vision of God.[44] Even in the case of Abraham, who is granted at least a partial vision of God, the human soul remains distinctly passive at the crucial stage. Philo concludes in this context that "our sight could not have borne the rays that pour from Him that is, since it is not even able to

---

[44] Philo stresses the importance of a mutual emission of light in the process of spiritual vision, see especially Praem. 44–6.

look upon the beams of the sun" (Abr. 76). He moreover insists that the eyes of the human soul cannot see God, because "it was contrary to holiness that the mortal should touch the eternal" (Abr. 76). Abraham does not therefore himself perceive God, but is granted a partial self-manifestation on the part of God (Abr. 79–80):

He in His love for mankind, when the soul approached Him, did not turn away His face, but came forward to meet him and revealed His nature, so far as the beholder's power of sight allowed. This is why we are told not that the Sage saw God, but that God was seen by him. For it were impossible that anyone should by himself apprehend the truly Existent, did not He reveal and manifest Himself.

Philo's Jacob experienced a similar vision (Praem. 37–9):

Earlier the eyes of his soul had been closed, but by means of continuous striving he began though slowly to open them … For a beam purer than ether and incorporeal suddenly shone upon them and revealed the conceptual world ruled by its charioteer. That charioteer, ringed with beams of undiluted light, was hard to see and guess, for the eye was dimmed by the dazzling beams, and yet in spite of the fiery stream which flooded it, his sight withstood in its unusual longing to see it. The Father and Saviour perceiving the sincerity of his yearning had pity and gave power to the visitation of his eyesight and did not grudge him the vision of Himself in so far as it was possible for mortal and created nature to approach Him. Yet the vision only showed that He is, not what He is.

This account of Jacob's vision highlights the limitations of the human soul, which is once more dazzled by the intensity of the Divine light. Philo insists that Jacob did not see God Himself, but merely apprehended His existence. This is necessarily so because God "cannot be discerned by anyone – to God alone is it permitted to perceive God".[45] The human soul thus remains ultimately blind to the nature of God and His thoughts. The vision of the word, on the other hand, can reach further. It is distinctly more active, radiating light and illuminating ethereal mysteries. Assuming the role of human eyes, the word is thus able to be in direct touch with the Divine Logos. Reading God's poetry, man gains access not only to the notion of God's existence, but also to His specific characteristics and wishes. Logo-vision is therefore superior to the vision of the soul. While the latter achieves only partial results, logo-vision indicates a distinctly Jewish path to the ultimate truth. This path is based on the assumption that the Torah is God's poetry and a perfect mimesis of His Logos which has formed nature. In the process of exegesis the human word can thus approach the congenial word of God.

---

[45] Praem. 40. Moses is perhaps the only exception. Philo says in Q.E. 2: 51 and 29 that Moses beheld God in the most intimate way, He causing His "incorporeal rays to shine" on him. Not surprisingly, Moses was at the same time said to be "akin to God and truly divine". On Moses as god, see above chapter three.

Philo bases his theory of logo-vision on LXX Ex. 20:18, where the children of Israel are said to see the voice of God. In Dec. 46–7 he describes the experience of the Israelites at Mt. Sinai in the following terms:

To their amazement a voice came forth from heaven, the blaze becoming utterly distinct discourse, familiar to the audience; and so clearly were the words formed by it that they seemed to see rather than to hear them. The Law confirms my statement, for it is written "all the people saw the Voice" (LXX Ex. 20:18).

Philo explains here that the Divine voice did not come out of the fire as an independent substance, but was the transformed fire itself. This fire-Logos had a beneficient effect, illuminating and instructing the Israelites without dazzling them (Dec. 48). God conveyed not only the general idea of His existence, but specific commands which were grasped by the Israelites through vision. Exposure to the Divine word has thus created a space where man can encounter God more intimately than anywhere else. While man's eyes, even the spiritual eyes of his soul, cannot directly behold Him, it is possible to see His voice and understand His essence through His word.

Philo's concept of logo-vision may have derived from his interest in dreams, a subject to which he devoted no less than three treatises.[46] As Philo well recognized, dreams are transcripts of Divine visions.[47] They combine the two elements crucial to his conception of the Torah, namely the textual dimension and the vision of God's message. Philo even highlights the visual role of words when interpreting Jacob's dream about the ladder. The stairway becomes an allegory for the human soul, while the angels moving on it represent the Divine words (Somn. 1:147):

Up and down throughout its [the stairway's] whole extent are moving incessantly the words of God, drawing it [the soul] up with them when they ascend and disconnecting it with what is mortal and showing it the sight of the only objects worthy our vision.

According to Philo, Jacob sees in his dream divine words which take him up to a vision of the ethereal realm. Strikingly, it is not Jacob's soul which initiates the spiritual ascent and enables him to see God, but the divine words which elevate him. Words are the vehicle which can bring man close to Him. Scripture is in Philo's view precisely the same kind of text as Jacob's dream. It contains divine words which can provide a vision of God and "the real nature of things" (Somn. 1:164). Enriching traditional oneirocriticism by Plato's physiology of human vision, Philo is thus able to suggest that the Biblical text bridges the gap between the human and the divine realm. It creates a space where true encounter is possible, human words matching and even touching the divine Logos.

---

[46] Only two of them have survived.

[47] For more details and bibliographical references, see: M. R. Niehoff, A Dream which is not Interpreted is like a Letter which is not Read, *JJS* 43.1 (1992) 58–84.

The seal is the last of the Philonic allegories which remains to be examined. This image is borrowed from Alexandrian Middle Platonism where it had become an established allegory for the Ideal Form and its shaping influence on the material world.[48] Philo uses it in a new sense, applying it for the first time to language and literary creativity. The seal now indicates how God's thoughts are expressed by His ποίησις in the double sense of the word.[49] This means that the Divine word functions like a seal, leaving both written signs in Moses' mind and structuring patterns on the material realm (Opif. 16–24). The creation of the world has thus simultaneously to do with the shaping of *hyle* and the composition of a written account. Moses' writing down of the Torah may furthermore be said to correspond to God's *poiesis*. In both cases, God's and Moses', the seal functions as a converter of ideas into letters which are legible to regular human beings.

Philo's allegory of the seal initially establishes language as the principle transmittor of the ideal archetypes. He applies to the image typically Middle-Platonic notions, speaking of it as an "archetypal seal" and an "incorporeal idea" as well as stressing that "the copy which is made by the impression is something else – a material something, naturally perceptible by the senses, yet not actually coming into relation with them" (Ebr. 133). Philo also says that the seal does not at all change while moulding "innumerable substances", which might later vanish, while the seal itself will retain its exact identity (Det. 76). Finally, the seal is said to provide the generic form from which specific examples derive (All. 1:22). All of these statements indicate Philo's familiarity with the discourse of the Middle-Platonists, who had elevated the seal to a much higher level than Plato himself. For the latter the seal had played only a subordinate function in the context of human memory. Plato explained human remembrance by analogy to the wax which receives imprints from the thoughts and perceptions "just as we make impressions from seal rings" (Theaet. 191d). The result is that "whatever is imprinted, we remember and know as long as its image lasts, but whatever is rubbed out or cannot be imprinted we forget and do not know".[50] The students of Plato, however, no longer interpreted the seal by

---

[48] The use of the image in this sense is first attested by Arius Didymus (Eus., Praep. Ev. 11:23). Theiler, Vorbereitung 489–99, argued that it may have developed earlier and that Philo may have become familiar with it through Eudoros of Alexandria.

[49] God's thoughts replace the Platonic Ideas, see also: A. N. M. Rich, The Platonic Ideas as the Thoughts of God, *Mnemosyne* N.S. 4.7 (1954) 123–33; H. A. Wolfson, Extradeical and Introdeical Ideas, in: idem, *Religious Philosophy. A Group of Essays.* (Cambridge MA 1961) 27–68; B. McGinn, Platonic and Christian: The Case of the Divine Ideas, in: R. Link-Salinger (ed.), *Of Scholars, Savants and their Texts: Studies in Philosophy and Religious Thought. Essays in Honor of Arthur Hyman* (New York 1989) 163–72; M. Jones, The Ideas of God as Thoughts of God, *CP* 21 (1926) 317–26.

[50] Theaet. 191d. In All. 1:100 Philo uses the metaphor of the wax in a perfectly Platonic way, applying it to the soul and its impressibility; see also: Immut. 43; Agr.166–7; Her. 181, 294.

reference to an impression made by virtually anything on the soul. They instead identified it with the transmission of ideal notions. Philo evidently accepted their ideas and regarded the seal as a translator of ethereal notions into human terms. At the same time, however, he added to the Middle-Platonic approach the dimension of language. Words were now for the first time identified with the seal. The significance of this step can initially be appreciated by the fact that Plato had assigned precisely the opposite role to language, which he had likened to impressionable, flexible and thus malleabable wax (Rep. 9:588d). Transferring language to the realm of the seal meant to enhance its status dramatically and to invest it with authentic existence, permanent character and creative power.

Philo elaborates upon the linguistic aspects of the seal metaphor mostly in his book *On the Creation of the World*. This treatise has so far been exclusively regarded as a book on ποίησις in the material sense.[51] Yet Philo apparently also meant it as a kind of *ars poetica*. He introduces this treatise by a discussion of Moses' literary activity when writing down the Torah. He uses the allegory of the seal to describe the process by which the ethereal ideas were translated into human language (Opif. 4–6):

Whether poet or speech writer, nobody could properly praise the beauty of the ideas [implied in] the creation of the world. For they exceed [our capacity of] speech and hearing, being too great and august to be adapted to the organs of any mortal. Yet one must not therefore keep silent, but loving God, venture beyond our power, saying – not on our own behalf – little instead of much, upon which the human mind will hit when possessed by love and longing for wisdom. For as the minutest seal when being engraved receives the impressions of colossal and great [figures], so apparently will be intimated through smaller characters the exceeding beauties of the creation of the world which is recorded in the laws – [beauties] which overshadow by their sparks the souls of the readers.

Philo indicates in this passage that he thought of the seal as a bridge between the absolute beauty of nature as fashioned by God and the human mind, which is limited in its capacity to absorb sublime notions. It furthermore emerges that Philo assigned to the Torah the function of a seal: it is a text which is on one side engraved by "colossal figures" and leaves on the other side miniature characters which reflect the contours of the original figures. Scripture thus adjusts ideas "too great and august" for human apprehension to the "organs" of man. Language is the best instrument for such a translation, because it can most

---

[51] See especially: Runia, Timaeus; G. D. Farandos, *Kosmos und Logos nach Philon von Alexandria, Elementa. Schriften zur Philosophie und ihrer Problemgeschichte* 4 (1976) 150–306; H. F. Weiss, *Untersuchungen zur Kosmologie des hellenistischen und palästinischen Judentums* (Berlin 1966) 18–74; R. P. C. Kannengiesser, Philon et les Pères sur la double Création de l'homme, in: *Philon d'Alexandrie. Lyon 11–15 Septembre 1966, Colloques Nationaux du Centre National de la Recherche Scientifique* (Paris 1967) 277–96.

accurately capture the Divine secrets of Nature. The Torah and Philo's interpretation of it therefore express ultimate truth. Unlike Plato's *Timaeus*, they are not just a likely story falling short of the vision of the Ideal Forms, but an accurate translation of God's colossal images.[52] Philo thus suggests a distinctly text-centred alternative to Plato's emphasis on vision: studying Scripture leads to a perfect understanding of the universe and man's place in it.

Philo continues to explain the role of the Divine Logos as a seal in the process of creation. He explains that the intelligible world, which God fashioned before the material cosmos, "is nothing else than the Word of God when He was already engaged in the act of creation" (Opif. 24). This Logos-intelligible word is at the same time His seal (Opif. 25). In Opif. 17–20 Philo uses the parable of the architect to describe its function in the creation of the world, which he likens to the foundation of a city:[53]

Whenever a city is being founded to satisfy the soaring ambition of some king or governor ... there comes forward now and again some trained architect who ... first sketches in his own mind wellnigh all the parts of the city that is to be wrought out ... Thus after having received in his own soul like in wax the figures of these objects severally, he carries about the image of a city, which is the creation of his mind. Then by his innate power of memory, he recalls the images of the various parts of this city, and imprints their types yet more distinctly in it: and like a good craftsman he begins to build the city of stones and timber, keeping his eye upon the pattern and making the visible and tangible objects correspond in each case to the incorporeal ideas ...
Exactly as the city which was fashioned beforehand within the mind of the architect held no place in the outer world, but had been engraved in the soul of the artificer as by a seal, in the same way the universe that consisted of ideas would have no other location than the Divine Logos, which was the author of this ordered frame. For what other place could there be for His powers sufficient to receive and contain, I say not all but any one of them whatever uncompounded and untempered?

The Logos is in this parable compared to an architect who translates the ambitious ideas of his king first into detailed plans and then into material constructions. In the process he sketches in his own mind the design of the future city, leaving in his soul such lasting impressions that he can build the city in their image.[54] This intelligible model, Philo insists, plays the same role as a seal

---

[52] Regarding Plato's views on the status of text, which he himself has composed in the *Timaeus*, see: Tim. 29d, 28a; see also: Cornford, Plato's Cosmology 21–32; Runia, Timaeus 412–6, 433–6.

[53] For the full text of the parable and a detailed analysis of it, see next chapter.

[54] Philo thus suggests that they are not ideal in the Platonic sense of external Forms; cf. Tim. 28a, where the architect is said to "keep his gaze fixed on that which is uniform"; and Tim. 29a, where the demiurge is said to have "fixed his gaze on the eternal". Philo's emphasis on the internal fashioning of the scheme might in fact be regarded as the foundation of an expressionistic notion of art, which is no longer thought to imitate external reality, but mostly internal images – a notion which was subsequently elaborated in Seneca's *Epistles*, whence it exercised seminal influence on literary theory in Western civilization; on mimetic theories

which renders colossal figures into small characters. The Logos thus tran-
scribes the grand plans of the transcendent God and shapes material reality in
accordance with them. Philo identified this transcript at least occasionally with
the written text of the Torah. This emerges from his interpretation of LXX Gen.
2:4, which adds to the Hebrew term תולדות the word βίβλος (All. 1:19–21):

"This is the book of creation of the heaven and the earth, when it came into being"
(LXX Gen. 2:4). The Logos ... is the primal origin both of the mind ordering itself after
the ideas and of sense-perception in the domain of the mind (if the expression is
permissible) ordering itself after the ideas. "Book" is Moses' name for God's Logos, in
which have been inscribed and engraved the composition of all else ... Above he has
called this day a book, because he indicates the creation of heaven and earth as fashioned in both. For God makes (ποιεῖ) both of them through His own supremely manifest and radiant Logos.

This passage beautifully explores the double meaning of the Greek term ποίησις
which implies both material and literary creativity. Philo suggests that for God
both aspects are identical, because He creates the world through His written
word. Engraving by a seal and writing Scripture thus become synonymous
terms. Both of them describe the effects of the Divine Logos on the material
realm. This is possible because the Logos functions like a seal translating
colossal, ideal figures into minute and concrete characters which can be grasped
by man.

The Torah thus emerges as the text which reflects most accurately the nature
of the universe as well as God's own *poesis* and character. Reading this text one
gains access to the highest truth. Writing it down, as Moses did, and interpreting
it, transfers man to the realm of *Imitatio Dei*.[55] For Philo the unique status of the
Torah moreover implied both the privileged status of the Jews among the
nations and the distinctly textual orientation of Jewish culture. Jewish life
should to a considerable extent revolve around Scripture. Philo himself devoted
most of his intellectual efforts to interpreting this text which he believed to have
achieved canonical status. He describes it as the "sacred books" which Moses
composed "under the instruction of God".[56] Unlike the law codes of other

---

of literature in Antiquity, see especially: D. A. Russell, *Criticism in Antiquity* (Berkeley
1981) 99–113; E. Auerbach, *Mimesis. The Representation of Reality in Western Literature*
(Princeton 1953, Germ. orig.) 3–23.

[55] Cf. Kabbalistic writers who attempted to imitate God by using the words of the Hebrew
Bible to create new material objects; on these activities, see especially: M. Idel, *Golem.
Jewish Magical and Mystical Traditions on the Articifial Anthropoid* (Albany 1990 = SUNY
Series in Judaica: Hermeneutics, Mysticism, and Religion); Y. Liebes, Golem Reconsidered
(Hebrew), *Kiryat Sefer* 63.4 (1990–1) 1305–22, especially 1309–12.

[56] Mos. 2:11. In Cont. 25 Philo mentions "the laws and oracles delivered through the
mouth of the prophets, and psalms and anything else which fosters and perfects knowledge
and piety". While this statement indicates Philo's awareness of additional writings, it does
not suggest their canonical status. Indeed, the formulation "anything else which fosters and

nations, the Biblical ordinances "truly come from God" and "omit nothing that is needful" (Mos. 2:12). As a transcript of God's own Logos, Moses' legislation thus contains everything essential a Jew ever needs to know. This text is all-encompassing and perfect, containing an answer to any question that may arise. This notion closely corresponds to the words of the Mishnaic teacher Ben Bag Bag, who famously formulated it thus: "turn it [Scripture] and turn it for everything is contained in it" (Avot 5:5).

In the same vein Philo also believed the Biblical text to be eternal and unchanging. While the external fortune of the Israelites often undergoes surprising reversals and radically changes, the spiritual centre of their life always remains the same. Philo emphatically argues that the Mosaic legislation differs on these grounds from that of all the other nations (Mos. 2:14–5):

> But Moses is alone in this, that his laws, firm and unmoved, unshakable, stamped as it were with the seals of nature herself, remain secure from the day when they were first enacted to now, and we may hope that they will remain for all future ages as though immortal ... Thus, though the nation has undergone so many changes, both to increased prosperity and the reverse, nothing – not even the smallest part of the ordinances – has been removed, [57] because all have clearly paid high honour to their venerable and godworthy character.

Philo elaborates here on formulations of the Deuteronomist, who had described the status of the Torah in more tentative terms. The latter referred to a time when the Israelites had returned to their land. Many of them took this normalization of their nationality as a sign that they were no longer obliged by the laws enacted in exile. The Deuteronomist vehemently opposed this approach and argued that even though the Israelites now live in the "land of milk and honey", they must continue to remember the God who has led them out of Egypt and respect His ordinances.[58] In this context he urged his readers not to "add to the word which I command you, nor take from it; that you may keep the commandments of the Lord your God" (Deut. 4:2). What was for the Deuteronomist only a programme, however, was for Philo a reality. He claimed that the laws of

---

perfects knowledge and piety" seems to refer to a broad range of not clearly defined books, which the Therapeutae cherished and preserved in a consecrated room of the house. It is therefore not surprising that Philo himself hardly ever refers to the prophetic books which obviously did not require the same kind of commentary as the canonical Torah.

[57] Colson's translation *ad.loc.* of ἐκινήθη as "disturbed" does not reflect the verb's original meaning of motion. Herodotus and Aristotle had already used this term in the context of removing laws and ancestral traditions (Hdt., 3:80; Arist., Pol. 1268b28). Philo thus elaborates here on an idea which he had already introduced earlier in this passage by the expressions ἀσάλευτα and μένει παγίως. Philo repeats this idea in Mos. 2:34 where he says that the translators of the Torah into Greek knew that they "could not add or take away or transfer anything, but must keep the original form and shape".

[58] On Deuteronomistic position, see: M. Weinfeld, *Deuteronomy and the Deuteronomistic School* (Oxford 1972) 161–4; Assmann, Gedächtnis 212–28.

Moses had indeed never been changed. Neither had their legitimacy ever been challenged. The Jews had instead always recognized their unique value and respected even the minutest part of the ordinances. Philo presents this as an obvious and natural state of affairs. This is so, he argues, because the text of the Torah authentically reflects the Divine Logos and is "stamped as it were with the seals of nature herself".[59] Philo's theory of language has thus provided a philosophical justification for the canonical status of Scripture. Given the specific roots of this text in the Divine Logos, one cannot but relate to it as the ultimate and unchanging source of truth to which the Jews had privileged access.

Given these views, it might come as a surprise that Philo did not prefer the original Hebrew text of the Bible. On the contrary, the LXX enjoyed in his eyes the same canonical status. Unlike Aristeas, he described the process of this translation as a revelational event similar to Moses' original experience on Mt. Sinai. Aristeas had spoken of the work of translation in remarkably factual terms. He mentioned how the translators had completed "their several tasks, reaching agreement among themselves on each by comparing versions" (Ar. 302). The precise language of the LXX was therefore the result of human judgement and convention. Its accuracy was confirmed by the community of the Jews, who praised this version and consequently demanded that no amendments or other translations be made (Ar. 311). Aristeas thus thought of the LXX as a felicitous translation which must be carefully preserved. For Philo, however, is was much more than this. The translation of the Torah into Greek reinacted in his view the original composition of the canonical text. He initially insists that the translators worked under similar circumstances as Moses, having nothing but the elements of nature before their eyes (Mos. 2:37). They did not execute a regular translation, but engaged in an authentic religious experience which resulted in a perfectly mimetic text (Mos. 2:37–9):

> ... they became as it were possessed and under inspiration wrote, not each several scribe something different, but the same word for word, as though dictated to each by an invisible prompter. Yet who does not know that every language, and especially Greek, abounds in terms and that the same thought can be put in many shapes by changing single words and whole phrases and suiting expressions to the occasion? This was not the case, we are told, with this law of ours, but the Greek words used corresponded literally with the Chaldean, exactly suited to the things they indicated ... these writers arrived at a wording which corresponded with the matter and alone, or better than any other, would bring out clearly what was meant.

Philo suggests here that the LXX was directly dictated by God. Like Moses, the human translators were instruments moved "by an invisible prompter". The results of their translation were therefore identical and perfectly corresponded

---

[59] Mos. 2:14. For further details on the connection between Torah and Nature, see below chapter nine.

to the original text. The Greek expressions chosen suited the nature of the things they indicated and rendered their meaning in a flawless way. As far as Philo was concerned, the mimetic value of the LXX was equal to that of the Hebrew text. Not a shadow of meaning was lost in the process of translation. While Philo occasionally used Hebrew etymologies to highlight the significance of the text, he generally relied on the Greek version of the Bible.[60] The emanation of God's Logos in the Hebrew Scriptures was thus perfectly translatable into Greek. This notion of the translatability of languages, terms and ultimately of cultures is remarkable and will be the focus of the next chapter.

---

[60] See also: S. Sandmel, Philo's Knowledge of Hebrew, SP 5 (1978) 107–12; Y. Amir, Philo and the Bible, *SP* 2 (1973) 1–8; D. Gooding and V. Nikiprowetzky, Philo's Bible in the *De Gigantibus* and *Quod Deus*, in: D. Winston and J. Dillon (eds.), *Two Treatises of Philo of Alexandria. A Commentary on De Gigantibus and Quod Sit Immutabilis* (Chico 1983 = Brown Judaic Studies 25) 119–25; cf. R. Marcus, A Textual-Exegetical Note on Philo's Bible, *JBL* 69 (1950); H. D. Mantel, Did Philo Know Hebrew? (Hebrew), *Tarbiz* 32.1 (1962) 98–9; idem, "Did Philo know Hebrew" – Additional Note (Hebrew), *Tarbiz* 32.4 (1963) 395; J.-G. Kahn, Did Philo know Hebrew? The Testimony of the "Etymologies" (Hebrew), *Tarbiz* 34.4 (1965) 337–45.

# 8. Parables as Translators of Culture

"we shall know if we carefully attend to some
comparison supplied by the things of our world"
(Opif. 17)

Parables played an important role in Philo's construction of Jewish culture in first century Alexandria. As fictional illustrations, which reflect common experience, they created a meaningful bridge between the Ancient Scriptures and contemporary life. They outlined Jewish culture by juxtaposing the Biblical text with the mundane reality of the Greco-Roman world. A space was thus created where different cultures could meet and engage with each other. A reciprocal process of cultural translation began: while Biblical stories were translated into contemporary language, the experience of the surroundings was transformed into Scriptural and thus distinctly Jewish terms.[1] A cultural discourse emerged which was embedded in the Biblical and the contemporary world, while transcending both of them. In this way the parable enabled Philo to construct a topical and meaningful type of Jewish culture.

The very existence of parables in Philo's work has so far either been overlooked or even explicitly denied. H. Thyen contrasted him in an influential book to the rabbis: while the latter were famous for their parables, Philo did not use them at all.[2] A number of factors contributed to the oversight of Philo's parables.[3] Initially, they may simply have been overlooked because they were

---

[1]  The intepretation of the parable as a translator of culture is based on D. Boyarin's analysis of rabbinic parables in: idem, *Intertextuality and the Reading of Midrash* (Bloomington 1990) 80–92. For more details on his theory and its relevance to Philo, see below. See also J. Levinson, Fatal Fictions (Hebrew), *Tarbiz* 68.1 (1998) 61–86, who analyses R. Shimon Ben Yochai's famous parable in G.R. 4:10 from the viewpoint of cultural discourse.

[2]  H. Thyen, *Der Stil der Jüdisch-Hellenistischen Homilie* (Göttingen 1955 = Forschungen zur Religion und Literatur des Alten und Neuen Testaments N.F. 47) 55.

[3]  D. Flusser came closest to recognizing parables in Philo's work, see especially: *Die rabbinischen Gleichnisse und der Gleichniserzähler Jesus* (Bern 1981 = Judaica et Christiana 4) 1:105, where he referred in passing to Philo's "comparisons" between athletes and philosophers, which resemble in his view those later used by Epictetus. Flusser refrained, however, from a proper analysis of the Philonic material and did not realize that Philo actually employed parables like the rabbis. Flusser probably avoided such an approach because of his general agument that rabbinic parables are unique and original. Neither Philo nor the New Testament could thus be seriously considered as a source of rabbinic parables. Furthermore, C. Thoma and S. Lauer, *Die Gleichnisse der Rabbinen* (Bern 1991 = *Judaica et Christiana* 13) occasionally refer to Philo's "Gleichnisse" without, however, appreciating

not introduced by the technical term παραβολή. Scholars have become accustomed to relying on such formal indications and ignore parables lacking them, because the parables in the Synoptic Gospels are usually thus designated. The term παραβολή is a standard introductory formula in these Gospels. Total confidence in such linguistic conventions should have been shaken, however, by the discovery of the Gospel of Thomas. This Gospel is generally no longer considered a Gnostic reworking of synoptic material, but rather as an independent, if not original source of Jesus traditions.[4] While preserving close parallels to most Synoptic parables, Thomas never used a term equivalent to παραβολή. Rather he told his parables in a strikingly informal and unmediated way, lacking any technical or introductory formulas. Whereas the Synoptic writers explicitly pointed to the parabolic nature of the illustration they were about to provide, Thomas typically limited himself to such short statements as "Jesus said: look the sower went out, took a handful of seeds ..." (Saying 9). His parables often follow the simple pattern of "x is like y" and lack any real application.[5] Even though scholars have noticed the minimalistic structure of Thomas' parables, they have failed to recognize that other writers of the first century may equally have told parables without naming them.[6] This possibility becomes more likely in view of the fact that even in the Synoptic Gospels, the terminology is still somewhat fluid. While the Synoptics established the παραβολή as a distinct genre of Jesus' teaching, they still referred to particular examples of parables in a variety of ways.[7] A parable could thus be identified in

---

their nature and contribution to the development of the parable. In Gleichnisse 2:37 they conclude, for example, the following: "Anderseits bringt das philonische Bild gegenüber Platons Timaios keine neuen Aspekte".

[4] See especially: G. J. Riley, The Gospel of Thomas in Recent Scholarship, *Currents in Research: Biblical Studies* 2 (1994) 227–52; F. T. Fallon and R. Cameron, The Gospel of Thomas: a Forschungsbericht and Analysis, *ANRW* II.25.6 (1988) 4195–4251; H. Koester and S. J. Patterson, The Gospel of Thomas – Does It Contain Authentic Sayings of Jesus?, *Bible Review* 6.2 (1990) 28–39; W. D. Stroker, Extracanonical Parables and the Historical Jesus, *Semeia* 44 (1988) 95–120. S. L. Davies, *The Gospel of Thomas and Christian Wisdom* (New York 1983); idem, The Christology and Protology of the Gosepl of Thomas, *JBL* 111.4 (1992) especially 665, has placed the Gospel of Thomas into the context of first century wisdom literature and even Philonic exegesis. With regard to the latter, he suggests that Thomas interpreted Gen. chaps. 1–2 in a similar way as Philo did. Focusing on the ethical principles of Thomas, Davies has not noticed that Philo also used parables.

[5] See especially: Sayings 57, 96, 97, 107, 109. On the issue of applications, or Nimshal, see further below.

[6] On the structure of Thomas' parables, see especially: R. Cameron, Parable and Interpretation in the Gospel of Thomas, *Forum* 2 (1986) 4–14, where he compares the structure of Thomas' parables to those in the Apocryphon of James. Thomas' parables have predominantly been interpreted with a view to contents and lack of allegorical application, see also summary discussion by B. B. Scott, *Hear Then the Parable. A Commentary on the Parables of Jesus* (Minneapolis 1989) 30–35.

[7] Regarding the establishment of the parable as a distinct literary genre, see especially: Mt. 13:1–52; Mk. 4:1–34.

the same Gospel both as λόγος and παραβολή (Mt. 15:12–5); or be called
parable in one Gospel, while simply being introduced by the term ὥσπερ in
another (Lk. 19:11; Mt. 25:14). Luke especially is less consistent in his terminology. He often lacks the term "parabole" where the other Synoptics use it;
instead he tends to introduce his parables simply by the verb ὁμοιόω. Occasionally he tells a parable as though it were an actual event.[8] It therefore seems that
even for the Synoptic narrators the parable has not yet become a completely
established literary genre with definite terminology and strict formal requirements. Philo's failure to use the term παραβολή can thus not be held against
him. It is evident that he could hardly have conformed to the norms of a genre
whose form only became standardized after his time.

Philo's parables may moreover have gone unnoticed because they are not
easily accommodated within the interreligious polemics which often accompany scholarly research on the parables.[9] Usually focusing on the canonical
works of their respective traditions, scholars mainly argued over issues of historical precedence and religious authenticity. The central question was whether
the rabbis copied from Jesus or, *vice versa*, Jesus from the rabbis. It was
assumed that the original parable was also religiously more valuable. Both
Christians and Jews claimed priority, each community regarding the parable as
its own original method of homiletics and moral instruction.[10] While confes-
sional boundaries have recently been crossed, especially in the circle around
Clemens Thoma, the parable is still linked to the question which religion
possesses the more authentic tradition of spirituality. In this context Philo may
appear rather irrelevant, because his work stands outside the canon of rabbinic
literature which became formative for subsequent Judaism. Insight into his
parables can hardly solve the problem of possible Christian influence on rab-

---

[8] See: Scott, Parable 28–9; without any introductory formula: Lk. 14:16–24; 15:11–32;
16:1–13.

[9] Regarding interreligious polemics in the history of parable research, see especially:
Scott, Parable 7–62; L. C. Gaughy, A Short History of Parable Interpretation, *Forum* 8 (1992)
229–45.

[10] See e.g.: W. Bousset, Jesus (Halle 1904) 21–2; Flusser, Gleichnisse *passim*, who as-
sumes that the Christian parables emulated rabbinic models; he is followed by his student
B. H. Young, *Jesus and His Jewish Parables. Rediscovering the Roots of Jesus' Teaching*
(New York 1989 = Theological Inquiries. Studies in Contemporary Biblical and Theological
Problems) 236–81; D. Stern, *Parables in Midrash. Narrative and Exegesis in Rabbinic
Literature* (Cambridge MA 1991) professes to avoid historical questions of cross-cultural
dependence (1–2), but actually assumes the priority of the rabbinic parable which developed
in his view the original and classical form of the Mashal only on the basis of Scripture and
without Christian models (9–10, 188–206); Thoma and Lauer, Gleichnisse 1:43–51, consider
only Biblical, Greek and Oriental, but not Christian influences on rabbinic parables; similarly their student P. Dschulnigg, *Rabbinische Gleichnisse und das Neue Testament. Die
Gleichnisse der PesK im Vergleich mit den Gleichnissen Jesu und dem Neuen Testament*
(Bern 1988 = Judaica et Christiana 12), uses the rabbinic material only as a background to the
New Testament, but not *vice versa*.

binic parables. The fact that some of Philo's parables were, as we shall see, apparently known to the rabbis does not exclude the possibility of New Testament influence. On the contrary, the rabbis may in addition to Philo's parables have adopted also the style and the themes of Christian parables. It is even likely that they would respond more to the Gospels than to Philo, because only the former became historically important and significantly challenged Jewish identity.[11] It was moreover in the Gospels that the parable became a tool for religious polemics. Matthew especially often used his parables as invective against Jewish leaders who rejected the authority of Jesus. While he himself still conceived of this conflict in inter-Jewish terms, his hostile tone anticipated the "Verus Israel" ideology of the Church from Justin Martyr onwards.[12] Not surprisingly, the rabbis were familiar with such parables and understood them in light of the sharpened discourse of their own time. In other words, Matthean parables originally directed against the Pharisaic leadership could in later centuries no longer be isolated from the "Verus Israel" doctrine of the Church and were thus understood as direct invective against all Jews. What could be more natural for the rabbis than to respond to Matthean parables in later Christian garb by telling inverse parables which countered the Christian message?[13]

Can Philo, on the other hand, illuminate the Jewish background of the Synoptic parables? His parables can with certainty be dated to pre-Christian times. This is an enormous advantage over rabbinic parables which are notorious for

---

[11] The significance of the Early Church for the formation of rabbinic Judaism has recently become an important subject of scholarly discussion, see especially: Boyarin, Two Synods; G. Hasan-Rokem, Narratives in Dialogue: A Folk Literary Perspective on Interreligious Contacts in the Holy Land in Rabbinic Literature of Late Antiquity, in: A. Kofsky and G. G. Stroumsa (eds.), *Sharing The Sacred. Religious Contacts and Conflicts in the Holy Land First-Fifteenth Centuries CE* (Jerusalem 1998) 109–29; M. Hirshman, *A Rivalry of Genius. Jewish and Christian Biblical Interpretation in Late Antiquity* (New York 1996, Hebr. orig. = SUNY Series in Judaica: Hermeneutics, Mysticism, and Religion). I. J. Yuval has gone furthest in suggesting the rabbis' direct dependence on Christian models, see especially: The Haggadah of Passover and Easter (Hebrew), *Tarbiz* 65.1 (1995) 5–28; idem, Easter and Passover As Early Jewish-Christian Dialogue, in: P. F. Bradshaw and L. A. Hoffman (eds.), *Passover and Easter: Origin and History to Modern Times* (Notre Dame 1999) 5:98–124.

[12] Among the Gospels Matthew's parables show both the most standardized form and the greatest animosity towards the Pharasaic leaders; see also: Scott, Parable 25–30; D. Guthrie, *New Testament Introduction* (Leicester 1970, 3rd. ed.) 21–52; the "Verus Israel" ideology seems to have developed gradually and later than originally assumed, see especially: G. D. Dunn, Tertullian and Rebekah: a Re-reading of an "Anti-Jewish" Argument in Early Christian Literature, *Vigiliae Christianae* 52.2 (1998) 119–45; Harvey, True Israel 1–10, 234–8; B. Przybylski, The Setting of Matthean Anti-Judaism, in: P. Richardson with D. Granskon (eds.), *Anti-Judaism in Early Christianity* (Waterloo, Ont. 1986 = Studies in Christianity and Judaism 2) 1:181–200, emphasizes the more general anti-Jewish orientation of Matthew's polemics; cf. also the traditional view of an early splitting of the ways in: M. Simon, *Verus Israel. A Study of the relations between Christians and Jews in the Roman Empire* (Oxford 1986, Fr. orig. 1964) 65–97.

[13] See e.g. Sifre Deut., Pisqa 312 which responds to Mt. 21:28–46, Mk. 12:1–12, Lk. 20:9–19. For other examples, see below.

their undatability. While cautious scholars have therefore been reluctant to consider them as a potential source for the New Testament, Philo is a far safer point of reference. At the same time, however, he is somewhat problematic on other grounds. Initially, he is geographically and, some would argue, culturally removed from Palestine. His influence on the New Testament is still a subject of scholarly inquiry. So far only the Gospel of John, Paul's writings and the Epistle to the Hebrews have been interpreted as depending on Philo.[14] All of these, however, lack parables in the proper sense.[15] The Synoptic Gospels, on the other hand, are generally considered to differ more significantly from the spirit of Philo's work. Even those scholars who place the Gospel of Matthew in a Philonic context do not argue for its direct dependence on him, but for the exposure of both authors to the same Hellenistic world.[16]

In addition, the very nature of Philo's parables calls for caution in comparing them to the Synoptics. Most strikingly, Philo's parables completely lack the apocalyptic dimension of many Synoptic parables in their extant form. He never talks about the kingdom to come. His parables are generally less allegorical and tend to deal in rather concrete fashion with God's works and the wise man. Yet this difference between Philonic and Synoptic parables also holds great promise. If significant parallels can nevertheless be established between some of them, Philo's version might indicate the embryonic form of the Christian parables before they were redacted by the Church.[17] Philo could potentially play a similar role as the Gospel of Thomas in elucidating the origins of early Christianity.[18] Furthermore, Philo's parables predominantly appear in exegeti-

---

[14] D. T. Runia, *Philo in Early Christian Literature. A Survey* (Assen 1993 = Compendia Rerum Judaicarum ad Novum Testamentum 3) 63–86; S. Sandmel, *Philo of Alexandria. An Introduction* (New York/Oxford 1979) 150–54; P. Borgen, Early Christianity; idem, Philo, Luke and Geography.

[15] As Scott, Parable 21, n. 72 has pointed out, the author of Heb. 9:9 uses the term παραβολή in the sense of a symbol and figurative speech.

[16] P.L. Shuler, Philo's Moses and Matthew's Jesus: A Comparative Study in Ancient Literature, *SPhA* 2 (1990) 86–103; D. Zeller, Jesus als vollmächtiger Lehrer (Mt. 5–7) und der hellenistische Gesetzgeber, in: L. Schenke (ed.), *Studien zum Matthäusevangelium. Festschrift für Wilhelm Pesch* (Stuttgart 1988) 301–17.

[17] On the redaction of the Synoptic Gospels in an apocalyptic spirit, see especially: A. Jülicher, *Die Gleichnisreden Jesu* (Tübingen 1910) 1:51–68, who criticized the allegorical interpretation of the Jesus parables, arguing that they originally established a similarity between two situations both of which were to be taken in their concrete, literal sense. J. Jeremias, *The Parables of Jesus* (London 1972, Germ. Orig. 3rd rev. ed.), followed Jülicher and highlighted the agricultural *Sitz-im-Leben* of the original Jesus parables. In his view the Jesus parables originally conveyed simple wisdom teachings before they were allegorized by the Church. Jülicher's and Jeremias' conclusions are by now generally accepted, see: Scott, Parables 42–6.

[18] The lack of allegory and Nimshal in Thomas' parables has often been recognized as an indicator of early material. The parable of the Sower, for example, simply ends with the details of the crops falling on different grounds (Saying 9; cf. Mt. 13:18–23; Mk. 4:14–20; Lk. 8:11–15); see especially: K. King, The Kingdom in the Gospel of Thomas, *Forum* 3.1 (1987) 48–97; Koester, Gospel of Thomas 37; R. Valantasis, *The Gospel of Thomas* (London

cal contexts – a feature which was foreign to the New Testament parables, even in Matthew, but was later shared by the rabbis.[19] This difference is significant. The question arises whether it is likely that the Synoptic writers extracted a parable from an exegetical context in order to use it in a more general sermon. Alternatively, both Philo and the Synoptics could independently have adopted general themes from Greco-Roman culture, each for his own purpose. Caution is thus called for. If similarities between Philonic and Synoptic parables are nevertheless so conspicuous that Philo's influence on the Synoptic writers suggests itself, one must still consider the adaptation of the parable to the specific theological and cultural setting of early Christianity.

This chapter primarily aims at examining Philo's parables in their own right. Their structure, message and contribution to Philo's overall construction of Jewish culture will be the focus of our attention. For this purpose they will also be considered in their historical context, namely as an important witness to the development of the parable before it became a fairly standardized genre in the Gospels. Philo provides a crucial glimpse into the early stage of the parable when Greco-Roman figures of comparison were for the first time applied to the Biblical heritage. Philo's importance at this juncture can hardly be overestimated. His contribution is properly appreciated if we pause for a moment and consider his predecessors in the discourse of comparison.

Initially, the Biblical Mashal demands attention. In Scripture the term Mashal refers to a rather broad range of phenomena which have little to do with the later parable: anonymous proverbs, wisdom sayings and occasionally a coded prophecy.[20] The Biblical Mashal still lacks the most important characteristic of the later parable, namely an explicit comparison between a fictional situation, on

---

and New York 1997 = New Testament Readings) 67; Cameron, Parable and Interpretation 14–23; R. Doran, A Complex of Parables: G. Th. 96–98, *NT* 29.4 (1987) 347–52. The very few applications which are nevertheless found in the GTh are of a surprisingly short and directly exhortatory nature. They usually amount simply to a call to the readers, such as: "anyone here with two good ears had better listen!" (Sayings 8, 63, 65, 76, 96). One expanded Nimshal of four lines is preserved in Saying 21. It similarly instructs the readers: "as for you then, be on guard against the world, prepare yourselves with great strength … anyone here with two good ears had better listen!".

[19] On the exegetical context of the rabbinic parable, see: *Song of Songs Rabbah* 1.1.8; Boyarin, Intertextuality 80–92; Stern, Parables 37–45, 63–71, 196–7; Scott, Parable 16–7. In the New Testament only the parable of the Wicked Husbandman seems to have a somewhat exegetical dimension (Mk. 12:1–12; Mt. 21:33–46; Lk. 20:9–19). The parable of the Sower furthermore alludes to Scripture (Mk. 4:3–20; Mt. 13:3–23; Lk. 8:5–15). The general absence of an exegetical context in Matthew's parables is striking, because this is the most Midrashic of the Gospels.

[20] See especially: Prov. 1:6; Ps. 49:4–5; Ez. 17:2–10. Nathan's speech to David is also of interest in this context (2 Sam. 12:1–14). While it lacks the technical term "Mashal" it presents a fictional story which is subsequently applied to David's sin with Batsheva. It therefore approaches the standard structure, but does not fully qualify as a parable in the later sense because it is a prophecy. The Nimshal is God's word, as quoted by Nathan.

the one hand, and Scripture or a subject of instruction on the other. Comparisons between different situations are usually only implied and their real *Sitz-im-Leben* is emphasized.[21] Philo is obviously familiar with this wisdom tradition, as he occasionally quotes from it.[22] But he does not limit himself to "the proverbs of Solomon". He has instead developed his own style of parable which was based on Greco-Roman figures of comparison. This style anticipates to a striking degree Synoptic and especially rabbinic parables. In light of the Biblical Mashal it is remarkable that Philo consistently divides his parables into their two standard parts, namely the Mashal proper, or story, and Nimshal, or application.[23] He regularly introduces the Mashal by terms like καθάπερ and ὥσπερ, while the Nimshal is indicated by such terms as οὕτως and τὸν αὐτὸν τρόπον.

To search for the roots of Philo's parables in ancient pagan literature is an awesome task. It is particularly complex because pagan authors used a variety of terms for comparison, including in Greek παραβολή, εἰκών and εἰκασία and ὁμοίωσις and in Latin *similitudo, collatio, comparatio* and *imago*.[24] Ancient pagans were less interested in the formal aspects of comparative figures, aiming instead at defining their rhetorical purpose, method and general structure. Aristotle's careless phrasing of his example of παραβολή has often been noted in this context.[25] This fluidity of form is attested not only by the master of rhetorics, but also by his successors in the Hellenistic period. It provides an important background for understanding Philo, whose terminology can be similarly fluid.

Three moments in Ancient pagan literature deserve closer attention: Aristotle's definition of παραβολή, the *similitudo per conlationem* in the anonymous treatise *Ad Herennium* and Stoic usage of the parable. Aristotle has previously been associated with the Synoptic parables. Adolf Jülicher already pointed to the similarity between Aristotle's παραβολή and the Synoptic parable in its original form.[26] He stressed in this way the concrete character of the early Christian parables before they were allegorized. Aristotle discussed the parable as a means of persuasion and proof, similar to the historical example. The

---

[21] On the Biblical *Parallelismus Membrorum* in Prov., see especially: G. v. Rad, Wisdom in Israel (London 1972, Germ. orig.) 26–9.

[22] Philo called the Book of Proverbs by the LXX name παροιμίαι, occasionally quoting (Ebr. 31, 84; Congr. 177) and alluding to it (Vir. 62); see also: J. Laporte, Philo in the Tradition of Biblical Wisdom Literature, in: R. Wilken (ed.), *Aspects of Wisdom in Judaism and Early Christianity* (Notre Dame 1975) 114–119.

[23] For a clear description of the parable's structure, see: C. Thoma, Literary and Theological Aspects of the Rabbinic Parables, in: idem and M. Wyschogrod (eds.), *Parable and Story in Judaism and Christianity* (N.J. 1989 = Studies in Judaism and Christianity) 37–41.

[24] M. H. McCall, *Ancient Rhetorical Theories of Simile and Comparison* (Cambridge MA 1969) IX.

[25] See especially: McCall, Theories 27, commenting on *Rhetoric* 2.20.1393b-1394a; Scott, Parables 20, who argued on these grounds that the parable was not yet a genre in Greek literature.

[26] Jülicher, Gleichnisreden 1:70–2.

difference between the two was only their historical authenticity: while the parable was a story invented by the speaker, the example refers to an event which actually happened. Both, however, are defined as an illustration of the argument by means of invoking a similar situation. Aristotle's own example of a parable suggests just how similar and concrete the two situations could be: "public officials must not be selected by lot, for that is like just as if (ὅμοιον γὰϱ ὥσπεϱ ἂν εἴ) choosing as representative athletes not those competent to contend, but those on whom the lot falls" (Rhet. 2.20.1393b). The argument about the proper selection of officials is thus reenforced by comparison to a more familiar and extreme case. Aristotle's παϱαβολή bears significant resemblance to the later genre of parable. Its proximity to the historical *exemplum* is particularly important because both Philo and the Synoptics blurred the difference between the two.[27]

At the same time, however, Aristotle's parable also lacks some of the characteristics of the later Jewish and Christian genre. Conspicuously absent are: a full-length story in the Mashal, a Nimshal and the typical gap between the mundane situation of the Mashal and the spiritual dimension of the Nimshal. These differences really amount to two major disparities: length and context of application. Brevity was not an accidental feature of Aristotle's parable. He insisted on it for the purpose of greater clarity. The type of comparison, which he called εἰϰών, was in his eyes inferior precisely because it was longer and therefore pedagogically less effective.[28] The Aristotelian parable could in principle not develop a whole narrative and subsequently explain its relevance in a Nimshal. Aristotle instead considered a parable to be successful if its meaning was immediately obvious. While the Synoptics and especially the rabbis usually engaged in long and often narratologically sophisticated *Meshalim*, Philo occupies an intermediate position in this regard. Some of his parables are almost as concise as Aristotle's, whereas others provide full stories replete with embellishing detail. The Nimshal, however, is a regular feature of his parables. More importantly, Aristotle applied the parable in a distinctly secular context. It therefore operated on one and the same level of culture. In the above example both the officials and the athletes play certain public roles in the polis. Their particular function is quite different, to be sure, yet both are real functionaries in Aristotle's world. Philo's parable, by contrast, operates not on one, but on two different levels, namely the mundane and the religious. The most common situation of daily life could thus be used to explain aspects of God Himself. The encounter between these seemingly opposite realms permitted an innovative hermeneutics which produced unexpected and entirely new meanings.

---

[27] Among post-Aristotelian theoreticians of parabolic discourse, Cicero in particular placed the comparison near the *exemplum*, see: McCall, Theories 98–112.

[28] McCall, Theories 40–2.

*Ad Herennium* was composed between 86–82 BCE by an unknown author and was later ascribed to Cicero.[29] It is the first detailed discussion of comparison after Aristotle and indicates the involvement of Rome in these literary matters. The author initially defines a *similitudo* as "a manner of speech, which carries over one element of likeness from one thing to a different" (4:59). The author is moreover aware of the great variety of realms from which the components of a *similitudo* can be taken. He lists an impressive number of them in oppositional pairs, insisting, however, that one must choose them carefully so that there is sufficient ground for comparison (4:59; 2:46). The most interesting type of *similitudo* from a Philonic perspective is the form of detailed parallel which serves to vivify the argument (*similitudo per conlationem*). Its "Mashal" consists of an extended narrative; it possesses a "Nimshal" and compares two things from conspicuously different areas. Its relevance to Philo demands that the example from *Ad Herennium* be quoted in detail (4:60):

Let us image a player on the lyre who has presented himself on the stage, magnificently garbed, clothed in a gold-embroidered robe, with purple mantle interlaced in various colours, wearing a golden crown illumined with large gleaming jewels, and holding a lyre covered with golden ornaments and set off with ivory. Further, he has a personal beauty, presence and stature that impose dignity. If, when, by these means he has roused a great expectation in the public, he should in the silence he has created suddenly give utterance to a rasping voice, and this should be accompanied by a repulsive gesture, he is the more forcibly thrust off in derision and scorn, the richer his adornment and the higher the hopes he has raised.

In the same way ("item"), a man of high station, endowed with great and opulent resources and abounding in all the gifts of fortune and the emoluments of nature, if he yet lacks virtue and the arts that teach virtue, will so much the more forcibly in derision and scorn be cast from all association with good men, the richer he is in the other advantages, the greater his distinction, and the higher the hopes he has raised.

The author of *Ad Herennium* celebrates this example for "bringing into relation by a method of parallel description the one man's ineptitude and the other's lack of cultivation" (ibid.). He moreover stresses that "all like elements are related" (ibid.), the components of each part corresponding to those of the other. We may add that this *similitudo* also contains an allegorical dimension which bridges the gap between the two different realms. The theatre thus corresponds to society, while lack of eloquence and repulsive gestures stand for lack of virtue and culture. The various ornaments represent opulence. A concrete story, which could actually have happened in daily life, has thus been translated into the language of ethics and culture. It is striking that Philo engages in a similar process of cultural translation. Applying the structure of the *similitudo per*

---

[29] On the background of this author, see: McCall, Theories 57; G. A. Kennedy, *The Art of Rhetoric in the Roman World 300 B.C. – A.D. 300* (Princeton 1972) 109–13.

*conlationem* to the Biblical text, he engages in a discourse on two levels, namely the mundane and the ethical.

Finally, the Stoics have to be considered as significant precursors of Philo's parable. Unfortunately they have left virtually nothing in terms of a theory of comparison. Yet this school seems to have been known in antiquity for its parabolic discourse. Cicero accused them of being "so fond of employing" those "extremely false analogies" (De Fin. 4:64). He complained that the Stoics justified their stringent theory of ethics by comparison to people under water who all drown, whether they are close to the surface or far removed from it.[30] This analogy was meant to explain the Stoic position that there is no intermediate ground between sin and virtue: anything less than perfectly good action is as sinful as a deliberately committed crime. Everybody except the wise man drowns in his immorality. Some of the Stoic comparisons have survived intact. Diogenes Laertes reports a Stoic analogy that conveys the same ethical teaching as the one Cicero referred to: "For say the Stoics just as (ὡς) a stick must be either straight or crooked, so (οὕτως) man must be either just or unjust" (D.L. 7:127). Zeno is moreover said to have "proved his argument by one of his favourite comparisons, as follows" (Cic., N.D. 2:22):

if flutes playing musical tones grew on an olive-tree, surely you would not question that the olive-tree possessed some knowledge of the art of flute-playing ... why then should we not judge the world to be animate and endowed with wisdom, when it produces animate and wise off-spring?

Cicero mentions another Stoic comparison in De Fin. 4:76:[31]

A skipper ... commits an equal transgression if he loses his ship with a cargo of straw and if he does so when laden with gold, similarly ("item") a man is an equal transgressor if he beats his parent or slave without due cause.

Two late contemporaries of Philo living in Rome made rather frequent use of the parable – Seneca and Musonius both of whom stood in the Stoic tradition. Seneca used the skipper, the physician and other figures in his comparisons. In view of Philo – and indeed the New Testament – his parable of the fertile ground is of particular interest:[32]

Certain qualities are innate only in better natures, just as rich ground, although it is neglected, produces a strong growth and a tall forest is the mark of fertile soil. And so (itaque) natures that have innate vigour like produce ...

---

[30] Cicero does not quote the Stoic comparison, but only paraphrases it.
[31] For additional examples, see especially: De Fin. 3:22, 3:46.
[32] Ira 2.15:1; also see: De Ira 2.10:8 (the skipper), 2.18:1 (health).

Musonius used the physician, the musician and the horseman as figures of comparison explaining his moral teaching.[33] These examples may suffice to show that the Stoics were in Antiquity known for a style of discussion based on frequent comparisons. This is not altogether surprising because they engaged in an overall re-interpretation of the world around them. Ancient myth was translated into stories about physical processes in nature, the polis was interpreted as a universal kingdom of wise men and biological ties were replaced by spiritual ones. On the whole, the Stoics referred to a reality which was not readily visible to the eyes of the average man. *Similitudines* could convey their position more easily precisely because they invoked a concrete experience familiar to the audience. Philo undoubtedly stood in this tradition of cultural translation, leaving his own distinct imprint on it.

Philo's parable of the provider of a banquet is especially rich and may serve as the starting point of our discussion. This parable is inserted in Opif. 78 where Philo dwells on Gen. 1:26 and inquires why man was created last. Is it possible, he seems to ask, that the chronological order of creation implies a hierarchy of values? This could suggest that man is not only the last, but also the least of God's creations. Such a reading of the Genesis account, however, did not meet with Philo's approval. After all Gen 1:26 explicitly states that man was created in the image of God and that he should rule over the other creatures whose similarity to God was nowhere mentioned. Why then was man nevertheless created after his subordinates? By thus problematizing a particular verse in the sequence of creation, Philo has created a gap in the Biblical text. Gen. 1:26 no longer simply describes the last stage of creation, but implies a paradox which requires an exegetical solution. Responding to these new issues, Philo asserts that those who have "immersed themselves more deeply than others into the laws of Moses"[34] have discovered insights unknown to the casual reader. Such interpreters suggested that man's position at the end of creation resulted precisely from his striking similarity to God. When He made man a "partaker of kinship with Himself in mind and reason ..., He did not begrudge him the other gifts either, but made ready for him beforehand all things in the world, as for a living being dearest and closest to Himself".[35] The notion of man's likeness to God with regard to his rational soul is a well-known theme in Philo's work. Since God was in his view incorporeal, man's creation in His image could refer only to man's divinely rational soul.[36] In the present context this idea is applied

---

[33] Musonius, fragm. 6 apud Stobeaus, Anth. 3.29:78 = ed. Lutz 52–3; fragm. 8 apud Stobaeus, Floril. 46.67 = ed. Lutz 66–7.

[34] οἱ τοῖς νόμοις ἐπὶ πλέον ἐμβαθύναντες (Opif. 77). It is not clear to which exegetes Philo is referring. He does not call them allegorists as he does on other occasions. Yet he obviously agreed with their understanding of Gen. 1:26 and his phrase may indeed be nothing but a general introduction to his own interpretation.

[35] ὡς οἰκειοτάτῳ καὶ φιλτάτῳ ζῴῳ (Opif. 77).

[36] See especially Opif. 69–71; and also Helleman, Deification 59–61.

to the issue of man's place in the sequence of creation. Philo has to explain the connection between man's likeness to God and his reception of the world as a gift and livelihood. For this purpose a parable is introduced (Opif. 78):

Just as (καθάπερ) givers of a banquet (ἑστιάτορες) then do not send out the summonses to supper until they have put everything in readiness for the feast, and those who provide gymnastic and theatrical contests, before they gather the spectators into the theatre or the stadium, have in readiness a number of combatants and performers to charm both eye and ear,
exactly in the same way (τὸν αὐτὸν τρόπον) the Ruler of all things, like some provider of contests and of a banquet, when about to invite man to the enjoyment of a feast and a spectacle, made ready beforehand the material for both. He desired that upon coming into the world man might at once find both a banquet and a most sacred display (συμπόσιον καὶ θέατρον ἱερώτατον), the one full of all things that earth and rivers and sea and air bring forth for use and enjoyment, the other of all sorts of spectacles, most impressive in their substance, most impressive in their qualities and circling with most wondrous movements.

This text clearly is a parable even though Philo has not explicitly identified it as such. The Mashal and Nimshal are easily recognizable and the terminology corresponds to the one used in Stoic and New Testament parables. Philo's introductory term καθάπερ parallels the Stoic and Synoptic use of ὡς and ὥσπερ at the opening of parables, while the phrase τὸν αὐτὸν τρόπον corresponds to the Stoic and Synoptic οὕτως as a marker of the Nimshal.[37] The Mashal proper moreover plays the Classical role of introducing a familiar and stereotypical situation from daily life.[38] Three scenes are invoked here: a banquet, gymnastic contests and the theatre. This variety of items in the Mashal anticipates the multiplicity of *Meshalim* connected with one single verse in rabbinic literature.[39] The narrative quality of Philo's Mashal, on the other hand, is rather poor. It is evidently inferior to the usually dramatic stories in rabbinic parables and rather borders on a simple observation from life. Yet the concision and realistic nature of this Mashal precisely identify it as a rather typical product of its time. It is characteristic of the early stage of the parable which still echoes Aristotle's παραβολή. Synoptic parables sometimes also refer to observable processes of nature. One of them is indeed nothing but a direct lesson from a fig-tree which corresponds to similar observations in the *Book of*

---

[37] See especially: Mt. 24:32; Mk. 4:26, and also: Mt. 24:11, Mt. 18:35; 20:16; Mk 4:31. The expressions καθάπερ and τὸν αὐτὸν τρόπον are not used in the Synoptic parables.

[38] Flusser, Gleichnisse 31–49, especially emphasized the "pseudo-realistic" character of the Mashal which often appears as though taken straight from daily life, but was not; Boyarin, Intertextuality 84–6; Stern, Parables 63–101; cf. also I. Ziegler, *Die Königsgleichnisse des Midrasch beleuchtet durch die römische Kaiserzeit* (Breslau 1903), who assumed the historical reality of virtually all parables and attempted to identify their precise *Sitz-im-Leben* at the Roman court.

[39] See e.g. the famous parables on Cain's murder of Abel in G.R. 22:9.

*Proverbs*.[40] Finally, the Nimshal in Philo's above-quoted parable fulfills its regular function of applying the mundane situation of the Mashal to the spiritual realm of God. Philo emphasizes the correlation between Mashal and Nimshal by explicitly stating in the Nimshal that the Ruler of all things acted "like some provider of contests and of a banquet".

Philo's Mashal invokes three mundane situations with which he and his readers were thoroughly familiar. Everyone could easily grasp the significance of these descriptions because they had all been in similar situations. The three stories share one masterplot about a generous host preparing in advance for his guests. Philo initially speaks about the ἑστιάτωρ making arrangements for the feast before sending invitations. This term is no longer used in its Classical sense of a provider of a meal for the citizens of a polis, but in the broader sense of someone arranging a rich symposion for friends and acquaintances.[41] Philo himself attended many such banquets and became rather cynical about their value and ostentation.[42] He certainly expected his readers to know what he was complaining about. As members of the upper-classes they would also have attended such parties. Philo had even encouraged them to avoid decadent luxury and keep the feasts modest as befits Mosaic law. The very value of a symposion, however, was never questioned by Philo. The reality of this cultural convention was so self-evident and socially accepted that it could easily become an icon in a Mashal.

The same holds true for the "gymnastic and theatrical contests". Two decades ago H. A. Harris showed Philo's enthusiastic approval of athletics and his intimate familiarity with the rules of the different sports.[43] Philo undoubtedly attended the games regularly. The gymnasium was so important that he mentioned it as the first item on his list of educational benefits which parents owe their children.[44] The theatre was similarly a self-evident part of Philo's cultural environment. He himself often seems to have attended it and occasionally recalls his experience (Ebr. 177). Specific playwrights and their *bon mots* are equally mentioned by Philo.[45] His readers were obviously expected to share this cultural code. Philo's Mashal about the different providers of entertainment thus reflects the values and stereotypical situations of his cultural environment. The threefold repetition of the plot highlights the schematic nature of the

---

[40] The "parabole" of the fig-tree is told in Mt. 24:32–5; Mk. 13:28–31 and Lk. 21:29–33; for other examples, see: Mt. 13:31–2; Mk. 4:30–2; Lk. 13:18–9, G.Th. 20.

[41] On the Classical Greek sense of ἑστίασις, see: P.-W. vol. 16 col. 1315.

[42] See esp. Cont. 52–3 where Philo mocks the self-conceit of both guests and hosts (ἑστιάτωρ). For more details on Philo's views on the banquet, see above chapter five.

[43] H. A. Harris, *Greek Athletics and the Jews* (Cardiff 1976) 51–101.

[44] Spec. 2:230; for more details on the gymnasium in the context of education, see above chapter five.

[45] For details on Philo's attitude towards theatre and known playwrights in the context of his construction of the Greek Other, see above chapter five.

narrative. Philo's Mashal thus fulfills exactly the function which Daniel Boyarin has identified as the main characteristic of the Mashal in rabbinic parables.[46] He argued that the Mashal provides Scripture with the ideological framework of the culture in which it is interpreted. In this way the Mashal defines the parameters within which exegesis can take place. By adducing a stereotypical situation from contemporary culture it suggests that Scripture should be understood in accordance with the masterplot of that society.

Boyarin furthermore suggested that the Mashal provides a narrative structure to which the Biblical account is assimilated in the Nimshal.[47] Philo's Nimshal performs exactly this function. It uses the cultural images of the Mashal as an intertext for a new reading of Gen 1:26. This means that Philo rewrites Gen 1:26 in light of the plot in the Mashal, thus adapting Scripture to the language of his own time. In this process of translation, God is assimilated to a provider of banquets and spectacles. Philo stresses that when creating the world, He acted just as a good host in first century Alexandria would have done. In this way God's behaviour and motivation have become intimately clear. He can now be easily understood because He has become part of the reader's cultural experience. God behaves according to the codes and norms of the reader's own society.

At the same time, however, Philo's Nimshal transcends the normal reality of a banquet. The general setting is applied to a specifically Jewish context and God offers His guest not merely some regular delights, but the whole world. The dimensions of hospitality have thus radically changed. Philo's Mashal suggests a completely new perspective on the creation of the world. He implies that the earth can be understood as a banquet in the concrete sense of the word: man is invited to feast on all the products of nature. The fruits, animals, waters etc. are nothing but a Divine gift to man. By consuming them man joins God's table-fellowship. Philo indeed assumes that God shared table community with man. Eating together has always been an expression of partnership and mutual trust in the Ancient world.[48] Philo himself emphasized elsewhere that table fellowship presupposes congeniality, especially if celestial participants are involved. When the three angels came to visit Abraham, Philo dwelt on the nature of their common ἑστίασις. Abraham could serve as the angel's host, he insists, precisely because he was "their kinsman and fellow-servant who had sought refuge with their master" (Abr. 116). The priests similarly shared God's table-fellowship at the altar in His Temple (Spec. 1:242). Sharing God's food in

---

[46] Boyarin, Intertextuality 85–92; Boyarin suggests that the cultural codes and ideological structures conveyed by the Mashal inform any process of reading, but remain unconscious to the readers themselves, while the rabbis have brought them to the surface (ibid. 92).

[47] Boyarin, Intertextuality 87–8.

[48] I. Nielsen and H. S. Nielsen (eds.), *Meals in a Social Context: Aspects of the Communal Meal in the Hellenistic and Roman World* (Aarhus 1998).

the form of sacrifices, the priests had become God's partners.[49] Philo's Nimshal in the above parable thus suggests the same type of table-fellowship between God and Adam. God shared food not only with the priests, but on a much grander scale with man *per se*. Eating the products of nature, man has become God's intimate partner.

Philo's parable about the provider of symposiac and other entertainments has thus filled the gap in Gen. 1:26. It explains the paradox of man's creation as the last, but most precious of God's creatures. Adducing a stereotypical situation from daily life, Philo has translated this Biblical verse into the terms of contemporary culture. At the same time he has transformed a mundane image into language about God. The result is a particularly complex discourse, which defines Jewish culture in light of both the Bible and the contemporary environment. Philo suggests that the Jews belong in their own particular way to both of these two worlds. Yet while being a part of them, they are not entirely absorbed. Philo and his readers have transcended Scripture by assimilating God to a typical host of their own time, yet also differ from pagan culture by having applied the image of the banquet to the Genesis account. Philo's parable thus constructs almost invisible boundaries in a remarkably irenic fashion. These boundaries are both permeable, as Jews participate in the culture of their environment, and distinct, as they reinforce a Biblical story. The peaceful, yet assertive nature of Philo's parable is especially noteworthy in view of the antagonistic and divisive spirit which characterizes its parallels in both the New Testament and rabbinic literature.

The significance of Philo's parable can indeed be appreciated by comparing it to its parallels in the Gospels and rabbinic literature. The parable of the banquet appears twice in the Synoptics, the more original version in Lk. 14:16–24 and the eschatologically redacted one in Mt. 22:1–14.[50] The Gospel of Thomas moreover preserves a version close to Luke, placing the banquet in the context of a polemic against commerce.[51] While Matthew explicitly introduced his story as a parable, Luke and Thomas simply have Jesus tell a story. Unlike Philo, they do not even use comparative adverbs such as καθάπερ. Nor do the

---

[49] The idea of sacrifice as table fellowship with God is also found in other nearly contemporary sources, see especially Dio Chrys., Or. 3:97; 1 Cor. 10:18; G. Mussies, *Dio Chrysostom and the New Testament* (Leiden 1972 = Studia ad Corpus Hellenisticum Novi Testamenti 2) 162.

[50] On the scholarly reconstruction of the original version of the parable, see especially: Jülicher, Gleichnisreden 2:418–33, who assumes that Lk. and Mt. independently used an original version, which Mt. allegorized far more than Lk., incorporating even the experience of the destruction of the Temple in 70 CE; Jeremias, Parables 50–3, who characterizes Mt.'s revision by both a far greater degree of allegorization and a missionary invitation of the Gentiles as extended by the early Church; similarly Scott, Parable 166–8; F. H. Borsch, *Many Things in Parables* (Philadelphia 1988) 47–55.

[51] Saying 64; see also: Valantasis, Thomas 142–3.

Early Christian versions preserve a clearly structured Nimshal. At most they have one sentence of instruction at the end of the Mashal, while Luke integrates his message into the speech of the host in the Mashal itself. The early Christian parables are furthermore devoid of any exegetical context. Their meaning emerges both from the text of the Mashal itself and from the narrative context. On purely formal grounds the early Christian versions of the parable are thus far more embryonic than Philo's. It is, on the other hand, immediately clear that they appeal to the same cultural experience as he had done. They share Philo's *Erfahrungshorizont* and are familiar with the practices of arranging and celebrating a banquet. Like him they assumed that a meal is prepared before sending the invitations. Matthew even mentions the details of such arrangements: "Behold, I have made ready my dinner, my oxen and my fat calves are killed, and everything is ready; come to the marriage feast" (Mt. 22:4).

Yet the Gospels look at the same cultural situation from a very different angle. Rather than focusing on the host's generosity, they dwell on the guests' reactions to his invitation. Those initially called, their story goes, excused themselves and refused to come. The host could thus not enjoy the banquet as expected, but had to search rather humbly for guests willing to join him. The end, however, was a happy one: the second round of guests arrived and the banquet actually took place. The Gospels moreover indicate who the persons were who accepted or refused the invitation. The general impression is that the poor, the handicapped and casual passers-by joined the banquet, while the rich did not. Thomas drew a clear social message from this and declared that "buyers and merchants [will] not enter the place of my Father" (Saying 64). Luke has the host say that "none of those men who were invited shall taste my banquet" (Lk. 14:24). Matthew further expands the Mashal. He highlights that anybody in the streets, even the wicked (πονηρούς), was invited at the second round (Mt. 22:10). Yet even among those who arrived at the banquet some were not worthy. The "man who had no wedding garment (ἔνδυμα γάμου)" was thus cast out and severely punished for his disrespect of the occasion (Mt. 22:11–4). Matthew concludes that "many are called, but few are chosen" (Mt. 22:14).

In the Gospels the parable of the banquet is about the kingdom of God. Both Matthew and Luke say so (Mt. 22:2; Lk. 14:15). This context suggests a distinctly more allegorical meaning of the Mashal than Philo had implied. The Synoptic Mashal no longer speaks about consuming food in the literal sense, but about salvation through Jesus' words. The image of table-fellowship has lost its concrete implications and refers primarily to spiritual companionship. The Mashal now defines the boundaries between "us", who have accepted His call in the form of Jesus, and the Others who have not. While Luke and Thomas seem to think of this opposition mostly in social terms, Matthew reads more into it. He claims that the first guests actually killed the servants who summoned them. In this way he imposes on the Mashal the same narrative pattern as the parable of the vineyard owner.[52] He even places the two side by side, thus suggesting for the banquet the same context of Jesus' imminent death against the background of rising tension between him and the Pharisaic leadership. The guests who killed the king's servants symbolically represent those Jews who killed the prophets, John the Baptist and, forshadowing the future, also Jesus himself. The guests following the king's call, on the other hand, are those Jews who accept the authority of Jesus. To be sure, Matthew does not yet identify "us" as Christians in contrast to Jews. He still thinks in terms of different groups within Judaism and the notion of "Verus Israel" is not yet available to him.[53] The hostile tone of his parable, however, clearly anticipates such later polemics. One group is defined not only in contrast to the other, but as a complete replacement of the other. Philo's irenic version of the parable, with its remarkably inclusive gesture, seems to have been long forgotten – if it was indeed ever known in Synoptic circles.

The rabbis, it seems, were familiar with the parable of the banquet both in the Philonic and the Matthean version. A distinctly Philonic version of the parable is preserved in G.R. 8:9. It appears here in exactly the same exegetical context, namely as an explanation of the paradox that man was created in the image of God, but after all the other creatures. G.R. formulates this paradox in the form of angelic opposition to man's creation and solves this exegetical problem in exactly the same way as Philo.[54] It is in other words suggested that Adam was deliberately created later so that the world could provide his sustenance. As R. Huna put it: "He [God] created him [Adam] with due deliberation: He first created his food requirements, and only then did He create him".[55] In light of the angels' continued opposition God is urged to further justify his decision to create Adam. For this purpose he tells a "Mashal of a king who had a tower full of good things and no guests – what pleasure has its owner in having filled it?!"[56] Instead of a Nimshal, G.R. reports the enthusiastic reaction of the angels: they are convinced now and praise the Lord. This rabbinic Mashal casts God in the same role as Philo had done, namely the role of a host who invites man to share His goods. The rabbis also focus on His generosity and commitment to

---

[52] Mt. 22:6; cf.Matthew's version of the parable of the vineyard tenants in Mt. 21:35, 38–9.

[53] See also: Harvey, True Israel 234–8.

[54] On the angels' opposition to man's creation, see also: A. Altmann, The Gnostic Background of the Rabbinic Adam Legends, in: idem, *Essays in Jewish Intellectual History* (Hanover, N. Hampshire 1981) 1–16.

[55] G.R. 8:6, English translation by H. Freedman, in: *Midrash Rabbah. Genesis* (London and Bournemouth 1951) 58.

[56] Only the printed edition of Venice explicitly identifies this text as a Mashal, see: J. Theodor and Ch. Albeck, *Midrash Bereshit Rabba. Critical Edition with Notes and Commentary* (Jerusalem 1965) 61, Ms Venecia ... משל למלך שהיה לו מגדל. Freedman follows the majority of manuscripts and translates: "A tower full of good things and no guests – what pleasure has its owner in having filled it?" (Freedman, Genesis Rabbah 59)

man. At the same time, however, some details here differ from Philo's version. A banquet is not explicitly mentioned. The rabbis instead speak generally about a tower full of good things. More importantly, G.R. echoes the New Testament motif of a host without guests. Yet the absence of the guests is raised here only as a theoretical possibility. The very suggestion, however, indicates the rabbis' awareness of the Christian version of the parable. While such an awareness remains marginal in the present context, it had a formative influence on other rabbinic versions of the parable.

Both b. Shab. 153a and Koheleth Rabbah interpret Koh. 9:8 in light of the Mashal of the banquet.[57] The verse "let your garments be always white; let not oil be lacking on your head" is in both works associated with a king who summoned to a banquet (סעודה). As in the New Testament there are two groups of guests: those who respond to the call and those who do not. The version of the parable in K.R. 9:8 is especially interesting:

"Let thy garments be always white; let no oil be lacking on your head" (Koh. 9:8). R. Johanan b. Zakkai said: if Scripture speaks of white garments, how many of these have the peoples of the world; and if it speaks of good oil, how much of it do the peoples of the world possess! Behold, it speaks only of Mitzvot, good deeds and Torah. R. Judah ha-Nasi said: to what may this be likened (משל למה הדבר דומה)? To a king who made a banquet to which he invited guests. He said to them: go wash yourselves, brush up your clothes, anoint yourselves with oil, wash your garments and prepare yourselves for the banquet, but he fixed no time when they were to come to it. The wise among them walked about by the entrance of the king's palace, saying: does the king's palace lack anything? The foolish among them paid no regard or attention to the king's command. They said: we will in due course notice when the king's banquet is to take place, because can there be a banquet without preparation and company? So the plasterer went to his plaster, the potter to his clay, the smith to his charcoal, the washer to his laundry. Suddenly the king ordered: Let them all come to the banquet. They hurried the guests so that some came in their splendid attire and others came in their dirty garments. The king was pleased with the wise ones who had obeyed his command and also because they had shown honour to the king's palace. He was angry with the fools who had neglected his command and disgraced the palace ... the king said:... the former shall recline and eat and drink, while these shall remain standing, be punished and look on and be grieved. Similarly in the world to come ...

This parable strikingly resembles Matthew's version: it makes a fine garment a precondition for participation in the banquet, places the feast in an eschatological context and suggests a severe punishment for those who have not prepared themselves adequately. The rabbis moreover emphasize with all New Testament versions the difference between two groups of guests, suggesting

---

[57] I am referring here to the rabbinic text in its present, redacted form without going into the details of its historical development. This means that if two interpretations have been placed next to each other by the redactor, they belong together even if they are attributed to two different authorities. This methodological approach has important implications for our analysis of the parable in *Koheleth Rabbah*.

that "we" followed the invitation, while the Others did not and busied themselves instead with daily matters. This rabbinic version of the parable differs significantly from Philo's. It has adopted the Christian interpretation of the banquet as an eschatological event which decisively defines identity and sharply divides groups.[58] The language of the New Testament has thus been internalized by the rabbinic interpreters. It became natural to think of the banquet in the terms coined by the New Testament parable. While the rabbis had in this way joined the Christian discourse, they wished to inverse its implications. The criteria for joining the banquet were no longer said to be Christian, but distinctly rabbinic values. While Matthew made salvation dependent on one's acceptance of Jesus, the rabbis demanded "Mitzvot, good deeds and Torah". In K.R. the parable is moreover introduced by an explicit reference to the nations of the world, who lack precisely these virtues even though they possess other seemingly redeeming qualities. This statement is a particularly clear response to Christian polemics. Yet the whole parable, with its Matthean structure and inversion of the Christian message, has its *Sitz-im-Leben* in Jewish-Christian relations. It is possible that the rabbis formulated their position especially in view of Jerome's authoritative commentaries. At the end of the fourth or the beginning of the fifth century, Jerome had interpreted Mt. 22:9 as God's invitation to the Gentiles and Koh. 9:8 as a call to repentance in view of the imminent judgement day.[59] The rabbis countered such exegesis by associating Koh. 9:8 with a parable, which inversed Mt. 22:1–14 and insisted that only the specifically Jewish way was the path to salvation in the world to come.

The Synoptic and rabbinic versions highlight the significance of Philo's parable. They especially show that just after Philo the terms of the discussion radically changed. From the New Testament onwards the parable of the banquet increasingly became a tool for religious polemics, which defined boundaries in highly oppositional terms. After Matthew it was difficult to think of the banquet in other than distinctly eschatological and competitive terms. Philo, on the other hand, could still construct Jewish culture in a most peaceful and complementary way. Applying Greco-Roman figures of comparison to Scripture, he translated Ancient Jewish tradition into contemporary language. In this way he embedded Alexandrian Jewish culture in the Biblical as well as the pagan discourse, while transcending both of them.

Other examples of Philo's parables suggest a similar dynamics of cultural translation and an equally complex *Rezeptionsgeschichte*. Let us first consider

---

[58] *Contra* Flusser, Gleichnisse 125, 182, who assumes *vice versa* that the New Testament versions of the parable depend on the rabbinic material. Both the dates of the sources and the content of the versions render this conjecture highly implausible.

[59] Jerome, Comment. in Evang. Mattheum, *CCSL* 77:199–202; idem, Comment. in Eccl., *CCSL* 72:324–7. On the possible contacts between Jerome's commentary and Midrash Koheleth Rabbah, see more generally: Hirshman, Rivalry 95–108.

the parables of the sower and the field. Philo uses them in two halachic contexts with distinctly cultic connotations. The parable of the sower appears in his interpretation of Lev 18:19, which forbids a man to "approach a woman to uncover her nakedness while she is in the impurity of her menstruation". Both the Masoretic text and the LXX indicate that this law has to do with ritual impurity (טמאתה, ἀκαθαρσία). Its cultic dimension is stressed in Lev. 15:19–24, which discusses the transmission by touch of the woman's impurity to other persons and objects. In this context it is determined that a menstruating woman must be kept in isolation for seven days, which were probably terminated with ablutions.[60] The state of menstrual impurity is thus defined here more rigorously than in Lev. 18:19, which explicitly refers only to abstention during the days of a woman's bleeding. Philo relates only to Lev. 18:19, while ignoring Lev. 15:19–24. He furthermore interprets the prohibition of intercourse during menstruation in a completely new light. His paraphrase of Lev. 18:19 indicates the direction of his exegesis: "whenever the menstrual issue occurs, a man must not touch a woman, but must during that period refrain from intercourse and respect the law of Nature".[61] Philo has glossed the Biblical text, adding the explanatory phrase "and respect the law of Nature". As far as he is concerned, Lev. 18:19 has to do with the ideal of a life in harmony with the universal laws of Nature.[62] These principles determine, he explains, that "the generative seeds should not be wasted fruitlessly for the sake of gross and untimely pleasure" (Spec. 3:32). The Mosaic legislation has thus been interpreted to deal not with the cultic impurity of menstrual blood, but with the limitation of sex to strictly reproductive purposes. The parable of the sower suggests in which sense this might actually be a natural virtue (Spec. 3:32–3):

For this [intercourse during menstruation] is just as if (ὅμοιον γὰρ ὡς εἴ) a husbandman should in drunkeness or madness sow wheat and barley in ponds or mountain-streams instead of in the plains, since the fields should become dry before the seed is lain in them.
Now Nature also each month purges the womb as if it were a cornfield, a field with mysterious properties over which, like a good husbandman, he must watch for the right time to arrive. So while the field is still inundated he will keep back the seed, which otherwise will be silently swept away by the stream ... But if the menstruation ceases, he may boldly sow the generative seeds, no longer fearing that what he lays will perish.

This text clearly is a parable. It is divided into two parts, one referring to a fictional and stereotypical situation, the other applying this situation to the verse in question. As in the previously discussed parable, Philo stresses also here the connection between Mashal and Nimshal by stating in the latter that the

---

[60] J. Milgrom, *Leviticus. The Anchor Bible* (New York 1991) 934–5.

[61] νόμον φύσεως (Spec. 3:32).

[62] For more details on the Stoic ideal of living in harmony with nature and Philo's application of it to Jewish customs, see chapter nine below.

man should behave "like a good husbandman". The introductory phrase ὅμοιον γὰϱ ὡς εἶ moreover echoes the expression ὅμοιον γὰϱ ὥσπεϱ ἄν εἶ in Aristotle's parable and, more generally, the wide use of the term ὁμοίωσις for parables from the late second century BCE onwards.[63] Philo's expression also anticipates New Testament terminology. Mark introduces the parable of the growing seed in a similar fashion. Instead of using the term "parabole", he simply has Jesus say: οὕτως ἐστὶν ἡ βασιλεία τοῦ θεοῦ ὡς ἄνθϱωπος βάλῃ τὸν σπόϱον ... (Mk. 4:26). Even though the parable of the growing seed is "a curiosity item" without parallel in the other Synoptics, modern scholars have never doubted that it is indeed a parable.[64] It is moreover significant in this context that the Synoptics, especially Matthew and Luke, often use both the adjective ὅμοιος and the verb ὁμοιόω as an introductory formula of parables in cases where these are not explicitly identified as a "parabole".[65]

The parable of the sower interprets Lev. 18:19 by invoking a mundane situation familiar to Philo and his readers. While Philo himself lived in one of the biggest urban centres of antiquity, he cherished an almost romantic attachment to the countryside. He stressed that the Bible had been translated into Greek on the island of Pharos just outside Alexandria, because the translators wished to escape from the unhealthy and noisy city (Mos. 2:34–5). They were instead looking for an "open and unoccupied spot" where they could find "peace and tranquility" necessary for the pursuit of their spiritual goals (Mos. 2:34–6). A similar combination of countryside and spirituality dominates Philo's accounts of the two exemplary communities of Jews. While the Therapeutae lived on an agricultural estate or farm (χωϱίον) a little outside Alexandria, the Essenes had chosen a remote desert spot.[66] Both communities were devoted to a life of the mind and both were engaged in agricultural work. It seems that among the Therapeutae only the younger apprentices were responsible for the maintenance of the gardens and the actual plowing of the fields, whereas the Essenes performed these tasks at all levels of the community.[67] Being associated with the Therapeutae, Philo was certainly familiar with their farm. The basic work of a sower cannot have remained foreign to him and would resonate in his readers,

---

[63] On the increasing use of the term ὁμοίωσις for parables, see: McCall, Theories 130–1.

[64] Scott, Parable 363–71, quotation from p. 363.

[65] E.g.: Mt. 11:16; 13:44, 45, 47; 20:1; Lk. 6:48; 7:31–2; 13:18–21; Mk. 4:30.

[66] On the agricultural significance of the word χωϱίον and the precise location of the Therapeutic community, see: Taylor and Davies, Therapeutae 10–4. The authors stress that the community was situated in a rural yet not isolated or desert spot, which was probably a popular resort area for rich Alexandrians. This is one of the numerous differences between the Therapeutae and the Essenes which shows the separate identity of the two groups.

[67] Regarding the Therapeutae, see: Cont. 19–20, 36; Taylor and Davies, Therapeutae 16–24; regarding the Essenes, see: Lib. 76 where Philo stresses that "some of them labour the land", using the same term for husbandman (γεωπονοῦντες) as in the above parable of the sower.

especially if they themselves were Therapeutae. Anyone living in Egypt could in fact be expected to have some idea about the sowing of wheat and barley, because Egypt was the granary of antiquity exporting to many Mediterranean countries.[68]

Philo's Mashal invokes the image of a sower gone mad. Only someone who has lost his senses or is drunken would waste seeds on ponds and mountain streams. Anybody in his right mind would instead throw them on fertile ground where he could expect them to grow into a rich harvest. This reference to agricultural experience is remarkably compelling. None of Philo's readers would doubt its logic. Most of them probably nodded their heads, joining Philo in his scorn of the foolish husbandman. The terms μέθη and φρενοβλάβεια are strong indeed and convey a polemical invective, which is probably directed against Jews who ignore Lev. 18:19 and have intercourse during menstruation. Yet Philo's comparison between the sower and the husband rests on one crucial assumption without which his comparison does not hold. It is the assumption that all seed, whether agricultural or human, serves nothing but reproductive purposes. Only on this premise can the husband, who has intercourse during menstruation, be accused of wasting his seed on infertile ground. This, however, is in a way precisely the point Philo has to prove. By interpreting Lev. 18:19 in analogy to the sower, he has conflated two rather different situations. The comparison itself thus implies an important hermeneutical step – a step which was made considerably easier by the widely known, Classical association of the female with the earth and the field.[69]

In the Nimshal Philo rewrites Lev. 18:19 in light of the Mashal and assimilates the husband to the sower. He initially establishes that the womb functions like a field. It possesses the same mysterious qualities and is fertile when dried up, yet sterile when inundated. Philo implies that the womb must be treated in the same way as a field and should consequently not be inseminated while flooded with blood. He moreover stresses that Nature determined these rhythms of sowing and abstention. The "law of Nature" mentioned above in the paraphrase of Lev. 18:19 thus does not remain an abstract principle, but is given concrete meaning. Given the experience of the sower, it would be clear, Philo

---

[68] Fraser, Ptolemaic Alexandria 1:148–84; Bowman, Egypt 676–702. Under Roman rule, Egypt's agriculture became especially important as she supplied a large portion of the wheat consumed in Rome.

[69] Regarding the association in Classical literature between the female and the earth, see especially: *Homeric Hymn to Demeter* 54, 192, 469; Plato, Men. 237c–238b; Tim. 49a–52e; Plutarch, De Is. et Os. 363d–365c, 372e–374d; see also: F. M. Cornford, *Plato's Cosmology. The Timaeus of Plato translated with a running Commentary* (London 1937) 177–88; J. G. Frazer, *The Worship of Nature* (London 1926) 318–27; Ch. R. Downing, The Mother Goddess among the Greeks, in: C. Olson (ed.), *The Book of the Goddess. Past and Present. An Introduction to Her Religion* (New York 1990) 49–54. These Classical motifs are also echoed in Philo, Ebr. 61; Opif. 38, 132–3.

hoped, that intercourse during menstruation was a violation of the "law of Nature". The reader should, in other words, identify with the sower to the extent of abstaining from intercourse during menstruation. The Nimshal concludes with the suggestion that once menstruation has ceased, the husband should "boldly sow the generative seeds". Philo thus seems to think of abstention periods of a length depending on the particular biology of each woman. While faithful to Lev. 18:19, he blatantly ignores the categorical injunction of Lev. 15:19 to refrain from any form of touch for seven days. While Biblical law was concerned with reducing society's contact with sources of ritual impurity which might infect it on a larger scale Philo is concerned to limit sex to strictly reproductive purposes. As soon as intercourse can potentially lead to impregnation, it is in his eyes permissible, if not mandatory.[70]

Philo has in this parable invoked an ideal masterplot from agricultural life and suggested that it is the basis of the Biblical prohibition. While retaining the literal meaning of Lev. 18:19, he has thus radically changed the deep structure of the verse and its overall purpose. A law concerning the ritual impurity of menstrual blood has been translated into a law of Nature. Philo has once more defined Jewish culture in a remarkably irenic and inclusive manner. On the one hand, the Jew who implements Lev. 18:19 appears now like a universal sower. On the other hand, however, the Biblical custom is justified and its importance brought home to Alexandrian Jews who might otherwise have ignored it. The example of the sower has thus been used to reformulate an ancient Jewish script in more modern language.

Philo returns to agricultural images in another discussion of Biblical ritual. This time he provides a fresh interpretation for the sin offering mentioned in Lev. 6:25–9. Philo assimilates this verse to a Mashal, which subsequently became very influential, and shows that this Biblical injunction also deals with natural virtue. The exegetical impetus for the Mashal is the sacrifical ceremony which privileges certain families among the Israelites. One might infer that social status determined the Temple ritual. This was, however, an idea of which Philo could not approve. Priestly privilege, he argues, is not to do with family pedigree, but with moral distinction. The priests are the best qualified persons to act as intermediaries between God and the sinners. In order to stress the absolute moral superiority of the priests, Philo suggests that "the sins of the greatly virtuous and the truly sacred are such as to be regarded as acts of righteousness if done by others" (Spec. 1:245). A parable is now inserted to explain this point further (Spec. 1:246):

---

[70] The time immediately after menstruation was considered, from Hippocrates onwards, to be a particularly fertile time, see: Hippocrates, Women's Diseases 1.17 (ed. Littré 8.56); idem, The Nature of the Child 15 (ed. Littré 7.494); idem, The Eight Months Fetus 13 (ed. Littré 7.458). For further details on Philo's views on human reproduction, see above chapter one, three and six.

For as (καθάπερ) the fields where the soil is deep and rich, even if they are sometimes unproductive, bear more fruit than those where it is naturally thin and poor, in the same way (τὸν αὐτὸν τρόπον) we find in virtuous and God-loving persons that their unproductiveness of goodness is better than the fortuitous righteous actions of the bad whose nature does not allow them to act intentionally in an honest way.

This parable appeals to the frustrating experience of trying to make naturally poor fields productive. Philo counts on the natural preference everybody will have for the deep and rich soil. All of his readers will easily agree that it is better to invest in the good field and rely on it for a rich harvest. Why bother with sterile soil? The same holds true, Philo suggests, for the sacrifical ritual. It is natural to leave the main part of it to the priests and reduce the part of Israel to a minimum.

This parable is in a way the mirror image of the previous one. While Philo focused there on the right time of sowing, he considers now the quality of the different fields and their receptivity to the seed. While the previous parable referred to the seed in the most concrete and literal sense, the present Mashal operates on a more allegorical level. The field now represents the human heart and is no longer inseminated in a biological sense. Its products are therefore neither edible fruits nor human babies, but good deeds. The seed is not directly mentioned in this context, but it would appear to be the word of God. The image of the field in this allegorical sense has probably been inspired by a famous Stoic εἰκών. Diogenes Laertes reports that the Stoics likened "philosophy to a fertile field: Logic being the encircling fence, Ethics the crop, Physics the soil or the trees".[71] By applying this εἰκών to Lev. 6:25–9, Philo has achieved a remarkable translation of cultures. Biblical ritual has been transformed into a moral principle. The priests are described as virtuous men who received the seed of ethics and produced a rich crop of moral action. Once again agricultural experience is said to be the masterplot underlying Biblical ritual. Again Philo has at the same time translated a general image of his environment into distinctly Jewish language. The universal features of a field, which the Stoics applied to their system of philosophy, are now used to justify the Jewish Temple cult. Almost invisible boundaries are thus constructed and contemporary Jewish culture becomes embedded both in Scripture and general culture. Philo's parable indeed suggests a way of identifying with these two worlds without, however, becoming entirely absorbed in either of them.

The significance of Philo's agricultural parables emerges with particular clarity in comparison to the New Testament where the image of the sower assumes central importance. In the Synoptics as well as the Gospel of Thomas, a parable appears which greatly resembles Philo's Mashal of the fruitful field.

---

[71] D.L. 7:40; Diogenes continues here a list of comparisons which he introduced at the beginning of the paragraph by the term εἰκάζουσι.

The version in Thomas is minimalistic to the extent that its meaning remains rather obscure. Thomas simply has a sower go out and cast the seeds on diverse types of ground. Only one of them produces fruits. End of story (Saying 9). In the absence of any narrative context the meaning of the Mashal is not self-evident. Some allegorical significance may have been implied, especially if the parable referred to the kingdom of God or the word of Jesus, as some scholars have suggested.[72] The Synoptics made the allegorical dimension of the parable explicit and directly associated the sower with Jesus's teaching (Mt. 13:1–23; Mk. 4:1–20; Lk. 8:4–15). Exceptionally detailed *Nimshalim*, which were prompted by the disciples' lack of understanding, explain that the seed represents the word of God as transmitted by Jesus. The productive field stands for those who receive his teaching, believe in it and remain steadfast even in times of tribulation. The different types of sterile ground, on the other hand, refer to those who have for one or another reason not accepted Jesus' authority and thus fail to live with the secrets of God's kingdom on their mind.

These early Christian parables obviously share Philo's cultural code. They are familiar with the εἰκών of the field and follow Philo's distinction between good and bad soil. Both Philo and the Synoptics furthermore use this parable for social demarcation. While Philo sought to justify the privileged position of the priests, the Synoptics distinguished the followers of Jesus. If the Synoptic writers did indeed borrow Philo's parable, they gave it their own characteristic twist. The emphasis has shifted from virtuous action in Philo's parable to the right belief and endurance in the Christian parable. While Philo sought to explain a Biblical ritual in contemporary language, the Synoptics were concerned with strengthening their own emerging group. Their story reflects the difficulties of a sect not recognized by the majority of Jews. They therefore dwell on the different ways in which their followers may desert the new creed. They emphasize Jesus' exclusive access to the word of God and heavenly kingdom which were not open to other Jewish groups. This controversy about Jesus was obviously foreign to Philo. His parable of the field reflects a rather more irenic atmosphere. Instead of engaging in polemics against other Jewish groups, he explains Biblical law in terms relevant to contemporary Alexandrian Jews like himself. In this way he created a culture which was both distinctly Jewish and part of the environment.

It is now appropriate to appreciate Philo's king parables. They form a special group within his work because, unlike the figures so far discussed, the king is a rather more frequent protagonist. This accumulation is highly significant. It indicates the incipient standardization of the genre of parable, which subsequently led to the establishment of a number of stock characters in rabbinic

---

[72] Valantasis, Thomas 67–9; Scott, Parable 344.

literature.[73] Philo is a crucial figure of transition in this respect. Familiar with the Stoic king analogies, he developed for the first time king parables about the Jewish God. The Stoics began in the Hellenistic era to project the concrete experience of the polis onto a universal and spiritual plain. They no longer focused on earthly organisations, but discussed the ideal city of perfectly wise men living in accordance with the laws of Nature.[74] In this context they also spoke about the wise man as a king. Diogenes Laertes reports that "according to them [the Stoics] not only are the wise men free, they are also kings".[75] Philo is clearly familiar with the Stoic interpretation of kingship and repeats it sometimes almost *verbatim*. In Somn. 2:244 he says, for example, that the doctrine that "the sage alone is a ruler and king" was laid down for "the students of philosophy", while in Mut. 152 he stresses the Mosaic origin of this idea.[76] On other occasions Philo uses the figure of the king as an analogy to the wise man, the mind and the soul.[77] It is highly significant that in these secular contexts the analogies remain simple comparisons between the king's authority and the mind's control over the emotions and bodily functions. They do not develop into fully structured parables. This only happens in a religious context, when Philo speaks about Him who "alone is king in real truth".[78]

The richest of Philo's king parables is a famous text which has so far not been discussed as a parable. It appears in Opif. 17–20 and explains the nature and place of the intelligible world in the process of creation.[79] The exegetical impetus for the parable is Gen 1:5 "and there was evening and there was morning, day one" (Opif. 15). Philo attributes special importance to the fact that Scripture identifies this day not as "the first day", but as "day one", while the following days of creation are all described by ordinal rather than cardinal numerals. Philo creates a gap in the Biblical text by suggesting that the first day of creation was singular in a deeper sense. Scripture is thus taken to allude to the cardinal role of this day. It was then that the intelligible world was created which served as a model for the entire world. As Philo put it, God created the intelligible world "in order that He might have the use of a pattern wholly God-

---

[73] On the latter, see also: Stern, Parables 93–7.

[74] Schofield, Stoic City 57–92.

[75] D.L. 7:122; the Stoics did not mean this in Plato's sense of a philosopher king, who actually ruled over a country and was at the same time versed in philosophy. They rather referred to the wise man of the universal city, who was a king over his emotions and his actions.

[76] See also: Abr. 261.

[77] See: Sacr. 49; Det. 23; All. 3:115; Spec. 3:111, 3:184, 4:92, 4:123; Somn. 1:32.

[78] Immut. 159; see also Conf. 170; Migr. 146; Somn. 2:99–100.

[79] I myself have discussed the opening passages of Opif. from other perspectives, see: M.R. Niehoff, What is in a Name? Philo's Mystical Philosophy of Language, *JSQ* 2.3 (1995) 243–8 (see also bibliography there); the most comprehensive commentary of Opif. is still Runia, Timaeus *passim*.

like and incorporeal in producing the material world" (Opif. 16). At this point, however, Philo encounters a difficulty because he had just stressed that there exists an unbridgeable gap between God, the unoriginate and invisible cause of all, and the visible and passive world of the material (Opif. 12). How then can God create an invisible world which is both God-like and a model for the material world? The parable of the king suggests an answer (Opif. 17–20):

(A) To speak of or conceive of that world which consists of ideas as being in some place is illegitimate; how it consists [of these ideas] we shall know if we carefully attend to some comparison supplied by the things of our world.[80] Whenever (ἐπειδάν) a city is being founded to satisfy the soaring ambition of some king or governor, who lays claim to absolute authority and also being magnificent in his ideas, and wishes to add to his good fortune,[81] there comes forward now and again some trained architect who, observing the favourable climate and convenient position of the sight, first sketches in his own mind wellnigh all the parts of the city that is to be wrought out – temples, gymnasia, town-halls, market-places, harbours, docks, streets, walls to be built, dwelling-houses as well as public buildings to be set up. Thus after having received in his own soul like in wax the figures of these objects severally, he carries about the image of a city, which is the creation of his mind. Then by his innate power of memory, he recalls the images of the various parts of this city, and imprints their types yet more distinctly in it: and like a good craftsman he begins to build the city of stones and timber, keeping his eye upon the pattern and making the visible and tangible objects correspond in each case to the incorporeal ideas.

Just such must be our thoughts about God (τὰ παραπλήσια δὴ καὶ περὶ θεοῦ δοξαστέον), namely when He was minded to found the one great city, He conceived beforehand the models of its parts, and out of these He constituted and brought to completion a world discernable only by the mind, and then, with that for a pattern, the world which our senses can perceive.

(B) Exactly as (καθάπερ) the city which was fashioned beforehand within the mind of the architect held no place in the outer world, but had been engraved in the soul of the artificer as by a seal, in the same way (τὸν αὐτὸν τρόπον) the universe that consisted of ideas would have no other location than the Divine Logos, which was the author of this ordered frame. For what other place could there be for His powers sufficient to receive and contain, I say not all but any one of them whatever uncompounded and untempered?

This passage contains two parts: the first (A) is an extended Mashal focusing on God's modelling of the world, while the second (B) is a complementary parable highlighting the role of the Divine Logos. While the first Mashal uses the

---

[80] My translation of εἰκών as 'comparison' follows the ancient use of this word (see McCall, Theories especially 11–2, 31–56); cf. F.H. Colson, Philo 1:15, who translates 'image'. The Hebrew translators were especially sensitive to Philo's intention and translated מָשָׁל (Philo, Writings 2:18).

[81] Philo expresses more sympathy about this king than the standard English translation would have us believe. I have therefore changed Colson's translations in Philo, 1:17, replacing the expression "tyrannical rule" by "absolute authority" (αὐτοκρατοῦς ἐξουσίας) and the expression "would fain add a fresh lustre to his good fortune" by "wishes to add to his good fortune" (τὴν εὐτυχίαν συνεπικοσμοῦντος).

somewhat old-fashioned term εἰκών and introduces the Nimshal by an informal phrase, the second employs the rather standard phrases καθάπερ and τὸν αὐτὸν τρόπον.

Philo initially explains the Biblical verse by a comparison to a known situation from life. He invokes a hypothetical and stereotypical case rather than a specific historical event. This clearly emerges from Philo's conspicuously general phrases "whenever", "some king or governor" and "some trained architect". Each of the characters and actions in the Mashal is typical. The king strives, as one would expect, for absolute rule and ostentatious architecture. The architect equally executes his work according to the known principles of his profession. Philo invokes these characters precisely because they are so familiar. It is moreover remarkable that this Mashal tells a far longer story than the previous parables. Philo almost seems to have been carried away and provides many embellishing details which are not necessary for the plot. His astonishingly long list of buildings renders the Mashal especially concrete. The more houses Philo mentions the more likely it is that his readers will recall their own experience of construction sites. They may even have been reminded of the foundation of Alexandria.[82] The main point of the Mashal, however, is to indicate that a worthwhile city can only be built according to a preconceived plan. If no blueprint exists, chaos prevails and the actual city will fail to live up to the king's expectations. Indeed, the more ambitious the king's ideas are, the more careful the architect must be in the outline of his plans. The multiplicity of buildings highlights the logic of this point. Philo's readers would instantly agree that the construction of "temples, gymnasia, town-halls, market-places, harbours, docks, streets, walls to be built, dwelling-houses as well as public buildings" could not be executed and coordinated unless there was an overall plan.

This cultural experience is in the Nimshal applied to Gen. 1:5. Philo suggests once more that a typical masterplot of his own society underlies a particular Biblical verse. In this case he assimilates the creation account to the story of the king who has his city built according to detailed architectural plans. At this point Philo focuses on the two-stage translation of God's intention to create the world: initially a model is created and then in its image the material world. In this way Philo has presented his own rather revolutionary interpretation of the Genesis account as corresponding to a regular procedure known in everyday life. While the Biblical God was simply said to create the world, Philo's God follows Platonic premises and creates material things according to an ideal model. Yet in contrast to the demiurge in the *Timaeus*, Philo attributes utmost authority to the creator God. He Himself is responsible for the creation of the model and acts like a king commissioning subordinate assistants.

---

[82] See also: D. T. Runia, Polis and Megalopolis: Philo and the Founding of Alexandria, *Mnemosyne* 42.3–4 (1989) 398–412; Sly, Philo's Alexandria 32–3.

The complementary parable in the above-quoted text further explores the relationship between God and the ideal model of the world. This time the role of the architect is emphasized and an analogy is drawn to the Divine Logos. While Philo had already in the first Mashal said that the architect "received in his own soul like in wax the figures of these objects severally", he now emphasizes that the city "which was fashioned beforehand within the mind of the architect held no place in the outer world".[83] Philo thus stresses that the design of the city was the architect's spiritual creation, neither a material body nor a copy from some external thing. He moreover suggests a parallel between the architect's soul and the Divine Logos. Both play a mediating role between the superior king and the material world. Both translate the ideas of the highest and transcendent institution into the lower realm of mundane reality. Philo's readers were expected to accept these novel ideas, and especially the notion of a Divine Logos, because they all were so familiar with the procedures of building a city. Given the pervasive use of architects and architectural designs, what would be more natural than to assume that God initially created the intelligible world as a plan for the material cosmos?

Philo's enormous contribution to the development of the king parable can best be appreciated by considering his direct influence. While the king parables of Opif. 17–20 do not appear in the New Testament, they resurface in Genesis Rabbah. The shorter and complementary Mashal appears in the context of Gen. 1:26. This verse, beginning with the loaded expression "let us make man in our image and in our likeness", has given rise to many speculations. Genesis Rabbah dwells at length on the plural form נעשה and suggests that the angels were also involved, initially even opposing God's plan to create man. While most rabbinic interpreters do not seem to have been disturbed by this plurality of heavenly beings, R. Ammi suggested an exegetical solution which confined the celestial powers to God Himself. Philo's king parable is now used to explain the role of God's heart in the process of creation (G.R. 8:3):

R. Ammi said: He took counsel with His own heart.
It may be compared to a king (משל למלך) who had a palace built by an architect, but when he saw that it did not please him: with whom is he to be indignant? surely with the architect!
Similarly, "and it grieved Him at His heart" (Gen. 6:6).

Genesis Rabbah has moreover adopted Philo's extended parable of Opif. 17–20 and integrated it into the first *Peticha* on Gen. 1:1. The opening of the Creation account is now interpreted in light of Prov. 8:30 "then I was by Him, as a nurseling (אמון) and I was daily all delight". Towards the end of the *Peticha* an anonymous exegete uses Philo's Mashal to explain how God created the world by looking into the Torah as His blue-print:

---

[83] On Philo's use of the metaphor of the seal, see above chapter seven.

Another interpretation: "amon" is a workman ("uman"). The Torah declares: "I was the working tool of the Holy One, blessed be He". In human practice, when a mortal king builds a palace, he builds it not with his own skill but with the skill of an architect. The architect moreover does not build it out of his head, but employs plans and diagrams to know how to arrange the chambers and the wicket doors.

Similarly, God consulted the Torah and created the world, while the Torah declares "In the beginning God created" (Gen. 1:1), "beginning" referring to the Torah.

This rabbinic parable betrays unmistakably Philonic traces: the same exegetical context, the same idea of creation according to an overall model, the same figures of king and architect. Even the introductory phrase of Philo's Mashal "some comparison supplied by the things of our world" is echoed in the rabbinic expression "according to the custom of the world" (בנוהג שבעולם).[84] At the same time, however, the process of cultural translation has continued and the rabbis have adapted the Mashal to their own values. Most conspicuously, they have transformed Philo's Divine Logos into the figure of the Torah. They have thus made explicit an aspect, which Philo may have implied in his parable, but made manifest only in other contexts.[85] The rabbis were also less concerned about the intricacies of Platonic models. For them the Torah was primarily a concrete book which could be opened. Their architect therefore does not act upon his creative imagination, but looks directly into written diagrams and plans.

Philo wrote other king parables. One of them discusses God's superior status and authority.[86] It appears in the context of the Decalogue where Philo stresses that God alone must be worshipped by the Jews. The meaning of Ex. 20:3 "do not have any other gods besides me" seems plain and Philo is primarily concerned with reinforcing the message of the verse. His readers obviously needed not only to grasp the words, but to be convinced by them and act accordingly. Initially Philo illuminates the absurdity of polytheism by ridiculing the worship of the elements. He dwells at length on the names of the different gods and on the religious blindness involved in acknowledging them. He moreover laments that "incapacity for instruction or indifference to learning prevents them from knowing the truly Existent, because they suppose that there is no invisible and conceptual cause outside what the senses perceive" (Dec. 59). At this point a king parable is inserted in order to strengthen the argument by appeal to a well-known situation (Dec. 61):

---

[84] This expression is also preserved in the parallel in Yalq. Shim. Gen. 1:1. Thoma and Lauer, *Gleichnisse* 2:34–8 rightly mention Philo's parable in the context of G.R. 1:1 without, however, appreciating its meaning and the significance of the connection between the two.

[85] For a more detailed discussion of this point, see below chapter seven.

[86] This point is also discussed in analogies between God and the sun, see especially: Spec. 1:40; Somn. 1:239–40.

So just as (καθάπερ) anyone who rendered to the subordinate satraps the honours due to the great king have seemed to reach the height not only of unwisdom but of foolhardiness, by bestowing on slaves what belonged to their master, in the same way (τὸν αὐτὸν τρόπον) anyone who pays the same tribute to the creatures as to their Maker may be assured that he is the most senseless and unjust of men in that he gives equal measure to those who are not equal, though he does not thereby honour the meaner but deposes the one superior.

This Mashal invokes the experience of the Persian governor in the provinces. Philo indicates that he has constructed a hypothetical case on the basis of a stereotypical situation. Given the social and political reality of the time, honouring the satraps like the great king himself would amount to folly. This is so, as everybody knows, because the satrap is merely a representative of higher power. Philo clearly expects his readers to be familiar with this image of absolute hierarchy. He appeals to an audience which has for centuries lived in the province of great empires and is used to the sight of governors. The Persian king was especially known for his aloofness from average human beings and his employment of vast administrative machinery mediating between him and the world.[87] Philo further highlights these hierarchical structures by referring to the satraps as "slaves".

The Nimshal underlines the significance of Ex. 20:3 by assimilating it to the hierarchical structures of the political world. God is thus cast in the role of a great king, who would be offended by the adoration of his subordinates. Philo criticizes such mistaken respect as senseless and "unjust", because it "deposes the one superior". Anyone living in a world where governors are a pervasive reality would easily understand that. Ex. 20:3 has thus been translated into the language of political hierarchy and social propriety. A uniquely Jewish injunction has been rendered more meaningful by embedding it in the surrounding world. Jews implementing Ex. 20:3 need therefore not feel complete outsiders in a polytheistic society, but should see themselves as consistently abiding by accepted principles of conduct.

This king parable also resurfaces in Genesis Rabbah. It appears in the context of Gen 1:26 and explains the nature of man's creation "in our image and in our likeness". R. Hoshaya uses the parable to insist on Adam's subordination to God (G.R. 8:10):

R. Hoshaya said: When the Holy One, Blessed be He, created Adam, the ministering angels mistook him and wished to exclaim "Holy" before him.
What does this resemble (משל למלך)?[88] A king and a governor who sat in a chariot, and his subjects wished to say to the king "Domine", but they did not know which it was.

---

[87] On Philo's views of the Persians, see above chapter two.
[88] Thus Venice and Ms Oxford 147; MS London, which Albeck used for his criticial edition, however, reads למה הדבר דומה.

What did the king do? He pushed the governor out of the chariot and so they knew who was the king.
Similarly, when the Lord created Adam, the angels mistook him. What did the Holy One, Blessed be He do? He caused sleep to fall upon him and so all knew that he was human.

This rabbinic Mashal bears close resemblance to Philo's parable. It invokes the same image of political hierarchy and shows that the adoration of subordinates is a grave error (בו טעו). Only the object of the invective has changed. While Philo criticized polytheistic idols and especially the deification of the elements of nature, R. Hoshaya directs his parable against the adoration of man. The details of his story moreover indicate that the worship of man is about to take place. The angels actually mistook Adam for God and wished to exclaim "Holy" before him. Rather drastic measures are taken to clarify this mistake and to minimize its negative effects. These features of the rabbinic parable suggest that R. Hoshaya spoke in a distinctly Christian context. He used the parable to counter Christian claims of Jesus' divine status.[89] Philo's parable thus seems to have been adapted in Genesis Rabbah to the dominant issue of later centuries.

A third and last example may illustrate the nature of Philo's king parables. This time the figure of the king explains how God may visit the human soul. Unlike all the previous *Meshalim*, this parable is not directly integrated into an exegetical context. It only continues in a more general way the discussion of Gen. 4:1 which led Philo to contemplate the nature of true festivity. He criticizes feasts of only material pleasures and stresses that real happiness derives from encounters with God. One should therefore prepare one's soul so that it can serve as "a lodging fit for God", lest He will "pass silently into some other home, where He judges that the builders' hands have wrought something worthier" (Cher. 98). A parable of the king now suggests how God may take His lodging in the human soul (Cher. 99–100):

When we are about to entertain kings we brighten and adorn our own houses. We despise no embellishment, but use all such freely and ungrudgingly, and make it our aim that their lodging shall have every delight and the honour withal that is their due. What house shall be prepared for God the King of kings, the Lord of all, who in His tender mercy and loving-kindness has deigned to visit created being and come down from the boundaries of heaven to the utmost ends of earth, to show His goodness to our race? Shall it be of stone and timber? Away with the thought, the very word is unlawful. For though the whole earth should suddenly turn into gold, or something more precious than gold, though all that wealth should be expended by the builders' skill on porches and porticos, on chambers, vestibules and shrines, yet there would be no place where

---

[89] *Contra* Thoma and Lauer, *Gleichnisse* 11–16, who identify only Gnostic motifs in the parable, cf. also J. Neusner, *Confronting Creation. How Judaism Reads Genesis. An Anthology of Genesis Rabbah* (Columbia 1991) 59–64, who argues that this Mashal testifies to the idea of God in human form, while ignoring its polemical tone.

His feet could tread. One worthy house there is: the soul that is fitted to receive Him. Justly and rightly then shall we say that in the invisible soul the invisible God has His earthly dwelling-place.

This text lacks the explicit terminology of comparison which we regularly encountered in previous examples. The standard structure of a parable is nevertheless discernible here too: the first part invokes a concrete situation, while the second part applies this image to the discussion of God. This time Philo refers to a thoroughly hypothetical, upper-class experience. He considers proper preparations for a royal visit, stressing that "we" would neglect no effort to render the lodgings as pleasant as possible. This cultural expectation is in the Nimshal applied to the religious realm. God is now cast into the role of a king visiting the house of one of his friends. For the king of the whole world, however, who "in His tender mercy and loving-kindness has deigned to visit created being and come down from the boundaries of heaven to the utmost ends of earth", common houses are not appropriate. Philo rejects the thought that houses of timber and stone would honour Him. Only the soul is worthy of receiving His presence and may therefore play the role of a hostess.

The significance of Philo's king parable may again be appreciated by considering the fact that a similar version resurfaced in later rabbinic Midrash. It is now adapted to rabbinic values and gives emphasis to Mt. Sinai as the historical encounter between God and the Jews:[90]

(This may be compared) to a king (לְמֶלֶךְ) who had a friend. He sent to him, saying: prepare yourself, because I shall visit you on a certain day. His friend did not believe him, then he thought, even if he comes, he will come as a private person or at night. The king knew what his friend had said and sent to him, saying: by your life, during the day I shall come to you, in public, riding on the horse which I was riding when I was anointed king and wearing the purple, which I wore when I was made Augustus,[91] so that everyone will know how great is my love for you.
In the same way, when the Holy One, Blessed be He revealed Himself on Sinai, He revealed Himself in a cloud …

These three examples of king parables suggest Philo's central importance in the history of the genre. He developed for the first time a parabolic discourse in which the king regularly represents God. This is a clear sign of the emergence of stock characters, which subsequently became a distinct feature in rabbinic literature. More importantly, Philo has adapted the secular Stoic king analogies to a distinctly religious and Jewish framework. The obvious gap between the mundane and the Divine realm have prompted an innovative hermeneutics

---

[90] Beit HaMidrasch (ed. A. Jellinek, Jerusalem 1938, 2nd ed.) 6:89, Yalq. Shim. Numb. 723; Ziegler, Königsgleichnisse 171.
[91] I have retained the flavour of the rabbinic text, which reads אוגוסטוס.

which laid the foundation for the widespread use of political language in Judaism and Christianity.

Similar features characterize Philo's parables of the charioteer and helmsman. They also form a distinct group of parables within his work. They too indicate a significant transfer of secular analogies to God. The figures of the charioteer and helmsman had already been used by Plato as illustrations in his moral and political theories. In the famous Phaedrus passage, for example, Plato compares the rational part of the soul to the charioteer, who controls horse-like senses and passions (246e). In his political treatises Plato moreover compared the philosopher king to a helmsman, who safely guides the ship of society through stormy times. In Pol. 296e–297a Plato even used comparative terms which subsequently became standard for the parable: ὥσπερ as an introduction of the comparison and τὸν αὐτὸν τρόπον at the beginning of the application. In Rep. 487e he presented his analogy of the helmsman as an εἰκών.

Philo is obviously familiar with these Platonic analogies. Sometimes he seems to borrow them directly. He interprets Gen. 3:17, for example, by a comparison to the helmsman. Initially Adam and Eve are allegorized as mind and sense-perception. Adam's eating of the fruit at Eve's suggestion thus appears as the mind's submission to the senses. God punished Adam because the mind must remain superior. A parable of the charioteer and helmsman now illustrates the chaos which prevails when inferior forces take over (All. 3:223–4):

This is just like (ὥσπερ) a charioteer, when he commands and guides his horses with the reins, the chariot goes the way he wishes, but if the horses have become unruly and got the upper hand, it has often happened that the charioteer has been dragged down and that the horses have been precipitated into a ditch by the violence of their motion, and that there is a general disaster. A ship again keeps her straight course, when the helmsman grasping the tiller steers accordingly, but capsizes when a contrary wind has sprung up over the sea, and the surge has settled in it.

Just so (οὕτως), when the Mind, the charioteer or helmsman of the soul, rules over the whole living being as a governor does a city, the life holds a straight course, but when irrational sense gains the chief place, a terrible confusion overtakes it, just as when slaves have risen against masters.

Philo's Mashal closely resembles Plato's analogies of the charioteer and the helmsman. He applies these figures to the same subject of rational control over the emotions and expresses a similar anxiety about unruly forces within man. Philo has at the same time added a dramatic dimension of his own. He especially points out that "it has often happened that the charioteer has been dragged down and that the horses have been precipitated into a ditch by the violence of their motion". Vivid appeal is thus made to the fears of the readers who might have witnessed similar incidents. The Nimshal of Philo's parable applies these mundane situations to his allegorical interpretation of Gen. 3:17. The stories about the charioteer and the helmsman reinforce God's admonition of Adam and suggest that He demands rational control over the senses.[92]

Yet Philo went beyond the Platonic analogies and applied the images of the helmsman and the charioteer also to the God of the Jews. In this way he has created parables with the characteristic two dimensions of the religious and the mundane. In Det. 141–2 he easily moves from the secular to the religious significance of the helmsman and charioteer:

"And Cain said to the Lord: the burden of being sent away is too great for me" (LXX Gen. 4:13). The character of this cry will appear from a comparison of like cases (ἀπὸ τῶν ὁμοίων φανεῖται). If the helmsman should abandon a ship at sea, must not all arrangements for sailing the ship go wrong? Again, if a charioteer quit a horse-chariot during the race, does it not necessarily follow that the chariot's course will lose all order and direction? And again, when a city has been abandoned by rulers or laws ... does not that city become a prey to two very great evils, anarchy and lawlessness?
Need I add that it is a law of nature (πέφυκε) that the body perishes if the soul quit it, and the soul if reason quit it, and reason if it be deprived of virtue?
Now if each of the figures I have named becomes an occasion of loss and damage to those abandoned by it, how great a disaster must we infer that those will experience who have been forsaken by God – men whom He rejects as deserters, false to the most sacred ordinances, and sends them into banishment, having tested them and found them unworthy of His surveillance and governance? For, to say it all in a word, it is certain that he who is left by a benefactor far greater than himself is involved in charges and accusations of the most serious kind.

The significance of this and similar parables is considerable.[93] Philo has trans-lated general secular images into distinctly religious language, without how-ever abandoning their secular use. The dimensions coexist and indicate the proximity between God and the human mind, both of which can be alluded to by the same image. Unlike the king parables, however, the helmsman and charioteer do not resurface in later parables. Neither the New Testament nor the rabbis seem to have taken them into account. This might have to do with the differences in geographical and cultural reality: in Palestine horse races and ships were obviously a far greater rarity than in Alexandria, where a writer like Philo could easily count on his audience's familiarity with them.

The last category of parables I wish to discuss can be characterized as follows: secular images which reflect Alexandrian life and Classical literature and are generally not mentioned in the Palestinian sources.[94] These Philonic parables invoke the figures of the physician, athlete, wooer and hound. The

---

[92] For another secular parable of the charioteer, see Sacr. 49.
[93] In Vir. 61, Praem. 34 Philo constructs similar parables, which compare God to the pilot of a ship.
[94] None of these figures appear in New Testament parables. They are also virtually absent in rabbinic parables, for a rare example of athletes, see G.R. 22:9.

physician appears mainly in the context of politics and rhetoric.[95] As I have discussed elsewhere, this figure explains in a Platonic mode the diversity of treatment a good politician needs to administer in face of the changing situations of the state.[96] More interesting are those parables which compare teachers to a physician choosing from his vast learning the right medicament for a specific patient. Emphasis is now given to the gap between practice and theory – an issue which might reflect the reality of Alexandrian medical schools. In Post. 141 Philo says the following:

> The man, on the other hand, who is setting out to teach, is like a good physician, who with his eyes fixed not on the vastness of his science, but on the strength of his patient, applies not all that he has ready for use from the resources of his knowledge – for this is endless – but what the sick man needs, seeking to avoid defect and excess.

In Det. 43 the figure of the physician explains the situation of the man who is virtuous, but has no practice in rhetoric and will therefore fail in public:

> For this is just as (καθάπερ γὰρ) in medicine there are some practicioners who know how to treat almost all afflictions and illnesses and cases of impaired health, and yet are unable to render any scientific account either true or plausible of any of them, and some, on the other hand, who are brilliant as far as theories go, admirable exponents of symptoms and causes and treatment, the subject matter of science, but no good whatever for the relief of suffering bodies, incapable of making even the smallest contribution to their cure;
> in just the same way (τὸν αὐτὸν τρόπον) those who have given themselves to the pursuit of the wisdom that comes through practice and comes out in practice have often neglected expression, while those who have been thoroughly instructed in the arts that deal with speech have failed to store up in the soul any grand lesson they may have learnt.

Another protagonist in Philo's secular parables is the athlete. He appears frequently and reflects Philo's passionate interest in sports. The athlete generally stands for the struggles of the wise man for virtue and endurance in an adverse world. Three examples among many may suffice here. In Lib. 26–7 Philo provides an extensive comparison between the virtuous man and the athlete who does not give in to the blows:

> I have observed in a contest of pancratiasts how one of the combatants will strike blow after blow both with hands and feet …. and leave nothing undone that might secure his victory, and yet he will finally quit the arena without a crown in a state of exhaustion and collapse, while the object of his attack, a mass of closely packed flesh rigid and solid, full of the elasticity of the true athlete … will yield not a whit to the blows, but by his stark and stubborn endurance will break down utterly the strength of his adversary and end by winning a complete victory.

---

[95] At first sight it may appear surprising that the physician is not used as a figure for God. His benevolence and wisdom could easily lend themselves to such an analogy.

[96] Jos. 33–4; Niehoff, Joseph 73–4.

Much the same as it seems to me is the case of the virtuous man (ὅμοιον δή τι τούτῳ πεπονθέναι): his soul strongly fortified with a resolution firmly founded on reason, he compels the employer of violence to give up in exhaustion, sooner than submit to do anything contrary to his judgement.

In Mut. 84 Philo moreover compares the practitioner of virtue, who takes a break to resume the struggle for morality, to athletes who anoint their bodies when they are weary with exercise. In the case of Moses the image of the athlete illustrates the swiftness of spiritual and intellectual progress. Indeed, Moses who learns virtually by himself, is said to be "just as bodies robust and agile in every part, [which] free their trainers from care, and receive little or none of the usual attention" (Mos. 1:22). These parables evidently translate the culture of sports into the realm of ethics and philosophy. They create a special context for the interpretation of Scripture, which is now embedded in the general environment. It is interesting that Epictetus engaged just after Philo in exactly the same type of parables, comparing athletes with man's moral struggle.

Finally, the parables of the wooer and the hounds illustrate man's erotic fascination with learning. In the context of Deut. 20:5–7 Philo uses the parable of the wooer to show that true happiness derives only from spiritual acquisitions. Closely following Aristippus' parable of mistress philosophy and her suitors (D.L. 2:79), Philo says in Agr. 158:

Beginnings are seen in a wooer, for just as (καθάπερ) he who is wooing a woman has wedlock still in futurity not being already a husband,
in the same way (τὸν αὐτὸν τρόπον) the well-constituted man looks forward to one day marrying *paideia* a high-born and pure maiden, but for the present he is her wooer.

The same message is conveyed in Somn. 1:49 through the image of the hounds:

For just as (καθάπερ) we are told that hounds used in the chase have by nature the sense of smell especially keen, so that by following the scent they can track out and find the dead bodies of wild animals at greatest distance,
in the same way (τὸν αὐτὸν τρόπον) does the man who is enamoured of *paideia* follow the path of the sweet effluvium given forth by justice and other virtues.

These parables fulfil the same role as the others we have considered in this chapter. They associate mundane images and common experience with spiritual issues, thus creating a meaningful bridge between Scripture and contemporary life in the Greco-Roman world. In this way Philo has created a cultural discourse which is both distinctly Jewish and remarkably inclusive. He suggests that Biblical terms can be translated into the language of contemporary culture and *vice versa*. Jews are thus part of the Biblical world as well as the pagan environment. Indeed, the Greco-Roman world was an integral part of Jewish culture.

# 9. Inscribing Jewish Culture into Nature

> "the race, following nature and the whole dispensation of heaven, reckoned the seasons similarly and in harmony with the months and years"
>
> (Q.E. 1:1)

In this last chapter we will be concerned with the connection between Nature and the Jewish way of life. This is a central subject in Philo's overall work and will be interpreted here for the first time in the context of his construction of Jewish culture.[1] We shall investigate Philo's discussion on the basis of Geertz's work. He drew attention to the fact that religions strive to objectivize their moral and aesthetic preferences "by depicting them as the imposed conditions of life implicit in a world with a particular structure". "Religion", Geertz furthermore explained, "tunes human actions to an envisaged cosmic order and projects images of cosmic order onto the plane of human experience".[2] By arguing for a basic congruence between a particular lifestyle and a metaphysical plane, religions claim normative value for their teachings. Philo enthusiastically employed this strategy. He devised three arguments to inscribe Jewish customs into nature, suggesting that Mosaic law is grounded in the law of nature, that Jewish customs preserve health and that the Jewish holidays reflect the structure of the universe. These three claims converge into Philo's overall argument for an intrinsic connection between the Jewish way of life and Nature. They ultimately argue that living according to Jewish customs is not a matter of personal and subjective preference, but of objective value.

Philo's most prominent strategy is his association of Mosaic law with the law of nature. The Torah, he insists, transmits nothing but natural law because Moses refrained from the ways of legislating customary among other nations. He derived his laws from a more reliable source than either those who have "drawn up a code of the things held to be right among their people" or those who, "dressing up their ideas in much irrelevant and cumbersome matter, have befogged the masses and hidden the truth under their fictions" (Opif. 1). Such legislation was merely based on convention and proved too superficial for Moses who sought

---

[1] The subject is indeed so central that φύσις has become one of the most frequently used terms in Philo's overall work.

[2] Both of the above quotations are taken from Geertz, Interpretation of Cultures 90.

ultimate truth and aimed at a genuine education of his people. He therefore drew
up a law-code based on the highest principles engraved in nature (Opif. 3):

His [Moses'] exordium ... is one that excites our admiration in the highest degree. It
consists of an account of the creation of the world, implying that the world is in
harmony with the law and the law with the world (τοῦ κόσμου τῷ νόμῳ καὶ τοῦ νόμου
τῷ κόσμῳ συνᾴδοτος), and that the man who observes the law is constituted thereby a
loyal citizen of the world, regulating his doings by the purpose and will of Nature (πρὸς
τὸ βούλημα τῆς φύσεως τὰς πράξεις ἀπευθύνοντος) in accordance with which the
entire world itself is also administered.

This passage and a similar one in Mos. 2:48 have often been interpreted in the
context of Philo's alleged apologetics which led him to claim universal significance for Mosaic law. Philo is said to have sought a compromise between
Jewish particularism and Hellenistic universalism.[3] Such an interpretation,
however, is problematic because it overemphasizes the conflict between Gaius
Caligula and the Jews which allegedly served as an overall context for Philo's
apologetic discussion on natural law. His Jewish audience, on the other hand,
has usually been ignored.[4] In the above-quoted passage there is indeed no sign
that Philo was defensive about his tradition. He is neither concerned to dispel
prejudices of misanthropy nor to bridge oppositional cultures and integrate the
Jews among the majority. He is, on the contrary, proud of the excellence of
Mosaic legislation and praises its superiority over all other law codes. His
statements were clearly meant for a Jewish audience who would identify with
his self-confident position. They must therefore be understood in the context of
constructing a distinctly Jewish discourse on culture.

The above-quoted passage evidently deals with the nature and sources of
Mosaic law. Philo stresses that, contrary to other legislations, it is not based on
human convention, but on the very structure of the world which has been
shaped at the time of the creation. It is thus not an invention of the human mind,
but a reflection of unchanging realities. As Philo put it, "the law [is in harmony]
with the world" and "the man who observes the law ...[is] regulating his doings
by the purpose and will of Nature" (Opif. 3). Only this type of law can,
according to Philo, be considered proper law, while legislation based on convention lacks any real value, amounting in fact to "non-law".[5] He stresses this
distinction on various occasions, once praising true law thus (Ebr. 142):

---

[3] See especially: H. Najman, The Law of Nature and the Authority of Mosaic Law, *SPhA*
11 (1999) 55–73; H. Koester, ΝΟΜΟΣ ΦΥΣΕΩΣ: The Concept of Natural Law in Greek
Thought, in: J. Neusner (ed.), *Religions in Antiquity. Essays in Memory of Erwin Ramsdell
Goodenough* (Leiden 1968 = *Numen* Suppl. Ser. 14 = *Studies in the History of Religions*)
521–41; and the rather confused discussion of F. Calabi, *The Language and the Law of God.
Interpretation and Politics in Philo of Alexandria* (Atlanta 1998) 36–8.

[4] This insight guides the present book throughout, for further details on its methodological assumptions and implications, see above especially Introduction and chapter one.

[5] ἀνομία (Sobr. 25); see also: Spec. 4:46; Jos. 30–1; Ebr. 34–40.

A statute which is a law in the true sense (τὸ πϱὸς ἀλήθειαν νόμιμον) is thereby eternal, since right reason, which is identical with law (ὁ ὀϱθὸς λόγος ὅς δὴ νόμος ἐστίν), is not destructible; for that its opposite, the unlawful (παϱάνομον), is ephemeral and of itself subject to dissolution is acknowledged by men of good sense.

In this passage Philo characterizes authentic law by two qualities: right reason and eternity. Its opposite is mainly identified by transitoriness. These features are intrinsically connected. Since true law is grounded in the rational structure of nature, it is as unchanging as the latter. *Vice versa*, unauthentic law or lawlessness are based on limited human insight and thus amount to a fleeting script in a changing world. Philo's argument is clear and forceful. Its cultural significance must be appreciated in the context of Stoic thought on which it was modelled.[6] The Stoic traditions preserved in Cicero's writings are especially important for a proper understanding of Philo because they indicate that this school had already applied the notion of natural law to a written law code. A solution had thus been suggested for problems raised by Classical Greek philosophy concerning the nature and objectivity of virtue.[7] In particular, the Stoic theory of natural law overcame the ancient dichotomy between the unchanging rights of nature and man-made ordinances which were always to some extent imperfect and arbitrary. It was for the first time argued that virtue consists in the knowledge and imitation of nature's rational order. The latter was considered objective, perfect and unchanging because it had been created by the divine reason. Human conduct was consequently judged to be good to the extent that it conformed to this transcendental and distinctly religious standard.[8]

More importantly, the Stoics had applied the notion of natural law to specific human legislation. As far as Cicero was concerned, the perfect ruler was no longer someone above the law who is limited by artificially crafted rules, but a translator of absolute justice into human ordinances. "Law", Cicero insisted, "is the highest reason implanted in Nature, which commands what ought to be done and forbids the opposite. This reason when firmly fixed and fully developed in the human mind is law" (Leg. 1:18). Certain human legislation conformed to natural law, while law in the vulgar sense was any decree written up

---

[6] R. A. Horsley, The Law of Nature in Philo and Cicero, *HTR* 71.1–2 (1978) 35–59, pointed already to some basic parallels between Philo's and Cicero's notions of natural law. Even though Horsley's article has often been quoted, it surprisingly lacked influence on Philonic scholarship.

[7] G. Striker, *Essays on Hellenistic Epistemology and Ethics* (Cambridge MA 1996) 209–20, stressed the Stoic contribution without, however, paying particular attention to the written text.

[8] See especially D.L. 7:88 where the Stoics are said to have based their moral philosophy on the notion of "living in agreement with nature". While animals necessarily live by their natural constitution and automatically seek self-preservation, man as a rational being has to choose whether or not to organize life according to nature. The truly rational man will do so, the Stoics insisted, because nature provides the best rational order. Imitating the harmony of the cosmos will render man both happy and virtuous. "Befitting acts" are thus defined as acts commanded by reason (D.L. 7:108).

by human whim (Leg. 1:19). The distinction between these two types of legislation was crucial. Cicero considered only such ordinances as proper law which
recognize "things just and unjust, made in agreement with that primal and most
ancient of all things, Nature" (Leg. 2:13). Roman law, he was convinced,
reflected nature and eternal justice, while the legislation of other nations is
generally dismissed as undeserving of the very title (Leg. 2:10–3). True law is
in fact nothing but an extension of "the right reason of supreme Jupiter".[9]
Instead of responding to the needs of the moment, such law is anchored in the
divine realm and in the unchanging, rational structure of the universe.

While the Stoics did not provide precise answers to the question of how the
divine order of the universe can be known and imitated by man, they assumed
the possibility of such imitation and focused on its significance for the individual and society at large.[10] Cicero especially insisted that proper law which
conforms to the order of nature "can neither be repealed nor abrogated" (Leg.
2:14). Grounding a specific law code in nature thus implied a claim not only to
its moral superiority but also to its absolute stability. Cicero characteristically
presented new contemporary laws as a continuation of ancestral customs, tracing them back to the earliest and most perfect stage of legislation (Leg. 2:23).
Roman law was moreover assigned a unique status and potentially applied, as
Cicero formulated it, to "all virtuous and stable nations" (Leg. 2:35).

Cicero's discussion of Roman law provides important insights into Philo's
background. It suggests that he may have had similar objectives in mind when
grounding Mosaic law in nature. Like Cicero, Philo was indeed concerned to
establish the superiority and absolute stability of Jewish customs. He praised
Moses for being "the best of all lawgivers in all countries, better in fact than any
that have ever arisen among either the Greeks or the barbarians" (Mos. 2:12).
The excellence of Mosaic law was in his view based on the fact that it "truly
come[s] from God" (ibid.). It therefore omits "nothing that is needful" and
survives all historical changes (Mos. 2:14). This point was particularly important for Philo. He insisted that Mosaic law differs in this respect from all other
legislation. While the institutions of other nations have been unsettled and
influenced by external events, Mosaic law has for ever remained the same
(Mos. 2:14–5):

But Moses is alone in this, that his laws, firm, unmoved and unshaken, stamped as it
were with the seals of nature herself, remain firm from the day when they were first
enacted until now, and we may hope that they will remain for all future ages as though
immortal, so long as the sun and the moon and the whole heaven and universe exist.
Thus, though the nation has undergone so many changes, both to increased prosperity

---

⁹ Leg. 2:10; see also Leg. 2:15–6, where the transcendental, religious dimension of true
law is stressed. Cf. also D.L. 7:88 where the Stoics are said to identify the rational principle
of the cosmos with the highest god Zeus.
¹⁰ See also: Striker, Essays 221–80.

and the reverse, nothing – not even the smallest part of the ordinances – has been disturbed, because all have clearly paid high honour to their venerable and godlike character.

Philo's argument of natural law amounts in this passage to an emphatic claim for the canonicity of Scripture. We saw already in chapter seven that he described the text of the Torah as an emanation of the divine Logos, which therefore contains the whole truth and needs to be preserved in all its minutiae. Philo now complements this argument by suggesting an intrinsic congruence between Mosaic law and the structure of nature. The permanence of the Biblical ordinances is guaranteed by their being "stamped as it were with the seals of nature herself". Philo suggests that permanence is the main consequence of the intrinsic connection between Mosaic law and nature. He emphasizes that Mosaic law is in this way provided with a stability that transcends political power and historical fortune. The Jewish people thus has a permanent point of reference which never loses its meaning.

The Jewish context of Philo's argument emerges especially from the last sentence in the above-quoted passage. Philo asserts here that "all have clearly paid high honour to their venerable and godlike character". It is evidently the Jews who would recognize the divine character of the Pentateuch and guarantee the permanence of its legislation by actually observing it. The Jews' veneration for the law is moreover distinguished from pagan respect for it. Only the latter is voluntary and deserving of special attention.[11] Philo's presentation of the Jews as completely united behind the letter of the text is an ideal image which does not reflect historical reality, but his own notion of Jewish culture. On other occasions he himself criticized those Jews who read Scripture in an exclusively allegorical way and rejected its normative claims on their life. He equally opposed those who compared the Pentateuch to the foundational literature of other nations.[12] Both groups of Jews obviously had a different understanding of the text. Philo set a particular accent by anchoring the Bible in unchanging realities which guaranteed its uniqueness and permanence.

The Jewish context of Philo's discussion is furthermore highlighted by the remarkable fact that Philo's immediately following treatment of the LXX does not contain any reference to the law of nature.[13] Philo dwells here on the reception of the Hebrew Bible among the Greek-speaking nations, suggesting that it spread over the entire *oikoumene*. This process did not, as far as Philo was concerned, involve any bridging or compromise between different cultures. Nor did he attempt to make Mosaic prescriptions more attractive for outsiders

---

[11] Mos. 2:17, 25–7.

[12] For an example see Philo's interpretation of Abraham, discussed above in chapter six.

[13] Mos. 2:17–44. The first paragraphs (27–26) introduce the circumstances of the translation by discussing the wide-spread admiration of the Torah among pagans. The interest of the latter, Philo insisted, made a Greek rendition of the Hebrew Scriptures necessary.

by translating them into terms which would be familiar to them. On the contrary, pagans were expected to embrace the Jews' particular way of life and gradually join the community. Philo reports that, impressed by the "daily, unbroken regularity of practice exercised by those who observe them [the laws]" (Mos. 2:27), they began to observe the Sabbath and Yom Kippur (Mos. 2:21–3). Spreading the Torah definitely did not imply a universalization of its principles, but an assimilation of others. Parallel to the best Greek philosophers who had in Philo's view become some kind of converts to Judaism, the whole Greek-speaking world would, at least potentially, accept the specific ordinances of Mosaic law.[14]

Philo returns, after his excursus on the LXX, to further praises of Mosaic law and its intrinsic connection to nature. This time he focuses on the significance of creation. Explaining the order of the Biblical books, he makes the following observations (Mos. 2:48–52):

> he [Moses] wished to show two most essential things: first that the Father and Maker of the world was in the truest sense also its Lawgiver, secondly that he who would observe the laws will accept gladly the duty of following nature and live in accordance with the orderings of the universe, so that his deeds are attuned to harmony with his words and his words with his deeds ... Thus whoever will carefully examine the nature of the particular enactments will find that they seek to attain to the harmony of the universe and are in agreement with the principles of the eternal nature (τῷ λόγῳ τῆς ἀιδίου φύσεως συνᾳδούσας).

Philo suggests here that Mosaic law and nature are like two sides of the same coin deriving from the same source. God both created the world and ordained the particular laws of the Jews.[15] This is so not only in a general sense, but with regard to every single ordinance which is said to be "in agreement with the principles of the eternal nature". Philo illustrates his understanding of Mosaic law by some historical examples mentioned in the Book of Genesis. He stresses that Israelite heroes were awarded or punished for their actions by Nature which served as an extension of God's judgement. The impious thus perished in the deluge and the devastating fire in the cities of Sodom and Gomorrah, while Noah and Lot were blessed with well-being (Mos. 2:53–64). These cases were meant to show the intrinsic connection between Mosaic law and Nature.

The second strategy Philo employs to inscribe Jewish customs into Nature is to argue for their healthiness. We saw already in previous chapters that Philo used the language of hygiene and health to characterize Others. The Egyptians emerged in his work as a sick nation which perverted all standards of nature, health and civilization. Their food was described by Philo as appalling and

---

[14] For details of Philo's views on Greek philosophers, see above chapter five.

[15] The connection between creation and Mosaic law has also been stressed by A. Myre, La loi de la nature et la loi mosaique selon Philon d'Alexandrie, *ScEs* 28.2 (1976) 178–9.

disgusting, provoking a shudder in any cultured person.[16] Their sexual customs were similarly considered to be the product of "the poisonous bane of incontinence" which upsets what has been carefully arranged by nature.[17] Philo furthermore showed how the pathology of the Egyptians produced turmoil in every aspect of life, spreading also to religion and politics. Most unfortunately, as far as he was concerned, they also infected two central Roman figures: Gaius Caligula and Flaccus who both succumbed to the Egyptian *malaise*. Gaius literally fell ill with a "severe disease" and "exchanged the more moderate, and therefore healthier, mode of life which he had followed while Tiberius was still alive ... for a life of luxury".[18] Gaius consequently lost self-control in three central areas: food, sex and religion.[19] His body and soul were destroyed, giving way to "weakness and mental illness bordering on death" (Leg. 14). Gaius gave himself over to "savagery" and became an altogether different person, unrecognizable to those who had known him before.[20] Becoming a true despot, Gaius generally "brought disease to the healthy" (Leg. 107). Flaccus fared similarly. He succumbed after Tiberius' death to a "constant depression and ... the stream of tears which poured ceaselessly from him as from a fountain" (Flac. 9). When hearing of the murder of Tiberius' grandson, Flaccus "threw himself down and lay speechless" and "his reasoning powers deteriorated".[21] Philo has Flaccus later recognize his state as a case of mental derangement. His mind, he admitted, had been clouded by a "phantom" and he had been "asleep and dreaming", seeing "figments of a soul which recorded as we may suppose things which had no existence as though they were" (Flac. 164). Flaccus professes to have been utterly "deluded" (Flac. 165). In his case, as well as that of Gaius and the Egyptians, Philo associates incontinence and physical disease with cultural and political turmoil. The illness of a person or community began with lack of *enkrateia*, leading to general decline and disruption of nature's order. The negative characteristics of Philo's Others were thus the direct result of their departure from the norms of nature which guarantee health and welfare. The Jews, on the other hand, emerge in Philo's construction as their exact mirror image. They established a culture grounded in nature and health, thus providing stability and authenticity.

---

[16] Her. 79; for an interpretation of this passage in the context of the Egyptian national character, see above chapter two.

[17] Spec. 3:23–4; Philo specifically refers here to the Egyptian twin-marriages which united what had been separated by Nature. For more details on the sexual norms of the Egyptians, see above chapter two and three.

[18] Leg. 14. On the conflicting Philonic evidence concerning the role of Gaius' disease, see above chapter four.

[19] Leg. 14, 76–114.

[20] Leg. 22; Flac. 14.

[21] Flac. 10, 18.

In a well-known passage towards the end of *De Praemiis et Poenis* Philo formulates the connection between Mosaic law and health in ostensibly Biblical language. Emphasizing divine providence, he says (Praem. 119):

He promises that those who take pains to cultivate virtue and set the holy laws before them to guide them in all they do or say in their private and in their public capacity will receive as well the gift of complete freedom from disease, and if some infirmity should befall them it will come not to do them harm, but to remind the mortal that he is mortal, to humble his over-wheening spirit and to improve his moral condition.

Health is in this passage presented as one of the material benefits of law observance. God uses his creation as a means of executing judgement, giving health to the pious and infirmity to the wicked. Man's physical condition is thus nothing but an expression of divine providence. Philo is aware that reality may challenge this traditional Biblical doctrine. Some are obviously ill but not wicked and thus undeserving of punishment, while others fare well even though they are not righteous. Koheleth formulated this painful insight in his famous outcry: "there is a righteous man who perishes in his righteousness, and there is a wicked man who prolongs in his wickedness" (Koh. 7:15). Philo had an answer to such criticism. He insisted that disease must sometimes be interpreted as an educational tool which ultimately leads to moral improvement. Philo's discussion so far is thoroughly Biblical and rooted in traditional theodicy.[22] He has not yet spoken in this context about either Nature or culture. His immediately following explanations, however, indicate a new approach which transcends Biblical notions.

In Praem. 120 Philo embarks on a broader explanation of the relationship between body and soul. He insists that God granted "as a privilege to the man of worth that his body, the congenital house of the soul, should be a house well built and well compacted from foundation to roof". Man would thus be provided with the things "necessary or useful for life" and his mind would not be distracted from spiritual concerns. For, Philo explains (Praem. 121–2):

if anything over-chills or over-heats it, the house becomes warped and dried up or contrarywise wet and damp, and all these make the mind incapable of guiding the course of its own life aright. But if it resides in a healthy body it will have full ease to live there devoting its leisure to the lore of wisdom, thus gaining a blessed and happy life.

In this passage Philo has moved from a purely theological discourse to medical language. Man's physical condition is no longer presented as an expression of divine providence, but as a function of man's care and responsibility. One is happier if one leads a healthy life. This is so because there is an intrinsic

---

[22] On the issue of theodicy in wisdom literature, see especially: v. Rad, Wisdom 124–37, 190–239.

physical connection between body and soul. The body must have the right temperature and humidity, otherwise it will disturb the mind and prevent it from engaging in wisdom. Philo mentions in this context the Israelites who have been led out of Egypt and liberated from "the yoke of many pleasures and many lusts and the innumerable distresses which its vices and lusts entail" (Praem. 124). Health and spiritual well-being have thus been associated with both *enkrateia* and the national character of the Jews. Abstinence from pleasure is in Philo's view the foundation of physical and mental health as well as of the Israelites' particular life-style.

Philo moreover grounded the connection between health and *enkrateia* in the laws of nature. Observing Mosaic law, leading a healthy life and exercising self-control have become virtually identical. As Philo put it in Ebr. 140–1:

For as in our bodies disease is the cause of dissolution, while health is responsible for their preservation, in the same way in our souls the life-preserving element is prudence, which is in some sense mental health (ὑγεία γὰρ τις αὕτη διανοίας), while the destroying element is folly inflicting incurable malady (νόσον ἀνίατον). This, he [Moses] says, is "an eternal statute" and the words mean what they say. For he holds that there is a deathless law engraved in the nature of the universe (νόμον ἀθάνατον ἐν τῇ τοῦ παντὸς ἐστηλιτεῦσθαι φύσει) which lays down this truth, that instruction is a thing which gives health and safety, while its absence is the cause of disease and destruction.

Physical and mental health appear in this passage as two sides of the same coin. Mosaic legislation is based on the recognition that there is a "deathless law engraved in the nature of the universe" according to which prudence and instruction guarantee the same kind of health as in the body. Both have life-preserving effect and prevent the dissolution of a system laid down by nature. In this sense virtue has a real ontological impact, adjusting man to eternal statutes.[23] For Philo this mainly involved a cultivation of the self, controlling

---

[23] Philo applied medical language to Jewish culture in more than a merely metaphorical sense, as Plato had done. He rather suggested that Mosaic law literally produces health. This construct of Jewish culture involves a translation of physical into spiritual terms. Towards physical health Philo was ambivalent. He sometimes saw it as a merely external good without intrinsic value which is shared even by the wicked and the beasts (See especially: Post. 159; Sobr. 67; Abr. 266–7). Health, he moreover insisted, is unstable and can easily be ruined (Jos. 130). Spiritual values are far more lasting and superior (Spec. 1:283–4, 2:197). At the same time, however, Philo showed respect for the medical profession, contrasting it to the cooks' merely ingratiating work and admiring its efforts to restore health (Jos. 62–3). The physician is in his view blessed by God. While He directly bestowed health in its original state, He acts through the medical profession when man needs to be cured from some ailment (All. 3:177–8; see also: Spec. 1:252). Philo continues in this respect the line taken by Ben Sira, on which see: S.J. Noorda, Illness and Sin, Forgiving and Healing. The Connection of Medical Treatment and Religious Beliefs in Ben Sira 38, 1–15, in: M.J. Vermaseren (ed.), *Studies in Hellenistic Religions* (Leiden 1979) 215–24. Philo moreover assumes a parallel between physical and mental processes. Body and soul require the same kind of cultivation and health. Virtue and knowledge thus fulfil a role corresponding to physical well-being (Sacr. 39; Her. 286; Mut. 230).

the passions and developing an austere life-style. "Continence and self-re-straint, together with simplicity and frugality", he insisted, promote "sound health and well-being".[24] On another occasion he stated that (Vir. 14):

> The special name of this health is temperance, that is σωφροσύνη or "thought-preserv-ing", for it creates a preservation of one of our powers, namely that of wise-thinking. For often when that power is in danger of being submerged by the tide of the passions, this spiritual health prevents it from being lost in the depths and pulls it up and lifts it on high, vitalizing and quickening it ...".

Philo calls for manly strength to cultivate these qualities and defeat at the same time their opposite, namely feminine submission to the vices of gluttony and licentiousness.[25] For him *enkrateia* is indeed a "medicine against licentious-ness (Agr. 98), producing "strength and health" (Leg. 14). He recommends self-cultivation and healing of the soul from youth onwards, when the innocence of childhood has been lost and man's passions are "fanned into a flame".[26] Instruc-tion must then serve as a healing art which rescues the soul and restores it to its original vigour.[27]

We saw already in chapter three that Philo was convinced of the superior quality of Mosaic legislation. It promoted in his view the virtue of *enkrateia* like none other, thus distinguishing the Jews on account of their austerity and self-cultivation. Philo formulated this insight also in medical language and argued for the healthiness of Mosaic legislation. Moses, he explained, is "the best of physicians for the distempers and maladies of the soul, [who] set before himself one task and purpose, to make a radical excision of the diseases of the mind and leave no root to sprout again into sickness which defies cure" (Immut. 67). Moses indeed acted as "good physicians [do, in order to] preserve their sick folk" (Dec. 12). Since the latter do not allow their patient any food and drink until the cause of disease has been eradicated, Moses initially led the Israelites out of the cities into the desert. Only after this cleansing did he provide them with healthy nourishment which was none other than the "laws and words of God" (Dec. 13). By thus associating Mosaic law with health Philo has inscribed it into Nature and suggested its objective value. Jewish customs, he insisted, command the same authority as dietary or medical instructions. They also require the same kind of self-cultivation and care.

---

[24] εἰς ὑγείαν ἄνοσον καὶ εὐεξίαν (Mos. 2:185).

[25] On the manly qualities of *enkrateia* in Philo's construction of Jewish values, see above chapter three. See similarly Philo's statement that virtue has the power to "bring health and safety", while a licentious life leads to their opposite, namely serious harm." (Det. 72); the verb ἀποφαίνω indicates the intrinsic power of virtue to render man healthy; it is not given as a reward for a previous performance of good deeds; see also Agr. 98.

[26] Her. 296; for further details on the innocence of childhood, see above chapter six.

[27] Her. 297–8; this point has been emphasized by L. Hogan, *Healing In The Second Temple Period*, PhD Thesis at the Hebrew University of Jerusalem 1986, 181–5.

Philo's explanation of Mosaic law in terms of health reflects the concerns of his time. Medicine was no longer used merely in a metaphorical sense as Plato had done, but as a concrete entity.[28] Ethics was increasingly interpreted as a therapy and cure. Philo's late contemporary, the Stoic philosopher Musonius, formulated this connection with particular precision:[29]

... those who want to be in health should spend their lives taking care of themselves. For unlike hellebore, reason (τὸν λόγον) should not be cast forth with the illness after it has effected a cure, but it should be allowed to remain in the soul to keep and guard the judgement. For the power of reason should not be compared to drugs but to health-giving foods, since it produces (ἐμποιοῦσα) a good and healthy habit of mind in those to whom it becomes habitual.

Musonius speaks here of a life-long therapy which employs reason to cure desire. If man habitually takes care of himself, he will gain a healthy condition of mind which cannot easily be ruined by the diseases of the soul. Philo evidently shares this medical interpretation of ethics and expresses himself in almost identitical terms. In one important respect, however, he differs from Musonius: he applied current medical language to the specifically Jewish way of life. For him, this was the best cure for both physical and mental diseases. Philo highlighted this point in various contexts. When discussing *enkrateia* he characteristically began with food, suggesting that a proper (kosher) diet is the first condition for general self-control (Spec. 4:96). This in turn leads to cure from disease, because "gluttony begets indigestion which is the source and origin of all distempers and illnesses" (Spec. 4:100). A proper diet thus implies the right mental disposition. Care of the physical self, as proscribed by Mosaic law, leads to mental health as well. Circumcision, Philo insists in the same spirit, insures hygiene and fertility, exempting at the same time from "the severe and most incurable malady of the prepuce called anthrax" (Spec. 1:4). The quintessential Jewish philosophers, the Therapeutae, have made healing their life-long profession:[30]

The vocation of these philosophers is at once made clear from their title of Therapeutae and Therapeutrides, a name derived from θεραπεύω, either in the sense of "cure" because they profess an art of healing better than that current in the cities which cure only the bodies, while theirs treats also the souls oppressed by grievous and well-nigh incurable diseases, inflicted by pleasures and desires and griefs and fears, by acts of covetousness, folly and injustice and the countless host of the other passions and vices ...

---

[28] See also: F. Wehrli, Der Arztvergleich bei Platon, in: idem, *Theoria und Humanitas. Gesammelte Schriften zur Antiken Gedankenwelt* (Zürich 1972) 206–14.

[29] Frgm. 36 apud Plut., De cohibenda ira 453 D,E = ed. Lutz 134–5.

[30] Cont. 2; regarding the Therapeutae as quintessential Jewish philosophers, see above chapter five.

The Therapeutics significantly set up their centre in a region with healthy climate where they cultivated a frugal life-style.[31] In their case, too, care of the physical self led to spiritual health. The intrinsic connection between these two realms suggested that Jewish customs conform to Nature and adjust the Jew to objective, unchanging realities.

Philo's third strategy of inscribing Jewish culture into nature involves a new interpretation of the holidays which derived to some extent from their original agricultural significance. Following the regular luni-solar calendar, Philo highlighted the correspondence between special positions of the sun and the dates of important Jewish holidays.[32] He thus suggested that the rhythm of the Jewish year imitates the eternal movement of the planetary system. Their precise correspondence was in his view indicated by their identical numerical structure. Philo himself mentioned as the source of his number theory the Pythagoreans, and especially Philolaus, who were known in Antiquity for describing transcendental realities in terms of numbers.[33] The latter were not held to be identical with material things, as Aristotle sometimes led his readers to believe, but represented in their view the unchanging structure of the universe according to

---

[31] Cont. 23–5; the frugality of the Therapeutae is mentioned on numerous other occasions in the treatise.

[32] The lunar basis of Philo's calendar emerges from such passages as Opif. 101; Spec. 2:142–4. He thus differed from the author of the *Book of Jubilees* and the Qumranites, who polemicized against a reckoning according to the moon which in their view corrupts the appointed times (see especially Jub. 6:36–8); regarding the solar calender used during the Second Temple Period, see especially: H. Cazelles, Sur les origins du calendrier des Jubilés, *Biblica* 43 (1962) 202–12; A. Jaubert, *La date de la cene: calendrier biblique et liturgie chretienne* (Paris 1957) 30–59; eadem, Le Calendrier des Jubilés et de la Secte de Qumran: Ses origines bibliques, *VT* 3 (1953) 250–64; J.M. Baumgarten, The Calender of the Book of Jubilees and the Bible (Hebrew), *Tarbiz* 32.4 (1962–3) 317–28.

[33] In Opif. 100 Philo attributes to the Pythagoreans the comparison between the hebdomad and the sovereign of the universe and to Philolaus a monotheistic conception of the supreme deity who is represented by the seven, while "other philosophers" are said to liken this number to the "motherless and virgin Nike". In All. 1:15 Philo speaks of the Pythagoreans as likening seven "to the motherless and ever-virgin maiden" (namely Athena). While P. Boyancé, Études Philoniennes, *REG* 76 (1963) 91–5, considers Opif. 100 a somewhat confused, but probably authentic Philolaus tradition, H. Thesleff, *The Pythagorean Texts Of The Hellenistic Period* (Abo 1965) 151 n. 10, suggests that Philo either misunderstood his source or himself invented the attribution to Philolaus. Both W. Burkert, *Lore and Science in Ancient Pythagoreanism* (Cambridge MA 1972, Germ. orig.) 249; and C. A. Huffman, *Philolaus of Croton: Pythagorean and Presocratic* (Cambridge 1993) 334–9, reject Philo's reference to Philolaus in Opif. 100 as a misunderstanding of his source which is better preserved in a later writer. Burkert and Huffman base their argument on an Aristotelian fragment preserved by Alex. of Aphrod., Met. 39.3–5, which speaks only of a Pythagorean comparison between seven and Athena. This evidence, however, is problematic given the loss of most of Aristotle's discussion on the Pythagoreans. Moreover, Lydus, De Mens. 2:12 resembles Philo, associating the number seven both with the monad and the motherless virgin maiden, see also: A. Delatte, *Études sur la littérature Pythagoricienne* (Genève 1974) 157–9.

which earthly bodies had been composed.[34] This primarily meant for the Pythagoreans that reliable knowledge can only be gained by investigating the mathematical composition of the world.[35] Such an investigation had important practical implications as well. The Pythagoreans insisted that the best way of life was the one that attunes the human soul to the harmonious structure of the cosmos.[36] Spiritual contemplation and frugality became imperative in this context. Familiar with these Pythagorean principles, Philo interpreted the Jewish calendar in view of transcendental numbers and suggested that by observing the Jewish holidays the soul is attuned to the universe.

The central element in Philo's cosmological interpretation of the Jewish calendar is the number seven. He attributed exceptional significance to it, regarding its properties as beautiful "beyond all words" (Opif. 89). Philo nevertheless attempted a description of the number seven and listed a catalogue of its superior qualities. Initially it is praised for being perfect and unique among the numbers of the first decad, because it is neither begotten nor begets (Opif. 99). Philo thus suggested with the Pythagoreans that seven is neither derived by the multiplication of other prime numbers nor does its own multiplication produce a number within the first decad.[37] This fact indicated a rather unique role for this number and the things associated with it. Philo argued that seven is the numerical value which informs the structure of the whole universe. This emerges in his view from a simple observation of known phenomena: lunar movement is characterized by septenal intervals; heaven is divided into seven zones; the number of fixed stars and other planetary constellations amounts to

---

[34] Aristotle left contradictory accounts of how the Pythagoreans saw the relationship between number and thing. In Met. 986a he stressed their identity, while in Met. 987b he characterized the relationship as one of imitation. Huffman, Philolaus 55–61 (Phil. Fragm. 20), convincingly argued that the statements of identity between number and thing must be attributed to Aristotle himself, who thus interpreted the more cautious approach of the Pythagoreans. Ar., Met. 1083b is of particular importance in this respect, because Aristotle qualifies here his own description by a comment to the effect that the Pythagoreans "apply mathematical theories to bodies as if they consisted of those numbers". See also: B. Sandywell, *Presocratic Reflexivity: The Construction of Philosophical Discourse c. 600–450 BC* (London and New York 1996) 197–203, who argued for a degree of misunderstanding on Aristotle's part; J. Burnet, *Early Greek Philosophy* (London 4th ed. 1930) 285–90, 307–9; and W. A. Heidel, The Pythagoreans and Greek Mathematics, *AJP* 61.1 (1940) 12–3, pointed to the inconsistencies in Aristotle's accounts without resolving them; while Burkert, Ancient Pythagoreanism 28–31; W. K. C. Guthrie, *A History of Greek Philosophy* (Cambridge 1962) 1:233–40; and Barnes, Presocratic Philosophers 381–3, preferred Aristotle's account of the identity between thing and number in Pythagorean theory and joined the Aristotelian criticism of it.

[35] Phil., frgm. 3 apud Iamblichus, *In Nic.* 7:8; frgm. 4 apud Stobaeus, *Eclogae* 1.21:7b; translation and commentary in Huffman, Philolaus 113–23, 172–7.

[36] See especially: F. M. Cornford, Mysticism and Science in the Pythagorean Tradition, *CQ* 16.3–4 (1922) 142–50; J. S. Morrison, Pythagoras of Samos, *CQ* N.S. 6.3–4 (1956) 152–6.

[37] On the Pythagorean background of this interpretation, see bibliography cited above in footnote 22.

seven.[38] Human body, life-cycle and soul testify to the septenal structure of the world, since they are all divided into seven parts.[39] Grammar and music as well are informed by structures of seven (Opif. 126–7). Philo concluded his praise by acknowledging:[40]

the very high honour which that number has attained in Nature, [and] the honour in which it is held by the most approved investigators of the science of Mathematics and Astronomy among Greeks and other nations.

Moses, however, surpassed these philosophers and scientists. He not only recognized the significance of the number seven, but also grounded the Jewish calender in it (Opif. 128). Jewish feasts are thus shown to coincide with the dates when the number seven recurs in the annual cycle. They are thus not holidays by human consent or historical circumstance, but by virtue of their correlation with seasons "appointed by nature" (Praem. 153).

Philo distinguishes several holidays as giving special honour to the recurrence of the number seven. These are the Sabbath, the Feast of Unleavened Bread and the Feast of Tabernacles.[41] The former celebrates the seventh day of every week, while the latter two occur each in a seventh month of the year, counted once from the spring and once from the autumn.[42] Philo stresses the centrality of these holidays, taking them as indicators of the overall cosmological basis of the Jewish calender. He once explicitly said that "all the yearly

---

[38] Opif. 101, 112, 113–5.

[39] Opif. 102–5, 117–25.

[40] Opif. 128; see also Dec. 102 where Philo speaks of the "precedence awarded" the number seven which is investigated and explained by "the students of mathematics".

[41] Originally the Feast of Unleavened Bread was completely separate from Passover (Ex. 23:14–5, 17, 34:23; see also: Levinson, Deuteronomy 53–97). The Feast of Passover involved a highly unusual type of sacrifice, which was carried out within the context of the clan, not on an altar, and had to do with smearing blood on the doorposts in order to protect the house against demons (Ex. 12:3–23). The Week of Unleavened Bread, on the other hand, involved in the Priestly Code a pilgrimage to a local sanctuary and was subsequently taken to commemorate the Exodus from Egypt (Lev. 23:36; Num. 28:17; Ex. 13:3–10, 23:15). The idea of a pilgrimage to a local sanctuary was based on Ex. 20:24 which explicitly spoke about sacrifices on altars "in every place where I cause my name to be remembered". For the Deuteronomist the very idea of sacrifices either in private homes or local sanctuaries was anathema (Deut. 12:13–4; on the exegetical transformation of Ex. 20:24 in Deut. 12:13–4, see: Levinson, Deuteronomy 27–30). The Deuteronomist therefore amalgamated the two holidays and commanded a pilgrimage to the central sanctuary in Jerusalem (Deut. 16:1–8). Philo ignored these Deuteronomistic innovations and remained faithful to the original conception of a separate Feast of Unleavened Bread. For details on his interpretation of the Feast of Passover, see above chapter three.

[42] While Philo dates the beginning of the year with Scripture to the spring, he also acknowledges the alternative reckoning according to which the year begins in the autumn. His discussion in Spec. 2:150 suggests that he considered the former to be specifically Jewish, while the latter was the generally accepted calender. Josephus similarly accepted both reckonings, distinguishing a religious and specifically Jewish count beginning in the spring from a secular, more widely acknowledged count beginning in the autumn (A.J. 1:80–2).

feasts prove to be as it were the children of that number [seven] which stands as a mother" (Spec. 2:214). The Sabbath celebrating the weekly recurrence of the number seven gives greatest honour to it. It therefore serves as Philo's paradigm and provides the basis of his overall discussion of the holidays. His interpretation of the other feasts is in fact nothing but an extension of his treatment of the Sabbath. Concerning this exemplary feast he summarily explains that Moses (Opif. 128):

inscribed its beauty [i.e. of the number seven] on the most holy tables of the law and impressed it on the minds of all who were set under him by bidding them at intervals of six days to keep a seventh day holy.

The Feasts of Unleavened Bread and Tabernacles are also praised because they occur in a seventh month of the year, thus coinciding with the summer and the winter equinoxes (Opif. 116):

The sun, too, the great lord of the day, bringing about two equinoxes each year, in spring and in autumn, the spring equinox in the constellation of the Ram, and the autumn equinox in that of the Scales, supplies very clear evidence of the sacred dignity of the seventh number, for each of the equinoxes occurs in a seventh month and during them there is enjoined by law the keeping of the greatest national festivals, since at both of them all fruits of the earth ripen, in the spring the wheat and all else that is sown, and in autumn the fruit of the vine and most of the other fruit-trees.

The above two passages are in several ways remarkable. They initially show Philo's consistency in defining the septenal principle as the basis of the Jewish calendar. Holidays conforming to this principle are highlighted and celebrated as "the greatest national festivals", while other holidays, such as Passover, Shavuot and the New Year, recede rather more into the background. Philo's interpretation follows to some extent Biblical legislation which had without much ado placed the Feasts of Unleavened Bread and of Tabernacles at the time of the equinoxes.[43] Biblical writers, however, had in this context stressed the agricultural significance of the holidays, explaining especially the Feast of Tabernacles as an expression of gratitude for the just completed harvest. The number seven and cosmological structures played no role in the Biblical discussion. This dimension was first introduced by Aristobulus who discussed the Sabbath by reference to the fact that "all the cosmos of all living beings and growing things revolves in series of sevens".[44] It is the widely acknowledged "sevenfold principle", he insisted, which determined the occurrence of the Sabbath on the seventh day of the week.[45] Aristobulus equally pointed to the

---

[43] The solar basis of the Biblical calendar has been pointed out by: Z. Shua, Sun Worship in Ancient Temples and Israelite Festivals (Hebrew), *Studies in Jewish Festivals* 5 (1994) 107–21.

[44] Apud Eus., Praep. Ev. 13.12:13.

[45] Apud Eus., Praep. Ev. 13.12:15; see also Aristobulus apud Eus., Praep. Ev. 13.13:3–8.

importance of the two equinoxes, stressing that the Passover sacrifice occurs at the time of the vernal equinox.[46] Philo clearly followed this interpretative line. He, too, wished to show that the Jewish calendar conforms to cosmological structures and especially to the septenal principle of the universe. Philo elaborated Aristobulus' approach which is preserved only fragmentarily and provided more detailed cosmological explanations for each holiday.

Philo advanced his own interpretation of the Sabbath amidst a variety of well-known Biblical conceptions which did not, however, restrict him. This emerges from his passing remarks on the nature of the Sabbath. Repeating Biblical legislation he says that it is a day of rest when one "abstains from work and profit-making crafts and professions" as well as from lighting fire and employing slaves.[47] Philo moreover mentions Gen. 2:2–3 where the seventh day of the week is for the first time distinguished as a day of Divine rest after the six days of creation.[48] The literal meaning of this verse was rather unacceptable to Philo because he conceived of God in transcendental terms and rejected distinctly anthropomorphic notions.[49] The idea of man imitating the deity by resting on the seventh day was equally problematic for him.[50] These Biblical conceptions of the Sabbath played virtually no role in his own interpretation. They were not even mentioned in his halachic discussion of the holiday. The historical explanation of the Sabbath, introduced in Deut. 5:15, is similarly played down. Philo obviously did not wish to connect the most central Jewish holiday to the memory of the Israelites' menial status in Egypt.[51]

Philo's own interpretation is based on the laws of nature. He argues that the sanctification of the seventh day is necessary because its "marvellous beauty" is "stamped upon heaven and the whole world and enshrined in nature itself".[52]

---

[46] Apud Eus., Ec. Hist. 7.32:16–8.

[47] Mos. 2:211; Spec. 2:65, 69; cf. Ex. 20:10, 31:14–17, 34:21, 35:1–3; Lev. 23:3; Deut. 5:13–4; regarding the influence of the Holiness Code on the development of the Sabbath and its centrality in Biblical times, see: Y. Knohl, The Sabbath and the Festivals in the Priestly Code and in the Laws of the Holiness School (Hebrew), *Shnaton. An Annual for Biblical and Ancient Near Eastern Studies* 7–8 (1983–4) 114–7.

[48] Post. 64. Note that Gen. 2:2–3 does not yet oblige man to hold a similar day of rest. Man's imitation of the Divine rest in the form of the Sabbath is a later Biblical interpretation which subsequently became standard.

[49] Ex. 20:10–1, 31:16–7. In Cher. 86–7 Philo interprets the Divine rest in a philosophical sense, namely as an expression of the "absolute ease" and effortlessness of God's permanent activity.

[50] Man's imitation of God was in Philo's view restricted to developing the rational aspects of the mind and controlling the passions. For further details and bibliography, see above chapter three.

[51] Such a conception of the Sabbath undermines his overall construction of Jewish identity which was, as we saw in the first part of the book and especially in chapter two, based on the notion of an abysmal contrast between Egyptians and Jews.

[52] Mos. 2:209; in the same context Philo stresses that Moses had ordained the celebration of the Sabbath for those who "followed the laws of nature" (Mos. 2:211).

The seventh day of the week is said to be celebrated by heaven and earth who "rejoice and exult in the full harmony of the sacred number" (Mos. 2:210). Moses recognized this day as the "birthday of the world" on which the creation was completed and revealed in its perfection.[53] Contrary to Ex. 31:17 Philo does thus not regard the Sabbath as an exclusive covenant between God and Israel, but as a truly public holiday belonging to all the nations and the whole universe (Opif. 89). The Jews, however, remained special, because only they honoured this holiday appropriately. Moses alone completely adjusted the calendar of his nation to the septenal structure of the cosmos.[54]

Philo moreover derived specific cultural significance from the cosmological roots of the Sabbath. Repeating that this day is called a virgin, he stressed that it is motherless as well. This had important implications for his construction of gender. Philo insisted that this day is "begotten by the father of the universe alone, the ideal form of the male sex with nothing of the female" (Spec. 2:56). The Sabbath is thus considered special because it is not spoilt by any female element and instead belongs entirely to the male deity. As the son of God it stands in the sign of the "manliest and bravest number, well gifted by nature for sovereignty and leadership" (Spec. 2:56). Philo has thus anchored the Sabbath not only in Nature, but also in virility. These are intrinsically connected because the creator God is also "the ideal form of the male sex". Nature thus provides objective and unchanging male standards which create a meaningful reality for human life. Feminity is construed in this context as a departure from those standards or as a detrimental addition to them. The observance of the Sabbath which is rooted in that transcendental reality has important implications. It adjusts the Jew to the rhythm and structure of nature, cultivating in him an

---

[53] ἡ τοῦ κόσμου γενέθλιος (Mos. 1:207). In Opif.89 and Mos. 2:210 Philo speaks of the Sabbath as the "birthday of world" following the creation on the previous six days. In Spec. 2:58–9 Philo explains more precisely what he meant: six is "the number under which the parts of the universe came into being, seven is that under which they were perfected". Seven thus "reveals as completed what six has produced, and therefore it may be quite rightly entitled the birthday of the world". These discussions echo the theme of a special proximity between the numbers one and seven, which we have observed above in Philo's explanation of the hebdomad.

[54] Philo's interpretation of the Sabbath contrasts with that of the author of the *Book of Jubilees*. While the latter spoke in a seemingly universal sense about the Jewish holidays being celebrated in heaven (e.g. Jub. 6:18), he grounds each holiday in a specific event of Israelite history. The Sabbath has in the author's view been instituted as a covenant between God and His people (Jub. 2:17–22); the Feast of Weeks as God's covenant with Noah (Jub. 6:17), the Feast of Tabernacles on the occasion of Abraham's rejoicing over Isaac's birth (Jub. 16:29) and the Day of Atonement on the occasion of the brother's remorse over their plot against Joseph (Jub. 34:18–9). While Gilat, Sabbath 62–3; and Goldenberg, The Jewish Sabbath 429, have pointed to the difference between Philo's universal interpretation of the Sabbath and the particularistic approach in the *Book of Jubilees* as well as rabbinic literature, they have overlooked the distinction of the Jewish nation which Philo implied when stressing that Moses gave exceptional honours to the universal structure of seven.

orientation towards manliness and sovereignity. These two virtues are, as we have seen in previous chapters, necessary to develop *enkrateia* and become an authentic Jew.[55] Philo stressed the correlation between the cosmological roots of the Sabbath and the human customs attached to it by suggesting that the Jews devote part of that day to "the contemplation of things pertaining to nature" (Mos. 2:216). Such contemplation would enhance their awareness of the structure of the universe in accordance with which Moses instructed them to live.

The Feast of Unleavened Bread is interpreted in a similar vein. While Philo mentions its specific national significance as described in the Biblical *Holiness Code* and the book of Deuteronomy, he gives clear priority to its cosmological dimension.[56] He praises the holiday primarily for "being in accordance with the lead of nature and the general cosmic order" (Spec. 2:150). This is so, he insists, because it occurs in a month which is both the seventh month of the year according to solar calculation and the first month of the Mosaic calendar.[57] The date of the Feast of Unleavened Bread thus involves the two most important and potent numbers of the first decad. It moreover occurs in the month of the spring equinox and lasts for seven days. Both of these features have in Philo's view special cosmic significance (Spec. 2:155–6):

> The feast begins at the middle of the month, on the fifteenth day, when the moon is full, a day purposely chosen because then there is no darkness, but everything is continuously lighted up … Again the feast is held for seven days to mark the precedence and honour which the number holds in the universe, indicating that nothing which tends to cheerfulness and public mirth and thankfulness to God should fail to be accompanied with memories of the sacred seven which He intended to be the source and fountain to men of all good things.

Philo has adopted the original date of the Feast of Unleavened Bread, namely the 15th of Nissan, as given in Lev. 23:6 and Num. 28:17.[58] This date is important for him, because it coincides with the new moon and thus with the climax of the lunar cycle which is divided into four periods of seven days (Opif. 101). The occurrence of the Feast of Unleavened Bread is thus perfectly attuned to the movement of the planets and the eternal rhythm of nature. The seven-day duration of the holiday is furthermore said to correspond to the honour given in the universe to the number seven. Philo explains the nature of the holiday by

---

[55] Regarding the role of *enkrateia*, manliness and sovereignity in Philo's construction of Jewish values, see especially chapter three.

[56] Spec. 2:150, 158; cf. Deut. 16:3; Ex. 23:15, 34:18, 12:16–20. The latter passage associates the Feast of Unleavened Bread with the Passover and for the first time rigorously forbids the eating of *Chametz* during the holiday; see also: Knohl, The Sabbath and the Feasts 117–20.

[57] Spec. 2:150; Q.E. 1:1; note that Ex. 12:2 defines the month of the Passover Feast as the first month.

[58] Ex. 12:18, on the other hand, marks the evening of the 14th of Nissan as the beginning of the Feast of Unleavened Bread.

suggesting that it occurs during the first month in order to remind "us of the creation of the world by setting before our eyes the spring when everything blooms and flowers" (Spec. 2:152). Occuring at the spring equinox, the Feast of Unleavened Bread stands in the sign of "birth and increase to animals and fruits and plants" (Spec. 2:154). Man's most essential food, the corn, is about to be ripe at this time and indicates imminent perfection. This state of Nature is directly mirrored in the unleavened bread which is also short of perfection. The dietary customs of the Jews on this holiday thus turn out to be a close imitation of nature. They are modelled on unchanging cosmic structures rather than on particular historical events.[59]

Finally, the Feast of Tabernacles is significant in Philo's eyes because it occurs on the day of the winter equinox. Its cosmological meaning thus corresponds to that of the Feast of Unleavened Bread. Philo stressed this correlation (Spec. 2:210):

Again, the beginning of this feast [of Tabernacles] comes on the fifteenth day of the month for the same reason as was given when we were speaking of the season of spring, namely that the glorious light which nature gives should fill the universe not only by day but also by night, because on that day the sun and moon rise in succession to each other with no interval between their shining, which is not divided by any borderland of darkness.

Complementing the cosmological dimension of the feast, Philo stressed also its agricultural significance which had been prominent in the early layers of the Biblical legislation.[60] He called it "the autumn festival" (Spec. 2:213) and explained that this feast teaches gratitude towards God for the harvest which is just brought in at this time of the year.[61] Philo moreover justifies the custom of dwelling in tents mainly by reference to agriculture. It is said to indicate the end of the season when the husbandman has to live outside in the fields in order to protect the harvest (Spec. 2:206–7). The historical interpretation of the Feast of Tabernacles, as described in Lev. 23:43, is mentioned only in passing. Philo suggests that "another reason [for the custom of dwelling in tents] may be that it should remind us of the long journeyings of our forefathers in the depths of the desert, when at every halting-place they spent many a year in tents" (Spec. 2:208). This historical reminiscence, however, serves only as a spring-board for

---

[59] In Spec. 2:160 Philo also associated the Feast of Unleavened bread with the food in the Garden of Eden; for more details on this interpretation in the context of Jewish self-restraint, see above chapter three.

[60] In Ex. 34:22 the feast is called "the feast of ingathering" – a clear reference to the completion of the agricultual work. Even in Deut. 16:13–5 where the feast is called "feast of booths" the agricultural meaning of the feast is preserved and no historical dimension is mentioned yet. In the priestly legislation the feast was then connected with the Exodus from Egypt (Lev. 23:43).

[61] Spec. 2:204–7; Philo stresses additional aspects of the feast's agricultural setting in his concluding remarks in Spec. 2:213.

more general observations. Philo enthusiastically explains how important it is to remember poverty in times of wealth, the dangers of war in times of peace, hardship in times of prosperity and illness in times of health (Spec. 2:208–9). The universal and cosmological significance of the Feast of Tabernacles clearly has the same overriding importance for Philo as that of the Sabbath and the Feast of Unleavened Bread. He consistently argues that the Jewish holidays were not grounded in a particular and thus to some extent arbitrary course of history, but in the unchanging structure of the universe.

Philo's interpretation of the Jewish calendar confirms conclusions we have reached above in the context of Mosaic law: his overall strategy is to inscribe the Jewish way of life in Nature. He does so by three complementary arguments which suggest that observance of Jewish law adjusts to the law and structure of the cosmos and also provides health. Living as a Jew was thus not a matter of personal preference, but of objective value recommended to any wise person aspiring to an authentic life. This construction of Jewish culture asserted the sense of superiority we have encountered before in Philo's discussions of identity. He firmly believed that the Jewish way of life according to Nature was perfect and distinguised the Jews from the culture of lower-minded nations. Philo made this point with particular clarity in the context of the calender, insisting that the Israelites were instructed by God to follow determined seasons "lest they follow the Egyptians with whom they are mixed and be seduced by the customs of the land in which they dwell" (Q.E. 1:1).

# Bibliography

G. Alföldy, La politique provinciale de Tibère, *Latomus* 24.4 (1965) 824–44. [Alföldy, Politique provinciale]

J. M. Alonso-Núñez, Die Abfolge der Weltreiche bei Polybios und Dionysios von Halikarnassos, *Historia* 32.4 (1983) 411–26.

A. Altmann, The Gnostic Background of the Rabbinic Adam Legends, in: idem, *Essays in Jewish Intellectual History* (Hanover, N. Hampshire 1981) 1–16.

Y. Amir, Philo and the Bible, *SP* 2 (1973) 1–8.

–, Philo's Version of Pilgrimage to Jerusalem (Hebrew), in: A. Oppenheimer *et al.* (eds.), *Jerusalem in the Second Temple Period. A. Schalit Memorial Volume* (Jerusalem 1980) 154–65 (reprinted in: Y. Amir, *Die hellenistische Gestalt des Judentums bei Philon von Alexandrien* (Neukirchen 1983 = *Forschungen zum jüdisch-christlichen Dialog* 5) 52–64).

–, *Die hellenistische Gestalt des Judentums bei Philon von Alexandrien* (Neukirchen 1983).

–, Monotheistic Problem of Hellenistic Jewry (Hebrew), *Da'at* 13 (1984) 13–27.

B. Anderson, *Imagined Communities. Reflections on the Origin and Spread of Nationalism* (London 1991, 2nd revised ed.). [Anderson, Imagined Communities]

J. Annas, Knowledge and Language: the Thaetetus and the Cratylus, in: M. Schofield and M. C. Nussbaum (eds.), *Language and Logos. Studies in ancient Greek philosophy presented to G. E. L. Owen* (Cambridge 1982) 95–114.

V. Aptowitzer, Asenath, The Wife of Joseph, *HUCA* 1 (1924) 239–306.

–, Spuren des Matriarchats im Jüdischen Schrifttum, *HUCA* 4–5 (1927–8) 207–240, 261–297.

P. Ariès, *Centuries of Childhood: A Social History of Family Life* (New York 1962, Fr. original 1960).

J. Assmann, Der Zweidimensionale Mensch: das Fest als Medium des kollektiven Gedächtnisses, in: idem and Th. Sundermeier (eds.), *Das Fest und das Heilige. Religiöse Kontrapunkte zur Alltagswelt* (Gütersloh 1991) 13–30.

–, *Das Kulturelle Gedächtnis. Schrift, Erinnerung und politische Identität in frühen Hochkulturen* (München 1992). [Assmann, Gedächtnis]

–, *Moses the Egyptian. The Memory of Egypt in Western Monotheism* (Cambridge MA 1997). [Assman, Moses]

A. E. Astin, *Cato The Censor* (Oxford 1978). [Astin, Cato]

E. Auerbach, *Mimesis. The Representation of Reality in Western Literature* (Princeton 1953, Germ. orig.).

M. Baar, *Das Bild des Kaisers Tiberius bei Tacitus, Sueton und Cassius Dio* (Stuttgart 1990 = Beiträge zur Altertumskunde 7).

J. P. V. D. Balsdon, Notes concerning the Principate of Gaius, *JRS* 24 (1934) 13–24.

–, *The Emperor Gaius* (Caligula) (Oxford 1934). [Balson, Gaius]

–, *Romans and Aliens* (Chapel Hill 1979). [Balsdon, Aliens]

J.M.G. Barclay, *Jews in the Mediterranean Diaspora. From Alexander to Trajan (323 BCE – 117 CE)* (Edinburgh 1996). [Barclay, Mediterranean Diaspora]

–, The Jews in the Diaspora, in: idem and J. Sweet, *Early Christian Thought in its Jewish Context* (Cambridge 1996) 27–40.

–, Judaism in Roman Dress: Josephus' Tactics in the *Contra Apionem*, in: J.U. Kalms (ed.), *Internationales Josephus- Kolloquium Aarhus 1999* (Münster 2000 = MJSt 6) 231–45.

M. Bar-Ilan, Children's Games in Antiquity (Hebrew), *Proceedings of the Eleventh World Congress of Jewish Studies* (Jerusalem 1994) 2:1:23–30.

–, "Childhood" and its Status in Biblical and Talmudic Society (Hebrew), *Beit Mikra* 40.1 (1994–5) 19–32.

–, Medicine in Eretz Israel during the First Centuries CE (Hebrew), *Cathedra* 92 (1999) 31–78.

J. Barnes, *The Presocratic Philosophers* (London 1982). [Barnes, Presocratic Philosophers]

J. Barr, *Holy Scripture. Canon, Authority, Criticism* (Oxford 1983).

R. Barraclough, Philo's Politics. Roman Rule and Hellenistic Judaism, *ANRW* II.21.1 (1984) 417–553. [Barraclough, Politics]

A.A. Barrett, *Caligula. The Corruption of Power* (London 1989). [Barrett, Caligula]

–, *Agrippina. Sex, Power, and Politics in the Early Empire* (New Haven 1996).

F. Barth, Introduction, in: idem (ed.), *Ethnic Groups and Boundaries. The Social Organization of Culture Difference* (Oslo/London 1969) 9–38. [Barth, Introduction]

J.M. Bassler, Philo on Joseph. The Basic Coherence of *De Josepho* and *De Somniis II*, *JSJ* 16.2 (1985) 240–55.

J.M. Baumgarten, The Calender of the Book of Jubilees and the Bible (Hebrew), *Tarbiz* 32.4 (1962–3) 317–28.

H. Baumgarten, Vitam brevem esse, longam artem. Das Proömium der Schrift Senecas *De brevitate vitae*, *Gymnasium* 77 (1970) 299–323.

T.M.S. Baxter, *The Cratylus. Plato's Critique of Naming* (Leiden 1992).

I. Becher, Oktavians Kampf gegen Antonius und seine Stellung zu den ägyptischen Göttern, *Das Altertum* 11.1 (1965) 40–7.

S. Belkin, *Philo and the Oral Law. The Philonic Interpretation of Biblical Law in Relation to the Palestinian Halakah* (Cambridge MA 1940).

H.I. Bell, Alexandria, *JEA* 13.3–4 (1927) 171–84.

W. Bergmann and Ch. Hoffmann, Kalkül oder "Massenwahn"? Eine soziologische Interpretation der antijüdischen Unruhen in Alexandria 38 n. Chr., in: R. Erb and M. Schmidt (eds.), *Antisemitismus und jüdische Geschichte. Studien zu Ehren von Herbert A. Strauss* (Berlin 1987) 15–46. [Bergmann and Hoffmann, Kalkül]

R. Bernhardt, *Imperium und Eleutheria. Die römische Politik gegenüber den freien Städten des griechischen Ostens* (Hamburg 1971).

K. Bertholet, The Use of Greek and Roman Stereotypes of the Egyptians by Hellenistic Jewish Apologists, with special reference to Josephus' Against Apion, in: J.U. Kalms (ed.), *Internationales Josephus- Kolloquium Aarhus 1999* (Münster 2000 = MJSt 6) 87–123.

P. Bilde, The Roman Emperor Gaius (Caligula)'s Attempt to Erect his Statue in the Temple of Jerusalem, *Studia Theologica* 32 (1978) 67–93. [Bilde, Gaius' Attempt]

– *et al.* (eds.), *Ethnicity in Hellenistic Egypt* (Aarhus 1992). [Bilde, Ethnicity in Egypt]

–, The Essenes in Philo and Josephus, in: F. H. Cryer and T. L. Thompson (eds.), Qumran between the Old and the New Testament (Sheffield 1998 = *JSOT* Ser. 290) 32–64.

E. Birnbaum, *The Place of Judaism in Philo's Thought.: Israel, Jews, and Proselytes* (Atlanta 1996 = Brown Judaic Studies 290, Studia Philonica Monographs 2) summarized also in *SBLSP* 32 (1993) 54–69.

H. Bloch, *Die Quellen des Flavius Josephus in seiner Archäologie* (Leipzig 1879).

F. Blumenthal, Der ägyptische Kaiserkult, *Archiv für Papyrusforschung und verwandte Gebiete* 5 (1913) 317–345.

F. Bömer, *P. Ovidius Naso. Die Fasten* (Heidelberg 1958).

G. Bohak, *Joseph and Aseneth and the Jewish Temple in Heliopolis* (Atlanta 1996 = *SBL* Early Judaism and its Literature 10). [Bohak, Joseph and Aseneth]

B. M. Bokser, *The Origins of the Seder. The Passover Rite and Early Rabbinic Judaism* (Berkeley 1984).

P. Borgen, Logos was the True Light, *NT* 14 (1972) 115–30.

–, Philo of Alexandria, in: M. E. Stone (ed.), *Jewish Writings of the Second Temple Period. Apocrypha, Pseudepigrapha, Qumran Sectarian Writings, Philo, Josephus* (Assen 1984 = *Compendia Rerum Judaicarum ad Novum Testamentum II*) 233–82.

–, Philo, Luke and Geography, in: idem, *Philo, John and Paul. New Perspectives on Judaism and Early Christianity* (Atlanta 1987 = *Brown Judaic Studies* 131) 273–85. [Borgen, Philo, Luke and Geography]

–, Some Hebrew and Pagan Features in Philo's and Paul's Interpretation of Hagar and Ishmael, in: idem (ed.), *The New Testament and Hellenistic Judaism* (Aarhus 1995). 151–164.

–, *Early Christianity and Hellenistic Judaism* (Edinburgh 1996). [Borgen, Early Christianity]

–, Emperor Worship and Persecution in Philo's *In Flaccum* and *De Legatione ad Gaium* and the Revelation of John, in: H. Cancik, H. Lichtenberger, P. Schäfer (eds.), *Geschichte – Tradition – Reflexion. Festschrift für Martin Hengel zum 70. Geburtstag* (Tübingen 1996) 3.493–509.

–, Moses, Jesus and the Roman Emperor. Observations in Philo's Writings and the Revelation of John, *NT* 38 (1996) 145–59.

–, *Philo of Alexandria: An Exegete for His Time* (Leiden 1997 = *Suppl. NT* 86). [Borgen, Philo of Alexandria an exegete]

–, The Crossing Of The Red Sea As Interpreted By Philo. Biblical Event – Liturgical Method – Cultural Application, in: J. V. Hills et al. (eds.), *Common Life in the Early Church. Essays Honoring Graydon F. Snyder* (Harrisburg 1999) 77–90.

–, Two Philonic Prayers and Their Contexts: An Analysis of *Who is the Heir of Divine Things* (*Her.*) 24–29 and *Against Flaccus* (*Flac.*) 170–75, *NTS* 45.3 (1999) 291–309.

–, Philo's *Against Flaccus* As Interpreted History, in: K.-J. Illman *et al.* (eds.), *A Bouquet of Wisdom. Essyas in Honour of Karl-Gustav Sandelin* (Abo 2000) 41–57.

F. H. Borsch, *Many Things in Parables* (Philadelphia 1988).

A. B. Bosworth, The Death of Alexander the Great: Rumour and Propaganda, *CQ* 21.1 (1971) 112–36.

–, *A Historical Commentary on Arrian's History of Alexander* (Oxford 1980).

–, *Alexander and the East. The Tragedy of Triumph* (Oxford 1996). [Bosworth, Alexander and the East]

A. Le Boulluec et P. Sandevoir, *La Bible d'Alexandrie. L'Exode* (Paris 1989).

W. Bousset, Jesus (Engl. tr. New York and London 1911).

G. W. Bowersock, *Augustus and the Greek World* (Oxford 1965). [Bowersock, Augustus]

–, *Greek Sophists in the Roman Empire* (Oxford 1969).

–, The Imperial Cult: Perceptions and Persistence, in: B. F. Meyer and E. P. Sanders (eds.), *Jewish and Christian Self-Definition in the Graeco-Roman World.* (London 1982) 3:171–82, repr. in: Bowersock, Studies, 327–42.

–, Augustus and the East: The Problem of the Succession, in: Millar and Segal, Caesar Augustus 169–88 (repr. in: Bowersock, Studies 27–46). [Bowersock, The Problem of the Succession]

–, *Studies on the Eastern Roman Empire. Social, Economic and Administrative History. Religion. Historiography* (Goldbach 1994). [Bowersock, Studies]

–, *Martyrdom and Rome* (Cambridge 1995 = Wiles Lectures 1993).

–, Greek Intellectuals and the Imperial Cult in the Second century A.D., in: *Le Culte des Souverains 179–206*; repr. in: Bowersock, Studies 293–320.

A. K. Bowman, Egypt, *CAH* (Cambridge 1996, 2nd ed.) 10:676–702.[Bowman, Egypt]

– and D. Rathbone, Cities and Administration in Roman Egypt, *JRS* 82 (1992) 107–27. [Bowman/Rathbone, Cities]

P. Boyancé, Etudes Philoniennes, *REG* 76 (1963) 64–110.

D. Boyarin, *Intertextuality and the Reading of Midrash* (Bloomington 1990).

–, *Carnal Israel. Reading Sex in Talmudic Literature* (Berkeley 1993 = The New Historicism: Studies in Cultural Poetics 25).

–, *Unheroic Conduct. The Rise of Heterosexuality and the Invention of the Jewish man* (Berkeley 1997).

–, A Tale of Two Synods: Nicea, Javneh, and Ecclesiology, *Exemplaria* 12.1 (2000) 21–62. [Boyarin, Two Synods]

–, *Making a Difference: How Christianity created the Jewish Religion*, forthcoming at Stanford University Press.

–, Justin Martyr invents Judaism, forthcoming in the *Journal of Church History.*

M. Braun, *History and Romance in Graeco-Oriental Literature* (Oxford 1938). [Braun, History and Romance]

H. R. Breitenbach, Der Alexanderexkurs bei Livius, *MH* 26.3 (1969) 146–57.

J. N. Bremmer, Adolescents, *Symposion,* and Pederasty, in: O. Murray, *Sympotica. A Symposium on the Symposion* (Oxford 1990) 135–48.

A. Brenner, *The Israelite Woman. Social Role and Literary Type in Biblical Narrative* (Sheffield 1985 = *JSOT Suppl. Ser.* 21).

C. A. Brown, *No Longer Be Silent. First Century Jewish Portraits of Biblical Women* (Westminster 1992).

T. S. Brown, Onesicritus. A Study in Hellenistic Historiography (Berkeley 1949).

J. Brunschwig, The cradle argument in Epicureanism and Stoicism, in: M. Schofield and G. Striker (eds.), *The Norms of Nature. Studies in Hellenistic Ethics* (Cambridge and Paris 1986) 113–44.

P. A. Brunt and J. M. Moore (eds.), *Res Gestae Divi Augusti. The Achievements of the Divine Augustus* (Oxford 1967).

R. Bultmann, Zur Geschichte der Lichtsymbolik im Altertum, *Philologus* 97 (1948) 1–36 (repr. in: *idem, Exegetica* (Tübingen 1967) 323–55).

W. Burkert, *Lore and Science in Ancient Pythagoreanism* (Cambridge MA 1972, Germ. orig.). [Burkert, Ancient Pythagoreanism]

J. Burnet, *Early Greek Philosophy* (London 4th ed. 1930).

M. F. Burnyeat, Aristotle on Learning to Be Good, in: A. Oksenberg Rorty (ed.), *Essays on Aristotle's Ethics* (Berkeley 1980) 69–92.

F. Calabi, *The Language and the Law of God. Interpretation and Politics in Philo of Alexandria* (Atlanta 1998) 36–8.

R. Cameron, Parable and Interpretation in the Gospel of Thomas, *Forum* 2 (1986) 4–14.

H. Cancik, H. Lichtenberger, P. Schäfer (eds.), *Geschichte – Tradition – Reflexion. Festschrift für Martin Hengel zum 70. Geburtstag* (Tübingen 1996). [Cancik *et al.*, Geschichte – Tradition – Reflexion]

W. Capelle, Griechische Ethik und römischer Imperialismus, *Klio* 25 (1932) 86–113.

P. Carny, Biblical Egypt as a Symbol in Philo's Allegory (Hebrew), *Shnaton. An Annual for Biblical and Ancient Near Eastern Studies* 5–6 (1982) 197–204.

P. Cartledge, *The Greeks. A Portrait of Self and Others* (Oxford 1993). [Cartledge, Greeks]

J. Cazeaux, 'Nul n'est prophète en son pays': Contribution à l'étude de Joseph d'après Philon, in: J. P. Kenney, (ed.), *The School of Moses. Studies in Philo and Hellenistic Religion. In Memory of Horst R. Moehring* (Atlanta 1995 = Brown Judaic Studies 304) 41–81.

H. Cazelles, Sur les Origins du Calendrier des Jubilés, *Biblica* 43 (1962) 202–12.

M. P. Charlesworth, Gaius and Claudius, *CAH* 10 (1934, 1st ed.) 653–701.

–, The Refusal of Divine Honours. An Augustan Formula, *PBSR* 15 (1939) 1–10. [Charlesworth, Divine Honours]

D. Chidester, *Word and Light. Seeing, Hearing, and Religious Discourse* (University of Illinois Press 1992). [Chidester, Word]

G. W. Clarke, Seneca the Younger under Caligula, *Latomus* 24.1 (1965) 62–9.

D. Cohen, *Law, Sexuality, and Society. The enforcement of morals in classical Athens* (Cambridge 1991).

–, The Augustan Law on Adultery: The Social and Cultural Context, in: D. I. Kertzer and R. P. Saller (eds.), *The Family In Italy from Antiquity to the Present* (New Haven and London 1991) 109–26.

–, Seclusion, Separation, and the Status of Women in Classical Athens, in: I. McAuslan and P. Walcot (eds.), *Women in Antiquity* (Oxford 1996 = *Greece and Rome Studies* III) 134–45.

J. Cohen, *"Be Fertile and Increase, Fill the Earth and Master It". The Ancient and Medieval Career of a Biblical Text* (Ithaca and London 1989).

N. G. Cohen, *Philo Judaeus. His Universe of Discourse* (Frankfurt 1995).

S. J. D. Cohen, Alexander the Great and Jaddus the High Priest according to Josephus, *AJS Review* 7–8 (1982–3) 41–68.

–, Solomon and the Daughter of Pharaoh: Intermarriage, Conversion, and the Impurity of Women, *JANES* 16–17 (1984–5) *Ancient Studies in Memory of Elias Bickerman*, 23–37.

–, The Origins of the Matrilineal Principle in Rabbinic Law, *AJS Review* 10.1 (1985) 19–53. [Cohen, Matrilineal Principle]

–, Crossing the Boundary and Becoming a Jew, *HTR* 82.1 (1989) 13–33. [Cohen, Crossing the Boundary]

–, Religion, Ethnicity, and 'Hellenism' in the Emergence of Jewish Identity in Maccabean Palestine, in: P. Bilde *et al.* (eds.), *Religion and Religious Practice in the Seleucid Kingdom* (Aarhus 1990) 204–23. [Cohen, Religion]

–, 'Ιουδαῖος τὸ γένος' and Related Expressions in Josephus, in: F. Parente and J. Sievers (eds.), *Josephus and the History of the Greco-Roman Period. Essays in Memory of Morton Smith* (Leiden 1994) 23–38.

–, *The Beginnings of Jewishness. Boundaries, Varieties, Uncertainties* (Berkeley 1999). [Cohen, Jewishness]

L. Cohn, Philo von Alexandria, *Neue Jahrbücher für das Klassische Altertum, Geschichte und Deutsche Literatur und Pädagogik* 1 (1898) 514–40.

–, Einleitung und Chronologie der Schriften Philos, *Philologus Suppl. Bd.* 7 (1899) 387–435. [Cohn, Einleitung]

A. Yarbro Collins, Aristobulus, in: J.H. Charlesworth (ed.), *The Old Testament Pseudepigrapha* (New York 1985) 2.831–42.

J.J. Collins, *Between Athens and Jerusalem* (New York 1983). [Collins, Athens and Jerusalem]

–, Sibylline Oracles, in: J.H. Charlesworth (ed.), *The Old Testament Pseudepigrapha* (New York 1983) 317–472.

–, A Symbol of Otherness: Circumcision and Salvation in the First Century, in: J. Neusner and E.S. Frerichs (eds.), *"To see Ourselves as Others see Us". Christians, Jews,"Others" in Late Antiquity* (Chico 1985) 163–86.

–, The Exodus and Biblical Theology, *Biblical Theology Bulletin* 25.4 (1995) 152–60.

–, Marriage, Divorce, and Family in Second Temple Judaism, in: L.G. Perdue *et al.* (eds.), *Families in Ancient Israel* (Westminster 1997) 104–62.

F.M. Cornford, Mysticism and Science in the Pythagorean Tradition, *CQ* 16.3–4 (1922) 137–50.

–, *Plato's Cosmology. The Timaeus of Plato translated with a running commentary* (London 1937). [Cornford, Plato's Cosmology]

G.P. Corrington, The Defense of the Body and the Discourse of Appetite: Continence and Control in the Graeco-Roman World, *Semeia* 57 (1992) 65–74.

H.M. Cotton, A Cancelled Marriage Contract From The Judean Desert (XHev/Se Gr.2), *JRS* 84 (1994) 64–86.

–, The Archive Of Salome Komaise Daugher Of Levi: Another Archive From The 'Cave Of Letters', *Zeitschrift für Papyrologie und Epigraphik* 105 (1995) 171–208.

–, The Rabbis and the Documents, in: Goodman, Jews in a Graeco-Roman World 167–79.

F. de Coulanges, *The Ancient City. A Study on the Religion, Laws, and Institutions of Greece and Rome* (Boston 1901).

I.M. Crombie, *An Examination of Plato's Doctrines* (London 1963). [Crombie, Examination]

P.R. Davies and B.D. Chilton, The Aqedah: A Revised Tradition History, *CBQ* 40.4 (1978) 514–46.

P.S. Davies, The Meaning of Philo's Text about the Gilded Shields, *JThS* 37.1 (1986) 109–14.

S.L. Davies, *The Gospel of Thomas and Christian Wisdom* (New York 1983).

–, The Christology and Protology of the Gosepl of Thomas, *JBL* 111.4 (1992) 663–682.

D. Dawson, *Allegorical Readers and Cultural Revision in Ancient Alexandria* (Berkeley 1992). [Dawson, Allegorical Readers]

P.L. Day (ed.), *Gender and Difference in Ancient Israel* (Minneapolis 1989).

J. Deininger, *Der politische Widerstand gegen Rom in Griechenland 217–86 v.Chr.* (Berlin and New York 1971).

A. Delatte, *Etudes sur la littérature Pythagoricienne* (Genève 1974).

G. Delling, *Paulus' Stellung zu Frau und Ehe* (Stuttgart 1931 = Beiträge zur Wissenschaft vom Alten und Neuen Testament 5).

–, Philons Enkomium auf Augustus, *Klio* 54 (1972) 171–192. [Delling, Enkomium]

–, Alexander der Grosse als Bekenner des Jüdischen Gottesglaubens, *JSJ* 12.1 (1981) 1–51. [Delling, Bekenner]

–, The "One Who Sees God" in Philo, in: Greenspahn, Nourished with Peace 27–41.

A.-M. Denis, *Fragementa Pseudepigraphorum quae supersunt Graece* (Leiden 1970).

J. M. Dillon, *The Middle Platonists, 80 B.C. to A.D. 220* (New York 1977). [Dillon, Middle Platonists]

S. Dixon, *The Roman Family* (Baltimore 1992). [Dixon, Roman Family]

R. Doran, A Complex of Parables: Gospel of Thomas 96–98, *Nov.Test.* 29.4 (1987) 347–52.

K. Dowden, Grades in the Eleusinian Mysteries, *Revue de l'Histoire des Religions* 197.4 (1980) 409–27.

Ch. R. Downing, The Mother Goddess among the Greeks, in: C. Olson (ed.), *The Book of the Goddess. Past and Present. An Introduction to Her Religion* (New York 1990) 49–59.

A. J. Droge, *Homer or Moses? Early Christian Interpretations of the History of Culture* (Tübingen 1989). [Droge, Moses]

P. Dschulnigg, *Rabbinische Gleichnisse und das Neue Testament. Die Gleichnisse der PesK im Vergleich mit den Gleichnisses Jesu und dem Neuen Testament* (Bern 1988 = Judaica and Christiana 12).

P. duBois, *Sowing the Body* (Chicago 1988).

D. Dueck, *The Geography of Strabo as an Augustan Work* (Jerusalem 1996, Diss. in Hebrew). [Dueck, Strabo]

G. D. Dunn, Tertullian and Rebekah: a Re-reading of an "Anti-Jewish" Argument in Early Christian Literature, *Vigiliae Christianae* 52.2 (1998) 119–45.

S. K. Eddy, *The King is Dead. Studies in the Near Eastern Resistance to Hellenism 334–31 B.C.* (Lincoln 1961). [Eddy, King]

L. M. Epstein, *Sex Laws and Customs in Judaism* (New York 1948). [Epstein, Sex Laws]

E. H. Erikson, *Identity. Youth and Crisis* (New York 1968).

–, *Childhood and Society* (New York 1950, 2nd. rev. ed. 1963).

J. K. Evans, *War, Women, and Children in Ancient Rome* (London and New York 1991).

J. Ch. Exum, *Fragmented Women. Feminist (Sub)versions of Biblical Narratives* (Sheffield 1993 = *JSOT* Suppl. Ser. 163).

F. T. Fallon and R. Cameron, The Gospel of Thomas: a Forschungsbericht and Analysis, *ANRW* II.25.6 (1988) 4195–4251.

E. Fantham, *Stuprum*: Public Attitudes and Penalties for Sexual Offenses in Republican Rome, *Echos du Monde Classique* 35 (1991) 267–91.

G. D. Farandos, Kosmos und Logos nach Philon von Alexandria, *Elementa. Schriften zur Philosophie und ihrer Problemgeschichte* 4 (1976).

J. R. Fears, The Stoic View of the Career and Character of Alexander the Great, *Philologus* 118.1 (1974) 113–30. [Fears, Alexander the Great]

–, The Cult of Virtues and Roman Imperial Ideology, *ANRW* II.17.2 (1981) 827–948.

D. M. Feldman, Marital Relations, Birth Control, and Abortion in Jewish Law (New York 1974).

L. H. Feldman, The Orthodoxy of the Jews in Hellenistic Egypt, *JSS* 22.4 (1960) 215–37.

–, The Sources of Josephus' 'Antiquities', Book 19, *Latomus* 21.2 (1962) 320–33.

–, Hebraism and Hellenism Reconsidered, *Judaism* 43.2 (1994) 115–26.

–, *Josephus' Interpretation of the Bible* (Berkeley 1998).

R. Feldmeier, Weise hinter 'eisernen Mauern'. Tora und Jüdisches Selbstverständnis zwischen Akkulturation und Absonderung im Aristeasbrief, in: M. Hengel and A. M. Schwemer (eds.), *Die Septuaginta zwischen Judentum und Christentum* (Tübingen 1994 = *WUNT* 72) 20–37.

J.-L. Ferrary, *Philhellénisme et Impérialisme. Aspects Idéologiques de la Conquete Romaine Du Monde Hellénistique, de la Seconde Guerre de Macédoine à la Guerre contre Mithridate* (Rome 1988). [Ferrary, Philhéllenisme]

A. Ferrill, *Caligula. Emperor of Rome* (London 1991).

J. A. Fishman, Language and Ethnicity, in: H. Giles (ed.), *Language, Ethnicity and Intergroup Relations* (London 1977) 15–57.

D. Fishwick, Genius and Numen, *HTR* 62 (1969) 356–67.

D. Flusser *Die rabbinischen Gleichnisse und der Gleichniserzähler Jesus* (Bern/Frankfurt 1981 = Judaica et Christiana 4).

B. Forte, *Rome and the Romans as the Greeks saw them* (Rome 1972 = *Pap. Mon. Am. Ac. Rome* 24). [Forte, Rome]

M. Foucault, *The Use of Pleasure* (New York 1980, Fr. orig. = *The History of Sexuality* vol. 2). [Foucault, Use of Pleasure]

–, *The Care of the Self* (New York 1986 = *The History of Sexuality* vol. 3). [Foucault, Care of Self]

S. D. Fraade, *From Tradition to Commentary. Torah and Its Interpretation in the Midrash Sifre to Deuteronomy* (Albany 1991 = SUNY: Series in Judaica: Hermeneutics, Mysticism, and Religion).

P. M. Fraser, The Alexandrine View of Rome, *Bull. Soc. Arch. Alex.* 42 (1967) 1–16. [Fraser, Alexandrian View]

–, *Ptolemaic Alexandria* (Oxford 1972). [Fraser, Ptolemaic Alexandria]

J. G. Frazer, *The Worship of Nature* (London 1926).

H. Freedman, *Midrash Rabbah. Genesis* (London and Bournemouth 1951).

S. Freud, *Der Mann Moses und die monotheistische Religion* (1934–38, available also in the Engl. Standard transl. of Freud's works by J. Strachey (New York and London 1966).

J. Freudenthal, *Hellenistische Studien* (Breslau 1875 = Jahresbericht des jüdisch-theologischen Seminars "Fraenkel'scher Stiftung").

R. A. Freund, *Understanding Jewish Ethics* (San Francisco 1990).

L. Friedländer, *Darstellungen aus der Sittengeschichte Roms in der Zeit von Augustus bis zum Ausgang der Antonine* (Leipzig 1922).

P. Friedländer, *Plato* (New York 1964, Germ. orig.).

H. Fuchs, *Der Geistige Gegenstand gegen Rom* (Berlin 1938).

E. Gabba, The Historians and Augustus, in: Millar and Segal, Caesar Augustus 61–88. [Gabba, Historians]

–, *Dionysius and The History of Archaic Rome* (Berkeley 1991). [Gabba, Dionysius]

K. L. Gaca, Philo's Principles of Sexual Conduct and their Influence on Christian Platonist Sexual Principles, *SPhA* 8 (1996) 21–39. [Gaca, Sexual Conduct]

–, Paul's Uncommon Declaration in Romans 1:18–32 and Its Problematic Legacy for Pagan and Christian Relations, *HTR* 92:2 (1999) 165–98.

I. M. Gafni, *Land, Center and Diaspora. Jewish Constructs in Late Antiquity* (Sheffield 1997 = *JSP* Suppl. Ser. 21).

K. Galinsky, *Augustan Culture. An Interpretative Introduction* (Princeton 1996).

J. F. Gardner, *Women in Roman Law and Society* (London and Sydney 1986). [Gardner, Women]

R. Garland, *The Greek Way of Life. From Conception to Old Age* (New York 1990). [Garland, Way of Life]

L. C. Gaughy, A Short History of Parable Interpretation, *Forum* 8 (1992) 229–45.

C. Geertz, *The Interpretation of Cultures. Selected Essays* (New York 1973). [Geertz, Interpretation of Cultures]

J. Geiger, The Ruler Cult as an Ideology of the Roman Empire (Hebrew), in: I. Gafni and G. Motzkin (eds.), *Priesthood and Monarchy. Studies in the Historical Relationships of Religion and State* (Jerusalem 1987) 51–60.

–, Herod and Rome: New Aspects, in: I. M. Gafni *et al.* (eds.), *The Jews in the Hellenistic-Roman World. Studies in Memory of Menahem Stern* (Jerusalem 1996) 133–45.

–, Cleopatra the Physician (Hebrew), *Cathedra* 92 (1999) 193–8.

E. Gellner, *Nations and Nationalism* (Oxford 1983). [Gellner, Nation and Nationalism]

–, *Culture, Identity, and Politics* (Cambridge 1987). [Gellner, Culture, Identity, and Politics]

A. C. Van Geytenbeek, *Musonius Rufus and Greek Diatribe* (Assen 1963).[Geytenbeek, Musonius]

Y. D. Gilat, The Sabbath Laws in the Writings of Philo, in: R. Link-Salinger (ed.), *Torah and Wisdom. Studies in Jewish Philosophy, Kabbalah, and Halacha. Essays in Honor of Arthur Hyman* (New York 1992) 61–73. [Gilat, Sabbath]

Ch. Gill, The question of character-development: Plutarch and Tacitus, *CQ* 33.2 (1983) 469–87. [Gill, The question of character-development]

–, The Question of Character and Personality in Greek Tragedy, *PT* 7 (1986) 251–73. [Gill, The Question of Character]

S. L. Gilman, *Difference and Pathology. Stereotypes of Sexuality, Race, and Madness* (Ithaca and London 1985). [Gilman, Difference and Pathology]

D. D. Gilmore, *Manhood In The Making. Cultural Concepts Of Masculinity* (New Haven and London 1990).

J. Glucker, God and Gods in Stoicism (Hebrew), forthcoming in: M. Kister (ed.), title to be determined.

R. K. Gnuse, *No Other Gods. Emergent Monotheism in Israel* (Sheffield 1997 = *JSOT* Suppl.Ser. 241).

H. E. Goldberg, Torah and Children: Symbolic Aspects of the Reproduction of Jews and Judaism, in: idem (ed.), *Judaism Viewed from Within and from Without. Anthropological Studies* (New York 1987) 107–30.

M. Golden, *Children and Childhood in Classical Athens* (Baltimore and London 1990). [Golden, *Childhood in Classical Athens*]

R. Goldenberg, The Jewish Sabbath in the Roman World up to the Time of Constantine the Great, *ANRW* II. 19.1 (1979) 414–447. [Goldenberg, The Jewish Sabbath]

J. Goldstein, Jewish Acceptance and Rejection of Hellenism, in: E.P. Sanders *et al.* (eds.), *Jewish and Christian Self-Definition* (London 1981) 2:64–87. [Goldstein, Jewish Acceptance and Rejection]

E. R. Goodenough, Philo and Public Life, *JEA* 12.1–2 (1926) 77–9.

–, The Political Philosophy of Hellenistic Kingship, *Yale Classical Studies* 1 (1928) 55–102.

–, *The Politics of Philo Judaeus. Practice and Theory* (New Haven 1938). [Goodenough, Politics]

–, *An Introduction to Philo Judaeus* (Oxford 2nd ed. 1962).

–, *The Jurisprudence of the Jewish Courts in Egypt: Legal Administration by the Jews under the Early Roman Empire as Described by Philo Judaeus* (New Haven 1929). [Goodenough, Courts]

–, *By Light, Light; The Mystic Gospel of Hellenistic Judaism* (New Haven 1935). [Goodenough, Light]

D. Gooding and V. Nikiprowetzky, Philo's Bible in the *De Gigantibus* and *Quod Deus*, in: D. Winston and J. Dillon (eds.), *Two Treatises of Philo of Alexandria. A Commentary on De Gigantibus and Quod Sit Immutabilis* (Chico 1983 = Brown Judaic Studies 25) 89–125.

M. Goodman, Jewish Attitudes to Greek Culture in the Period of the Second Temple, in: G. Abramson and T. Parfitt (eds.), *Jewish Education and Learning. Published in Honour of Dr. David Patterson on the occasion of his Seventieth Birthday* (Chur 1994) 167–74. [Goodman, Jewish Attitudes]

–, Josephus as Roman Citizen, in: F. Parente and J. Sievers (eds.), *Josephus and the History of the Greco-Roman Period. Essays in Memory of Morton Smith* (Leiden 1994) 329–38.

–, *Mission and Conversion* (Oxford 1994). [Goodman, Mission]

–, The Roman Identity of Roman Jews, in: I. M. Gafni *et al.* (eds.), *The Jews in the Hellenistic-Roman World. Studies in Memory of Menahem Stern* (Jerusalem 1996) 85–99.

–, *The Roman World. 44 BC – AD 180* (London 1997). [Goodman, Roman World]

–, Jewish History and Roman History: Changing Methods and Preoccupations, in: Oppenheimer, Jüdische Geschichte 75–83.

–, The Function of Minim in Early Rabbinic Judaism, in: Cancik *et al.*, Geschichte – Tradition – Reflexion 1:501–10.

– (ed.), *Jews in a Graeco-Roman World* (Oxford 1998). [Goodman, Jews in a Graeco-Roman World]

–, The Emergence of Christianity, in: A. Hastings (ed.), *A World History of Christianity* (Michigan 1999) 7–24.

–, The Pilgrimage Economy of Jerusalem in the Second Temple Period, in: L. I. Levine (ed.), *Jerusalem – Its Sanctity and Centrality to Judaism, Christianity, and Islam* (New York 1999) 69–76.

K. Goudriaan, Ethnical Strategies in Graeco-Roman Egypt, in: Bilde, Ethnicity in Hellenistic Egypt 74–99. [Goudriaan, Ethnical Strategies]

P. Goukowsky, *Essai Sur Les Origines Du Mythe D'Alexandre (336–270 av. J.-C.)* (Nancy 1978).

G. Graesholt, Philo of Alexandria. Some Typical Traits of his Jewish Identity, *Classica et Mediaevalia* 43 (1992) 97–110.

A. J. Graham, *Colony and Mother City in Ancient Greece* (Chicago 1983, 2nd revised ed).

P. Green, Caesar and Alexander: Aemulatio, Imitatio, Comparatio, *Am. Jour. of Anc. Hist.* 3.1 (1978) 1–26.

–, *Alexander to Actium. The Historical Evolution of the Hellenistic Age* (Berkeley 1990).

F. E. Greenspahn *et al.* (eds.), *Nourished with Peace. Studies in Hellenistic Judaism in Memory of Samuel Sandmel* (Chico 1984). [Greenspahn et al., Nourished with Peace]

M. T. Griffin, *Seneca. A Philosopher in Politics* (Oxford 1976).

M. J. Gruber, The Hebrew qedeshah and Her Canaanite and Akkadian Cognates, in: idem, *The Motherhood of God And Other Studies* (Atlanta 1992) 17–47.

E. S. Gruen, *The Hellenistic World and the Coming of Rome* (Berkeley 1984). [Gruen, Hellenistic World]

–, The Imperial Policy of Augustus, in: K. A. Raaflaub and M. Toher (eds.), *Between Republic and Empire. Interpretations of Augustus and His Principate* (Berkeley 1990) 395–416.

–, *Culture and National Identity in Republican Rome* (New York 1992). [Gruen, Culture and National Identity]

–, The expansion of the empire under Augustus, *CAH* X (1996, 2nd ed.) 147–97.

–, Fact and Fiction: Jewish Legends in a Hellenistic Context, in: P. Cartledge *et al.* (eds.), *Hellenistic Constructs. Essays in Culture, History, and Historiography* (Berkeley 1997) 72–88.

–, The Origins and Objectives of Onias' Temple, *SCI* 16 (1997 = Studies in Memory of Abraham Wasserstein) 47–70.

–, *Heritage and Hellenism. The Reinvention of Jewish Tradition* (Berkeley 1998). [Gruen, Heritage]

–, Jews, Greeks, and Romans in the Third Sibylline Oracle, in: Goodman, Jews in a Graeco-Roman World 15–36. [Gruen, Third Sibylline Oracle]

–, Rome and the Myth of Alexander, in: T. W. Hillard et al. (eds.), *Ancient History in a Modern University* (Grand Rapids, Michigan and Cambridge 1998)1:178–91. [Gruen, Alexander]

–, *Diaspora as Construct and Reality. Jewish Experience in the Second Temple* (tentative title), forthcoming.

–, Jewish Constructs of Greeks and Hellenism, in: Gruen, Diaspora as Construct and Reality. [Gruen, Jewish Constructs of Greeks and Hellenism]

–, The Jews in Alexandria, unpublished paper forthcoming in: Gruen, Diaspora as Construct and Reality.

A. J. Guerra, The One God Topos in Spec. Leg. 1:52, SBLSP 29 (1990) 148–57.

V. Guignard, Le Rapport De Philon D'Alexandrie A La Philosophie Grecque Dans Le Portrait Des Empereurs, in: C. Levy (ed.), *Philon d'Alexandrie et le langage de la philosophie* (Brepols 1998) 459–69.

R. Gurval, *Actium and Augustus. The Politics and Emotions of Civil War* (Ann Arbor 1995). [Gurval, Actium and Augustus]

D. Guthrie, *New Testament Introduction* (Leicester 1970, 3rd. ed.).

W. K. C. Guthrie, *A History of Greek Philosophy* (Cambridge 1962).

Y. Gutman, *The Beginnings of Jewish-Hellenistic Literature* (Hebrew) (Jerusalem 1963) 2:109–35. [Gutman, Beginnings]

A. Gwynn, The Character of Greek Colonisation, *JHS* 38 (1918) 88–123.

G. Haaland, Jewish Laws for a Roman Audience: Toward an Understanding of Contra Apionem in: J. U. Kalms and F. Siegert (eds.), *Internationales Josephus-Kolloquium Brüssel 1998* (Münster 1999 = MJSt 4) 282–304. [Haaland, Jewish Laws for a Roman Audience]

Ch. Habicht, Die augusteische Zeit und das erste Jahrhundert nach Christi Geburt, in:

*Le Culte des Souverains dans l'Empire Romain* (Geneva 1972 = Entretiens sur l'Antiquité Classique 19) 41–88. [Habicht, Die augusteische Zeit]

Th. N. Habinek, *The Politics of Latin Literature. Writing, Identity, and Empire in Ancient Rome* (Princeton 1998). [Habinek, The Politics of Latin Literature]

M. Hadas, *Aristeas to Philocrates (Letter of Aristeas)* (New York 1951).

–, *Hellenistic Culture. Fusion and Diffusion* (New York and London 1959). [Hadas, Hellenistic Culture]

M. Hadas-Lebel, L'évolution de l'image de Rome auprès des Juifs en deux siècles de relations judéo-romaines – 164 à + 70, *ANRW* II.20.2 (1987) 784–812.

H. Hänlein-Schäfer, *Veneratio Augusti. Eine Studie zu den Tempeln des ersten römischen Kaisers* (Roma 1985 = Archaelogica 39). [Hänlein-Schäfer, Veneratio Augusti]

M. Halbertal, *Interpretative Revolutions in the Making. Values as Interpretative Considerations in Midrashei Halakhah* (Hebrew) (Jerusalem 1997).

E. Hall, *Inventing the Barbarian. Greek Self-Definition through Tragedy* (Oxford 1989). [Hall, Barbarian]

J. M. Hall, *Ethnic Identity in Greek Antiquity* (Cambridge 1997).

S. Hall, Cultural Identity and Diaspora, in: J. Rutherford (ed.), Identity. Community, Culture, Difference (London 1990) 222–37.

–, Ethnicity: Identity and Difference, in: G. Eley and R. G. Suny (eds.), *Becoming National. A Reader* (New York 1996) 339–351. [Hall, Ethnicity]

B. Halpern Amaru, Land Theology in Philo and Josephus, in: L. A. Hoffman (ed.), *The Land of Israel: Jewish Perspectives* (Notre Dame 1986 = Studies in Judaism and Christianity in Antiquity 6) 65–93.

R. J. Hankinson, Philosophy of Science, in: J. Barnes (ed.), *The Cambridge Companion to Aristotle* (Cambridge 1995) 109–39.

A. E. Hanson, The Medical Writers' Woman, in: D. M. Halperin *et al.* (eds.), *Before Sexuality. The Construction Of Erotic Experience in the Ancient Greek World* (Princeton 1990) 309–38.

P. R. Hardie, *Virgil's Aeneid. Cosmos and Imperium* (Oxford 1986).

H. A. Harris, *Greek Athletics and the Jews* (Cardiff 1976). [Harris, Greek Athletics]

W. V. Harris, Child-Exposure in the Roman Empire, *JRS* 84 (1994) 1–22.

F. Hartog, *The Mirror of Herodotus. The Representation of the Other in the Writing of History* (Berkeley 1988, Fr. orig. 1980 = The New Historicism. Studies in Cultural Poetics 5). [Hartog, Mirror]

G. Harvey, The True Israel. Uses of the Names Jew, Hebrew, and Israel in Ancient Jewish and Early Christian Literature (Leiden 1996 = Arbeiten zur Geschichte des Antiken Judentums und des Urchristentums 35). [Harvey, True Israel]

G. Hasan-Rokem, Narratives in Dialogue: A Folk Literary Perspective on Interreligious Contacts in the Holy Land in the Rabbinic Literature of Late Antiquity, in: A. Kofsky and G. G. Stroumsa (eds.), *Sharing The Sacred. Religious Contacts and Conflicts in the Holy Land First -Fifteenth Centuries CE* (Jerusalem 1998) 109–29.

A. Hastings, *The Construction of Nationhood. Ethnicity, Religion and Nationalism* (Cambridge 1997). [Hastings, Construction of Nationhood]

P. Hayman, Monotheism – A Misused Word in Jewish Studies?, *JJS* 42 (1991) 1–15.

R. D. Hecht, The Exegetical Context of Philo's Interpretation of Circumcision in: Greenspahn *et al.*, Nourished with Peace 51–79.

W. A. Heidel, The Pythagoreans and Greek Mathematics, *AJP* 61.1 (1940) 1–33.

I. Heinemann, Ursprung und Wesen des Antisemitismus im Altertum, in: *Festgabe zum zehnjährigen Bestehen der Akademie für die Wissenschaft des Judentums 1919–1929* (Berlin 1929) 76–91.

–, *Philons griechische und jüdische Bildung* (Breslau 1932). [Heinemann, Bildung]

–, Über die Einzelgesetze Buch I–IV, in: L. Cohn (ed.), *Die Werke Philos von Alexandria in deutscher Übersetzung* (Breslau 1910).

W. E. Helleman, Philo of Alexandria on Deification and Assimilation to God, *SPhA* 2 (1990 = Brown Judaic Studies 226) 51–71. [Helleman, Deification]

M. Hengel, Anonymität, Pseudepigrahie und Literarische Fälschung in der Jüdisch-Hellenistischen Literatur, *Entretiens sur l'Antiquité Classique XVIII,* Pseudepigrapha (1972) 1:229–39.

–, *Judaism and Hellenism. Studies in their Encounter in Palestine during the Early Hellenistic Period* (London 1974, Germ. orig.). [Hengel, Judaism and Hellenism]

–, Die Begegnung zwischen Judentum und Hellenismus im Palästina der vorchristlichen Zeit, in: idem, *Judaica et Hellenistica. Kleine Schriften I* (Tübingen 1996) 151–70.

A. Heuss, Alexander der Grosse und die politische Ideologie des Altertums, *Antike und Abendland* 4 (1954) 65–104. [Heuss, Alexander der Grosse]

E. Hilgert, Philo Judaeus et Alexandrinus: The State of the Problem, in: Kenney, School of Moses 1–15. [Hilgert, Philo Judaeus et Alexandrinus]

H. Hill, Dionysius of Halicarnassus and the Origins of Rome, *JRS* 51 (1961) 88–93.

M. Himmelfarb, Judaism and Hellenism in 2 Maccabees, *PT* 19.1 (1998) 19–40.

M. Hirshman, *A Rivalry of Genius. Jewish and Christian Biblical Interpretation in Late Antiquity* (New York 1996, Hebr. orig. = SUNY Series in Judaica: Hermeneutics, Mysticism, and Religion).

G. Hölscher, *Die Quellen des Josephus für die Zeit vom Exil bis zum Jüdischen Kriege* (Leipzig 1904).

W. Hoffmann, *Das literarische Porträt Alexanders des Grossen im griechischen und römischen Altertum* (Leipzig 1907).

L. Hogan, *Healing In The Second Temple Period*, PhD Thesis at the Hebrew University of Jerusalem 1986.

C. H. Holladay, *Theios Aner in Hellenistic-Judaism: A Critique of the Use of this Category in New Testament Christology* (Missoula 1977 = SBL Diss. Ser. 40). [Holladay, Theios Aner]

–, Fragments from Hellenistic Jewish Authors (Chico 1983 = *SBL* Texts and Translations 20) [Holladay, Fragments]

–, Jewish Responses to Hellenistic Culture, in: Bilde, Ethnicity in Egypt 139–63.

H. W. Hollander, *Joseph as an Ethical Model in the Testaments of the Twelve Patriarchs* (Leiden 1981).

M. Hombert et C. Préaux, *Recherches sur le Recensement dans l'Egypte Romaine* (Leiden 1952).

S. Honigman, The Birth of a Diaspora: The Emergence of a Jewish Self-Definition in Ptolemaic Egypt in the Light of Onomastics, in: S. J. D. Cohen and E. S. Frerichs (eds.), *Diasporas in Antiquity* (Atlanta 1993 = Brown Judaic Studies 288) 93–127.

W. Horbury and D. Noy, *Jewish Inscriptions of Graeco-Roman Egypt* (Cambridge 1992).

R. A. Horsley, The Law of Nature in Philo and Cicero, *HTR* 71.1–2 (1978) 35–59.

P. W. van der Horst, "Thou shalt not Revile the Gods": the LXX Translation of Ex. 22:28 (27), its Background and Influence, *SPhA* 5 (1993) 1–8.

C. A. Huffman, *Philolaus of Croton: Pythagorean and Presocratic* (Cambridge 1993). [Huffman, Philolaus]

L. W. Hurtado, *One God. One Lord. Early Christian Devotion and Ancient Jewish Monotheism* (London 1988).

M. Idel, *Language, Torah, and Hermeneutics in Abraham Abulafia* (New York 1989).

–, *Golem. Jewish Magical and Mystical Traditions on the Articifial Anthropoid* (Albany 1990 = SUNY Series in Judaica: Hermeneutics, Mysticism, and Religion).

T. Ilan, The Greek Names of the Hasmoneans, *JQR* 78.1–2 (1987) 1–20.

–, Notes on the Distribution of Jewish Women's Names in Palestine in the Second Temple and Mishnaic Periods, *JJS* 40.1 (1989) 186–200.

–, *Jewish Women in Greco-Roman Palestine. An Inquiry into Image and Status* (Tübingen 1995 = Texte und Studien zum antiken Judentum 44).

W. Jaeger, *Paideia. The Ideals of Greek Culture* (New York 1944, Germ. orig.) 3.3–45.

N. Janowitz, Rabbis and their Opponents: The Construction of the "Min" in Rabbinic Anecdotes, *Journal for Early Christian Studies* 6.3 (1998) 449–62. [Janowitz, Rabbis and their Opponents]

A. Jaubert, Le Calendrier des Jubilés et de la Secte de Qumran: Ses origines bibliques, *VT* 3 (1953) 250–64.

–, *La date de la cene: calendrier biblique et liturgie chretienne* (Paris 1957).

A. Jellinek, (ed.), Beit HaMidrasch (Jerusalem 1938, 2nd ed.) vol. 6.

J. Jeremias, *The Parables of Jesus* (Engl. tr. London 1972, 3rd rev. ed.).

A. H. M. Jones, review of E. R. Goodenough, The Politics of Philo Judaeus. Practice and Theory (New Haven 1938), *JThS* 40 (1939) 182–5.

–, *The Greek City. From Alexander to Justinian* (Oxford 1940).

C. P. Jones, *Plutarch and Rome* (Oxford 1971). [Jones, Plutarch]

M. Jones, The Ideas of God as Thoughts of God, *CP* 21 (1926) 317–26.

A. Jülicher, *Die Gleichnisreden Jesu* (Tübingen 1910) vol. 1.

J. Juster, *Les Juifs dans L'Empire Romain. Leur Condition Juridique, Economique et Sociale* (Paris 1914) vol. 1.

J.-G. Kahn, Did Philo know Hebrew? The Testimony of the "Etimologies" (Hebrew), *Tarbiz* 34.4 (1965) 337–45.

–, La Valeur et la Légimité des Activités politiques d'après Philon d'Alexandrie, *Méditerranées* 16 (1998) 117–27.

R. P. C. Kannengiesser, Philon et les Pères sur la double Création de l'homme, in: *Philon d'Alexandrie. Lyon 11–15 Septembre 1966, Colloques Nationaux du Centre National de la Recherche Scientifique* (Paris 1967) 277–96.

A. Kasher, Jerusalem as a 'Metropolis' in Philo's National Consciousness (Hebrew), *Cathedra* 11 (1979) 45–56.

–, *The Jews in Hellenistic and Roman Egypt. The Struggle for Equal Rights* (Tübingen 1985). [Kasher, Jews in Egypt]

R. S. Katz, The Illness of Caligula, *CW* 65 (1972) 223–5.

J. P. Kenney, (ed.), *The School of Moses. Studies in Philo and Hellenistic Religion. In Memory of Horst R. Moehring* (Atlanta 1995 = Brown Judaic Studies 304 = Studia Philonica Monographs 1). [Kenney, School of Moses]

D. Kienast, *Cato der Zensor* (Heidelberg 1954).

–, Augustus und Alexander, *Gymnasium* 76 (1969) 430–56. [Kienast, Augustus und Alexander]

K. King, The Kingdom in the Gospel of Thomas, *Forum* 3 (1987) 48–97.

M. Kister, Studies in 4QMiqsat Ma'ase Ha-Torah and Related Texts: Law, Theology, Language and Calender (Hebrew), *Tarbiz* 68.3 (1999) 317–71.

H. - J. Klauck, Die heilige Stadt. Jerusalem bei Philo und Lukas, *Kairos* 28.3–4 (1986) 129–51.

F. N. Klein, Die Lichtterminologie bei Philon von Alexandrien und in den hermetischen Schriften. Untersuchungen zur Struktur der religiösen Sprache der hellenistischen Mystik (Leiden 1962).

Y. Knohl, The Sabbath and the Festivals in the Priestly Code and in the Laws of the Holiness School (Hebrew), *Shnaton. An Annual for Biblical and Ancient Near Eastern Studies* 7–8 (1983–4) 109–46. [Knohl, The Sabbath and the Feasts]

–, On 'The son of God', Armillus and Messiah Son of Joseph (Hebrew), *Tarbiz* 68.1 (1998) 13–37.

H. Koester, ΝΟΜΟΣ ΦΥΣΕΩΣ: The Concept of Natural Law in Greek Thought, in: J. Neusner (ed.), *Religions in Antiquity. Essays in Memory of Erwin Ramsdell Goodenough* (Leiden 1968 = *Numen* Suppl. Ser. 14 = *Studies in the History of Religions*). [Koester, The Concept of Natural Law]

– and S. J. Patterson, The Gospel of Thomas – Does It Contain Authentic Sayings of Jesus?, *Bible Review* 6.2 (1990) 28–39.

E. Kornemann, Zur Geschichte der antiken Herrscherkulte, *Klio* 1 (1901) 51–146. [Kornemann, Herrscherkulte]

A. T. Kraabel, The Roman Diaspora: Six Questionable Assumptions, *JJS* 33.1–2 (1982) 445–64. [Kraabel, Roman Diaspora]

D. Kraemer, Images of Childhood and Adolescence in Talmudic Literature, in: idem (ed.), *The Jewish Family. Metaphor and Memory* (New York and Oxford 1989) 65–80.

R. S. Kraemer, Monastic Jewish Women in Greco-Roman Egypt: Philo Judaeus on the Therapeutrides, *Signs: Journal of Women in Culture and Society* 14.2 (1989) 342–70. [Kraemer, Monastic Jewish Women]

–, On the Meaning of the Term "Jew" in Greco-Roman Inscriptions, *HTR* 82.1 (1989) 35–53.

–, Women's Authorship of Jewish and Christian Literature in the Greco-Roman Period, in: Levine, "Women Like This" 221–42.

–, *Her Share of the Blessings. Women's Religions among Pagans, Jews, and Christians in the Greco-Roman World* (New York 1992).

–, *When Aseneth Met Joseph. A Late Antique Tale of the Biblical Patriarch and His Egyptian Wife, Reconsidered* (New York 1998) 245–93.

R. A. Kraft, Philo and the Sabbath Crisis: Alexandrian Jewish Politics and the dating of Philo's Works, in: B. A. Pearson *et al.* (eds.), *The Future of Early Christianity. Essays in Honor of Helmut Koester* (Minneapolis 1991) 131–41.

N. Kretzmann, Plato on the Correctness of Names, *Am. Philos. Quart.* 8 (1971) 126–38.

J. Laporte, Philo in the Tradition of Biblical Wisdom Literature, in: R. Wilken (ed.), *Aspects of Wisdom in Judaism and Early Christianity* (Notre Dame 1975).

–, The Ages of Life in Philo of Alexandria, *SBLSP* 25 (1986) 278–90. [Laporte, Ages of Life]

F. Lasserre, Strabon devant l'Empire romain, *ANRW* II. 30.1 (1982) 867–96.

H. Leisegang, Philons Schrift über die Gesandtschaft der Alexandrinischen Juden an den Kaiser Gaius Caligula, *JBL* 57 (1938) 377–405. [Leisegang, Legatio]

J. D. Levenson, *The Death and Resurrection of the Beloved Son. The Transformation of*

*Child Sacrifice in Judaism and Christianity* (New Haven 1993). [Levenson, Beloved Son]

B. M. Levick, *Tiberius The Politician* (London 1976).

A.-J. Levine (ed.), "Women Like This". New Perspectives on Jewish Women in the Greco-Roman World (Atlanta 1991 = Society of Biblical Literature. Early Judaism and its Literature 1). [Levine, "Women Like This"]

B. M. Levinson, *Deuteronomy and the Hermeneutics of Legal Innovation* (New York and Oxford 1997). [Levinson, Deuteronomy]

J. Levinson, Fatal Fictions (Hebrew), *Tarbiz* 68.1 (1998) 61–86.

N. Lewis, "Greco-Roman Egypt": Fact or Fiction?, *Proc. XII. Intern. Congr. Pap.* (Toronto 1970 = ASP 7) 3–14. [Lewis, "Greco-Roman Egypt"]

–, On Paternal Authority in Roman Egypt, *RIDA* 17 (1970) 251–58.

–, The Romanity of Roman Egypt: a Growing Consensus, Atti XVII Congr. Intern. Pap. (Naples 1984) 1077–84.

H. Lichtenberger, Lesen und Lernen im Judentum, in: A. T. Khoury and L. Muth (eds.), *Glauben Durch Lesen? Für Eine Christliche Lesekultur* (Freiburg 1990) 23–38.

Y. Liebes, Golem Reconsidered (Hebrew), *Kiryat Sefer* 63.4 (1990–1) 1305–22.

–, The Seven Double Letters *BGD KFRT*, On the Double *REISH* and the Background of Sefer Yezira (Hebrew), *Tarbiz* 61.2 (1992) 237–47.

H. Lindsay, *Suetonius. Caligula. Edited with Introduction and Commentary* (London 1993).

S. E. Loewenstamm, *The Evolution of the Exodus Tradition* (Jerusalem 1992, Heb. orig.).

A. A. Long and D. N. Sedley, *The Hellenistic Philosophers* (Cambridge 1987).

T. J. Luce, The Dating of Livy's First Decade, *TAPA* 96 (1965) 209–40.

D. Lührmann, The Godlessness of Germans Living by the Sea according to Philo of Alexandria, in: B. A. Pearson (ed.), *The Future of Early Christianity. Essays in Honor of Helmut Koester* (Minneapolis 1991) 57–63.

C. E. Lutz, Musonius Rufus "The Roman Socrates", *Yale Classical Studies* 10 (1947) 3–147. [Lutz, fragms.]

R. Mac Mullen, Nationalism in Roman Egypt, *Aegyptus* 44.3–4 (1964) 179–99.

M. Malaise, *Les Conditions de Pénétration et de Diffusion des Cultes Égyptiens en Italie* (Leiden 1972).

I. Malkin, *Religion and Colonization in Ancient Greece* (Leiden 1987 = SGRR 3).

F. Manns, Le symbole eau-Esprit dans le Judaisme ancien, *Studium Biblicum Franscis-canum Analecta* 19 (1983).

M. Manson, La 'Pietas' et le Sentiment de l'enfance à Rome d'après les monnaies, *Revue Belge de Numismatique et de Sigillographie* 121 (1975) 21–80.

–, *Puer bimulus* (Catulle, 17, 12–13) et l'image du petit enfant chez Catulle et ses prédécesseurs, *Mélanges de l'Ecole Française de Rome* 90.1 (1978) 247–91.

–, The Emergence of the Small Child in Rome (Third Century BC-First Century AD), *History of Education* 12.3 (1983) 149–59. [Manson, Small Child]

H. D. Mantel, Did Philo Know Hebrew? (Hebrew), *Tarbiz* 32.1 (1962) 98–9.

–, "Did Philo know Hebrew" – Additional Note (Hebrew), *Tarbiz* 32.4 (1963) 395.

J. Marböck, *Weisheit im Wandel. Untersuchungen zur Weisheitstheologie bei Ben Sira* (Bonn 1971, repr. 1999 in *BZAW* Bd. 272) 63–68.

I. G. Marcus, *Rituals of Childhood. Jewish Acculturation in Medieval Europe* (New Haven 1996).

R. Marcus, A Textual-Exegetical Note on Philo's Bible, *JBL* 69 (1950) 363–5.

A. Marmorstein, *The Old Rabbinic Doctrine of God* (London 1937 = Jews' College Publications 14).

H.I. Marrou, *A History of Education in Antiquity* (London 1956, Fr. orig.). [Marrou, Education].

F.B. Marsh, *The Reign of Tiberius* (Oxford 1931).

L. Massebieau and E. Bréhier, Essai sur la chronologie de la vie et des oeuvres de Philon, *RHR* 53 (1906) 25–64, 164–85, 267–89. [Massebieau, Chronologie]

S.L. Mattila, Wisdom, Sense Perception, Nature, and Philo's Gender Gradient, *HTR* 89.2 (1996) 103–29.

L. deMause, The Evolution of Childhood, in: idem (ed.), *The History of Childhood* (New York 1974) 1–73. [DeMause, Childhood]

M.H. McCall, *Ancient Rhetorical Theories of Simile and Comparison* (Cambridge MA 1969).

J.G. McConville, Deuteronomy's Unification of Passover and Massot. A Response to Bernard M. Levinson, *JBL* 119.1 (2000) 47–58.

D. McCrone, *The Sociology of Nationalism. Tomorrow's ancestors* (London and New York 1998).

B. McGinn, Platonic and Christian: The Case of the Divine Ideas, in: R. Link-Salinger (ed.), *Of Scholars, Savants, and their Texts: Studies in Philosophy and Religious Thought. Essays in Honor of Arthur Hyman* (New York 1989) 163–72.

–, *The Foundations of Mysticism* (New York 1992).

W.A. Meeks, Moses as God and King, in: J. Neusner (ed.), *Religions in Antiquity. Essays in Memory of Erwin Ramsdell Goodenough* (Leiden 1968 = Suppl. to Numen 14) 354–71.

–, The Divine Agent and His Counterfeit in Philo and the Fourth Gospel, in: E. Schüssler Fiorenza (ed.), *Aspects of Religious Propaganda in Judaism and Early Christianity* (Notre Dame 1976) 43–67.

J. [Mélèze-] Modrzejewski, La Règale de droit dans l'Egypte romaine, *Proc. XII Intern. Congr. Pap.* (Toronto 1970 = Brown Judaic Studies 288) 317–77.

–, How to Be a Greek and Yet a Jew in Hellenistic Alexandria, in: S.J.D. Cohen and E.S. Frerichs (eds.), *Diasporas in Antiquity* (Atlanta 1993 = Brown Judaic Studies 288) 65–92. [Mélèze-Modrzejewski, How to Be a Jew]

–, *The Jews of Egypt. From Ramses II to Emperor Hadrian* (Philadelphia 1995, Fr. orig.).

R. Mellor, The Goddess Roma, *ANRW* II, 17:2 (1981) 950–1030.

A. Mendelson, *Secular Education in Philo of Alexandria* (Cincinnati 1982 = Monographs of the Hebrew Union College 7). [Mendelson, Secular Education]

–, *Philo's Jewish Identity* (Atlanta 1988 = Brown Judaic Studies 161). [Mendelson, Identity]

R. Merkelbach, *Die Quellen des Griechischen Alexanderromans* (München 1954 = Zetemata 9). [Merkelbach, Alexanderroman]

A.C. Merriam, The Caesareum and the Worship of Augustus at Alexandria, *TAPA* 14 (1883) 5–35.

E.T. Merrill, The Expulsion of Jews from Rome under Tiberius, *CP* 14.4 (1919) 365–72.

T.N.D. Mettinger, *No Graven Image? Israelite Aniconism in Its Ancient Near Eastern Context* (Stockholm 1995 = Coniectanea Biblica Old Testament Series 2).

J. Milgrom, *Leviticus. The Anchor Bible* (New York 1991).

F. Millar, The Background to the Maccabean Revolution: Reflections on Martin Hengel's Judaism and Hellenism, *JJS* 29.1 (1978) 1–21.

–, Empire and City, Augustus to Julian: Obligations, Excuses and Status, *JRS* 73 (1983) 76–96.

– and E. Segal (eds.), *Caesar Augustus. Seven Aspects* (Oxford 1984). [Millar and Segal, Caesar Augustus]

J.G. Milne, Greek and Roman Tourists in Ancient Egypt, JEA 3 (1916) 76–80.

A. Momigliano, review of E.R. Goodenough, The Politics of Philo Judaeus. Practice and Theory (New Haven 1938) *JRS* 34 (1944) 163–5.

–, *Claudius. The Emperor and his Achievement* (Cambridge 1961; Engl. transl. of Ital. orig.).

–, Flavius Josephus and Alexander's Visit to Jerusalem, *Athenaeum* 57.3–4 (1979) 442–8.

–, Some Preliminary Remarks on the "Religious Opposition" to the Roman Empire, in: A. Giovannini (ed.), *Opposition et Résistances à l'Empire d'Auguste à Trajan* (Genève 1987 = *Fondation Hardt* 33) 103–129.

Th. Mommsen, Cornelius Tacitus und Cluvius Rufus, *Hermes* 4 (1870) 295–325.

C. Mondésert, Philo of Alexandria, in: W. Horbury *et al.* (eds.), *The Cambridge History of Judaism* (Cambridge 1999) 3:877–900.

D. Montserrat, *Sex and Society in Graeco-Roman Egypt* (London and New York 1996 = Cornell Studies in Classical Philology 52).

M.G. Morgan, Caligula's Illness again, *CW* 66 (1973) 327–9.

–, Once Again Caligula's Illness, *CW* 70 (1977) 452–3.

J. Morris, The Jewish Philosopher Philo, in: E. Schürer, *The History of the Jewish People in the Age of Jesus Christ (175 B.C.–A.D.135) new engl. version rev. and ed. by G. Vermes, F. Millar and M. Goodman* (Edinburgh 1987) 3.2:809–89.

J.S. Morrison, Pythagoras of Samos, *CQ* N.S. 6.3–4 (1956) 135–56.

R. Mortley, *From Word to Silence. The rise and fall of logos* (Bonn 1986).

C. Müller, (ed.), *Reliqua Arriani et Scriptorum de Rebus Alexandri M. Fragmenta (collegit); Pseudo-Callisthenis Historiam Fabulosam* (Paris 1877).

G. Mussies, *Dio Chrysostom and the New Testament* (Leiden 1972 = Studia ad Corpus Hellenisticum Novi Testamenti 2).

A. Myre, La loi de la nature et la loi mosaique selon Philon d'Alexandrie, *ScEs* 28.2 (1976) 163–81.

H. Najman, The Law of Nature and the Authority of Mosaic Law, *SPhA* 11 (1999) 55–73. [Najman, The Law Of Nature]

C.A. Nelson, *Status Declarations in Roman Egypt, ASP* 19 (Amsterdam 1979).

J. Neusner, *Confronting Creation. How Judaism Reads Genesis. An Anthology of Genesis Rabbah* (Columbia 1991).

C. Nicolet, *Space, Geography, and Politics in the Early Roman Empire* (Ann Arbor 1991 = *Jerome Lectures* 19 ). [Nicolet, Space]

M.R. Niehoff, Philo's Views on Paganism, in: G.N. Stanton and G.G. Stroumsa, *Tolerance and Intolerance in Early Judaism and Christianity* (Cambridge 1988)135–58. [Niehoff, Philo's Views on Paganism]

–, A Dream which is not Interpreted is like a Letter which is not Read, *JJS* 43.1 (1992) 58–84.

–, *The Figure of Joseph in Post-Biblical Jewish Literature* (Leiden 1992 = Arbeiten zur Geschichte des antiken Judentums und des Urchristentums 16). [Niehoff, Joseph]

–, Associative Thinking in the Midrash Exemplified by the Rabbinic Interpretation of the Journey of Abraham and Sarah to Egypt (Hebrew), *Tarbiz* 62.3 (1993) 339–59.

–, The Return of Myth in Genesis Rabbah on the Akeda, *JJS* 46. 1–2 (1995) 69–87.

–, What is in a Name? Philo's Mystical Philosophy of Language, *JSQ* 2.3 (1995) 220–52.

–, Two Examples Of Josephus' Narrative Technique in His "Rewritten Bible", *JSJ* 27.1 (1996) 31–45.

–, Philo's Views on Paganism, in: G. N. Stanton and G. G. Stroumsa (eds.), *Tolerance and Intolerance in Early Judaism and Christianity* (Cambridge 1998) 135–58.

–, Alexandrian Judaism in 19th Century *Wissenschaft des Judentums*: Between Christianity and Modernization, in: Oppenheimer, Jüdische Geschichte 9–28. [Niehoff, Alexandrian Judaism]

I. Nielsen and H. S. Nielsen (eds.), *Meals in a Social Context: Aspects of the Communal Meal in the Hellenistic and Roman World* (Aarhus 1998).

V. Nikiprowetzky, La Spiritualisation des Sacrifices et le Culte Sacrificiel au Temple de Jérusalem chez Philon d'Alexandrie, *Semitica* 17 (1967) 97–116.

–, Thèmes et traditions de la lumière chez Philon d'Alexandrie, *SPhA* 1 (1989) 6–33.

A. D. Nock, Religious Developments from the Close of the Republic to the Death of Nero, *CAH* 10 (1934) 465–511. [Nock, Religious Developments]

S. J. Noorda, Illness and Sin, Forgiving and Healing. The Connection of Medical Treatment and Religious Beliefs in Ben Sira 38, 1–15, in: M. J. Vermaseren (ed.), *Studies in Hellenistic Religions* (Leiden 1979) 215–24.

V. Nutton, The Beneficial Ideology, in: P. D. A. Garnsey and C. R. Whittaker (eds.), *Imperialism in the Ancient World* (Cambridge 1978) 209–221.

S. M. Olyan, Ben Sira's Relationship to the Priesthood, *HTR* 80.3 (1987) 261–86.

A. Oppenheimer (ed.), *Jüdische Geschichte in hellenistisch-römischer Zeit. Wege der Forschung: Vom alten zum neuen Schürer* (München 1999 = Schriften des Historischen Kollegs. Kolloquien 44). [Oppenheimer, Jüdische Geschichte]

U. Ortmann, Cicero und Alexander, in: W. Will (ed.), *Zu Alexander d. Gr. Festschrift G. Wirth zum 60. Geburtstag* (Amsterdam 1988) 2.801–63.

P. A. K. Otte, *Das Sprachverständnis bei Philo von Alexandrien* (Tübingen 1967).

I. Pardes, Imagining the Promised Land: The Spies in the Land of the Giants, *History and Memory* 6.2 (1994) 5–23.

S. Pearce, Belonging and Not Belonging: Local Perspectives in Philo of Alexandria, in: S. Jones and S. Pearce, *Jewish Local Patriotism and Self-Identification in the Graeco-Roman Period* (Sheffield 1998= *JSPS* Suppl. Ser. 31) 79–105. [Pearce, Belonging]

L. Pearson, *The Lost Histories of Alexander the Great* (Chico 1983 = reprint of 1960 ed. in Am. Phil. Assoc. Monogr. Ser. 20). [Pearson, Lost Histories]

Ch. Pelling, Childhood and Personality in Greek Biography, in: idem (ed.), *Characterization and Individuality in Greek Literature* (Oxford 1990) 213–44. [Pelling, Childhood and Personality]

–, The triumviral Period, *CAH* (Cambridge 1996, 2nd ed.) 10:54–67.

L. G. Perdue, *Wisdom and Cult. A Critical Analysis of the Views of Cult in the Wisdom Literature of Israel and the Ancient Near East* (Missoula 1977).

M. Petit, Exploitations non bibliques des Thèmes de Tamar et de Genèse 38. Philon d'Alexandrie; textes et traditions juives jusqu'aux Talmudim, in: *ΑΛΕΞΑΝΔΡΙΝΑ. (Hellénisme, judaisme et christianisme à Alexandrie) Mélanges offerts à P. Claude Mondésert S. J.* (Paris 1987) 77–115.

N. Petrochilos, *Roman Attitudes to the Greeks* (Athens 1972).

R. H. Pfeiffer, Canon of the Old Testament, in: G.A. Buttrick *et al.* (eds.), *The Interpreter's Dictionary Of The Bible. An Illustrated Encyclopedia* (Nashville 1962) 1:498–520.

V. Pirenne-Delforge, Apion, in: Der Neue Pauly (1996) 1:845–7.

J. Plescia, *Patria Potestas* and the Roman Revolution, in: S. Bertman (ed.), *The Conflict of Generations in Ancient Greece and Rome* (Amsterdam 1976) 143–69.

A. J. Podlecki, *The Persians by Aeschylus* (Englewood Cliffs 1970).

M. Pohlenz, Die Begründung der abendländischen Sprachlehre durch die Stoa, *Nachrichten von der Gesellschaft der Wissenschaften zu Göttingen*, philologisch-historische Klasse 1 N. F. 3.6 (1939) 151–98. [Pohlenz, Sprachlehre]

J. Pollini, Man or God: Divine Assimilation and Imitation in the Late Republic and Early Principate, in: K. A. Raaflaub and M. Toher (eds.), *Between Republic and Empire. Interpretations of Augustus and His Principate* (Berkeley 1990) 334–363.

S. B. Pomeroy, *Goddesses, Whores, Wives, and Slaves. Women in Classical Antiquity* (New York 1975).

–, *Women in Hellenistic Egypt. From Alexander to Cleopatra* (New York 1984).

R. Poole, *Nation and Identity* (London and New York 1999). [Poole, Nation and Identity]

B. Porten, *Archives from Elephantine* (Berkeley 1968).

– and H. Z. Szubin, The Status of the Handmaiden Tamet: A New Interpretation of Krealing 2 (TAD B3.3), *Israel Law Review* 29.1–2 (1995) 43–64.

C. Préaux, La singularité de l'Égypte dans le monde gréco-romain, *Chronique d'Égypte* 25 (1950) 110–23.

–, Le Statut de la Femme à l'époque hellénistique, principalement en Egypte, *Recueils de la Societé Jean Bodin* 11.1 (1959) 127–175.

J. Preuss, *Biblical and Talmudic Medicine* (Northvale and London 1993, Germ. orig. New York 1978, transl. and ed. by F. Rosner).

S. R. F. Price, *Rituals and Power. The Roman imperial cult in Asia Minor* (Cambridge 1984).

B. Przybylski, The Setting of Matthean Anti-Judaism, in: P. Richardson with D. Granskon (eds.), *Anti-Judaism in Early Christianity* (Waterloo, Ont. 1986 = Studies in Christianity and Judaism 2) 1:181–200.

M. Pucci Ben Zeev, New Perspectives on the Jewish-Greek Hostilities in Alexandria During the Reign of Emperor Caligula, *JSJ* 21 (1990) 226–35. [Pucci Ben Zeev, New Perspectives]

K. Raaflaub and M. Toher (eds.), *Between Republic and Empire. Interpretations of Augustus and His Principate* (Berkeley 1990). [Raaflaub and Toher, Between Republic and Empire]

G. v. Rad, Wisdom in Israel (London 1972, Germ. orig.) 26–9. [v. Rad, Wisdom]

T. Rajak, Moses in Ethiopia: Legend and Literature, *JJS* 29.2 (1978) 111–22.

–, Was there a Roman Charter for the Jews?, *JRS* 74 (1984) 107–23.

–, The Jewish Community and its Boundaries, in: J. Lieu *et al.* (eds.), *The Jews among Pagans and Christians In the Roman Empire* (London/New York 1992) 9–28.

B. Rawson, Adult-Child Relationships in Roman Society, in: eadem (ed.), *Marriage, Divorce, and Children in Ancient Rome* (Oxford 1991) 7–30.

A. Reinhartz, Philo On Infanticide, *SPhA* 4 (1992) 42–58. [Reinhartz, Infanticide]

–, Parents and Children: a Philonic Perspective, in: S. J. D. Cohen (ed.), *The Jewish*

*Family in Antiquity* (Atlanta 1993 = Brown Judaic Studies 289) 61–88. [Reinhartz, Parents and Children]

M. Reinhold, Roman Attitudes towards the Egyptians, *Ancient World* 3.3–4 (1980) 97–103.

–, The Declaration of War on Cleopatra *CJ* 77.2 (1981–2) 97–103.

A. N. M. Rich, The Platonic Ideas as the Thoughts of God, *Mnemosyne* N.S. 4.7 (1954) 123–33.

A. Richlin, Not before Homosexuality: The Materiality of the *Cinaedus* and the Roman Law against Love between Men, *Journal of the History of Sexuality* 3 (1993) 561–66.

J. M. Riddle, *Contraception and Abortion from the Ancient World to the Renaissance* (Cambridge MA 1992). [Riddle, Contraception].

Ch. Riedweg, *Mysterienterminologie bei Platon, Philon und Klemens von Alexandrien* (Berlin 1987). [Riedweg, Mysterienterminologie]

G. J. Riley, The Gospel of Thomas in Recent Scholarship, *Currents in Research: Biblical Studies* 2 (1994) 227–52.

W. Rösler, *Mnemosyne* in the *Symposion*, in: O. Murray (ed.), *Sympotica. A Symposium on the Symposion* (Oxford 1990) 230–7.

J. S. Romm, *The Edges of the Earth in Ancient Thought. Geography, Exploration, and Fiction* (Princeton 1992).

A. Rousselle, Personal Status and Sexual Practice in the Roman Empire, in: M. Feher (ed.), *Fragments of the Human Body* (New York 1989) 3:317–21.

D. T. Runia, *Philo of Alexandria and the Timaeus of Plato* (Leiden 1986). [Runia, Timaeus]

–, God and Man in Philo of Alexandria, *JThS* 39 (1988) 48–75.

–, Naming and Knowing. Themes in Philonic Theology with special reference to the *De Mutatione Nominum*, in: R. van den Broek *et al.* (eds.), *Knowledge of God in the Graeco-Roman World* (Leiden 1988 = Etudes preliminaires aux Religions orientales dans l'Empire Romain 112) 69–91. [Runia, Naming and Knowing]

–, Polis and Megalopolis: Philo and the Founding of Alexandria, *Mnemosyne* 42.3–4 (1989) 398–412.

–, *Philo in Early Christian Literature. A Survey* (Assen 1993 = Compendia Rerum Judaicarum ad Novum Testamentum 3).

–, Philo of Alexandria and the Greek *Hairesis*-Model, *Vigiliae Christianae* 53.2 (1999) 117–47.

D. A. Russell, *Criticism in Antiquity* (Berkeley 1981).

S. Safrai, Education and the Study of the Torah, in: idem and M. Stern (eds.), *The Jewish People in the First Century. Historical Geography, Political History, Social Cultural and Religious Life and Institutions* ( Philadelphia 1976)1:2: 945–70.

R. P. Saller, *Patriarchy, property, and death in the Roman family* (Cambridge 1994).

K.- G. Sandelin, The Danger of Idolatry according to Philo of Alexandria, *Temenos* 27 (1991) 109–150. [Sandelin, Idolatry]

S. Sandmel, Philo's Knowledge of Hebrew, SP 5 (1978) 107–12.

–, *Philo of Alexandria: An Introduction* (New York/Oxford 1979).

B. Sandywell, *Presocratic Reflexivity: The Construction of Philosophical Discourse c. 600 – 450 BC* (London and New York 1996).

N. M. Sarna, *The JPS Torah Commentary. Exodus* (Philadelphia – New York 1991).

M. Sartre, *L'Orient Romain. Provinces et sociétés provinciales en Méditerranée orien-*

*tale d'Auguste aux Sévères (31 avant J.- C. – 235 après J.- C.)* (Paris 1991). [Sartre, Orient]

M.L. Satlow, "Wasted Seed", The History of a Rabbinic Idea, *HUCA* 65 (1994) 137–75.

–, "Try To Be a Man": The Rabbinic Construction of Masculinity, *HTR* 89.1 (1996) 19–40.

–, Rhetoric and Assumptions: Romans and Rabbis on Sex, in: M. Goodman, Jews in a Graeco-Roman World 135–44.

C. Saulnier, Lois romaines sur les Juifs selon Flavius Josèphe, *RB* 88.2 (1981) 161–98.

P. Schäfer, *Judeophobia. Attitudes toward the Jews in the Ancient World* (Cambridge MA 1997). [Schäfer, Judeophobia]

G. Scarpat, Cultura ebreo-ellenistica e Seneca, *RB* 13.1 (1965) 3–30.

B. Schaller, Philon von Alexandreia und das "Heilige Land", in: G. Strecker (ed.), *Das Land Israel in biblischer Zeit* (Göttingen 1983) 172–187.

–, Philo, Josephus und das sonstige griechisch-sprachige Judentum in *ANRW* und weiteren neueren Veröffentlichungen, *Theologische Rundschau* 59 (1994) 186–214.

D.M. Schenkeveld and J. Barnes, Language, in: A. Keimpe *et al.* (eds.), *The Cambridge History of Hellenistic Philosophy* (Cambridge 1999) 177–225. [Schenkeveld and Barnes, Language]

L.H. Schiffman, Jewish Identity and Jewish Descent, *Judaism* 34.1 (1985) 78–84.

T.E. Schmidt, Hostility to Wealth in Philo of Alexandria, *JSNT* 19 (1983) 85–97.

M. Schofield, *The Stoic Idea of the City* (Cambridge 1991).[Schofield, Stoic City]

G. Scholem, Der Name Gottes und die Sprachtheorie der Kabbala, *Neue Rundschau* 83 (1972) 470–95, reprinted in: idem, *Judaica. Studien zur jüdischen Mystik* (2nd ed. Frankfurt 1977) 3.7–70, Engl. transl. in: *Diogenes* 79 (1972) 59–80; 80 (1972) 164–94.

W. Schubart, Rom und die Ägypter nach dem Gnomon des Idios Logos, *Zeitschrift für ägyptische Sprache und Altertumskunde* 56 (1920) 80–95.

D.R. Schwartz, Philo's Priestly descent, in: Greenspahn *et al.*, Nourished with Peace 155–71. [Schwartz, Priestly Descent]

–, Philonic Anonyms of the Roman and Nazi Periods: Two Suggestions, *SPhA* 1 (1989) 63–73.

–, On Drama and Authenticity in Philo and Josephus, *SCI* 10 (1989–90) 113 – 29. [Schwartz, Drama]

–, *Agrippa I. The Last King of Judaea* (Tübingen 1990 = *Texte und Studien zum Antiken Judentum* 23, revised Hebr. orig.). [Schwartz, Agrippa]

–, On Sacrifice by Gentiles in the Temple of Jerusalem, in: idem, *Studies in the Jewish Background of Christianity* (Tübingen 1992) 102–16.

–, Temple or City: What did Hellenistic Jews See in Jerusalem? in: M. Poorthuis and Ch. Safrai (eds.), *The Centrality of Jerusalem. Historical Perspectives* (Kampen 1996) 114–27. [Schwartz, City]

–, The Jews of Egypt between the Temple of Onias, the Temple of Jerusalem, and Heaven (Hebrew), *Zion* 62.1 (1997) 5–22.

–, On Luke-Acts and Jewish-Hellenistic Historiography, unpublished paper based on a lecture delivered at the European Conference of the SBL (Lausanne 1997). [Schwartz, Luke-Acts and Jewish-Hellenistic Historiography]

–, Rome and the Jews, Freedom and Autonomy, forthcoming in: A.K. Bowman *et al.* (eds.), *Rome and the Meditarrenean* (Oxford 2002).

J. Schwartz, Note sur la Famille de Philon d'Alexandrie, in: *Mélanges Isidore Lévy*

(Bruxelles 1955 = *Annuaire de l'Institut de Philologie et d'Histoire Orientales et Slaves 13*) 591–602.

–, L'Egypte de Philon, in: *Philon d'Alexandrie. Colloques Nationaux du Centre National de la Recherche Scientifique* (Paris 1967) 35–44.

B. B. Scott, *Hear Then the Parable. A Commentary on the Parables of Jesus* (Minneapolis 1989).

K. Scott, Octavian's Propaganda and Antony's *De Sua Ebrietate, CP* 24 (1929) 133–41.

–, The Political Propaganda of 44–30 B.C., *Mem. Am. Ac. in Rome* 11 (1933) 7–49.

R. Seager, *Tiberius* (London 1972). [Seager, Tiberius]

E. Seckel und W. Schubart, *Der Gnomon des Idios Logos* (Berlin 1919 = Ägyptische Urkunden aus den staatlichen Museen zu Berlin. Griechische Urkunden V. Band, Teil I).

T. Seland, *Establishment Violence in Philo And Luke. A Study of Non-Conformity to the Torah and Jewish Vigilante Reactions* (Leiden 1995).

Y. Shavit, *Athens in Jerusalem: Classical Antiquity and Hellenism in the Making of the Modern Secular Jew* (London 1997, Hebr. orig.). [Shavit, Athens in Jerusalem]

–, Up the River or Down the River? An Afrocentrist Dilemma, in: H. Erlich and I. Gershoni (eds.), *The Nile. Histories, Cultures, Myths* (London 2000) 79–104.

Z. Shavit, *Poetics of Children Literature* (Athen, Georgia 1986).

–, *A Past Without Shadow. The Construction of the Past Image in the German "Story" for Children* (Tel Aviv 1999).

A. N. Sherwin-White, *The Roman Citizenship* (Oxford 1973 2d ed.).

–, *Racial Prejudice in Imperial Rome* (Cambridge 1967). [Sherwin-White, Racial Prejudice]

D. Shotter, *Tiberius Caesar* (London and New York 1992).

Z. Shua, Sun Worship in Ancient Temples and Israelite Festivals (Hebrew), *Studies in Jewish Festivals* 5 (1994) 107–21.

P. L. Shuler, Philo's Moses and Matthew's Jesus: A Comparative Study in Ancient Literature, *SPhA* 2 (1990) 86–103.

D. Sills, Strange Bedfellows: Politics and Narrative in Philo, in: S. D. Breslauer, *The Seductiveness of Jewish Myth. Challenge or Response?* (New York 1997) 171–90.

M. Simon, *Verus Israel. A Study of the relations between Christians and Jews in the Roman Empire* (Oxford 1986, orig. Fr. ed 1964).

C. J. Simpson, The Cult of the Emperor Gaius, *Latomus* 40.3 (1981) 489–511. [Simpson, Cult]

M. B. Skinner, *Quod multo fit aliter in Graecia*, in: J. P. Hallett and M. B. Skinner (eds.), *Roman Sexualities* (Princeton 1997) 3–25.

D. Sly, *Philo's Perception of Women* (Atlanta 1990 = *Brown Judaic Studies* 209).

–, The Plight of Woman: Philo's Blind Spot?, in: W.E. Helleman (ed.), *Hellenisation Revisited. Shaping a Christian Response Within the Greco-Roman World* (Lanham and London 1994) 173–87.

–, *Philo's Alexandria* (London and New York 1996). [Sly, Philo's Alexandria]

E. M. Smallwood, Some Notes on the Jews under Tiberius, *Latomus* 15.3 (1956) 314–29.

–, *Philonis Alexandrini Legatio ad Gaium* (Leiden 1970). [Smallwood, Legatio]

–, *The Jews under Roman Rule* (Leiden 1981).

K. A. D. Smelik and E. A. Hemelrijk, "Who knows not what monsters demented Egypt worships?" Opinions on Egyptian animal worship in Antiquity as part of the ancient conception of Egypt, *ANRW* II 17.4 (1984) 1852–2000. [Smelik and Hemelrijk, Egyptian Worship]

R. Smend, *Die Weisheit des Jesus Sirach* (Berlin 1906).

A.D. Smith, *The Ethnic Origins of Nations* (Oxford 1986). [Smith, Origin of Nations]

J.Z. Smith, The Garments of Shame, *History of Religions* 5.2 (1966) 217–38.

–, Fences and Neighbors: Some Contours of Early Judaism, in: idem, *Imagining Religion. From Babylon to Jonestown* (Chicago 1982) 1–18.

M. Smith, Rome and the Maccabean Conversions – Notes on I Macc. 8, in: E. Bammel *et al.* (eds.), *Donum Gentilicium: New Testament Studies in Honour of David Daube* (Oxford 1978) 1–7.

L. Smolar and M. Aberbach, The Golden Calf Episode in Postbiblical Literature, *HUCA* 39 (1968) 91–116.

M. Sordi, Timagene di Alessandria: uno storico ellenocentrico e filobarbaro, *ANRW* II.30.1 (1982) 775–97. [Sordi, Timagene]

H. von Staden, *Herophilus. The Art of Medicine in Early Alexandria* (Cambridge 1989).[von Staden, Herophilus]

W. Steidle, *Sueton und die Antike Biographie* (München 1951 = Zetemata. Monographien zur klassischen Altertumswissenschaft 1) 76–80.

A. Stein, *Untersuchungen zur Geschichte und Verwaltung Aegyptens unter Römischer Herrschaft* (Stuttgart 1915). [Stein, Untersuchungen]

G. Stellin, Gotteserkenntnis und Gotteserfahrung bei Philo von Alexandrien, in: H.-J. Klauck (ed.), *Monotheismus und Christologie. Zur Gottesfrage im hellenistischen Judentum und im Urchristentum* (Freiburg 1992 = Quaestiones Disputatae 138) 19–21.

G.E. Sterling, *Historiography and Self-Definition. Josephus, Luke-Acts, and Apologetic Historiography* (Leiden 1992). [Sterling, Historiography].

–, Platonizing Moses: Philo And Middle Platonism, *SPhA* 5 (1993) 96–111.

–, Recluse or Representative? Philo and Greek-Speaking Judaism beyond Alexandria, *SBLSP* (1995) 595–616.

–, 'Thus are Israel': Jewish Self-Definition in Alexandria, *SPhA* 7 (1995) 1–18. [Sterling, Jewish Self-Definition]

–, Recherché or Representative? What is the Relationship between Philo's Treatises and Greek-speaking Judaism", *SPhA* 11 (1999) 1–30.

–, 'The School Of Sacred Laws': The Social Setting Of Philo's Treatises, *Vigiliae Christianae* 53.2 (1999) 148–64.

–, *The Jewish Plato. Philo of Alexandria, Greek speaking Judaism, and Christian origins*, forthcoming at Hendrikson.

D. Stern, *Parables in Midrash. Narrative and Exegesis in Rabbinic Literature* (Cambridge MA 1991).

S. Stern, *Jewish Identity in Early Rabbinic Writings* (Leiden 1994 = Arbeiten zur Geschichte des antiken Judentums und des Urchristentums 23).

Z. Stewart, Sejanus, Gaetulilus and Seneca, *AJP* 74 (1953) 70–85.

R. Stoneman, Jewish Traditions on Alexander the Great, *SPhA* 6 (1994) 37–53. [Stoneman, Jewish Traditions]

–, Who are the Brahmans? Indian Lore and Cynic Doctrine in Palladius' *De Bragmanibus* and its Models, *CQ* 44.2 (1994) 500–10.

–, Naked Philosophers: the Brahmans in the Alexander Historians and the Alexander Romance, *JHS* 115 (1995) 99–114.

–, *Alexander the Great* (London and New York 1997).

L. Storoni, *The Idea of the City in Roman Thought. From Walled City to Spiritual Commonwealth* (London 1970, Ital. orig. 1967).

S. K. Stowers, *A Rereading Of Romans. Justice, Jews, and Gentiles* (New Haven and London 1994). [Stowers, Romans]

H. Strasburger, Poseidonios on Problems of the Roman Empire, *JRS* 55 (1965) 40–53.

J. A. Straus, L'esclavage dans l'Egypte Romaine, *ANRW* II.10.1 (1988) 841–911.

G. Striker, *Essays on Hellenistic Epistemology and Ethics* (Cambridge MA 1996). [Striker, Essays]

A. Strobach, *Plutarch und die Sprachen. Ein Beitrag zur Fremdsprachenproblematik in der Antike* (Stuttgart 1997 = Palingenesia 64).

W. D. Stroker, Extracanonical Parables and the Historical Jesus, *Semeia* 44 (1988) 95–120.

J. Stroux, Vier Zeugnisse zur römischen Literaturgeschichte der Kaiserzeit, *Philologus* 86 (1931) 338–68.

–, Die Stoische Beurteilung Alexanders des Grossen, *Philologus* 88.2 (1933) 222–40.

Y. Sussman, The History of Halakha and the Dead Sea Scrolls – Preliminary Observations on Miqsat Ma'ase Ha-Torah (4QMMT) (Hebrew), *Tarbiz* 59.1 (1990) 11–76.

M. Swan, Josephus, *A.J.* XIX, 251–252: Opposition to Gaius and Claudius, *AJP* 91.2 no. 362 (1970) 149–64.

R. Syme, *Tacitus* (Oxford 1958).

–, The Crisis of 2 B.C., in: Roman Papers 3:912–36 (originally published in: *Baye-rische Akademie der Wissenschaften Phil.-Hist. Klas.* Sitzungsber. 7 (1974) 3–34).

–, The Greeks under Roman Rule, in: idem, *Roman Papers* (Oxford 1979) 2:566–81 (orig. Proceed. Mass. Hist. Soc. 72 (1957–63) 3–20). [Syme, Greeks]

H. Szesnat, 'Pretty Boys' in Philo's *De Vita Contemplativa*, *SPhA* 10 (1998) 87–107.

F. Taeger, *Charisma. Studien zur Geschichte des Antiken Herrscherkultes* (Stuttgart 1957).

R. Taubenschlag, Die Geschichte der Rezeption des römischen Privatrechts in Aegyp-ten, in: idem, *Opera Minora* (Warsaw 1959) 1:181–289.

–, Die *materna potestas* im gräko-ägyptischen Recht, in: ibid. 2:323–337.

–, Die *patria potestas* im Recht der Papyri, in: ibid. 2:261–321.

J. E. Taylor and Ph. R. Davies, The So-Called Therapeutae of *De Vita Contemplativa*: Identity and Character, *HTR* 91.1 (1998) 3–24. [Taylor and Davies, Therapeutae]

L. R. Taylor, Tiberius' Refusal of Divine Honours, *TAPA* 60 (1929) 87–101.

–, *The Divinity of the Roman Emperor* (Middletown 1931 = APA Monograph Ser. 1). [Taylor, Divinity]

V. A. Tcherikover, Jewish Apologetic Literature Reconsidered, *Eos* 48.3 (1956) 169–93. [Tcherikover, Apologetic Literature]

– and A. Fuks, (eds.), *Corpus Papyrorum Judaicarum* (Cambridge MA 1957–60) vol. 1 and 2. [*CPJ*]

–, The Ideology of the Letter of Aristeas, *HTR* 51.1 (1958) 59–85.

–, The Decline of the Jewish Diaspora in Egypt in the Roman Period, *JJS* 14.1–4 (1963) 1–32.

–, *Hellenistic Civilization and the Jews* (Philadelphia 1959; rep. New York 1970).

W. Theiler, *Die Vorbereitung des Neuplatonismus* (Berlin 1930). [Theiler, Vorberei-tung]

–, *Untersuchungen zur antiken Literatur* (Berlin 1970).

J. Theodor and Ch. Albeck, *Midrash Bereshit Rabba. Critical Edition with Notes and Commentary* (Jerusalem 1965).

H. Thesleff, *The Pythagorean Texts Of The Hellenistic Period* (Abo 1965).

C. Thoma, Literary and Theological Aspects of the Rabbinic Parables, in: idem and M. Wyschogrod (eds.), *Parable and Story in Judaism and Christianity* (N.J. 1989= Studies in Judaism and Christianity) 26–41.

– and S. Lauer, *Die Gleichnisse der Rabbinen* (Bern 1991 = *Judaica und Christiana* 13).

H. Thyen, *Der Stil der Jüdisch-Hellenistischen Homilie* (Göttingen 1955 = Forschungen zur Religion und Literatur des Alten und Neuen Testaments N.F. 47).

D. L. Tiede, *The Charismatic Figure as Miracle Worker* (Missoula 1972 = SBL Diss. Ser. 1). [Tiede, Charismatic Figures]

D. Timpe, Römische Geschichte bei Flavius Josephus, *Historia* 9 (1960) 474–502. [Timpe, Flavius Josephus]

T. H. Tobin, *The Creation of Man: Philo and the History of Interpretation* (Washington 1983 = The Catholic Biblical Quarterly Monograph Series 14).

S. Treggiari, *Roman Marriage. Iusti Coniuges from the Time of Cicero to the Time of Ulpian* (Oxford 1991).

F. Ullrich, Entstehung und Entwicklung der Literaturgattung des Symposion, *Programm des Kgl. Neuen Gymnasiums zu Würzburg* (Würzburg 1908–9) 1:3–49, 2:3–73.

N. Umemoto, Juden, "Heiden" und das Menschengeschlecht in der Sicht Philons von Alexandria, in: R. Feldmeier und U. Heckel (eds.), *Die Heiden. Juden, Christen und das Problem des Fremden*, (Tübingen 1994 = *WUNT* 70) 22–51.

W. C. van Unnik, *Das Selbstverständnis der jüdischen Diaspora in der hellenistisch-römischen Zeit* (Leiden 1993 = Arbeiten zur Geschichte des antiken Judentums und des Urchristentums 17).

St. Usher, The Style of Dionysius of Halicarnassus in the 'Antiquitates Romanae', *ANRW* II.30.1 (1982) 817–38.

R. Valantasis, *The Gospel of Thomas* (London and New York 1997 = New Testament Readings).

F. L. Vatai, *Intellectuals in Politics in the Greek World. From Early Times to the Hellenistic Age* (London 1984).

G. Vermes and M. D. Goodman (eds.), *The Essenes According to the Classical Sources* (Sheffield 1989).

F. Vittinghoff, Römische Kolonisation und Bürgerrechtspolitik unter Caesar und Augustus, Ak. d. Wiss. u. Lit., Abhandl. Geist. u. Soz. Wiss. Kl. (1951) 1217–1366.

C. J. De Vogel, *Pythagoras and Early Pythagoreanism. An Interpretation of Neglected Evidence on the Philosopher Pythagoras* (Assen 1966). [Vogel, Pythagoras]

B. Z. Wacholder, *Nicolaus of Damascus* (Berkeley 1962). [Wacholder, Nicolaus]

C. Wachsmuth, Timagenes und Trogus, *Rheinisches Museum für Philologie* 46 (1891) 465–79.

A. Wallace-Hadrill, *Suetonius. The Scholar and his Caesars* (London 1983/ New Haven 1984).

N. Walter, *Der Thoraausleger Aristobulos. Untersuchungen zu seinen Fragmenten* (Berlin 1964 = TUGAL 86).

J. Walters, Invading the Roman Body: Manliness and Impenetrability in Roman Thought, in: J. P. Hallett and M. B. Skinner (eds.), *Roman Sexualities* (Princeton 1997) 29–43. [Walters, Invading the Body]

M. Walzer, *Exodus and Revolution* (New York 1985).

P. R. C. Weaver, The Status of Children in Mixed Marriages, in: B. Rawson (ed.), *The Family in Ancient Rome. New Perspectives* (New York 1986) 145–169.

J. R. Wegner, Philo's Portrayal of Women – Hebraic or Hellenic?, in: Levine, "Women like This" 41–66.

F. Wehrli, Der Arztvergleich bei Platon, in: idem, *Theoria und Humanitas. Gesammelte Schriften zur Antiken Gedankenwelt* (Zürich 1972) 206–14.

M. Weinfeld, *Deuteronomy and the Deuteronomistic School* (Oxford 1972). [Weinfeld, Deuteronomy and the Deuteronomistic School]

H. Weiss, Philo on the Sabbath, *SPhA* 3 (1991 = *Heirs of the Septuagint. Philo, Hellenistic Judaism and Early Christianity. Festschrift for Earle Hilgert*) 83–105.

H. F. Weiss, *Untersuchungen zur Kosmologie des hellenistischen und palästinischen Judentums* (Berlin 1966).

P. Wendland, *Die Therapeuten und die Philonische Schrift vom Beschaulichen Leben. Ein Beitrag zur Geschichte des Hellenistischen Judentums* (Leipzig 1896).

T. Whitmarsh, The Birth of Prodigy: Heliodorus and the Genealogy of Hellenism, in: R. Hunter, *Studies in Heliodorus* (Cambridge 1998 = Cambr. Phil. Soc. Suppl. vol. 21) 93–124.

T. E. J. Wiedemann, Tiberius to Nero, *CAH* (Cambridge 1996, 2nd ed.) 10:198–255.

D. Wiggins, Heraclitus' conceptions of flux, fire and material persistence, in: Schofield and Nussbaum, Language and Logos 1–32.

U. v. Wilamowitz-Moellendorff und F. Zucker, Zwei Edikte des Germanicus auf einem Papyrus des Berliner Museums, *Sitzungsber. Kön. Pr. Akad. d. Wiss.* (1911) 794–821.

U. Wilcken, Alexander der Grosse und die indischen Gymnosophisten, *Sitzungsber. d. Preuss. Ak. d. Wiss. Phil.-Hist. Klasse* (1923) 150–83. [Wilcken, Indische Gymnosophisten]

–, *Alexander der Grosse* (Leipzig 1931).

–, *Alexander the Great* (New York 1967, transl. of Germ. orig.).

C. A. Williams, Greek Love at Rome, *CQ* 45.2 (1995) 517–39. [Williams, Greek Love]

H. Willrich, *Judaica. Forschungen zur hellenistisch-jüdischen Geschichte und Literatur* (Göttingen 1900). [Willrich, Judaica]

–, Caligula, *Klio* 3 (1903) 65–118; 288–317; 397–470. [Willrich, Caligula]

D. Winston, *Philo of Alexandria. The Contemplative Life, The Giants, and Selections* (New York 1981). [Winston, Philo of Alexandria]

–, Philo's Ethical Theory, *ANRW* II, 21.1 (1984) 372–416.

–, The Sage as Mystic in the Wisdom of Solomon, in: J. G. Gammie and L. G. Perdue (eds.), *The Sage in Israel and the Ancient Near East* (Winona Lake 1990) 383–97.

–, Aspects of Philo's Linguistic Theory, *SPhA* 3 (1991 = Heirs of the Septuagint. Philo, Hellenistic Judaism and Early Christianity. Festschrift for Earle Hilgert) 109–25. [Winston, Linguistic Theory]

–, review of W. C. van Unnik, *Das Selbstverständnis der jüdischen Diaspora in der hellenistisch-römischen Zeit* (Leiden 1993 = Arbeiten zur Geschichte des antiken Judentums und des Urchristentums 17) 127–37, *AJS Rev.* 20.2 (1995) 399–402.

–, Philo and the Rabbis on Sex and the Body, *PT* 19.1 (1998) 41– 62. [Winston, Philo and the Rabbis]

R. E. Witt, *Albinus and the History of Middle Platonism* (Cambridge 1937 = Transactions of the Cambridge Philological Society 7).

H. A. Wolfson, Extradeical and Introdeical Ideas, in: idem, *Religious Philosophy. A Group of Essays.* (Cambridge MA 1961) 27–68.

–, *Philo. Foundations of Religious Philosophy in Judaism, Christianity, and Islam* (Cambridge MA 1947). [Wolfson, Philo]

A.J. Woodman, *Velleius Paterculus. The Tiberian Narrative (2.94–131). Edited with an Introduction and Commentary* (Cambridge 1977).

O.L. Yarbrough, *Not like the Gentiles. Marriage Rules in the Letters of Paul* (Atlanta 1985 = *SBL* Diss. Ser. 80).

Z. Yavetz, The Res Gestae and Augustus' Public Image, in: Millar and Segal, Caesar Augustus 1–36. [Yavetz, Public Image]

–, *Julius Caesar. The Limits of Charisma* (Hebrew), (Tel Aviv 1992).

–, *Tiberius and Caligula. From Make-believe to Insanity* (Hebrew), (Tel Aviv 1995). [Yavetz, Tiberius and Caligula]

B.H. Young, *Jesus and His Jewish Parables. Rediscovering the Roots of Jesus' Teaching* (New York 1989 = Theological Inquiries. Studies in Contemporary Biblical and Theological Problems).

H.C. Youtie, ΑΠΑΤΟΡΕΣ: Law VS. Custom in Roman Egypt, in: J. Bingen *et al.* (eds.), *Le Monde Grec. Hommages à Claire Préaux* (Bruxelles 1975) 723–40. [Youtie, ΑΠΑΤΟΡΕΣ]

I.J. Yuval, The Haggadah of Passover and Easter (Hebrew), *Tarbiz* 65.1 (1995) 5–28.

–, Easter and Passover As Early Jewish-Christian Dialogue, in: P.F. Bradshaw and L.A. Hoffman (eds.), *Passover and Easter: Origin and History to Modern Times* (Notre Dame 1999) 5:98–124.

D. Zeller, Das Verhältnis der alexandrinischen Juden zu Ägypten, in: M. Pye and R. Stegerhoff (eds.), *Religion in fremder Kultur. Religion als Minderheit in Europa and Asien* (Saarbrücken 1987 = Schriften zur internationalen Kultur- und Geisteswelt 2) 77–85.

–, Jesus als vollmächtiger Lehrer (Mt. 5–7) und der hellenistische Gesetzgeber, in: L. Schenke (ed.), *Studien zum Matthäusevangelium. Festschrift für Wilhelm Pesch* (Stuttgart 1988) 301–17.

I. Ziegler, *Die Königsgleichnisse des Midrasch beleuchtet durch die römische Kaiserzeit* (Breslau 1903).

F. Zucker, Verfahrensweisen in der Einführung gewisser Einrichtungen des Augustus in Ägypten, *RIDA* 8 (1961) 155–64.

# Index of Sources

## Hebrew Bible

### Genesis (Gen.)

| | |
|---|---|
| 1:1 | 238–9 |
| 1:5 | 235, 237 |
| 1:26 | 220, 223–4, 238, 240 |
| 1:26–8 | 169, 186 |
| 1:27 | 191 |
| 2:2–3 | 262 |
| 2:10 | 194–5 |
| 3:17 | 243 |
| 4:1 | 241 |
| 6:6 | 238 |
| 12:13.16 | 56 n 47 |
| 12:18–9 | 56 n 47 |
| 16:1 | 25 |
| 17:12–3 | 26 |
| 21:11 | 24 |
| 21:12 | 24 |
| 30:3–13 | 28 |
| 37:3 | 181 |
| 38:15–6 | 99 n 98 |
| 39 | 65 |
| 39:7 | 66 |
| 49:43 | 67 |
| 50:19 | 66–7 |

### Exodus (Ex.)

| | |
|---|---|
| 2:11–2 | 70 |
| 2:14 | 70 |
| 2:15 | 70 |
| 2:21 | 23 n 25 |
| 3:17–19 | 55 n 40 |
| 4:1–5:2 | 55 n 40 |
| 4:10 | 193, 196 |
| 4:16 | 193 |
| 5:2 | 51 n 23 |
| 6:12 | 193 |
| 7:1 | 84 n 38, 85, 193 |
| 12:2 | 109, 264 n 57 |
| 12:3–23 | 260 n 41 |
| 12:16–20 | 264 n 56 |

| | |
|---|---|
| 12:18 | 264 n 58 |
| 13:3–10 | 260 n 41 |
| 14:25 | 57 |
| 20:3 | 239–240 |
| 20:10 | 262 n 49 |
| 20:14 | 24 n 28 |
| 20:24 | 260 n 41 |
| 21:22–3 | 163, 165 |
| 22:28 | 172 |
| 23:14–5 | 108 n 137, 260 n 41 |
| 23:15 | 260 n 41, 264 n 56 |
| 23:17 | 108 n 137 |
| 31:17 | 263 |
| 34:18 | 264 n 56 |
| 34:22 | 265 n 60 |
| 34:23 | 108 n 137 |

### Leviticus (Lev.)

| | |
|---|---|
| 6:25–9 | 232–3 |
| 15:19–24 | 229, 232 |
| 18:3–4 | 96 |
| 18:19 | 229–32 |
| 22:27 | 166 |
| 23:6 | 264 |
| 23:36 | 260 n 41 |
| 23:43 | 265 |

### Numbers (Num.)

| | |
|---|---|
| 23:19 | 85 |
| 28:17 | 260 n 41, 264 |

### Deuteronomy (Deut.)

| | |
|---|---|
| 4:1–8 | 188 |
| 4:2 | 207 |
| 5:15 | 262 |
| 12:13–4 | 260 n 41 |
| 12:31 | 173 |
| 16:3 | 264 n 56 |
| 16:13–5 | 265 n 60 |
| 20:5–7 | 246, 99 n 98 |

23:18

**Joshua (Josh.)**

2:1–21                    99 n 98

**Judges (Judg.)**

11:30–40                  173 n 46

**Sam. (Samuel)**

2:12:1–14                 215 n 20

**Kings (Kg.)**

2:22:2–13                 188

**Ezechiel (Ez.)**

17:2–10                   215 n 20
28:11–4                   197

**Psalms (Ps.)**

49:4–5                    215 n 20
65:10                     194

**Proverbs (Prov.)**

1:6                       215 n 20
3:11–2                    54
8:30                      238

**Kohelet (Koh.)**

7:15                      254
9:8                       227–8

**Nehemia (Neh.)**

8:1–8                     188

## LXX

**Genesis (Gen.)**

1:26                      164 n 10
2:4                       206
4:13                      244
8:21                      162 n 6
9:6                       164
22:10                     173 n 43

**Exodus (Ex.)**

4:14                      199
14:6–7                    55 n 37
20:18                     190, 202
20:22                     190
21:22–3                   164 n 10
22:27                     77
22:28                     172
34:20                     172
15:19                     229

**Leviticus (Lev.)**

18:19                     229

**Numbers (Num.)**

8:18                      172

**Deuteronomy (Deut.)**

4:12                      190
4:19                      77

**Jeremy (Jer.)**

19:5–6                    172

**Ezechiel (Ez.)**

20:25–6                   172

## New Testament

**Matthew (Mt.)**

11:16                     230 n 65
13:1–23                   234
13:1–52                   211 n 7
13:3–23                   215 n 19
13:18–23                  214 n 18

13:31–2                   222 n 40
13:44, 45, 47             230 n 65
15:12–5                   212
18:35                     221 n 37
20:1                      230 n 65
20:16                     221 n 37

| | |
|---|---|
| 21:28–46 | 213 n 13 |
| 21:33–46 | 215 n 19 |
| 21:35, 38–9 | 226 n 52 |
| 22:1–14 | 224, 228 |
| 22:2 | 225 |
| 22:4 | 225 |
| 22:6 | 226 n 52 |
| 22:9 | 228 |
| 22:10 | 225 |
| 22:11–4 | 225 |
| 22:14 | 225 |
| 24:11 | 221 n 37 |
| 24:32 | 221 n 37 |
| 24:32–5 | 222 n 40 |
| 25:14 | 212 |

*Mark (Mk.)*

| | |
|---|---|
| 4:1–20 | 234 |
| 4:1–34 | 211 n 7 |
| 4:3–20 | 215 n 19 |
| 4:14–20 | 214 n 18 |
| 4:26 | 221 n 37, 230 |
| 4:30 | 230 n 65 |
| 4:30–2 | 222 n 40 |
| 4:31 | 221 n 37 |

| | |
|---|---|
| 12:1–12 | 213 n 13, 215 n 19 |
| 13:28–31 | 222 n 40 |

*Luke (Lk.)*

| | |
|---|---|
| 6:48 | 230 n 65 |
| 7:31–2 | 230 n 65 |
| 8:4–15 | 234 |
| 8:5–15 | 215 n 19 |
| 8:11–15 | 214 n 18 |
| 13:18–9 | 222 n 40 |
| 13:18–21 | 230 n 65 |
| 14:15 | 225 |
| 14:16–24 | 224 |
| 14:24 | 225 |
| 19:11 | 212 |
| 20:9–19 | 213 n 13, 215 n 19 |
| 21:29–33 | 222 n 40 |

*Acts*

| | |
|---|---|
| 17 | 146 n 38 |
| 18:15 | 146 n 38 |

*Corinthians (Cor.)*

| | |
|---|---|
| 1:10:18 | 224 n 49 |

# Philo

*Abr. = De Abrahamo*

| | |
|---|---|
| 10 | 138 n 7 |
| 26 | 179 n 66 |
| 52–3 | 32 n 48 |
| 60 | 30 |
| 66–67 | 31 |
| 70 | 30 |
| 70–1 | 78 n 13 |
| 76 | 198 n 41, 201 |
| 79 | 30 |
| 79–80 | 201 |
| 83 | 194 n 26 |
| 95 | 56 |
| 112 | 178, 184 |
| 116 | 223 |
| 168 | 25 n 31, 181 |
| 176 | 173 n 43 |
| 177 | 173 n 43 |
| 178 | 173 n 42 |
| 179–81 | 173 |
| 196 | 173 n 46 |
| 250–1 | 25 |
| 258 | 57 |

| | |
|---|---|
| 266–7 | 255 n 23 |

*Aet. = De Aeternitate Mundi*

| | |
|---|---|
| 52 | 138 n 6 |
| 65 | 165 n 13 |
| 67 | 167 n 23 |
| 69 | 19 |

*Agr. = De Agricultura*

| | |
|---|---|
| 18 | 181 n 72 |
| 65 | 35 n 58 |
| 98 | 256, 256 n 25 |
| 158 | 246 |

*All. = Legum Allegoriae*

| | |
|---|---|
| 1:10 | 175 n 52 |
| 1:15 | 258 n 33 |
| 1:19–21 | 206 |
| 1:22 | 203 |
| 1:48–52 | 196 |
| 1:62 | 196 |
| 1:63–5 | 195 n 27 |

| | |
|---|---|
| 1:91–2 | 189 |
| 1:100 | 203 |
| 1:108 | 143 |
| 2:15 | 144 n 31 |
| 2:53 | 174 n 49 |
| 2:77 | 47 |
| 2:94 | 28 |
| 3:84 | 176 n 54 |
| 3:108 | 198 n 41 |
| 3:171 | 199 |
| 3:177–8 | 255 n 23 |
| 3:180 | 181 |
| 3:223–4 | 243 |

*Cher. = De Cherubim*

| | |
|---|---|
| 8 | 179 n 67 |
| 63 | 151 |
| 86–7 | 262 n 49 |
| 98 | 241 |
| 99–100 | 241 |
| 114 | 178 |

*Conf. = De Confusione Linguarum*

| | |
|---|---|
| 4 | 138 n 7 |
| 70 | 192 n 21 |
| 78 | 36 |

*Congr. = De Congressu quaerendae Eruditionis gratia*

| | |
|---|---|
| 15–6 | 181 n 72 |
| 74–6 | 181 |
| 79–80 | 182 |
| 81 | 162 n 5, 179 n 64 |
| 82 | 162 n 6 |
| 121 | 175 n 52 |
| 137 | 165 n 12 |
| 146–50 | 181 n 72 |
| 177 | 177 n 54, 180, 216 n 22 |

*Cont. = De Vita Contemplativa*

| | |
|---|---|
| 2 | 257 n 30 |
| 14 | 147 |
| 15 | 148 |
| 19–20 | 230 n 67 |
| 23–5 | 258 |
| 25 | 206 n 56 |
| 32–3 | 102 n 113 |
| 36 | 230 n 67 |
| 57 | 138 n 6 |
| 58–61 | 148 |
| 63 | 148 |
| 66 | 148 |

| | |
|---|---|
| 68 | 148 |
| 69 | 148 |
| 73–4 | 148 |
| 75 | 147, 155 |

*Dec. = De Decalogo*

| | |
|---|---|
| 12 | 256 |
| 13 | 256 |
| 46–7 | 202 |
| 48 | 202 |
| 52 | 76–7 |
| 52–71 | 143 n 28 |
| 59 | 239 |
| 61 | 239 |
| 76 | 143 n 28 |
| 79–80 | 48 |
| 96 | 107 n 132 |
| 98 | 108 n 136 |
| 102 | 260 n 40 |
| 119 | 170 n 36 |
| 119–20 | 170 |
| 130 | 24 n 28 |
| 132–4 | 169 |

*Det. = Quod Deterius Potiori insidiari soleat*

| | |
|---|---|
| 38–40 | 193 |
| 40 | 194 |
| 43 | 245 |
| 72 | 256 n 25 |
| 76 | 203 |
| 125–7 | 199 |
| 127 | 200 |
| 127–9 | 200 |
| 137–40 | 195 n 29 |
| 141–2 | 244 |
| 145 | 180 |
| 147 | 165 |
| 161 | 85 n 40 |
| 162 | 85 |

*Ebr. = De Ebrietate*

| | |
|---|---|
| 31 | 216 n 22 |
| 33 | 183 n 76 |
| 34 | 183 n 77 |
| 35 | 183 n 77 |
| 54–55 | 183 n 77 |
| 61 | 231 n 69 |
| 84 | 216 n 84 |
| 95 | 47, 176 |
| 128 | 197 |
| 133 | 203 |

| 140–1 | 255 |
| 142 | 248 |
| 177 | 222 |

*Flac. = In Flaccum*

| 2 | 134 |
| 9 | 134, 253 |
| 10 | 134, 253 n 21 |
| 14 | 133 |
| 17 | 59 |
| 18 | 134 |
| 19–20 | 61, 119 |
| 19–25 | 134 |
| 29 | 59, 60 n 63 |
| 33 | 59 |
| 34 | 59 n 58 |
| 36 | 61 |
| 37 | 59 n 58 |
| 41–2 | 61 |
| 46 | 34–6, 38 |
| 48–9 | 81 |
| 51 | 61 |
| 53–4 | 60 n 65 |
| 66 | 62 |
| 68 | 62 |
| 74 | 81 n 25 |
| 83 | 135 |
| 89 | 102 |
| 94 | 127 |
| 105–6 | 125 |
| 108–24 | 87 |
| 115 | 41 |
| 125–6 | 41 n 80 |
| 128 | 125 |
| 129 | 125 |
| 130 | 158 |
| 147 | 41, 135 n 77 |
| 152 | 41 |
| 159 | 135 n 76 |
| 164 | 134, 253 |
| 165 | 135, 253 |
| 166 | 119 |
| 170 | 41, 135 |
| 189 | 41 |
| 191 | 41, 135 n 77 |

*Fug. = De Fuga et Inventione*

| 29 | 184 |
| 108 | 84 |
| 180 | 51 |
| 195–202 | 195 n 29 |
| 212 | 27 |

*Gig. = De Gigantibus*

| 64 | 194 n 26 |

*Her. = Quis Rerum Divinarum Heres*

| 79 | 47, 106, 253 n 16 |
| 171 | 170 n 35 |
| 214 | 143, 155 |
| 286 | 255 n 23 |
| 294 | 162 n 5 |
| 295 | 162 n 4 |
| 295–6 | 162 n 6 |
| 296 | 256 n 26 |
| 297–8 | 256 n 27 |

*Hyp. = Hypothetica*

| 7:1 | 99 n 98 |
| 7:10–14 | 108 n 136 |

*Immut. = Quod Deus immutabilis sit*

| 67 | 256 |
| 173–5 | 157 |
| 175 | 113, 157 |

*Jos. = De Josepho*

| 4 | 181 |
| 33–4 | 245 n 96 |
| 42 | 66 |
| 42–8 | 94 n 83 |
| 43 | 99 |
| 130 | 255 n 23 |
| 135–6 | 113, 157 |
| 164 | 56 |
| 204 | 65, 179 n 68 |
| 254 | 65 |
| 257 | 65 |
| 258–9 | 65 |
| 262 | 65 |

*Lib. = Quod Omnis Probus Liber sit*

| 13 | 138 n 6 |
| 15 | 162 n 5 |
| 19 | 139 |
| 26–7 | 245 |
| 36 | 183 n 77 |
| 43 | 84 |
| 53 | 138 |
| 57 | 140 |
| 76 | 230 n 67 |
| 88 | 146 n 88, 155 |
| 93–5 | 152 |
| 96 | 155 |

| | |
|---|---|
| 133 | 53 |
| 141 | 139 |
| 143 | 139 |
| 160 | 162 n 5 |

*Leg. = De Legatione ad Gaium*

| | |
|---|---|
| 1–3 | 135 |
| 2:5–8 | 36 n 63 |
| 3 | 40 |
| 8 | 115 |
| 8–13 | 133 |
| 10 | 113, 115 |
| 11 | 127 |
| 14 | 133, 133 n 71.72, 253, 253 n 18, 256 |
| 18 | 133 |
| 22 | 133, 253 n 20 |
| 24 | 120 n 37 |
| 32–65 | 86, 93 |
| 33 | 120 |
| 34 | 120 |
| 44 | 134 |
| 48 | 134 |
| 51 | 134 |
| 63–5 | 134 |
| 67–73 | 40 n 34 |
| 76–7 | 86 n 43 |
| 76–114 | 133 |
| 78–85 | 87 |
| 78–93 | 86 n 47 |
| 92–8 | 87 |
| 107 | 253 |
| 115 | 162 |
| 116 | 87 n 52, 93, 120 |
| 117–8 | 80, 83 |
| 119 | 119, 133 |
| 138–9 | 86 |
| 141 | 126 |
| 141–2 | 120, 126–7 |
| 143 | 81 n 25, 128 |
| 144 | 54 n 34 |
| 144–5 | 128 |
| 146–7 | 129 |
| 147 | 115 |
| 149 | 81 n 25, 128 n 58, 130 |
| 149–51 | 131 n 66 |
| 150–1 | 81 n 26 |
| 153 | 131 |
| 154 | 93 n 78.79, 131 |
| 156 | 37, 108 n 136, 131–2 |
| 156–7 | 107 |
| 157 | 131–2 |
| 159–61 | 124, 133 |

| | |
|---|---|
| 161 | 127 |
| 162 | 60, 86 n 43.44, 119 |
| 163 | 61 |
| 167 | 127 n 55 |
| 167–9 | 119 |
| 170 | 62, 162 |
| 186 | 43 |
| 188 | 82 |
| 192–3 | 41 |
| 196 | 42, 135 |
| 201 | 80 n 23 |
| 203 | 86 n 45 |
| 205 | 62, 86 n 45 |
| 206 | 88 n 54 |
| 210 | 177 |
| 212 | 83 |
| 230 | 162 |
| 243 | 43 |
| 245 | 83 |
| 267 | 43 |
| 280 | 82 n 29 |
| 281–4 | 43 |
| 283 | 36 |
| 290 | 82 |
| 292 | 82 |
| 294–310 | 127 |
| 299 | 125 |
| 299–310 | 119 |
| 301 | 125 |
| 302 | 125 n 50 |
| 304–5 | 125 |
| 310 | 83 n 35, 132 |
| 312 | 132 |
| 313 | 37 |
| 318 | 83 n 35, 132, 132 n 69 |
| 319 | 132 |
| 324 | 124 |
| 333 | 42 n 82 |
| 333–7 | 79 n 21 |
| 334–5 | 42 n 82 |
| 337 | 42 n 82 |
| 338 | 60, 85 |
| 352–67 | 87 n 49 |
| 355 | 62 |
| 356 | 82 |
| 366 | 135 |
| 367 | 135 |
| 373 | 85 n 42 |

*Migr. = De Migratione Abrahami*

| | |
|---|---|
| 20 | 94 n 83 |
| 47–8 | 190 |
| 48–9 | 190 |

| | |
|---|---|
| 52 | 190 |
| 157 | 194 n 26 |
| 160 | 67 |
| 160–1 | 56 |

*Mos. = De Vita Mosis*

| | |
|---|---|
| 1:1–3 | 40, 158 |
| 1:2–3 | 173 n 42 |
| 1:2–4 | 69 n 82 |
| 1:6 | 50 |
| 1:9 | 55 n 41 |
| 1:10 | 54 |
| 1:15 | 167 n 23 |
| 1:18–20 | 178 |
| 1:20 | 69 |
| 1:21 | 69 |
| 1:22 | 246 |
| 1:24 | 69 |
| 1:25–9 | 69 n 112 |
| 1:26–9 | 102 n 112 |
| 1:27 | 69 |
| 1:30–3 | 69 |
| 1:36 | 55 n 43 |
| 1:45 | 71 |
| 1:49 | 56 n 48 |
| 1:84 | 196 |
| 1:86 | 55 |
| 1:88 | 51 n 23, 162 |
| 1:117 | 50 |
| 1:140 | 50 n 40 |
| 1: 147 | 25 |
| 1:148 | 71 |
| 1:149 | 76 n 6 |
| 1:156 | 84 n 37 |
| 1:158 | 95 n 84 |
| 1:168 | 55 n 37, 57 |
| 1:178 | 58 |
| 1:239 | 35 |
| 1:240–2 | 35 n 58 |
| 1:278 | 33 |
| 2:2 | 71 |
| 2:11 | 206 n 56 |
| 2:12 | 207, 250 |
| 2:14 | 208, 250 |
| 2:14–5 | 207, 250 |
| 2:17 | 251 n 11 |
| 2:17–20 | 140 n 15 |
| 2:17–44 | 251 n 13 |
| 2:20–1 | 140 |
| 2:21–3 | 252 |
| 2:23–4 | 150 n 48 |
| 2:27 | 139, 140 n 15, 252 |
| 2:31 | 141 n 16 |

| | |
|---|---|
| 2:34 | 207 n 57 |
| 2:34–5 | 230 |
| 2:34–6 | 230 |
| 2:37 | 208 |
| 2:37–9 | 208 |
| 2:48 | 248 |
| 2:48–52 | 252 |
| 2:53–64 | 252 |
| 2:127 | 190 n 12 |
| 2:185 | 256 n 24 |
| 2:193 | 31 n 46 |
| 2:194–5 | 51 |
| 2:209 | 262 n 52 |
| 2:210 | 263 |
| 2:211 | 262 n 47, 262 n 52 |
| 2:216 | 264 |
| 2:232 | 38 |

*Mut. = De Mutatione Nominum*

| | |
|---|---|
| 11–2 | 189 n 9.10 |
| 63–5 | 189 |
| 69 | 189 n 7 |
| 84 | 246 |
| 125–6 | 84 n 38 |
| 131 | 194 n 26 |
| 152 | 235 |
| 181 | 85 |
| 230 | 255 n 23 |

*Opif. = De Opificio Mundi*

| | |
|---|---|
| 1 | 247 |
| 3 | 248 |
| 4–6 | 204 |
| 8 | 140 |
| 12 | 236 |
| 15 | 235 |
| 16 | 236 |
| 16–24 | 203 |
| 17–20 | 205, 235–6, 238 |
| 21 | 139 n 13 |
| 24 | 205 |
| 25 | 205 |
| 38 | 231 n 69 |
| 69 | 169 n 34, 189 n 7 |
| 69–70 | 200 |
| 71 | 200 |
| 77 | 169 n 33, 220 n 34.35 |
| 78 | 220–1 |
| 79 | 169 |
| 89 | 259, 263 |
| 99 | 259 |
| 100 | 258 n 33 |
| 101 | 258, 264 |

| | |
|---|---|
| 116 | 261 |
| 124 | 19 n 6 |
| 126–7 | 260 |
| 127 | 111 n 3 |
| 128 | 260–1 |
| 132–3 | 231 n 69 |
| 133 | 167 n 19 |
| 134 | 191 |
| 145–6 | 189 n 7 |
| 149 | 194 n 26 |
| 149–50 | 189 n 8, 190 n 10 |
| 153 | 196 |
| 161 | 101 |
| 161–2 | 179 n 64 |

*Plant. = De Plantatione*

| | |
|---|---|
| 14 | 144 n 31 |
| 15 | 167 n 19 |
| 168 | 179 n 63 |

*Post. = De Posteritate Caini*

| | |
|---|---|
| 64 | 262 n 48 |
| 101–2 | 181 n 72 |
| 127–9 | 195 |
| 135–6 | 195 n 29 |
| 141 | 245 |
| 159 | 255 n 23 |

*Praem. = De Praemiis et Poenis*

| | |
|---|---|
| 34 | 244 n 93 |
| 37–9 | 201 |
| 40 | 201 n 45 |
| 44–6 | 200 n 44 |
| 54 | 71 |
| 110 | 170 |
| 119 | 254 |
| 120 | 254 |
| 121–2 | 254 |
| 124 | 255 |
| 153 | 260 |
| 162 | 176 |

*Prov. = De Providentia*

| | |
|---|---|
| 2:64 | 33 n 53 |

*Q.E. = Questiones et Solutiones in Exodum*

| | |
|---|---|
| 1:1 | 264 n 57, 266 |
| 1:7 | 103 n 115 |
| 2:29 | 201 n 45 |
| 2:51 | 201 n 45 |

*Q.G. = Questiones et Solutiones in Genesim*

| | |
|---|---|
| 2:6 | 140 |
| 2:54 | 162 n 6 |
| 2:62 | 78 |
| 3:47 | 170 n 37 |
| 3:48 | 170 n 36 |
| 4:14 | 179 n 66 |
| 4:188 | 84 n 38 |

*Sacr. = De Sacrificiis Abelis et Caini*

| | |
|---|---|
| 39 | 255 n 23 |
| 49 | 244 n 92 |
| 58–64 | 178 n 60 |
| 131 | 195 n 28 |

*Sobr. = De Sobrietate*

| | |
|---|---|
| 9 | 27 |
| 24 | 179 n 66 |
| 25 | 248 |
| 67 | 255 n 23 |

*Somn. = De Somniis*

| | |
|---|---|
| 1:49 | 246 |
| 1:58–9 | 144 |
| 1:60 | 145 |
| 1:72 | 198 |
| 1:75 | 198 |
| 1:106–7 | 165 n 13 |
| 1:115 | 198 |
| 1:127 | 191 |
| 1:147 | 202 |
| 1:164 | 202 |
| 2:9 | 184 |
| 2:10 | 179 |
| 2:98 | 67 |
| 2:98–100 | 66 |
| 2:106–8 | 66 |
| 2:117–8 | 53 |
| 2:119 | 53 n 29 |
| 2:120 | 53 |
| 2:124 | 107 n 131 |
| 2:126 | 107 n 130 |
| 2:178 | 163 |
| 2:204 | 179 |
| 2:242–5 | 194 |
| 2:244 | 235 |
| 2:258 | 192 n 21 |
| 2:259 | 193 |
| 2:260 | 193 |
| 2:262 | 193 n 22 |

*Spec. = De Specialibus Legibus*

| | |
|---|---|
| 1:4 | 257 |
| 1:28 | 143 n 28 |
| 1:51–53 | 30 n 43 |
| 1:53 | 77 |
| 1:67 | 35 |
| 1:76–78 | 37 n 65 |
| 1:138 | 172 |
| 1:139 | 172 |
| 1:242 | 223 |
| 1:245 | 232 |
| 1:246 | 232 |
| 1:252 | 255 n 23 |
| 1:283–4 | 255 n 23 |
| 1:313 | 162 |
| 1:314 | 177, 187 |
| 1:326 | 24 |
| 1:332 | 178 |
| 2:23–4 | 253 n 17 |
| 2:32–3 | 229 |
| 2:42–48 | 106 n 129 |
| 2:56 | 263 |
| 2:58 | 263 n 53 |
| 2:60 | 108 n 135 |
| 2:61–2 | 108 |
| 2:64 | 108 n 135 |
| 2:66–70 | 107 |
| 2:125 | 184 n 79 |
| 2:145 | 108 |
| 2:146 | 55 n 43, 108, 108 n 137 |
| 2:148 | 109 n 139 |
| 2:150 | 109 n 138, 260 n 42, 264 |
| 2:152 | 265 |
| 2:154 | 265 |
| 2:155–6 | 264 |
| 2:158 | 264 n 56 |
| 2:160 | 109 |
| 2:164–5 | 143 n 28 |
| 2:165 | 78 |
| 2: 166 | 95 |
| 2:167 | 76 |
| 2:195 | 94, 109 |
| 2:197 | 255 n 23 |
| 2:206–7 | 265 |
| 2:208 | 265 |
| 2:208–9 | 266 |
| 2:210 | 265 |
| 2:213 | 265 |
| 2:160 | 265 n 59 |
| 2:204–7 | 265 n 61 |
| 2:213 | 265 n 61 |
| 2:214 | 261 |
| 2:226–7 | 183 |
| 2:228 | 180 |
| 2:230 | 181, 183 |
| 2:232 | 176 |
| 2:233 | 180 n 69 |
| 2:236 | 163, 175 n 53, 180 n 71 |
| 3–4 | 95 n 84 |
| 3:3 | 8 |
| 3:8 | 95 |
| 3:9 | 95 |
| 3:11 | 96 |
| 3:15 | 97 |
| 3:15–22 | 150 n 48 |
| 3:17 | 97 |
| 3:22 | 98 |
| 3:22–5 | 98 |
| 3:23–4 | 47, 98 |
| 3:30 | 99 |
| 3:32–63 | 99 |
| 3:33 | 18 |
| 3:34 | 101 |
| 3:37 | 103 |
| 3:37–42 | 150 n 47 |
| 3:39 | 101 |
| 3:51 | 99 n 98 |
| 3:67 | 23 |
| 3:69 | 24 n 27 |
| 3:81 | 184 n 81 |
| 3:108 | 164 n 11 |
| 3:109 | 164 |
| 3:110 | 164 |
| 3:111–2 | 165, 169 |
| 3:113 | 101 |
| 3:114 | 171 |
| 3:117 | 168 n 32 |
| 3:119 | 174 n 49 |
| 3:138–9 | 55 n 42 |
| 3:163 | 115 n 20 |
| 3:169 | 184 |
| 3:171 | 102, 184 |
| 3:172–5 | 184 n 80 |
| 3:173–5 | 102 |
| 3:176 | 184 |
| 4:61 | 140 |
| 4:68 | 175 |
| 4:96 | 257 |
| 4:97 | 105 |
| 4:98–9 | 105 |
| 4:100 | 257 |
| 4:100–18 | 105 |
| 4:102 | 106 |
| 4:110 | 105 n 123 |
| 4:159 | 76 |
| 4:179 | 127 |
| 4:181 | 84 n 38 |

*Vir.* = *De Virtutibus*

| | |
|---|---|
| 14 | 256 |
| 61 | 244 n93 |
| 62 | 216 n22 |
| 110–4 | 24 n27 |
| 115 | 171 |
| 125–6 | 166 |
| 128 | 166 n18 |
| 128–33 | 166, 169 |
| 129–30 | 167 n19 |
| 130 | 167 |

| | |
|---|---|
| 132 | 168 n29 |
| 133 | 167 |
| 134 | 19 n7 |
| 134–8 | 170 |
| 178 | 175 n53, 180 n71 |
| 182 | 176 n56 |
| 197 | 180 |
| 208 | 183 n77 |
| 220–1 | 30, 77 n9 |
| 223–4 | 28 |

## Ancient Authors

### Aeschylus

*Pers.* = *Persae*

| | |
|---|---|
| 93–106 | 97 n94 |
| 213 | 55 n41 |
| 338–445 | 55 |
| 373 | 57 |
| 402–4 | 53 |
| 457–60 | 58 n56 |
| 465–70 | 58 n56 |
| 480–1 | 58 n56 |
| 595 | 56 n46 |
| 733 | 53 n29 |
| 749–50 | 53 |
| 782–6 | 57 |
| 909 | 53 n29 |

### Alexander Aphrodisiensis (Alex. of Aphrod.)

*Met.* = *Metaphysica*

| | |
|---|---|
| 39.3–5 | 258 n33 |

### Aristoteles (Arist.)

*G.A.* = *De Generatione Animalum*

| | |
|---|---|
| 2:1:734a | 166 n16 |

*Met.* = *Metaphysica*

| | |
|---|---|
| 986a | 259 n34 |
| 987b | 259 n34 |
| 1083b | 259 n34 |

*Nic. Eth* = *Nichomachea Ethica*

| | |
|---|---|
| 3.1118b | 95 n87 |

*Pol.* = *Politica*

| | |
|---|---|
| 1268b28 | 207 n57 |
| 1335b24–6 | 166 n16 |

*Rhet.* = *Rhetorica*

| | |
|---|---|
| 2.20.1393b | 217 |

### Arrianus (Arrian.)

*Anab.* = *Anabasis*

| | |
|---|---|
| 7.2:2 | 154 n62 |
| 7.2:2–4 | 154 |
| 7.2:4 | 153 |

### Augustinus

*De Cons. Evang.* = *De Consensu Evangelistarum*

| | |
|---|---|
| 1.22:30 | 78 n14 |

### Augustus (Aug.)

*R.G.* = *Res Gestae*

| | |
|---|---|
| 3:1 | 114 n15.16 |
| 6:1 | 90 n62 |
| 24:1 | 117 |
| 25:1 | 129 n59 |
| 26:4 | 114 n16 |
| 31–32 | 114 n16 |
| 34:1–3 | 90 n62 |

### Ben Sira (Sir.)

| | |
|---|---|
| 24:1–12, 23–34 | 197 n33 |
| 24:10–15 | 197 n34 |
| 24:30 | 197 |
| 30:13 | 180 n69 |
| 38: 1–15 | 18 n5 |

Cicero (Cic.)

*Ad Her. = Ad Herennium*
*(ascribed to Cicero)*

| | |
|---|---|
| 2:46 | 218 |
| 4:34 | 115 n 18 |
| 4:59 | 218 |
| 4:60 | 218 |

*De Div. = De Divinatione*

| | |
|---|---|
| 1:47 | 154 |

*De Fin. = De Finibus*

| | |
|---|---|
| 1:23 | 168 n 26 |
| 3:62 | 168 |
| 4:64 | 219 |
| 4:76 | 219 |

*De Ira*

| | |
|---|---|
| 2.10:8 | 219 n 32 |
| 2.15:1 | 219 n 32 |
| 2.18:1 | 219 n 32 |

*De Off. = De Officiis*

| | |
|---|---|
| 1:90 | 154 n 63 |
| 2.2:5 | 182 n 73 |

*De Rep. = De Republica*

| | |
|---|---|
| 3:24 | 154 n 63 |

*Leg. = De Legibus*

| | |
|---|---|
| 1:18 | 249 |
| 1:19 | 250 |
| 2:10–3 | 250 |
| 2:13 | 250 |
| 2:14 | 250 |
| 2:15–6 | 250 n 9 |
| 2:23 | 250 |
| 2:35 | 250 |

*N.D. = De Natura Deorum*

| | |
|---|---|
| 1:43 | 48 n 13 |
| 1:81–2 | 49 n 13 |
| 1:101 | 49 n 13 |
| 2:19 | 78 n 13 |
| 2:22 | 219 |
| 2:62 | 84 n 36 |
| 3:39 | 49 n 13 |

*Pro Rabiro Post. = Pro Rabiro Postumo*

| | |
|---|---|
| 34–5 | 59 n 60 |

*Pro Flac. = Pro L. Valerio Flacco*

| | |
|---|---|
| 69 | 37 |

*Tus. Disp. = Tusculanae Disputationes*

| | |
|---|---|
| 5:58 | 150 n 45 |
| 5:78 | 49 n 13 |

*Verr. = In Verrem*

| | |
|---|---|
| 2.1:140 | 104 n 120 |

Q. Curtius Rufus

*H.A. = Historia Alexandri Magni*

| | |
|---|---|
| 10.9:1–6 | 157 |

Dio Cassius (Dio)

*Roman History*

| | |
|---|---|
| 50.3:4–5 | 49 n 15 |
| 50.4:1 | 49 n 15 |
| 50.25:3 | 49 n 17.18 |
| 51.16:3–4 | 117 n 29 |
| 51.16:5 | 48 n 13, 117 n 30, 157 |
| 54.16:1–5 | 104 n 120 |
| 56.3:3–5 | 168 n 29 |
| 56.8:2–3 | 168 n 29 |
| 57:18 | 124 n 47 !!! |
| 59.26:8–9 | 87 n 49 |
| 60.5:1 | 89 |

Dio Chrysostomos (Dio Chr.)

*Or. = Orationes*

| | |
|---|---|
| 3:97 | 224 n 49 |

*Paus. =Pausanias*

| | |
|---|---|
| 10.24:3 | 141 n 21 |

Diodorus (Diod.)

*Bib. = Bibliotheces Historices*

| | |
|---|---|
| 1.55:2 | 72 |
| 1.180: 3–4 | 27 |
| 10.9:3 | 102 n 111 |

## Diogenes Laertius (D.L.)

*Vitae Philosophorum*

| | |
|---|---|
| Prol. 1:1–11 | 142 |
| 2:21 | 145 |
| 2:79 | 246 |
| 7:40 | 233 n 71 |
| 7:88 | 249 n 8, 250 n 9 |
| 7:108 | 249 n 8 |
| 7:122 | 235 n 75 |
| 7:127 | 219 |

## Dionysius of Halicarnassus

*A.R. = Antiquitates Romanae*

| | |
|---|---|
| 1.2:1 | 115 |
| 1.3:3 | 115 |
| 1.33:4 | 117 n 27 |
| 1.4:2 | 116 n 25 |
| 1.4:3 | 116 n 23 |
| 1.5:3 | 116 n 24 !!! (A.J.) |
| 1.5:3 | 116 |
| 1.10:1–2 | 116 n 26 |
| 7.70:5 | 117 n 27 |

## Eusebius (Eus.)

*Ec. Hist. = Ecclesiastes Historias*

| | |
|---|---|
| 7.32:16–8 | 262 n 46 |

*Praep. Ev. = Praeperatio Evangelica*

| | |
|---|---|
| 9.23:2–3 | 68 |
| 9.23:4 | 68 |
| 9.27:4 | 71, 73 |
| 9.27:5 | 71 |
| 9.27:6 | 73 |
| 9.27:7 | 71 |
| 9.27:9–10 | 72 |
| 9.27:21 | 72 |
| 11:23 | 191, 203 n 48 |
| 13.12:1 | 141 n 18 |
| 13.12:13 | 261 n 44 |
| 13.12:15 | 261 n 45 |
| 13.13:3–8 | 261 n 45 |

## Gaius

*Inst. = Institutiones*

| | |
|---|---|
| 1:104 | 20 n 14 |
| 1:55 | 20 n 14 |

## Herodotus (Hdt.)

*Historiae*

| | |
|---|---|
| 2:14 | 50 |
| 2:19 | 50 |
| 2:20–24 | 51 |
| 2:35 | 51 |
| 2:37–64 | 51 |
| 3:80 | 207 n 57 |

## Iamblichus

*Vit. Pyth. = De Vita Pythagorica*

| | |
|---|---|
| 211 | 101 n 110 |

## Jerome

*Comment. in Eccl.*

| | |
|---|---|
| CCSL 72:324–7 | 228 n 59 |

## Josephus (Jos.)

*A.J. = Antiquitates Judaicae*

| | |
|---|---|
| 1:80–2 | 260 n 42 |
| 1:154–7 | 78 n 13 |
| 1:223–4 | 174 n 47 |
| 2: 39–59 | 99 n 98 |
| 2:50–9 | 65 n 76 |
| 4:278 | 171 n 38 |
| 11:302–47 | 151 n 53 |
| 12:12–118 | 140 n 15 |
| 14:127–39 | 7 n 22, 112 n 5 |
| 15:328 | 130 |
| 15:329 | 130 |
| 15:339 | 130 |
| 16:43 | 108 |
| 16:163–71 | 37 |
| 16:361–2 | 177 n 57 |
| 18:81–4 | 123–4 |
| 18:168–78 | 122 |
| 18:172 | 122 |
| 18:179–89 | 126 |
| 18:188 | 123 |
| 18:205–10 | 120 n 37 |
| 18:225–37 | 123 |
| 18:226 | 122 |
| 18:259 | 8, 112 n 9 |
| 18:289–304 | 79 n 21 |
| 18:292 | 123 |
| 18:300–1 | 42 n 82 |
| 18:305–6 | 79 n 21 |
| 19:208 | 91 n 70 |

19:227          88
19:246          88
19:278–9        39
19:281          37 n 68

*B.J. = Bellum Judaicum*

1:534–43        177 n 57
2:208           88

*Contr. Ap. = Contra Apionem*

1:4             144
1:7             144
2:58–60         7 n 22
2:58–61         112 n 2
2:137           47 n 9
2:202           171 n 38

Juvenalis (Juv.)

*Sat. = Saturae*

6:82–104        105 n 122
15:44–6         48–49 n 13

Livius (Liv.)

*Ab Urbe Condita*

9.18:6          117 n 31
34.2:1–4:3      104 n 120
34.4:1–4        150 n 46

Lucianus

*Quomodo hist. conscrib. = Quomodo
historia conscribenda sit*

40              152 n 57

Johannes Lydos

*De Mens. = De Mensibus*

2:12            259 n 33

Cornelius Nepos

*Alc. =Alcibiades*

2:2             150 n 45

Ovid

*Ars Amat. = Ars Amatoria Fasti*

2:684           36, 115

Philolaus (Phil.)

*In Nic. = In Nicomachi Arithmeticam
Introductionem (apud Iamblichus)*

7:8             259 n 35

Plato

*Crat. = Cratylos*

400d–401a       191
424a–426b       188 n 4

*Hip. Mai = Hippias Maior*

283a            147 n 39

*Leg. = Leges*

1:636c          95 n 87
1:643d–644b     179 n 64
7:792a–797b     179 n 64
7:808d          175
8:838a–b        98

*Men. = Menon*

237c–238b       231 n 69

*Phaedo*

66e–69e         198 n 40
79a–84b         198 n 40

*Phaedrus*

246e            243

*Pol. = Politicus*

296e–297a       243

*Rep. = Respublica*

487e            243 ???
6:507d–517a     198 n 36
9:588d          204

*Symp. = Symposium*

206c–212a       149
212a            198 n 40

*Theaet. = Theaetetus*

191d            203
206d            194

*Tim.= Timaius*

| | |
|---|---|
| 28a | 205 n 52.54 |
| 29a | 205 n 54 |
| 29d | 205 n 54 |
| 49a–52e | 231 n 69 |

Plinius the Elder

*N.H. = Naturalis Historia*

| | |
|---|---|
| 7:112 | 146 n 34 |
| 29:14 | 146 n 35 |

Plutarchus (Plut.)

*Alex. = Alexanderus*

| | |
|---|---|
| 65:8 | 154 |

*Ant. = Antonius*

| | |
|---|---|
| 58:4 | 49 n 15 |
| 80:1 | 117 n 29 |

*Cato Mai = Cato Maior*

| | |
|---|---|
| 12:5 | 146 |
| 22:1–5 | 146 n 34 |
| 23:1 | 146 n 33 |
| 23:2 | 146 n 34 |

*De Is. et Os. = De Iside et Osiride*

| | |
|---|---|
| 363d–365c | 231 n 69 |
| 372e–374d | 231 n 69 |

*De Lib. Educ. = De Libris Educandis*

| | |
|---|---|
| 3 | 167 n 22 |

*Praec. Ger. Reip. = Praecepta Gerendae Reipublicae*

| | |
|---|---|
| 814d | 117 n 29 |

Polybios (Polyb.)

*Hist. = Historia*

| | |
|---|---|
| 31.25:4 | 150 |

Pseudepigrapha

*Ar. = Letter of Aristeas*

| | |
|---|---|
| 16 | 78 |
| 29–31 | 140 n 15 |
| 134–7 | 143 n 27 |

| | |
|---|---|
| 143–57 | 105 n 123 |
| 181 | 141 n 16 |
| 187–300 | 141 n 16 |
| 311 | 208 |

*G. Th. = Gospel of Thomas*

| | |
|---|---|
| Saying 9 | 211, 214 n 17, 234 |
| Saying 20 | 222 n 40 |
| Saying 64 | 224 n 51, 225 |

*Jub. = Jubilees*

| | |
|---|---|
| 2:17–22 | 263 n 54 |
| 6:17 | 262 n 54 |
| 6:18 | 263 n 54 |
| 6:36–8 | 258 n 32 |
| 11:14–12:21 | 30 n 42 |
| 16:29 | 263 n 54 |
| 34:18–9 | 263 n 54 |
| 39:6–8 | 65 n 76 |

*Jos. and As. = Jospeh and Aseneth*

| | |
|---|---|
| 24:1–10 | 28 n 38 |

*I Macc. = I. Maccabees*

| | |
|---|---|
| 8:1–32 | 112 n 6 |

*II Macc.= II. Maccabees*

| | |
|---|---|
| 4:10–7 | 143 n 29 |

*Sib. Or. = Sybelline Oracle*

| | |
|---|---|
| 2:281 | 171 n 38 |
| 3:171–4, 381–400 | 143 n 30 |

Pseudo-Phocylides

| | |
|---|---|
| 184 | 171 n 38 |

Rabbinic Sources

*Avot*

| | |
|---|---|
| 5:5 | 207 |

*b. Shab. = Talmud Bavli Shabbath*

| | |
|---|---|
| 153a | 227 |

*b. Yeb. = Talumd Bavli Yebamoth*

| | |
|---|---|
| 16b | 31 n 46 |
| 22b | 24 n 29 |
| 23a | 31 n 46 |
| 44b–45b | 31 n 46 |

*b. Kid. = Talmud Bavli Kidushin*

| | |
|---|---|
| 68a | 24 n 29 |
| 70a | 31 n 46 |

*G.R. = Genesis Rabbah*

| | |
|---|---|
| 4:10 | 210 n 1 |
| 8:3 | 238 |
| 8:6 | 226 n 55 |
| 8:9 | 226 |
| 8:10 | 240 |
| 13:9 | 52 n 24 |
| 22:9 | 221 n 39, 244 n 94 |
| 56:3–4 | 174 n 48 |

*K.R. = Kohelet Rabbah*

| | |
|---|---|
| 9:8 | 227 |

*m. Kid. = Mishna Kidushin*

| | |
|---|---|
| 3:12 | 31 n 46 |

*m. Yeb. = Mishna Yebamoth*

| | |
|---|---|
| 7:5 | 31 n 46 |

*t. Kid = Tosephta Kidushin*

| | |
|---|---|
| 4:16 | 31 n 46 |

*Sifre Deut. = Sifre Deuteronomy*

| | |
|---|---|
| Pisqa 312 | 213 n 13 |

*Yalq. Shim. Gen. = Yalqut Shimoni on Genesis*

| | |
|---|---|
| 1:1 | 239 n 84 |

*Yalq. Shim. Numb. = Yalqut Shimoni on Numbers*

| | |
|---|---|
| 723 | 242 n 90 |

Seneca the Elder

*Contr. = Controversiae*

| | |
|---|---|
| 1:9 | 146 n 36 |

Seneca the Younger (Sen.)

*Benef. = De Beneficiis*

| | |
|---|---|
| 2.16:1 | 156 n 66 |

*Cons. Helv. = Consolatio ad Helviam Matrem*

| | |
|---|---|
| 19:3–4 | 104 |
| 19:6 | 59 n 60, 104 |

*Cons. Pol. = Consolatio ad Polybium*

| | |
|---|---|
| 13:2–3 | 92 |
| 17:3 | 92 |
| 17:5 | 92 |

*De Ira*

| | |
|---|---|
| 1.20:8–9 | 92 |
| 3.17:1–18:1 | 156 |

*De Tranq. Anim. = De Tranquillitate Animi*

| | |
|---|---|
| 14:9 | 93 n 76 |

*N.Q. = Naturales Quaestiones*

| | |
|---|---|
| 6.22:2 | 156 |

Stobaeus

*Anth. = Anthologion*

| | |
|---|---|
| 2.31:123 | 185 n 83 |
| 2.31:126 | 167 n 22, 185 n 84 |
| 3.6:23 | 95 n 87 |
| 3.6:23 | 100 n 105 |
| 3.18:17 | 105 n 124.125 |
| 3.29:78 | 220 n 33 |

*Flor. = Florilegium*

| | |
|---|---|
| 46.67 | 93 n 77, 220 n 33 |
| 67.20 | 95 n 87 |
| 69.23 | 95 n 87 |
| 70.14 | 97 n 87 |
| 79.51 | 168 n 29, 180 n 71 |

Strabo

*Geogr. = Geographica*

| | |
|---|---|
| 1.4:9 | 118 |
| 2.5:26 | 118 |
| 3.3:8 | 119 n 36 |
| 3.4:19 | 146 |
| 6.4:2 | 114 n 14, 119 n 36 |
| 10.4:9 | 129 |
| 13.4:8 | 119 n 36 |
| 15.1:61 | 153 |
| 15.1:63–5 | 152 n 58 |

16.1:28    114 n 14
16.2:35–6    69 n 82
17.1:9    81 n 26, 130 n 65
17.3:2    114 n 14
17:801    49 n 13

**Suetonius (Suet.)**

*Aug. = Divus Augustus*

17:1    49 n 15
18:1    150, 157
52:1    90 n 66
53:1    90 n 66
70    88 n 53
89:1    132 n 69
93    132

*Claud. = Divus Claudius*

11:1–2    89
12:1    89

*Gaius*

22:2    91 n 68

*Tib. = Tiberius*

32:2    121
36:1    124 n 47
42:1    126
48    122 n 41
61:2–4    126
75:1    126

**Tacitus (Tac.)**

*Agr. = Agricola*

13    121

*An. = Annales*

1:172–77    126 n 51
2:59    121
2.85    124 n 47 !!!
3:33    105 n 122
3:38    121 n 40
3:44    121 n 40
3:69    122
4:38    89 n 60
6:50    126 n 53
6:51    126
12:8    91 n 70
14:20    150 n 45

*Hist. = Historiae*

1:11    48 n 13, 59 n 60
5:9    79

**Pompeius Trogus**

*Hist. Phil. = Historia Philippicae*

41.6:8    114 n 13

**Velleius Paterculus**

*The Tiberian Narrative*

2.103:5    121
2.114:1–2    121
2.126:3–4    121

**Vergilus (Verg.)**

*Aen. = Aeneis*

8:685–8    49 n 16.18
8:714–31    115 n 17

# Index of Names

Aaron 193–4, 19–7, 199
Abraham 24–6, 29–31, 56–7, 145, 172–4,
    181, 200–1, 223, 263 n 54
Adam 169, 175, 189, 224, 226, 240–1,
    243–4
Adelphoi 63
Aeschylus 52–3, 55–8
Aesop 141
Agrippa 22, 43, 60–1, 79, 82, 119, 123–4,
    127
Alexander the Alabarch 8, 157
Alexander the Great 8, 58, 63, 72–3, 92,
    113, 116–7, 138, 141, 150–7
Anaxagoras 147
Anderson, B. 2
Antony 49–50, 54, 104, 117, 129, 150
Apion 62, 158
Apis 48
Apollo 88
Aristeas 143, 208
Aristobulus 141–2, 144, 152–5, 261–2
Aristotle 18, 156, 166, 175, 178, 216–8,
    221, 230, 258, 259 n 34
Arius Didymus 117, 191
Arrian 153
Aristippus 246
Artapanus 10, 63, 68, 71–4, 141, 144,
    151, 187
Assman, J. 187
Aseneth 68
Augustus 6, 48–50, 52–4, 58–9, 81–3,
    88–93, 104, 114–19, 121, 125, 128–33,
    136, 150, 158, 185, 242

Balaam 27
Barth, F. 2–4, 17, 45, 75, 111, 137
Ben Bag Bag 207
Ben Sira 197
Bertholet, K. I
Boyarin, D. I, 11, 223

Caesar 6, 61, 130
Cain 244
Calanus 152–5

Callisthenes 92, 156
Carabas 61
Carneades 146
Castor 91
Cato 104 n 120, 137, 142, 146, 150
Cazeaux, J. 64
Chantethotes 72
Charlesworth, M.-P. 89
Chenephres 72–3
Chrysippus 175
Cicero 37, 59, 142, 150, 154, 167–8,
    218–9, 249–50
Claudius 39–40, 88–90, 92, 118, 128, 131
Cleanthes 143
Cleopatra 49, 54, 104, 185
Clitus 156
Curtius 157
Cohen, S.J.D. 18
Colson, F.H. 149
Collins, J.J. I
Cotton, H. I

Dan 28
Dandamis 154
Darius 57
David 24
DeMause 163 n 7
Demetrius 148
Democritus 147
Dio Cassius 48, 49 n 15, 117, 120, 124
Diodorus 27, 55, 72–73, 181
Diogenes Laertes 141, 219, 230, 235
Dionysus 61, 63, 87
Dionysius of Halicarnassus 115–8
Dorion the Jew 63
Dositheus 63
Diotema 149
Drimylos 63

Ephraim 32
Epictetus 246
Eppia 105 n 122
Erastothenes 118
Esau 140

Euergetai 63
Euergetes I 63
Euripides 139
Eve 175, 243
Ezechiel the Tragedian 23, 187

Flaccus 40–2, 61, 76, 87, 119, 133–6, 253
Foucault, M. 95

Gaca, K.L. 100
Gaius 8–9, 38–43, 59–62, 76, 79–80,
    82–3, 85–94, 110–2, 115, 118–20,
    123–4, 126–8, 133–6, 158, 248, 253
Galen 96
Geertz, C. 2–4, 161, 247
Gemellus 120 n 37, 123
Germanicus 89, 121
Glucker, J. I
Goodenough, E.R. 39
Goodman, M. I
Goudrian, K. 7
Gruen, E.S. I, 12, 22

Habicht, C. 89
Hadas, M. 141–2
Hagar 24–8
Hall, S. 1, 4f
Harris, H.A. 222
Hartog, F. 51
Heine, H. 138
Helicon 62, 86, 119–120, 162
Helleman, W.E. 84
Hengel, M. I
Heraclitus 143–4, 155
Hermes 73
Herod 6, 125, 130
Herodotus 50–1, 72, 96
Holladay, C. 85
Homer 92, 138, 141, 158
Honigman, S. I, 63

Isaac 24–5, 27, 179, 263 n 54
Ishmael 24, 27
Isidorus 61–2, 158
Isis 73, 103
Issachar 28–9

Jacob 28–9, 65, 140, 181, 201–2
Jerome 228
Jesus 211–2, 224–6, 228, 230, 234,
    241
Johanna (unknown) 32
John the Baptiste 226
Joseph 26, 32, 56, 63–9, 74, 99, 179, 181

Josephus 6, 8, 37, 78 n 13, 79 n 21, 122–6,
    128, 130, 142, 144, 151, 174, 260 n 42
Jülicher, A. 216
Jupiter 78, 91–2, 250
Julia Augusta 132
Juster, J. 80
Justin Martyr 213

Kasher, A. 22
Kister, M. I

Laius 97
Lampo 61, 158
Leah 28–29
Leisegang, H. 40
Levenson, J. 171–2
Liebes, Y. I
Livia 89
Livy 114, 150
Lot 252
Lucian 152
Lucius Vitellius 93
Luke 6, 212, 224–5, 230

Macro 86, 93, 120, 134
Mandanis 152–3
Manson, M. 175
Mark 230
Matthew 215, 224–8, 230
Megasthenes 153–5
Menasseh 32
Mendelson, A. 11
Moses 23, 35, 63, 69–74, 84–5, 94, 106,
    109–10, 132, 138–40, 144, 151, 158,
    172, 178–9, 187, 190, 192–4, 196, 199,
    203–4, 206–8, 220, 235, 246–8, 250,
    252, 256, 261, 263–4
Musonius (Rufus) 100, 105, 167–8, 185,
    219–220, 257

Nepos 150

Nicolaus of Damascus 8, 108
Noah 252, 263 n 54

Oedipus 97–8
Onesicritus 152–3
Orpheus 73, 141
Ovid 36, 115

Paul 214
Pericles 142
Petronius 43, 83, 133, 136
Pharaoh 55–7, 65, 67, 70–1, 85, 162
Philo as Community leader 9–10, 19, 23

Philolaus 258
Pilate 125
Plato 96, 98, 138–42, 147–50, 175, 188
    n 4, 189, 191, 194, 198, 200, 202–5,
    237, 239, 243–5, 257
Plutarch 8, 112, 154, 163, 167
Pollux 91
Polybius 55, 150
Pompeius Trogus 114 n 12
Pool, R. 5
Poseidon 53
Potiphar's wife 65, 67–8, 99
Price, J.J. I
Ptolemaios 63
Ptolemy E. 140
Pythagoras/Pythagorean 100–1, 141

R. Ammi 238
R. Hoshaya 240–1
R. Huna 226
R. Johannan b. Zakkai 227
R. Jehuda ha-Nasi 227
Rachel 28–9, 181
Renan, E. 5

Sarah 25–6, 57, 178, 184
Satran, D. I
Schäfer, P. I
Schwartz, D.S. I
Sejanus 124
Seneca the Younger 9, 59, 91–3, 104–5,
    142, 156, 185, 219
Sesostris 72–3, 151
Silanus 86, 93, 134
Smallwood, E.M. 120

Simpson 92
Smith, A. 4, 17
Socrates 140, 144–6
Sophocles 138–9
Strabo 81 n 26, 114, 117–8, 129–130, 146,
    153
Suetonius 89–91, 120, 124, 126, 132, 157

Tacitus 59, 79, 120, 122, 124–5, 150
Tamar 26, 29–32, 77
Tcherikover, V. 13, 21, 39
Terach 144–5
Themistocles 142
Theodotus 63
Thoma, C. 212
Thomas (Gospel of) 211, 224–5, 234
Thyen, H. 210
Tiberius 89, 118–28, 131, 133–34, 253
Tiede, D.L. 72
Timagenes 8, 117, 151, 156
Tobin, T.H. 191

Varro 78
Velleius 121
Virgil 49 n 16, 114

Weber, M. 3
Willrich 157
Winston, D. I

Xenophon 55, 148, 150
Xerxes 53, 55–7, 92

Zeno 138, 140, 142, 219
Zeus 82, 154, 168
Zilpah and Bilhah 28–9
Zipporah 23

# Subject Index

Abortion 163–6
Acculturation 68
*Acta Isodori* 22
*Ad Herennium* 218
Adultery 96, 99
Aesthetics 137–8
*Akedah* 172–4
Alexander Romance 152, 155
Alexandria/ns 1, 8, 13, 17, 19, 32, 38–42,
  59–61, 81, 86–7, 89, 103–4, 111–2,
  117–9, 123, 125, 128–31, 136, 152,
  156–8, 162, 181, 186, 203, 210, 223,
  228, 230, 232, 234, 237, 244–5
Allegory/allegorical 32, 64, 67, 165, 175,
  192–7, 199, 202–4, 214, 216, 218, 225,
  233–4, 243, 251
Aniconism 62, 82–3, 94
Anti-Semitism 60
Apologetics 13, 35, 40, 112, 118, 126, 248
Architect 205, 236–9
Asia 32, 36, 43, 82, 115, 128–9, 151–2
Assimilation 12, 29, 37, 50, 53–4, 58,
  64–8, 70, 85, 109, 132, 139, 143–4,
  155, 179, 223–4, 231–2, 237, 240, 252
Assyrians 115
Athos 68
Audience 5, 9, 13, 39–40, 50, 102, 111–2,
  117–8, 125, 128–9, 139, 196, 199, 202,
  220, 240, 244, 248

Bastard 21, 24–5, 27–9, 32
Barbarian 49, 52–4, 57–8, 62, 78, 92, 94,
  96–9, 115–8, 120, 126, 129–30, 139,
  142, 152, 155–6, 171, 250
Bible/Biblical 5, 11, 17, 23–4, 27–9,
  31–2, 34, 55–8, 63–7, 70, 76, 96,
  99–100, 105, 107–8, 139–40, 143,
  145, 171–3, 175, 177–8, 181, 187–8,
  192, 202, 204, 207, 209–10, 21–6,
  219–20, 223–4, 229–30, 232–5, 237,
  246, 251, 254, 261–2, 264–5, (see
  Scripture)
Biology/biological 17–8, 21, 24, 27, 29,
  33, 43–4, 166, 220, 228, 232–3

Birth 4, 17, 20, 22–3, 25, 28–9, 9–8,
  119–20, 127, 165–6, 168, 170
*Boof of Yezira* 189 n 5

Caesarea 130
*Caesareum* 81, 130–1
Canon/canonization 187, 206, 208, 212,
  251
Capri 120, 126
Child Exposure 101, 164–8, 171
Christian Church 11, 213–4
Citizen/ship 8, 20–2, 32, 36, 62, 89, 158,
  177, 187, 222, 248
Civil Rights 20, 22
Civilization 48, 52, 54, 58, 62, 73, 75, 94,
  96, 110, 115, 117, 130, 136, 138, 142,
  152, 157–8, 252
Colonization/Colony 34–6, 38, 44, 116
Community 2–3, 9–10, 13, 17, 19, 22, 25–6,
  36–7, 52, 87, 102, 112, 176–7, 187, 195,
  208, 212, 223, 230, 242–3, 252–3
Comparison/Competition 142–6, 156,
  215–220, 228, 231, 233, 235–7, 246
Construct/ion
– of Augustus 132
– of boundaries 139, 224, 233
– of counter image 68, 71
– of cultural discourse 183, 185
– of curriculum vitae 70
– of difference 5
– of Egyptian Other 48–9, 58, 60–2, 67
– of ethnic boundaries 3, 183
– of gender 263
– of the Greeks 97, 137–8, 148–50, 152,
  155
– of hierarchy 94
– of identity 3, 13
– of Isaac and Joseph 179
– of Jewish Childhood 170–1
– of Jewish Culture 185, 210, 215, 228,
  247–48, 266
– of Jewish descent 9, 22, 28, 32–3, 43, 75
– of Jewish identity 1, 6, 9, 11–2, 17, 42,
  45, 63, 71, 98–9, 103–4, 110–1, 161

– of Jewish values  75–6
– of language  191
– of the Other  45, 51–2, 75, 149, 155,
    253
– of the Persians  54, 97
– of the Romans  118–9, 127, 133
– Roman construct  86
– social contructs  2, 5, 45
*Contra Apionem*  144
Conversion  26, 29–31, 132, 252
Conubium  23–4, 32, (see Marriage)
Corruption  52, 125, 175
Cosmos/cosmic  30, 37, 113, 115, 205,
    238, 247, 259–66, (see Universe)
Creation  109, 164, 169–70, 189, 191,
    203–6, 220, 226, 235–40, 252, 262–3
Custom  4, 9, 31, 35, 40, 46–7, 49, 51, 54,
    62, 66–7, 70, 72 (– of circumcision),
    83, 96–7, 101, 117, 125, 130–2, 135,
    148, 163–4, 232, 239, 247, 250, 252–3,
    256, 258, 264–6

Day of Atonement  107, 109–10
*De Josepho*  64, 66–7
*De Migratione*  67
*De Praemiis et Poenis*  254
*De Somniis*  64, 66–7
Deification  60–1, 65, 76, 80, 82–3, 85–7,
    93, 241, (see Imperial cult)
Descent  9, 17, 23, 32–3, 43–4, 69, 92,
    111, 116, 158
Deuteronomist  207
Diaspora  10, 62
Discourse  1, 2, 5, 13, 83, 88, 142, 157,
    161, 183, 185, 187, 210, 213, 215, 219,
    224, 228, 242, 246, 248, 254
– Roman discourse  13, 49–50, 52, 76, 93,
    104, 149–50, 155–6
Divine
– Image  169–70, 186, 220, 226
– Language  189–92, 195
– Logos  188, 190–3, 195–6, 198–202,
    205–9, 236, 238–9, 251
– Omnipotence  178
– Order  174, 250
– Providence  40–2, 76, 133, 135–6, 184,
    254
– Voice  30, 190, 199, 202
– Word  84, 194–5, 197, 199, 202–3, 205,
    256
Divinity  60, 84, 91

East and West  41, 53–5, 58, 62, 121, 141,
    153

Education  120, 127, 163, 171, 174, 176–9,
    181–7
Egypt  7, 9–11, 13, 20–2, 24–8, 32, 35–6,
    38–9, 41, 44–75, 81, 85–7, 89, 94, 96,
    98–9, 103–8, 111, 119, 121, 128–9,
    132–5, 141, 151, 157–8, 162, 168, 176,
    179, 185, 187, 193, 207, 231, 252–3,
    255, 262, 266
Elephantine  22
Elite  8, 9, 32, 42, 44, 50, 102, 104, 106,
    110, 112, 116, 125, 129, 150, 158, 167,
    175, 181, 186, 242
Embassy  8, 38–9, 41, 43, 62
*Enkrateia*  94, 102, 105–10, 127, 131, 134,
    176, 178–9, 182, 185, 253, 255–7, 264,
    (see Self-control, Self-restraint, Manli-
    ness)
Environment  3–5, 17, 19, 30, 36, 45, 68,
    77–8, 103, 139, 157, 161–62, 186, 222,
    224, 233–4, 246
*Epikrisis*  20
*Epistle to the Hebrews*  214
Epistomology  188–9
Essenes  146–7, 155, 230
Ethics  75, 94, 110, 138, 140, 218–9, 233,
    246, 257
Ethiopia/ns  23, 71
Ethnicity/Ethnic  1–5, 9, 13, 17–8, 20–3,
    33, 36, 38, 41, 45–6, 58, 66–7, 70–1,
    75–6, 78, 96, 107, 111, 133, 137, 139,
    150, 155, 183, (see Other/ness)
Ethnographic  50–1
Euphrates  28, 113–4
Europe  32, 36, 43, 53, 82, 115, 128, 151–2
*Eusebeia*  81
Exegete/Exegesis  24–5, 31, 46, 63–4,
    6–9, 71, 165, 187, 196–7, 199, 201,
    214–5, 220, 223, 225–6, 228–9, 232,
    235, 238–9, 241
Exile  33, 41, 207
Exodus  33, 35, 47, 53, 55, 58, 63, 69, 74
    (mental), 109, 158

Fatherland  34–5
Fatherless  21, 24
Foetus/Embryo  163–4, 166
Freedom/Liberty  53, 5–6, 58, 62, 88, 93,
    105, 107, 120, 129, 154–5, 254
Frugality  105, 108–9, 148, 150, 256,
    258–9

*Genesis Apocryphon*  56
Geography  2, 50–2, 64, 214, 244
Germans  113–4

*Gnomon of the Idios Logos* 21
God/gods 26, 30–1, 35, 51, 53, 60, 65–7,
    73, 76–8, 82, 84–7, 90, 92–3, 95, 119,
    131–3, 135, 139, 142, 145, 151, 153,
    162–4, 170, 172–4, 176–8, 181–2, 184,
    189, 191, 193, 195, 198–9, 201, 207–8,
    220–5, 233–42, 244, 256, 26–3,
    (see Divine)
Godless 51–2
Golden Calf 46, 49, 134
Goshen 68
*Gospel of Thomas* 211, 214, 224, 233–4
Greek/s 35, 51, 55, 58, 76, 96–9, 113–5,
    118, 120, 129, 137–58, 168, 177, 181–3,
    208–9, 230, 250
Greek Culture 12, 95–6, 98, 116–8,
    137–9, 141–3, 149, 158, 183
Greek East 8, 9, 54, 112, 115, 117–8, 12–
    29, 158
Gymnosophist 152–4
*Gynaikon* 102–3, 184, (see Women's
    quarter)

Heliopolis 68
Halacha 96, 107, 150, 262
Handmaid 24, 28–30, 183
Haran 145
Health/iness 255–8, 266
Hellenism/Hellenistic 12–3, 27, 73, 100,
    103, 115, 117–8, 129–30, 137–8, 141–3,
    157–8, 187, 214, 216, 235, 248
Hermeneutics 124, 217, 231, 242
Hermopolis 72
High Priest 84, 89, 196
Hierarchy 18, 67, 99, 108–9, 127, 182,
    220, 240–1
Historiography 39, 116, 144
Homeland 33, 50, 52–3, 62, 153–5, 169
Homosexual 101, 103, 149 n 43
Humanism 12, 138
Humanity 47–8, 50, 52, 71, 105, 109, 131,
    148

Idolatry/Idol-Worshipper 30, 62, 65, 77,
    108, 143
Imperial Cult 79–82, 90, (see Deification)
*In Flaccum* 6, 37–40, 61, 111–2, 135
Influence 12
Integration 52, 60, 64, 67–9, 73–4, 77, 93,
    110
Interpretation/interpreter 3–4, 13, 24, 41,
    47, 53–4, 61, 63–5, 67–9, 71, 79, 81,
    83, 88, 90, 93–4, 97, 105, 107, 112,
    118, 122, 124, 134, 144, 155–6, 158,

169–70, 172–3, 178, 181, 183, 187,
    190, 192, 196–7, 199, 205–6, 220, 223,
    228–9, 231–2, 235, 237–9, 243, 246,
    248, 254, 258–9, 261–2, 265–6
Israel 94, 202, 233

Jamnia 59–60, 79
Jerusalem 33–4, 36–9, 52, 151
– as mothercity 17, 33–8, 42–4, 62, 75
*Jewish Antiquities* 122–3
Jewish *Politeia* 26, 29–30, 77
Jewishness 11–2, 18, 32
Judaism 12–3, 137–8, 212, 242, 252

Kosher food 105–6, 110, 257
Land 50–1, 113, 120, 126, 207, 266
– Promised Land 31–2
– of Israel 35
– native Land 36
– of residence 63
Language 2, 56, 72, 76–7, 93, 131, 139,
    161, 175, 187–210, 218, 223–4, 228,
    232–4, 240, 242, 244, 246, 254, 256–7
– meta-language 188
– theory of language 189 n 5, 191, 197,
    208
*Laographia* 20, 22
Law 17, 24, 27, 49, 66, 70, 97–9, 106,
    108, 115, 119, 141, 164, 177, 187, 202,
    206, 208, 222, 232, 234, 244, 247–52,
    254, 256–7, 261, 266
– of Nature 122, 145, 229, 231, 235, 249,
    251, 255, 262
Leader/ship 8, 19, 61, 63, 68–73, 105,
    117, 119, 139, 156, 213, 226, 263
Legal 20, 23–5, 29, 96
*Legatio* 6, 37–41, 61, 86–7, 93, 95 n 84,
    111–2, 118, 128, 131, 135
Legislation 18, 24, 27, 82, 94–8, 109–10,
    140–1, 207, 229, 247–51, 255–6,
    261–2, 265
Leontopolis 63
Life-Style 4, 25, 29, 116, 176, 179, 186,
    247, 255–9, 266
Logos 78, 193, 195, 200, 202, (see also
    Divine Logos)
– logo-centric 188
Loyalty 12, 31, 34–6, 43, 62, 70–1, 117,
    123, 145, 155
– Disloyalty 62, 79
*LXX* 163–4, 172, 208–9, 229, 25–2
Lybians 113, 157

Macedonians 113, 115, 117, 151, 154–7
*Mamzer* 24
Masculinity/manliness 103–4, 183, 263–4
Marriage 20–1, 23, 25, 29, 31–2, 48, 68, 95–101, 103, 172, 184, (see Conubium)
Mashal 215–18, 222–3, 225, 227, 229, 231–4, 236–9, 241
Materialism/material 47, 51–2, 75, 95, 98, 108, 148, 181, 189, 200, 205, 236, 238, 241, 254
Maternal 18
Matriarch 26, 32, 181
Matrilineality/matrilineal 18, 22, 27, 31
Medes 115
Medicine 18 n 4, 27, 137, 245, 254, 256–7
Metaphor 37, 52, 167, 190, 193, 197–8, 200, 204, 257
Metropolis 20, 35, 37
Minority 45
Modesty 71, 91–2, 104, 109, 131, 185, 196
Mother-son union 96–7
Monotheism 78–81, 83
Multi-ethnic 3, 13, 36, 39, 45, 111, 186
Mystery 201
Myth 17, 44, 58, 220
– of origins 4, 17, 33, 37–8, 41–3
Name/s 78, 94, 113, 135, 150, 188–9, 190, 239
Nation/hood 1–2, 4, 12, 23, 46, 50–1, 58, 60, 62, 75–7, 80, 86, 93–4, 96–9, 106, 110, 113, 115, 125, 127, 130–1, 135–6, 138, 141–5, 158, 164, 177, 182, 206–7, 228, 247, 250–2, 255, 263, 266
Nature 53, 77, 93, 95, 98, 99, 101, 164–9, 172, 199–20, 229, 231, 247–66
*New Testament* 213–4, 219, 221, 224, 227–8, 230, 233, 238, 244
Nile 50–1, 192–3
Nimshal 216–8, 221–3, 225–6, 229, 231–2, 234, 237, 240, 242–3

Objectivity 12
*Oikoumene* 33, 36, 53, 76, 81 n 25, 112, 128, 152, 251
Onias 68
Origins 17, 25–6, 29, 34–6, 50, 60, 69–70, 73, 75, 116–8, 141–2, 151, 194, 206, 214, 235, (see Myth of origins)
Orthodoxy 11, 78
Other/ness 3, 5, 9, 45–6, 48–9, 51–2, 58,

60, 62, 68–9, 71, 74–5, 78, 94, 96, 98, 107, 111, 139, 148–9, 155–6, 225, 228, 252–3, (see Construct, Ethnicity)

*Paideia* 177, 182, 186–7, 246
Palestine 6, 30, 43, 54, 63–4, 67, 125, 214, 244
Parable of the charioteer and helms-man 243
– of the physician, athlete, wooer and hound 244–246
– of the provider of a banquet 148, 220–8
– of the sower and the field 229–33
– of king 234–9, 242
Parthians 113–4
Passover 107–9, 178, 261–2
Patriarchal 18, 185
Patrilineality/patrilineal 18, 23–4, 27, 29
*Pax augusta* 121
Pentateuch 18
*Pergraecari* 149–50
Persians 52–8, 74, 96–8, 113, 115, 156–7, 240
Perversion 46, 48, 62–3, 97–8, 127, 252
*Phaedrus (Plato)* 243
Philosophy/philosophers 8, 10, 83, 132, 137–9, 141–2, 144–8, 150, 152–6, 165, 168, 181–5, 187, 191, 233, 235, 246, 249, 252, 257, 260
Platonic 190, 197–8, 237, 239, 243–5
– Forms 191, 197–8, 203, 205
– Ideas 191
– Middle-Platonism 191, 203–4
Pleasure/s 66, 95–6, 99–101, 104, 106, 109, 134, 174, 179, 241, 255
Pogrom 40, 60, 62, 111, 136
*Poiesis* 203–4, 206
Polemics 47, 101, 137, 174, 212–3, 228, 231, 234
*Praeparatio Evangelica* 11
Procreation 27, 99–101, 103, 168–9, 170
Proselytes 77
*Proskynesis* 56, 87
Ptolemies 20, 22, 61, 63, 68, 73, 98, 113, 150, 157
Pythagoreans 100–1, 103, 165, 258–9

Qumran 18 n 3

Rabbis/Rabbinic 5, 11, 24, 78, 100, 174, 210, 212–3, 215, 217, 221, 223–4, 227–8, 238–9, 241–2, 244
Rationality/rational 12, 95, 103, 105, 137–8, 147, 175, 193, 220, 243, 249

Reconciliation 66–7
Red Sea 53, 55, 57
Relativity 3, 5
Religion 31, 49, 51–2, 62–3, 73, 75–80,
    82–3, 86, 92, 110, 125, 131–4, 143,
    163, 166, 168, 170–1, 182, 188, 208,
    212, 228, 235, 239, 242, 244, 247, 253
*Republic (Plato)* 197
*Res Gestae (Augustus)* 114, 129
Return 34–5
Rhine 113–4
Rite of Passage 26, 77
Ritual 82–3, 178, 229, 232–4
Rome/Romans 6–9, 13, 19, 21, 37, 39,
    42, 44, 49–50, 54, 58, 75–6, 78, 85–9
    (Dea Roma), 90–1, 93, 99, 104–5, 107,
    110–38, 142–3, 145–9, 154–7, 175,
    185, 187, 218–9, 253
Roman Administration 7, 19–20, 23, 41,
    134
– Amicii 7, 9
– anti-Roman 39, 116, 155
– court 88
– culture 74, 83, 93–5, 215, 228
– Elite 9, 175
– Emperor 40, 61, 81–2, 85, 87–8, 90,
    92, 118–9, 123–8, 132–4
– Empire 8, 36–7, 92, 113, 115–7, 119,
    121, 126–9, 131–3, 136, 168
– Government 62, 86, 88–9, 92, 116, 128,
    134
– Institution 79
– Law 21, 23, 27–8, 32, 177, 250
– Policy 24, 91, 118, 168
– pro-Roman 112
– Rule 6, 22, 39, 59, 61, 68, 88, 91,
    111–5, 118–20, 128–31, 136
– World 58, 60, 210

Sabbath 82, 107–8, 131–2, 140, 252,
    260–4, 266
Sacrifices 46, 57, 82–3, 86, 108, 131–2,
    166, 196, 232–3, 262
– Child sacrifice 171–4
– Self-sacrifice 42
Sais 68
Salamis 53–4, 57–8
Sarmatians 113
Scripture 27, 109, 139–40, 142, 144,
    147, 170, 177, 182–3, 186–7, 190,
    192, 197, 199–200, 205–6, 208–10,
    215, 223, 227–8, 233, 235, 246, 251,
    (see Bible)
Scythians 114

Self
-awareness 2, 3, 9, 153, 170
-confidence 142, 144
-conscious 63, 67
-control 103, 106, 131, 133, 185, 253,
    255, 257, (see *Enkrateia*)
-cultivation 256
-definition 99, 112
-expression 4
-image 53, 90, 117, 131, 152
-knowledge 145
-perception 37
-restraint 94–6, 98–9, 103, 105–6, 110,
    182, (see *Enkrateia*)
Servant 24, 30–1, 67, 107, 170, 182,
    225–6
Sexuality/sexual 23, 47–8, 95, 99–103,
    105, 110, 133–4, 184, 232, 253, 263
Sibling union 98
*Similitudo* 216, 218, 220
Sin/Sinner 34, 41, 46, 65–6, 219, 232
Slave/Slavery 24–7, 29, 32, 49, 52, 55,
    62, 88, 148, 156, 162, 175, 240
Soul 30, 47–8, 65, 6–8, 108, 133–5, 148–9,
    155, 162, 166, 175, 177, 190, 195, 198,
    200–2, 204–5, 220, 235–6, 238, 241,
    243–4, 246, 253–7, 259–60, 262
Spiritualization/Spirituality 11, 26, 107–8,
    110, 178, 185, 189, 196, 198, 202, 212,
    220, 225, 230, 235, 238, 246, 258
Status 8, 17, 20–2, 24–5, 27–9, 31, 35, 38,
    93, 108, 118, 169, 204, 206–7, 239, 241
    Civil- 18, 38
    Legal- 19, 27
    Menial- 25–9, 262
    Social- 20, 22, 24, 107, 232
Stoicism 37, 57, 78, 140, 166–8, 182, 194,
    216, 219–1, 233, 235, 242, 249–50, 257
Subjectivity 3, 12
Succession 24
*Symbiosis* 63, 65, 68, 73
Symbol/symbolic 2–4, 12, 32–3, 35, 47,
    56, 89, 128, 137, 151, 156, 192, 196,
    226
Synagoge 32, 38, 42, 60–1, 81, 131–2,
    178
*Synoptic Gospels/Synopitcs* 211–4, 216–7,
    221, 224–6, 228, 230, 233–4
Syrians 21, 30, 141

Tax/taxation 20–3, 43, 82 (of Temple),
    105, 113, 157
Temple/Jerusalem Temple 24, 26, 30,
    33–5, 37–8, 42–3, 60, 63, 79–83, 86–7,

89–91, 110–1, 117, 123, 130–3, 136, 151, 172, 196–7, 223, 232–3
Terminology 25, 211–2, 216, 221, 230, 242
Theologoumena 10
Theology 10, 12, 33, 79, 83
*Therapeutae* 146–50, 155, 230–1, 257–8
*Timaeus(Plato)* 139–40, 205, 237
Tolerance 77, 132
Tradition 12–3, 33, 66–8, 70, 73, 80, 83, 93, 110, 116–7, 120, 129, 139, 142–3, 145, 147, 150, 152, 154–6, 168, 172, 176, 181, 185, 211–2, 216, 219–20, 228, 248–9, 254
*Treskeia* 83
True Israel/Verus Israel 46, 213, 226
Typology 54, 58
    Anti-type 90
    Archetype 52, 96, 138, 180, 188, 190, 198, 203
    Stereotype 48, 54–5, 58, 65, 97, 128, 137, 155, 221–4, 229, 237, 240
    Type 148, 175, 191, 199, 221, 224, 237

Tyranny/Tyrann 40, 54–5, 57, 88, 91–3, 122, 125–6, 129, 133, 154–5, 156

*Urbs / Orbis* 36, 113
Universe 4, 9, 51, 78, 109, 192, 205, 229, 232, 235, 248, 250, 255, 259, 262–4, 266, (see Cosmos)

Values 9, 17, 32, 43, 46, 48, 55, 62–65, 67, 70, 75–6, 82–3, 85, 93–4, 98–9, 104, 106, 110–2, 117, 127, 129, 131, 134–5, 137, 140, 142, 145–8, 153–4, 156, 162–3, 177, 179, 182–3, 185–7, 208–9, 220, 222, 228, 239, 242, 247–8, 252, 256, 259, 266
Violence 22, 38–9, 42, 62, 125, 155, 243, 246
Vision (of God) 30, 191, 198, 200–2, 205

Women's quarter 102–3, (see *Gynaikon*)
Worship 52, 73, 77–8, 80–4, 86–7, 90–1, 134

Zoolatry 48, 50, 62–3, 74

# Texts and Studies in Ancient Judaism

## Alphabetical Index

*Albani, M., J. Frey, A. Lange* (Ed.): Studies in the Book of Jubilees. 1997. *Volume 65.*

*Avemarie, Friedrich:* Tora und Leben. 1996. *Volume 55.*

*Becker, Hans-Jürgen:* Die großen rabbinischen Sammelwerke Palästinas. 1999. *Volume 70.*
- see *Schäfer, Peter*

*Cansdale, Lena:* Qumran and the Essenes. 1997. *Volume 60.*

*Chester, Andrew:* Divine Revelation and Divine Titles in the Pentateuchal Targumim. 1986. *Volume 14.*

*Cohen, Martin Samuel:* The Shi ur Qomah: Texts and Recensions. 1985. *Volume 9.*

*Crown, Alan D.:* Samaritan Scribes and Manuscripts. 2001. *Volume 80.*

*Doering, Lutz:* Schabbat. 1999. *Volume 78.*

*Ego, Beate:* Targum Scheni zu Ester. 1996. *Volume 54.*

*Engel, Anja:* see *Schäfer, Peter*

*Frey, J.:* see *Albani, M.*

*Frick, Peter:* Divine Providence in Philo of Alexandria. 1999. *Volume 77.*

*Gibson, E. Leigh:* The Jewish Manumission Inscriptions of the Bosporus Kingdom. 1999. *Volume 75.*

*Gleßmer, Uwe:* Einleitung in die Targume zum Pentateuch. 1995. *Volume 48.*

*Goldberg, Arnold:* Mystik und Theologie des rabbinischen Judentums. Gesammelte Studien I. Hrsg. von *M. Schlüter* und *P. Schäfer.* 1997. *Volume 61.*
- Rabbinische Texte als Gegenstand der Auslegung. Gesammelte Studien II. Hrsg. von *M. Schlüter* und *P. Schäfer.* 1999. *Volume 73.*

*Goodblatt, David:* The Monarchic Principle. 1994. *Volume 38.*

*Grözinger, Karl:* Musik und Gesang in der Theologie der frühen jüdischen Literatur. 1982. *Volume 3.*

*Gruenwald, I., Sh. Shaked* and *G.G. Stroumsa* (Ed.): Messiah and Christos. Presented to David Flusser. 1992. *Volume 32.*

*Halperin, David J.:* The Faces of the Chariot. 1988. *Volume 16.*

*Herrmann, Klaus* (Hrsg.): Massekhet Hekhalot. 1994. *Volume 39.*
- see *Schäfer, Peter*

*Herzer, Jens:* Die Paralipomena Jeremiae. 1994. *Volume 43.*

*Hezser, Catherine:* Form, Function, and Historical Significance of the Rabbinic Story in Yerushalmi Neziqin. 1993. *Volume 37.*
- The Social Structure of the Rabbinic Movement in Roman Palestine. 1997. *Volume 66.*
- Jewish Literacy in Roman Palestine. 2001. *Volume 81.*
- see *Schäfer, Peter*

*Hirschfelder, Ulrike:* see *Schäfer, Peter*

*Horbury, W.:* see *Krauss, Samuel*

*Houtman, Alberdina:* Mishnah und Tosefta. 1996. *Volume 59.*

*Ilan, Tal:* Jewish Women in Greco-Roman Palestine. 1995. *Volume 44.*
- Integrating Jewish Woman into Second Temple History. 1999. *Volume 76.*

*Instone Brewer, David:* Techniques and Assumptions in Jewish Exegesis before 70 CE. 1992. *Volume 30.*

*Ipta, Kerstin:* see *Schäfer, Peter*

*Jacobs, Martin:* Die Institution des jüdischen Patriarchen. 1995. *Volume 52.*

*Kasher, Aryeh:* The Jews in Hellenistic and Roman Egypt. 1985. *Volume 7.*
- Jews, Idumaeans, and Ancient Arabs. 1988. *Volume 18.*
- Jews and Hellenistic Cities in Eretz-Israel. 1990. *Volume 21.*

*Krauss, Samuel:* The Jewish-Christian Controversy from the earliest times to 1789. Vol.I. Hrsg. von *W. Horbury.* 1996. *Volume 56.*

*Kuhn, Peter:* Offenbarungsstimmen im Antiken Judentum. 1989. *Volume 20.*

*Kuyt, Annelies:* The 'Descent' to the Chariot. 1995. *Volume 45.*

*Lange, A.:* see *Albani, M.*

*Lange, Nicholas de:* Greek Jewish Texts from the Cairo Genizah. 1996. *Volume 51.*

*Lapin, Hayim:* Economy, Geography, and Provincial History in Later Roman Galilee. 2001. *Volume 85.*

*Leonhardt, Jutta:* Jewish Worship in Philo of Alexandria. 2001. *Volume 84.*

*Lohmann, Uta:* see *Schäfer, Peter*

*Loopik, M. van* (Übers. u. komm.): The Ways of the Sages and the Way of the World. 1991. *Volume 26.*

*Luttikhuizen, Gerard P.:* The Revelation of Elchasai. 1985. *Volume 8.*

*Mach, Michael:* Entwicklungsstadien des jüdischen Engelglaubens in vorrabbinischer Zeit. 1992. *Volume 34.*

*Mendels, Doron:* The Land of Israel as a Political Concept in Hasmonean Literature. 1987. *Volume 15.*

*Mutins, Georg von:* see *Schäfer, Peter*

*Necker, Gerold:* see *Schäfer, Peter*

*Niehoff, Maren:* Philo on Jewish Identity and Culture. 2001. *Volume 86.*

*Olyan, Saul M.:* A Thousand Thousands Served Him. 1993. *Volume 36.*

*Otterbach, Rina:* see *Schäfer, Peter*

*Prigent, Pierre:* Le Judaisme et l'image. 1990. *Volume 24.*

*Pucci Ben Zeev, Miriam:* Jewish Rights in the Roman World. 1998. *Volume 74.*

*Reeg, Gottfried* (Hrsg.): Die Geschichte von den Zehn Märtyrern. 1985. *Volume 10.*

– see *Schäfer, Peter*

*Renner, Lucie:* see *Schäfer, Peter*

*Reichman, Ronen:* Sifra und Mishna. 1998. *Volume 68.*

*Rohrbacher-Sticker, Claudia:* see *Schäfer, Peter*

*Salvesen, A.* (Ed.): Origen's Hexapla and Fragments.1998. *Volume 58.*

*Samely, Alexander:* The Interpretation of Speech in the Pentateuch Targums. 1992. *Volume 27.*

*Schäfer, Peter:* Der Bar-Kokhba-Aufstand. 1981. *Volume 1.*

– Hekhalot-Studien. 1988. *Volume 19.*

*Schäfer, Peter* (Hrsg.): Geniza-Fragmente zur Hekhalot-Literatur. 1984. *Volume 6.*

– see *Goldberg, Arnold*

– in Zusammenarbeit mit *Klaus Herrmann, Rina Otterbach, Gottfried Reeg, Claudia Rohrbacher-Sticker, Guido Weyer:* Konkordanz zur Hekhalot-Literatur. Volume 1: 1986. *Volume 12.* – Volume 2: 1988. *Volume 13.*

*Schäfer, Peter, Margarete Schlüter, Hans Georg von Mutins* (Hrsg.): Synopse zur Hekhalot-Literatur. 1981. *Volume 2.*

*Schäfer, Peter* (Hrsg.) in Zusammenarbeit mit *Hans-Jürgen Becker, Klaus Herrmann, Ulrike Hirschfelder, Gerold Necker, Lucie Renner, Claudia Rohrbacher-Sticker, Stefan Siebers:* Übersetzung der Hekhalot-Literatur. Volume 1: §§ 1–80. 1995. *Volume 46.* – Volume 2: §§ 81–334. 1987. *Volume 17.* – Volume 3: §§ 335–597. 1989. *Volume 22.* – Volume 4: §§ 598–985. 1991. *Volume 29.*

*Schäfer, Peter,* und *Hans-Jürgen Becker* (Hrsg.) in Zusammenarbeit mit *Anja Engel, Kerstin Ipta, Gerold Necker, Uta Lohmann, Martina Urban, Gert Wildensee:* Synopse zum Talmud Yerushalmi. Volume I/1–2: 1991. *Volume 31.* – Volume I/3–5: 1992. *Volume 33.* – Volume I/6–11: 1992. *Volume 35.* – Volume III: 1998. *Volume 67.* – Volume IV: 1995. *Volume 47.*

*Schäfer, Peter,* und *Shaul Shaked* (Hrsg.): Magische Texte aus der Kairoer Geniza. Volume 1: 1994. *Volume 42* – Volume 2: 1997. *Volume 64.* – Volume 3: 1999. *Volume 72.*

*Schäfer, Peter* (Ed.): The Talmud Yerushalmi and Graeco-Roman Culture. 1998. *Volume 71.* Volume II: 2000. *Volume 79.*

*Schäfer, Peter* und *Hezser, Catherine* (Ed.): The Talmud Yerushalmi and Graeco-Roman Culture II. 2000. *Volume 79.*

*Schlüter, Margarete:* see *Goldberg, Arnold*
– see *Schäfer, Peter*
*Schmidt, Francis:* Le Testament Grec d'Abraham. 1986. *Volume 11.*
*Schröder, Bernd:* Die 'väterlichen Gesetze'. 1996. *Volume 53.*
*Schwartz, Daniel R.:* Agrippa I. 1990. *Volume 23.*
*Schwemer, Anna Maria:* Studien zu den frühjüdischen Prophetenlegenden. Vitae Prophetarum Volume I: 1995. *Volume 49.* – Volume II (mit Beiheft: Synopse zu den Vitae Prophetarum): 1996. *Volume 50.*
*Shaked, Shaul:* see *Gruenwald, I.*
– see *Schäfer, Peter*
*Shatzman, Israel:* The Armies of the Hasmonaeans and Herod. 1991. *Volume 25.*
*Siebers, Stefan:* see *Schäfer, Peter*
*Spilsbury, Paul:* The Image of the Jew in Flavius Josephus' Paraphrase of the Bible. 1998. *Volume 69.*
*Stroumsa, G.G.:* see *Gruenwald, I.*
*Stuckenbruck, Loren T.:* The Book of Giants from Qumran. 1997. *Volume 63.*
*Swartz, Michael D.:* Mystical Prayer in Ancient Judaism. 1992. *Volume 28.*
*Sysling, Harry:* Tehiyyat Ha-Metim. 1996. *Volume 57.*
*Urban, Martina:* see *Schäfer, Peter*
*Veltri, Giuseppe:* Eine Tora für den König Talmai. 1994. *Volume 41.*
– Magie und Halakha. 1997. *Volume 62.*
*Weyer, Guido:* see *Schäfer, Peter*
*Wewers, Gerd A.:* Probleme der Bavot-Traktate. 1984. *Volume 5.*
*Wildensee, Gert:* see *Schäfer, Peter*
*Wilson, Walter T.:* The Mysteries of Rigtheousness. 1994. *Volume 40.*

*For a complete catalogue please write to the publisher*
*Mohr Siebeck · Postfach 2040 · D-72010 Tübingen.*
*Up-to-date information on the internet at http://www.mohr.de.*